Accelerating English Language Learning

Authors

Anna Uhl Chamot

Jim Cummins

Carolyn Kessler

J. Michael O'Malley

Lily Wong Fillmore

Consultant

George González

ScottForesman

A Division of HarperCollins*Publishers*

Editorial Offices: Glenview, Illinois

ional Offices: Sunnyvale, California • Atlanta, Georgia

enview, Illinois • Oakland, New Jersey • Dallas, Texas

man's Home Page at http://www.scottforesman.com

ISBN 0-673-19682-8
ISBN 0-673-19690-9 [Texas]

Scott, Foresman and Company,
1900 East Lake Avenue, Glenview, Illinois 60025.

1.800.554.4411
http://www.scottforesman.com

1 2 3 4 5 6 7 8 9 10 BB 05 04 03 02 01 00 99 98 97 96

CONTENTS

AUTHORS

ANNA UHL CHAMOT is an associate professor in the area of ESL teacher preparation at George Washington University. Previously Associate Director of the Georgetown University/Center for Applied Linguistics National Foreign Language Resource Center, she also managed two Title VII Special Alternative Instructional Projects in the Arlington, Virginia, Public Schools. She has co-authored two books with J. Michael O'Malley, *Learning Strategies in Second Language Acquisition* and *The CALLA Handbook: How to Implement the Cognitive Academic Language Learning Approach.* Other publications include content-ESL books in history and mathematics and a textbook series based on the CALLA model, *Building Bridges: Content and Learning Strategies for ESL.* Dr. Chamot holds a Ph.D. in ESL and applied linguistics from the University of Texas at Austin, and a Master's degree in foreign language education from Teachers College, Columbia University.

JIM CUMMINS is a professor in the Modern Language Centre and Curriculum Department of the Ontario Institute for Studies in Education. He has published several books related to bilingual education and ESL student achievement including: *Bilingualism and Special Education: Issues in Assessment and Pedagogy; Bilingualism in Education: Aspects of Theory, Research and Policy* (with Merrill Swain); *Minority Education: From Shame to Struggle* (with Tove Skutnabb-Kangas); and *Empowering Minority Students.* His latest and highly acclaimed work is *Brave New Schools: Challenging Cultural Illiteracy Through Global Learning Networks* (with Dennis Sayers). His current research focuses on the challenges educators face in adjusting to classrooms where cultural and linguistic diversity is the norm. Dr. Cummins received his Ph.D. from the University of Alberta, Canada.

CAROLYN KESSLER is a professor of ESL and Applied Linguistics at the University of Texas at San Antonio. She has extensive experience in teacher education for meeting the needs of linguistically and culturally diverse populations. Among recent books and monographs authored or co-authored are: *Cooperative Language Learning: A Teacher's Resource Book; Literacy con Cariño: A Story of Migrant Children's Success; Making Connections: An Integrated Approach to ESL* (a secondary program), *Parade* (a K-6 EFL program), and *Teaching Science to English Learners, Grades 4-8.* Her research interests include the integration of content area learning with second language and literacy development, adult and family literacy and language learning, and second language acquisition for both children and adults. Dr. Kessler holds both an M.S. and a Ph.D. from Georgetown University.

J. MICHAEL O'MALLEY is Supervisor of Assessment and Evaluation in Prince William County Public Schools in Virginia, where he is establishing a performance assessment program in grades K-12. He was previously Senior Researcher in the National Foreign Language Resource Center at Georgetown University and for six years was Director of the Evaluation Assistance Center at Georgetown University. Dr. O'Malley is co-developer with Anna Uhl Chamot of the Cognitive Academic Language Learning Approach (CALLA). CALLA was introduced by O'Malley and Chamot in 1986 and was the subject of both their 1994 work *The CALLA Handbook* and their earlier book on the research and theory underlying the approach. Dr. O'Malley is noted for his research on learning strategies in second language acquisition and for his work on assessment of language minority students. He received his Ph.D. in psychology from George Peabody College.

LILY WONG FILLMORE is a professor in the Graduate School of Education at the University of California, Berkeley. Her specializations are in the areas of second language learning and teaching, the education of language minority students, and socialization for learning across cultures. She is project director and principal investigator for the Family, Community, and the University Partnership, which prepares professionals to work in educational institutions in American Indian communities in the Southwest. She is also a major advisor to the Council of Chief State School Officer's LEP SCASS initiative, in which representatives from several states are working to develop ways to assess the conditions under which LEP students acquire English language skills at school. Dr. Wong Fillmore received her Ph.D. in linguistics from Stanford University.

CRITIC READERS

Sandra H. Bible
Elementary ESL Teacher
Shawnee Mission School District
Shawnee Mission, Kansas

Betty A. Billups
Dallas Independent School District
Dallas, Texas

María G. Cano
BIL/ESL Specialist
Pasadena Independent School District
Pasadena, Texas

Anaida Colón-Muñiz, Ed.D.
Director of English Language Development
and Bilingual Education
Santa Ana Unified School District
Santa Ana, California

Debbie Corkey-Corber
Educational Consultant
Williamsburg, Virginia

Lily Pham Dam
Instructional Specialist
Dallas Independent School District
Dallas, Texas

María Delgado
Milwaukee Public Schools
Milwaukee, Wisconsin

Dr. María Viramontes de Marín
Chair, Department of Education and Liberal Studies at the National
Hispanic University
San Jose, California

Tim Hart
Supervisor of English as a Second Language
Wake County
Raleigh, North Carolina

Lilian I. Jezik
Bilingual Resource Teacher
Colorna-Norco Unified School District
Norco, California

Helen L. Lin
Chairman, Education Program
Multicultural Arts Council of Orange County, California
Formerly ESL Lab Director, Kansas City, Kansas Schools

Teresa Montaña
United Teachers Los Angeles
Los Angeles, California

Loriana M. Novoa, Ed.D.
Research and Evaluation Consultants
Miami, Florida

Rosa María Peña
Austin Independent School District
Austin, Texas

Thuy Pham-Remmele
ESL/Bilingual K-12 Specialist
Madison Metropolitan School District
Madison, Wisconsin

Roberto San Miguel
Kennedy-Zapata Elementary School
El Cenizo, Texas

Jacqueline J. Servi Margis
ESL and Foreign Language Curriculum Specialist
Milwaukee Public Schools
Milwaukee, Wisconsin

Elizabeth Streightoff
ESL Magnet Teacher, Lamar Elementary School
Conroe Independent School District
The Woodlands, Texas

Susan C. VanLeuven
Poudre R-1 School District
Fort Collins, Colorado

Rosaura Villaseñor
(Educator)
Norwalk, California

Sharon Weiss
ESL Consultant
Glenview, Illinois

Cheryl Wilkinson
J.O. Davis Elementary School
Irving Independent School District
Irving, Texas

Phyllis I. Ziegler
ESL/Bilingual Consultant
New York, New York

The Philosophy of *ScottForesman ESL*

ScottForesman ESL accelerates English language learning through the use and application of the following principles.

Thematic Units

In theme- or topic-based lessons, curriculum content is presented thematically to provide the basis for language learning. Topic-related language and concepts are recycled over a period of time, ensuring their conceptualization and making students increasingly able to communicate their ideas on the topic. Each level of *ScottForesman ESL* contains six thematic units; each unit contains two related chapters. In each unit students are exposed to a rich array of language and activities based on the major topic. As students work through each unit, the variety of text types, formats, and activities enables them to master both the language and the concepts.

Balanced Skills

In each chapter of *ScottForesman ESL,* students develop all of the four language skills—listening, speaking, reading, and writing. This balanced approach ensures communicative proficiency. Authentic texts, both fiction and nonfiction, give ample reading practice. "Talk About It" and "Write About It" sections in each chapter offer practice in listening, speaking, and writing. The "Writer's Workshop" in Books 2-8 leads students through the writing process. These sections, along with the abundant optional activities, give students the time and opportunity to achieve communicative competence.

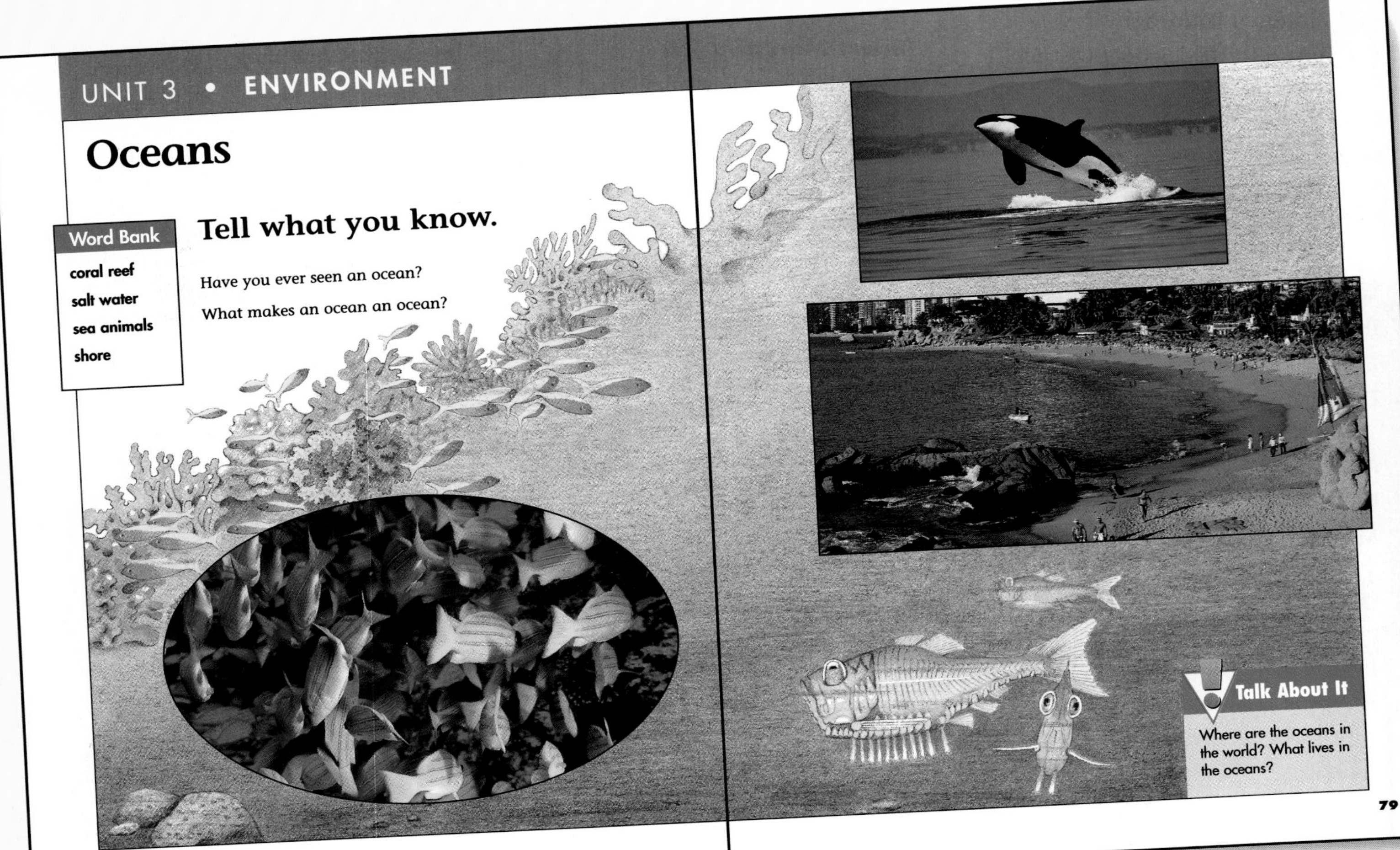

UNIT 3 • ENVIRONMENT
Oceans
Word Bank
coral reef
salt water
sea animals
shore
Tell what you know.
Have you ever seen an ocean?
What makes an ocean an ocean?
Talk About It
Where are the oceans in the world? What lives in the oceans?
78
79

The Cognitive Academic Language Learning Approach (CALLA)

ScottForesman ESL follows the principles of CALLA: it teaches grade-level topics from the major curriculum areas; it develops academic language skills; and it provides explicit instruction in learning strategies for both content and language acquisition.

Learning Strategies

Learning strategies are actions or thoughts that students can apply to challenging tasks. *ScottForesman ESL* integrates learning strategies instruction into each part of the learning process by providing guidelines for teaching the strategies and for helping students develop an awareness of their own learning processes.

Cooperative Learning

Throughout *ScottForesman ESL,* cooperative learning activities give students opportunities to work in groups to share what they know and to learn new information and skills. For a cooperative group to be successful, there should be a common, agreed upon goal and assigned individual roles for achieving that goal. In fact, cooperative learning activities are characterized by three components: (1) Positive interdependence—members rely on each other to achieve the end product; (2) Individual accountability—each member is responsible for information that is used to achieve the group's goal; (3) Face-to-face interaction—members work and talk together. In addition, cooperative learning may entail (4) Group processing—the group reviews what they did in terms of the group process or group mechanics; and (5) Development of social skills—members use group maintenance skills to keep the process going and task skills to perform what is required.

What is a volcano?

Volcanoes are openings in the earth's surface. Hot rock from deep under the earth bursts out, or erupts. The eruptions cause mountains to form. The hot liquid rock that comes out of a volcano is called lava. Pieces of rock also may come out of a volcano.

There are three kinds of volcanoes:

▲ Paricutin in Mexico is a cinder cone volcano.

1. Shield volcanoes form when lava slowly flows through several openings in the earth. Over the years, the lava forms a low mountain. When a shield volcano erupts, there is not a big explosion.

2. Cinder cone volcanoes form when rocks shoot out of an opening in the earth. The rocks fall back to earth as cinders or small pieces of burned rock. The cinders form a cone-shaped mountain.

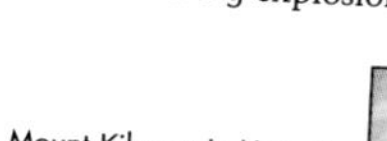
Mount Kilauea in Hawaii is a shield volcano. ▶

138 CONNECT LANGUAGE • SOCIAL STUDIES/SCIENCE

3. Composite volcanoes are a mixture of the two other kinds. They form when eruptions of lava and cinders pile up to make high mountains. Some composite volcanoes have violent eruptions. Mount Vesuvius is a composite volcano.

Mount Fuji in Japan is a composite volcano. ▶

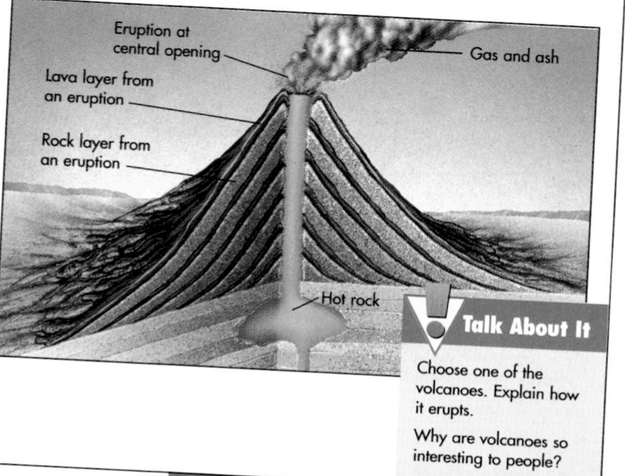

Talk About It

Choose one of the volcanoes. Explain how it erupts.

Why are volcanoes so interesting to people?

SOCIAL STUDIES/SCIENCE • CONNECT LANGUAGE 139

PROGRAM PHILOSOPHY

Integrated Curriculum

Each chapter in *ScottForesman ESL* develops language, concepts, and strategies related to a particular area of the curriculum. As students gain control over new material, it is vital that they understand how to transfer this knowledge and understanding to other areas of the curriculum and to "real life." In the Connect section of every chapter, students apply what they have learned to a new curriculum area and to the reading of authentic literature. Throughout the program, students learn how language and ideas cross the curriculum and how they can be applied in their content area classes.

Home/School Connections

ScottForesman ESL fosters a "community building" approach to education so teachers and parents can work together collaboratively as co-educators of children. In this approach, families are key participants in the academic success of children learning English, so learning communities develop in which the culture of hope, possibility, and promise can flourish.

Multicultural Understanding

Americans are a multicultural people. *ScottForesman ESL* recognizes the need to respect and preserve each group's culture, while at the same time acknowledging the interdependence of these cultures, the unity of our nation, and respect for others. Throughout the program, the variety of activities take into consideration students' different learning styles and backgrounds. And by presenting topics that are interesting and relevant to students, it helps them understand their different backgrounds and facilitates communication among them, their families, and the rest of society.

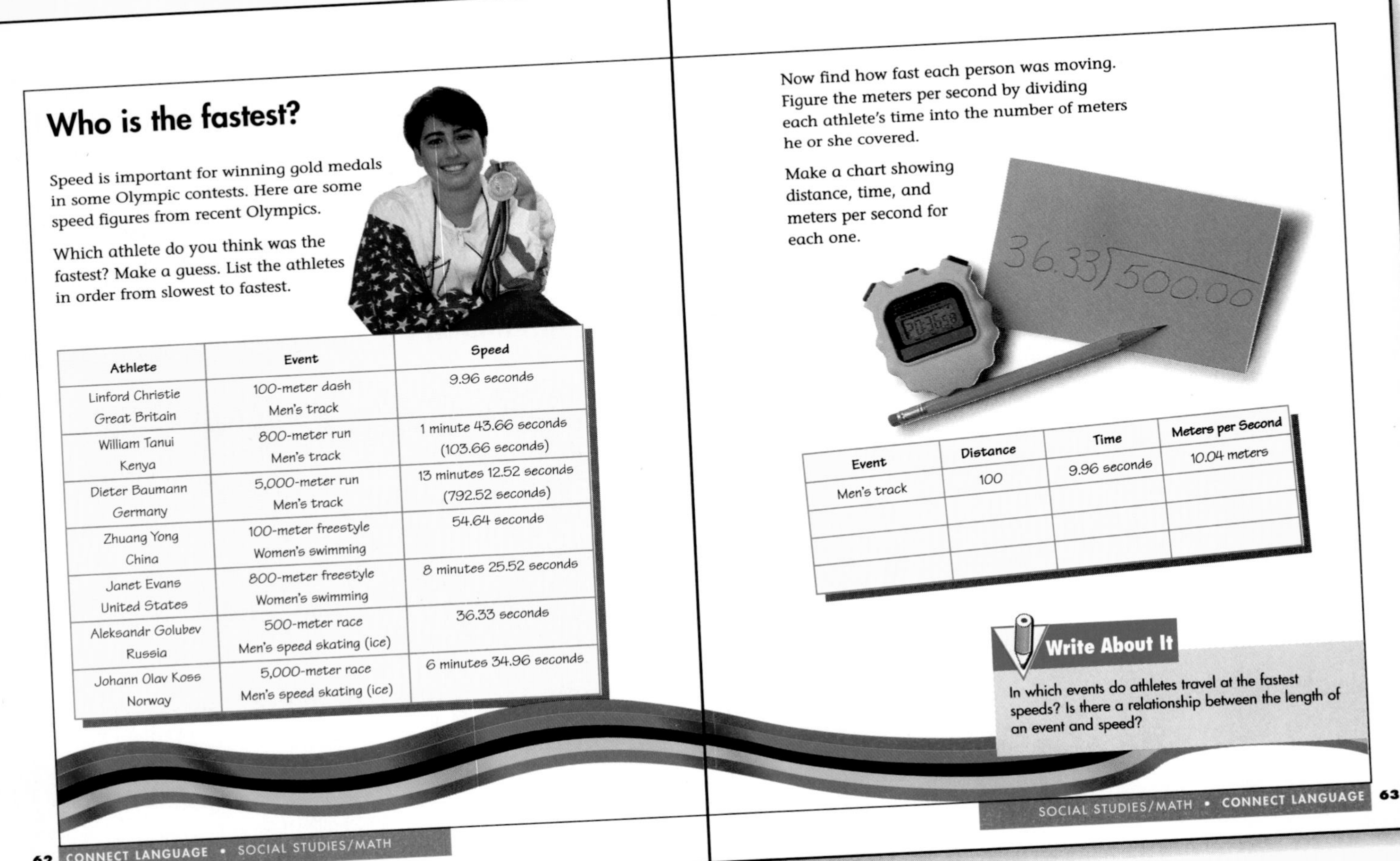

Who is the fastest?

Speed is important for winning gold medals in some Olympic contests. Here are some speed figures from recent Olympics.

Which athlete do you think was the fastest? Make a guess. List the athletes in order from slowest to fastest.

Athlete	Event	Speed
Linford Christie Great Britain	100-meter dash Men's track	9.96 seconds
William Tanui Kenya	800-meter run Men's track	1 minute 43.66 seconds (103.66 seconds)
Dieter Baumann Germany	5,000-meter run Men's track	13 minutes 12.52 seconds (792.52 seconds)
Zhuang Yong China	100-meter freestyle Women's swimming	54.64 seconds
Janet Evans United States	800-meter freestyle Women's swimming	8 minutes 25.52 seconds
Aleksandr Golubev Russia	500-meter race Men's speed skating (ice)	36.33 seconds
Johann Olav Koss Norway	5,000-meter race Men's speed skating (ice)	6 minutes 34.96 seconds

62 CONNECT LANGUAGE • SOCIAL STUDIES/MATH

Now find how fast each person was moving. Figure the meters per second by dividing each athlete's time into the number of meters he or she covered.

Make a chart showing distance, time, and meters per second for each one.

Event	Distance	Time	Meters per Second
Men's track	100	9.96 seconds	10.04 meters

Write About It

In which events do athletes travel at the fastest speeds? Is there a relationship between the length of an event and speed?

SOCIAL STUDIES/MATH • CONNECT LANGUAGE 63

Authentic Literature

Authentic children's literature such as that which appears in *ScottForesman ESL* is perhaps the most reliable and consistent source of academic English input children can have. By using such texts, teachers can help children develop the vocabulary, structures, and background knowledge they need to comprehend the intellectually challenging language of the classroom.

Authentic Assessment

Assessment is authentic when it enables students to communicate successfully their strengths and educational needs and when the results can be used to improve instruction based on accurate knowledge of students' progress. Authentic assessment activities in *ScottForesman ESL* include teacher observation, self assessment, peer assessment, performance assessment, and portfolio assessment. Traditional language and listening assessments are also included, as are standardized test instruction and practice.

Self Esteem

Children thrive in an atmosphere in which their language, culture, and values are acknowledged and respected and in which they can succeed. *ScottForesman ESL* encourages students to affirm their heritages and to celebrate them in the classroom. Activities are suggested throughout in which students demonstrate and explain aspects of their own and their families' lives and cultures. Optional activities provide opportunities for all students—from beginners through advanced—to be successful by demonstrating their accomplishments both individually and in cooperative groups.

Why the Sea Is Salty

Retold by Gail Sakurai

Reader's Tip
This folk tale is from Japan.

Language Tip
Vocabulary
Look at the words that tell about Ichiro and Jiro. *Poor* is the opposite of *wealthy*. *Greedy* is the opposite of *generous*. *Mean-spirited* is the opposite of *kind-hearted*.

Strategy Tip
Understand Plot
The words that tell about Ichiro and Jiro are opposites. The brothers are not alike. This is important in what will happen in the story.

A long time ago in Japan, there lived two brothers. Ichiro, the older brother, was wealthy, greedy, and mean-spirited. Jiro, the younger brother, was poor, generous, and kind-hearted.

88 CONNECT LANGUAGE • SCIENCE/LITERATURE

It had been a hard winter for Jiro. Now the new year was approaching, and poor Jiro did not have any food to feed his family. He hated to ask his stingy older brother for help, but Jiro couldn't let his wife and children go hungry. Reluctantly, he went off to Ichiro's house.

Language Tip
Vocabulary
A *stingy* person does not like to share things or spend money.

Language Tip
Vocabulary
Jiro went *reluctantly* to his brother's house. Jiro did not want to go to his brother's house.

Strategy Tip
Understand Characters
Why do you think Jiro went reluctantly to see his brother?

SCIENCE/LITERATURE • CONNECT LANGUAGE 89

COMPONENTS

Student Book

The 240-page, hard-cover *Student Book* contains six curriculum-based, thematic units of two chapters each. Each unit contains a full-length piece of authentic literature plus poems, songs, and other shorter literature pieces. Book 1 contains a Children's Reference Section. Books 2-8 contain a Writer's Workshop which leads students through the writing process.

Teacher's Edition

The spiral-bound *Teacher's Edition* contains reproduced student pages with complete instructions for presenting each page along with Options for Reaching All Students. Each unit features a planning guide, a list of resources, suggestions for a unit project, *Activity Book* and test answers, and wrap-up activities.

ACTIVITY BOOK

Language Development Activity Book with Standardized Test Practice

The *Activity Book* contains a variety of language practice along with instructions for and practice in taking standardized tests.

Name

Reading Objective 4: Perceive relationships and recognize outcomes in a variety of written texts.

Clues

1. When you take tests, look for special clue words such as *because* or *since*. These words often signal cause-and-effect relationships. Some questions may ask you to predict probable future actions and outcomes.
2. Make sure you know what the question is asking. Reread the passage to find the answer.

Sample

There is a lot of motion in our world. You start an object in motion by using an outside force. A force can be anything that starts an object moving, such as a push or a pull. When it is in motion, an object stays moving until another force stops it.

An object can't have motion without a force since

A. only a force moves

B. a force starts the object moving

C. objects move slowly

D. objects roll away

The correct answer is B. An outside force i

Name

Word Search

Circle these words in the puzzle.

CHEMICALS
GOVERNMENT
FACTORIES
HARMFUL
FARMERS
POLLUTION
FERTILIZER
PESTICIDE
OIL SPILL

53

BLACKLINE MASTER

Teacher's Resource Book

The reproducible pages in the *Teacher's Resource Book* contain scoring rubrics, checklists, and rating scales; graphic organizers; letters to families in Cambodian, Cantonese, English, Hmong, Spanish, and Vietnamese; and language and listening assessments for each chapter of the program.

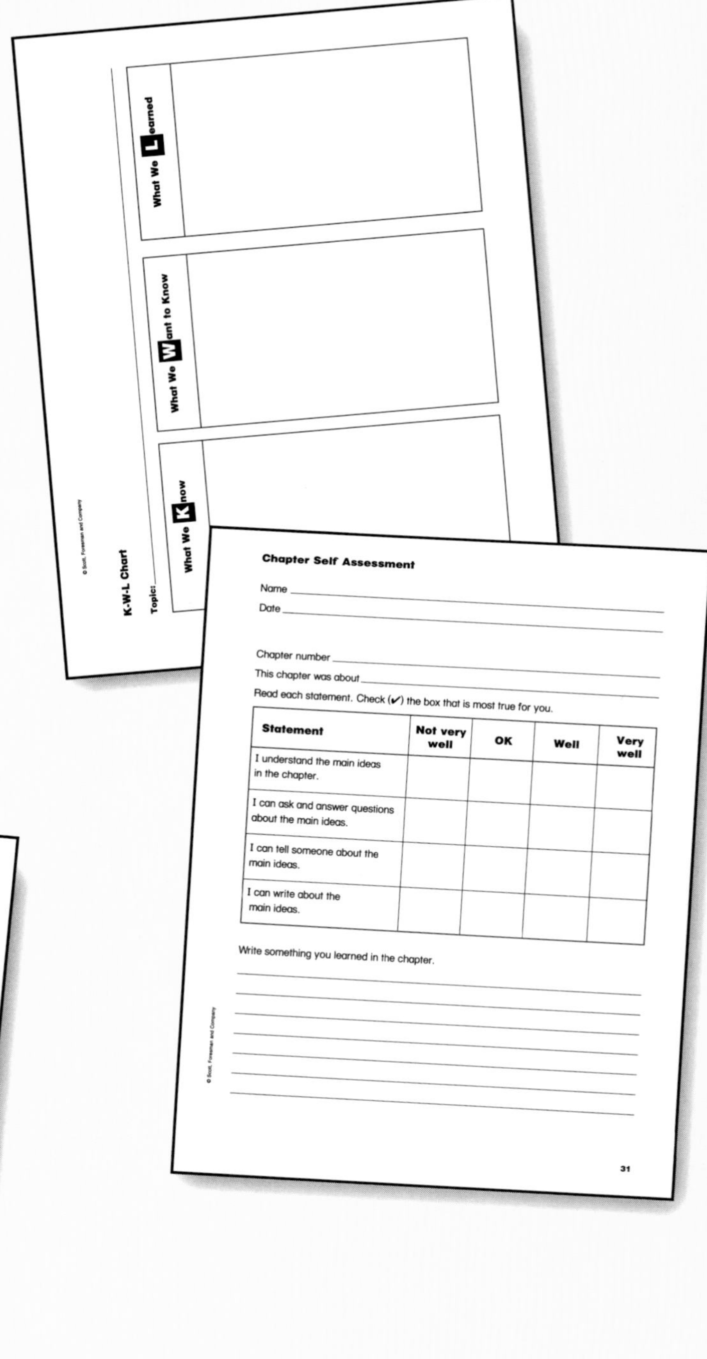

K-W-L Chart

Topic:

What We Know

What We Want to Know

What We Learned

Chapter Self Assessment

Name

Date

Chapter number

This chapter was about

Read each statement. Check (✓) the box that is most true for you.

Statement	Not very well	OK	Well	Very well
I understand the main ideas in the chapter.				
I can ask and answer questions about the main ideas.				
I can tell someone about the main ideas.				
I can write about the main ideas.				

Write something you learned in the chapter.

31

Audio Tapes

Eight audio tapes per level contain all the stories, songs, poems, and rhymes for that book plus a listening assessment for every chapter.

Picture Cards

Seventy-two full-color, labeled cards with 144 pictures can be used to introduce and reinforce vocabulary in a variety of games and exercises.

Videos

The video for each level contains a theme-related sequence that reinforces the language and concepts of each unit in the book.

Writer's Notebook

Writer's Notebook Software helps students explore their knowledge, thinking, and creativity by combining personal journal writing with computer technology. Writing prompts are included for each chapter and each major literature selection.

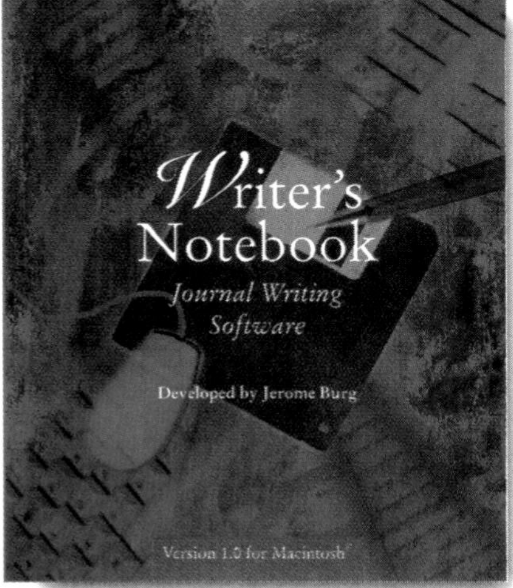

Writer's
Notebook
Journal Writing
Software
Developed by Jerome Burg
Version 1.0 for Macintosh

Newcomer Books

A (Grades 1-2),
B (Grades 3-5),
C (Grades 6-8)

These books, which contain age-appropriate lessons in survival English, were designed to ease new students into English and the American school system.

Write the secret words.

Number code

a	b	c	d	e	f	g	h	i
1	2	3	4	5	6	7	8	9

j	k	l	m	n	o	p	q	r
10	11	12	13	14	15	16	17	18

s	t	u	v	w	x	y	z
19	20	21	22	23	24	25	26

8 15 21 19 5
h o u s e

1. 19 20 18 5 5 20

2. 1 4 4 18 5 19 19

3. 1 18 5 1 3 15 4 5

Make an address book. page 23

PRACTICE 7

ORGANIZATION

The Teacher's Edition

Each level of *ScottForesman ESL* contains six thematic units; each unit contains two related chapters. Each unit of the *Teacher's Edition* contains these features.

Planning Guide

The Planning Guide lists the objectives and the vocabulary focus for each chapter. A chart for each chapter shows the content focus, language awareness objectives, and learning strategies for each lesson in the *Student Book*.

Resources

A list of Resources for each chapter includes Support Materials and Assessment Materials for the unit and a bibliography of books for extended reading and of related technology products.

UNIT 1 • DIGGING UP THE PAST

Planning Guide

Digging Up Fossils

Objectives

Describe dinosaurs.
Tell how scientists learn about dinosaurs.
Tell when dinosaurs lived.
Make fossils in the classroom.
Compare old and new ideas about dinosaurs.

Vocabulary Focus

Paleontology words, such as *fossil, bones, skeleton.*
Words describing dinosaurs, such as *fast, large, meat-eater.*
Words dividing history, such as *era, period.*

Lesson	Content Focus	Language Awareness Objectives	Learning Strategies
Preview pp. 2–3 Tell What You Know.			
Present pp. 4–5 How Do Scientists Learn About Dinosaurs?	Science	**Grammar** Plurals with -s and Irregular Plurals	Use headings.
Practice pp. 6–7 Dinosaur Fossils	Science	**Vocabulary** Idiom *Turn Into*	Recognize patterns.
Practice pp. 8–9 When Did Dinosaurs Live?	Science	**Grammar** *Before* and *After*	Read a chart.
Connect pp. 10–11 You Can Make Fossils.	Science/Art	**Phonics** Consonant *p*, Consonant Blends *pl, pr*	Use action words in directions.
Connect pp. 12–23 *The News About Dinosaurs*	Science/ Literature	**Grammar** Past Tense of the Verb *To Be* **Vocabulary** Antonyms **Grammar** Conjunctions *Or* and *And*	Remember details. Find details.
Connect p. 24 "Seismosaurus"	Science/ Literature	**Vocabulary** Synonyms	
Assess p. 25 Tell What You Learned.			

Resources

Chapter 1

Support Materials

numbers 6, 20, 23, 28, 31, 35, 46, 64

pages 2–11

Unit 1, Digging Up the Past

Side 1
News About the Dinosaurs, pages T12-T23

Side 2
"Seismosaurus," page T24

Writer's Notebook

Assessment Materials

Language Assessment, Blackline Master 40
Listening Assessment, Blackline Master 41

Side 1
Listening Assessment, page T25

Listen carefully. Dr. Paleo has just found some fossils for a new dinosaur. Circle the pictures that show what Dr. Paleo has discovered.

Wow! What a find! These new fossils are very interesting, and they really tell me a lot about my new dinosaur. I'm especially excited about the footprints. They are like big holes in the ground. There are quite a few of them—six in all. Then there are these teeth. They are very sharp! I'm going to have to think about all these fossils carefully to decide what my dinosaur was like.

Newcomer Book C

Survival language for absolute beginners. For overview, see pages xxviii–xxix.

For Extended Reading

Dinosaurs Walked Here and Other Stories Fossils Tell by Patricia Lauber, Bradbury Press, 1987
Learn how fossil bones, teeth, shells, leaf prints, eggs, insects, and animal tracks tell the stories of the earth's mysterious past.
Level: Average

Let's Go Dinosaur Tracking! by Miriam Schlein, Harper Collins, 1991
Tracks tell us all kinds of things about the creatures that made them. Travel along with the energetic characters in this book and discover the fun of being a paleontologist.
Level: Beginning

Living With Dinosaurs by Patricia Lauber, Bradbury Press, 1991
The time is 75 million years ago. The place is prehistoric Montana, which has a seashore. Come on in and discover the wondrous creatures that made this place their home.
Level: Advanced

The New Dinosaur Dictionary by Helen Roney Sattler, Lothrop, Lee & Shepard, 1990
A comprehensive collection of information about dinosaurs will be an excellent classroom resource.
Level: Advanced

Still Wait by Carol Carrick, Houghton Mifflin, 1980
Fifty-foot crocodiles with jaws six feet long have never been seen, but their bones have been found. This is the story of one of those giant crocodiles of long ago.
Level: Advanced

Related Technology

Dinosaur Westwind Media, 1993
Experience a paleontological dig and name a dinosaur.

Unit Project

This optional project is designed to be completed over the two chapters of the unit. Typically, this is a hands-on, cooperative project that results in a product students can share with friends and family. Letters to invite family participation in each project are provided in Cambodian, Cantonese, English, Hmong, Spanish, and Vietnamese. At the end of the project, family and friends are invited to school to share the results.

Activity Book Answers

The *Activity Book* pages for every chapter of the book are reproduced in mini format with the answers in place. Answers to the practice standardized tests can be found on the *Assess* page of each chapter.

Page-by-Page Teaching Suggestions

Student Book pages are reproduced in the *Teacher's Edition* with complete instructions for presenting each page, for developing language awareness, and for modeling learning strategies. *Options for Reaching All Students* suggest activities for beginning and advanced students and mixed-ability groups, as well as ideas for peer tutoring, cooperative learning, and home connections.

Wrap-Up

Following the page-by-page teaching, the Unit Wrap-Up contains suggestions for individual, small group, and class activities based on the unit theme. Suggestions are given for discussing what the students have learned in the unit and for sharing the unit project with family and friends. Signs of Success, a unit checklist, provides a quick way to assess students' progress.

Themes and Topics

The themes and topics for Book 6 of *ScottForesman ESL* are the following.

Unit 1:	**Ideas in Conflict—Digging Up the Past**
Chapter 1:	Digging Up Fossils
Chapter 2:	Digging Up Ancient Objects
Unit 2:	**Challenges—Good Sports**
Chapter 3:	Types of Fitness
Chapter 4:	Olympic Challenges
Unit 3:	**Environment—Oceans**
Chapter 5:	Life Underwater
Chapter 6:	Taking Care of the Oceans
Unit 4:	**Justice—The Ancient Romans**
Chapter 7:	The Roman Empire
Chapter 8:	Volcanoes in History
Unit 5:	**Relationships—The Physics of Fun**
Chapter 9:	What Makes Things Move?
Chapter 10:	The Physics of Roller Coasters
Unit 6:	**Change—Dealing with Change**
Chapter 11:	Handling Stress
Chapter 12:	Getting Information

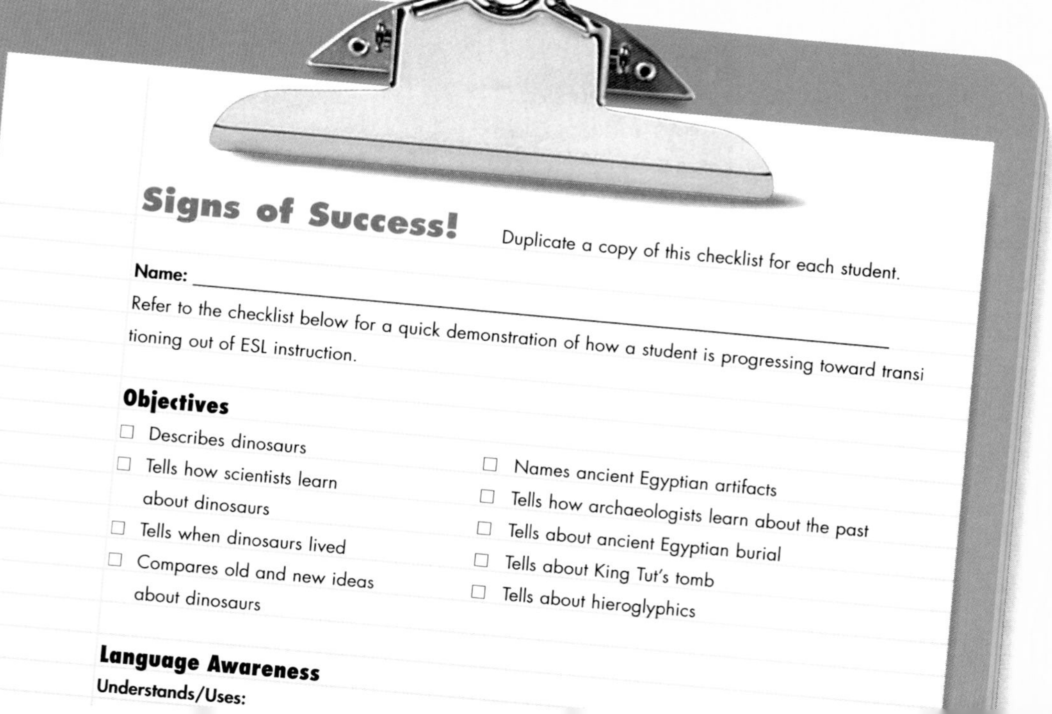

Signs of Success! Duplicate a copy of this checklist for each student.

Name: ______________________

Refer to the checklist below for a quick demonstration of how a student is progressing toward transitioning out of ESL instruction.

Objectives

- ☐ Describes dinosaurs
- ☐ Tells how scientists learn about dinosaurs
- ☐ Tells when dinosaurs lived
- ☐ Compares old and new ideas about dinosaurs
- ☐ Names ancient Egyptian artifacts
- ☐ Tells how archaeologists learn about the past
- ☐ Tells about ancient Egyptian burial
- ☐ Tells about King Tut's tomb
- ☐ Tells about hieroglyphics

Language Awareness

Understands/Uses:

The Lesson Plan

JIM CUMMINS

The five step instructional sequence of each chapter in *ScottForesman ESL* provides the means for teachers to implement effective instructional strategies in ways that affirm ESL students' developing sense of self.

Preview

There is general agreement among cognitive psychologists that we learn by integrating new input into our existing cognitive structures, or schemata. Our prior knowledge and experience provide the foundation for interpreting new information.

In a classroom of English language learners from diverse backgrounds, prior knowledge about a particular topic may vary widely. Simple transmission of the information or skill may fail to connect with the prior knowledge and experience of some students. Other students may have relevant information in their first language but not realize that there is any connection with what they are learning in English.

Every chapter in *ScottForesman ESL* begins with a *Preview* section, designed to activate students' prior knowledge through pictures and brainstorming as a whole class or in small groups or pairs. Finding out what students know about a particular topic allows the teacher to supply relevant concepts or vocabulary that some or all of the students may be lacking but which will be important for understanding the chapter. Building this context permits students to understand more complex language and to pursue more cognitively demanding activities.

In addition to making the learning process more efficient, activating prior knowledge also accelerates academic progress in other significant ways:

- It stimulates students to use the target language.
- It permits teachers to get to know their students as individuals with unique personal histories.
- It creates a classroom in which students' cultural knowledge is expressed, shared, and validated—thereby motivating students to participate more actively in the learning process.

Present

Input in English can be presented orally or through written text. In either case, comprehension can be facilitated through the use of photographs, illustrations, maps, graphs, diagrams, and other graphic organizers such as Venn diagrams, semantic webs, and time lines. This kind of scaffolding enables ESL students to participate effectively in instruction even when their knowledge of the language is still quite limited.

The *Present* section of every chapter in *ScottForesman ESL* introduces language and concepts through a wide variety of scaffolding devices and learning strategies. This linguistic and contextual support gives students access to the language of text, a language very different from the language of interpersonal conversation. In the language of text, the vocabulary usually consists of words that are less frequent than those in everyday conversation; grammatical constructions are more complex because meanings must be made more explicit; and meaning is not supported by the immediacy of context and interpersonal cues (e.g., gestures, intonation). A wide variety of learning strategies is presented to help students become independent interpreters of this language. (See pp. xxi-xxii.)

Academic success depends on students gaining access to and comprehending the language of books and school discourse. *ScottForesman ESL* provides the support students need as they learn school English as a source of comprehensible input.

Practice

Active language use in both oral and written modalities is important for both cognitive and linguistic growth. At a cognitive level, writing about or discussion of complex issues with the teacher and peers encourages students to reflect critically and refine their ideas.

Linguistic growth is stimulated by active language use in at least three ways.

- Students must try to figure out sophisticated aspects of the target language to express what they want to communicate.
- The effort to use language brings home to students (and their teachers) what aspects of language they need assistance with.
- Teachers are given the opportunity to provide corrective feedback to build language awareness and help students see how the language works.

The *Practice* section of every chapter in *ScottForesman ESL* gives students the active language use they need to develop both cognitive and linguistic competencies. Students are also encouraged to express *themselves*; in other words, to explore their own feelings, ideas, and experiences in a supportive context and thereby become more aware of their goals, values, and aspirations.

Among the instructional strategies that encourage this active language use are cooperative learning, drama and role playing, and peer tutoring. All of these strategies are used to promote creative writing and publishing of student work, which are of central importance in accelerating ESL students' academic growth.

Connect

An integrated curriculum crosses subject areas and connects various curriculum components into a meaningful whole. This leads students to a deeper understanding of both the concepts they are learning and the language used to describe those concepts.

The *Connect* section of every chapter in *ScottForesman ESL* gives students practice in applying the language and strategies they are learning to a new area of the curriculum. It also provides the opportunity for students to apply their expanding understanding of language and concepts to the reading of authentic literature. (See pp. xviii-xx.)

Assess

Instruction and assessment are closely linked. Assessment involves monitoring of students' content learning and oral and written language use in order to provide appropriate guidance and feedback to the students.

The *Assess* section of every chapter in *ScottForesman ESL* provides a wide variety of assessment tools. In the Student Book, "Tell What You Learned" checks understanding of content and provides self-assessment. In the Teacher's Edition, "Options for Assessment" provides ideas for language and writing assessment. The Audiotapes and *Teacher's Resource Book* contain a listening assessment for every chapter; the *Teacher's Resource Book* contains additional language assessment; and the *Activity Book* for each chapter contains instructions and practice for standardized tests.

In addition, the *Teachers Resource Book* contains a wide variety of rubrics, rating sheets, checklists, and forms for teacher, peer, and self assessment. (See pp. xxiii-xxv.)

King Tut's Tomb
King Tut lived more than 3,300 years ago. He became king of Egypt when he was 9 years old. He died when he was 18 years old. He lived a short life, but King Tut is one of the most famous pharaohs of all.
In 1922, an archaeologist named Howard Carter discovered King Tut's tomb in the Valley of the Kings.
▲ Howard Carter examining the mummy of King Tut.
32 USE LANGUAGE • SOCIAL STUDIES

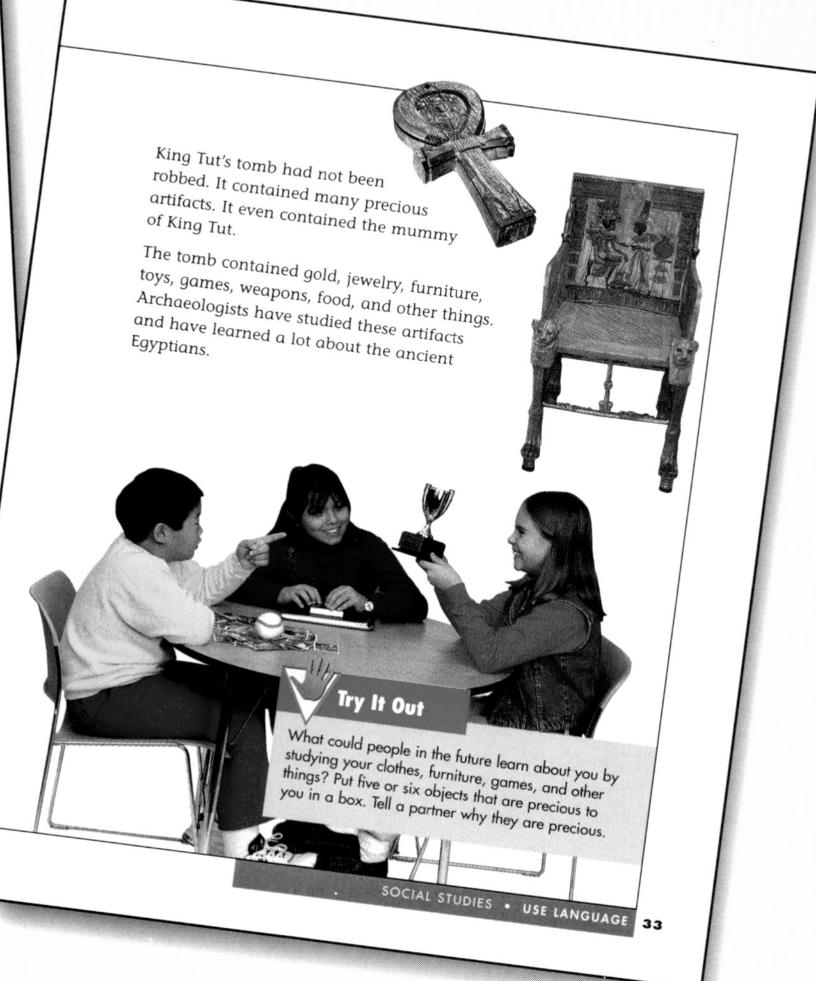

King Tut's tomb had not been robbed. It contained many precious artifacts. It even contained the mummy of King Tut.
The tomb contained gold, jewelry, furniture, toys, games, weapons, food, and other things. Archaeologists have studied these artifacts and have learned a lot about the ancient Egyptians.
Try It Out
What could people in the future learn about you by studying your clothes, furniture, games, and other things? Put five or six objects that are precious to you in a box. Tell a partner why they are precious.
SOCIAL STUDIES • USE LANGUAGE 33

Cognitive Academic Language in ESL Instruction

ANNA UHL CHAMOT & J. MICHAEL O'MALLEY

The Cognitive Academic Language Learning Approach (CALLA) is an instructional model for meeting the academic needs of ESL students in American schools. It is designed to assist ESL students to succeed by providing beginning or transitional instruction in either standard ESL programs or bilingual programs.

The CALLA model includes three components and instructional objectives in its curricular and instructional design:

- topics from the major school subjects,
- the development of academic language skills,
- explicit instruction in learning strategies for both content and language acquisition.

Content subjects are the primary focus of instruction in CALLA. Content, rather than language, drives the curriculum. Language modalities (e.g., listening, speaking, reading, writing) are developed for content-area activities as they are needed, rather than being taught sequentially. Academic language skills can be developed as the need for them emerges from the content. Language skills will be most meaningful when students perceive that they are needed in order to accomplish a communicative or academic task.

There are at least four reasons for incorporating curricular content into the ESL class.

- Students develop important knowledge in all subject areas. Throughout *ScottForesman ESL,* students learn grade level concepts and processes in science, social studies, mathematics, and other academic areas, thus providing a foundation for their content-area classes.
- Students learn the language functions and skills needed for success in content areas. Every lesson of the *Teacher's Edition* of *ScottForesman ESL* suggests language awareness activities designed to strengthen students' abilities to practice these functions and skills.
- Many students exhibit greater motivation when learning content than when they are learning language only. Students in *ScottForesman ESL* are motivated not only by the topics presented but also by knowing that they are developing the concepts and skills associated with science, mathematics, social studies, and literature. They perceive that they are doing "real" schoolwork instead of merely learning English.
- Students learn the strategies necessary for success in curriculum areas. These learning strategies are the mental processes and behaviors students use to access their learning. Extensive suggestions throughout *ScottForesman ESL* provide guidelines for learning strategy instruction. *Academic language* is the language that is used by teachers and students for the purpose of acquiring new knowledge and skills. This kind of language differs in many ways from social language, the language that is used for interaction in social settings. Academic language is more difficult and takes longer to learn than social language. It may be less interactive than social language and may provide fewer context clues, such as gestures, to assist comprehension. Academic language has very specific purposes, including imparting new information, describing abstract ideas, and developing conceptual understanding. These purposes are cognitively demanding, thus increasing the comprehension difficulties students experience.

Academic language consists primarily of the functions needed for authentic academic content. These functions include explaining, informing, justifying, comparing, describing, proving, debating, persuading, and evaluating. To accomplish these functions requires the use of both lower-order and higher-order thinking skills. *ScottForesman ESL* enables students to practice the functions and thinking skills needed to engage in specific content activities. Discrete language elements such as vocabulary, grammatical structures, spelling, and pronunciation are integrated into this practice.

Make a mosaic.

The ancient Romans decorated their homes with mosaics. Mosaics are pictures made with small pieces of stone or glass.

Make your own mosaic.

Things You Need

- a large piece of cardboard
- glue
- a pencil
- scissors
- small pieces of colored paper or colored peas and beans

1. Draw a picture or a pattern on the cardboard. Draw in lines for different colors you want to use.
2. Put some glue on a small area of your drawing. Paste the pieces of paper or the beans onto that area. Repeat this step until your mosaic is filled in.

128 CONNECT LANGUAGE • SOCIAL STUDIES/ART

There are at least five reasons for focusing on academic language skills in the ESL classroom.

- For ESL students, the ability to use academic language effectively is a key to success in grade-level classrooms.
- Academic language is not usually learned outside of the classroom setting.
- Grade-level teachers may assume that all of their students already know appropriate academic language, when, in fact, ESL students in their classes have often acquired only social language skills.
- Academic language provides students with practice in using English as a medium of thought.
- Students may need assistance in using learning strategies with academic language, just as they do with content knowledge and skills.

ScottForesman ESL responds to each of these reasons. In its content-based lessons, both teachers and students use academic language to communicate, analyze, and explain. It provides the exposure students need to develop academic language functions and thinking skills. It prepares students for transition into grade-level classrooms. Throughout the program, guidelines are given for:

- modeling academic language appropriate to content topic;
- providing practice in listening to information and answering higher level questions;
- creating opportunities for using academic language through cooperative activities;
- having students describe, explain, justify, evaluate, and express understanding of and feelings about topics and processes;
- having students read and write in every major curriculum area.

Learning Strategies, the third key element in CALLA instruction, are important for language learning and for learning academic content. Learning strategies are the mental processes and overt behaviors students use to assist their learning. Strategies are taught explicitly in CALLA to help students develop metacognitive awareness of their own learning and to become self-directed learners. Knowing how and when to use learning strategies is especially important for ESL students who are learning both a new language and challenging academic content.

In *ScottForesman ESL,* learning strategies are taught in every lesson. Students are prompted to use various learning strategies for language and content activities. The Teacher's Edition contains suggestions for introducing, modeling, practicing, extending, and assessing learning strategies. (See pp. xxi-xxii.)

ScottForesman ESL incorporates the major principles from CALLA, which are based on cognitive research and learning theory. The CALLA model has been successful in accelerating ESL students' academic achievements in school districts nationwide.

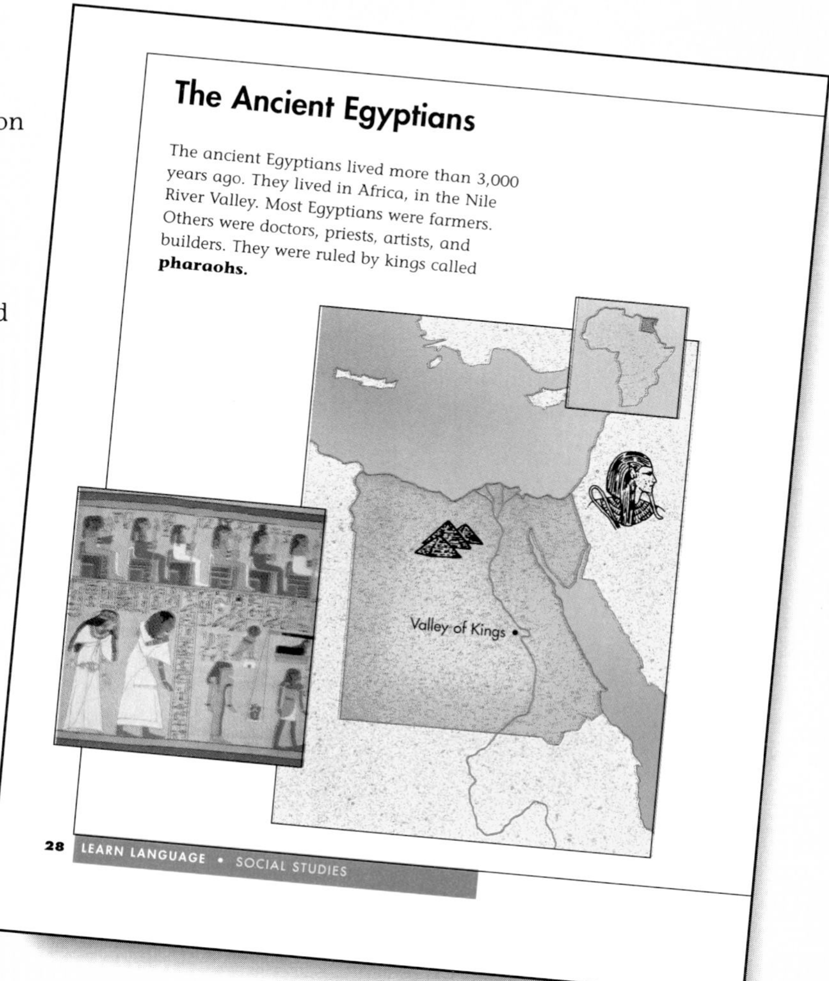

The Ancient Egyptians
The ancient Egyptians lived more than 3,000 years ago. They lived in Africa, in the Nile River Valley. Most Egyptians were farmers. Others were doctors, priests, artists, and builders. They were ruled by kings called **pharaohs.**
Valley of Kings
28 LEARN LANGUAGE • SOCIAL STUDIES

Authentic Literature in ESL Instruction

LILY WONG FILLMORE

How do children acquire those aspects of language knowledge and proficiency that figure in intellectual demanding communication? Few children, whether native speakers of English or learners of English, are fully proficient in this type of language when they first enter school. Children who have had books read to them at home, or who have learned to read in their primary languages, will have some familiarity with the language of written texts. But all will need to develop it further to handle the language demands of school. For most, authentic children's literature such as that appearing in *ScottForesman ESL* is a major source of input for academic language, whether in the native or a second language.

Let us look at a piece of literature, "The Night of the Stars" by Douglas Gutierrez. The story tells of a man who did not like the night because there was no light. He goes to the mountain top from which he thinks night comes and tries to get it to stop obscuring the light of day. But the man is told that nothing can be done, because the light is hidden behind the night. The man thinks about this, and eventually comes up with a solution:

> "Once more he went to the mountain. The night was like an immense awning, covering all things. When at last he reached the highest point on the mountain, the man stood on his tiptoes, and with his finger poked a hole in the black sky. A pinprick of light flickered through the hole. The man who did not like the night was delighted. He poked holes all over the sky. Here, there, everywhere, and all over the sky little points of light appeared. Amazed now at what he could do, the man made a fist and punched it through the darkness. A large hole opened up, and a huge round light, almost like a grapefruit, shone through. All the escaping light cast a brilliant glow at the base of the mountain and lit up everything below . . . the fields, the street, the houses. Everything."

Now one might wonder how a piece of literature such as this one, offering a mythic account of how the stars and the moon came to be, might figure in the interpretation of language such as that found in a science text. Isn't an account like this one contradictory to the science materials that the students are reading? The answer is this: texts like this delightful piece of literature give children access to the language itself. The language of stories gives access to vocabulary, structures, phrasings, and discourse processes that children, whether they are native speakers of English or learners of English, must eventually learn. Let us look at what the readers of "The Night of the Stars" will find as input in this passage:

Vocabulary: Among the words the readers will encounter are nouns such as *mountain, awning, point, tiptoes, pinprick, light,* and *glow*; verbs such as *reach, flicker, shine, poke, amaze,* and *delight*; adjectives such as *brilliant, immense, huge, round,* and *highest*; and adverbials such as *everywhere* and *below*. Notice that this vocabulary is specific and precise—it tells the reader where the man went and what he did and more. It tells the reader about the event in language that evokes images and feelings and qualities.

According to some experts, vocabulary size and breadth are crucial determinants of reading and overall academic performance. School-age children acquire much of the new vocabulary they learn by reading books. Children reading a text such as the one we are looking at may or may not learn all the words that they do not already know. Whether they do or do not understand every word is not usually critical to the understanding of the story. But having read it, they will have encountered the words used in it. This gives them a passing acquaintance with the ones that are new to them, and of how they are used in this particular text. The next time they encounter these words, they will have some usage information available in memory that may just help them figure out what they mean. The point is, it takes a great deal of reading to learn the words that are crucial to the understanding of texts with real meaning payloads.

Structure: Our story has a relatively simple past narrative—all of the events take place in past time. Most of the verbs are in the simple past tense. But the time relations among the parts of this story are not all that simple. The first two sentences might appear to be a simple sequence of events: The man went to the mountain. Once there, he checks out the night-time sky, and likens it to an immense awning. It is somewhat more complex than that, however.

"Once more" indicates that the man has gone to the mountain before, and "he went to the mountain" describes what he was doing in this event, but not necessarily the completion of the activity. The next sentence—"the night was like an immense awning, etc.," is a description of what the man perceived or thought while he was on his way to the mountain, rather than what he saw once he arrived. How do readers know that? Because in the next sentence, the temporal clause, "when at last he reached the highest point on the mountain" tells them that only then was the journey completed. This then suggests that the second sentence describes the man's observations before the completion of the journey. Does this make any difference to the readers? It probably doesn't—at least in terms of their understanding and enjoyment of the story. However, when readers figure out or are helped to see how the events described in this story relate, they pick up a bit more information about how English works with respect to temporal relations.

Background knowledge: Just as readers must apply their linguistic knowledge to the interpretation of the texts they read, so too must they make use of their knowledge of the world and their prior experiences in reading. No text contains every bit of information needed to understand it fully. Writers generally assume a level of prior language knowledge and cultural and real world experience when they write. If they believe that the intended readers are unlikely to be familiar with certain words or concepts, they will define or discuss them. Otherwise, they simply presuppose that the readers will be able to apply their knowledge of language and of how it works to the reading and interpretation of the text, and that they will draw on their knowledge of the world and on their experiences to fill in the gaps in the text. The ideal reader then is one who has the cultural background, experience, and linguistic knowledge to do just what the writer hopes the readers of the text will be able to do when they read it.

That fact presents a special problem to educators who are concerned with finding or preparing appropriate instructional materials and texts for children from diverse cultural and linguistic backgrounds. How can these children deal with texts that are as complex as those used for mainstream students? How can they possibly comprehend materials that presuppose cultural background, knowledge, and experiences that they don't already have? Shouldn't they be given materials that are culturally familiar, that deal with the world as they know and have experienced it?

I will argue that the education of children irrespective of their background would be greatly diminished if educators were to choose materials for them that were in any way narrowed or lowered in level because of putative deficiencies in the children's backgrounds. Such decisions must take into account the role authentic and challenging materials play in building children's background knowledge and in supporting language development. Authentic literature gives English learners access to the vocabulary, grammar, and discourse conventions of the language they are learning. Children also gain the very kind of background knowledge that they need to have to deal with materials they read in school from the literature and textbooks they have already read. This argument might seem rather circular, at first glance. How do children get the background they need in the first place? And what kind of useful background could they possibly get from a story like "The Night of the Stars"?

Consider the cognitive skills it takes to make sense of such scientific ideas as supernovas or the time it takes light to travel from a star to earth. How does anyone understand concepts like these without actually having experienced them? How do scientists and theorists come up with ideas like brown dwarfs and black holes? I will argue that this kind of thinking begins with the development of the imagination. One way to develop the imagination is by reading and thinking about stories like "The Night of the Stars." The ability to conceptualize possible worlds is not entirely unrelated to the ability to create and consider impossible ones, of the sort involved in that story. There may be nothing in our story that leads directly to knowledge that will enable a reader to understand a newspaper story about the discovery of a new black hole. Yet, the reader who, as a child, was able to imagine someone standing on top of a mountain, poking holes in the nighttime sky thereby creating stars will no doubt find it easier than one without such early experiences.

Authentic texts such as those in *ScottForesman ESL* are perhaps the most reliable and consistent source of academic English input children can have. However, texts do not by themselves reveal how the language in them works, nor do they provide many clues as to what the words that appear in them mean or how they are used. Such materials work as input when teachers do the following:

- provide the support learners need to make sense of the text;
- call attention to the way language is used in the text;
- discuss with learners the meaning and interpretation of sentences and phrases within the text;
- point out that words in one text may have been encountered or used in other places;
- help learners discover the grammatical cues that indicate relationships such as cause and effect, antecedent and consequence, comparison and contrast, and so on.

In short, teachers help written texts become usable input—not only by helping children make sense of the text, but by drawing their attention, focusing it, in fact, on how language is used in the materials they read. Done consistently enough, the learners themselves will soon come to notice the way language is used in the materials they read. When they can do that, everything they read will be input for learning.

Presenting Stories in ESL Instruction

GEORGE A GONZÁLEZ

Reading authentic literature presents special challenges to ESL students. Some students may understand details, but not see the big picture. Others may grasp the gist of a story, but not have the language to explain their understanding.

Sentences

Choosing and presenting the important sentences of a story can convey the most significant and salient ideas of the selection and represent critical story elements. These sentences can form a story map that includes related story elements, such as characters, events, problems, feelings and opinions, setting, time, and conclusion. The important sentences can also convey knowledge and information such as linguistic patterns.

Words

Children who cannot understand and use a wide repertoire of words in their oral language often encounter problems with reading comprehension. For these children, idioms and words that represent new concepts or new labels can be especially challenging. Throughout *ScottForesman ESL* are suggestions for words and terms to be presented to these students.

The following six methods for oral teaching of new vocabulary in context help make words meaningful, relevant, and enjoyable.

Personalization

Relate the word to a situation familiar to children.

example: <u>bad mood</u>

The baby is in a <u>bad mood;</u> he is not happy; he has been crying all day.

Demonstration

Demonstrate the action implied by the word, stating what you are doing as you do it.

example: <u>kneel</u>

I <u>will kneel</u> on the floor; I <u>am kneeling</u> on the floor; I <u>have knelt</u> on the floor.

Dramatization

Act out a situation illustrating the meaning of several words.

example: <u>shake</u>, <u>fall</u>, <u>shuffled</u>, <u>collapsed</u>, <u>couch</u>

Exemplification

Recite several examples of sentences in which a particular word or expression could be used.

example: <u>unpleasant</u>

The weather today is <u>unpleasant</u>. It is <u>unpleasant</u> to be scolded. The odor near the garbage cans was <u>unpleasant</u>.

Illustration

Guide children to draw pictures or to manipulate picture cards that depict the objects or concepts.

Definition

Define words or terms through description followed by a repetition of the word.

example: <u>decision</u>

I have decided to go to Nashville to visit friends.
It is my <u>decision.</u>

Sounds

Children who cannot perceive, discriminate, or produce the sounds of English may experience difficulties with word attack skills and spelling. Throughout *ScottForesman ESL*, the "Language Awareness" sections contain lessons on pronunciation and sound/letter relationships that are exemplified in the text. As students become acquainted with the sounds in context, they will develop a sensitivity to and an awareness of the English sound system and at the same time improve their comprehension.

The *ScottForesman ESL* Audio Tapes afford the opportunity for children to listen to the sounds of English within the context of authentic literature—over and over again.

Gestures and Body Language

Children who cannot express in English their ideas about a story will often be able to show their understanding by pantomiming elements of the plot or the emotions of the characters. Help them by pointing out the body language and facial expressions of characters in the illustrations. Demonstrate with students the way people in different cultures use gestures and other paralinguistic language. Compare, for example, the ways people wave hello or good-by, the distance people stand from one another when conversing, and the ways people show deference or respect.

Activities throughout *ScottForesman ESL* suggest ideas for helping students use pantomime, gestures, and body language to help convey what they want to get across in English.

LEARNING STRATEGIES

Learning Strategies in ESL Instruction

ANNA UHL CHAMOT

Learning strategies are actions or thoughts that students can apply *on their own* to a challenging task. Learning strategies can be applied with language-related tasks, such as listening to or reading a text, speaking, or writing, or with tasks related to subject matter content, such as information and processes in science, mathematics, social studies, literature, art, and music.

ScottForesman ESL integrates learning strategies throughout and provides guidelines for teaching the strategies and helping students develop an awareness of their own learning processes. The intent of the learning strategies instructional component of *ScottForesman ESL* is to help all students develop their ability to learn independently.

ScottForesman ESL teaches students how to apply a number of useful learning strategies for school subjects. Students are encouraged to make use of their own background knowledge through discussions and brainstorming activities. They are taught to make a plan for carrying out an activity, for monitoring themselves as they work, and for evaluating their own achievements. Other learning strategies taught in *ScottForesman ESL* include predicting, making inferences, classifying, summarizing, note-taking, using picture clues, cooperating with classmates, and asking questions for clarification. Each chapter of *ScottForesman ESL* presents learning strategies that assist in preparing for a task (INTO strategies), for working on a task (THROUGH strategies), and for evaluating and extending a task (BEYOND strategies).

ScottForesman ESL integrates learning strategies instruction into each part of the learning process. The *Teacher's Edition* provides specific suggestions for presenting learning strategies throughout the *ScottForesman ESL* instructional sequence.

Preview

The purpose of this step in learning strategies instruction is to help students become more aware of their own learning processes, thus developing their metacognition, or understanding of their own thinking. The teacher begins by helping students identify their prior knowledge about strategies already familiar to them. The types of strategies students are already using can be quite diverse, especially in the case of students whose previous schooling has been in other countries. Most students are quite interested in finding out about their classmates' varying approaches to learning, and teachers can capitalize on this natural interest in suggesting new learning strategies to try.

Ways to identify students' prior knowledge about learning strategies include class or small group discussions in which students compare their individual approaches to working on a particular task, such as reading a story or following directions for a science experiment. More formal ways to identify existing learning strategies are through student interviews, questionnaires, or personal journals.

Present

In presenting a learning strategy, teachers need to be explicit and direct in their explanation, as this helps students develop awareness of strategic thinking. One of the most effective ways to present a strategy is through teacher modeling, in which teachers think aloud about their own use of the strategy. *ScottForesman ESL* provides examples of think-aloud scripts *(Model a Strategy)* which teachers can use or adapt to demonstrate different strategies.

In addition to modeling the strategy, teachers should also name it, tell students how it will help them learn, and explain when to use it. Naming a strategy makes it more concrete for students and helps focus class discussions about strategy use. Posters of learning strategies associated with easily remembered icons are helpful in reminding students about the names and uses of the strategies they are learning.

Can a taller coaster give you a longer ride?

The chart shows the height and length of four roller coasters. Compare these numbers.

Roller Coaster	Place	Height of First Hill	Length of Track
American Eagle	Six Flags, IL	39 meters	1,400 meters
Colossus	Six Flags, CA	35 meters	1,300 meters
The Twister	Blitch Gardens, CO	30 meters	900 meters
The Riverside Cyclone	Riverside Park, MA	33 meters	1,000 meters

Answer these questions:

1. How long is the longest roller coaster?
2. How long is the roller coaster with the shortest first hill?
3. How does the height of the hill affect the length of the track?

182 CONNECT LANGUAGE • SCIENCE/MATH

Students also need to understand that the purpose of learning strategies is to provide them with tools that they can use to help themselves in learning. Finally, teachers need to be sure that students understand that knowing *when* to use a strategy is as important as knowing *which* strategy to use.

Practice

As with any type of process or procedure, students need ample practice opportunities in applying learning strategies to their language development and subject matter learning. Learning strategies can be practiced with any task or activity that presents a challenge or a problem to be solved—very easy tasks can be accomplished successfully without consciously using learning strategies!

The rich variety of activities in *ScottForesman ESL* provides extensive opportunities for practicing the learning strategies presented. For example, stories, poems, and informational articles provide opportunities for using different kinds of reading strategies. Projects, reports, experiments, and other hands-on activities can be enhanced with planning, monitoring, and self-assessment strategies. Group discussions and cooperative learning activities are excellent vehicles for developing strategic competence in cooperation and questioning for clarification.

Connect

When students extend a strategy to a new context or connect two or more strategies in a unique approach to a problem, they are well on their way to becoming independent and self-regulated learners. Teachers can assist this process by asking students to brainstorm new ways to use a strategy or combine strategies and by suggesting that they try a strategy in another class or in a setting outside of school.

Another activity that connects learning strategies to students' own lives is to have students interview family members about their learning strategies or teach a favorite learning strategy to a younger sibling. When upper grade students read biographies, they may find it interesting to look for clues about the types of learning strategies that a famous person may have used. Finally, students can learn about strategies used by athletes, artists, dancers, musicians, actors, writers, and other contributors to students' life experiences.

Assess

Students need to evaluate how well different strategies are working for them so that they can build their own repertoire of effective learning strategies. Debriefing discussions after practicing one or more strategies can help students think through their use of strategies and pinpoint moments when a strategy really worked—or did not work—for them.

More formal ways for students to evaluate their own strategy use is through checklists, learning logs, or journals in which they describe their use of different learning strategies. Some teachers have also found that having students compare their performance on similar tasks with and without using a learning strategy is an effective strategy evaluation activity. The most important contribution that teachers can make in student self-evaluation of strategies is to provide many opportunities for students to reflect on, discuss, and write about their insights into their own learning processes.

Learning strategies are fun to teach and fun to learn. Students enjoy talking about their thinking, and teachers gain deeper insights by listening to their students' thoughts. Students who have already developed effective learning strategies should be encouraged to share them with classmates and to continue using them even as they are acquiring additional strategies. Eventually, students will take the responsibility for choosing their own personal repertoire of learning strategies and making their own decisions about when and how to apply the strategies.

The approach to learning strategies instruction in *ScottForesman ESL* helps students deal with challenging tasks, gain an appreciation of their own learning process, and develop both their language skills and their knowledge and understanding of content area subjects.

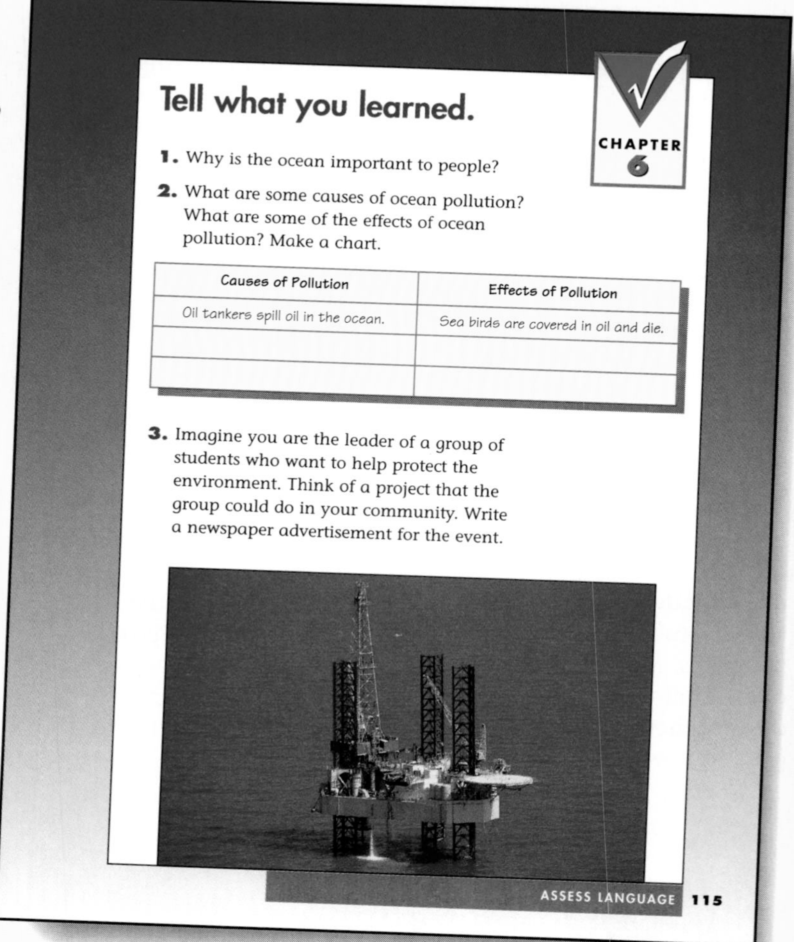

Tell what you learned.

CHAPTER 6

1. Why is the ocean important to people?
2. What are some causes of ocean pollution? What are some of the effects of ocean pollution? Make a chart.

Causes of Pollution	Effects of Pollution
Oil tankers spill oil in the ocean.	Sea birds are covered in oil and die.

3. Imagine you are the leader of a group of students who want to help protect the environment. Think of a project that the group could do in your community. Write a newspaper advertisement for the event.

ASSESS LANGUAGE 115

Authentic Assessment in ESL Instruction

J. MICHAEL O'MALLEY

Assessment is authentic when it enables students to communicate successfully their strengths and educational needs, and when the results can be used to improve instruction based on accurate knowledge of student progress. Such assessment mirrors good classroom instruction, and it gives students ongoing feedback that enables them to reflect on their accomplishments, identify future learning needs, and develop goals and strategies for attaining them. As a result, this type of assessment empowers students to become self-directed learners and empowers teachers to use assessment information for instructional improvement.

The authentic assessment activities in *ScottForesman ESL* are integrated with and complement instruction. Because the assessment is part of instruction, it should not require significant additional time to prepare and conduct. Students do not need to stop learning for authentic assessment to occur.

The approach to assessment taken in *ScottForesman ESL* addresses four major issues: *who* conducts the assessment, *when* assessment occurs, *what* is assessed, and *how* assessment is accomplished. Each of these is important to ensure that assessment is authentic:

- Who—Assessment is conducted by students, teachers, and parents working in partnership to improve instruction and learning.
- When—Assessment is ongoing and enables both teachers and students to maintain a continuous record of student progress.
- What—The processes and strategies involved in learning as well as the products of learning are assessed.
- How—The assessment is designed to assist students with all levels of proficiency in English to communicate what they know and can do.

Three critical components of authentic assessment in *ScottForesman ESL* are the use of *scoring rubrics, benchmark standards,* and *informed judgment.*

Scoring rubrics are holistic scoring scales that identify what students know and can do at different levels of performance on classroom tasks. Typically, there may be four or five levels of proficiency or achievement defined on a scoring rubric.

Benchmark standards identify clearly for students and teachers the expected levels of performance based on specific tasks. That is, you might determine that all students should be performing at level 4 or 5, the highest levels of performance, on oral proficiency. With rubrics and benchmarks, students understand the nature of the performance expected as they progress through each level of proficiency and achievement toward mastery.

Informed judgment is based on scoring rubrics and benchmark standards. The judgment may be expressed by the teacher, the student, peers, or parents. This aspect of authentic assessment assures that responsibility for educational judgments about students is assumed by those in the classroom and others most closely associated with the child.

The assessment procedures in *ScottForesman ESL* assess students' knowledge through all four language skills—listening, speaking, reading, and writing. And because *ScottForesman ESL* integrates language development with literature and other academic content—including math, science, and social studies—the assessment provides information on the knowledge and procedural skills students use in all subjects.

Assessment activities in *ScottForesman ESL* are contained in the *Student Book,* the *Teacher's Edition,* the *Activity Book,* and the *Teacher's Resource Book. ScottForesman ESL* also provides sample forms, checklists, rubrics, and other guidelines to be used or adapted for assessment. (For additional forms, checklists, and rubrics, see *Authentic Assessment for English Language Learners: Practical Applications for Classroom Teachers* by J.M. O'Malley & L. Valdez Pierce, Addison-Wesley [forthcoming].)

A key element in authentic assessment is the use of multiple assessments, providing students with varied opportunities to demonstrate their learning and accomplishments. *ScottForesman ESL* includes all of the following: *teacher observation, self-assessment, peer assessment, performance assessment,* and *portfolio assessment.*

Teacher Observation

Teachers often make daily classroom observations to check on a student's progress or to plan for instruction. *ScottForesman ESL* provides suggestions on how to conduct observations through sample checklists, rating scales, and forms on which to note student behaviors that are directly relevant to the lesson.

Checklists identify specific behaviors to be observed and provide a form on which to indicate that the behavior occurred or how frequently it occurred. Examples of behaviors that might appear on a checklist are: scanning to find information while reading, using various cues for word meaning in context, making an outline or graphic organizer to plan an essay, or explaining successfully a problem-solving approach to a peer. A checklist of unit objectives appears at the end of each unit of *ScottForesman ESL.*

Rating scales are similar to checklists but provide an opportunity to indicate the degree to which a particular behavior occurred. For example, you can use a 3-point scale to indicate the level of control the student exhibited over specific aspects of writing, such as sentence formation—consistent control, reasonable control, or little or no control. A rating scale might also enable you to indicate if the student behavior occurred independently or with peer or adult support. Several examples of rating scales appear in the *ScottForesman ESL Teacher's Resource Book.*

Anecdotal records are notes describing behaviors that provide a rich indication of student progress when reviewed over the course of a school year. You can describe a specific behavior along with the learning materials, setting, student grouping, and time and place the behavior occurred. An example of a form for an anecdotal record appears in the *ScottForesman ESL Teacher's Resource Book.*

ScottForesman ESL provides varied procedures to observe student learning and performance as learning is taking place. You can identify individual students to observe in advance and plan the occasion when you will conduct the observation. In this way, you can manage the observations efficiently.

Self-assessment

The importance of self-assessment cannot be overstated. Self-assessment is the key to student empowerment because it gives students an opportunity to reflect on their own progress toward instructional objectives, to determine the learning strategies that are effective for them, and to develop plans for their future learning. With self-assessment, students are active participants in deciding what and how much to learn and in setting the criteria by which their learning is evaluated.

To encourage self-assessment, you should share scoring rubrics with students and elicit their input on improving the rubrics. You can also share *anchor papers,* i.e., samples of student work that represent each point on the scoring rubric. After students review the anchor papers, they can then rate their own work or the work of their peers. Additional ways to encourage self-assessment include *K-W-L Charts, Reading Logs, Journals,* and *Self Ratings.*

K-W-L Charts are charts students complete using three columns to reflect what they *Know* about a topic before an instructional activity, what they *Want* to know from the lesson, and what they *Learned* from the lesson after its completion. The rows on the chart can reflect specific topics covered. For example, a lesson on Plants We Eat might cover Parts of the Plant, Types of Plants, and How Plants Grow. Suggestions for K-W-L Charts appear throughout *ScottForesman ESL.*

Reading Logs are records students keep of the reading they have completed. These might be categorized by genre and include the title, author, topics, and date on which the reading was completed, as well as the student's personal response to the reading and important concepts or information to remember. A Reading Log form appears in the *ScottForesman ESL Teacher's Resource Book.*

Tell what you learned.

CHAPTER 10

1. How do roller coasters work? What makes them move?
2. How can friction and gravity affect how a roller coaster works?
3. You are going to plan a roller coaster. How would it look? Draw a picture. Explain how it works.
4. Tell about one thing you learned about motion that you did not know before.

ASSESS LANGUAGE 191

Journals are students' narrative diaries of what they have learned in each subject area. The journal may be kept daily and might mention the topics, what was difficult, what was easy, what strategies helped in learning, and what the student wants to know next.

Self Ratings are the students' use of a scoring rubric to rate their own performance. For example, the use of a rubric for writing might include composing, style, sentence formation, word usage, and mechanics (spelling, capitalization, and punctuation).

ScottForesman ESL provides opportunity for self assessment at the end of each chapter in the *Student Book* (page 35 in the *Teacher's Resource Book*). In addition, the *Teacher's Resource Book* contains a variety of forms and logs that students can use to monitor their own progress (pages 10-14).

Peer Assessment

In addition to rating their own products and learning processes, students can rate the work of their peers as readers, writers, and learners. Students can rate the oral and written work of their peers, identifying areas that can be improved as well as areas that are presented effectively. These ratings can be based on scoring rubrics that students develop themselves or on rubrics provided by teachers. Students may need both guidance and assurance that peer feedback will be stated positively. One of the main advantages of self and peer assessment is that students internalize the standards for learning more readily than they would from teacher assessment alone. Another advantage concerns time management for teachers, who need only spot-check student performance rather than spend time rating every single product from each student. See page 18 in the *ScottForesman ESL Teacher's Resource Book* for a sample peer assessment form.

Performance Assessment

This type of assessment includes exhibitions of student-constructed work such as written products, science demonstrations, oral presentations, retellings, pair interactions, discussions, drawings, and graphic organizers. Some student products can be exhibited in the classroom, presented and described by the student or by groups that worked together, or documented by video or audio recorder. The student work can be evaluated by the teacher, the student, and by peers using a scoring rubric that reflects different levels of performance. Rubrics used in performance assessment typically integrate language and content in a holistic scoring procedure that may also reflect the processes used in solving problems or in reaching conclusions.

Portfolio Assessment

A portfolio is a collection of student work that shows growth over time. The portfolio may contain written products, worksheets, self-assessments, or audio tapes. It is useful to document learning, to identify student strengths and needs, to help in making instructional decisions, and to provide evidence of student progress in student and parent conferences. The keys to a successful portfolio are student involvement and self-assessment. Students should play a major role in deciding what goes into the portfolio and how the work is evaluated, so they can feel ownership over their learning.

There are at least three different types of portfolios: a *collections portfolio,* containing virtually everything the student has produced; a *showcase portfolio,* focusing on the student's best work; and an *assessment portfolio,* illustrating growth with respect to specific instructional objectives. *ScottForesman ESL* encourages the use of assessment portfolios, a type which is efficient for assisting students and teachers in planning for future learning activities. For all portfolios, we suggest using a *portfolio cover sheet* that identifies specific portfolio entries, the date of each entry, and the type of each entry (e. g., written product, tape, peer assessment, checklist). A variety of forms and checklists are provided in the *Teacher's Resource Book* for teacher, self, and peer portfolio assessment (pages 15-20).

The multiple forms of assessment included in *ScottForesman ESL* provide students with varied opportunities to communicate what they know and can do, what learning processes work effectively for them, and what progress they have made over time. Such opportunities put students in a better position to manage their learning and to become self-directed learners.

To take advantage of assessment information, you need to periodically review the student portfolios, your own anecdotal records and ratings, and other evidence of student progress in light of goals established for instruction. The scoring rubrics and benchmark standards are essential parts of authentic assessment that give you indications of how successful students have been in learning and what worked and did not work in your own instruction. Use this information in planning your instructional activities, in student conferences, and in communicating with parents. You can also use it to assist in placement decisions, to communicate with other teachers, to report to administrators, and to anticipate the results of end-of-year testing. By using the assessment information in *ScottForesman ESL* effectively, you can help to ensure that all your students enjoy maximum learning success!

Home/School Connections in ESL Instruction

CAROLYN KESSLER

Parents are children's first teachers; the home the first learning community. Here children acquire their first language and develop a world view shaped by the community of which they are a part. Their experiences as they grow in this community provide a wealth of knowledge about what they believe, value, do in daily encounters, and what they perceive about how the world around them works. As children whose home language is other than English enter the schooling process, they not only meet new teachers and a different community, but often a new world view. Connecting home and school in light of this linguistic and cultural diversity is a challenge for both parents and teachers.

ScottForesman ESL provides the means for teachers and parents to work together collaboratively as co-educators of their children. Educating children so that they can succeed academically in an English-speaking environment is the goal of this collaboration.

Home-school partnerships as developed in *ScottForesman ESL* integrate life at home with that of the school in a "community-building" approach. In this approach, collaborative work between children and parents at home finds an audience at school. The teacher's role is to draw on the funds of knowledge that children have from their home and life experiences and to connect what happens inside the classroom to what happens outside. Under these conditions learning English takes on real meaning.

This community-building approach encourages students to develop their own voices as they interact with others, including family and community members. The home-school connection draws extensively on resources from the home. Among them are the support and encouragement parents give for their children's educational undertakings, frequent parent-child conversations, the exchange of ideas and information about concrete situations or problems children experience, and taking action to solve problems.

Because of the power of family stories in transmitting cultural values and attitudes that can contribute to school success, *ScottForesman ESL* encourages the telling of family stories. In this participatory approach, teachers learn about the community with which their students are identified and work towards building communities of learners in their classrooms where cultural and linguistic differences brought from home are understood and valued.

In the *ScottForesman ESL* community-building approach, the many dimensions of a student's life, including culture and the social context of the home and community, are viewed as rich resources for learning. Teachers value, use, and build on children's prior knowledge through tapping into the funds of knowledge that learners bring to school.

Children from diverse backgrounds have a wealth of cultural capital—experiences, knowledge, attitudes, beliefs, aspirations, and skills that are passed from one generation to another. Activities designed to incorporate children's cultural capital in the classroom validate the home culture. Approaches and strategies, however, that recognize and build on culturally different ways of learning and seeing the world rely on teachers making efforts to know about and understand the socio-cultural contexts of their students' lives. When efforts are made, teachers are in a much stronger position to join parents as full partners in their children's schooling.

ScottForesman ESL provides many opportunities for the development of this partnership. Each unit of the program suggests a unit project to be carried out by the students as a class. Letters to family members inviting their participation in the project are provided in six different languages (Cambodian, Cantonese, English, Hmong, Spanish, and Vietnamese). At the completion of each project families are invited to visit the classroom to see what the children have accomplished.

In addition, *ScottForesman ESL* provides suggestions throughout each chapter for ways to build community. These suggestions include:

- children reading aloud at home to parents in either the home language or English;
- children carrying out research with family members on their family's social history through interviews of parents, grandparents, and other family members;
- parents and children collaborating on writing projects, such as publishing books about their family history, making timelines of family history, making a map of family migrations, keeping portfolios of their work together;
- families telling stories that transmit family beliefs, cultural values, attitudes, aspirations, self-images;
- children telling their stories at school, sometimes in their first language with explanations given in English by the children or a bilingual staff member or volunteer;
- teachers inviting parents to school to read a book in their home language or provide a presentation drawing on some particular area of interest or expertise.

Families are key participants in the academic success of children learning English. When families join in a partnership with the school, learning communities can develop in which the culture of hope, possibility, and promise can flourish.

BIBLIOGRAPHY

Anderson, R.C., and P. Freebody. "Vocabulary Knowledge" in J. T. Guthrie, ed. *Comprehension and Teaching: Research Reviews*. International Reading Association, 1981.

Auerbach, Elsa R. *Making Meaning, Making Change*. Delta Systems, 1992.

Bachman, L.F., & A.S. Palmer. "The Construct Validation of Self-ratings of Communicative Language Ability." *Language Testing* 6 (1), 1989.

Bartlett, F. *Remembering*. Cambridge University Press, 1932.

Brown, J.D. "Classroom-centered Language Testing." *TESOL Journal* 1(4), 1992.

Chamot, A.U., & J.M. O'Malley. *The CALLA Handbook: Implementing the Cognitive Academic Language Learning Approach*. Addison-Wesley, 1994.

Clemmons, J., et al. *Portfolios in the Classroom, Grades 1-6*. Scholastic Professional Books, 1993.

Cummins, Jim, & Dennis Sayers. *Brave New Schools: Challenging Cultural Illiteracy Through Global Learning Networks*. St. Martin's Press, 1995.

Cummins, Jim. *Negotiating Identities: Education for Empowerment in a Diverse Society*. California Association for Bilingual Education, 1996.

Cummins, Jim. "Linguistic Interdependence and the Educational Development of Bilingual Children." *Review of Educational Research*, 49 (2), 1979.

El-Dinary, P.B. "Framework for Strategies Instruction." Available from Language Research Projects, Georgetown University, Washington, DC.

Enright, D. Scott, & Mary Lou McCloskey. *Integrating English: Developing English Language and Literacy in the Multilingual Classroom*. Addison-Wesley, 1988.

Fathman, A.K., M.E. Quinn, & C. Kessler. *Teaching Science to English Learners, Grades 4-8*. National Clearinghouse for Bilingual Education, 1992.

Fillmore, C.J. "Ideal Readers and Real Readers" in D. Tannen, ed. *Analyzing Discourse: Text and Talk. Georgetown Round Table on Languages and Linguistics 1981*. Georgetown University Press, 1982.

Freeman, David E., & Yvonne S. Freeman. *Between Worlds: Access to Second Language Acquisition*. Heinemann, 1994.

Gándara, P. *Over the Ivy Walls: The Educational Mobility of Low Income Chicanos*. State University of New York Press, 1995.

Genesee, Fred, ed. *Educating Second Language Children: The Whole Child, the Whole Curriculum, the Whole Community*. Cambridge University Press, 1994.

Glazer, S.M., & C.S. Brown. *Portfolios and Beyond: Collaborative Assessment in Reading and Writing*. Christopher-Gordon, 1993.

Hays, C.W., R. Bahruth, & C. Kessler. *Literacy con cariño: A Story of Migrant Children's Success*. Heinemann, 1991.

Hudelson, Sarah. *Write On: Children Writing in ESL*. Prentice Hall Regents, 1989.

Kessler, Carolyn, ed. *Cooperative Language Learning: A Teacher's Resource Book*. Prentice Hall Regents, 1992.

Larsen-Freeman, Diane, & Michael H. Long. *An Introduction to Second Language Acquisition Research*. Longman, 1991.

Lightbown, Patsy, & Nina Spada. *How Languages Are Learned*. Oxford University Press, 1993.

McCaleb, Sudia P. *Building Communities of Learners: A Collaboration Among Teachers, Students, Families, and Community*. St. Martin's Press, 1994.

Miller, G. "How School Children Learn Words" in F. Marshall, ed. *Proceedings of the Third Eastern States Conference on Linguistics*. The Ohio State University, 1987.

Ogle, D. "K-W-L Group Instruction Strategy" in A.S. Palincsar, et al., eds. *Teaching Reading as Thinking*. Association for Supervision and Curriculum Development, 1986.

O'Malley, J.M., & A.U. Chamot. *Learning Strategies in Second Language Acquisition*. Cambridge University Press, 1990.

O'Malley, J.M., & L. Valdez Pierce. *Authentic Assessment for English Language Learners: Practical Applications for Classroom Teachers*. Addison-Wesley, (forthcoming).

Pressley, M., V. Woloshy, & Associates. *Cognitive Strategy Instruction That Really Improves Children's Academic Performance*, 2nd ed. Brookline Books, 1995.

Richard-Amato, Patricia A., & Marguerite Ann Snow. *The Multicultural Classroom: Readings for Content-area Teachers*. Longman, 1992.

Rigg, Patt, & Virginia G. Allen, eds. *When They Don't All Speak English: Integrating the ESL Student into the Regular Classroom*. National Council of Teachers of English, 1989.

Routman, R. *Invitations: Changing as Teachers and Learners K-12*. Heinemann, 1994.

Rumelhart, De.E. "Schemata: The Building Blocks of Cognition" in Spiro, R.J., B.C. Bruce, & W.J. Brewer, eds. *Theoretical Issues in Reading Comprehension*. Erlbaum, 1980.

Scarcella, Robin. *Teaching Language Minority Students in the Multicultural Classroom*. Prentice Hall Regents, 1990.

Short, D.J. "Assessing Integrated Language and Content Instruction." *TESOL Quarterly*, 27 (4),1993.

Spangenberg-Urbschat, Karen, & Robert Pritchard, eds. *Kids Come in All Languages: Reading Instruction for ESL Students*. International Reading Association, 1994.

Sternberg, R.J., and J.S. Powell. "Comprehending Verbal Comprehension." *American Psychologist* 8, 1983.

Tierney, R.J., M.A. Carter, & L.E. Desai. *Portfolio Assessment in the Reading-Writing Classroom*. Christopher-Gordon, 1991.

Yancey, K. B. *Portfolios in the Writing Classroom*. National Council of Teachers of English, 1992.

Professional Associations

National Association for Bilingual Education, 1220 L Street NW, Suite 605, Washington, DC 20005

National Center for Research on Cultural Diversity and Second Language Learning, Center for Applied Linguistics, 1118 22nd Street NW, Washington, DC 20037

Teachers of English to Speakers of Other Languages, 1600 Cameron Street, Suite 300, Alexandria, VA 22314-2751

Newcomer Book C was designed for students in grades 6, 7, and 8 who are new to the English language. All of the activities in this book represent real-life situations centered around school themes that are age- and grade-level appropriate. Pictures, games, and opportunities for artistic creativity stimulate communication and motivate students to use language and vocabulary in a variety of settings. The activities provide many opportunities for students to work in small groups or with partners to facilitate cooperation and establish a community atmosphere.

Each lesson is divided into four types of activities: *Preview/Present* allows students to focus on situations they are familiar with that will activate prior knowledge of words, concepts, and language. Prior to using this book, review simple directions at the beginning of each lesson and model how to find the correct page or how to use a pencil when necessary. Then begin the lesson by focusing students' attention on the illustration and by reading the lesson title aloud to them. Have students say all they can about each picture on the first page of each lesson using as many words as they know. Model the new words and language by showing students pictures or real items. Use TPR to model new vocabulary by saying sentences such as "Point to the (pencil)."

Present/Practice and *Practice* give students the opportunity to practice the new language. Model the directions and the activities, then have partners complete the activities.

Use *Assess* to check understanding and to review or reteach any material students may have found difficult. These activities review key vocabulary as well as provide opportunities for students to write about themselves. Self-evaluation objectives give students opportunities to checkmark the objectives they feel they have successfully mastered.

Build on students' language development by allowing them to practice conversations and vocabulary words. See the Options labeled *Beginning* throughout this Teacher's Edition for additional activities.

Lesson 1 *My Class*

Preview/Present page 1

Tell what you know and *Name the items.* Encourage students to talk about the picture. Have students act out the conversation in groups. Show picture cards or realia to present the vocabulary. Have students identify items in their classroom.

Present/Practice page 2

Say the numbers. Help students read and say the number words. Have them practice counting with partners.

Write the numbers. Say the numbers. Model the activity for students. Then have students complete it with partners.

How many? Count the items in the picture. Write the number words. Have students count the chairs in the picture *(five).* Have them count the objects. Continue, having students count classroom objects with partners.

Practice page 3 and page 21

Count the items in your classroom. List classroom objects on the board. Have students count how many of each item is in the classroom. Have partners make their own lists.

Ask a friend. What do you have? Have students choose classroom objects and act out the conversation with partners.

Play the matching game. Have students cut out the pictures on page 21. Have partners place their cards face down and mix them. Each student will choose two cards. When the numbers match, they can keep the cards if they can say "I have (four) (books) and (four) (chairs)." The student with the most cards at the end of the game wins.

Assess page 4

Read and model the activities. Have students complete them independently.

Lesson 2 *About Me*

Preview/Present page 5

Tell what you know and *Name the items.* Encourage students to talk about the picture. Have students practice naming the vocabulary with partners.

Present/Practice page 6

Say the alphabet. Present the alphabet by using alphabet flash cards. If students need additional help recognizing and writing the alphabet, use the Blackline Masters on pages xxx and xxxi as practice.

Say the numbers. Help students read and say the number words. Have them practice counting from 11 to 21.

What numbers? Write and say. Help them fill in the missing numbers. Have them practice counting to 26.

Draw a line. Help students read the words and decide where they go on the form. Have partners complete the activity.

Ask a friend. Write. Draw a student form on the board, and fill out the information about yourself. Have students fill out the forms with partners.

Practice page 7 and page 23

Write the secret word. Read the number code with students. Write an example on the board, and help students write the secret word. Have partners complete the code.

Make an address book. Show students a completed address book from page 23. Model the language, and have students work in small groups.

Assess page 8

Read and model the activities. Have students complete them independently.

Lesson 3 *On Time*

Preview/Present page 9

Tell what you know and *What time is it? Say the times.* Encourage students to talk about the picture. Have students act out the conversation. Use a toy clock to model the times. Have students practice saying the times in pairs.

Present/Practice page 10

Say the colors. Have students identify objects in the classroom by name and color. Have students practice saying the color words with partners.

Say the shapes. Show items in the shapes of the shape vocabulary. Have students identify classroom objects by name, shape, and color with partners.

Write and say the times. Help students say the times on the clocks. Have students complete the activity with partners.

Circle the word. Have partners complete the activity.

Practice page 11 and page 25

Draw and color. Make a pattern. Draw a pattern on the board and help students complete it. Have students complete the activity with partners.

Measure the shapes. Write the numbers. Draw a shape on the board. Measure it and write the measurements in inches next to it. Have students cut out the ruler on page 25 and complete the activity with partners.

Play the matching game. Model the activity using the cards on the page 25. Have students cut out the cards, mix them up, and place them facedown on a table or desk. Partners take turns choosing two cards. If they match, he or she must say the time, then keep the cards. The student with the most cards at the end of the game wins.

Assess page 12

Read and model the activities. Have students complete them independently.

Lesson 4 *My Week*

Preview/Present page 13

Tell what you know and *Say the days of the week.* Encourage students to talk about the picture. Use a calendar to present the days of the week.

Present/Practice page 14

Say the months. Have students practice saying the months. Talk about any important dates or holidays they may know. Teach the rhyme: "Thirty Days Have September."

It's Wednesday. Put the pictures in order. Help students decide which picture came first. Have them put the pictures in chronological order with partners.

Practice page 15 and page 27

Circle the word. Help students read the days and months. Help them decide which word is missing from the sequence. Have students complete the activity with partners.

Write. Use the words in the box. Model the activity. Have students talk about the pictures and read the words in the box. Have partners complete the activity.

Make a schedule. Have students cut out and complete the schedules. Have them compare and contrast their schedules with partners. They may want to tape their schedules to their notebooks for reference.

Assess page 16

Read and model the activities. Have students complete them independently.

Lesson 5 *My School*

Preview/Present page 17

Tell what you know. Encourage students to talk about the picture and read the sentences. Walk them through school and point out places like those in the pictures.

Present/Practice page 18

Say the times. Use a toy clock to practice the times one thirty through twelve thirty. Have students practice saying the times with partners.

Who are they? Say. Help students identify the people. If possible, introduce actual school personnel.

Circle the word. Help them identify the places. Have partners complete the activity.

Practice page 19 and page 29

Write the word. Help students identify the pictures by comparing them to the picture on page 17. Have them complete the activity with partners.

Who are the people in your school? Write names of school personnel on the board and read them aloud. Then have partners complete the activity.

Write about your classes. Help students read the column titles and complete one item orally before completing the activity.

Play the game. Help students read the words and identify the pictures on page 29. Have them cut out the game board and cards. Use small objects (paper clips, erasers) as game pieces. Place the cards in a stack. Students take turns choosing a card and identifying the items or completing the command. If correct, they move the number of spaces shown on the card. The student to reach finish first wins.

Assess page 20

Read and model the activities. Have students complete them independently.

Name: ______________________________

A A

a a

B B

b b

C C

c c

D D

d d

E E

e e

F F

f f

G G

g g

H H

h h

I I

i i

J J

j j

K K

k k

L L

l l

M M

m m

Name: ______________________________

N N n n

O O o o

P P p p

Q Q q q

R R r r

S S s s

T T t t

U U u u

V V v v

W W w w

X X x x

Y Y y y

Z Z z z

Planning Guide

Digging Up Fossils

Objectives

Describe dinosaurs.

Tell how scientists learn about dinosaurs.

Tell when dinosaurs lived.

Make fossils in the classroom.

Compare old and new ideas about dinosaurs.

Vocabulary Focus

Paleontology words, such as *fossil, bones, skeleton.*
Words describing dinosaurs, such as *fast, large, meat-eater.*
Words dividing history, such as *era, period.*

Lesson	Content Focus	Language Awareness Objectives	Learning Strategies
Preview pp. 2–3 Tell What You Know.			
Present pp. 4–5 How Do Scientists Learn About Dinosaurs?	Science	**Grammar** Plurals with *-s* and Irregular Plurals	Use headings.
Practice pp. 6–7 Dinosaur Fossils	Science	**Vocabulary** Idiom *Turn Into*	Recognize patterns.
Practice pp. 8–9 When Did Dinosaurs Live?	Science	**Grammar** *Before* and *After*	Read a chart.
Connect pp. 10–11 You Can Make Fossils.	Science/Art	**Phonics** Consonant *p*, Consonant Blends *pl, pr*	Use action words in directions.
Connect pp. 12–23 *The News About Dinosaurs*	Science/ Literature	**Grammar** Past Tense of the Verb *To Be* **Vocabulary** Antonyms **Grammar** Conjunctions *Or* and *And*	Remember details. Find details.
Connect p. 24 "Seismosaurus"	Science/ Literature	**Vocabulary** Synonyms	
Assess p. 25 Tell What You Learned.			

Digging Up Ancient Objects

Objectives

Name ancient Egyptian artifacts.

Tell how archaeologists learn about the past.

Tell about ancient Egyptian burial.

Tell about King Tut's tomb.

Tell about hieroglyphics.

Vocabulary Focus

Names of artifacts, such as *furniture, toys, weapons.*

Archaeology words, such as *explore, photograph, study.*

Words about ancient Egypt, such as *mummy, pharaoh, pyramid, hieroglyphics.*

Lesson	Content Focus	Language Awareness Objectives	Learning Strategies
Preview pp. 26–27 Tell What You Know.			
Present pp. 28–29 The Ancient Egyptians	Social Studies	**Phonics** Letters *f* and *ph*	
Practice pp. 30–31 The Pharaohs' Tombs	Social Studies	**Grammar** Past Tense	Use diagrams for meaning.
Practice pp. 32–33 King Tut's Tomb	Social Studies	**Grammar** Expressions *Years Old/ Years Ago*	
Connect pp. 34–35 Hieroglyphics	Social Studies/ Language Arts	**Writing** Numbers	
Connect pp. 36–37 New Discovery in Egypt Announced	Social Studies/ Reading	**Grammar** Quantity Words *All, Most, Many, Several*	Keep track of chronolgy.
Connect p. 38 "The Crocodile"	Social Studies/ Literature	**Phonics** Rhyme.	
Assess p. 39 Tell What You Learned.			

Resources

Chapter 1

Support Materials

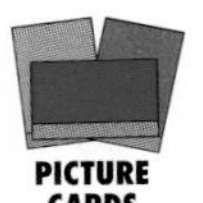
PICTURE CARDS

numbers 6, 20, 23, 28, 31, 35, 46, 64

ACTIVITY BOOK

pages 2–11

VIDEO

Unit 1, Digging Up the Past

RED TAPE

Side 1

News About the Dinosaurs, pages T12-T23

RED TAPE

Side 2

"Seismosaurus," page T24

DISK

Writer's Notebook

Assessment Materials

BLACKLINE MASTER

Language Assessment, Blackline Master 40

Listening Assessment, Blackline Master 41

WHITE TAPE

Side 1

Listening Assessment, page T25

Listen carefully. Dr. Paleo has just found some fossils for a new dinosaur. Circle the pictures that show what Dr. Paleo has discovered.

Wow! What a find! These new fossils are very interesting, and they really tell me a lot about my new dinosaur. I'm especially excited about the footprints. They are like big holes in the ground. There are quite a few of them—six in all. Then there are these teeth. They are very sharp! I'm going to have to think about all these fossils carefully to decide what my dinosaur was like.

Newcomer Book C

Survival language for absolute beginners. For overview, see pages xxviii–xxix.

For Extended Reading

Dinosaurs Walked Here and Other Stories Fossils Tell by Patricia Lauber, Bradbury Press, 1987

Learn how fossil bones, teeth, shells, leaf prints, eggs, insects, and animal tracks tell the stories of the earth's mysterious past.

Level: Average

Let's Go Dinosaur Tracking! by Miriam Schlein, Harper Collins, 1991

Tracks tell us all kinds of things about the creatures that made them. Travel along with the energetic characters in this book and discover the fun of being a paleontologist.

Level: Beginning

Living With Dinosaurs by Patricia Lauber, Bradbury Press, 1991

The time is 75 million years ago. The place is prehistoric Montana, which has a seashore. Come on in and discover the wondrous creatures that made this place their home.

Level: Advanced

The New Dinosaur Dictionary by Helen Roney Sattler, Lothrop, Lee & Shepard, 1990

A comprehensive collection of information about dinosaurs will be an excellent classroom resource.

Level: Advanced

Still Wait by Carol Carrick, Houghton Mifflin, 1980

Fifty-foot crocodiles with jaws six feet long have never been seen, but their bones have been found. This is the story of one of those giant crocodiles of long ago.

Level: Advanced

Related Technology

Dinosaur Westwind Media, 1993

Experience a paleontological dig and name a dinosaur.

Chapter 2

Support Materials

pages 12–21

Side 2

"The Crocodile," page T38

Writer's Notebook

Assessment Materials

Language Assessment, Blackline Master 42

Listening Assessment, Blackline Master 43

Side 1

Lesson Text

Here is a pyramid in Egypt. Draw an artifact inside the pyramid. The artifact could be a toy, furniture, or something else you learned about in this chapter. Also draw a mummy in the pyramid. Remember that mummies were the way ancient Egyptians preserved the dead bodies of people. Now check your drawing. You should have drawn an artifact and a mummy in the pyramid.

For Extended Reading

Ancient Egypt by Laurence Santrey, Troll Associates, 1985

A nonfiction book about life in ancient Egypt and the accomplishments of its civilization.

Level: Beginning

The Children of Egypt by Matti A. Pitkänen, Carolrhoda Books, Inc., 1991

A nonfiction book about the children of today's Egypt and their connection to their civilization's past.

Level: Advanced

Egyptians by Rachel Wright, Franklin Watts, 1992

A nonfiction book about ancient Egyptian culture, including crafts that represent the time.

Level: Beginning

Mummies, Masks, & Mourners by Margaret Berrill, E.P. Dutton, 1989

Discover how archaeologists and historians act as detectives, finding clues to reconstruct ancient civilizations.

Level: Average

The Pharaohs' Curse by Susan Dudley Gold, Crestwood House, 1990

A nonfiction book about the life and customs of the pharaohs, how they were discovered, and legends that surround them.

Level: Average

The Riddle of the Rosetta Stone by James Cross Giblin, HarperTrophy, 1990

The history behind and the importance of the discovery of this key to ancient Egypt.

Level: Advanced

Related Technology

Ancient Egypt and the Middle East, Queue Inc., 1994

Checks for understanding and keeps records for each student.

Project

Museum Displays

This optional project can be completed over the next two chapters. In this project, students will create museum displays consisting of models of dinosaurs and pictures of ancient Egyptian artifacts. See the Unit Wrap-Up, page T39a, for more ideas on sharing the project with family members.

What You'll Need

Collect the following items for the project:

Art Materials
- clay
- paints
- markers
- ruler
- tape

Research Materials
- books with pictures of dinosaurs
- a dinosaur dictionary
- books with pictures of ancient Egypt

Picture Sources
- old magazines, such as travel magazines
- photocopiable materials, from the library, on ancient Egypt or travel to Egypt
- materials about Egypt from travel agencies

Display Materials
- cardboard on which to mount photos
- table on which to display dinosaur models

Beginning the Project

Explain to students that they will be making museum displays as part of the unit about the work of scientists who study dinosaurs and ancient peoples. They will be using clay to make models of dinosaurs. They will be obtaining pictures of ancient Egyptian artifacts to put on display. Discuss museum displays with students. If possible, take a trip to a natural history or historical museum to see the way that items are displayed.

Home Involvement

Send the Letter to the Family, Blackline Masters 34–39, to families to explain that students will be taking part in a project in connection with their study of scientists who study the past. Encourage family members to supply art materials for the project. Also encourage family members to discuss the project with their children during the course of the unit.

Preparing the Displays

Have students work in groups to look through materials on dinosaurs. Have the groups choose a dinosaur and make a model of it out of clay and paint it. Encourage groups to choose dinosaurs from different periods shown in the chart in the Student Book. Also suggest that students keep the idea of scale in mind. Have the groups work together to decide on a method of display. One possibility would be a horizontal time line based on the chart in the Student Book. Make sure that they include a labeling system of some sort. Encourage students to make a card of information about each dinosaur to put into the display.

At the same time, students can be collecting pictures of artifacts from ancient Egypt. Students can look at old magazines, travel brochures, library resources, and other such sources to obtain pictures of Egyptian artifacts. Groups of students may want to focus on a specific tomb, such as King Tut's tomb, or a historic site, such as a temple. Have students decide what to include, organize the pictures, and prepare displays with labels.

Daily Discussion

Take a few minutes each day for discussion to practice vocabulary learned in conjunction with the museum displays. At the end of the unit, have students summarize the information they learned about dinosaurs, ancient Egyptians, and the work of scientists. Here are some key concepts about the two areas of study covered in the unit.

Paleontology

- Scientific study
- A paleontologist studies the forms of life in prehistoric or geologic times through the analysis of plant and animal fossils.
- A principal source of information in reconstructing the earth's history

Archaeology

- Scientific study
- An archaeologist studies material evidence, such as buildings, tools, and pottery, of human life and activities.
- A principal source of information about prehistoric and ancient cultures

See page T39a for ideas about sharing the museum displays with families and friends when the unit is completed.

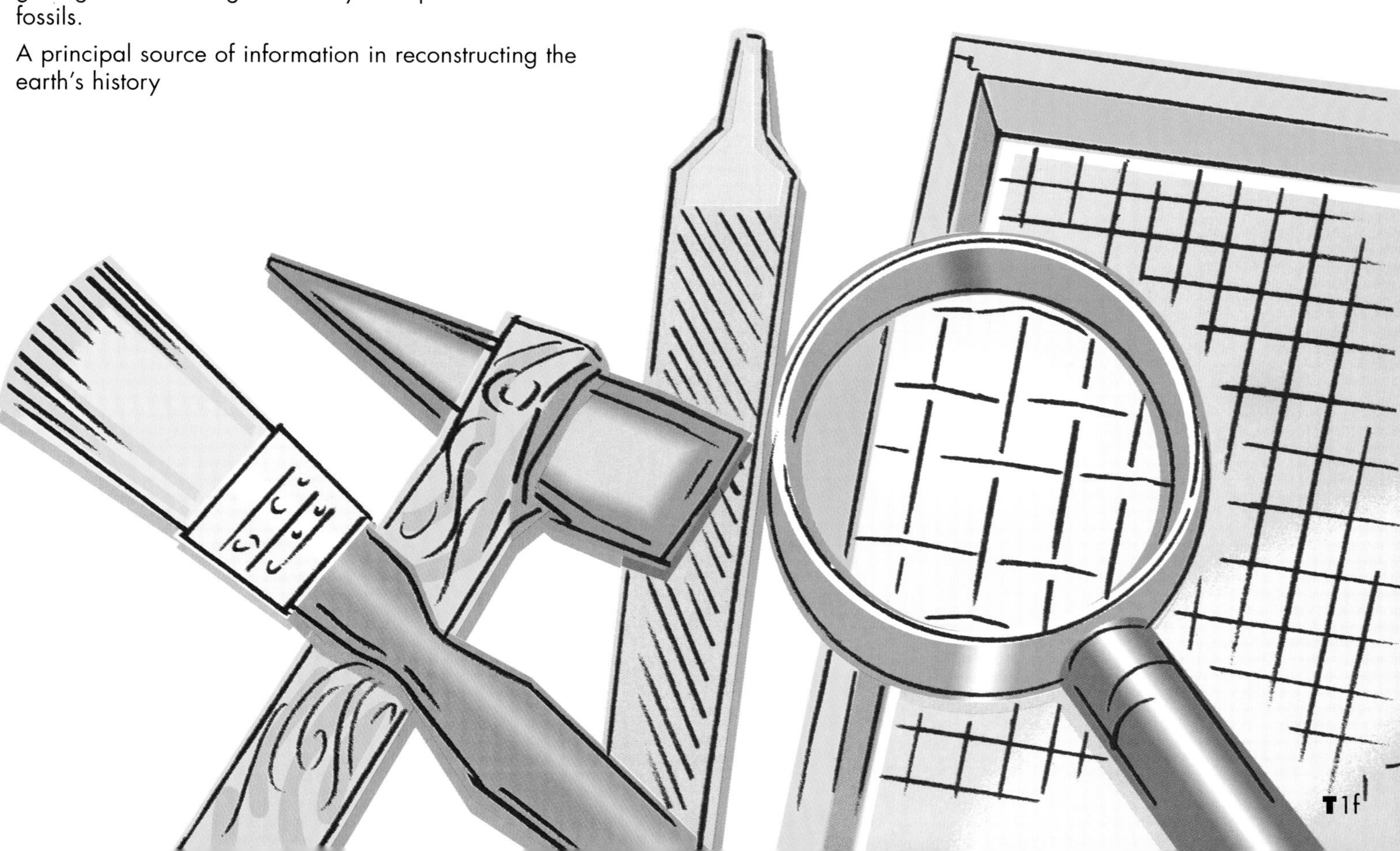

Activity Book

Chapter 1

Name ______________________

Classifying Body Parts

Write each word under the correct heading.

bones	neck	claws
teeth	feet	skeleton
legs	tail	eyes

Hard Body Parts	Soft Body Parts
bones	legs
teeth	neck
claws	feet
skeleton	tail
	eyes

Which body parts could turn into fossils?
hard body parts (or the hard body parts listed above)

What did this dinosaur eat? Plants or meat? meat

Why do you think so? Answers will vary.

Name ______________________

More Than One

Use these words to complete the sentences. Change the words so they say *more than one*.

fossil	scientist	bone	skeleton	tooth	foot

1. The bones are fossils. (fossil)
2. Dinosaurs have many bones. (bone)
3. Some scientists study fossils. (scientist)
4. Meat-eaters have sharp teeth. (tooth)
5. Scientists use dinosaur bones to make skeletons. (skeleton)
6. Some dinosaurs walked on four feet. (foot)
7. Plant-eaters have teeth. (tooth)
8. Some dinosaurs walked on two feet. (foot)

Name ______________________

Dinosaur Puzzle

Fill in the puzzle with the words in the dinosaur footprint.

bones	faster	fossils	teeth
dinosaur	feet	meat-eaters	slow
eggs	footprints	skeleton	

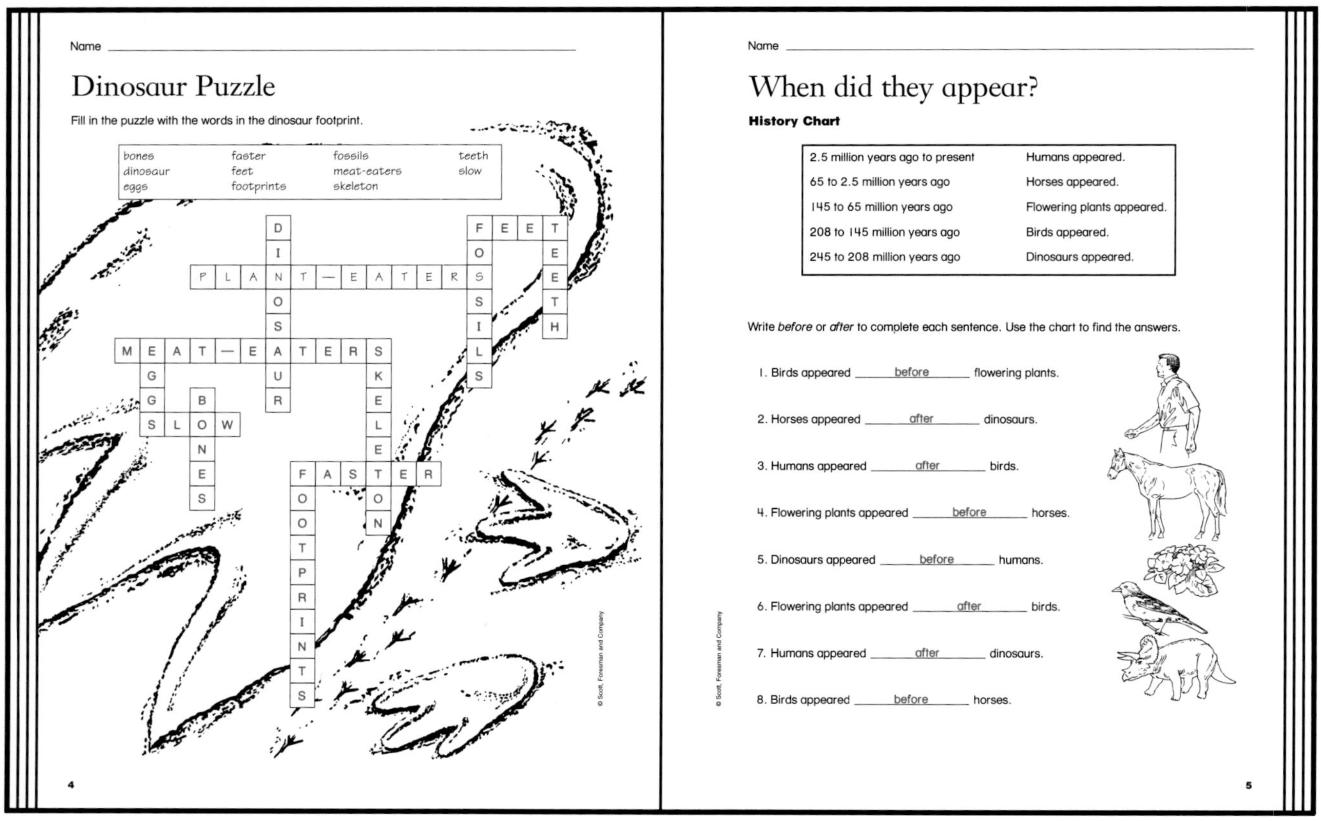

Name ______________________

When did they appear?

History Chart

2.5 million years ago to present	Humans appeared.
65 to 2.5 million years ago	Horses appeared.
145 to 65 million years ago	Flowering plants appeared.
208 to 145 million years ago	Birds appeared.
245 to 208 million years ago	Dinosaurs appeared.

Write *before* or *after* to complete each sentence. Use the chart to find the answers.

1. Birds appeared before flowering plants.
2. Horses appeared after dinosaurs.
3. Humans appeared after birds.
4. Flowering plants appeared before horses.
5. Dinosaurs appeared before humans.
6. Flowering plants appeared after birds.
7. Humans appeared after dinosaurs.
8. Birds appeared before horses.

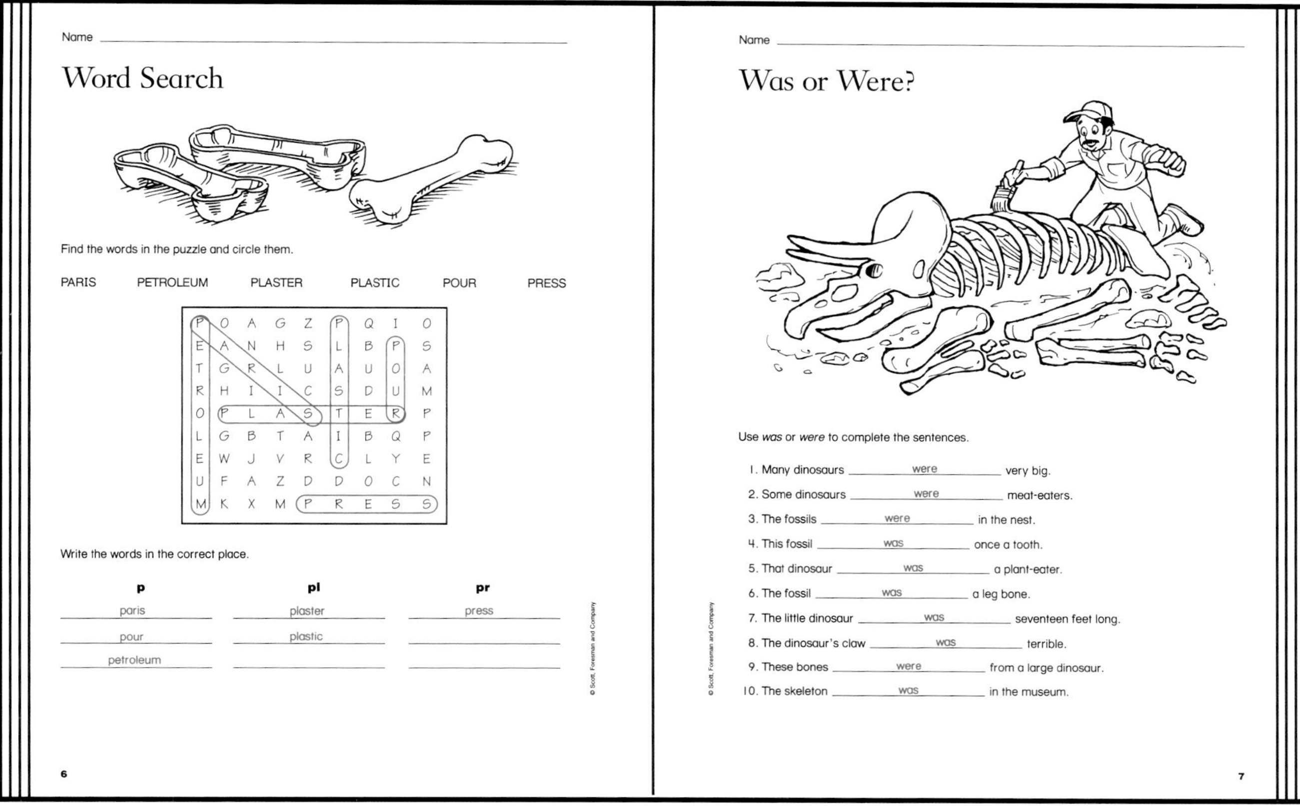

Name

Word Search

Find the words in the puzzle and circle them.

PARIS PETROLEUM PLASTER PLASTIC POUR PRESS

P	O	A	G	Z	P	Q	I	O
E	A	N	H	S	L	B	P	S
T	G	R	L	U	A	U	O	A
R	H	I	I	C	S	D	U	M
O	P	L	A	S	T	E	R	P
L	G	B	T	A	I	B	Q	P
E	W	J	V	R	C	L	Y	E
U	F	A	Z	D	D	O	C	N
M	K	X	M	P	R	E	S	S

Write the words in the correct place.

p	pl	pr
paris	plaster	press
pour	plastic	
petroleum		

Name

Was or Were?

Use *was* or *were* to complete the sentences.

1. Many dinosaurs were very big.
2. Some dinosaurs were meat-eaters.
3. The fossils were in the nest.
4. This fossil was once a tooth.
5. That dinosaur was a plant-eater.
6. The fossil was a leg bone.
7. The little dinosaur was seventeen feet long.
8. The dinosaur's claw was terrible.
9. These bones were from a large dinosaur.
10. The skeleton was in the museum.

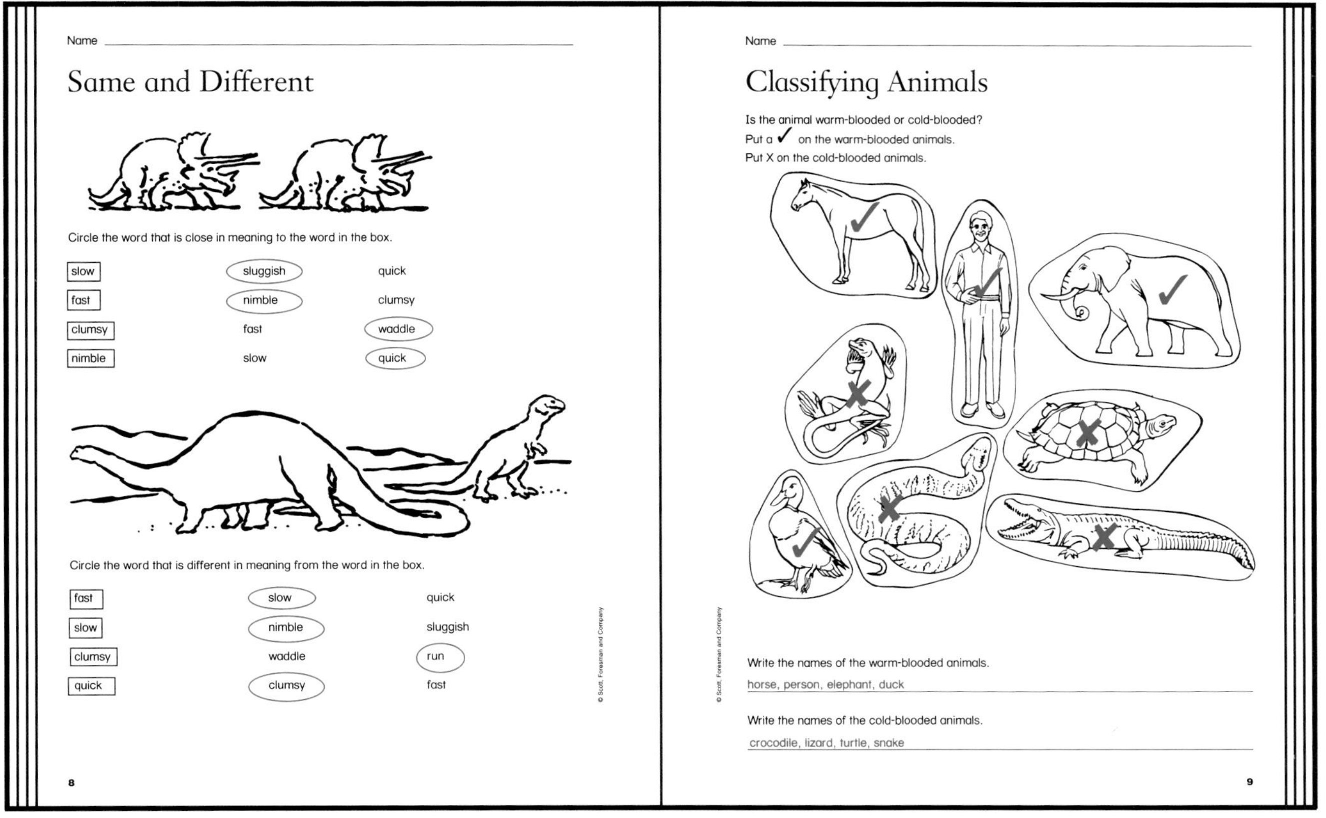

Name

Same and Different

Circle the word that is close in meaning to the word in the box.

slow	sluggish	quick
fast	nimble	clumsy
clumsy	fast	waddle
nimble	slow	quick

Circle the word that is different in meaning from the word in the box.

fast	slow	quick
slow	nimble	sluggish
clumsy	waddle	run
quick	clumsy	fast

Name

Classifying Animals

Is the animal warm-blooded or cold-blooded?
Put a ✓ on the warm-blooded animals.
Put X on the cold-blooded animals.

Write the names of the warm-blooded animals.

horse, person, elephant, duck

Write the names of the cold-blooded animals.

crocodile, lizard, turtle, snake

Activity Book

Chapter 2

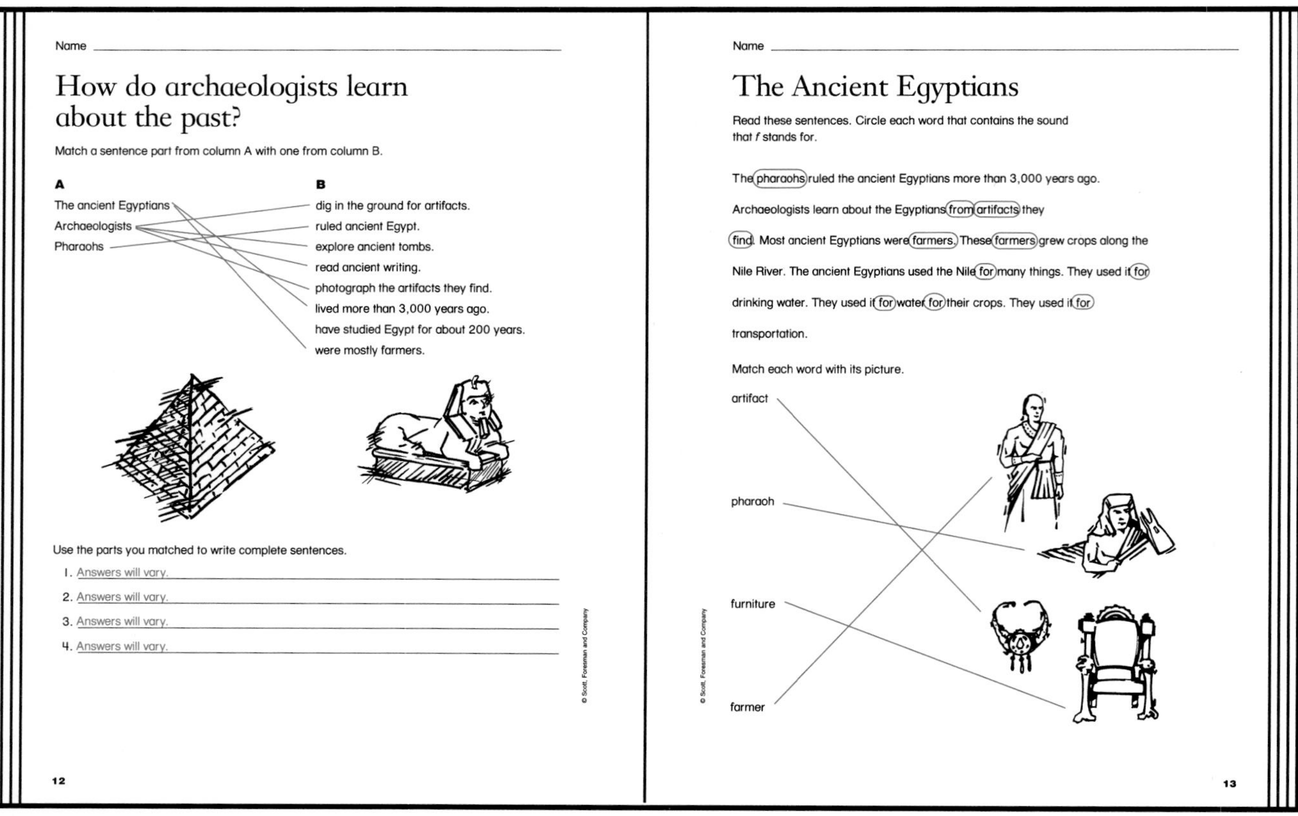

Name

How do archaeologists learn about the past?

Match a sentence part from column A with one from column B.

A

The ancient Egyptians
Archaeologists
Pharaohs

B

dig in the ground for artifacts.
ruled ancient Egypt.
explore ancient tombs.
read ancient writing.
photograph the artifacts they find.
lived more than 3,000 years ago.
have studied Egypt for about 200 years.
were mostly farmers.

Use the parts you matched to write complete sentences.

1. Answers will vary.
2. Answers will vary.
3. Answers will vary.
4. Answers will vary.

Name

The Ancient Egyptians

Read these sentences. Circle each word that contains the sound that *f* stands for.

The pharaohs ruled the ancient Egyptians more than 3,000 years ago. Archaeologists learn about the Egyptians from artifacts they find. Most ancient Egyptians were farmers. These farmers grew crops along the Nile River. The ancient Egyptians used the Nile for many things. They used it for drinking water. They used it for water for their crops. They used it for transportation.

Match each word with its picture.

artifact
pharaoh
furniture
farmer

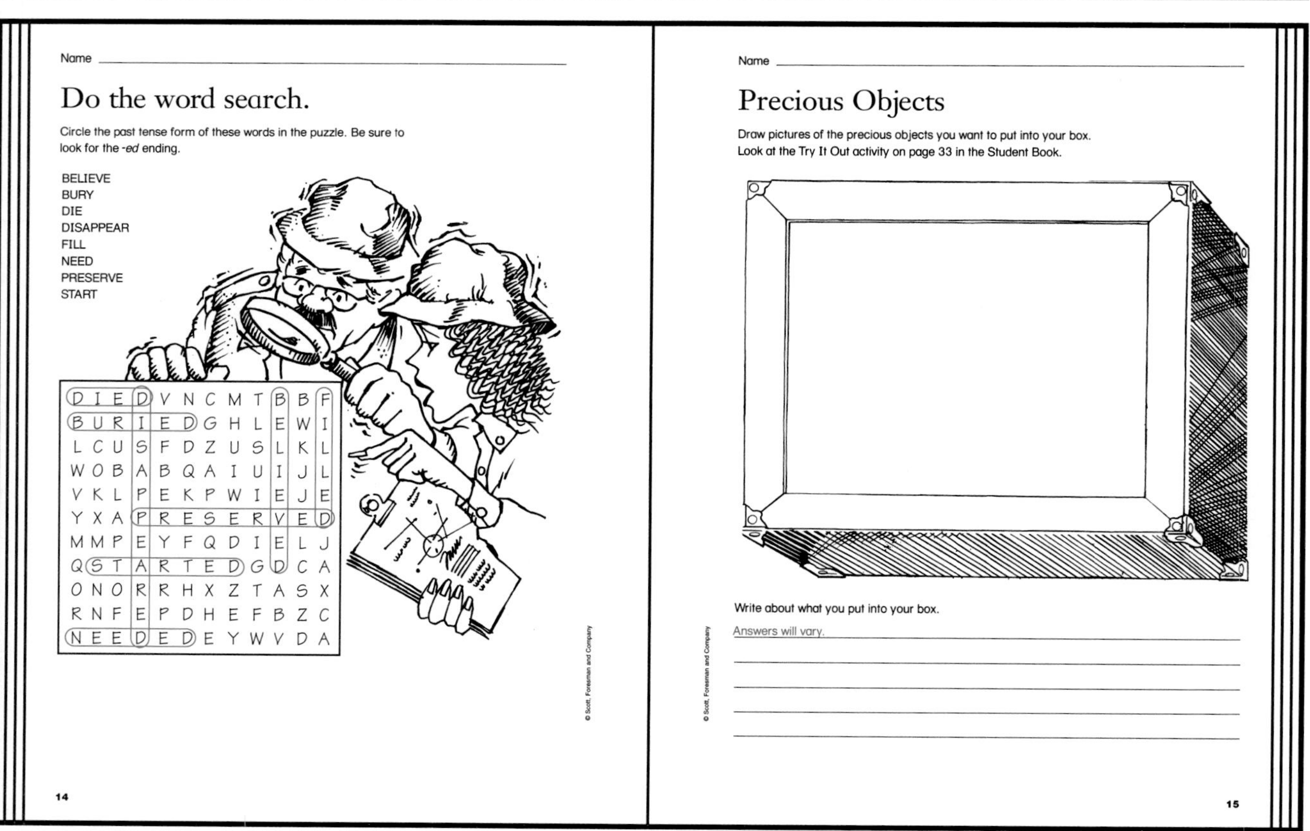

Name

Do the word search.

Circle the past tense form of these words in the puzzle. Be sure to look for the *-ed* ending.

BELIEVE
BURY
DIE
DISAPPEAR
FILL
NEED
PRESERVE
START

D	I	E	D	V	N	C	M	T	B	B	F
B	U	R	I	E	D	G	H	L	E	W	I
L	C	U	S	F	D	Z	U	S	L	K	L
W	O	B	A	B	Q	A	I	U	I	J	L
V	K	L	P	E	K	P	W	I	E	J	E
Y	X	A	P	R	E	S	E	R	V	E	D
M	M	P	E	Y	F	Q	D	I	E	L	J
Q	S	T	A	R	T	E	D	G	D	C	A
O	N	O	R	R	H	X	Z	T	A	S	X
R	N	F	E	P	D	H	E	F	B	Z	C
N	E	E	D	E	D	E	Y	W	V	D	A

Name

Precious Objects

Draw pictures of the precious objects you want to put into your box. Look at the Try It Out activity on page 33 in the Student Book.

Write about what you put into your box.

Answers will vary.

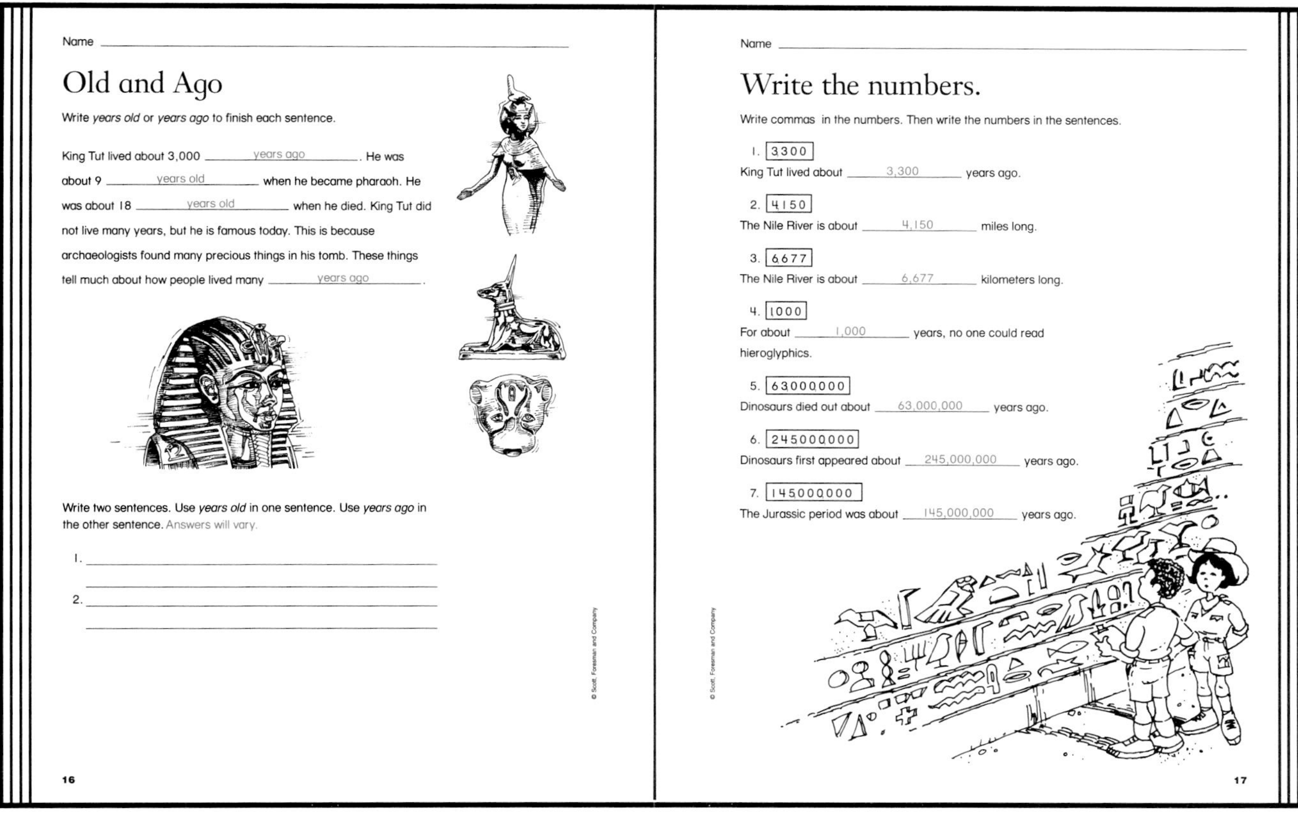

Name ____________________

Old and Ago

Write *years old* or *years ago* to finish each sentence.

King Tut lived about 3,000 ___years ago___. He was about 9 ___years old___ when he became pharaoh. He was about 18 ___years old___ when he died. King Tut did not live many years, but he is famous today. This is because archaeologists found many precious things in his tomb. These things tell much about how people lived many ___years ago___.

Write two sentences. Use *years old* in one sentence. Use *years ago* in the other sentence. Answers will vary.

1. ____________________

2. ____________________

Name ____________________

Write the numbers.

Write commas in the numbers. Then write the numbers in the sentences.

1. 3300
King Tut lived about ___3,300___ years ago.

2. 4150
The Nile River is about ___4,150___ miles long.

3. 6677
The Nile River is about ___6,677___ kilometers long.

4. 1000
For about ___1,000___ years, no one could read hieroglyphics.

5. 63000000
Dinosaurs died out about ___63,000,000___ years ago.

6. 245000000
Dinosaurs first appeared about ___245,000,000___ years ago.

7. 145000000
The Jurassic period was about ___145,000,000___ years ago.

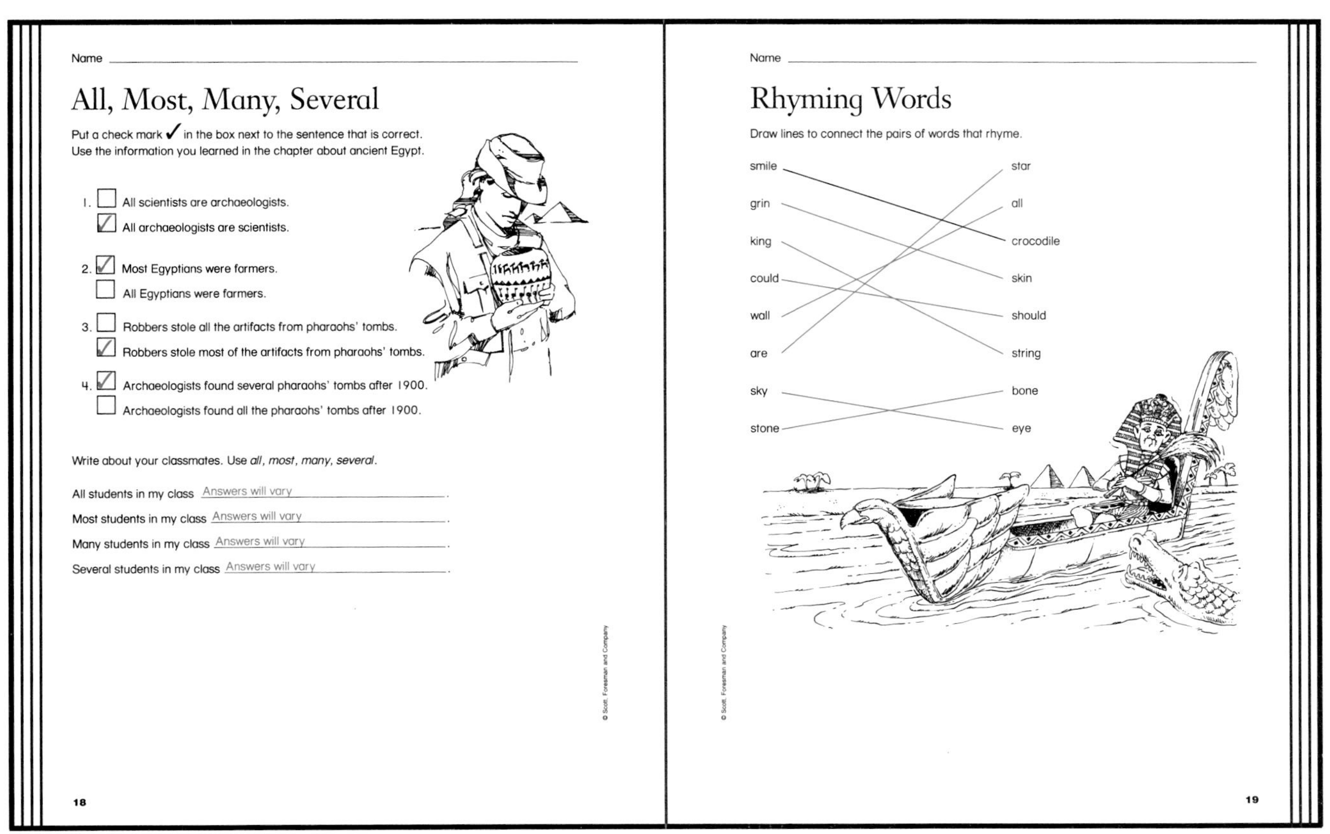

Name ____________________

All, Most, Many, Several

Put a check mark ✓ in the box next to the sentence that is correct. Use the information you learned in the chapter about ancient Egypt.

1. ☐ All scientists are archaeologists.
   ☑ All archaeologists are scientists.

2. ☑ Most Egyptians were farmers.
   ☐ All Egyptians were farmers.

3. ☐ Robbers stole all the artifacts from pharaohs' tombs.
   ☑ Robbers stole most of the artifacts from pharaohs' tombs.

4. ☑ Archaeologists found several pharaohs' tombs after 1900.
   ☐ Archaeologists found all the pharaohs' tombs after 1900.

Write about your classmates. Use *all*, *most*, *many*, *several*.

All students in my class ___Answers will vary___.

Most students in my class ___Answers will vary___.

Many students in my class ___Answers will vary___.

Several students in my class ___Answers will vary___.

Name ____________________

Rhyming Words

Draw lines to connect the pairs of words that rhyme.

smile	star
grin	all
king	crocodile
could	skin
wall	should
are	string
sky	bone
stone	eye

Preview

Activate Prior Knowledge
Make a K-W-L Chart

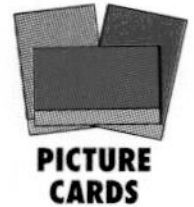
PICTURE CARDS

Start discussion of dinosaurs by showing students pictures such as Picture Cards 23 dinosaurs and 46 museum. Introduce the word *dinosaur.* Ask students what they know about dinosaurs. Start a K-W-L chart:

K: What We Know	Many dinosaurs were big.
W: What We Want to Know	When did dinosaurs live?
L: What We Learned	

Add to the chart throughout the chapter.

Develop Language and Concepts
Present Pages 2 and 3

Invite students to look at the pictures and name as many dinosaurs as they can. Point to the name of each dinosaur and say it.

Read the questions from page 2 with students. Use TPR to check their understanding of *fast, slow,* and *eat.* Use pictures to introduce *meat* and *plants.* Ask students to talk about the dinosaurs. Start a list of words that tells what dinosaurs were like.

Ask students the Talk About It question. Talk about their interest in dinosaurs. Add things they want to learn to the K-W-L chart.

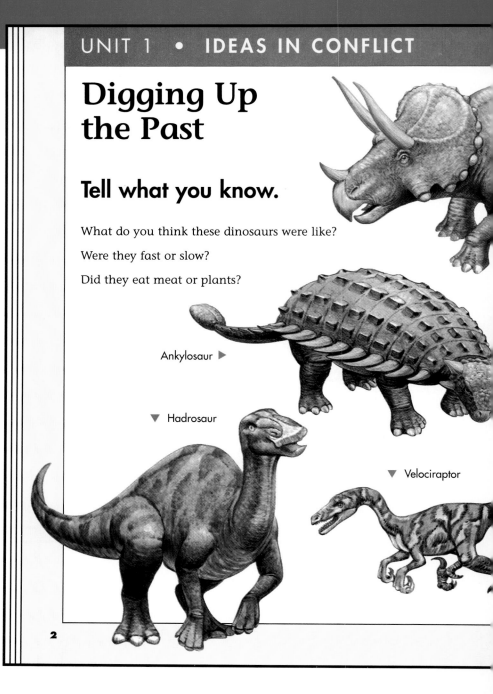

Digging Up the Past

Tell what you know.

What do you think these dinosaurs were like?

Were they fast or slow?

Did they eat meat or plants?

Ankylosaur ▶

▼ Hadrosaur

▼ Velociraptor

Options for Reaching All Students

Beginning
Language: Location Words

Write the following words on the board and read them with the students: *top, bottom, left, right.* Illustrate their meaning by pointing to a page in the Student Book. Give locations and ask students to point to the dinosaur being described; for example, "This dinosaur is at the top. It is at the left."

Advanced
Language: Dinosaur Guessing Game

Have students work in pairs. One student chooses one dinosaur from the pictures on the page and describes it orally to a partner, leaving out the name of the dinosaur. The partner then must guess which dinosaur is being described. For example, one student might say, "This dinosaur has a big head and big body, and a long tail. It probably ate meat," prompting the response "tyrannosaurus rex" from the partner.

Triceratops

Deinonychus

Tyrannosaurus rex

Talk About It

Why are people interested in dinosaurs?

3

THEME/KEY CONCEPTS

Scientists and archaeologists learn new things about the past. They keep discovering new things as they dig up fossils and artifacts. Sometimes these new discoveries lead to new ideas that conflict with what people have believed for a long time.

Chapter 1

- Scientists learn about dinosaurs by studying fossils.
- Scientists learn new things that change what people believe. For example, scientists are discovering new dinosaurs, although some scientists thought that there were no new dinosaurs to be found.

Chapter 2

- Archaeologists learn about ancient Egypt by studying tombs and artifacts from the past.
- Archaeologists thought that all royal tombs had been discovered, but recently a new tomb was found.

FYI

Here is the pronunciation of the dinosaur names:

Ankylosaur—ang-KYLE-o-sawr
Deinonychus—dyne-ON-ik-us
Hadrosaur—HAD-ro-sawr
Triceratops—try-SAIR-uh-tops
Tyrannosaurus rex—tye-RAN-uh-sawr-us rex
Velociraptor—veh-lossd-ih-RAP-tor

Mixed Ability

Video: Digging up the Past

Show the Unit 1 portion of the video to give students an overview of the unit. You may want to replay the tape several times throughout the unit for language and concept reinforcement and development.

Cooperative Learning

Science: Draw a Dinosaur

Have students work in groups to draw a dinosaur that interests them. Then have students write words that describe their dinosaur. Encourage them to use the list of words they have made in the whole class activity.

Present

Activate Prior Knowledge

Brainstorm Vocabulary

TPR

Do a TPR activity, with students naming the parts of the body that they know. Have students look at pages 2 and 3 and name the body parts of a dinosaur. Be sure to include *bones, teeth,* and *claws.*

Develop Language and Concepts

Present Pages 4 and 5

ACTIVITY BOOK

Introduce students to new vocabulary before reading. Use a picture of a scientist to introduce the word *scientist.* Explain that people who study dinosaurs are scientists.

Use a small rock and a cotton ball to present the concepts of *hard* and *soft.* Ask students to identify things in the classroom that are hard or soft. Then ask them what parts of a dinosaur were hard or soft. Use the pictures of dinosaurs on pages 2 and 3 to illustrate sharp and flat teeth. Read the text with students. Use Activity Book page 2.

Model a Strategy

Use Headings

Model how to use headings to understand main ideas:

I can use the question at the beginning of the lesson to help my reading. As I read the selection and look at the pictures, I try to answer the question How do scientists learn about dinosaurs?

CHAPTER 1

Digging Up Fossils

How do scientists learn about dinosaurs?

Dinosaurs died millions of years ago. After millions of years, the hard parts of the animals, like bones and teeth, turned into stone. They became **fossils.**

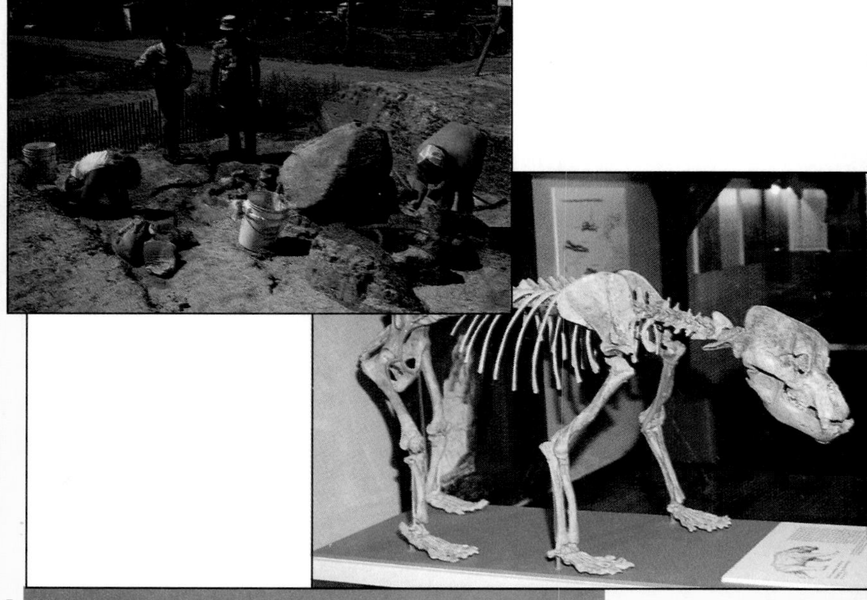

Options for Reaching All Students

Beginning

Language: Words and Pictures

Review the words *teeth, sharp, flat, meat-eater,* and *plant-eater.* Have students fold a piece of paper in half and write plant-eaters and meat-eaters at the top of each column. Have them draw teeth that might go with each heading and something that the dinosaur might eat.

Advanced

Language: Summarizing

Have students orally summarize what they learned about dinosaurs from the page. Invite them to answer the question *How do scientists learn about dinosaurs?* Then ask students why dinosaurs needed different kinds of teeth.

Cooperative Language Experience

Read About Dinosaurs

Provide students with books about dinosaurs or have them bring in dinosaur books that interest them. Read passages from books and show pictures.

As a class, write down facts you learned about dinosaurs from the books and pictures.

Scientists study fossil bones. They put an animal's bones together to make a skeleton. They can tell how tall the animal was. They can tell how fast the animal walked.

Scientists study fossil teeth too. They can tell what the animal ate. Meat-eaters had sharp teeth. Plant-eaters had flat teeth.

Talk About It

What parts of an animal can become fossils? What parts of an animal can't become fossils?

Language Awareness

Grammar
Plurals with *-s* and Irregular Plurals

TPR

Talk with students about one and more than one, singular and plural. Start with words that form plurals by adding *-s:* for example, body parts such as *bone, bones; finger, fingers; leg, legs.* Then point out words that form plurals irregularly (not using *-s),* such as *tooth, teeth; foot, feet.*

Have students do actions as you give commands involving singular and plurals, such as "Touch one foot, Touch two feet; Raise one arm, Raise two arms."

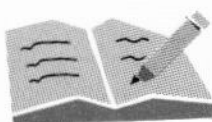

ACTIVITY BOOK

Use Activity Book page 3.

Assess

Use students' responses to Talk About It for assessment. Students should be able to

- name two parts of dinosaurs that became fossils (teeth, bones)
- tell something that scientists know from studying dinosaur fossils

LOOK**AHEAD**

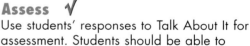

In the next section, students will learn how scientists use fossils to develop knowledge about dinosaurs.

QuickCheck

Names of Body Parts

Ask students to identify hard and soft body parts.

Practice

Activate Prior Knowledge

Review K-W-L Chart

Review the K-W-L chart with students. Ask what students know about dinosaur fossils. Ask questions such as these:

- What parts of dinosaurs turned into fossils?
- What do scientists do with these fossils?

Add the information to the K-W-L chart. Ask students if they want to make any additions to the things they want to learn.

Develop Language and Concepts

Present Pages 6 and 7

ACTIVITY BOOK

Read the text with students. Have students add words to the K-W-L chart *(eggs, nest, baby dinosaurs, footprints.)*. Read the Word Bank. Encourage students to use the Word Bank words as they answer the questions in Think About It. Ask students to analyze what each kind of fossil tells scientists about dinosaurs. Use Activity Book page 4.

Model a Strategy

Recognize Patterns in English

Model using patterns to aid reading:

On this page, each paragraph follows a pattern. The first sentence tells about a part of a dinosaur that turned into a fossil. The second sentence tells what scientists do. Since the paragraphs are similar, reading the first one will give me some clues to help me with the rest of the reading.

Dinosaur Fossils

This dinosaur's bones turned into fossils. Scientists put the fossil bones together to make a skeleton.

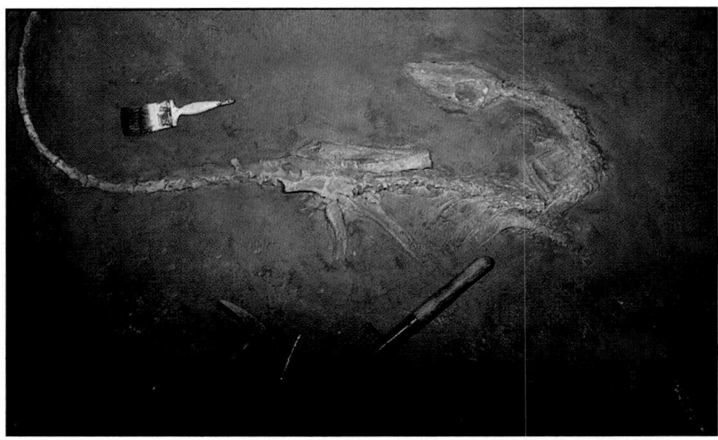

A dinosaur laid eggs in this nest. The eggs and baby dinosaurs turned into fossils. Scientists study the fossils.

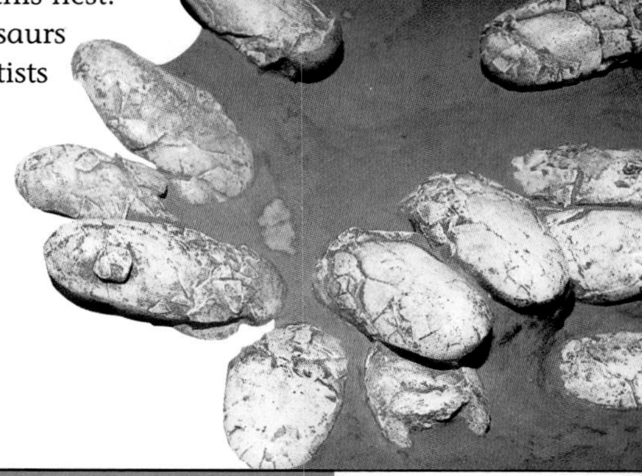

Options for Reaching All Students

Beginning

Language: Words and Pictures

Review key kinds of dinosaur fossils with students. Write these words on the board: *bones, teeth, eggs, footprints*. Have students fold a piece of paper into fourths. Have the students copy one word in each of the four sections and illustrate it.

Advanced

Science: Think Like a Paleontologist

Tell students that a scientist who digs for fossils is called a *paleontologist*. Challenge students to think like a paleontologist by guessing what a paleontologist can learn from each kind of fossil. For example, Teeth fossils tell us _____ (what kinds of food dinosaurs ate).

Have them complete sentences like the following:

Bone fossils tell us_____.
Fossil skeletons tell us_____.
Egg fossils tell us_____.
Dinosaur footprints tell us_____.

A dinosaur walked through mud and left these footprints. The mud turned into stone. Scientists study the footprints.

Dinosaur teeth turned into fossils. Scientists study the dinosaur teeth.

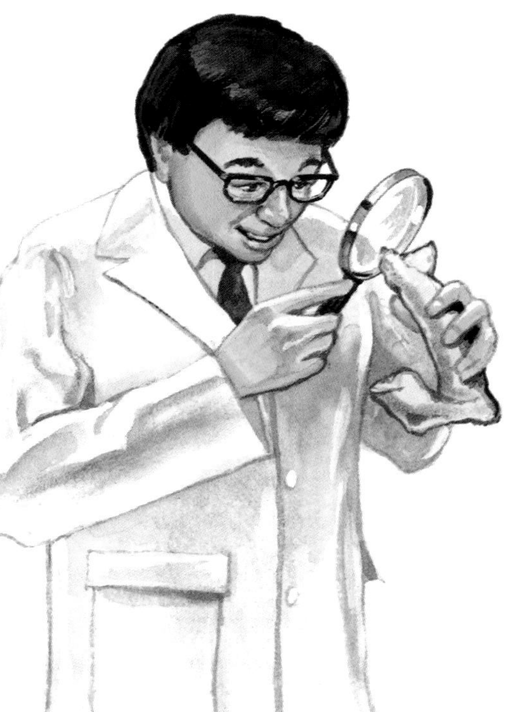

Word Bank

- fast
- large
- meat-eater
- plant-eater
- slow
- small

Think About It

What kinds of fossils have scientists found? What can scientists learn about dinosaurs from each kind of fossil?

Language Awareness

Vocabulary
Idiom *turn into*

To help students understand the phrase *turn into,* bring in an ice cube to show how the solid cube *turns into* water.

Have students find examples of *turn into* in the text and name the things that turn into fossils. Then have the students make sentences, using prompts such as the following:

bones/stone
ice cubes/water
teeth/fossils

Assess 

Use the K-W-L chart and students' responses to Think About It for assessment. Students should be able to

- list at least three kinds of dinosaur fossils *(bones, teeth, eggs, footprints)*
- tell something scientists learn from fossils

LOOK **AHEAD**

In the next section, students will learn about geologic time and the appearance of species, including dinosaurs and humans.

Mixed Ability

Art: What Can Footprints Tell?

Ask students in groups to think about what makes footprints look different. Have students move like different kinds and sizes of dinosaurs. Ask them to look for how they place their feet if

they are moving very fast
they are moving slowly
they are very heavy

Ask them to think about how their footprints might change.

Provide pairs of students with paper and stamp pads or fingerpaints. Have them make dinosaur tracks by using their fingertips to make "footprints." Each pair should produce footprints for several different kinds of dinosaurs, for example:

fast-moving
slow-moving
walked on four legs
walked on two legs
very heavy

Then pairs should exchange prints and try to draw conclusions about the prints produced by others.

Practice

Activate Prior Knowledge

Review Time and Numbers

Use clocks and calendars to check students' understanding of units of time *(minute, second, hour, day, week, month, year)*. Encourage them to name the smallest unit they know (*second*) and the longest *(year)*. Check their understanding of a *million* by writing numbers on the board. Explain that these pages will introduce them to long units of time.

Develop Language and Concepts

Present Pages 8 and 9

Read the text with students. Help students look at the chart for any words they recognize. Go through the chart pronouncing the names. Have students read the numbers. Explain that one meaning of .5 is *one-half*. Make sure students understand the meaning of *ago*.

Model a Strategy

Read a Chart

Model how to read the chart:

On this chart, the events that are newer are on the top. The events that are older are on the bottom. When I look at charts, I need to figure out how they are organized.

When did dinosaurs live?

Scientists divide history into long numbers of years called **eras.** Eras are divided into **periods.**

The chart shows the era and periods when dinosaurs lived.

Are the oldest events at the top or the bottom of the chart?

Era	Period	
Cenozoic	Quaternary	2.5 million years ago to present
	Tertiary	65 to 2.5 million years ago
Mesozoic	Cretaceous	145 million to 65 million years ago
	Jurassic	208 to 145 million years ago
	Triassic	245 to 208 million years ago

Options for Reaching All Students

Beginning

Critical Thinking: Classify Animals

Have students work in pairs to name the animals. They can use Picture Cards 6 bird, 20 crocodile, 28 elephant, 31 giraffe, 35 hippopotamus, 64 snake. Invite them to classify the animals as birds, reptiles, or mammals.

Advanced

Math: Measurements

Present students with a chart such as the following:

Brachiosaurus, 82 feet
Triceratops, 9 meters
Plateosaurus, 27 feet

Have them figure which dinosaur is the longest. Present the formula for converting meters to feet, which is to multiply by 3.281.

Peer Tutoring

Science: Read Charts

Have pairs of students of mixed ability ask and answer questions using the chart. Questions might be:

Which dinosaur lived first, allosaurus or tyrannosaurus?

Which came first, birds or flowering plants?

Which dinosaur was bigger, tyrannosaurus or allosaurus?

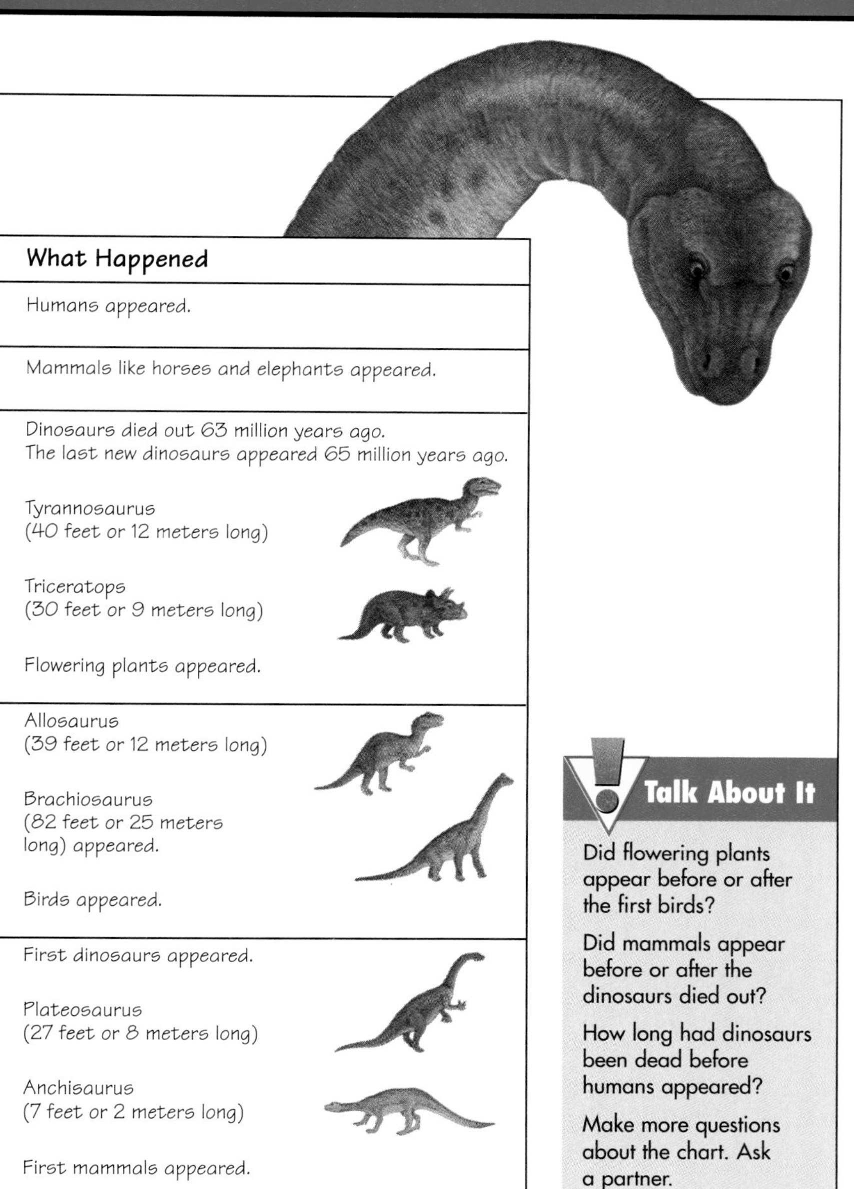

What Happened
Humans appeared.
Mammals like horses and elephants appeared.
Dinosaurs died out 63 million years ago. The last new dinosaurs appeared 65 million years ago. Tyrannosaurus (40 feet or 12 meters long) Triceratops (30 feet or 9 meters long) Flowering plants appeared.
Allosaurus (39 feet or 12 meters long) Brachiosaurus (82 feet or 25 meters long) appeared. Birds appeared.
First dinosaurs appeared. Plateosaurus (27 feet or 8 meters long) Anchisaurus (7 feet or 2 meters long) First mammals appeared.

Talk About It

Did flowering plants appear before or after the first birds?

Did mammals appear before or after the dinosaurs died out?

How long had dinosaurs been dead before humans appeared?

Make more questions about the chart. Ask a partner.

SCIENCE • USE LANGUAGE 9

Language Awareness

Grammar
Before and *After*

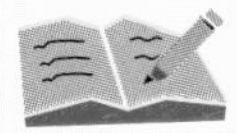

Help students understand the meaning of *before* and *after* by discussing what happens in a school day. Discuss what students do before lunch. Then discuss what they do after lunch. Help students make sentences describing activities, such as the following:

We study math *before* we eat lunch.
We eat lunch *after* we study math.

Have students use the chart to make sentences.

The first dinosaurs appeared before birds appeared.

Use Activity Book page 5.

Assess √

Use students' responses to Talk About It for assessment. Students should be able to

- use the chart to compare when dinosaurs lived to other events in geologic time
- explain how long ago dinosaurs and humans appeared by using the chart

LOOK **AHEAD**

In the next section, students will use common materials to make "fossil" molds and casts.

Cooperative Learning

Make a Time Line

Have students make a large vertical time line using the information in the chart. They should write number cards with numbers for 50-million-year periods starting with 250 million years ago until now. They can use masking tape or adding machine tape for the line. Put it on a wall where the students can keep it for a while. Work with students to figure out the distance between each 50 million year periord. Help them to understand why the size for each period needs to be the same.

Using construction paper, students can make and add labels for each of the living things on the chart. Have them attach their labels to the time line in the correct places.

Have students do research to add other dinosaurs and species to the time line.

Home Connection

Personal Time Lines

Have students gather dates and facts from their lives and the lives of family members to arrange on personal time lines. Important dates might include parents' wedding date, birthdates, or arrival in the U.S. Photos might be used to illustrate the time lines. Have students record the events and dates and then display their time lines.

Connect

Activate Prior Knowledge

Review Vocabulary

Review the fossils that students have seen in previous pictures: bones, footprints, eggs, and skeletons. Tell students they will be making a mold and a cast, the way some fossils were formed. Introduce the concept of mold by bringing in a jello mold or a cookie cutter. If possible, demonstrate making jello to help students make the analogy between mold and cast (jello).

Develop Language and Concepts

Present Pages 10 and 11

Read the list of ingredients and directions with students. Point out that the activity will not be finished in one day. Have the students act out each action word to reinforce understanding. Ask students to retell each step before doing it. Encourage students to color their fossils. After they do the activity, help them understand that the hard parts of dinosaurs' bodies formed a mold in the earth. Then minerals slowly filled the mold, making a cast. The "casts" are fossils. Then have students complete the Write About It activity.

You can make fossils.

Things You Need

shell · petroleum jelly · plaster of Paris · water · jar · plastic spoon · clay

To make a mold:

1. Make the clay into a circle.
2. Cover the seashell with petroleum jelly. Cover the clay with petroleum jelly.
3. Press the outside of the seashell into the clay.
4. Remove the shell from the clay.

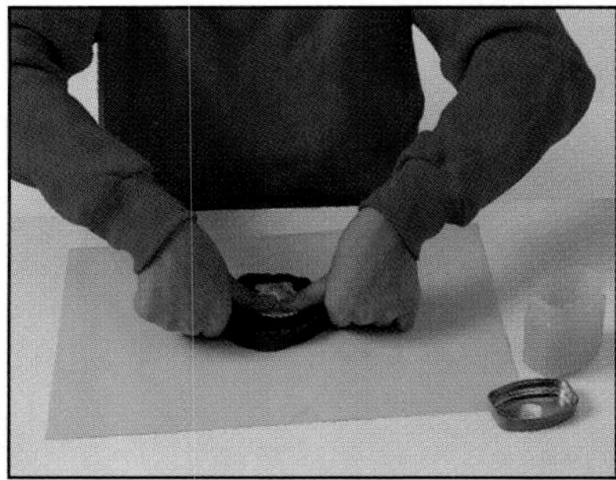

Options for Reaching All Students

Beginning

Language: Charades

TPR

Help students use the action words from the activity to make a game. Have them write each word on an index cards. Examples might be *press, pour, remove, mix.* Shuffle the cards and have students take turns choosing a card and acting out the word for the other students to guess.

Advanced

Language: Research

Have students work in groups to describe and illustrate the process by which dinosaur bone fossils were formed. Have them look into books that describe dinosaurs. Have them present their results to the class.

Cooperative Language Experience

Field Trip

If possible, arrange a field trip to a natural history museum or an institution that has fossils or dinosaur skeletons on exhibit. After the trip, write an experience story about the trip with the students. If this is not possible, show a video about dinosaurs and have students write about the experience.

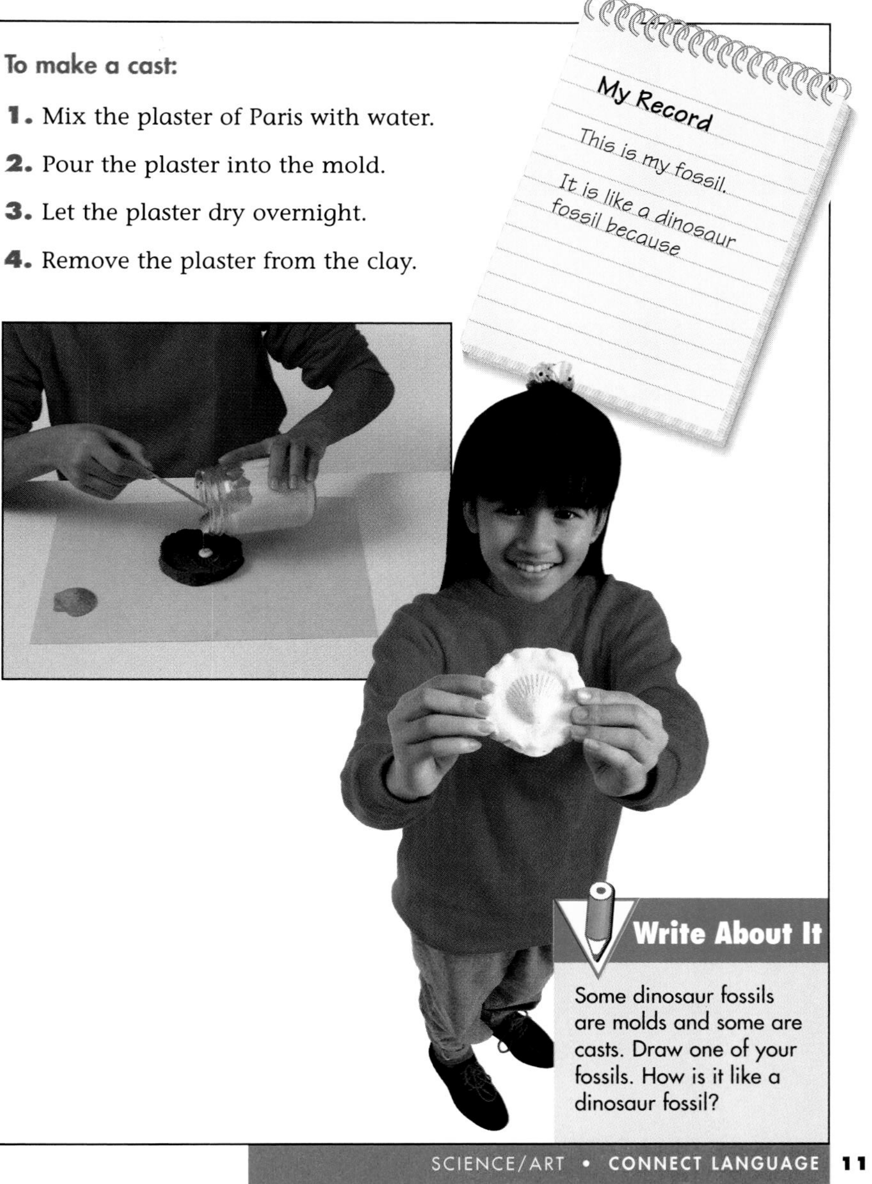

To make a cast:

1. Mix the plaster of Paris with water.
2. Pour the plaster into the mold.
3. Let the plaster dry overnight.
4. Remove the plaster from the clay.

My Record

This is my fossil.

It is like a dinosaur fossil because

Write About It

Some dinosaur fossils are molds and some are casts. Draw one of your fossils. How is it like a dinosaur fossil?

SCIENCE/ART • **CONNECT LANGUAGE** **11**

Language Awareness

Phonics

Consonant *p*, Consonant Blends *pl*, *pr*

ACTIVITY BOOK

List the words *plaster, Paris, pour, petroleum,* and *press* on the board. Model the sounds. Invite students to find the words in the text and read sentences. Also invite them to come up with some other examples of words that use the blends, such as *page, please,* and *practice.*

Use Activity Book page 6.

Model a Strategy

Use Action Words in Directions

Model using action words in directions:

I see in this activity, each numbered step begins with an action word, such as make or pour. The action word tells me what to do. If I am not sure what an action word means, I look at the pictures or ask for help before doing it.

Assess

Students should be able to

- tell what they learned from the activity
- compare their "fossils" to dinosaur fossils

LOOK **AHEAD**

In the next section, students will read a literature selection with changing ideas about dinosaurs.

Home Connection

Share Learning

Encourage students to share what they are learning about dinosaurs with family members. They might bring their fossils home to share with their families.

Writer's Workshop

Write About Assisting a Paleontologist

Refer students to the Writer's Workshop on pages 230 to 236. Have students imagine they are assisting a paleontologist on a dig. Have them use the pictures and what they have learned to tell about what they would be doing.

Connect

Activate Prior Knowledge

Review Vocabulary

Show students a newspaper. Ask them where they usually get news. Ask them what news is. Develop the idea that news can be something you did not know before. Show students pictures of present-day reptiles such as turtles and crocodiles. Ask them how these animals are like dinosaurs. Review the K-W-L chart with them to recap what they know about dinosaurs and what they want to find out.

Introduce the Selection

Help students locate the title and author of this selection. Connect what you have said about news with the title of the book. Ask them to predict what news they might expect to find. Explain that this article tells how ideas about dinosaurs have been changed by new discoveries.

Read the Selection

RED TAPE

Read the selection with the students. Read it with them a second time, using the Reader's Tips. Play the selection on Side 1 of the Red Tape several times.

Language Awareness

Grammar

Past Tense of the Verb *be*

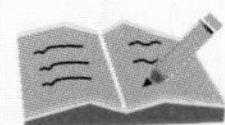
ACTIVITY BOOK

Point out that the past tense tells about something that already happened. Introduce *was* and *were* in sentences that relate to students' experiences, such as

We were in the cafeteria at lunch.
I/He/She was in the cafeteria at lunch.

Prompt students to say sentences about the dinosaurs, using *was* and *were*. The pictures in the text can be used as prompts:

This dinosaur *was* a plant-eater. This dinosaur *was* slow.
These dinosaurs *were* meat-eaters. These dinosaurs *were* fast.

Use Activity Book page 7.

Model a Strategy

Remember Details

Model how to remember details:

When I read, I use a Basket of Facts to help me keep track of what I need to remember. The text has information about three new dinosaurs in picture captions. I chose one as the name of my Basket of Facts. Then I wrote each fact I found about the dinosaur on a strip of paper to put on the basket. This helps me remember what I have read. My "basket" can be a box or a bag or just a piece of paper.

Options for Reaching All Students

Beginning

Language: Recognize Vocabulary

The beginning of this selection uses many words found elsewhere in this chapter. Have students locate five words they are sure they know the meaning of, and draw a picture or write a sentence to illustrate their understanding.

Advanced

Science: Discover a New Dinosaur

Have students pretend they have discovered the fossils of a new dinosaur. Have them describe their discovery and tell how the fossils helped them know what this dinosaur was like. Have students assign their dinosaur a name. Then have them illustrate their discovery, with a drawing of the dig or of the dinosaur as they imagine it.

Cooperative Learning

Describe Dinosaurs

Have groups of students chart the information about newly discovered dinosaurs from this selection. The chart might include:

Name
Where Found
Length
Food
Other Information

The News About Dinosaurs

by Patricia Lauber

Strategy Tip
Read On to Get Meaning
The author uses the word reptile. Read on to find examples of reptiles. What examples of reptiles does the author give?

Dinosaurs were discovered in the early 1800s. Until then, no one had even guessed that once there were dinosaurs.

Scientists studied the big teeth and bones they had found. They wondered what kind of animals these belonged to. Finally they decided the animals were reptiles—relatives of today's crocodiles, turtles, snakes, and lizards. In 1841 the animals were named *dinosaurs,* meaning "terrible lizards."

Dinosaur hunters dug for bones. They found giant dinosaurs, dinosaurs the size of chickens, and many in-between sizes. They gave each kind a name. They fitted bones together and made skeletons. After a hundred or more years, this work seemed to be ending. Scientists began to think they had discovered nearly every kind of dinosaur that ever walked the earth.

▼ *Mamenchisaurus* was a giant plant-eating dinosaur, 72 feet long. Its 33-foot neck is the longest of any known animal. The dinosaur is named for the place in China where it was found.

Strategy Tip
Read to Understand the Big Idea
Don't try to remember or pronounce all the dinosaurs' names. Read to find out what ideas scientists have about dinosaurs.

THE NEWS IS:

The work was far from finished. Today new kinds of dinosaurs are found all the time. And scientists think there must be hundreds more that they haven't discovered yet. Four of the new kinds they have found are *Baryonyx*, *Mamenchisaurus*, *Deinonychus*, and *Nanotyrannus*.

▼ *Nanotyrannus* was a pygmy tyrannosaur, a small relative of *Tyrannosaurus rex.* Its name means "pygmy tyrant." This small meat-eating dinosaur looked like its big relative but was only one-tenth as heavy and one-third as long—it weighed about 1,000 pounds and was 17 feet long. *Nanotyrannus* was discovered in a museum, where it had earlier been mistaken for another meat-eater, a gorgosaur, also known as *Albertosaurus*. Here its jaws are about to close on a smaller dinosaur.

▲ *Deinonychus* was found in Montana. It was fairly small, about 9 feet long, and walked on its hind legs. Each hind foot had a big claw, shaped like a curved sword. The dinosaur's name means "terrible claw." Like other meat-eaters, *Deinonychus* spent much of its time resting or sleeping and digesting its last meal. This pair has just awakened, hungry and ready to hunt.

Connect

Develop Language and Concepts

Present Pages 16 Through 19

Tell students that sometimes authors make their point by using *opposites*. Help them to understand the idea of differences. Use pairs of words such as *big/small, tall /short, and old/new*. Find examples in students' experience. Ask them to find things in the classroom that show contrasts. Examples might be an old pencil and a new one.

Help the students to connect the idea of opposites to the way the author has written this piece of literature. She gives the old ideas and then the new ideas that have changed them.

Language Awareness

Vocabulary
Antonyms

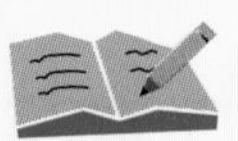
ACTIVITY BOOK

Explain to students that *antonyms* are words that have opposite meanings. Pages 16 through 19 describe the movement of dinosaurs with words that are opposites. Give students the words *slow* and *clumsy*. Then find the words *quick* and *nimble*. Tell students that these words are opposites of *slow* and *clumsy*. They are antonyms. Have students move in ways that are quick and nimble and slow and clumsy.

Use Activity Book page 8 to review synonyms and antonyms.

Model a Strategy

Keep Track of Details That Relate to Main Idea

Model keeping track of ideas that relate to the main topic:

I can look at a part of the reading to find information. I want to look at pages 17 through 20 to find words that tell how dinosaurs moved. I see one example right near the beginning: "Dinosaurs are good walkers." I will read through the rest of the selection to find some more. I'll keep a list of the examples I find.

FYI

Albertosaurus—al-BER-tuh-sawr-us
Allosaurus—AL-uh-sawr-us
Apatosaurus—ah-PAT-uh-sawr-us
Baryonyx—BAR-ee-ON-is
camarasaur—KAM-uh-ruh-sawr
camptosaur—KAMP-tuh-sawr
Deinonychus—dyne-PM-ik-us
Mamenchisaurus—mah-MEN-chee-sawr-us
Nanotyrannus—NAN-o-tie-ran-us
tryrannosaur—tye-RAN-uh-sawr

Options for Reaching All Students

Beginning

Math: Measurement

Have students select one of the three "new" dinosaurs described in the selection. Have students measure out the length of that dinosaur. Then they can cut a strip of paper the same length as the dinosaur and write a label for it giving its name and length.

Advanced

Math: Measure Dinosaurs

Have students use the descriptions of the dinosaurs provided in the selection to make a bar graph of their relative lengths. Each half-inch on the graph could represent 5 feet in length.

Mixed Ability

Social Studies: Locate Dinosaur Discoveries

Have students use the text and a world map to locate the discoveries of the three dinosaurs described in the selection. For enrichment, students might also use reference material to locate major sites where dinosaur fossils were discovered, such as Dinosaur National Park on the Colorado-Utah border.

Language Tip
Synonyms
Waddling and *dragging* mean "moving slowly."

Strategy Tip
Predict
Here you read that the old idea was that dinosaurs were slow and clumsy. What will the new idea about dinosaurs be?

Most reptiles walk with their knees bent and their feet wide apart. Scientists used to think dinosaurs must have walked the same way. They pictured dinosaurs as slow and clumsy, waddling along with their tails dragging on the ground. So that was how dinosaurs were made to look in books and museums.

▲ For many years, people thought of dinosaurs as slow-moving and slow-witted. That is how they appear in this 1870s painting by Benjamin Waterhouse Hawkins. He was the first artist to work closely with scientists who were studying dinosaurs.

THE NEWS IS:

Dinosaurs didn't look like that at all. They were good walkers. They held their tails up. And many kinds were quick and nimble. Today's scientists have learned this by studying dinosaur footprints.

▼ *Camarasaurs* (foreground) and *camptosaurs* are crossing a recently flooded area and leaving footprints. Preserved in rock, such tracks have revealed much about dinosaurs.

Strategy Tip
Synonyms
When you read, look for words that mean the same.
quick—nimble
mud—wet sand
footprints—tracks

When dinosaurs walked in mud or wet sand, they left footprints. Most of these tracks washed or oozed away. But in some places the tracks hardened. Later they were buried under mud or sand that turned to rock. The tracks were preserved in the rock—they became fossils.

▼ Today dinosaurs are shown as lively and active. These huge, horned plant-eaters are driving off *Albertosaurus,* a fierce meat-eater.

Connect

Develop Language and Concepts

Pages 20 Through 23

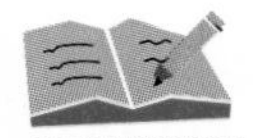
ACTIVITY BOOK

Show students pictures of mammals and reptiles that are alive today. Ask them to name the animals in English. Focus on the concepts of warm-blooded and cold-blooded. Tell students that one difference between reptiles and mammals is that reptiles are cold-blooded and mammals are warm-blooded. Read page 21 with students to find differences between cold-blooded and warm-blooded animals.

Use Activity Book page 9 to review understanding of cold-blooded and warm-blooded animals.

Language Awareness

Grammar
Conjunctions *or* and *and*

Explain to students that little words like *or* and *and* are very important in English. Help students locate these words in the selection (near the end of the deinonychus description). Explain that *and* usually means *both things* and *or* usually means *one thing or the other.*

TPR

To check for understanding, have students follow commands such as:

Raise your left hand and your right hand.

Raise your left hand or your right hand.

Invite students to give commands.

Response Activities

Personal Response

Ask students these questions: *If you had a chance to spend a day with living dinosaurs, would you take it? Why or why not? What would you most want to do or see?*

Critical Response

Ask students these questions: *What would happen if scientists stopped looking for new information? What if they had remained satisfied that they had discovered all kinds of dinosaurs that ever existed?*

Creative Response

Have students work in groups to prepare a TV news interview about a new dinosaur that has been found. One person should be the interviewer. The others can be a scientific team that made the discovery. Have them prepare a list of questions to ask and a description telling about the new dinosaur. The description should be divided so that each "scientist" contributes something. Have them share their presentation with the class.

Options for Reaching All Students

Beginning

Science: Classify Animals

Have students make lists of cold-blooded and warm-blooded animals. Then have them share one animal from their list with the class, explaining how they know it is warm- or cold-blooded.

Advanced

Language: Explain Reasons

Have students read the description of deinonychus near the end of the selection. Then have them work in pairs to role-play a discussion where they take on the role of a scientist trying to convince a colleague that not all dinosaurs were cold-blooded.

Mixed Ability

Language: Summarize

Have students use the selection to find four ideas about dinosaurs that have changed in recent years. Have them explain the old idea, the new idea, and the reason for the change by forming sentences like:

Scientists used to think _____, but now they think _____. They changed their minds because _____.

Tracks show that dinosaurs walked in long, easy strides. Their legs and feet were under their bodies, not out to the side. Their bodies were high off the ground. Big plant-eaters walked at 3 or 4 miles an hour. Some small meat-eaters could run as fast as 35 or 40 miles an hour.

▼ At least some dinosaurs could swim. *Apatosaurus* has tried to escape a pack of *Allosaurus* by taking to the water—but the meat-eaters can swim, too.

▶ A splash of color would call attention to the spiny neck frill of this horned dinosaur, which may have frightened meat-eaters.

All of today's reptiles are cold-blooded. Their bodies do not make much heat. To be active, reptiles need an outside source of heat—sunlight, warm air, sun-warmed water. When reptiles are cool, they are sluggish and slow-moving.

Mammals and birds are warm-blooded. They make their own heat, and they can be active by day or by night, in warm weather or in cool. They have much more energy than reptiles do and can stay active for hours at a time.

Scientists long thought that dinosaurs, like today's reptiles, were cold-blooded animals.

Strategy Tip
Antonyms
When you read, look for words that mean the opposite.
warm—cool
active—sluggish

Language Tip
Vocabulary
Animals that are hunted and eaten are called prey. An animal's hind legs are its back legs.

THE NEWS IS:

Some dinosaurs may have been warm-blooded. *Deinonychus*—"terrible claw"—is one of those dinosaurs.

Deinonychus was fairly small. It had the sharp teeth of a meat-eater, hands shaped for grasping prey, and powerful hind legs. It also had a huge, curved claw on one toe of each hind foot. This was a claw shaped for ripping and slashing.

▼ Three *Deinonychus* work together to bring down *Iguanodon,* which was too old or too sick to defend itself with its thumb spike or tail.

To attack, *Deinonychus* must have stood on one hind foot and slashed with the other. Or it must have leaped and attacked with both hind feet. Today's reptiles are not nimble enough to do anything like that. And as cold-blooded animals, they do not have the energy to attack that way. Warm-blooded animals do. That is why some scientists think *Deinonychus* must have been a warm-blooded dinosaur. They also think that many of the small, meat-eating dinosaurs were warm-blooded.

▲ *Deinonychus* and other small meat-eaters may have had feathers.

Study Tips
Compare and Contrast
When you compare and contrast you tell how two things are alike and how they are different. As you read, think of ways you can compare and contrast dinosaurs. One way is by what they ate.

Connect

Activate Prior Knowledge

Review Vocabulary

Have students look at the picture of seismosaurus. Ask students to name other dinosaurs that are like seismosaurus. Ask them to answer these questions: *Do you think seismosaurus was a meat-eater or a plant-eater? Why? What size words would you use to tell about seismosaurus?*

Develop Language and Concepts

Present Page 24

Read the poem with students several times. Then play the poem on Side 2 of the Red Tape several times. Have students read it chorally. Help students do the Write About It activity and share poems.

Language Awareness

Vocabulary
Synonyms

Explain that many of the words in the poems mean "big." Locate the words with students. Explain that the words are called *synonyms.* They are words that have similar meanings.

Seismosaurus

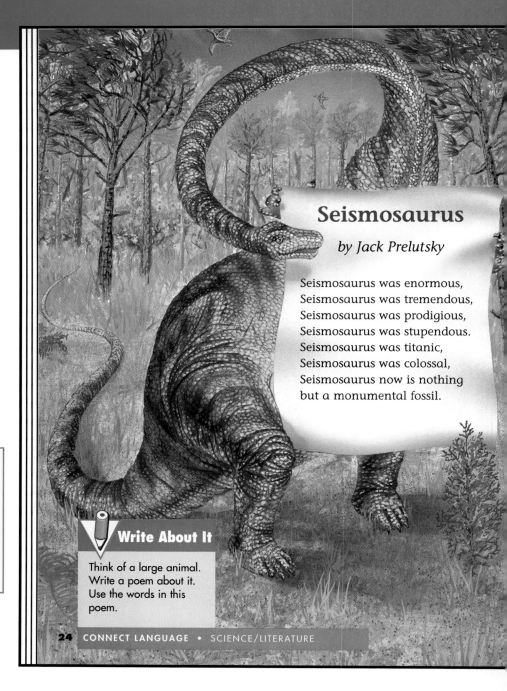

by Jack Prelutsky

Seismosaurus was enormous,
Seismosaurus was tremendous,
Seismosaurus was prodigious,
Seismosaurus was stupendous.
Seismosaurus was titanic,
Seismosaurus was colossal,
Seismosaurus now is nothing
but a monumental fossil.

Write About It

Think of a large animal. Write a poem about it. Use the words in this poem.

Options for Reaching All Students

Beginning

Language: Synonyms

Many of the words in the poem are synonyms for *big*. Tell students that seismosaurus was the biggest dinosaur ever found, but there are other very large dinosaurs. Have students make a list of other dinosaurs that are very large and describe their sizes, using the words in the poem.

Advanced

Language: Relative Sizes

Many of the words in the poem are synonyms for *big*. Have students look at the chart, at the reading, and other sources. Ask them to rank dinosaurs according to size.

Home Connection

Animals from Native Countries

Have students ask a family member to help them make a list of animals that are native to the country they come from. Encourage students to bring in pictures or drawings of some of the animals to share with the class.

CHAPTER 1

Tell what you learned.

1. What are fossils? What parts of animals become fossils?

2. Think of scientists' ideas about dinosaurs. Make a chart.

Old Ideas	New Ideas
Scientists know about every kind of dinosaur.	
Dinosaurs moved slowly.	
Dinosaurs were cold-blooded.	

3. What was the most interesting thing you learned about dinosaurs? Why do you think it's interesting?

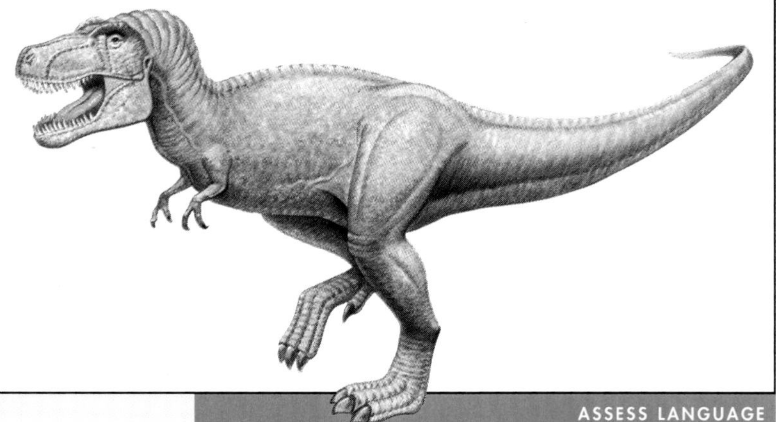

Assess ✓

Activity 1: Evaluate conceptual understanding of *fossil* (hard part of animal or trace of an animal turned into stone) and awareness of which animal parts become fossils (bones, teeth, eggs, footprints).

Activity 2: Evaluate whether students have understood the major ideas of the literature selection by their ability to fill in the chart with opposites of old ideas.

Activity 3: Ask students to share their responses with the group.

Have students complete the Chapter Self-Assessment, Blackline Master 31. Have students choose the product of one of the activities to place in their portfolios. Add results of rubrics, checklists, self-assessments, or portfolio assessments, Blackline Masters 2–18 and 31.

Listening Assessment

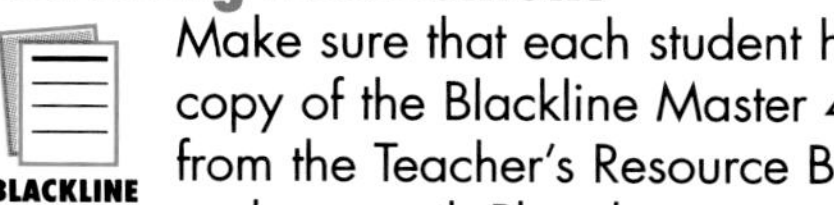

Make sure that each student has a copy of the Blackline Master 41 from the Teacher's Resource Book, and a pencil. Play the tape several times and have students complete the activity.

See page T1c for the tapescript.

Options for Assessment

Vocabulary Assessment

Matching Game

Have students work in pairs to create matching pairs of cards about dinosaurs. Then have them use these cards to play a concentration game. Matches might include any vocabulary from the chapter, such as:

sharp teeth	meat-eater
skeleton	bones
era	period

Writing Assessment

Student Report: My Favorite Dinosaur

Have students use information from the text or other sources to write and illustrate a brief report about one dinosaur they find interesting. Make sure they include as much information about size, food, and body shape as they can find.

Language Assessment

Use Blackline Master 40 in the Teacher's Resource Book.

Standardized Test Practice

Use pages 10 and 11. Answers: **1.** 65 million years ago **2.** dinosaurs died out before humans appeared **3.** scientists divide history into eras **4.** when dinosaurs lived

Preview

Activate Prior Knowledge

Review Vocabulary

Present the words in the Word Bank and help students give examples of each: furniture (for example, chair, table), jewelry and clothing, toys, and weapons. Have students give examples from their daily life. Help with vocabulary as needed.

Develop Language and Concepts

Present Pages 26 and 27

To introduce the concept that clothing and other everyday things change over time, you might want to show pictures of you or your family wearing old-fashioned clothes or pictures of the local area fifty or one hundred years ago.

Have students look at the pictures in the text. Then read aloud the Word Bank words to the students. Help students relate the Word Bank words to the appropriate pictures by pointing to a picture and saying the corresponding word aloud. The chair is an example of furniture. Ask volunteers to say the correct object name and class word as you point to a picture.

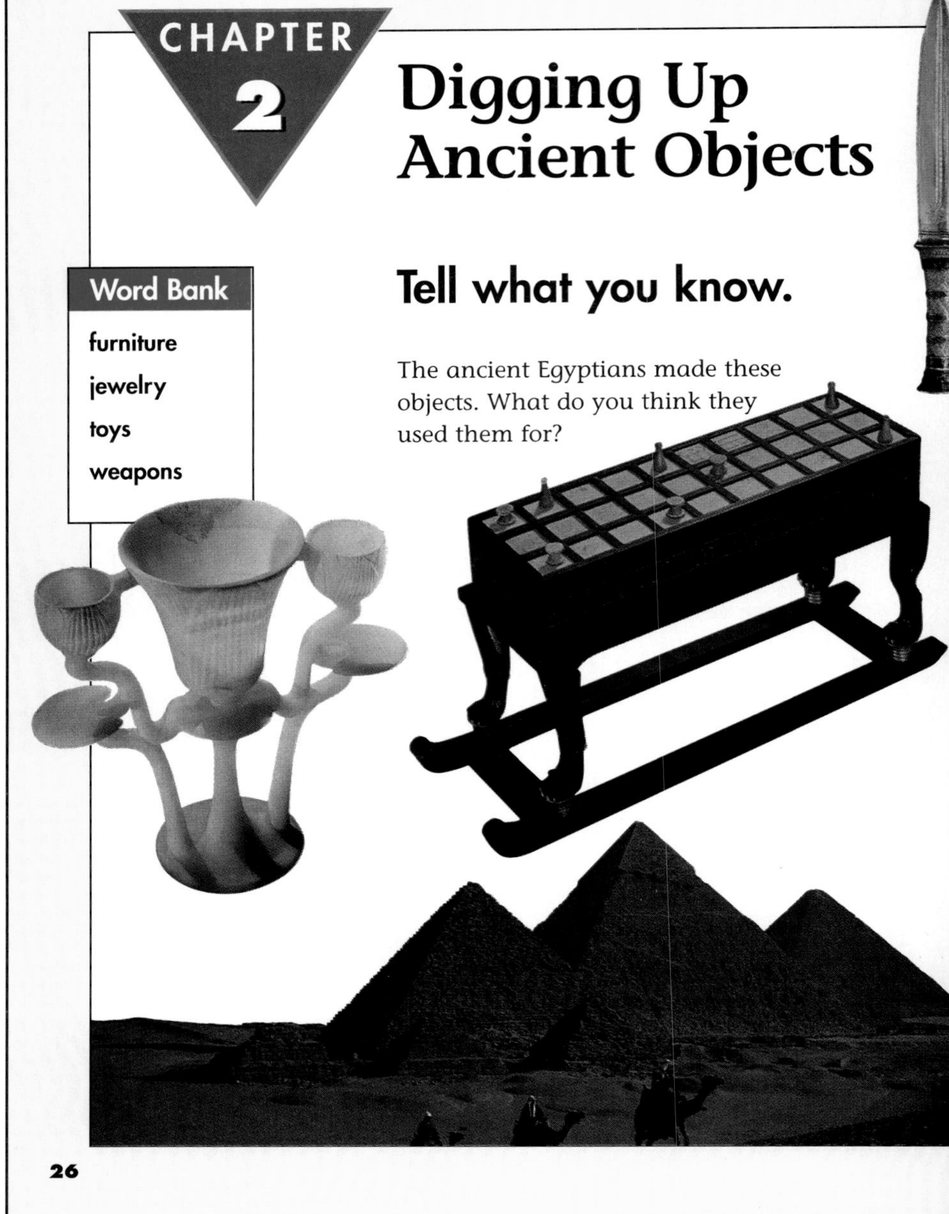

CHAPTER
2
Digging Up Ancient Objects
Word Bank
furniture
jewelry
toys
weapons
Tell what you know.
The ancient Egyptians made these objects. What do you think they used them for?
26

Options for Reaching All Students

Beginning

Language: Use New Words

Have students look in magazines and find examples of words in each of the categories in the Word Bank. Help students label the words.

Advanced

Language: Class Bee

Have a word bee in which you give a general class word for everyday items, and students have to name something from the class; for example, things in the kitchen—stove.

Mixed Ability

Language: Classify Objects

Have students work in pairs to list the pictured objects by category. They might make a chart labeled *Toys, Furniture, Personal Items*. Then have them add items of their own to each category.

Talk About It

How was life the same for ancient Egyptians as for people today?

How was life different for ancient Egyptians than for people today?

27

Explain that all the objects on the page were made more than three thousand years ago in ancient Egypt. Introduce the word *ancient*, making sure that students understand that this civilization flourished a very long time ago. Point out that compared to the dinosaurs, however, the ancient Egyptians lived just a short while ago.

Guide students in answering the questions in Tell What You Know.

Have students do the Talk About It. List ideas on the board.

Help students classify ideas into groups such as household items, clothing, entertainment, and so on.

Cooperative Language Experience

Learn About the Past

If possible, have students visit a historic site or building in your area or look at pictures of life in your area in the past. With the class, write a story about what you saw.

Home Connection

Things in the Past

Have students ask family members to tell about life in their native land when they were growing up. Ask them if there are photos available. Invite students to tell about similarities and differences.

Present

Activate Prior Knowledge

Brainstorm Vocabulary

Ask students to name some important jobs that people have in our society. List student responses on the board. Have students explain why each job is important. Guide the discussion to include job categories similar to those listed in the passage on ancient Egypt (farmers, doctors, priests, artists, builders, and rulers).

Develop Language and Concepts

Present Pages 28 and 29

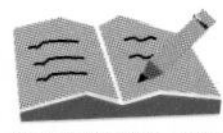

Talk about the map and the illustrations with students before you read the text. Help students locate Egypt on the map on the locator map of Africa. If possible, have students also locate Africa and Egypt on a world map or a globe.

Read the text with students. Help students pronounce the word *archaeologist.* Then help students use the pictures and the words in the Word Bank to describe the work of an archaeologist. Point out that archaeologists have been studying ancient Egypt for a very long time (200 years). Also point out that just like scientists who study dinosaurs, there is always something new to find out about ancient Egypt.

Use Activity Book page 12.

The Ancient Egyptians

The ancient Egyptians lived more than 3,000 years ago. They lived in Africa, in the Nile River Valley. Most Egyptians were farmers. Others were doctors, priests, artists, and builders. They were ruled by kings called **pharaohs.**

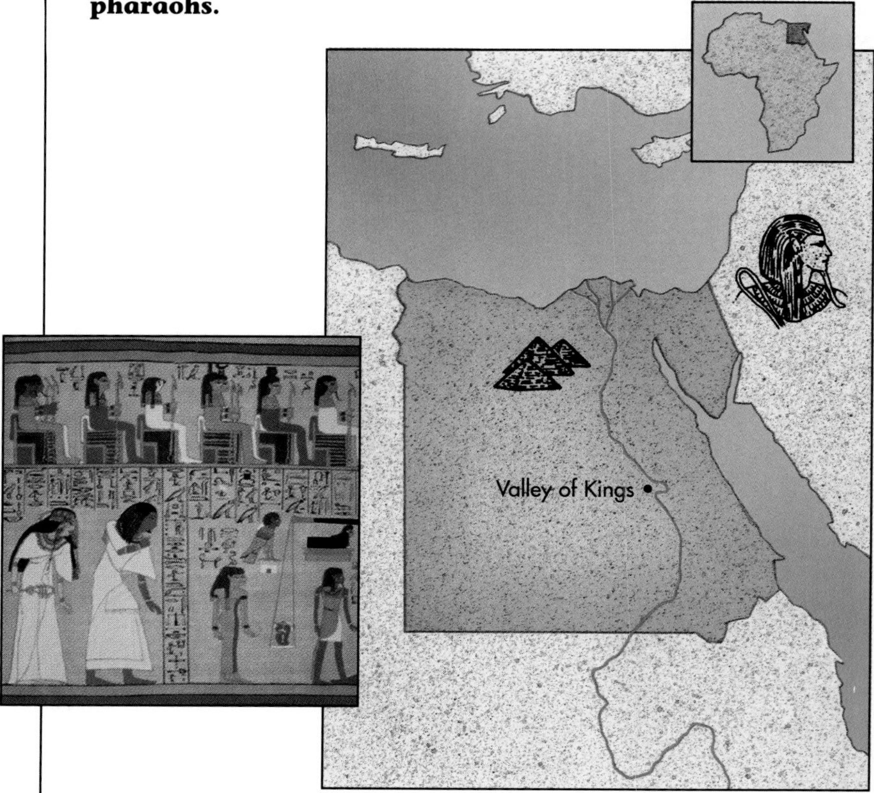

Options for Reaching All Students

Beginning

Social Studies: Careers

Have students list jobs in the United States today but that did not exist in ancient Egypt, such as bus driver, computer programmer, telephone salesperson, and cable TV installer. Be sure students recognize that these jobs all involve technology that was not available in ancient times.

Advanced

Language: Write a Journal Entry

Have students create an imaginary diary or field journal entry for an archaeologist. Refer students to the pictures, text, and Word Bank for ideas about what an archaeologist does.

Cooperative Learning

Writing: Understand Artifacts

Give groups of students objects or pictures of four or five everyday items that archaeologists might find if they were studying our civilization many years from now. Have students work in groups to describe each item, without naming it. Have them tell what archaeologists might find out about our life now by studying these items. Groups working with different artifacts could

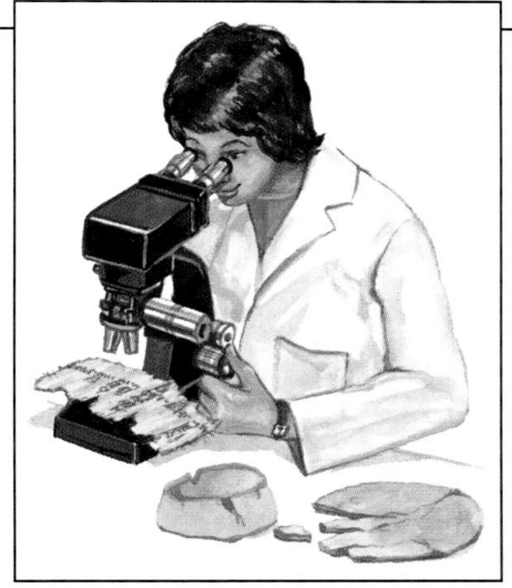

Archaeologists are scientists who study about ancient people. Archaeologists have studied the ancient Egyptians for about two hundred years. They have studied their jewelry, furniture, clothing, weapons, toys, and other **artifacts.**

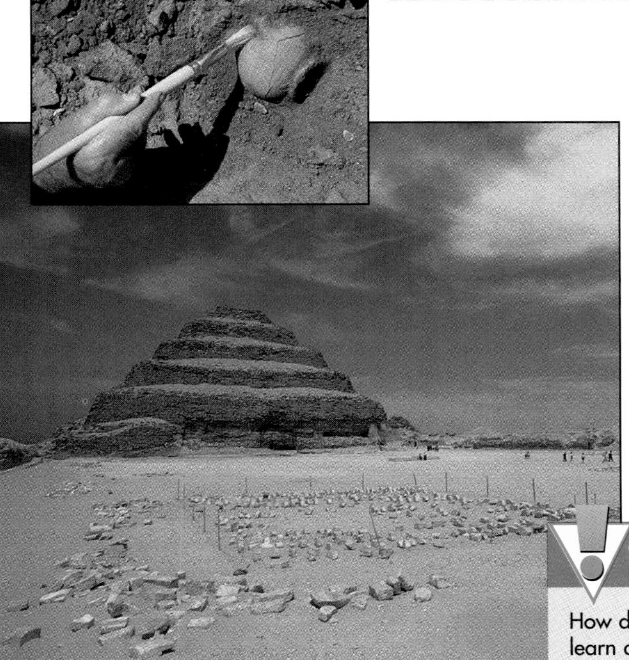

Word Bank

- dig
- explore
- find
- photograph
- read
- study

Talk About It

How do archaeologists learn about the past?

Language Awareness

Phonics
Letters *f* and *ph*

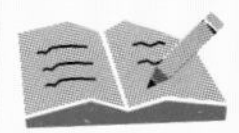

ACTIVITY BOOK

Write the following words on the board: *farmers, furniture, artifacts*. Explain that to pronounce the sound the letter *f* stands for they should touch their top teeth with their lip and blow out air. Ask students to repeat the words after you. Then tell students that the letter combination *ph* is sometimes pronounced like the sound the letter *f* usually stands for.

Use Activity Book page 13.

Assess

Use students' responses to Talk About It for assessment. Students should be able to

- name a few facts about the ancient Egyptians
- describe how archaeologists find out about the past (dig up artifacts)

LOOK**AHEAD**

In the next section, students will learn about the ancient Egyptians' beliefs about death.

exchange descriptions and try to guess the names of items being described. Here is an example:

This is a small, shiny, flat disk. It has numbered titles of songs on it. From studying this artifact, archaeologists in the future will know what kind of music we listened to. *(compact disk)*

Practice

Activate Prior Knowledge

Relate Personal Experience

Have students look at the pyramids on page 31 and ask them if they have ever seen pictures or visited these or other pyramids. If students have seen or visited the Egyptian pyramids or the ones in Mexico, for example, ask them to tell the rest of the class about them.

Develop Language and Concepts

Present Pages 30 and 31

Have students look at the pictures of a tomb and a mummy. Read the text with students. Have the class study the drawing of the interior of the pyramid on page 31. Refer to the pyramid drawing again to point out where the mummy would be located in the central chamber. Point out the tunnels so that students recognize exactly what part of the drawing that word refers to.

Have students Discuss what ancient Egyptians believed they needed in the spirit world after life and how their ideas differ from other peoples and other times.

Have students talk about things that are precious to them and do the Write About It activity.

The Pharaohs' Tombs

Ancient Egyptians believed that their spirits lived after their bodies died. The Egyptians believed that they needed their bodies in the spirit world. They preserved dead bodies as **mummies.**

The Egyptians believed that they needed things from the earth in the spirit world. They filled their tombs with useful and precious artifacts.

Mummies were preserved with special oils and wrapped with special cloth.

30 USE LANGUAGE • SOCIAL STUDIES

Options for Reaching All Students

Beginning

Social Studies: Build a Tomb

Divide students into teams of four. Tell them they are to pretend that the pharoah commanded them to build a pyramid tomb for him. Tell students to design the tomb and fill it with precious objects that they think will please the pharaoh. Students should draw a diagram of the tomb with the objects labeled.

Advanced

Social Studies: Write About Exploration

Have students write a first-person account of exploring an Egyptian tomb. Tell students to use the pictures in the chapter and the diagram. They should pretend that they are the first people to go inside the tomb in 2,000 years. Have them speculate what things were used for: "The pharaoh must have used this chair to sit in when his subjects came to see him."

Mixed Ability

Language: Vocabulary Discovery

Have pairs of students of mixed ability make a vocabulary list from these pages. They should select all the unfamiliar words and make an alphabetical list. Have students use pictures, context clues, and discussion to come up with the meaning of unfamiliar words as well as looking up some of the words in a dictionary.

Some pharaohs were buried in tombs that were hidden in huge **pyramids.** They filled the tombs with gold, jewelry, clothes, toys, furniture, and other precious things. But robbers found the tombs and stole the precious artifacts.

When archaeologists started studying the ancient Egyptians, most of the artifacts from the tombs had disappeared.

The tomb was in the middle of the pyramid. Tunnels went from the tomb to the outside. When the tomb was finished, the tunnels were filled with rocks.

Make a list of things we think of as precious today. Why do we think of these things as precious?

Language Awareness

Grammar
Past Tense

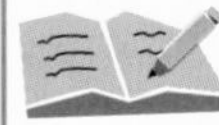

Point out that many verbs have past tense forms that end in *-ed.* Have students find examples in the text in this chapter, such as *lived, died, believed, filled, started.* Invite students to tell some facts that they learned about the ancient Egyptians, using the past tense.

Use Activity Book page 14.

Model a Strategy

Use Diagrams for Meaning

Model using diagrams for meaning:

As I read, I like to look at the diagrams to see if they can help me understand what I'm reading. Diagrams often show things that cannot be shown in a photograph. The diagram of the pyramid shows how the inside of it looks. The words on a diagram are called labels. Labels often appear in the text and help me understand it.

Assess ✓

Students should be able to

- tell some facts about Egyptian pyramids

LOOK **AHEAD**

In the next section, students will learn about a very special tomb, that of King Tut.

Cooperative Learning

The Pyramids and the Valley of the Kings

Have students work in groups to investigate how the tombs were built, what building materials were used, and how the materials got to the site. Have them divide up topics and resources. Ask groups to choose a mural or a dramatization to share their information.

Home Connection

Precious Objects

Invite families to help students decide on "precious" objects for the Write About It activity. Invite families to share objects that are precious to the story of the family. These may be photographs or things that they brought with them from their native countries.

Practice

Activate Prior Knowledge

Review Prior Learning

Have students recall what they have learned about the ancient Egyptians: where they lived, and how they buried their pharaohs.

Develop Language and Concepts

Present Pages 32 and 33

ACTIVITY BOOK

Study the artifact pictures together. Help students name each item, such as chair and mummy.

Read the text with students. Help them make conclusions about King Tut from the objects pictured.

Have students do the Try It Out activity in pairs. For their boxes, students may want to make drawings of precious objects that are too large or too valuable to bring to class. Use Activity Book page 15.

FYI King Tut

- **King Tut's full name was Tutankhamen.**
- **Tut was relatively unknown until the discovery of his tomb in 1922. This is probably due to the shortness of his reign and religious differences with his successors, who tried to eliminate all references to his rule.**

King Tut's Tomb

King Tut lived more than 3,300 years ago. He became king of Egypt when he was 9 years old. He died when he was 18 years old. He lived a short life, but King Tut is one of the most famous pharaohs of all.

In 1922, an archaeologist named Howard Carter discovered King Tut's tomb in the Valley of the Kings.

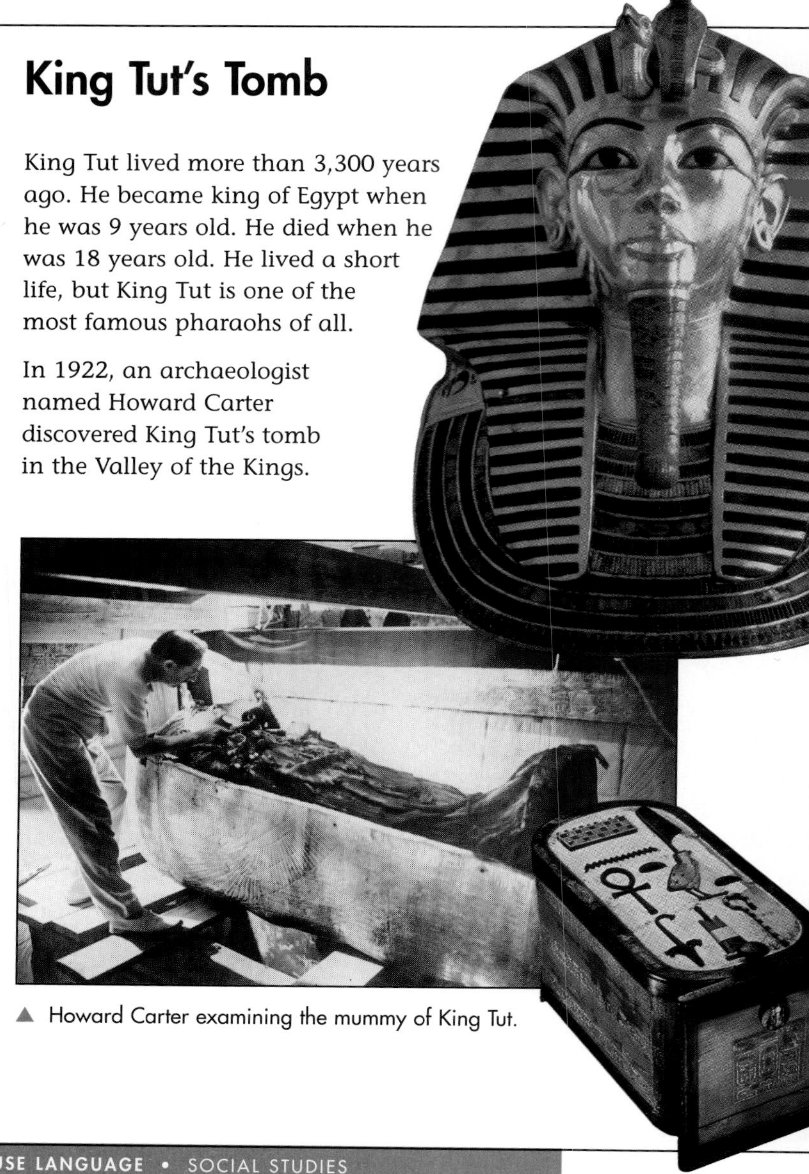

▲ Howard Carter examining the mummy of King Tut.

Options for Reaching All Students

Beginning

Math: Identify Numbers

Have students each write on a separate sheet of paper three or more numbers that relate to their lives. They might include their ages, the dates they were born, the number of brothers and sisters they have, their house numbers, and so on. Then ask a volunteer to write his or her list of numbers on the board. Other students should then say aloud what those numbers are. The student that says all the numbers correctly gets to go to the board to write out his or her numbers.

Advanced

Language: Compare and Contrast

Have students work in pairs. Each pair should begin by separately writing down four or more items they would include in a personal pyramid tomb. Then the two students should compare their lists and determine which things they both put in the tomb. Have pairs share their results.

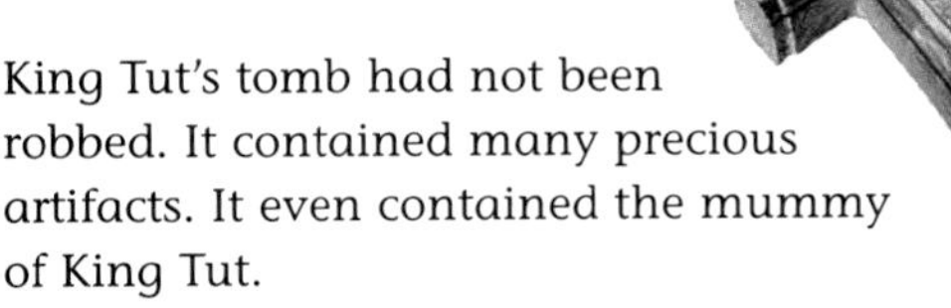

King Tut's tomb had not been robbed. It contained many precious artifacts. It even contained the mummy of King Tut.

The tomb contained gold, jewelry, furniture, toys, games, weapons, food, and other things. Archaeologists have studied these artifacts and have learned a lot about the ancient Egyptians.

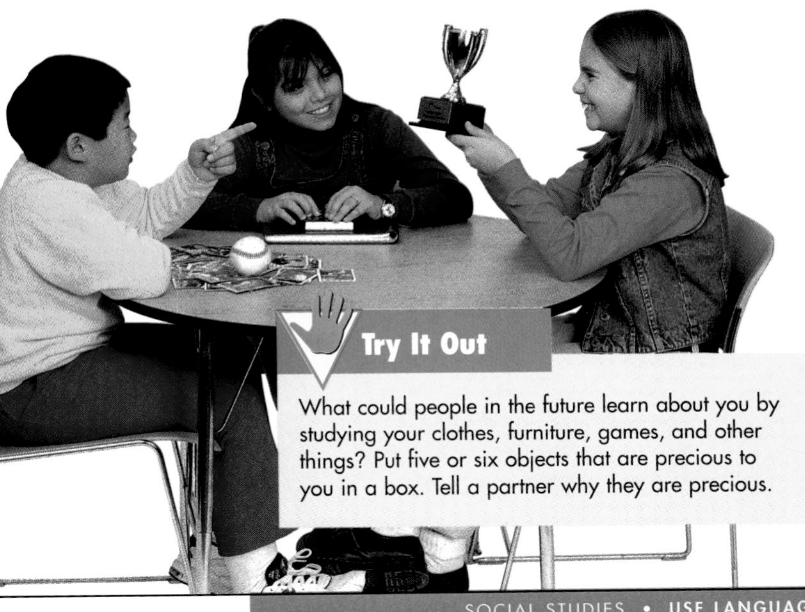

Try It Out

What could people in the future learn about you by studying your clothes, furniture, games, and other things? Put five or six objects that are precious to you in a box. Tell a partner why they are precious.

Language Awareness

Grammar
Expressions *Years Old/Years Ago*

ACTIVITY BOOK

Reread the first three sentences in the text. Point out the expressions *years old* and *years ago.* Help students make sets of personal statements that use *years old* and *years ago.*

I came to the United States two years ago.
I was ten years old.

I came to this school one year ago.
I was eleven years old.

Use Activity Book page 16.

Assess

Students should be able to

- tell who King Tut and Howard Carter were
- name the objects from Tut's tomb shown on the page

LOOK **AHEAD**

In the next section, students will learn about hieroglyphics—the written language of the ancient Egyptians.

Cooperative Learning

Research

Provide students with books about King Tut. Have them work in pairs and write three or four additional facts about King Tut, the discovery of his tomb or things found in his tomb.

QuickCheck

Numbers

Check that students can read numbers and say the numbers either before or after a number you say aloud.

Writer's Workshop

Objects That Tell About You

Refer students to the Writer's Workshop on pages 230 to 236. Have students write about the objects that tell about them. Encourage them to list the objects and tell why the objects are important to them.

Connect

Activate Prior Knowledge

Use Pictures

Write a short sentence on the board. Then have several students from different backgrounds copy the sentence on the board in their native languages. Then say to students: *Could a person who knows only one of the languages shown here figure out the other ones? Why or why not? How?*

Develop Language and Concepts

Present Pages 34 and 35

Read the text with students. Have them look at the pictures of hieroglyphics. Say: *Some hieroglyphics use pictures. Look at the hieroglyphics for water, eye, and star. How do these hieroglyphics use pictures?*

Make sure that students understand that the Rosetta Stone was the key to understanding hieroglyphics because it included the same words in other languages that could be read by modern archeologists.

Explain the concept of an alphabet with students and how the English alphabet has twenty-six letters. Encourage students to exchange information about their languages.

FYI Rosetta Stone

• The Rosetta Stone was found by an officer in Napolean's army in 1799 near the Rosetta mouth of the Nile River.

(Continued on page T35)

Hieroglyphics

The ancient Egyptians used a kind of picture writing called **hieroglyphics.** They wrote in hieroglyphics on the walls of their tombs.

After a time, people forgot how to read hieroglyphics. For 1,000 years, no one in the world could read hieroglyphics.

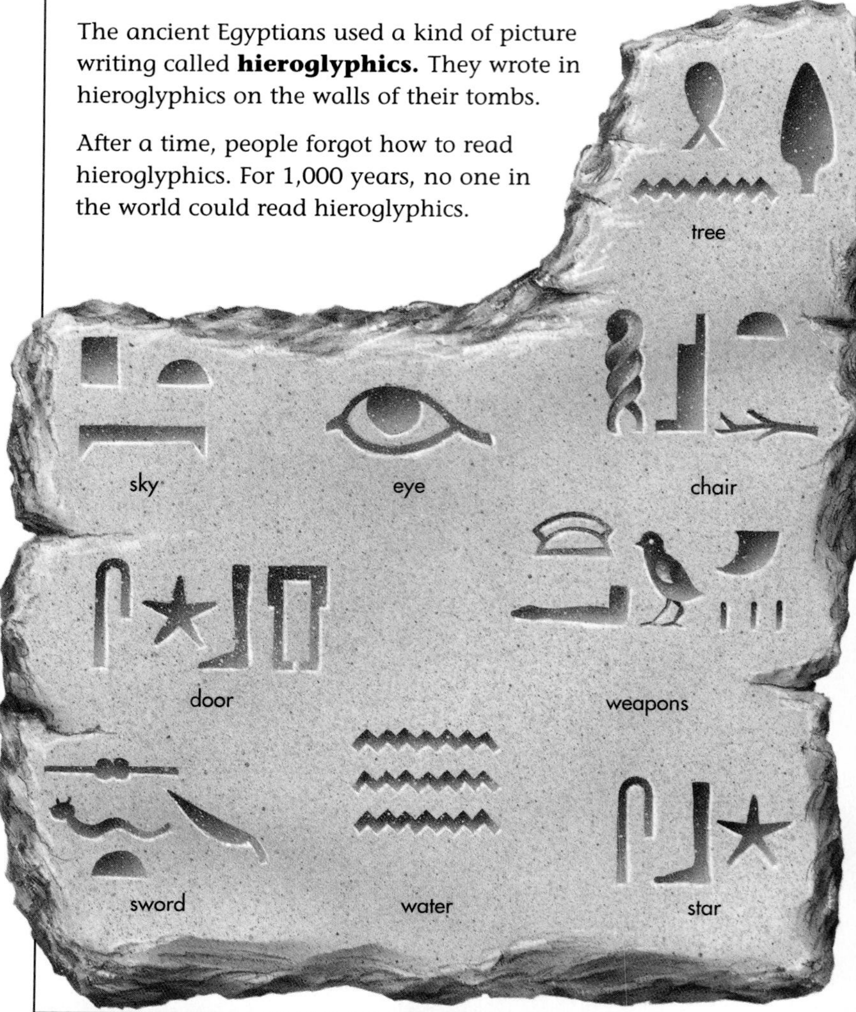

Options for Reaching All Students

Beginning

Language: Picture Writing

Have students write down a simple message in picture language, such as inviting someone to the cafeteria for lunch. Have students trade messages and try to figure them out.

Advanced

Language: Vocabulary in Two Languages

Have students study the words in this lesson to select three or more words that they can write in both English and their native language. Students should write the pairs of words on a sheet of paper and, if possible, draw pictures to illustrate what the pairs mean.

Cooperative Language Experience

A Trip to the Library

Take a class trip to the school library. Have each student choose a topic from this or the previous lessons on Egypt and have them look for books or encyclopedia entries on their topics. Don't overlook CD-ROMs and on-line encyclopedias.

Then in 1799, a soldier found a rock called the Rosetta Stone. There was writing on the Rosetta Stone in three different languages. All three languages said the same thing. One of the languages was hieroglyphics.

After almost 25 years, archaeologists learned how to read the hieroglyphics. Now they could read about the lives of the ancient Egyptians.

Talk About It

What other languages besides English can you read?

How are the written forms of these languages like English? How are they different?

Language Awareness

Vocabulary
Large Numbers

ACTIVITY BOOK

Point out to students that in American English, numbers are grouped in sets of three digits that are set off by commas for ease of understanding: 1,000. Write some other examples on the board and ask students to add commas in the appropriate places. Be sure to include some items that would not use commas.

Use Activity Book page 17.

• The Rosetta Stone contains a decree commemorating the crowning of Ptolemy V Epiphanes as king of Egypt in 203 B.C. The stone shows the decree in three languages: hieroglyphiocs, Greek, and Demotic, the popular language of Egypt at the time.

Assess

Use student's responses to Talk About It for assessment. They should be able to

- tell what languages they speak
- discuss the written forms of the languages they speak

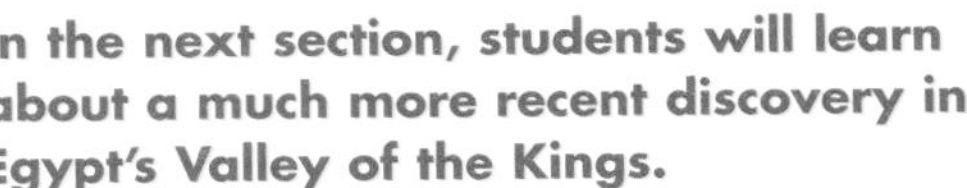

In the next section, students will learn about a much more recent discovery in Egypt's Valley of the Kings.

QuickCheck

Alphabet

Check that students can say the English alphabet and write the letters.

Connect

Activate Prior Knowledge

Use Known Facts to Make Hypotheses

Ask students to name things they already know about ancient Egypt. As students list things, write them on the board. Then ask students: *Do you think all the tombs and artifacts in ancient Egypt have been found already? Why or why not?*

Develop Language and Concepts

Present Pages 36 and 37

Read the text with students and talk about the pictures with them. Help them to identify the main ideas in the article: the *who, what, where,* and *when.* Help them to see how this newspaper article might influence their responses to the questions asked above. Point out that Weeks has created some new ideas about what may or may not remain to be found in the Valley of the Kings. Ask students: *How might Weeks's discoveries change our ideas about our knowledge of the ancient Egyptians?*

New Discovery in Egypt Announced

Egypt, 1995— American archaeologist Kent Weeks has discovered a tomb in Egypt's Valley of the Kings. Most archaeologist believed that all the important tombs there had been discovered. Weeks disagreed, and today the world knows he was correct.

In 1820, archaeologists found a large room in the Valley of the Kings, but they did not think it was important. In 1988, Weeks decided to explore it.

Weeks and his team explored for seven summers. Finally they found a door. Behind the door, they found many more rooms. They had found a large tomb!

Options for Reaching All Students

Beginning

Language: *Many, Most, All, Several*

Have students work individually to write one or more sentences that use the words *many, several,* and *all* and that describe classroom or school situations.

Advanced

Social Studies: More About Ancient Egypt

Have students research and report on other things that remain from ancient Egypt such as the Sphinx and temples. Encourage them to include sizes of monuments and locations of the sites.

Mixed Ability

Language: Write Newspaper Headlines

Have students pretend they are newspaper reporters and editors. Have each group of students review this chapter and make up newspaper story headlines that talk about the things in this chapter as though they had just been discovered. Have students exchange headlines, write them on the board, and work to improve the

Hieroglyphics in the rooms say that several sons of the pharaoh Ramses II were buried in the tomb about 3,000 years ago.

Long ago robbers found the tomb and stole many objects. However, Weeks hopes to find many artifacts as he explores the tomb.

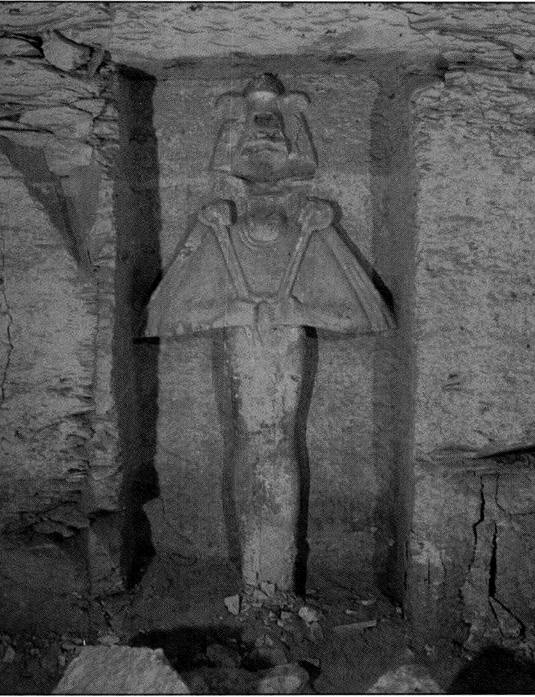

▲ A statue of the god Osiris from the tomb

Think About It

How have ideas about ancient peoples changed?

How did Weeks show that other archaeologists were wrong?

Language Awareness

Grammar
Quantity Words—*All, Most, Many, Several*

ACTIVITY BOOK

Write the words *all, most, many, several* on the board. Illustrate each word in turn using the classroom situation; for example, All the students are sitting. Most students are wearing black shoes. Many students are wearing white shirts. Several students have blue backpacks. Illustrate the words with a diagram: *All* is 100%, *most* is over 50-90%, *many* is 40–70%, *several* is 10%.

Use Activity Book page 18.

Model a Strategy
Keep Track of Chronology

Model how to keep track of the order of events:

When I read an article, I sometimes make a chart to keep track of the events and order in which they happened. I look for important dates. Here I can write 1820, when the room was discovered, 1988, when Weeks started to dig, and 1995, when he found the tomb.

reporters' words by working on such things as appropriate length, understandability, and word choice.

Cooperative Learning
Research

Find out more about Weeks. Have students work in groups. Have them make a Basket of Facts with what they know about Weeks' discovery. Ask them to come up with questions they would like to ask him. Work with the school librarian to find more information, if possible.

Multicultural Connection
Monuments Around the World

Bring in information about monuments in places around the world, such as the Mayan pyramids in Guatemala and the Great Wall of China. Focus on places in countries where students may have lived. Encourage students to invite family members to tell about visits to any of the places.

Connect

Activate Prior Knowledge
Use Pictures

Read the headnote aloud with students. Say to them: *Crocodiles are very ancient animals. They lived in the Nile River Valley long before the first ancient Egyptians lived there. Crocodiles lived near the time of the dinosaurs.*

Develop Language and Concepts
Present Page 38

Read the poem aloud with students at least once before playing Side 2 of the Red Tape. Then play the poem twice for students. Explain the meaning and humor of the poem.

Language Awareness

Phonics
Rhyme

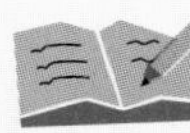

Say to students: *When some words or the end parts of words sound the same, we say that these words rhyme. Some words that rhyme in this poem are Nile, crocodile, smile, and while. They all end in -ile.* Help students find the other *-ile* rhyming words. Discuss the phrases *dishonest, guile,* and *treacherous reptilian style.*

Use Activity Book page 19.

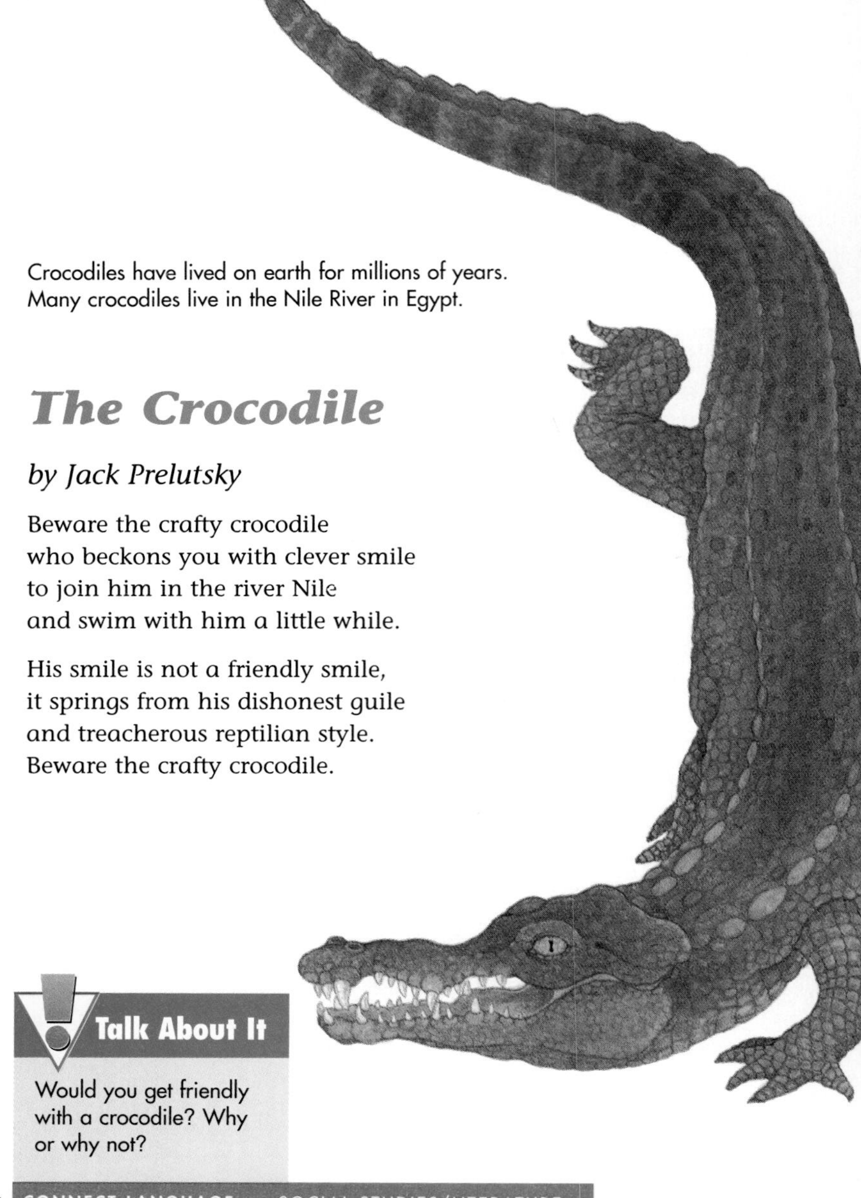

Crocodiles have lived on earth for millions of years. Many crocodiles live in the Nile River in Egypt.

The Crocodile

by Jack Prelutsky

Beware the crafty crocodile
who beckons you with clever smile
to join him in the river Nile
and swim with him a little while.

His smile is not a friendly smile,
it springs from his dishonest guile
and treacherous reptilian style.
Beware the crafty crocodile.

Talk About It

Would you get friendly with a crocodile? Why or why not?

Options for Reaching All Students

Beginning
Language: Rhyming Words

Have students review this unit to find three or more pairs of words that rhyme. They should write down the pairs of words they find. Later, the pairs of students may want to share their findings with each other.

Advanced
Science: Crocodile Report

Have students use encyclopedias to find more information about crocodiles and report to the class. They can answer the question *Are crocodiles really dangerous to people?*

Tell what you learned.

CHAPTER 2

1. How have archaeologists learned about ancient Egypt?
2. Do you think that archaeologists should keep looking for even more tombs in the Valley of the Kings? Why or why not?
3. You are an archaeologist working in Egypt. What artifact would you most like to find? Why?

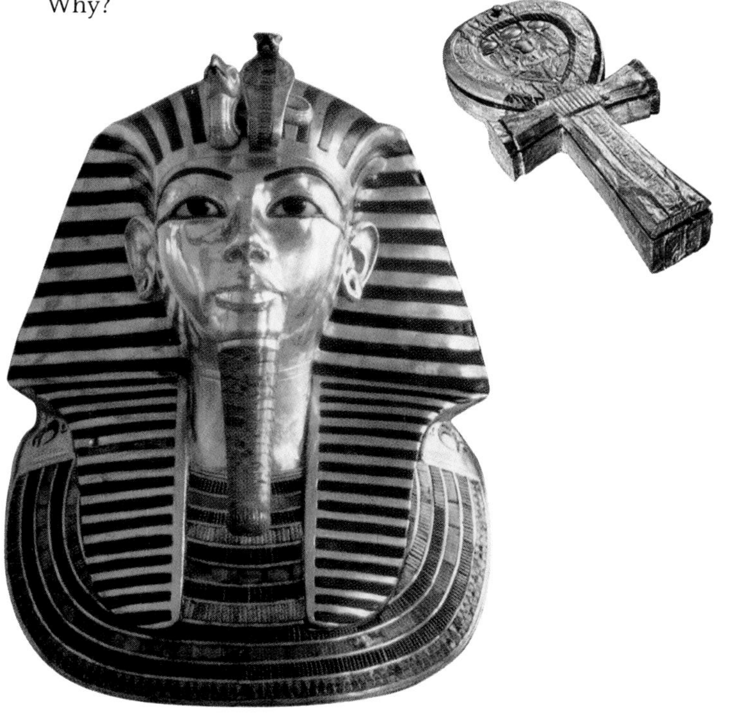

ASSESS LANGUAGE 39

Assess

Activity 1: Evaluate students' understanding of what archaeologists do to learn about ancient peoples.

Activity 2: Check that students realize that Weeks's discovery came a long time after many other archaeologists had long since decided all the major finds in the Valley of the Kings had been made. Students' answers should reflect knowledge of this fact, whether they answer pro or con.

Activity 3: Give students some time to look through the chapter to get ideas of what artifact they would most like to find. Then ask them to tell why they would like that one. Evaluate their reasons.

Have students complete the Chapter Self-Assessment, Blackline Master 31. Have students choose the product of one of the activities to place in their portfolios. Add results of rubrics, checklists, self-assessments, or portfolio assessments, Blackline Masters 2–18 and 31.

Listening Assessment

BLACKLINE MASTER

Make sure that each student has a copy of Blackline Master 43, from the Teacher's Resource Book. Tell students that you will play the tape several times and they should follow the directions for drawing.

WHITE TAPE

See page T1d for the tapescript.

Options for Assessment

Vocabulary Assessment

Alphabet Book for Egyptians

Have students make an alphabet book with words and definitions about ancient Egypt. Have them include as many letters as they can; for example, M is for a mummy. A mummy is a preserved body. P is for pharaoh. The pharaoh was the ruler of Egypt.

Writing Assessment

Facts About Ancient Egypt

Have students make a book with facts about ancient Egypt.

Language Assessment

BLACKLINE MASTER

Use Blackline Master 42 in the Teacher's Resource Book.

Standardized Test Practice

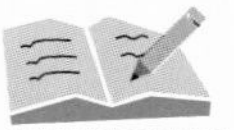

ACTIVITY BOOK

Use pages 20 and 21.
Answers: **1.** 1,402,300 **2.** 80% **3.** N **4.** green

Wrap-Up

Activities

Archaeologist Biography

Have students work in pairs to research an archaeologist such as Howard Weeks or Howard Carter. Ask them to summarize the archaeologist's work and share the information with the class. As a follow-up, have students write a journal for a day in the life of the archaeologist; for example, the day that Weeks found the new tomb mentioned in the book or that Carter first looked into King Tut's tomb.

Report on Digging Up the Past

Encourage advanced students to research the process of an archaeology dig. You might put them in contact with a local university or college that is involved with a local dig. Ask them to find out how a dig site is researched, established, and maintained. Have students report back to the class on their findings.

News Conference

Have students act out a news conference with the "news" about the dinosaurs and ancient Egypt. Several students take the role of a "panel" of expert paleontologists and archaeologists. Other students question them about recent dinosaur discoveries (students can use the information about dinosaurs from the selection in the Student Book) and information they collected about ancient Egypt. Encourage students to read the rest of Patricia Lauber's book to get more "new" information about dinosaurs.

Discussing the Theme

Have students work in small groups to discuss their understanding of the history of dinosaurs and archaeology. Choose from the following activities that will demonstrate to them how much they have learned and how useful that information is to them.

- Have students tape-record a list of new words learned.
- Have students draw or find pictures that represent words they have learned and create a bulletin board display. Ask more advanced students to work with beginning students to label the pictures appropriately.
- Have groups discuss situations in which the words they have learned will be useful, for example, in social studies and science classes. Invite the groups to role-play classroom discussions that incorporate the new words.
- Lead a dinosaur fact conversation trail game: ask a basic question about a dinosaur and then help a student who can answer that question formulate a new question. Assist students as they follow the trail to more dinosaur facts.

Sharing the Project

Use the invitation from Blackline Masters 32 and 33 in the Teacher's Resource Book to invite family members to school to see the museum displays students have prepared as the unit project.

Assign students in pairs to be tour guides. When family members arrive, gather them in groups of 4 to 6 and have a pair of tour guides—one paleontologist and one archaeologist—show them the exhibits.

You might want to assemble the visitors and present the dinosaur fact trail game for them.

Signs of Success!

Duplicate a copy of this checklist for each student.

Name: ______________________________

Refer to the checklist below for a quick demonstration of how a student is progressing toward transitioning out of ESL instruction.

Objectives

- ☐ Describes dinosaurs
- ☐ Tells how scientists learn about dinosaurs
- ☐ Tells when dinosaurs lived
- ☐ Compares old and new ideas about dinosaurs
- ☐ Names ancient Egyptian artifacts
- ☐ Tells how archaeologists learn about the past
- ☐ Tells about ancient Egyptian burial
- ☐ Tells about King Tut's tomb
- ☐ Tells about hieroglyphics

Language Awareness

Understands/Uses:

- ☐ uses headings
- ☐ idiom *turn into*
- ☐ *before* and *after*
- ☐ past tense of the verb *to be*
- ☐ synonyms and antonyms
- ☐ conjunctions *or* and *and*
- ☐ expressions *years old/years ago*
- ☐ past tense

Hears/Pronounces/Reads:

- ☐ consonant *p,* blends *pl, pr*
- ☐ letters *f* and *ph*

Learning Strategies

- ☐ Uses headings
- ☐ Recognizes patterns in English
- ☐ Reads a chart
- ☐ Uses action words in directions
- ☐ Uses diagrams for meaning
- ☐ Finds details
- ☐ Remembers details
- ☐ Keeps track of chronology

Comments

____

____

Planning Guide

Types of Fitness

Objectives

Name various types of physical fitness.

Describe steps one must take to be fit.

Identify body parts.

Understand and use commands in exercises.

Make a fitness plan.

Tell about different games played around the world.

Vocabulary Focus

Kinds of exercise, such as *gymnastics, softball, jogging, swimming.*
Types of fitness, such as *cardiovascular, muscular endurance, flexibility, strength.*
Various aerobic exercise movements, such as *bending, jumping, stretching.*

Lesson	Content Focus	Language Awareness Objectives	Learning Strategies
Preview pp. 40–41 Tell What You Know.			
Present pp. 42–43 How Fit Are You?	Health	**Grammar** When Clauses	
Practice pp. 44–45 Steps to Fitness	Health	**Vocabulary** Numbers Expressed as Words	Rehearse steps.
Practice pp. 46–47 Make a Fitness Plan.	Health	**Grammar** Gerund forms	Read a chart.
Connect pp. 48–49 Games from Many Cultures	Health/ Social Studies	**Grammar** Present Tense	Use reference resources.
Connect pp. 50–51 Jump Rope Rhymes	Health/ Literature	**Phonics** Initial Consonants *b* and *f*	Use techniques to memorize.
Connect p. 52 "Take Me Out to the Ball Game"	Health/ Literature	**Spelling** Contractions	
Assess p. 53 Tell What You Learned.			

Olympic Challenges

Objectives

Describe the history of the Olympic Games.

Explain how the modern games differ from the ancient Olympics.

Name various Olympic events.

Identify skills Olympic athletics need.

Explain the nature of Greek myths.

Vocabulary Focus

Olympic sports, such as *weight lifting, diving, track and field.*

Sport skills Olympic athletes need, such as *balance, coordination, speed, agility.*

Lesson	Content Focus	Language Awareness Objectives	Learning Strategies
Preview pp. 54–55 Tell What You Know.			
Present pp. 56–57 The Olympic Games	Social Studies	**Grammar** Irregular Past Tense	Use a map.
Practice pp. 58–59 Compare the Games	Social Studies	**Grammar** Expression *Such As*	
Practice pp. 60–61 Interesting "Firsts"	Social Studies	**Vocabulary** Ordinal Numbers	Categorize information.
Connect pp. 62–63 Who Is the Fastest?	Social Studies/ Math	**Grammar** Superlatives	
Connect pp. 64–75 *Atalanta and the Golden Apples*	Social Studies/ Literature	**Grammar** Subject Pronouns **Grammar** Real Conditional Sentences **Grammar** Regular Past Tense	Predict before and during reading.
Connect p. 76 "I Am the Running Girl"	Social Studies/ Literature	**Spelling** Basic Punctuation Rules	
Assess p. 77 Tell What You Learned.			

Resources

Chapter 3

Support Materials

ACTIVITY BOOK

pages 22–31

VIDEO

Unit 2, Good Sports

ORANGE TAPE

Side 2
"Hey Little Girl," page T50
"Miss Mary Mack," page T51
"Take Me Out to the Ball Game," page T52

DISK

Writer's Notebook

Assessment Materials

BLACKLINE MASTER

Language Assessment, Blackline Master 50
Listening Assessment, Blackline Master 51

WHITE TAPE

Side 1
Listening Assessment, page T53

Listen carefully. You will hear the steps for an exercise. Write down the steps. You will hear the directions once. Then you will hear them again more slowly. Begin to write. Then you will hear the directions one more time. Check what you wrote.

1. Raise your arms up.
2. Touch your head.
3. Touch your shoulders.
4. Bend your knees.
5. Jump four times.
6. Take one hop forward.

Newcomer Book C

Survival language for absolute beginners. For overview, see pages xxviii–xxix.

For Extended Reading

Bicycle Rider by Mary Scioscia, Harper & Row, 1983

Champion bicyclist Marshall Taylor wins his first race!

Level: Beginning

Joe Montana: Comeback Quarterback by Thomas R. Raber, Lerner Publications Company, 1989

The story of the exciting career, from college to Super Bowl, of retired quarterback, Joe Montana.

Level: Average

Michael Jordan: The Bulls' Air Power by Mike Herbert, Childrens Press, 1987

The story Michael Jordan, star of the Chicago Bulls and the NBA.

Level: Beginning

Running a Race: How You Walk, Run, and Jump by Steve Parker, Franklin Watts, 1991

Students read about what happens to the body while running and learn proper techniques for warming up and breathing.

Level: Average

Sport: Players, Games & Spectacle by Norman Barrett, Franklin Watts, 1993

Diagrams and illustrations help chronicle sporting events from the beginning of time until today.

Level: Advanced

25 Great Moments by Geoffrey C. Ward and Ken Burns, Alfred A. Knopf, 1994

Exciting accounts of great moments in baseball history.

Level: Advanced

Related Technology

Sports Illustrated for Kids: Sports Encyclopedia, Creative Multimedia, 1994

Lots of good information about all sports, written especially for kids.

Chapter 4

Support Materials

pages 32–41

Side 1

Atalanta and the Golden Apples: A Greek Myth, pages T64–75

Side 2

"I Am the Running Girl," page T76

Assessment Materials

Language Assessment, Blackline Master 52

Listening Assessment, Blackline Master 53

Side 1

Listening Assessment, page T77

Listen carefully. Circle the sports you hear mentioned.

The Olympic games are a popular event watched by millions of people around the world. One of the most-watched sports of all is women's gymnastics. This sport is beautiful to look at. It requires much agility and balance on the part of its participants. One person who helped to make the sport popular was Nadia Comaneci, who scored a perfect 10 in the 1976 Olympics. One of the best-known events in the Olympics is the marathon. This twenty-six mile race is the last event in the Summer Olympics. The runners cross the finish line in the Olympic stadium. In the Winter Olympics, the most popular sport is skiing. The most spectacular event is the downhill race, in which skiers go down a steep hill at speeds of seventy to eighty miles an hour.

For Extended Reading

Greek Myths by Geraldine McCreaught,

Classic stories of the ancient Greeks retold by the author.

Level: Average

Jesse Owens by Wayne Coffey, Blackbirch Press, Inc., 1992

The spectacular life of this four-time Olympic gold medalist, who overcame racial prejudice and other hardships to achieve his goal.

Level: Average

Journey to Olympia: The Story of the Olympic Games by Tessa Duder, Scholastic Inc., 1992

A detailed look at the history of the Olympic games.

Level: Average

The Olympians: Great Gods and Goddesses of Ancient Greece by Leonard Everett Fisher, Holiday, 1984

Learn about the gods and goddesses who inspired the first Olympic games in ancient Greece.

Level: Average

The Olympic Games by Julian May, Creative Education, 1975

An overview of the Olympic games from their beginning to the present.

Level: Average

The Winter Olympics by Caroline Arnold, Franklin Watts, 1983

Learn about the origins of the winter Olympics and its events.

Level: Average

Related Technology

Myths of Ancient Greece, Queue, Inc., 1995

Well-illustrated and narrated.

Project

Class Olympics

This optional project can be completed over the next two chapters. In this project, students will participate in sports and other kinds of competitions. See the Unit Wrap Up, page T77a, for more ideas on sharing the project with family members.

What You'll Need

Arrange special access to:

- the school gym or yard
- sports equipment from the physical education department (including balls, jump ropes, mats, and so on)

Collect the following materials:

- a stopwatch or watch with a second hand
- a camera or video camera
- a notebook for recording information
- yellow, blue, and green construction paper or other materials for awards
- cardboard
- string or yarn
- sheets of oak tag
- scissors
- felt-tipped markers

Beginning the Project

Tell students that the class will be organizing its own Olympic games and that students will be choosing which events to include. Review with them the five kinds of fitness (cardiovascular, flexibility, muscular endurance, strength, and body fatness) and the six sports skills (coordination, agility, fast reaction time, speed, strength, and balance) that they have considered in the unit. Encourage them to come up with games that relate top the fitness or sports skills. If possible, enlist the help of someone from the physical education department to help with ideas for games.

Encourage students to name games from their countries of origin that they could teach to other students. Be aware of any physically challenged students, prompting them to develop creative physical activities at which they might excel, such as throwing a Frisbee as far as possible for a student who is confined to a wheelchair. Game choices should be appropriate for all members of the class.

Possibilities might be a three-legged race (coordination), dodge ball (agility and fast reaction time), a potato and spoon relay (balance).

In addition, include two or three nonphysical activities to include in the Olympics such as activities related to the study of English; for example, a spelling bee, a game in which students are given English words and draw them or use them in sentences, and word unscrambling games.

Hold a class vote to choose ten events for the class Olympics, and help students make a large chart featuring each activity as a heading.

Home Involvement

Send the Letter to the Family, Blackline Masters 44–49, to families, explaining that the class will be organizing its own Olympic games and that students will be "training" for their events for at least a few minutes each day. Encourage families to discuss games and sports in their native countries.

Daily Discussion

Use discussion time each day to plan the details of the Olympic events. There are some items to consider:

- event selection
- rules must be clear, fair, and written
- space availability and requirements for the events
- schedule of events: how will the space be used and set up
- judges
- awards
- sign-ups

Encourage each student to participate in at least one event, allowing students who do not want to compete to serve as counters for events or as set-up crew only as a last resort. After students have decided in which events they will compete, ask them how they plan to train for their events. Help each student develop a training schedule: for example, a student competing in a ball-bouncing event might plan to bounce a ball for two ten-minute sessions each day. If possible, schedule extra times in the gym when students can train.

The Class Olympics

Hold the Class Olympics in the school yard or gym.

Prepare for the day of the games by helping students make a large sign announcing each event. Post the sign and change it as each game is completed. Physical events should be organized according to categories of fitness, and signs should include both the type of fitness and the name of the event, for example, "Strength: The Frisbee Throw." Other events can be organized in subject areas or other appropriate categories.

Set up an area for judges, who will be responsible for measuring times and determining the results: first place (gold), second place (silver), and third place (bronze) for each event. People from the physical education department or the administration might be willing to act as judges.

Take pictures during the games; if possible, use a videocamera.

When the games are over, fill in the class chart with the names of the winners.

Activity Book

Chapter 3

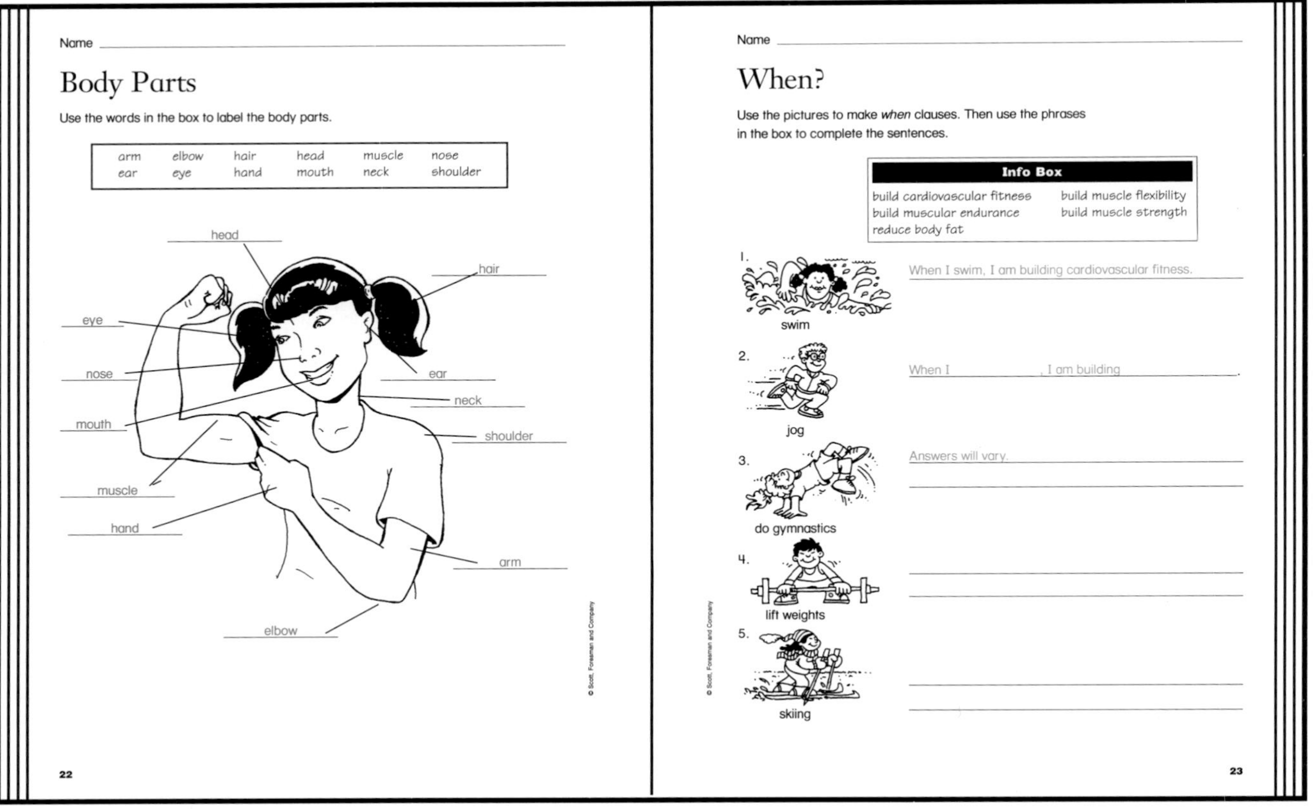

Name ____________________

Body Parts

Use the words in the box to label the body parts.

arm	elbow	hair	head	muscle	nose
ear	eye	hand	mouth	neck	shoulder

© Scott, Foresman and Company

22

Name ____________________

When?

Use the pictures to make *when* clauses. Then use the phrases in the box to complete the sentences.

Info Box

build cardiovascular fitness
build muscular endurance
reduce body fat
build muscle flexibility
build muscle strength

1. swim — When I swim, I am building cardiovascular fitness.
2. jog — When I ________, I am building ________.
3. do gymnastics — Answers will vary.
4. lift weights
5. skiing

© Scott, Foresman and Company

23

Name ____________________

Practice with Numbers

Write the missing numbers in the blanks. Say the numbers. Check them with a partner.

1. Count by fives from 25 to 75.
   25, 30, 35, 40, 45, 50, 55, 60, 65, 70, 75
2. Count by tens from 80 to 150.
   80, 90, 100, 110, 120, 130, 140, 150
3. Count by fifties from 200 to 500.
   200, 250, 300, 350, 400, 450, 500
4. Count backwards from 65 to 55.
   65, 64, 63, 62, 61, 60, 59, 58, 57, 56, 55
5. Count backwards by fives from 30 to 0.
   30, 25, 20, 15, 10, 5, 0

Write the numbers.

22 twenty-two
100 one hundred
19 nineteen
75 seventy-five
56 fifty-six
12 twelve

Write your personal numbers.

My Personal Numbers

My street number is Answers will vary.
My favorite number is ____________
My age is ____________
The year I was born was ____________

© Scott, Foresman and Company

24

Name ____________________

My Plan

Use this chart for the Write About It activity on page 47 in the Student Book.

Physical Activities I Do	How Often?	Kind of Fitness the Activity Builds

Complete the sentences.

I would like to improve this fitness area: Answers will vary.
I will use this activity: ____________
I will do it ________ times a week.
This is the time I plan to do it: ____________

© Scott, Foresman and Company

25

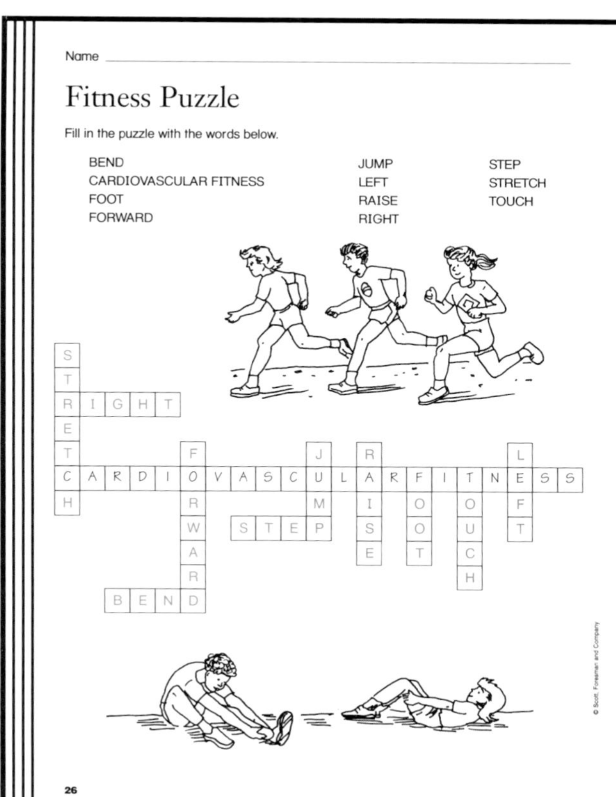

Name ______________________

Fitness Puzzle

Fill in the puzzle with the words below.

BEND	JUMP	STEP
CARDIOVASCULAR FITNESS	LEFT	STRETCH
FOOT	RAISE	TOUCH
FORWARD	RIGHT	

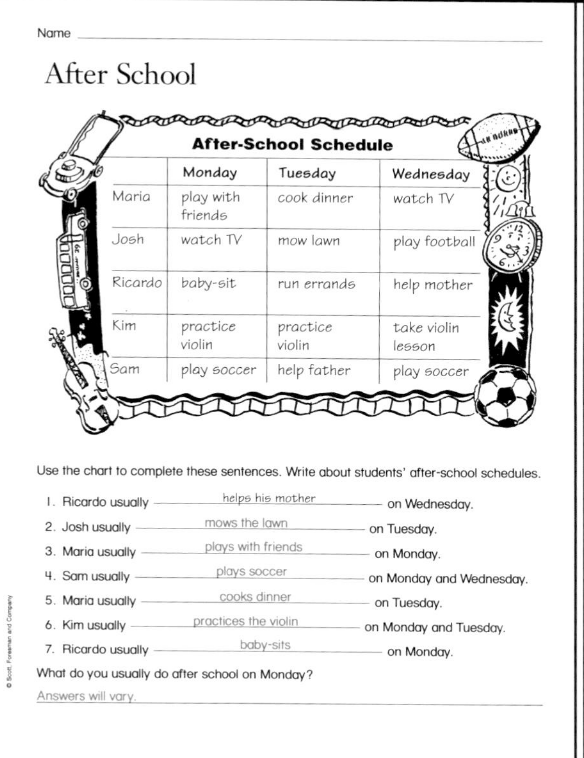

Name ______________________

After School

After-School Schedule

	Monday	Tuesday	Wednesday
Maria	play with friends	cook dinner	watch TV
Josh	watch TV	mow lawn	play football
Ricardo	baby-sit	run errands	help mother
Kim	practice violin	practice violin	take violin lesson
Sam	play soccer	help father	play soccer

Use the chart to complete these sentences. Write about students' after-school schedules.

1. Ricardo usually helps his mother on Wednesday.
2. Josh usually mows the lawn on Tuesday.
3. Maria usually plays with friends on Monday.
4. Sam usually plays soccer on Monday and Wednesday.
5. Maria usually cooks dinner on Tuesday.
6. Kim usually practices the violin on Monday and Tuesday.
7. Ricardo usually baby-sits on Monday.

What do you usually do after school on Monday?

Answers will vary.

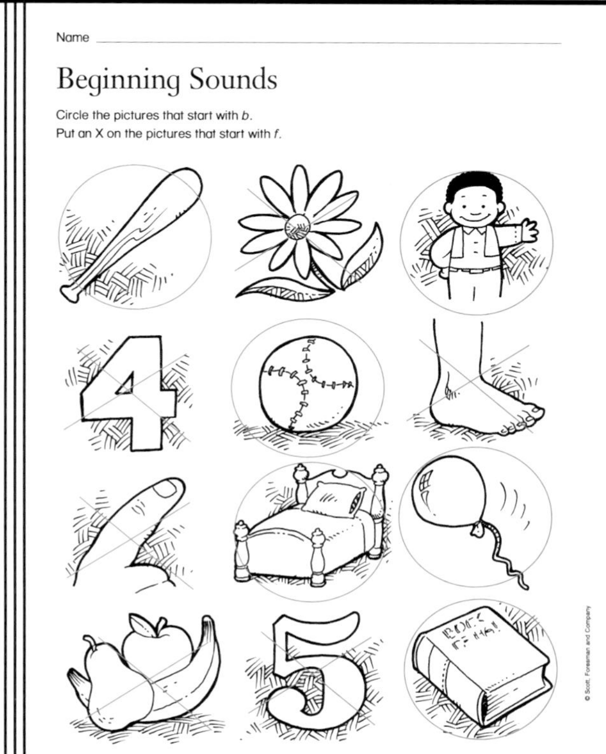

Name ______________________

Beginning Sounds

Circle the pictures that start with *b*.
Put an X on the pictures that start with *f*.

Name ______________________

Contractions

Fill in the blanks with words from the box.

Info Box

did not / didn't
do not / don't
have not / haven't
he is / he's
is not / isn't
they are / they're
we are / we're
you are / you're

	Contraction	Long Form
1.	isn't	is not
2.	you're	you are
3.	don't	do not
4.	they're	they are
5.	he's	he is
6.	we're	we are
7.	didn't	did not
8.	haven't	have not

Write contractions in the blanks.

1. We're (We are) going to a party.
2. He isn't (is not) going to the party.
3. You're (You are) going with us.
4. They haven't (have not) gotten a present yet.
5. She didn't (did not) know what to bring as a present.

Activity Book

Chapter 4

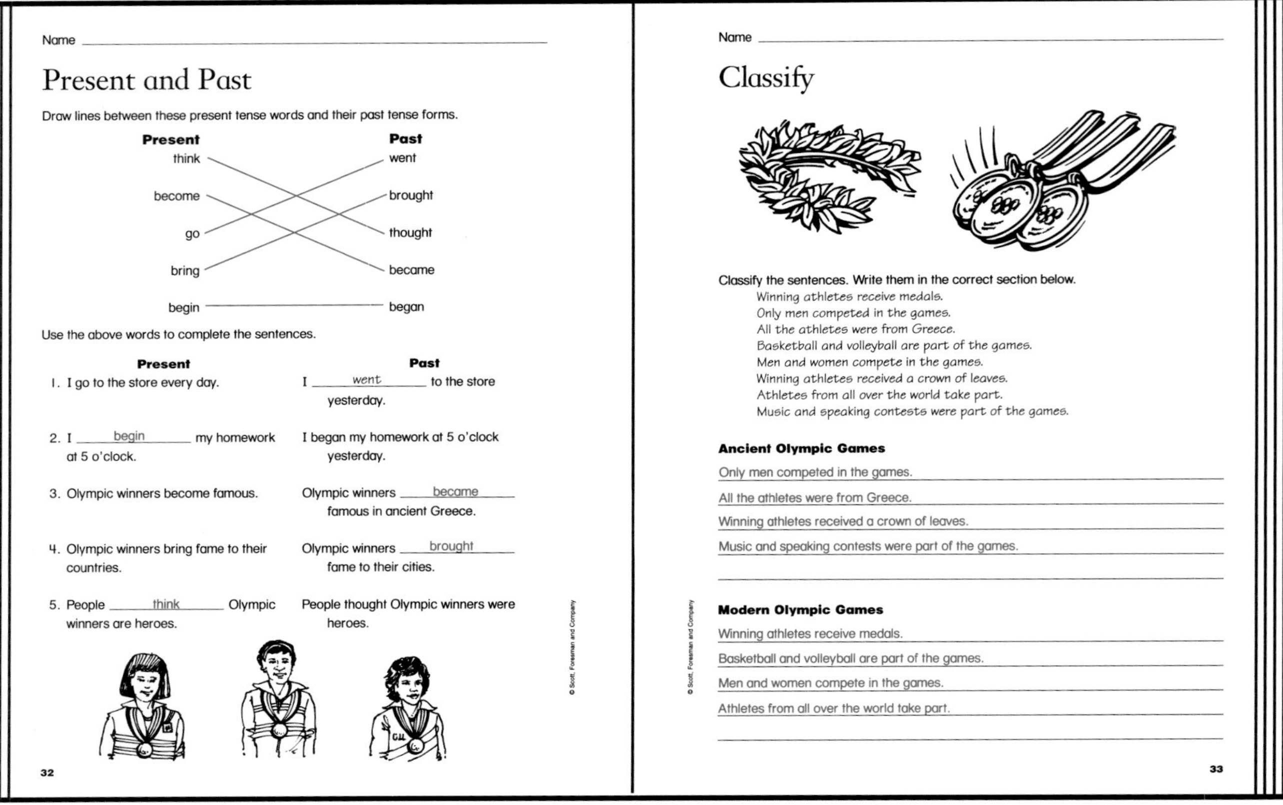

Name ______________________

Present and Past

Draw lines between these present tense words and their past tense forms.

Present	Past
think	went
become	brought
go	thought
bring	became
begin	began

Use the above words to complete the sentences.

Present	Past
1. I go to the store every day.	I ___went___ to the store yesterday.
2. I ___begin___ my homework at 5 o'clock.	I began my homework at 5 o'clock yesterday.
3. Olympic winners become famous.	Olympic winners ___became___ famous in ancient Greece.
4. Olympic winners bring fame to their countries.	Olympic winners ___brought___ fame to their cities.
5. People ___think___ Olympic winners are heroes.	People thought Olympic winners were heroes.

Name ______________________

Classify

Classify the sentences. Write them in the correct section below.

Winning athletes receive medals.
Only men competed in the games.
All the athletes were from Greece.
Basketball and volleyball are part of the games.
Men and women compete in the games.
Winning athletes received a crown of leaves.
Athletes from all over the world take part.
Music and speaking contests were part of the games.

Ancient Olympic Games

Only men competed in the games.
All the athletes were from Greece.
Winning athletes received a crown of leaves.
Music and speaking contests were part of the games.

Modern Olympic Games

Winning athletes receive medals.
Basketball and volleyball are part of the games.
Men and women compete in the games.
Athletes from all over the world take part.

Name ______________________

Which Floor?

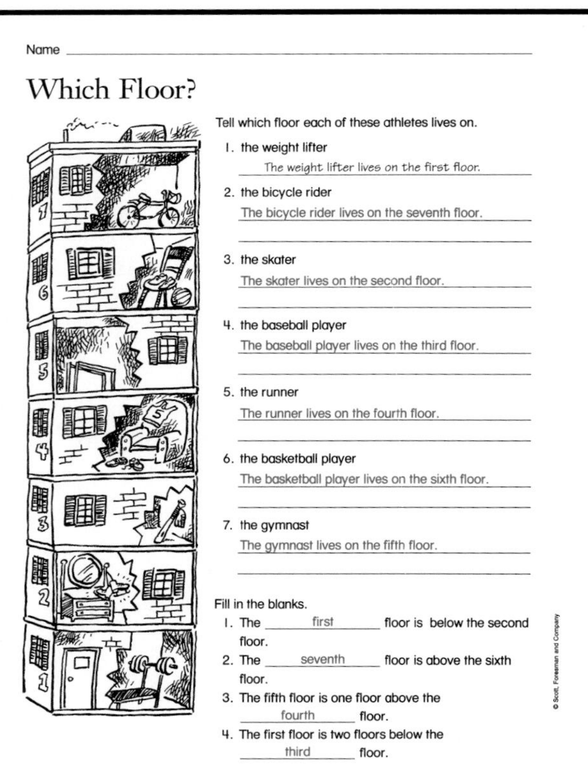

Tell which floor each of these athletes lives on.

1. the weight lifter
   The weight lifter lives on the first floor.
2. the bicycle rider
   The bicycle rider lives on the seventh floor.
3. the skater
   The skater lives on the second floor.
4. the baseball player
   The baseball player lives on the third floor.
5. the runner
   The runner lives on the fourth floor.
6. the basketball player
   The basketball player lives on the sixth floor.
7. the gymnast
   The gymnast lives on the fifth floor.

Fill in the blanks.

1. The ___first___ floor is below the second floor.
2. The ___seventh___ floor is above the sixth floor.
3. The fifth floor is one floor above the ___fourth___ floor.
4. The first floor is two floors below the ___third___ floor.

Name ______________________

Chart

Use this chart for the activity on pages 62 and 63 of the Student Book.
Show distance, time, and meters per second for each event.

Event	Distance	Time	Meters per Second
Men's track	100	9.96 seconds	10.04 meters
Men's track	800	103.66 seconds	7.72 meters
Men's track	5,000	792.52 seconds	6.31 meters
Women's swimming	100	54.64 seconds	1.83 meters
Women's swimming	800	505.52 seconds	1.58 meters
Men's speed skating	500	36.33 seconds	13.76 meters
Men's speed skating	5,000	394.96 seconds	12.66 meters

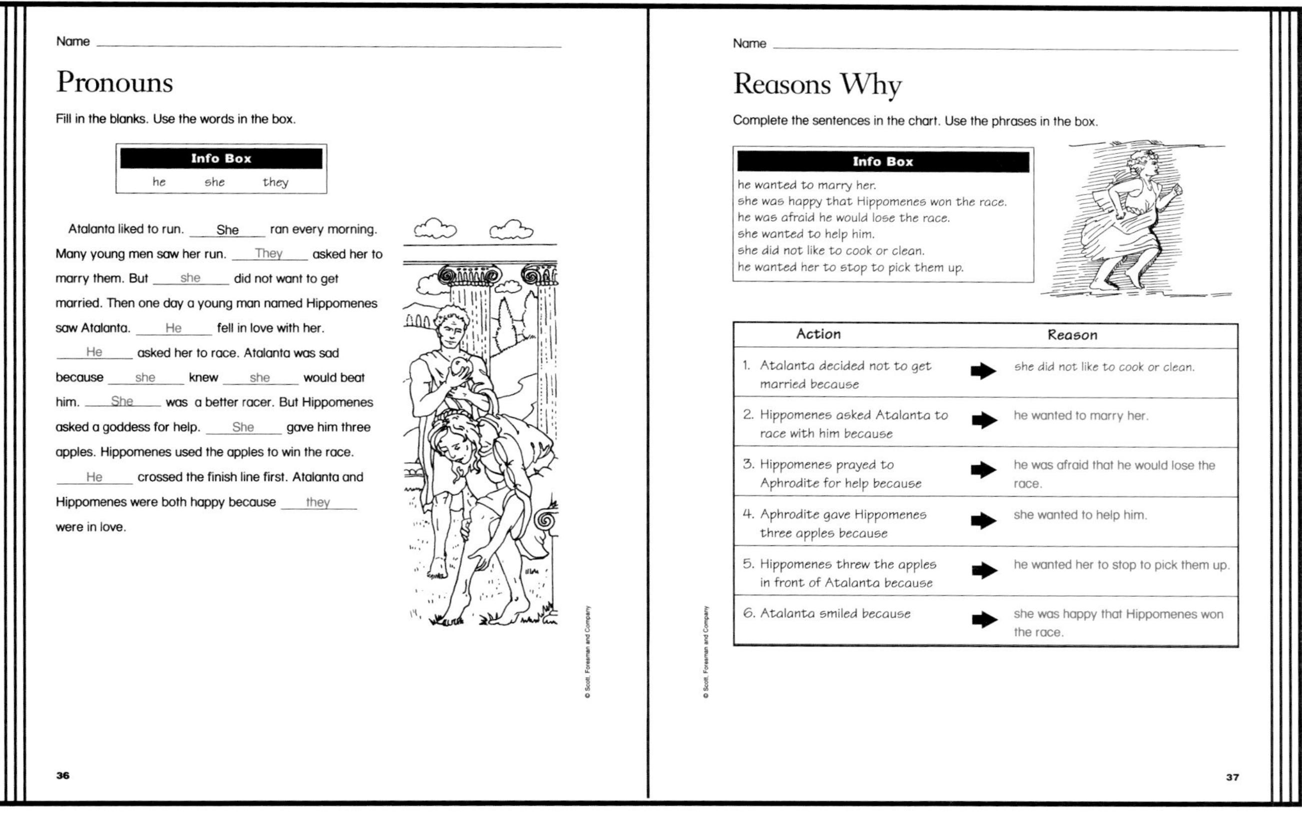

Name ______________________

Pronouns

Fill in the blanks. Use the words in the box.

Info Box

he she they

Atalanta liked to run. __She__ ran every morning. Many young men saw her run. __They__ asked her to marry them. But __she__ did not want to get married. Then one day a young man named Hippomenes saw Atalanta. __He__ fell in love with her. __He__ asked her to race. Atalanta was sad because __she__ knew __she__ would beat him. __She__ was a better racer. But Hippomenes asked a goddess for help. __She__ gave him three apples. Hippomenes used the apples to win the race. __He__ crossed the finish line first. Atalanta and Hippomenes were both happy because __they__ were in love.

Name ______________________

Reasons Why

Complete the sentences in the chart. Use the phrases in the box.

Info Box

he wanted to marry her.
she was happy that Hippomenes won the race.
he was afraid he would lose the race.
she wanted to help him.
she did not like to cook or clean.
he wanted her to stop to pick them up.

Action		Reason
1. Atalanta decided not to get married because	➡	she did not like to cook or clean.
2. Hippomenes asked Atalanta to race with him because	➡	he wanted to marry her.
3. Hippomenes prayed to Aphrodite for help because	➡	he was afraid that he would lose the race.
4. Aphrodite gave Hippomenes three apples because	➡	she wanted to help him.
5. Hippomenes threw the apples in front of Atalanta because	➡	he wanted her to stop to pick them up.
6. Atalanta smiled because	➡	she was happy that Hippomenes won the race.

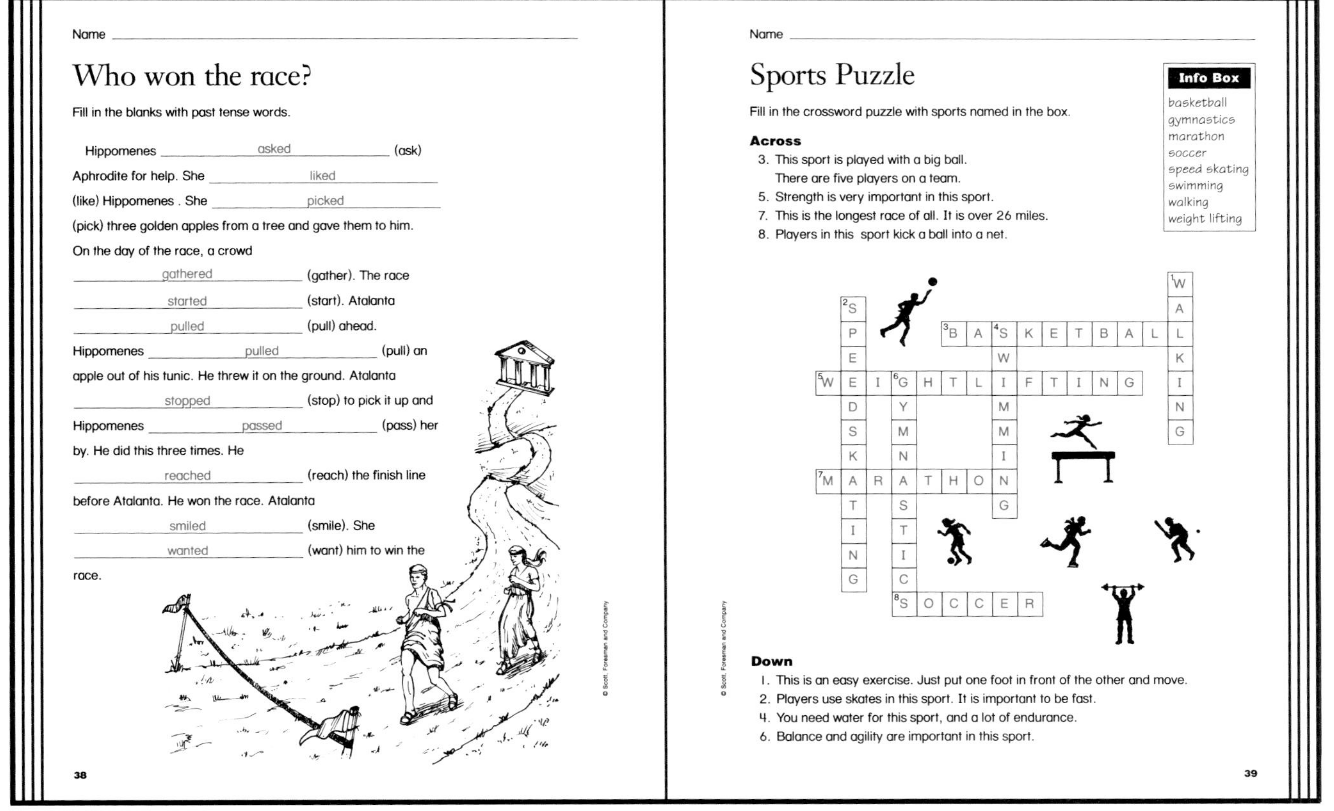

Name ______________________

Who won the race?

Fill in the blanks with past tense words.

Hippomenes __asked__ (ask) Aphrodite for help. She __liked__ (like) Hippomenes . She __picked__ (pick) three golden apples from a tree and gave them to him. On the day of the race, a crowd __gathered__ (gather). The race __started__ (start). Atalanta __pulled__ (pull) ahead. Hippomenes __pulled__ (pull) an apple out of his tunic. He threw it on the ground. Atalanta __stopped__ (stop) to pick it up and Hippomenes __passed__ (pass) her by. He did this three times. He __reached__ (reach) the finish line before Atalanta. He won the race. Atalanta __smiled__ (smile). She __wanted__ (want) him to win the race.

Name ______________________

Sports Puzzle

Fill in the crossword puzzle with sports named in the box.

Info Box

basketball
gymnastics
marathon
soccer
speed skating
swimming
walking
weight lifting

Across

3. This sport is played with a big ball. There are five players on a team.
5. Strength is very important in this sport.
7. This is the longest race of all. It is over 26 miles.
8. Players in this sport kick a ball into a net.

														1 W
	2 S													A
	P				3 B	A	4 S	K	E	T	B	A	L	L
	E						W							K
5 W	E	I	6 G	H	T	L	I	F	T	I	N	G		I
	D		Y				M							N
	S		M				M							G
	K		N				I							
7 M	A	R	A	T	H	O	N							
	T		S				G							
	I		T											
	N		I											
	G		C											
			8 S	O	C	C	E	R						

Down

1. This is an easy exercise. Just put one foot in front of the other and move.
2. Players use skates in this sport. It is important to be fast.
4. You need water for this sport, and a lot of endurance.
6. Balance and agility are important in this sport.

UNIT 2

Preview

Activate Prior Knowledge

Use Pictures

Collect several sports magazines and distribute them among students. Let students examine them in groups. Help students name the sports in the pictures and comment on them. List vocabulary on a large piece of chart paper.

Have students talk about the kinds of exercise they do and the sports they play. Add the names to the list.

Ask students why people exercise and play sports. Discuss fitness and the role sports play in keeping people fit at all ages.

Develop Language and Concepts

Present Pages 40 and 41

Help students describe the activities in the pictures on pages 40 and 41: playing softball, doing gymnastics, walking, jogging, and swimming. Have them suggest other sports activities. Introduce the Word Bank, relating the words to the illustrations.

Have students answer the questions in Tell What You Know. Finally, have students answer the questions in Talk About It activity in small groups.

Good Sports

Word Bank

- do gymnastics
- jog
- play softball
- run
- swim
- walk

Tell what you know.

What is fitness?

What are some ways to get fit?

Options for Reaching All Students

Beginning

Language: Words and Pictures

TPR

Write the following words on the board and read them with the students: *do gymnastics, jog, run, play softball, swim, walk*. Then have the students play an action/mime game such as "Simon Says" to practice using the words and reinforce meaning with movement.

Advanced

Writing: Sports Sentences

Use the same six words as in the beginning students' activity, but have the students illustrate and write sentences to go with the illustrations; for example, *The girl likes to do gymnastics*, or *My father likes to jog.*

Mixed Ability

Video: Good Sports

VIDEO

Show the Unit 2 portion of the video to give students an overview of the unit. You may want to replay the tape several times throughout the unit for language and concept reinforcement and development.

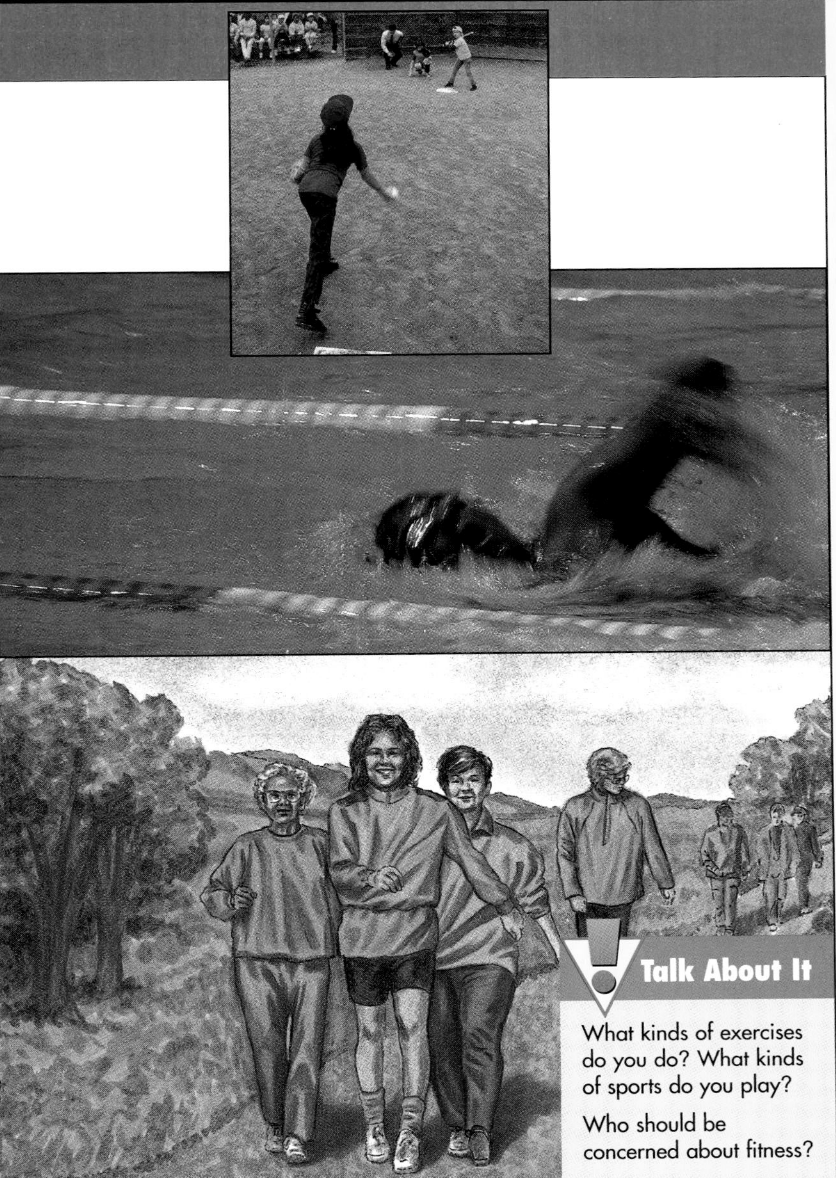

Talk About It
What kinds of exercises do you do? What kinds of sports do you play?
Who should be concerned about fitness?
41

THEME/KEY CONCEPTS

In this unit, students examine sports and fitness. They will learn about the history of the Olympic games. Both keeping fit and competing in sports tie in with the theme of challenges.

Chapter 3

- There are various types of fitness, such as cardiovascular fitness.
- Different kinds of physical activities contribute to different types of fitness, as well as to overall fitness.
- Students make a personal plan for regular exercise.

Chapter 4

- Sports were important to the ancient Greeks, as evidenced in their setting up the original Olympic Games.
- The ancient and modern Olympics are alike in some ways, but different in many ways.
- A literature selection introduces ancient Greek mythology in the context of a story about a runner.

Cooperative Learning

Use a Graphic Organizer

Distribute copies of the Idea Web, Blackline Master 20 in the Teacher's Resource Book to pairs of students. Have students write the name of a sport in the center and fill in the web. Here are some ideas for categories:

Who plays?
Who wins?
What equipment?

Home Connection

Talk About Sports

Have students work with family members to make a list of sports played in their home countries. If they have pictures to illustrate the sports, they should bring them to class. Have all students practice *In my home country, the people play . . .* or *In my home country, the people (ski, bowl).* List the sports and countries.

Present

Activate Prior Knowledge

Use Pictures

Have students look at the pictures on page 43 and identify what the people are doing in each of the pictures. Have them discuss the sports they participate in, or those they like to watch. As each sport is named, have the students tell which parts of their bodies they use in that particular sport.

Develop Language and Concepts

Present Pages 42 and 43

ACTIVITY BOOK

Help students name and locate parts of the body in the diagram. Read the text with students. With the class, make a chart similar to the following for the five types of physical fitness and related activities.

Type of Fitness	Activities That Promote It
Cardiovascular	swimming, bike riding, jogging, hiking

Explain that some activities develop more than one type of fitness. You might want to consult a health book to ensure accuracy of information.

Use Activity Book page 22 to review parts of the body.

CHAPTER 3

Types of Fitness

How fit are you?

Physical fitness is important for good health. When you are physically fit, your body is in good condition. When you are healthy, your body lets you do the things you want to do and need to do.

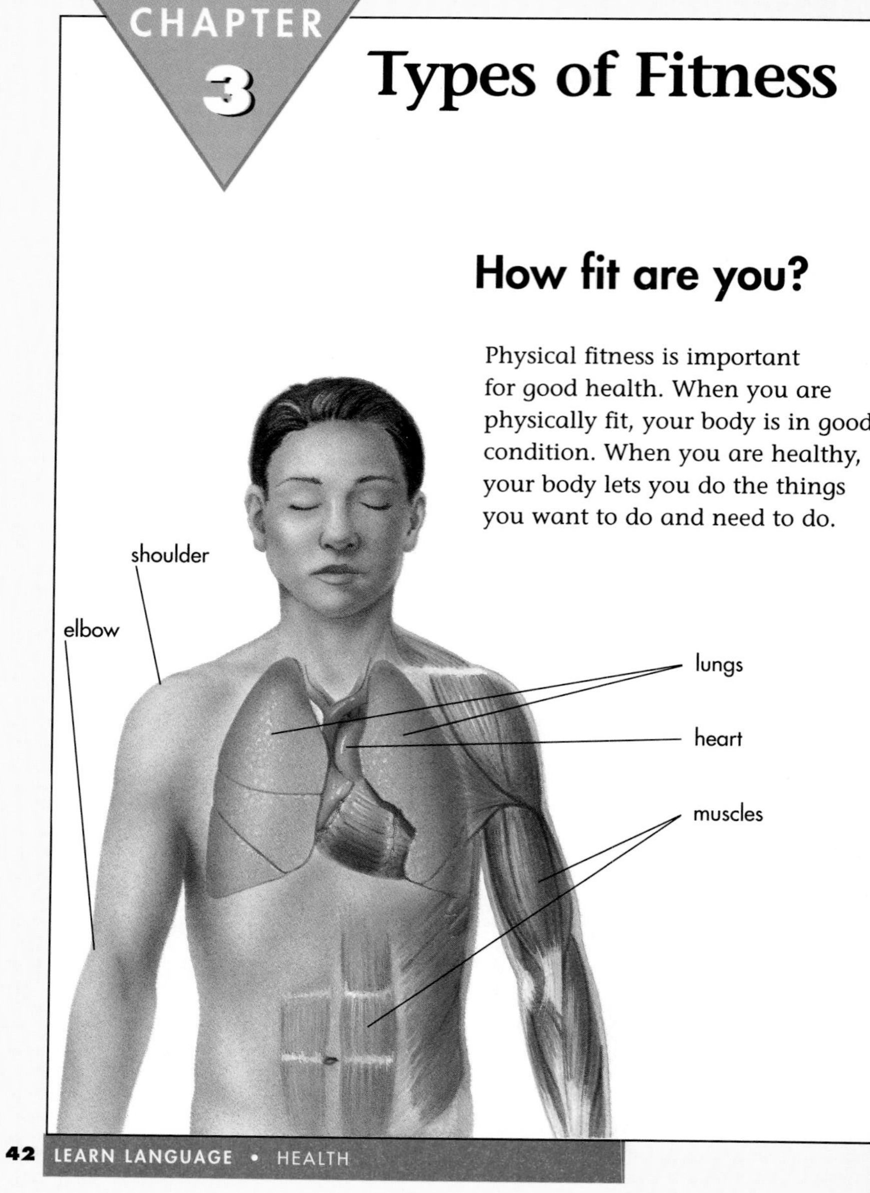

Options for Reaching All Students

Beginning

Health: Make a Chart

Have students create a wall chart, writing the five kinds of fitness on paper strips and label cards for the activities that develop each one. Have them illustrate each activity.

Advanced

Language: *When* Clauses

Have students create their own sentences with *when* clauses. Tell them to make their sentences reflect what they know about fitness. Have them fold a piece of paper in half, and write their sentences with the *when* clause on one side and result clause on the other. Make sure students use a comma at the end of the *when* clause.

Peer Tutoring

Language: Parts of the Body

Pair students of mixed ability and have them review the parts of the body on page 42. Following the review, have students take turns with one student naming a body part and the other student pointing to the part of the body in the illustration. A final review could be to play a modified game of "Simon Says," focusing on the vocabulary from this section of the unit, for example,

Five different kinds of fitness are important for good health.

Cardiovascular fitness means that your heart and lungs are strong. When you ride a bicycle or swim, you are building your cardiovascular fitness.

Muscular endurance means that you can use your muscles for a long time without tiring. When you hike or go jogging, you are building your muscular endurance.

Flexibility means that you can move your joints easily. Your knees, elbows, and shoulders are joints. When you dance or do gymnastics, you are building flexibility.

Strength is the amount of force your muscles can produce. When you lift weights, you are building muscle strength.

Body fatness is the amount of fat in your body. Everyone needs some body fat. But if you have too much body fat, your body has to work harder to carry its weight. You have a greater risk of heart disease. When you go cross-country skiing, you are helping to reduce your body fat.

Think About It

Why do people exercise?

HEALTH • LEARN LANGUAGE 43

Language Awareness

Grammar
When Clauses

ACTIVITY BOOK

Point out to students that *when* clauses are groups of words that describe an event that happens together with another event. Point out the two events in sentences such as the following:

When I go to the park, I play soccer.

Sometimes the event in the *when* clause results in the event in the other clause:

When I read books in English, I am learning a lot of new words.

Underline the *when* clause and point out that it is followed by a comma. Ask which is the result, and circle it.

Have the students find the other *when* clauses in the text on these pages. Use Activity Book page 23.

Assess 

Students should be able to

- name various kinds of fitness and activities that promote that kind of fitness

LOOK**AHEAD**

In the next section, students will test their cardiovascular fitness.

Simon Says touch your shoulder, Simon Says bend your elbow.

QuickCheck

Parts of the Body

Make sure that students can name the parts of the body.

Practice

Activate Prior Knowledge

Demonstrate Exercises

Demonstrate a simple exercise like the ones on the pages in the Student Book; for example, touching one's toes, hips, and head in sequence. Give commands for the exercise. Ask students to give commands for any simple exercise they know.

Develop Language and Concepts

Present Pages 44 and 45

Help students look for words on the pages that express ways to move: *run, step, hop, kick*. Also help them find words that indicate directions: *forward, backward, right, left*. Have students act out the words. Read the text with students.

Tell students they are going to learn how to check their cardiovascular fitness. Make sure that each student can feel his or her own pulse. Explain and demonstrate that the first step is *running in place*. Then have the students practice running in place. Have them take one another's pulses before and after running in place, and record the results.

Then present the aerobic exercise. Have students follow each step slowly and then do the steps quickly to music.

Introduce the words in the Word Bank and have students act them out. Help students with any additional words they need to do the Talk About It activity, in which they present their own exercises.

Steps to Fitness

Test your cardiovascular fitness.

Cardiovascular fitness increases your energy level. It helps you stay active for longer periods of time without tiring.

Do this activity to test your cardiovascular fitness.

Things You Need

a watch or clock with a second hand, or a stopwatch

1. Run in place for 1 minute. Take 2 steps each seconds. This is 120 steps in all.
2. Rest for 1 minute.
3. Feel your pulse. Count your heart rate for 30 seconds.

If you are fit, you will count fewer than 75 heartbeats.

Do an aerobic exercise.

Many people do **aerobic exercises** to build cardiovascular fitness. Your heart is a muscle. Aerobics help exercise your heart.

Read the directions for Step Hop and try it.

1. On count 1, step forward with your right foot.

1

Options for Reaching All Students

Beginning

Language: Follow Directions for Exercises

TPR

Give directions for exercises. Use the words *bend, jump, raise, stretch,* and *touch* and the numbers in your directions to the students. For example, *Bend your knees. Jump ten times. Raise your hand three times. Stretch your leg. Touch your nose.*

Advanced

Language: Instruct Exercises

Have advanced students find other simple exercises in health books and explain them for beginning students to do.

Peer Tutoring

Language: Work with Numbers

Have students work in pairs of mixed ability. Give each pair a tens sequence, such as twenties, forties, eighties and so on. Have them write the numbers in that tens sequence and say the words for the numbers. Expand the activities to sequences of fives or even and odd number sequences.

2. On count 2, step forward with your left foot.

3. On count 3, step forward with your right foot.

4. On count 4, hop on your right foot, kick with your left leg, and clap your hands.

5. Repeat the four counts, but start with your left foot.

Word Bank

bend
jump
raise
stretch
touch

6. Do the exercise quickly in time with music.

Talk About It

What other exercises do you know? Show them and explain how to do them.

Language Awareness

Vocabulary
Numbers Expressed as Words

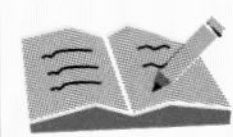
ACTIVITY BOOK

Practice counting to 120 with the students. While many languages use Arabic numerals, the spoken or written expression of numbers beyond ten may be different. Demonstrate spelling of numbers to 120. Point out the use of hyphens in numbers such as twenty-one. Have "number bee" activities in which students give the number before or after the number you say, count by fives, write numbers you say, and so on. Use Activity Book page 24.

Model a Strategy

Rehearse Steps

Model how to rehearse steps:

When I see a numbered list of steps I try to go through them in my mind or act them out slowly before I actually do the activity. This helps me to avoid mistakes.

Assess 

Students should be able to

- follow and give directions for exercises

LOOK **AHEAD**

In the next section, students will make a personal fitness plan.

Home Connection

Cardiovascular Fitness Test

Each student is to perform the cardiovascular fitness test on at least three people outside of the classroom. Have all students make a chart with two columns. In column 1, students list three family members or friends. In column 2, have students list the results of the "test."

Name	Pulse
1.	
2.	
3.	

Practice

Activate Prior Knowledge

Relate Personal Experience

Ask students about how they use schedules and then about schedules for sports and exercises. Discuss how planning helps organize activities and maintain motivation.

Develop Language and Concepts

Present Pages 46 and 47

ACTIVITY BOOK Have students name the sports objects and related sports on the pages: cycling, hiking, weight lifting, and jogging. Read the text with students. Focus attention on the chart. Write the words *excellent, good, fair, poor* on the board in random order. Help students put them in order from very good to least good. Have students answer questions based on the chart such as these:

What are the two best ways to build muscular strength?
Does bicycling build flexibility?

Write on the board: *I like to hike. It is good for building cardiovascular fitness. It is excellent for building muscular endurance.* Ask students to create similar statements.

Have students complete the Write About It activity. Have students use Activity Book page 25 to organize their responses. Use Activity Book page 26 to review vocabulary.

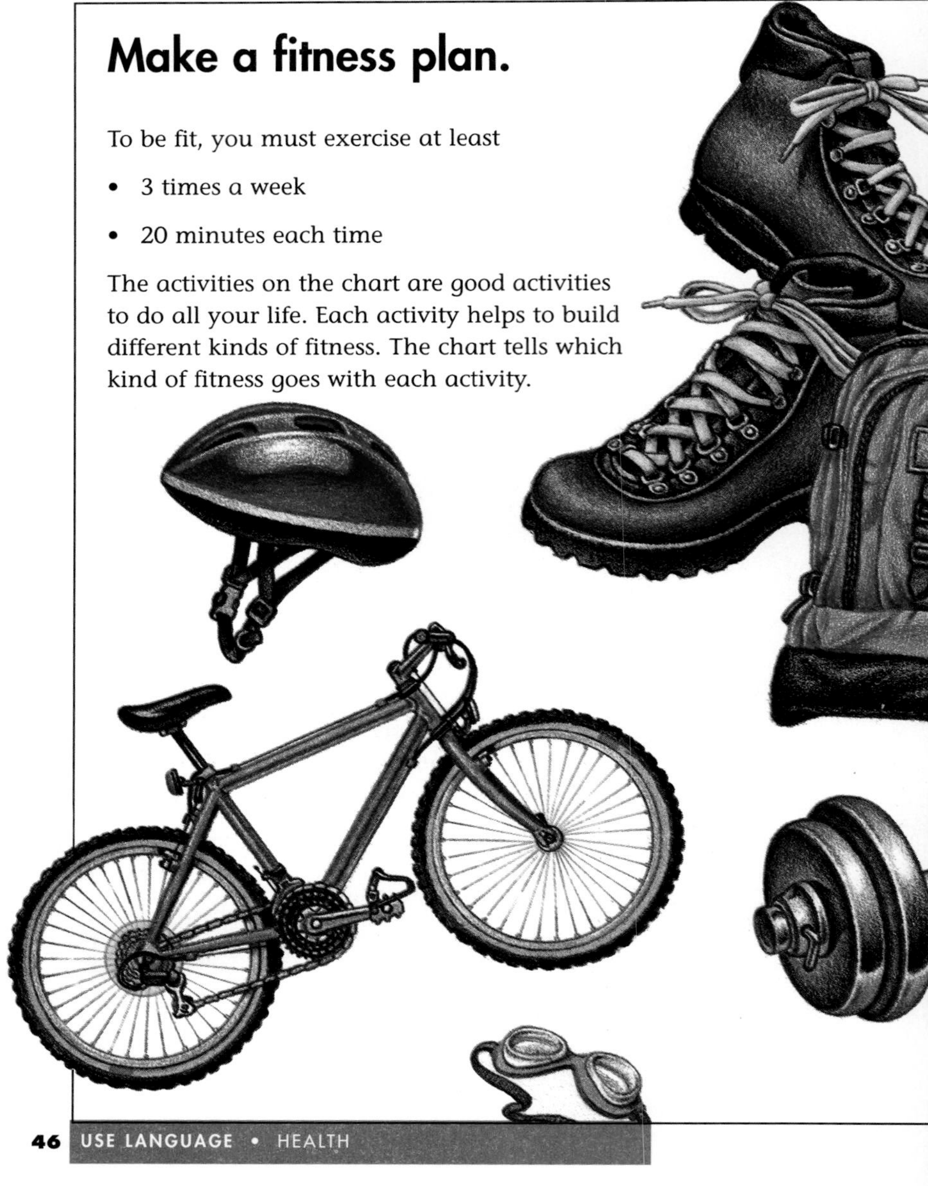

Make a fitness plan.
To be fit, you must exercise at least
• 3 times a week
• 20 minutes each time
The activities on the chart are good activities to do all your life. Each activity helps to build different kinds of fitness. The chart tells which kind of fitness goes with each activity.
46 USE LANGUAGE • HEALTH

Options for Reaching All Students

Beginning

Language: Writing

Review physical activities from page 47. Ask students which one they like best or would most like to do. Have them act out the activity for the others to guess. Encourage them to make word cards for the physical activities on page 47 and add them to the wall chart of sports.

Advanced

Critical Thinking: Evaluate Physical Activity

Advanced students should develop five or more questions for an interview that they will conduct with others in the group about personal fitness. Prompt with questions such as *What kinds of physical activities do you do? How does (physical activity) help you stay fit?* and so on. Have each student report results and write down his or her responses.

Cooperative Learning

Survey

Poll students to find out what physical activity they like best. Ask them which of the activities on the chart on pages 46 and 47 they would most like to try. Record their answers on the board. Ask students to make a bar graph showing results. Then have students analyze how many students prefer activities with a good or excellent rating in their fitness area. Have students talk about the results.

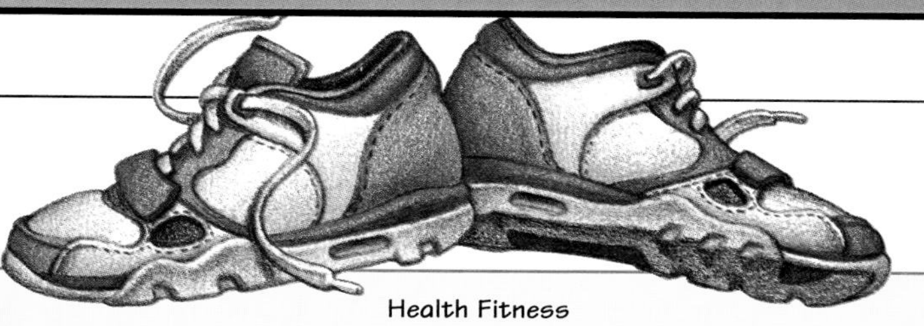

Health Fitness

'hysical ctivities	Builds Cardiovascular Fitness	Builds Muscular Strength	Builds Muscular Endurance	Builds Flexibility	Helps Control Fatness
cling	excellent	fair	good	poor	excellent
ce, Aerobic	excellent	fair	good	good	excellent
nastics	fair	excellent	excellent	excellent	fair
g	good	fair/good	excellent	fair	good
ging	excellent	poor	good	poor	excellent
/Karate	poor	fair	fair	fair	poor
r Skating	fair/good	poor	fair	poor	fair/good
nming	excellent	fair	good	fair	excellent
ht Lifting	poor	excellent	good	fair	fair

List the physical activities you do. Write how often you do them. Next to each, write the kind of fitness it helps to build.

Look at your list. Is there one fitness area you need to improve? Plan an activity or exercise that will help build that kind of fitness. Decide how often you will do the activity and when you will do it.

Language Awareness

Grammar
Gerund Forms

Help students list the names of sports. Use the list to teach verb and gerund (noun) forms:

to hike	hiking
to jog	jogging

Have students make sentences: *I like to roller skate. Roller skating is my favorite sport.*

Point out spelling rules for adding *-ing*: dropping *e* and doubling the final letter for short words ending in vowel + consonant.

Model a Strategy

Read a Chart

Model how to read a chart:

I know that a chart summarizes information. I look carefully at any chart to see how it presents information. In this chart, the sports are listed in the left column. Kinds of fitness are listed at the tops of the other columns. To tell what kind of fitness a sport builds, I read across the rows.

Assess 

Students should be able to

- relate the kinds of fitness to sports

LOOK **AHEAD**

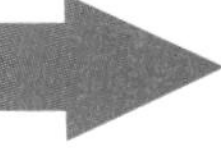

In the next section, students will learn about games from different cultures.

Writer's Workshop

Favorite Sports

Refer students to Writers' Workshop on pages 230 to 236 of the Student Book. Have students review the physical activities they listed in the Write About It on page 47. Ask them to write about their favorite sports and why they enjoy doing them.

Connect

Activate Prior Knowledge
Relate Personal Experiences

Ask students to name games they played in their native countries. Ask, *Why do people play games?* You may want to talk about the role of fun in maintaining physical and mental health.

Develop Language and Concepts
Present Pages 48 and 49

TPR Have students look at the illustrations on pages 48 and 49. Point out the antelope, the dragon, and steeple. Explain that the games shown are named for something familiar to people in a particular country.

Introduce action words: *chase, tag, play, stand, walk*. Have students act out the words. Read the text with students. Then invite them to pantomime the games. Have teams of students come to the front of the room to show how the games are played. If possible, play the game outside on the playground.

Model a Strategy
Use Reference Resources

Model using resources to find more information:

When I want to find out more about a topic, I can go to other resources. I can look in an atlas to see where a country is located. I can use an encyclopedia to see pictures of life in that country.

Games from Many Cultures

People from different cultures play many similar games. Children all over the world play tag. Tag is a game in which players chase each other and try to tag, or touch, another player.

Beware the Antelope

In Central Africa, tag is called "Beware of the Antelope." The leader, or antelope, chases and tags other players. Then they, too, become antelopes. The game continues until everyone has been tagged.

Options for Reaching All Students

Beginning
Study Skills: Use Information Resources

Have students point out on a world map the countries that you name. Begin with the names of the countries on pages 48 and 49. Have students use atlases to locate the areas where the games are played. Have them look at encyclopedias to find pictures of those areas.

Advanced
Language: State Rules

Have students work in groups to explain games that they know from their native countries and explain the rules. Have each member give directions so that the other members of the group can play the game.

Cooperative Language Experience
Take a Field Trip

If possible, arrange a field trip to a local Y or other fitness center to look at their fitness programs. Have someone from the center show students the workout equipment and the pool. Ask personnel at the center to talk about activities and the kinds of fitness they promote. Perhaps someone from the center could demonstrate the equipment.

Catch the Dragon's Tail

In China, children play a kind of tag called "Catch the Dragon's Tail." The leader, or dragon, is at the head of a line. The leader tries to tag the tail, or last person in line.

Bell in the Steeple

In Russia, children play tag with a bell. The game is called "Bell in the Steeple." A "guard" stands in a small square and holds a box. The other players walk around the guard and pass a bell from one to another. When the guard claps, the player with the bell puts it into the guard's box. The other players chase the guard and try to get the bell.

GUARD'S SQUARE

Talk About It

Have you ever played a game like tag? What were the rules?

Language Awareness

Grammar
Present Tense

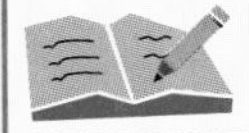

ACTIVITY BOOK

Use the action words from the lesson. Work with students to make sentences about things they do every day or regularly. For example:

I play tag at recess.
I walk to school every day.
I play soccer every Tuesday.

Then have students talk about things they do as a class, with the pronoun *we*. Finally, have students tell information about individual class members.

Kayla exercises every morning.
Roberto plays soccer on Tuesday.

Point out the addition of *s* for the third person singular present tense. Use Activity Book page 27.

Assess

Students should be able to

- describe the game of tag and explain one version of it

LOOK**AHEAD**

In the next section, students will learn about jump rope rhymes.

Following the trip, write a language experience story with students.

Multicultural Connection

Games Around the World

Have students share games from around the world that they know. Have them interview family members about games. Also have them interview other children in the school or neighborhood. Encourage students to share games in both words and pictures.

QuickCheck

Third Person Singular in the Present Tense

Check to see that students understand the use of the present tense with third person singular. Have them work in pairs and find out what sports their partner plays and report back. Check for the use of *s* with *he* or *she*.

Connect

Activate Prior Knowledge

Discuss Jumping Rope

Ask students if they jump rope. If possible, bring in a jump rope and arrange for a demonstration. Ask for volunteers who may be able to demonstrate "double Dutch jumping." Ask, *What kind of physical fitness does it develop?* (cardiovascular) Point out that jumping rope is popular with children in the United States.

Develop Language and Concepts

Present Pages 50 and 51

ORANGE TAPE

Read the jump rope rhymes with students. Point out the rhyming words. Repeat the rhymes emphasizing the rhythm. Have students clap the rhythm of the rhyme. Ask if they know why the *rhythm* is important. Ask them what kinds of physical activity are made easier when a rhythm is used. (Figure skating or dance are possibilities.) Play the rhymes on Side 2 of the Orange Tape several times and invite students to say the words.

Explain that the words of the rhymes do not really make much sense but the repeated sounds add to the rhythm of the rhymes.

Encourage students to do the Try It Out activity. You should provide jump ropes and arrange for students to do the activity on the playground or at the gym.

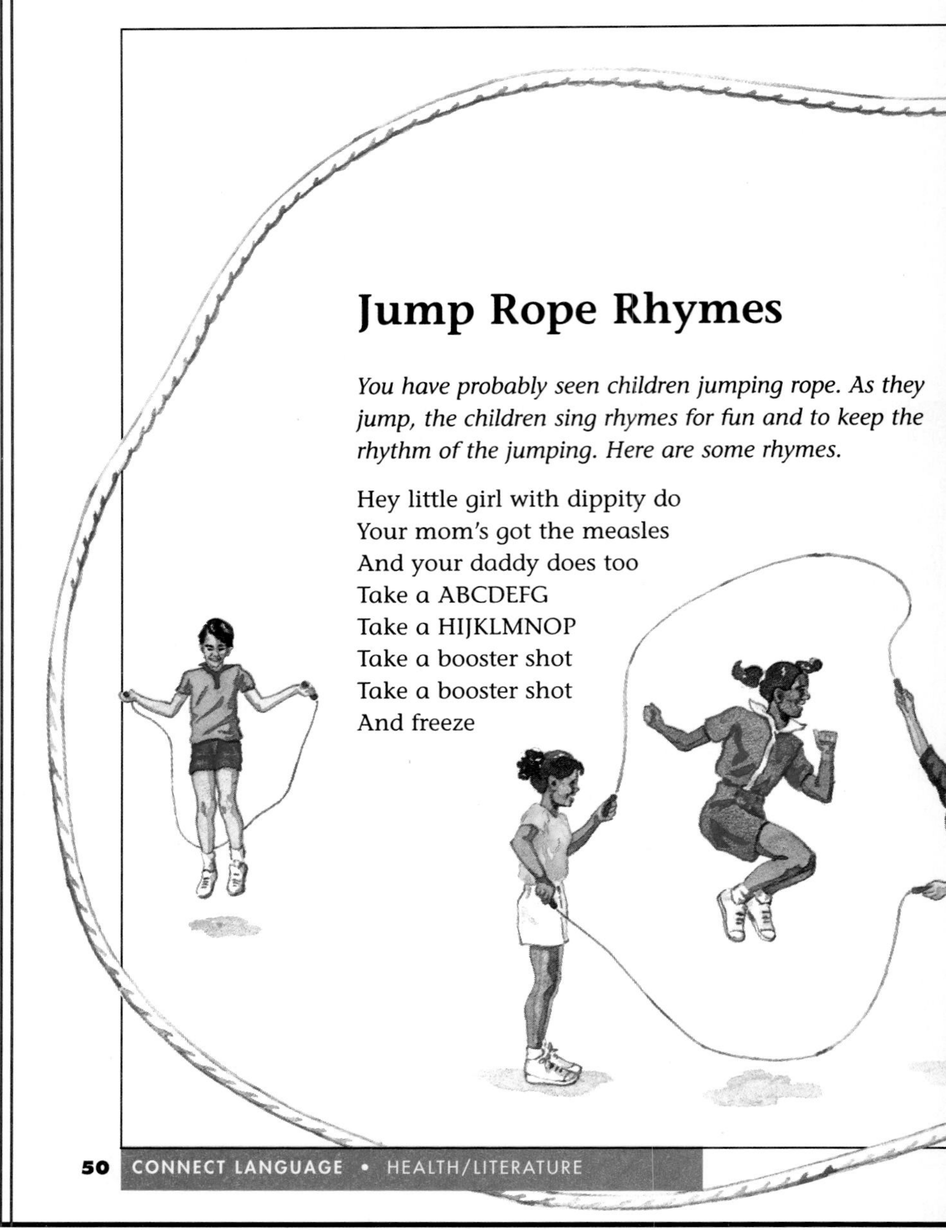

Jump Rope Rhymes

You have probably seen children jumping rope. As they jump, the children sing rhymes for fun and to keep the rhythm of the jumping. Here are some rhymes.

Hey little girl with dippity do
Your mom's got the measles
And your daddy does too
Take a ABCDEFG
Take a HIJKLMNOP
Take a booster shot
Take a booster shot
And freeze

50 CONNECT LANGUAGE • HEALTH/LITERATURE

Options for Reaching All Students

Beginning

Language: Initial *b* and *f*

Have students find pictures in old magazines that illustrate the beginning sounds of *b* and *f*. Have students use the pictures to make a collage and a word list. Help students make alliterative sentences with the words that could be part of jump rope rhymes; for example; *David does dirty dishes.*

Advanced

Language: More Jump Rope Rhymes

Have students find books with jump rope rhymes in the library. Have groups of two or three select a rhyme, learn it, and perform it for the class.

Mixed Ability

Language: Rhyming Words

Have students work in pairs of mixed ability. Ask students to find and list rhyming words in the jump rope rhymes. Ask them to add any other rhyming words they can think of.

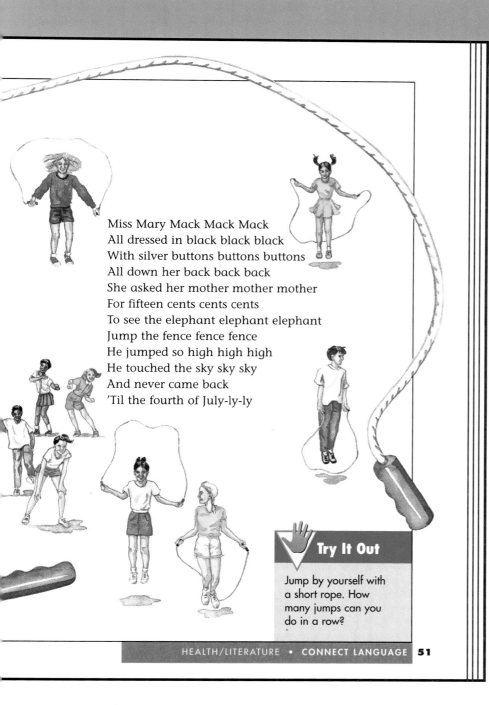

Miss Mary Mack Mack Mack
All dressed in black black black
With silver buttons buttons buttons
All down her back back back
She asked her mother mother mother
For fifteen cents cents cents
To see the elephant elephant elephant
Jump the fence fence fence
He jumped so high high high
He touched the sky sky sky
And never came back
'Til the fourth of July-ly-ly

Try It Out

Jump by yourself with a short rope. How many jumps can you do in a row?

Language Awareness

Phonics
Initial Consonants *b* and *f*

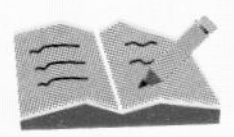
ACTIVITY BOOK

Present initial sounds of *b* and *f* to students. Have them find words in the rhyme that start with those sounds. List them in two columns on the board (for example, *freeze, fifteen, fence* and *black, back, buttons*). Ask students for other words they know that start with the same sound. Use prompts such as suggesting they think of color words, action words, number words, and so on. Add them to the list.

Use Activity Book page 28 for more practice.

Model a Strategy

Use Techniques to Memorize

Model how using rhyme and rhythm can help in memorizing things more easily:

When I recognize rhymes, I think about the rhyming sounds. As I memorize the words, the same sounds of the rhyming words help me to remember them. The rhythm stays in my mind and also helps me remember words.

Cooperative Learning

Art

Have groups of students work together to make a poster on butcher paper for each of the jump rope rhymes.

Home Connection

Traditional Rhymes

Have students ask family members about rhymes or sayings that are common in their home countries. Students should write them down in their primary language and translate if possible. They should make a report to the class.

QuickCheck

Alphabet and Months

Check that students can name the letters of the alphabet. Also check that they can name the months of the year in English and spell them.

Connect

Activate Prior Knowledge

Use Pictures

Have students name the sport in the picture. Ask if any of them have been to or played in a baseball game. Have students name sports people watch in their native countries.

Develop Language and Concepts

Present Page 52

ORANGE TAPE

Read the lyrics of the song and explain words such as *root, Cracker Jack,* and "1, 2, 3 strikes, you're out!" Explain that this song is commonly sung at baseball games. Play the songs on Side 2 of the Orange Tape several times and invite students to sing along.

Language Awareness

Spelling
Contractions

ACTIVITY BOOK

Explain that a contraction results when two words are put together and some letters are taken out. Write *do + not* on the board. Strike out the second *o* and then write *don't.* Show how an apostrophe takes the place of the missing letter. Repeat the procedures with *you're.* Point out that *n't* stands for *not* and *'re* for *are.* Have students find other examples of contractions in their book. Use Activity Book page 29.

Take Me Out To The Ball Game

Take me out to the ball game,
Take me out to the crowd,
Buy me some peanuts and Cracker Jack,
I don't care if I ever get back.
So it's root, root, root for the home team,
If they don't win it's a shame,
For it's one, two, three strikes, "You're out!"
At the old ball game.

Talk About It

Baseball is a popular game in this country. What sports were popular in the country you or your family came from?

Options for Reaching All Students

Beginning

Language: Sequencing

Make sentence strips with the lines from "Take Me Out to the Ball Game." Mix them up and give them to the teams. Time them to see which team can put the song in the correct order first. Have the winning team read or sing it out loud.

Advanced

Writing: Research

Have students identify one sport that they would like to know more about. Arrange for them to have time at the school library or borrow resources they could use from a local public library. Have students look at pictures and books and write down basic facts about the sport.

Tell what you learned.

CHAPTER 3

1. Why is it important to be physically fit? Why is cardiovascular fitness so important?

2. Tell about two exercises you do. How do they help you keep fit?

3. Tell about one new thing you learned about fitness.

Assess

Activity 1: Evaluate student's knowledge of the importance of fitness. Evaluate their understanding of what cardiovascular fitness is and why it is important.

Activity 2: Evaluate student's ability to associate an activity with an appropriate fitness goal.

Activity 3: Evaluate the understanding of fitness that students show in their responses.

Have students complete the Chapter Self-Assessment, Blackline Master 31. Have students choose the product of one of the activities to place in their portfolios. Add the results of any rubrics, checklists, self-assessments, or portfolio assessments, Blackline Masters 2–18 and 31.

Listening Assessment

BLACKLINE MASTER

Make sure that each student has a copy of Blackline Master 51 from the Teacher's Resource Book. Play the tape and have students complete the dictation.

WHITE TAPE

See page T40c for the tapescript.

Options for Assessment

Vocabulary Assessment

Sports and Fitness

Create a set of cards that have the name of a sport or physical activity on them. Choose activities that have been featured in the chapter. Ask students to classify them under the kinds of fitness that they strengthen.

Writing Assessment

Physical Activity: A Personal Book

Have students make their own personal books in which they illustrate and write about different physical activities they do and kinds of sports they play.

Language Assessment

BLACKLINE MASTER

Use Blackline Master 50 in the Teacher's Resource Book.

Standardized Test Practice

ACTIVITY BOOK

Use pages 30 and 31.
Answers: **1.** it is important to build cardiovascular fitness **2.** Tag and jump rope are exercises young people do.

Preview

Activate Prior Knowledge

Use Pictures

Ask students if they have ever seen the Olympic Games on television. Use pictures of past Olympic Games from a library picture file, on videos, or on a CD. Explain the symbols of the Olympics: the flag (the five circles on the flag symbolize the five continents), the lighting of the Olympic flame, and the parade of athletes from the various nations. Encourage students to tell what they know about any of the sports or athletes. Make a list of the sports events.

Call attention to the two seasons when the games are held. Have students identify summer sports and winter sports.

Develop Language and Concepts

Present Pages 54 and 55

Have students look at the pictures on the page and identify the sports. Have them match the words in the Word Bank to the pictures. Have students answer the questions in Tell What You Know.

TPR Then introduce the sports skills named on pages 54 and 55 (balance, coordination, and so on). Use pictures and TPR to help students understand the meaning of these terms. It might be helpful to discuss animals that possess these qualities to help students understand them. For example, a cheetah has

(Continued on page T55)

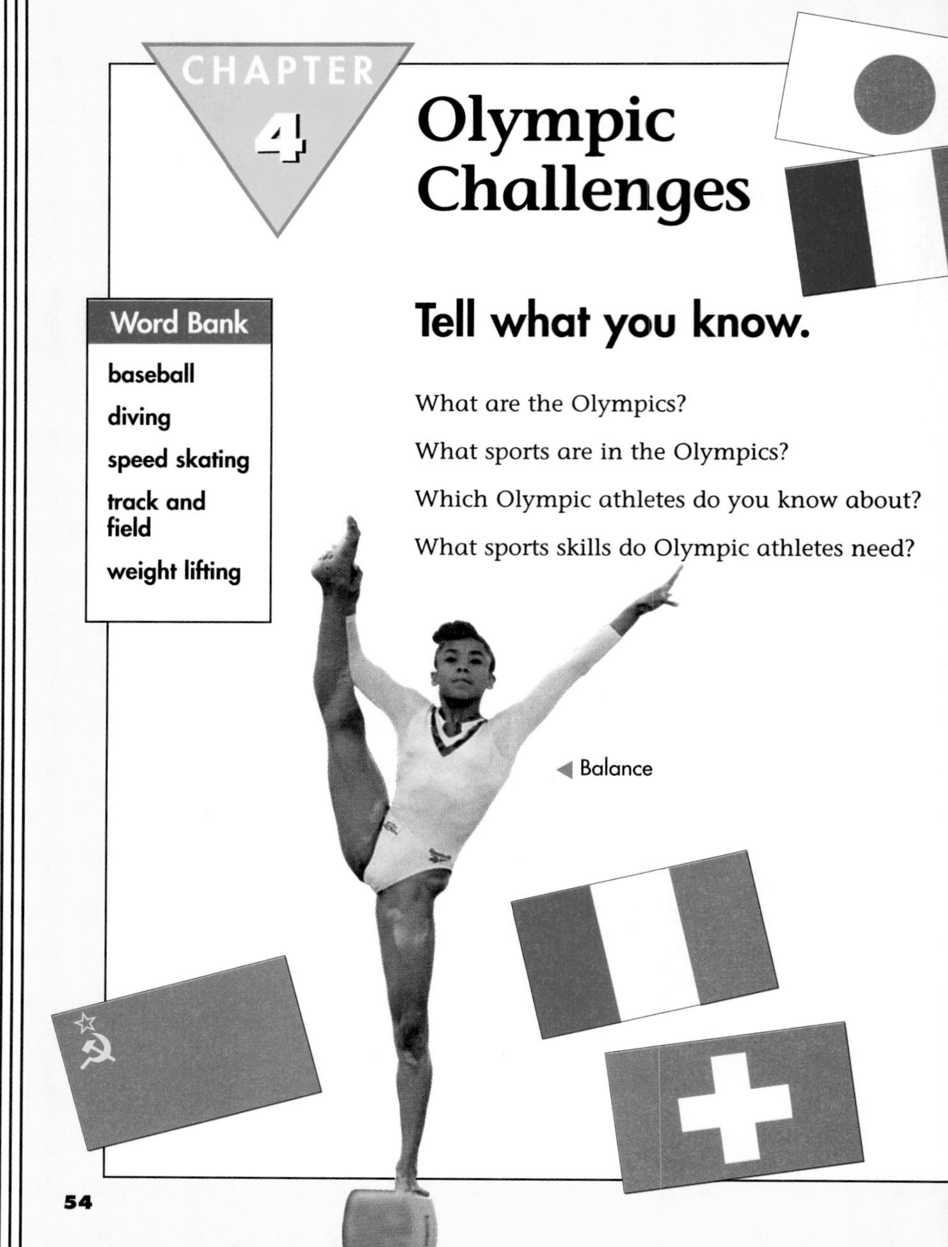

CHAPTER 4
Olympic Challenges
Word Bank
baseball
diving
speed skating
track and field
weight lifting
Tell what you know.
What are the Olympics?
What sports are in the Olympics?
Which Olympic athletes do you know about?
What sports skills do Olympic athletes need?
◀ Balance
54

Options for Reaching All Students

Beginning

Critical Thinking: Classify Sports

Provide students with lists and pictures of Olympic sports. Have students classify the sports in various ways (e.g., team sports vs. individual sports, outdoor vs. indoor, summer vs. winter, skills required).

Advanced

Geography: Olympic Countries

List some of the Olympic countries. Have students pick a country and have them draw the flag of that country. Encourage them to use picture resources in encyclopedias. Then have each student give a brief presentation about that country or about its flag.

Cooperative Learning

Interview

Have students work in small groups to act out interviews between reporters and Olympic athletes pictured on the page. Help students brainstrom a list of questions such as the following: How did you get into the Olympics Games? How often do you practice? Why do you like your sport? How do you feel about being in the Olympics? Encourage the groups to look at sports

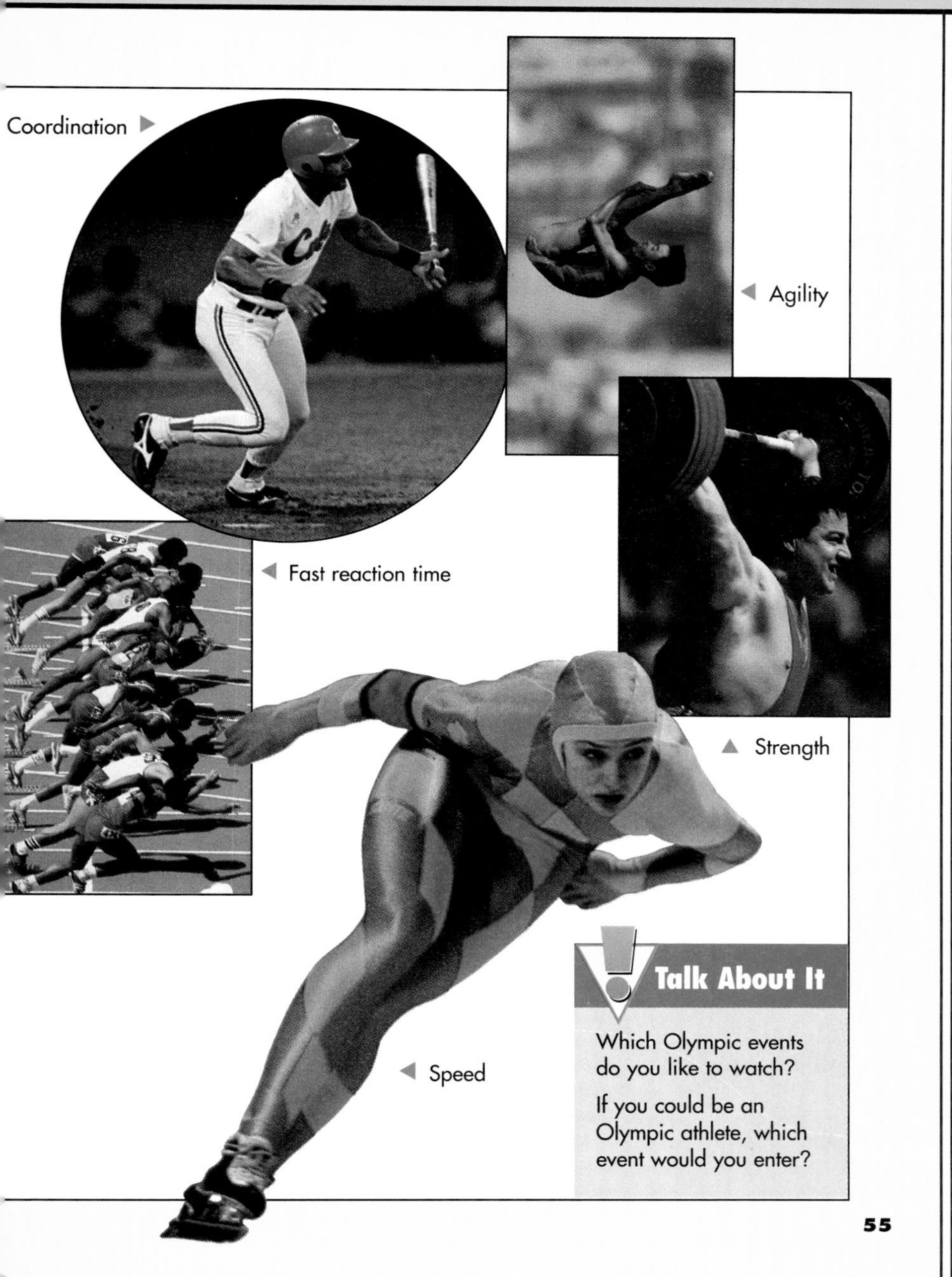
Coordination
Agility
Fast reaction time
Strength
Speed
Talk About It
Which Olympic events do you like to watch?
If you could be an Olympic athlete, which event would you enter?
55

speed and a fast reaction time; monkeys are flexible; squirrels can balance well. Have students look at the different sports illustrated on the page and comment on the skills required. Talk about why each skill is important.

Have students complete the Talk About It activity in small groups.

magazines to get more information about the sports. Have the groups present interviews to the class.

Home Connection

Interview

Have students ask if anyone in their home or a family acquaintance has ever attended or participated in the Olympics. Have students report back to the class any interesting anecdotes they discover.

Present

Activate Prior Knowledge

Discuss Meaning of Heroes

Help students understand the meaning of the word *hero.* Ask them to name people whom they see as heroes. Make a list. Ask, *Are athletes heroes for you?*

Develop Language and Concepts

Present Pages 56 and 57

Use pictures to help students understand the difference between *ancient* and *modern.* Draw a time line on the board to show "ancient" times.

Read the text with students. Direct students' attention to the map of ancient Greece. Help them locate Olympia. Discuss with them how the name of this sports event came from its original location.

Have students do the Think About It activity in small groups.

Model a Strategy

Use a Map

Model how to use maps in textbooks:

When I start to study a new place in a social studies book, it is important that I look on a map to better understand what I am reading. When I look at a map, I can tell where the place is located in relation to other cities, countries, or bodies of water.

The Olympic Games

The Olympic Games began in ancient Greece about 2,700 years ago. Every four years, athletes from Greek cities went to Olympia. At Olympia, they competed in sports to honor the god, Zeus.

The Olympic Games were very important to the Greeks. Armies even stopped fighting so the soldiers could compete. Many Olympic events tested skills that were important for soldiers, such as wrestling, throwing the javelin, or racing chariots.

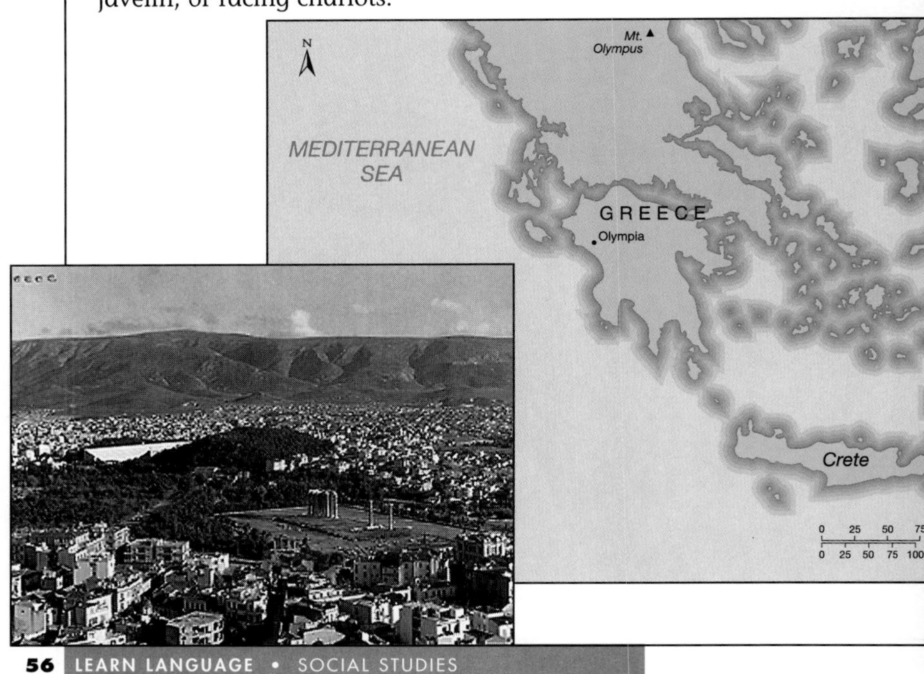

Options for Reaching All Students

Beginning

Language: Past Tense Forms

Have students make separate word cards with present and past tense words from the lesson: *bring/brought, think/thought, go/went, become/became.* Have students shuffle the past tense cards, draw one, match it with the present tense card, say the words, and use them in sentences.

Advanced

Social Studies: Time Line

Have groups of students work together to make a time line showing the ancient Egyptians, the ancient Greeks, and modern times. Encourage them to add other historical periods that they know about and to use reference books.

Mixed Ability

Studies Skills: Research

Have students use the library and encyclopedias to find pictures of ancient Olympic events that were included in the ancient games, such as javelin throwing, chariot racing, and discus throwing. Have them draw pictures and write a sentence about each event.

Winners received only a crown of leaves for a prize. But winners became heroes in their cities. They brought fame and honor to their cities because people thought a city with many Olympic heroes was a strong city.

The Olympic Games became famous in other countries. People from other places went to see the games, but only Greek athletes could compete. Foreigners could watch, but they could not compete.

Think About It

In modern Olympics, we count how many medals each country wins. Why?

Are sports important to you? Which ones? Why?

Language Awareness

Grammar
Irregular Past Tense

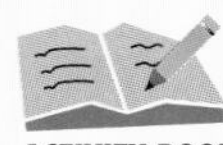

ACTIVITY BOOK

Help students see the difference between present and past tenses. Help them see that the verbs in the spread are all in the past tense since the text is describing the ancient Greeks. Explain the regular way of forming the past tense, by adding *-ed*. Tell students that English has some verbs that form the past tense in different ways. Point out the past tense forms of words in the text: *began, became, brought,* and *thought.* Help students list the present tense form of the verbs. Use Activity Book page 32.

Assess

Students should be able to

- name two or three facts about the ancient Greek Olympic games

LOOK AHEAD

In the next section, students will compare and contrast ancient and modern Olympic Games.

Peer Tutoring

Social Studies: Remember Basic Facts

Pair students of mixed ability. Ask them to think of three things they remember about sports of the ancient Olympic Games. Ask them to think of something they might like to learn more about.

Cooperative Learning

The Ancient Greeks

Start an ongoing project in which students research information about the ancient Greeks, focusing on their contributions to Western civilization. Students can use books about the ancient Greeks for students, as well as textbooks. The result of the project should be a poster about the ancient Greeks including contributions such as language, democracy, or philosophy.

Practice

Activate Prior Knowledge

Compare and Contrast

Have students look at the illustrations of sports on pages 56 and 57. Compare them to the illustrations on pages 58 and 59. Have them describe differences and similarities in sports.

Develop Language and Concepts

Present Pages 58 and 59

ACTIVITY BOOK

Tell students that the ancient and modern games are different in some ways and similar in other ways. Read the text with students. Ask students how the ancient and modern games are different and how they are similar. Tell them that they will be making a chart that shows similarities and differences. Draw a large circle on the board. Ask students to list what was different in the ancient games from the modern games. List their responses on the left side of the circle. Then draw a second big circle overlapping the first circle. Ask stuidents to list the differences in the modern games. List their responses on the right side of the second circle. Next ask students to list similarities. List those in the overlapping section. Help students see how this graphic organizer helps them to show similarities and differences at the same time. Tell students that this diagram is called a *Venn diagram.* Use Activity Book page 33 to further compare the games.

Have students discuss the questions in Talk About It.

Compare the games.

The modern Olympic Games are similar to the ancient Olympic Games in many ways.

- Athletes in ancient games competed in wrestling, foot races, discus throwing, javelin throwing, and long jumping. Athletes in modern games compete in the same events.
- Winning athletes in the ancient games became heroes. Winning athletes still bring honor and fame to their countries.

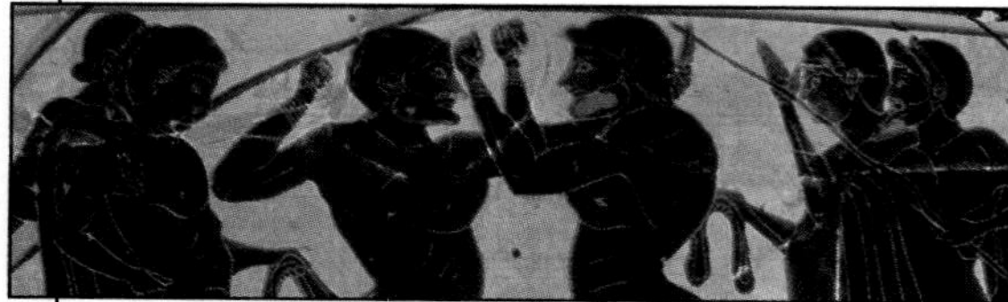

The ancient games were different from the modern games in many ways.

- The ancient games included music and speaking contests.
- The ancient games originally took place on one day. Over the years they grew to four days.
- The first ancient games had only one foot race about 200 meters long.

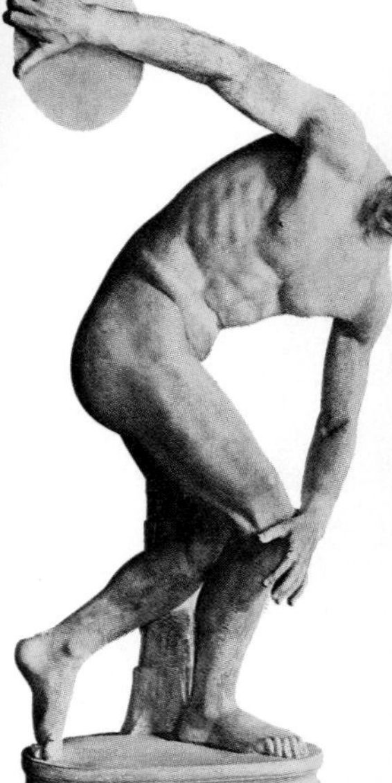

58 USE LANGUAGE • SOCIAL STUDIES

Options for Reaching All Students

Beginning

Language: Practice with *such as*

Make cards listing categories such as animals, sports, foods, and games. Students pick a card and work with a simple sentence structure: *I like (food) such as _____.* Students write sentences filling in the blanks. Have students share what they have written in small groups.

Advanced

Study Skills: Sports

Have students work in groups. Have groups research and illustrate five Olympic sports. Coordinate so that groups do not do the same sports.

Mixed Ability

Language: Sports Vocabulary

BLACKLINE MASTER

Help groups of students make idea webs to list vocabulary associated with various sports. Use Blackline Master 20 in the Teacher's Resource Book. Have them use the following categories: equipment, actions (hit a ball, run), scoring. Have groups share their webs.

The modern Olympic Games are different from the ancient games in many ways.

▲ Modern Olympic medal

- The winners in today's games receive medals, not crowns of leaves.
- There are summer and winter games and many more events. There are many team sports such as basketball and volleyball.
- Today both men and women compete in the games. People from all over the world take part.
- There are events for people with disabilities.

Talk About It

How would the modern games be different if athletes came from just one country? What are the good things about international games?

Language Awareness

Grammar
Expression *such as*

Write this sentence on the board, *There are many team sports such as basketball and volleyball.* Show students that *such as* points the way to examples to follow. Ask students if they can think of other team sports that are played at the Olympics. Have them repeat the sentence using their examples after *such as.* Use this example for more practice: *Olympics have athletes from many countries such as _____.*

Model a Strategy
Use a Graphic Organizer

Model how to use a graphic organizer:

When I read, I often try to keep track of important information by writing it down in a graphic organizer. For this lesson, I used a Venn diagram, which is good to compare and contrast. Another organizer is an idea web, which can have categories and related words.

Assess 

Students should be able to

- name similarities and differences between the ancient and modern Olympic games

In the next section, students will read about interesting Olympic "firsts."

Cooperative Learning
More About Venn Diagrams

Have students complete Blackline Master 23 in the Teacher's Resource Book with information on the Olympic games. Then suggest other topics on which students can complete Venn diagrams. These may be ones that relate to sports; for example, soccer vs. baseball (both are played with a ball; in soccer the ball is hit with foot or head; in baseball, the ball is hit with a bat; both are team sports; soccer has eleven players on a team; baseball has nine).

Practice

Activate Prior Knowledge

"First" Discussion

Ask students what they think the title *Interesting "Firsts"* means. What is an interesting "first" for them? Ideas would be the first time they did something important by themselves; for example, the first time they rode a bike.

Develop Language and Concepts

Present Pages 60 and 61

Read each of the paragraphs with students and have them identify the "first."

Compare Bikila's marathon time to a morning at school. Ask what it would be like to run 26 miles before lunch.

Have students respond to the Think About It question. Answers should include ideas such as regular training.

Model a Strategy

Categorize Information

Model how to categorize information:

As I read the short paragraphs on these pages, I notice that each paragraph gives the name of the athlete, the event, the year, and where the Olympics were held, and why the person's achievement was important. Once I see the pattern, I can predict that the next paragraphs will have the same information. Looking for patterns helps me to read better.

Interesting "Firsts"

At each Olympic Games, some winning athletes capture the attention of the world.

The first modern Olympic Games were held in ▶ Greece in 1896. The first event was the triple jump. James Connolly of the United States won this event by jumping 13.71 meters.

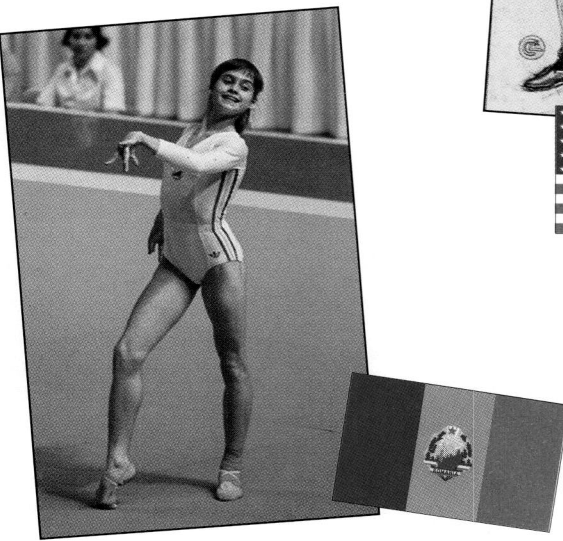

▲ At the 1976 Games in Montreal, Canada, Nadia Comaneci of Romania won her place among the firsts for her gymnastic performances. In all Olympic history, no one had earned a perfect 10 from the judges. Nadia earned seven perfect 10's for her performances in Montreal.

Options for Reaching All Students

Beginning

Writing: Personal Firsts

Brainstorm a list of "firsts" that are in the students' experience; for example, the first time they roller-skated, the first time they ate a certain food. List these on the board. Have students use the list to write a list of personal firsts using the items on the board and the sentence frame *I first* _____ *when I was* _____ *years old.*

Advanced

Social Studies: Research

Have students get books on the Olympics and add to the list of Olympic firsts or interesting events or athletes in the Olympics. Have them use the paragraphs in the Student Book as a model to report back to the class.

Mixed Ability

Language: Listen to an Athlete's Schedule

Find some information on a recent Olympic winner whose life is the subject of magazine articles. Look for one with a training schedule. Gymnasts, track stars, or figure skaters might be good choices. Return to the question in the Think About It, *What do Olympic winners do to prepare for competition?* Read the article to students. Tell students

Jamaica has no snow. But in 1988 a team from Jamaica wanted to enter the bobsled event during the Winter Olympics in Calgary, Canada. Some people thought that they were not taking a skillful sport seriously. But the team learned to deal with snow and cold weather. They passed the test that allowed them to take part in the Olympics. It was the first time anyone from Jamaica had competed in the winter games. ▶

▲ The marathon is the longest foot race of all. It covers 42,195 meters—over 26 miles! In Rome in 1960, Ethiopian Abebe Bikila became the first African to win the race. He completed it in 2 hours, 15 minutes, and 16.2 seconds. He was also the first runner to run barefoot.

Think About It

What do you think these athletes did to prepare for their "firsts"?

Language Awareness

Vocabulary
Ordinal Numbers

ACTIVITY BOOK

Tell students that ordinal numbers show the order or position of a number in a series of numbers. Explain that *first* is an ordinal number. It corresponds to the number one. List the ordinal numbers to ten on the board as well as the corresponding number: *second, third, fourth, fifth, sixth, seventh, eighth, ninth,* and *tenth*. Ask students to suggest a pattern in the formation of the ordinal numbers. Help them recognize that after *first, second,* and *third* ordinals, numbers end with *-th*. You might want to introduce ordinals through one hundred and help students see the pattern of formation. Use Activity Book page 34.

Assess 

Students should be able to

- discuss one or two of the athletes on the pages and why their achievements were important

In the next section, students will be calculating speeds of athletes in various Olympic events.

that they will compare their daily schedule with that of an Olympic athlete. Ask them to listen very carefully for details. Read the article again. Ask students to give the athlete's schedule. Write the athlete's schedule on the board and talk about it. Then have students make comparisons with their own schedules.

Home Connection
Interview

Ask students to ask family members to tell them about "firsts" that were important in their own personal lives. Students should report back to the class.

QuickCheck

Nationalities

Check that students can name countries and related nationalities. Explain that *-n* or *-an* is added to the name of many places; for example, *Africa, African*. Another common suffix is *-ese*.

Connect

Activate Prior Knowledge

Discuss Distance and Time

Ask students what speed is. If possible, have volunteers run a short, set distance and compare times. Students need to measure both distance (feet or meters) and time. Then have students run longer distances. Have them compare their speeds on the two distances. Help them calculate their distance per second by dividing the distance by their time.

Develop Language and Concepts

Present Pages 62 and 63

ACTIVITY BOOK

Have students look at the chart and read the headings. Read the text with students. Have them guess the rank order of the speed of the athletes.

Review with students English words for division, such as *into* and *divided by*. Do a few division problems on the board, including division with decimals. Explain methods for moving the decimal to the right and methods for rounding. Have students calculate the meters per second of the athletes on the chart on page 62 and complete the chart on page 63. Students can use the chart on Activity Book page 35. Have students answer the questions *Who was the fastest?* and *Are the speeds in shorter races faster or slower than the longer races?* Ask them why they think that happens.

Who is the fastest?

Speed is important for winning gold medals in some Olympic contests. Here are some speed figures from recent Olympics.

Which athlete do you think was the fastest? Make a guess. List the athletes in order from slowest to fastest.

Athlete	Event	Speed
Linford Christie Great Britain	100-meter dash Men's track	9.96 seconds
William Tanui Kenya	800-meter run Men's track	1 minute 43.66 seconds (103.66 seconds)
Dieter Baumann Germany	5,000-meter run Men's track	13 minutes 12.52 seconds (792.52 seconds)
Zhuang Yong China	100-meter freestyle Women's swimming	54.64 seconds
Janet Evans United States	800-meter freestyle Women's swimming	8 minutes 25.52 seconds
Aleksandr Golubev Russia	500-meter race Men's speed skating (ice)	36.33 seconds
Johann Olav Koss Norway	5,000-meter race Men's speed skating (ice)	6 minutes 34.96 seconds

Options for Reaching All Students

Beginning

Language: Classify

Have students research and find icons for the Olympic sports. Review the six sports skills from the beginning of the chapter, and ask students to classify the icons under the skills they think the sports require. Discuss their choices.

Advanced

Math: Speed Comparisons

Have students select other sports that interest them, look in record books, and compare speeds at which athletes travel.

Mixed Ability

Language: Records

Have students look through books of sport records, both with statistics and ones that describe athletes' performance. Have students write the three most interesting facts they learned.

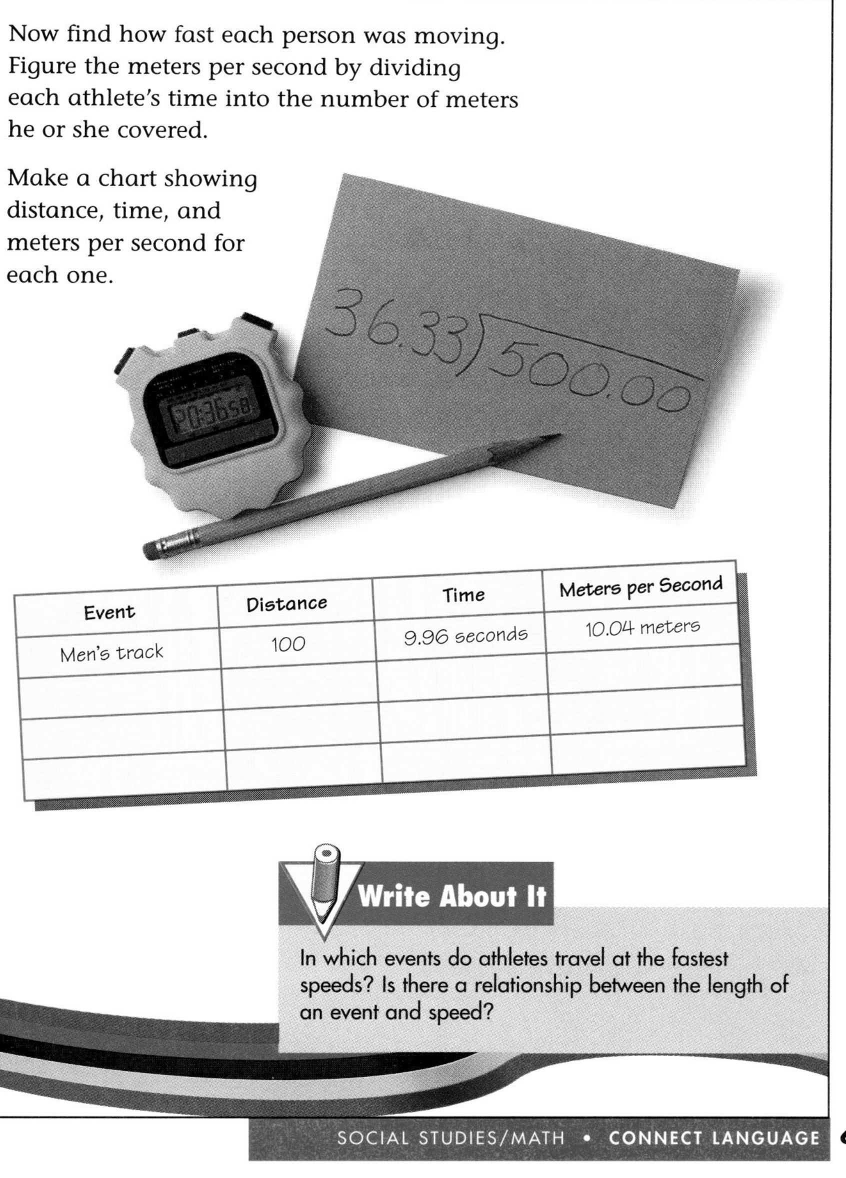

Now find how fast each person was moving. Figure the meters per second by dividing each athlete's time into the number of meters he or she covered.

Make a chart showing distance, time, and meters per second for each one.

Event	Distance	Time	Meters per Second
Men's track	100	9.96 seconds	10.04 meters

Write About It

In which events do athletes travel at the fastest speeds? Is there a relationship between the length of an event and speed?

Language Awareness

Grammar
Superlatives

Call attention to the words *slowest* and *fastest* in the text. Point out that the ending *-est* is added to words to form the superlative. The superlative ranks something at the top. Also point out the *most* (*most miles)* and *best* (*best runner)* are also superlatives. Help students to create sentences based on the results in the chart. For example:

Christie was the fastest runner. Golubev was the fastest person.

Help them use sports results and record books to create more superlative sentences.

Assess 

Use students' responses to the Write About It for assessment. Students should be able to

- explain the results about comparative speeds from the chart they prepared in the lesson

LOOK **AHEAD** 

In the next section, the students will read an ancient Greek myth about a speedy runner.

Multicultural Connection
International Sports

Have students discuss sports that are popular internationally, such as soccer and basketball, as well as ones that are popular in specific countries around the world. Also discuss athletes who are popular internationally. Have students make lists.

Home Connection
Sports in Native Lands

Have students ask family members if any particular Olympic sport is popular in the country they came from. Ask if any particular winner has received widespread fame. Ask students to find out as much as they can and share it with the class.

Writer's Workshop
An Olympic Sport

Refer students to pages 230 to 236 in the Student Book. Ask students to write about the Olympic sport that interests them the most. In prewriting activities, encourage students to brainstorm reasons why they might be attracted to a sport and include them.

Connect

Activate Prior Knowledge

Recall and Review

Ask students to recall what they learned about the ancient Greeks. Review with them the importance of athletic events and of the gods.

Introduce the Selection

Help students read the title and the name of the reteller. Discuss with students that Greek myths are very old stories. No one really knows who made them up originally. They have been told and retold by many different people. Some myths have been retold in different ways.

Read the background information with students on pages 64 and 65 about myths in general and this particular myth. Have them look through the pictures and ask them what they think will happen in this myth.

Read the Selection

ORANGE TAPE

Read the story with students. Reread the story and present the Reader's Tips. Have students listen to the selection on Side 1 of the Orange Tape several times.

Language Awareness

Grammar
Subject Pronouns

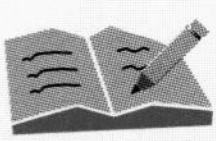
ACTIVITY BOOK

Introduce the subject pronouns *I, you, he, she, it, we,* and *they*. Show students how pronouns *he, she,* and *they* replace nouns in text. Read a sample passage from the myth using only nouns, without pronouns. Then read the passage again with the pronouns.

Show students that the word the pronoun replaces determines which pronoun to use. For example: <u>Atalanta</u> loved to run. *She* was happiest when she was running. The <u>young men</u> wanted to marry Atalanta. *They* thought she was beautiful.

Use Activity Book page 36 for practice.

Model a Strategy

Predict Before and During Reading

Model using prediction to help reading:

When I am getting ready to read a story, I look at the title and the pictures. Then I read the first sentences. Doing this gives me an idea of what the story is about and about where the story is taking place. As I continue reading, I assess my predictions about characters and events. I ask, "How does what is happening compare with my prediction? What have I learned about the characters?" Sometimes as I read, I have to change my prediction.

Options for Reaching All Students

Beginning

Language Arts: Character Study

BLACKLINE MASTER

Call students' attention to the sentence in the story, *But Atalanta had a problem.* Ask them what the problem was (Young men wanted to marry her, and she didn't want to get married). Ask students to recall information that they already have about Atalanta. Help them start an idea web about Atalanta and add to it as they read the story. Talk with them about ways they learn about a character in a story. Have them look at pictures, at things Atalanta says or does, at what the author says about her. With Atalanta's name in the center, have them fill in some circles with information about Atalanta. Students can use Blackline Master 20.

Advanced

Language Arts: Character Study

BLACKLINE MASTER

Have students complete a character trait chart for Atlanta. Help students understand what a character trait is and explore with them what they know about Atalanta and how they found it out. Have students add to the chart as they read the story. Students can use Blackline Master 27.

Atalanta and the Golden Apples: A Greek Myth

Retold by Margot Biersdorf

About Ancient Greek Myths

The ancient Olympic Games were a religious festival. The Greeks played the games to honor their chief god, Zeus.

The Greeks had many gods and goddesses. They believed their gods lived on top of Mount Olympus. From there, Zeus ruled not only the people but the other gods as well.

Gods and goddess were more powerful than people. They often acted to help people they liked. They sometimes punished people they did not like.

Stories about the gods and goddesses are called myths. Some myths explain why people are the way they are or why the world is the way it is. Myths may tell why the seasons change. They may tell why there are thunderstorms. They may tell why two people love each other.

Aphrodite was the Greek goddess of love and beauty. She could use her power to help people love each other. As you read the myth about a girl named Atalanta, you will find out how Aphrodite could do this.

Language Tip
Idiom
Atalanta knew her own mind. This means that she knew what was important to her.

Reader's Tip
Stop and Think
Do you think Atalanta was like most other young women? Why or why not?

Atalanta loved to run. She was happiest when she was running. She was the fastest runner anyone had ever seen.

Atalanta was a young woman who knew her own mind. She hated to be inside away from the sun and the wind. She did not like to cook or clean.

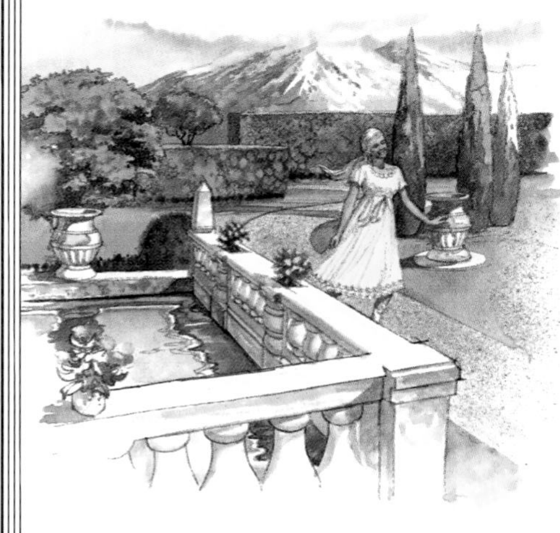

"I shall never get married," she promised herself. "I could not be myself. I would have to stay inside and cook and clean."

But Atalanta had a problem. Young men saw her running, and they fell in love with her. She did not know how beautiful she was as she raced by.

The young men followed Atalanta around. Each one asked her to marry him. Atalanta refused, but the young men still kept asking.

Language Tip
Vocabulary
Refuse means to say no.

Connect

Develop Language and Concepts

Present Pages 68 Through 71

Have students retell the story. Ask them to predict what will happen next. Then read on with them to see if their predictions are correct.

Ask students to identify the main characters. Focus their attention on Atalanta. Have them review what they know about her from the first pages. Ask them to notice how she feels about her promise at the end of this section.

Language Awareness

Grammar

Real Conditional Sentences

Discuss conditional sentences. Point out that on page 68, Atalanta tells the young men, "If you win the race, I will marry you." Explain that the first event needs to happen for the second event to happen. Introduce other conditional sentences that relate to classroom experiences: *If the weather is good on friday, we will run our races outdoors.* Help students identify the condition and the possible result. Have students complete sentences such as:

If I exercise every day, I will _____.
If I practice shooting basketballs every day, _____.
If the weather is good on Saturday, _____.

Teachable Moment

Story Elements: Conflict

Ask the students to state the problem in this story. Tell students that conflict in a story builds interest.

The conflict or problem in this story is that Atalanta has promised herself never to marry, and now she likes Hippomenes. She must decide if she is going to be true to herself and try to win the race. Readers are left wondering how this problem will be resolved. Will Atalanta try not to win the race? Will Hippomenes die because he loses the race against Atalanta? Conflict makes the reader want to read on to find out what will happen.

Options for Reaching All Students

Beginning

Language: Sentence Strips

Have pairs of students list five events in the story to this point and write them on separate sentence strips. Have them mix up the strips and give them to another pair, whose task is to put the strips in order.

Advanced

Social Studies: Research the Gods

Have students research Greek gods and heroes, such as Aphrodite, Zeus, Athena, or Hercules, and make brief presentations about them.

Mixed Ability

Language Arts: Greek Myths

Read to the students other Greek myths, which are available in a wide variety of books. Have students summarize the stories.

Reader's Tip
Look for Clues
What was Atalanta's plan? Why did she think it would work?

Finally, Atalanta had a plan. She told the young men, "I will marry the man who can win a race with me. If you win the race, I will marry you. But beware," she added. "If I win the race, you will die."

Atalanta hoped that the young men would go away. "I can beat any of them in a race," she thought to herself. "Surely no one will want to race me. If they race me, they know they will die."

She was wrong. Several young men chose to race her. Atalanta ran faster. She won all the races, and all those young men died.

A young athlete, Hippomenes, heard the news of the races. "How could anyone be willing to die for such a stupid dare?" he wondered. "I must go and see for myself."

When he saw Atalanta running as fast and free as the wind, he changed his mind. "I am going to marry her," he promised himself.

Strategy Tip
Understand Plot
Atalanta made a promise to herself. Hippomenes made a promise to himself. What were their promises?

Hippomenes asked Atalanta to give him running lessons. She liked the looks of the young man. She decided to help him. "I run every morning at seven o'clock," she said. "If you want to run with me, I will teach you."

So Atalanta and Hippomenes ran together every day. She showed him how to use his arms. She showed him how to make his stride longer. They were a beautiful sight running together in the early morning sun. Atalanta liked Hippomenes very much.

Language Tip
Vocabulary
A *stride* is the length of a step from one foot to the other.

Reader's Tip
Make Inferences
Why do you think Hippomenes took running lessons from Atalanta?

One day Hippomenes told Atalanta that he wanted to marry her. He asked to race with her. Atalanta was very sad. She liked Hippomenes, but she knew she could run faster. She wished that he would win the race.

Then she remembered that she had promised never to get married. She had to do her best to win. Sadly she agreed to race him the next day.

Study Tip
Find the Conflict
A conflict happens when two things do not go together. Characters can have conflicts because they want something that does not fit with another thing they want. Atalanta has a conflict. What is it?

Connect

Develop Language and Concepts
Present Pages 72 Through 75

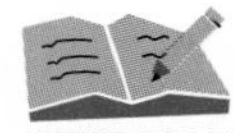
ACTIVITY BOOK

Have students retell the story to this point. Have them recall what the problem was in this story and describe and discuss how it was solved.

To check comprehension, have students use Activity Book page 37.

Have students dramatize the myth. They can make and dress up in costumes or use stylized puppets to represent the characters. Have students make a backdrop for their presentation.

Language Awareness

Grammar
Regular Past Tense

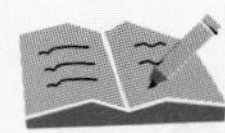
ACTIVITY BOOK

Review that regular past verbs end in *-ed*. Help students look through the story and find examples of past tense verbs. Have them put the verbs into two columns of regular and irregular verbs. Then have students work in small groups and retell the story. Encourage them to refer to the lists of verbs.

Use Activity Book page 38.

Teachable Moment
Literary Elements: Similes

On page 73, both Atalanta and Hippomenes are described a running *as fast as the wind*. The author compared their speed to the speed of the wind. Ask students to find another simile on page 69 *(as fast and as free as the wind)*. These comparisons use *as*. Similes can also use *like*. *(For example: She ran like the wind.)* Explain that similes help the reader to get clear pictures of what the writer is saying.

Response Activities
Personal Response

Ask students these questions:

Atalanta was happiest when she was running. When are you happiest? What do you like to do best?

Critical Response

Ask students these questions:

How did Hippomenes solve his problem? He knew he was slower than Atalanta, but he found a way to beat her in the race. How did he do that?

Creative Response

Ask students to guess what happened next for Atalanta and Hippomenes. Have them tell what their life was like after they were married.

Options for Reaching All Students

Beginning
Critical Thinking: Make Inferences

Have students act out the race as it was told in the story. Ask them to tell why they think Atalanta stopped to pick up the apples. Ask them what might have happened if she had not stopped to pick them up.

Advanced
Critical Thinking: Consider Alternatives

Ask students to think about what would have happened if Aphrodite had not helped Hippomenes. Have them come up with at least two different alternatives and act them out.

Cooperative Learning
Greek Myths

Have students work in pairs and find books on Greek myths and read stories about the gods. Have students choose a way to report the stories back to class, by drawings or summaries. Encourage them to read other versions of the myth about Atlanta.

Strategy Tip
Predict
How do you think the three golden apples will help Hippomenes?

Hippomenes was worried. He knew Atalanta was a faster runner. He prayed to Aphrodite, the goddess of love. "You made me love her. Help me to win the race." Aphrodite heard him. She liked Hippomenes. She was angry at Atalanta for refusing to get married.

Aphrodite took Hippomenes to a magic place. There he saw a beautiful tree with yellow leaves and shining golden apples. Aphrodite picked three apples from the tree. She gave them to Hippomenes. "I will tell you what to do with them," she said. She whispered to him how to use the apples.

The next day a crowd gathered to watch the race. Atalanta and Hippomenes lined up at the starting line. "Ready, steady, go!" said the starter. Off they went.

At first Hippomenes and Atalanta ran side by side. They were both running as fast as wind. Atalanta began to pull ahead. Hippomenes reached inside his tunic and pulled out a golden apple. He threw it in front of Atalanta. Atalanta saw the beautiful apple. She stopped to pick it up. Hippomenes passed her.

Reader's Tip
Make Inferences
Why do you think Atalanta was interested in the golden apples?

Strategy Tip
Understand Patterns
Myths often have a pattern—the same thing happens two or three times. Look for a pattern in the race.

Before long, Atalanta caught up with him. Again she began to pull ahead. Hippomenes threw the second golden apple. Again he passed her as she stopped to pick it up.

The race went on. Hippomenes was getting tired. As Atalanta pulled ahead, he threw the third golden apple off to the side of the race track.

Would Atalanta run off the track to get the third apple? Hippomenes knew he could only win if she went to pick up the apple. Atalanta thought she could get the third apple and still catch up to Hippomenes. She ran off to get the apple.

In the blink of an eye, she was back running on the track. Hippomenes put on a last burst of speed. Gasping for breath, he reached the finish line just before Atalanta. He had won the race!

Atalanta stopped at the finish line and smiled. It was the first time she was happy to lose a race.

Reader's Tip
Understand Character
How did Atalanta change since the beginning of the story? Why was she so happy after losing a race?

Connect

Activate Prior Knowledge

Relate Personal Experiences

ACTIVITY BOOK

Have students discuss the sports they like to do. Ask whether they prefer individual sports or team sports and why. Follow with Activity Book page 39.

Develop Language and Concepts

Present Page 76

ORANGE TAPE

Read the poem to the class and play Side 2 of the Orange Tape several times. Then discuss the Think About It questions, including how the arrangement of the poem reinforces the idea that the girl is different from people who engage in other sports and activities.

Language Awareness

Spelling
Basic Punctuation Rules

Look at the poem with the students and point out that the poet has not used capital letters for the word "I." Also the poet does not use periods at the end of sentences. Help students "rewrite" the poem in correct English. Explain that poems sometimes break rules of standard English to put emphasis on certain ideas or words.

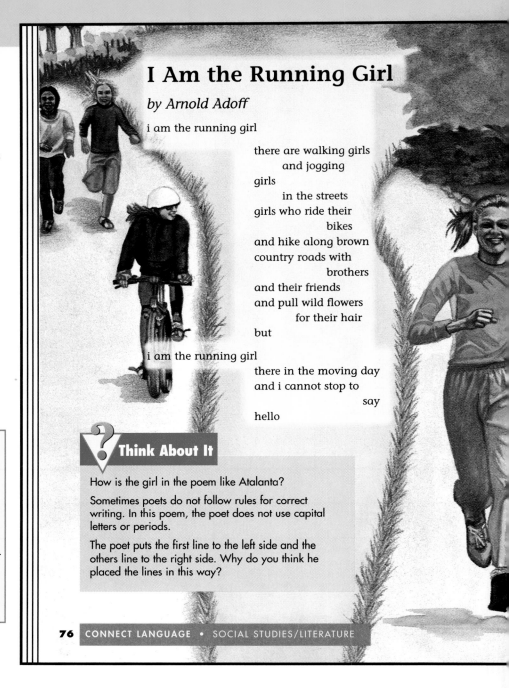

I Am the Running Girl

by Arnold Adoff

i am the running girl
there are walking girls
and jogging
girls
in the streets
girls who ride their
bikes
and hike along brown
country roads with
brothers
and their friends
and pull wild flowers
for their hair
but
i am the running girl
there in the moving day
and i cannot stop to
say
hello

Think About It

How is the girl in the poem like Atalanta?

Sometimes poets do not follow rules for correct writing. In this poem, the poet does not use capital letters or periods.

The poet puts the first line to the left side and the others line to the right side. Why do you think he placed the lines in this way?

Options for Reaching All Students

Beginning

Language: Action Verbs

TPR

Help students find the action verbs in the poem (*running, jogging, ride, hike, pull, moving, stop, say*). Ask, *which actions can be illustrated in a picture?* Have students act out the action verbs.

Advanced

Writing: Personal "Poems"

Have students write personal poems based on the format of the poem in the text. Have students choose activities or hobbies that characterize them and write about the actions they do in the sport. For example, "I am a soccer-playing boy. I run, I kick, I score goals. Other people like baseball or football, but I am the soccer-playing boy."

Mixed Ability

Language: Sports Vocabulary

Have students find pictures of sports in magazines. Have them write all the action words that they can that are associated with the sport.

Tell what you learned.

CHAPTER 4

1. How are today's Olympic Games different from the ancient games? How are they like the ancient games?
2. What did you learn about the Olympic Games that you did not know before? What would you like to learn more about?
3. What was Hippomenes' problem? How did he resolve it?

   What was Atalanta's problem and how did she resolve it?

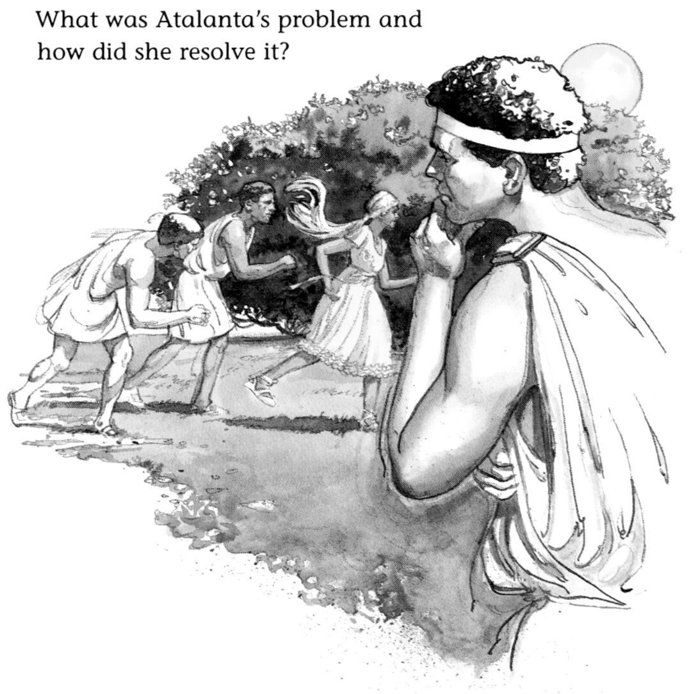

Assess ✓

Activity 1: Students should be able to list at least two ways the games are alike and two ways they are different.

Activity 2: Evaluate students' understanding of the Olympics and the depth of their responses.

Activity 3: Evaluate students' understanding of the characters' problems: Hippomenes wanted to marry a girl who didn't want to get married. Atalanta's problem was that she didn't want to marry, but men wanted to marry her. Then she met a man that she liked.

Have students complete the Chapter Self-Assessment, Blackline Master 31. Have students choose the product of one of the activities to place in their portfolios. Add the results of any rubrics, checklists, self-assessments, or portfolio assessments, Blackline Masters 2–18 and 31.

Listening Assessment

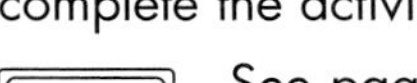

BLACKLINE MASTER

Make sure each student has a copy of Blackline Master 53, from the Teacher's Resource Book. Play the tape several times and have students complete the activity.

WHITE TAPE

See page T40d for the tapescript.

Options for Assessment

Strategy Assessment

Use a Graphic Organizer

Have students use a graphic organizer of their choice to summarize important information about any of the lessons in the chapter, the ancient vs. modern games, comparisons of two sports, or information about one sport.

Writing Assessment

Fact Booklet

Ask students to make a booklet with important facts about the Olympics or the ancient Greeks.

Language Assessment

BLACKLINE MASTER

Use Blackline Master 52 in the Teacher's Resource Book.

Standardized Test Practice

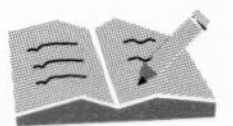

ACTIVITY BOOK

Use pages 40 and 41.
Answers: **1.** $3.00 **2.** 1,097 **3.** 5.14 minutes **4.** Not here

UNIT 2

Wrap-Up

Activities

A Fitness Collage

Have students cut pictures from magazines of people doing activities that increase fitness. Encourage students to include all kinds of activities, even ones that are not usually considered "sports"; a picture of a woman walking a dog or a house painter painting a wall would be appropriate. Discuss with students how each activity increases fitness. Hang the collage in the classroom.

Fitness Exercises

Plan a time for students to demonstrate exercises or fitness activities that they have been doing. All or part of the group might polish the aerobic exercise and perform it. Take time to talk about the kinds of fitness that these activities build.

Chart

Ask students to name popular games or sports from their countries of origin and explain how they are played. Help them create a chart to present their information.

tennis	
aerobics	
swimming	
basketball	

Discussing the Theme

Review with students the importance of fitness for a healthy life. Choose from the following activities that will demonstrate to students how much they have learned and how useful these types of information are to them:

- Have students tape-record a list of new words learned.
- Have students complete and share their fitness charts, reviewing their initial goals and the progress they have made. Display the charts of those who followed through with them.
- Play a game with students. Call out the following words and ask students to try to be the first to name an activity for each: balance, agility, speed, strength, fast reaction time, coordination. Present the words in different combinations until the class runs out of answers.
- Discuss games in different countries, encouraging students to recall the games from the unit as well as to name and describe games they enjoyed in their countries of origin.
- Have students discuss situations in which the words they have learned will be useful, such as in gym class, at sporting events, or when reading the sports section of a newspaper.

Sharing the Project

Use the invitation form, Blackline Masters 32 and 33, to invite family members to school for the Olympic awards ceremony.

You should prepare a gold, silver, and bronze medal for each activity. Cut them out of cardboard and cover them with colored paper: yellow for gold, blue for silver, and green for bronze. Write the category, the event, the name of the winner, and the date on each medal. Punch holes and hang the medals on necklaces of string or yarn.

Students could present a demonstration of fitness exercises and activities. These students should receive award recognition for their efforts well.

If there are students who did not win any medals, create special awards for them based on activities where you know—from personal observation or discussion with another teacher—that they have made progress. An example would be a "Special Award for Achievement in Swimming."

When family members arrive, post the signs for the events one by one and present the medals by hanging them around the students' necks. Take photographs of students receiving medals, or video tape the event.

Serve healthful refreshments, such as unsweetened fruit juice and raw vegetables with a yogurt-based dip. Help students make a sign for the refreshment table: "These foods promote low body fat."

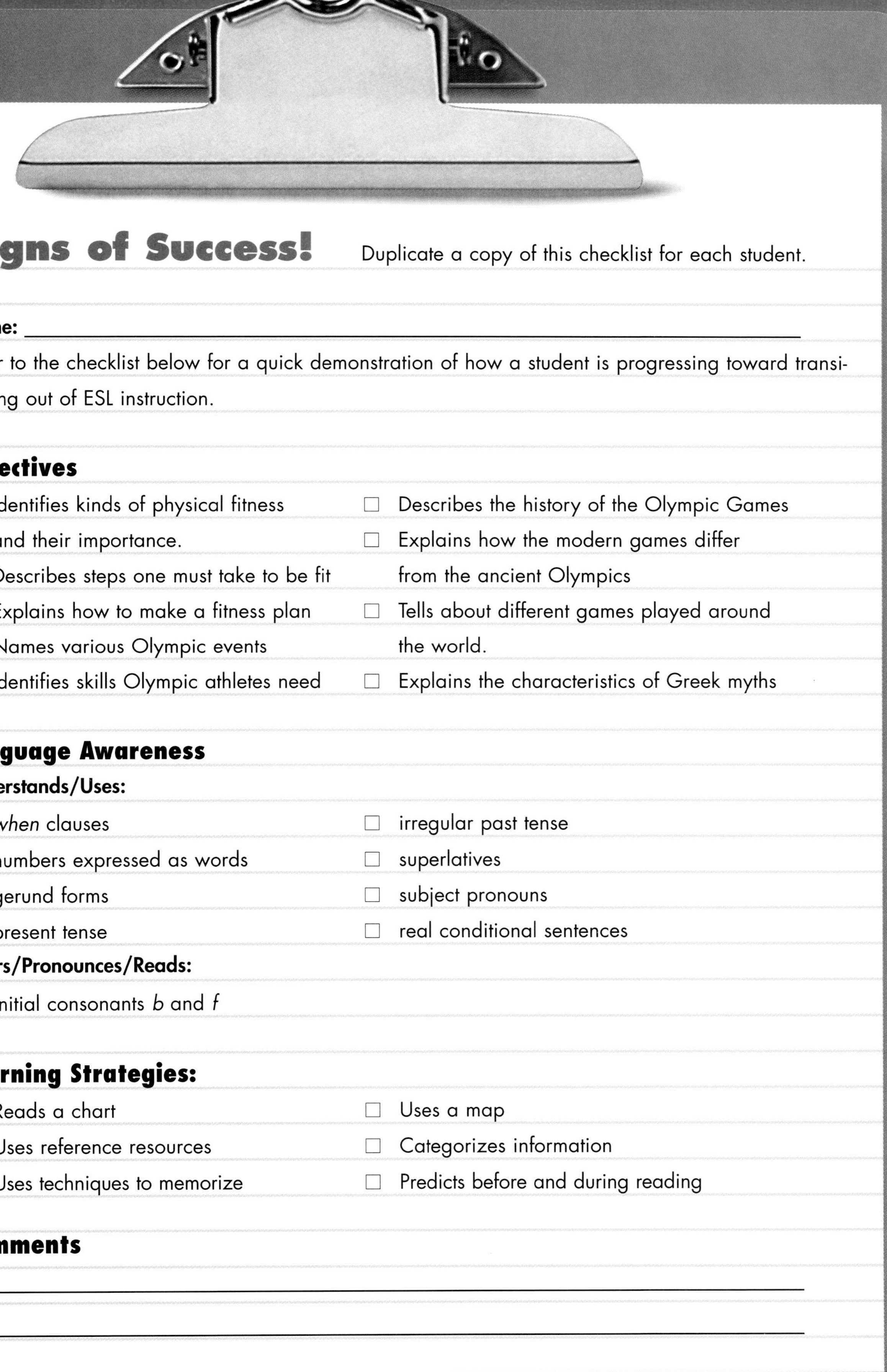

Signs of Success!

Duplicate a copy of this checklist for each student.

Name: ______________________________

Refer to the checklist below for a quick demonstration of how a student is progressing toward transitioning out of ESL instruction.

Objectives

- ☐ Identifies kinds of physical fitness and their importance.
- ☐ Describes steps one must take to be fit
- ☐ Explains how to make a fitness plan
- ☐ Names various Olympic events
- ☐ Identifies skills Olympic athletes need
- ☐ Describes the history of the Olympic Games
- ☐ Explains how the modern games differ from the ancient Olympics
- ☐ Tells about different games played around the world.
- ☐ Explains the characteristics of Greek myths

Language Awareness

Understands/Uses:

- ☐ *when* clauses
- ☐ numbers expressed as words
- ☐ gerund forms
- ☐ present tense
- ☐ irregular past tense
- ☐ superlatives
- ☐ subject pronouns
- ☐ real conditional sentences

Hears/Pronounces/Reads:

- ☐ initial consonants *b* and *f*

Learning Strategies:

- ☐ Reads a chart
- ☐ Uses reference resources
- ☐ Uses techniques to memorize
- ☐ Uses a map
- ☐ Categorizes information
- ☐ Predicts before and during reading

Comments

____

____

Planning Guide

Life Underwater

Objectives

Name the areas of the ocean.

Name the things found in the ocean.

Compare the areas of the ocean.

Tell why things float.

Name the oceans of the world.

Vocabulary Focus

Words related to oceans, such as *salt water, shore.*
Areas of the ocean, such as *light zone, dark zone, trenches.*
Things found in the ocean, such as *sea animals, islands.*
Words comparing the areas of the ocean, such as *colder, darker, lighter.*

Lesson	Content Focus	Language Awareness Objectives	Learning Strategies
Preview pp. 78–79 Tell What You Know.			
Present pp. 80–81 The Ocean Floor	Science	**Grammar** Comparatives with *-er*	
Practice pp. 82–83 Coral Reefs, Light Zones, and Dark Zones	Science	**Grammar** Adjectives—Position and Agreement	Identify main topics.
Practice pp. 84–85 Why Do Things Float?	Science	**Grammar** Articles *A* and *An*	Follow order in an experiment.
Connect pp. 86–87 Oceans of the World	Science/ Social Studies	**Grammar** Expressions *Surrounds/ Is Surrounded By*	
Connect pp. 88–99 *Why the Sea Is Salty*	Science/ Literature	**Language Function** Greetings/ Farewells **Vocabulary** Antonyms **Grammar** Irregular Past Tense Verbs	Use dialogue to evaluate characters. Use pictures for meaning.
Connect p. 100 "Shells"	Science/ Literature	**Phonics** Long *e*, Vowel Digraphs *ea/ee*	
Assess p. 101 Tell What You Learned.			

Taking Care of the Oceans

Objectives

Tell how people use the ocean.

Tell how people pollute ocean.

Name some solutions to pollution.

Tell how students can help the environment.

Tell about aquaculture.

Vocabulary Focus

Uses of the ocean, such as *food, fun, research.*
Ways to help the environment, such as *reduce, reuse, recycle.*
Words about farming the land, such as *agriculture, tractor, plow.*
Words about farming the water, such as *aquaculture, boat, fish.*

Lesson	Content Focus	Language Awareness Objectives	Learning Strategies
Preview pp. 102–103 Tell What You Know.			
Present pp. 104–105 How Do People Pollute the Oceans?	Social Studies	**Grammar** Questions with *How/* Answers with *By* and *-ing*	
Practice pp. 106–107 Some Pollution Solutions	Social Studies	**Grammar** *Stop/Start* + *-ing*	Use a graphic organizer.
Practice pp. 108–109 What Can You Do to Help the Environment?	Social Studies	**Grammar** Expressions *Less* or *More*	
Connect pp. 110–111 Farming the Water	Social Studies/ Science	**Phonics** Consonant Digraph *sh*	
Connect pp. 112–113 "Neighborhood News"	Social Studies/ Reading	**Grammar** *Wh* Questions in the Past Tense	Find information in a newspaper article.
Connect p. 114 "Yellow Submarine"	Social Studies/ Literature	**Phonics** Consonant *s*	
Assess p. 115 Tell What You Learned.			

Resources

Chapter 5

Support Materials

ACTIVITY BOOK

pages 42–51

VIDEO

Unit 3, Oceans

YELLOW TAPE

Side 1

Why the Sea Is Salty, pages T88–T99

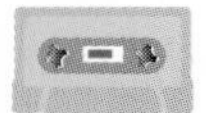
YELLOW TAPE

Side 2

"Shells," page T100

DISK

Writer's Notebook

Assessment Materials

BLACKLINE MASTER

Language Assessment, Blackline Master 60

Listening Assessment, Blackline Master 61

WHITE TAPE

Side 2

Lesson Text

Listen carefully. Circle the places in the oceans that you hear talked about. Also circle the numbers you hear.

People are interested in the oceans. Many people swim in the warm water of coral reefs. They see colorful fish. People also take trips on boats to see coral reefs. The bottoms of the boats are glass. People can see the fish of the reefs below the boats. Not many people have visited the bottom of the ocean. This is the dark zone. There temperatures are below thirty-five degrees Fahrenheit. The water can be 19,500 feet deep. There is very little life on the bottom of the ocean. It is difficult for fish to live in the dark zone. It is also difficult for people to visit there.

Newcomer Book C

Survival language for absolute beginners. For overview, see pages xxviii–xxix.

For Extended Reading

Animals of the Sea by Millicent E. Seslam, Four Winds Press, 1975

Learn about many creatures that live in our oceans.

Level: Beginning

Corals by Lili Ronai, Thomas Y. Crowell, 1976

The physical characteristics and life cycles of coral.

Level: Average

How Did We Find Out About Life in the Deep Sea? by Isaac Asimov, Walker and Company, 1982

About oceanography and discovering life in the deep sea.

Level: Advanced

The Magic Schoolbus on the Ocean Floor by Joanna Cole, Scholastic Inc., 1992

Join Ms. Frizzle's class as they learn about the ocean firsthand!

Level: Beginning

The Oceans by David Lambert, The Bookwright Press, 1983

A nonfiction look at all aspects of oceans, including their important resources, waves and tides, and currents.

Level: Advanced

What's in the Deep? by Alese and Morton Pechter, Acropolis Books Ltd., 1989

Nelson and Patricia go snorkeling with their older cousin, a marine biologist, and learn about the ocean, its inhabitants, and keeping it clean and healthy.

Level: Average

Related Technology

Oceans, Microsoft Home, 1995

Intuitive, highly motivating encyclopedia of information.

Chapter 6

Support Materials

numbers 26, 29, 56

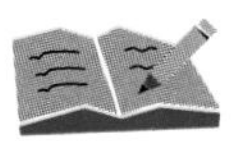

pages 52–61

Side 2

"Yellow Submarine," page T114

Writer's Notebook

Assessment Materials

Language Assessment, Blackline Master 62

Listening Assessment, Blackline Master 63

Side 2

Lesson Text

Listen carefully and circle the projects that the school is doing to protect the environment.

Our school started some projects to help protect the environment. We decided to recycle paper. In every classroom, there are two big wastebaskets. When we want to throw out paper, we use those baskets. The paper in the baskets is taken to our community recycling center.

We also decided to reuse plastic. We keep plastic cups in our lockers. When it is time for lunch, we each bring our own plastic cup to the cafeteria. We use the cup to drink. Then we wash the cup and put it back into our lockers. This way we are using less plastic, and so we are making less garbage.

For Extended Reading

Endangered Ocean Animals by Dave Taylor, Crabtree Publishing Company, 1993

A nonfiction book detailing how ocean pollution, oil spills, and hunting have led many marine mammals, birds, and fish to become endangered.

Level: Average

Finsetkind O'Day by Bruce McMillan, J.B. Lippincott Company, 1977

Young Brett's first experience as a sternman on a Maine lobster boat teaches him a lot about this industry.

Level: Advanced

Jack, the Seal and the Sea, English adaptation by Joanne Fink, Silver Burdett Press, 1988

Fisherman Jack is oblivious to the polluted conditions of the sea's water until he meets an ailing seal and receives a very special message from the sea.

Level: Beginning

Oil Spills by Jane Walker, Gloucester Press, 1993

A nonfiction book that describes specific oil spills, examines their effects on the environment, and discusses efforts to prevent future disasters.

Level: Advanced

The Story of the New England Whalers by Conrad Stein, Children's Press, 1982

Learn how whales were a major resource for the people of New England until oil was discovered in the mid-nineteenth century.

Level: Beginning

Related Technology

In the Company of Whales, Discovery Communications, 1993

Discovery Channel's beautiful exploration of the giants of the deep.

Project

Ocean Model

This optional project can be completed over the next two chapters. The project involves making a model of the ocean on chart paper, including light and dark zones, a coral reef, and a shoreline. See the Unit Wrap-Up, page T115a, for more ideas on sharing the project with family members.

What You'll Need

Collect the following items for the project:

Art Materials

- chart paper
- paints
- markers
- construction or other colored paper
- mixed media materials, which might include cellophane wrap, waxed paper, or other clear or translucent materials

Research Materials

- books that show photos, maps, and diagrams of the ocean

Beginning the Project

Explain to students that they will be making a diagram of the ocean as part of the unit on oceans. They will be using chart paper and art markers to make their diagram.

Home Involvement

Send the Letter to the Family, Blackline Masters 54–59 in the Teacher's Resource Book, to families to solicit their participation in collecting mixed media materials for the ocean diagram/model and to begin discussing home-recycling procedures.

Creating the Ocean Model

Have students review the maps, diagrams, and information that show various aspects of the ocean in the Student Book. Then encourage them to use resource books that provide more information that they can draw upon.

Divide the class into two groups. One group should create a cross-section diagram of the ocean to include the ocean floor, dark and light zones. This can be done on a large piece of chart paper. Encourage students to add or attach pictures or drawings of fish and other animals that inhabit the zones. The other group should create a diagram of a shoreline with a coral reef. Have each group create an overlay out of clear plastic that can be used to show the effects of pollution.

Each group should create a chart that elaborates and explains their diagram. On it, they should provide information about how people use the ocean. Encourage them to find out what resources come from the ocean. They should be able to explain their model or diagram to visitors.

Daily Discussion

Take a few minutes each day for discussion to practice vocabulary learned in conjunction with the ocean model. At the end of the unit, have students discuss ways the oceans affect their lives and ways to protect oceans. See page T115a for ideas about sharing the ocean model with families and friends when the unit is completed.

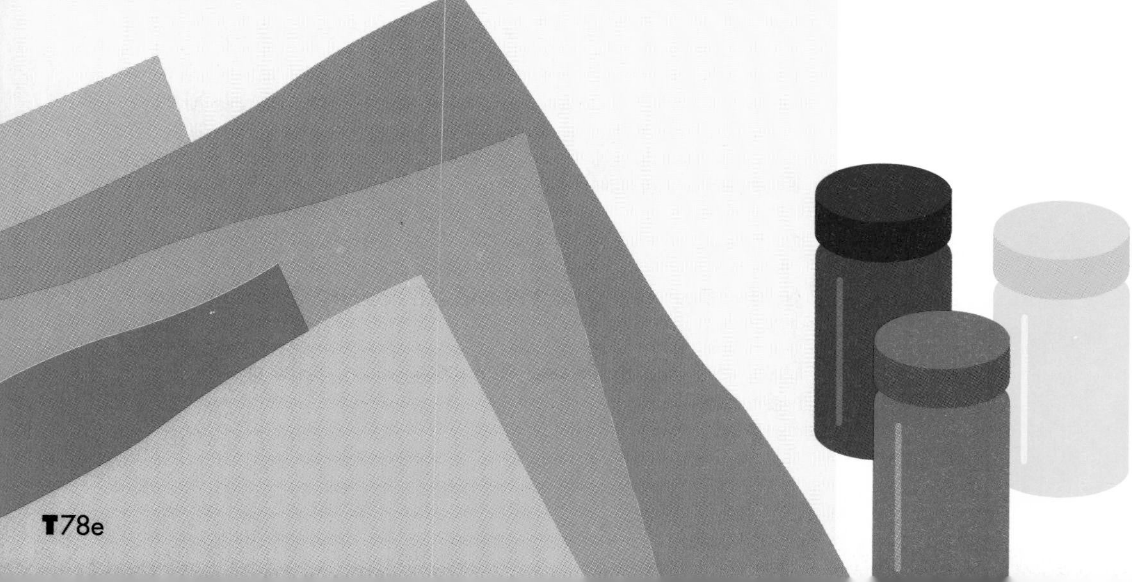

Here are some suggested activities for the discussion to accompany and complement the information in the Student Book during daily discussion.

- Have small groups of students do research on whales or sharks and report back to class.
- Have students research the Great Barrier Reef off Australia. They should report not only on the great variety of fish that live there but also on the importance of the reef and threats to it.
- Have students report on kelp. What is its importance to the ocean environment? How do people use kelp?
- If possible, have students report on and bring in examples of different kinds of sand and rocks from different beaches.
- Obtain a selection of music related to the sea to play thought the unit, from sea shanties to "La Mer."
- Have a group of students research and report on Jacques Costeau and his many contributions to informing people about the importance of marine life.

Here is some specific information about oceans to review during the project:

Pacific Ocean

- The largest of the oceans
- Mostly a warm body of water
- Tropical and subtropical climate
- Important mineral source of salt, bromine, magnesium, and oil

Atlantic Ocean

- The saltiest of the oceans
- Contains many dissolved minerals
- The youngest of the oceans
- Most heavily used trade route in the world
- Important source of fish as food

Indian Ocean

- Third largest ocean
- Tropical to temperate climate
- Annual, predictable monsoons make trade routes possible.

Arctic Ocean

- The smallest of the oceans
- The coldest of the oceans
- Has one large ice pack floating in the center
- Has limited marine and plant life
- Oil spills are an environmental concern.

Activity Book Chapter 5

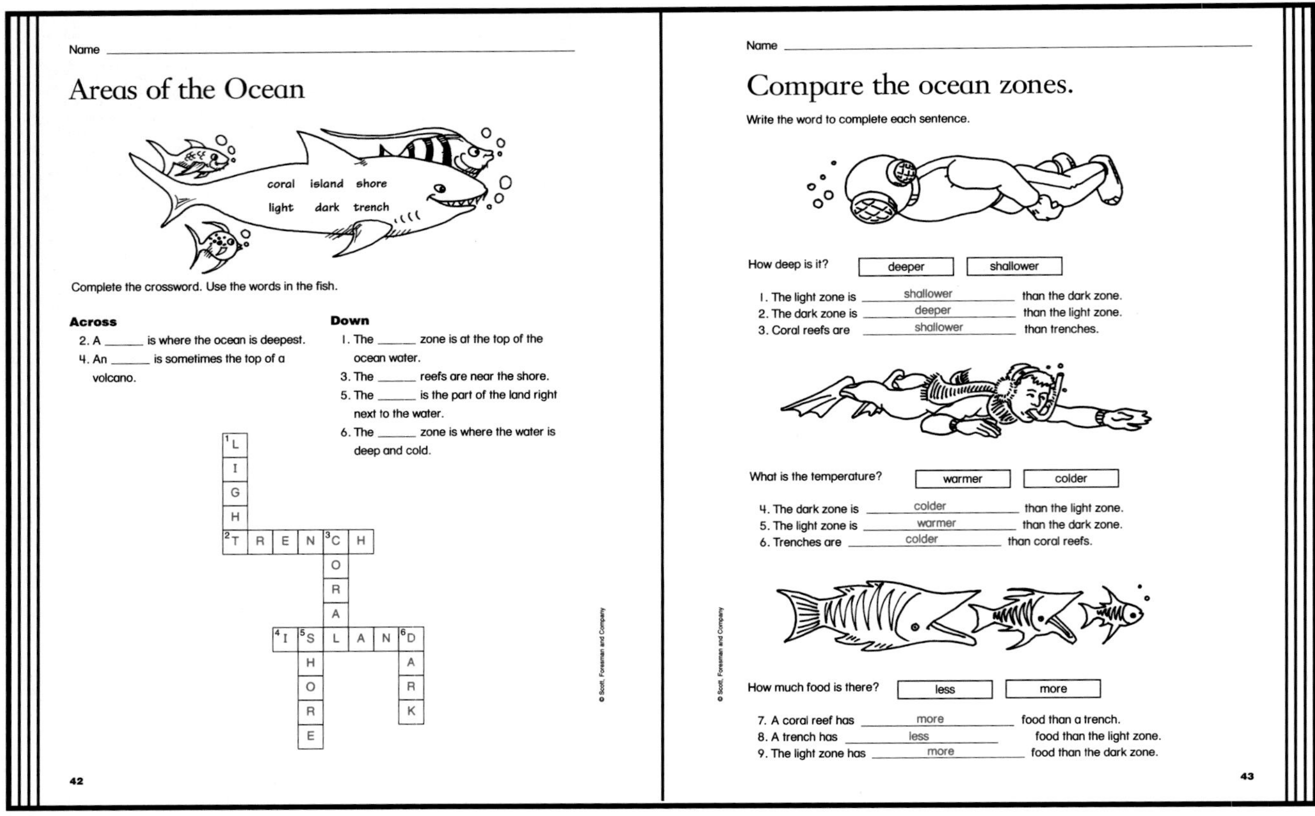
Name

Areas of the Ocean

coral island shore
light dark trench

Complete the crossword. Use the words in the fish.

Across

2. A ______ is where the ocean is deepest.
4. An ______ is sometimes the top of a volcano.

Down

1. The ______ zone is at the top of the ocean water.
3. The ______ reefs are near the shore.
5. The ______ is the part of the land right next to the water.
6. The ______ zone is where the water is deep and cold.

1 LIGHT (down)
2 TRENCH (across)
3 CORAL (down)
4 ISLAND (across)
5 SHORE (down)
6 DARK (down)

© Scott, Foresman and Company

42

Name

Compare the ocean zones.

Write the word to complete each sentence.

How deep is it? deeper shallower

1. The light zone is shallower than the dark zone.
2. The dark zone is deeper than the light zone.
3. Coral reefs are shallower than trenches.

What is the temperature? warmer colder

4. The dark zone is colder than the light zone.
5. The light zone is warmer than the dark zone.
6. Trenches are colder than coral reefs.

How much food is there? less more

7. A coral reef has more food than a trench.
8. A trench has less food than the light zone.
9. The light zone has more food than the dark zone.

© Scott, Foresman and Company

43

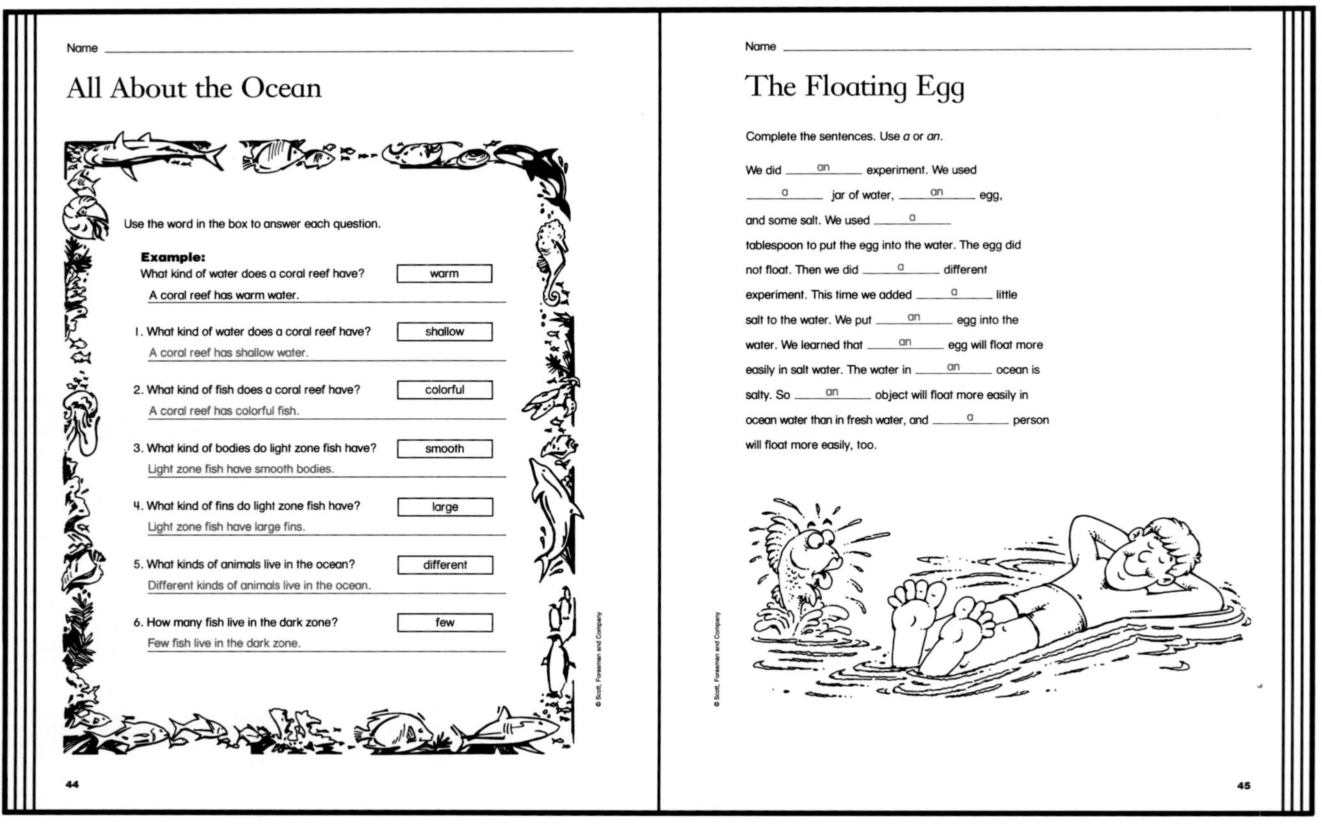
Name

All About the Ocean

Use the word in the box to answer each question.

Example:
What kind of water does a coral reef have? warm
A coral reef has warm water.

1. What kind of water does a coral reef have? shallow
A coral reef has shallow water.
2. What kind of fish does a coral reef have? colorful
A coral reef has colorful fish.
3. What kind of bodies do light zone fish have? smooth
Light zone fish have smooth bodies.
4. What kind of fins do light zone fish have? large
Light zone fish have large fins.
5. What kinds of animals live in the ocean? different
Different kinds of animals live in the ocean.
6. How many fish live in the dark zone? few
Few fish live in the dark zone.

© Scott, Foresman and Company

44

Name

The Floating Egg

Complete the sentences. Use *a* or *an*.

We did an experiment. We used a jar of water, an egg, and some salt. We used a tablespoon to put the egg into the water. The egg did not float. Then we did a different experiment. This time we added a little salt to the water. We put an egg into the water. We learned that an egg will float more easily in salt water. The water in an ocean is salty. So an object will float more easily in ocean water than in fresh water, and a person will float more easily, too.

© Scott, Foresman and Company

45

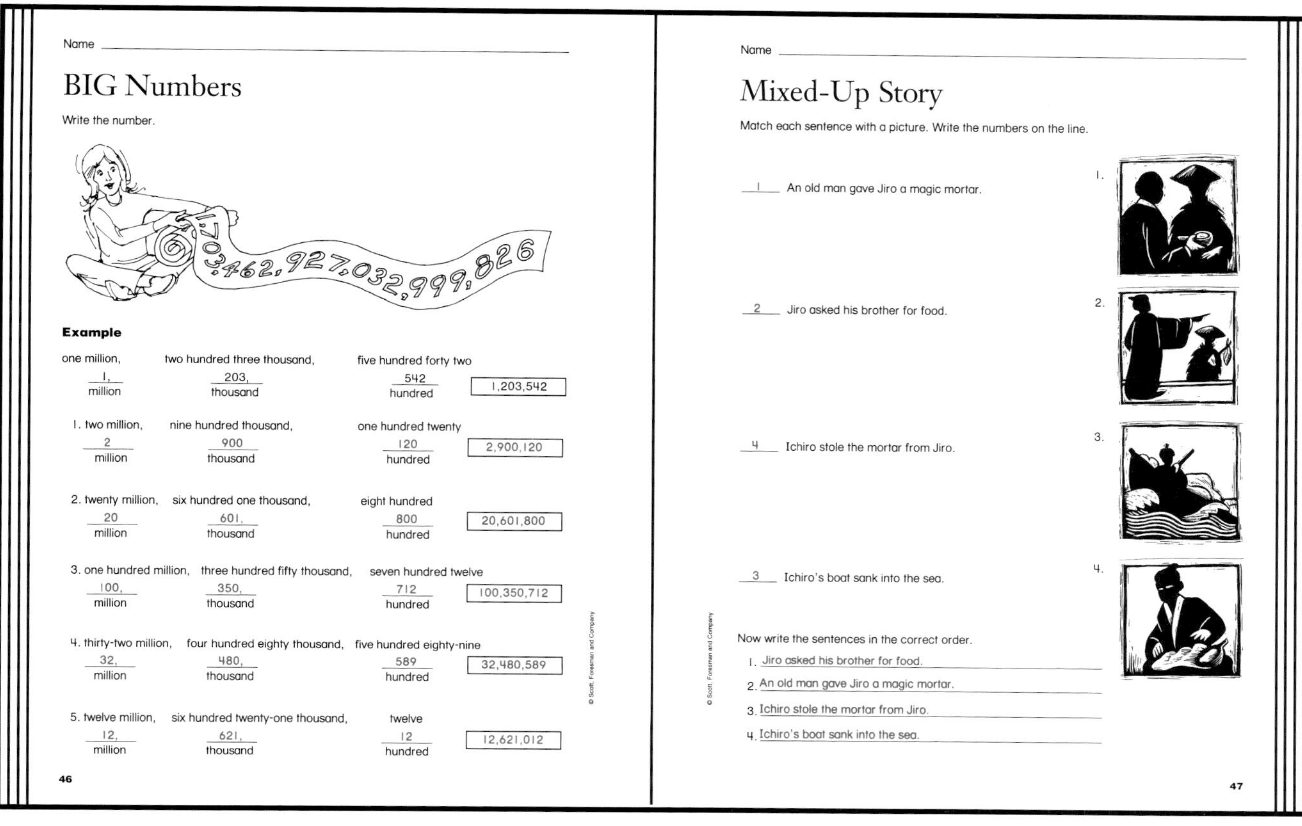

Name

BIG Numbers

Write the number.

Example

one million,	two hundred three thousand,	five hundred forty two	
1, million	203, thousand	542 hundred	1,203,542
1. two million,	nine hundred thousand,	one hundred twenty	
2 million	900 thousand	120 hundred	2,900,120
2. twenty million,	six hundred one thousand,	eight hundred	
20 million	601, thousand	800 hundred	20,601,800
3. one hundred million,	three hundred fifty thousand,	seven hundred twelve	
100, million	350, thousand	712 hundred	100,350,712
4. thirty-two million,	four hundred eighty thousand,	five hundred eighty-nine	
32, million	480, thousand	589 hundred	32,480,589
5. twelve million,	six hundred twenty-one thousand,	twelve	
12, million	621, thousand	12 hundred	12,621,012

Name

Mixed-Up Story

Match each sentence with a picture. Write the numbers on the line.

1 An old man gave Jiro a magic mortar. 1.

2 Jiro asked his brother for food. 2.

4 Ichiro stole the mortar from Jiro. 3.

3 Ichiro's boat sank into the sea. 4.

Now write the sentences in the correct order.

1. Jiro asked his brother for food.
2. An old man gave Jiro a magic mortar.
3. Ichiro stole the mortar from Jiro.
4. Ichiro's boat sank into the sea.

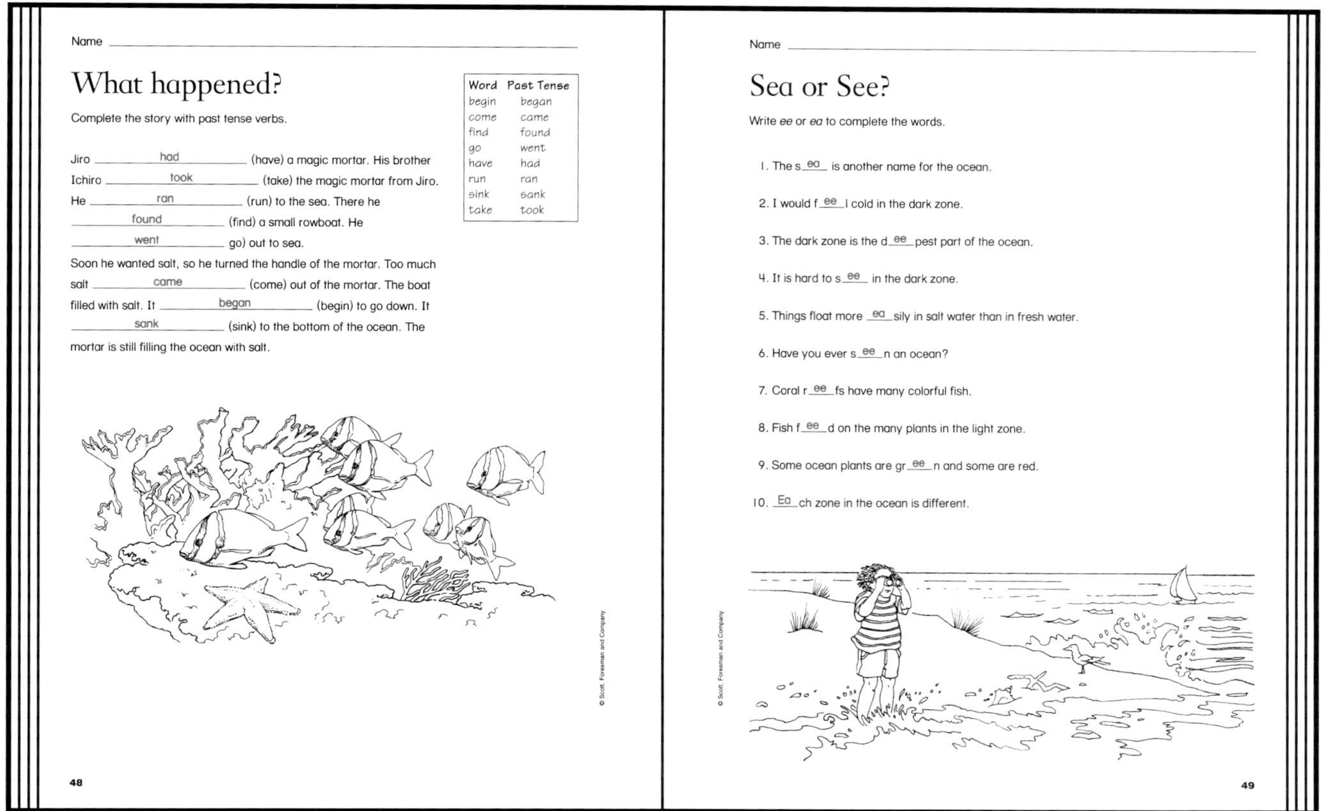

Name

What happened?

Complete the story with past tense verbs.

Word	Past Tense
begin	began
come	came
find	found
go	went
have	had
run	ran
sink	sank
take	took

Jiro had (have) a magic mortar. His brother Ichiro took (take) the magic mortar from Jiro. He ran (run) to the sea. There he found (find) a small rowboat. He went go) out to sea. Soon he wanted salt, so he turned the handle of the mortar. Too much salt came (come) out of the mortar. The boat filled with salt. It began (begin) to go down. It sank (sink) to the bottom of the ocean. The mortar is still filling the ocean with salt.

Name

Sea or See?

Write *ee* or *ea* to complete the words.

1. The s ea is another name for the ocean.
2. I would f ee l cold in the dark zone.
3. The dark zone is the d ee pest part of the ocean.
4. It is hard to s ee in the dark zone.
5. Things float more ea sily in salt water than in fresh water.
6. Have you ever s ee n an ocean?
7. Coral r ee fs have many colorful fish.
8. Fish f ee d on the many plants in the light zone.
9. Some ocean plants are gr ee n and some are red.
10. Ea ch zone in the ocean is different.

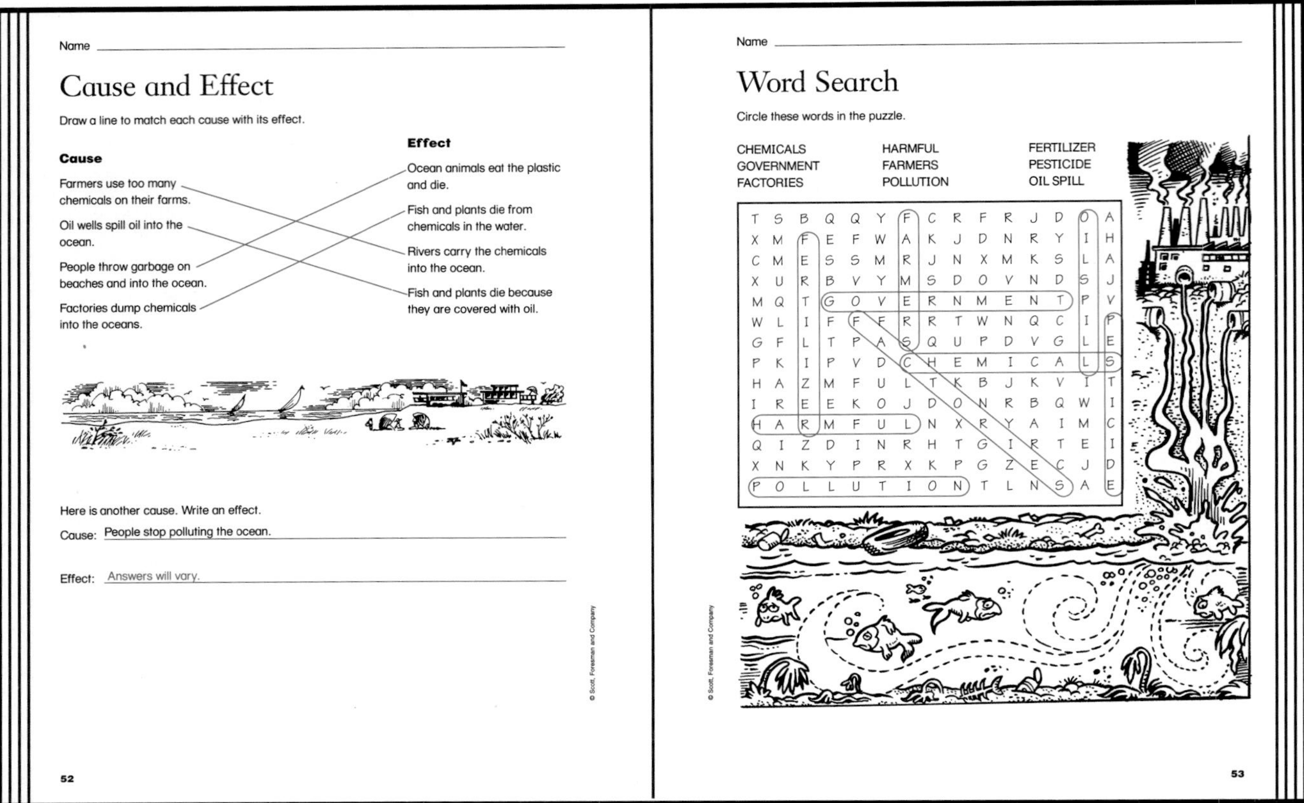

Name

Cause and Effect

Draw a line to match each cause with its effect.

Cause

Farmers use too many chemicals on their farms.

Oil wells spill oil into the ocean.

People throw garbage on beaches and into the ocean.

Factories dump chemicals into the oceans.

Effect

Ocean animals eat the plastic and die.

Fish and plants die from chemicals in the water.

Rivers carry the chemicals into the ocean.

Fish and plants die because they are covered with oil.

Here is another cause. Write an effect.

Cause: People stop polluting the ocean.

Effect: Answers will vary.

Name

Word Search

Circle these words in the puzzle.

CHEMICALS	HARMFUL	FERTILIZER
GOVERNMENT	FARMERS	PESTICIDE
FACTORIES	POLLUTION	OIL SPILL

T	S	B	Q	Q	Y	F	C	R	F	R	J	D	O	A
X	M	F	E	F	W	A	K	J	D	N	R	Y	I	H
C	M	E	S	S	M	R	J	N	X	M	K	S	L	A
X	U	R	B	V	Y	M	S	D	O	V	N	D	S	J
M	Q	T	G	O	V	E	R	N	M	E	N	T	P	V
W	L	I	F	F	F	R	R	T	W	N	Q	C	I	P
G	F	L	T	P	A	S	Q	U	P	D	V	G	L	E
P	K	I	P	V	D	C	H	E	M	I	C	A	L	S
H	A	Z	M	F	U	L	T	K	B	J	K	V	I	T
I	R	E	E	K	O	J	D	O	N	R	B	Q	W	I
H	A	R	M	F	U	L	N	X	R	Y	A	I	M	C
Q	I	Z	D	I	N	R	H	T	G	I	R	T	E	I
X	N	K	Y	P	R	X	K	P	G	Z	E	C	J	D
P	O	L	L	U	T	I	O	N	T	L	N	S	A	E

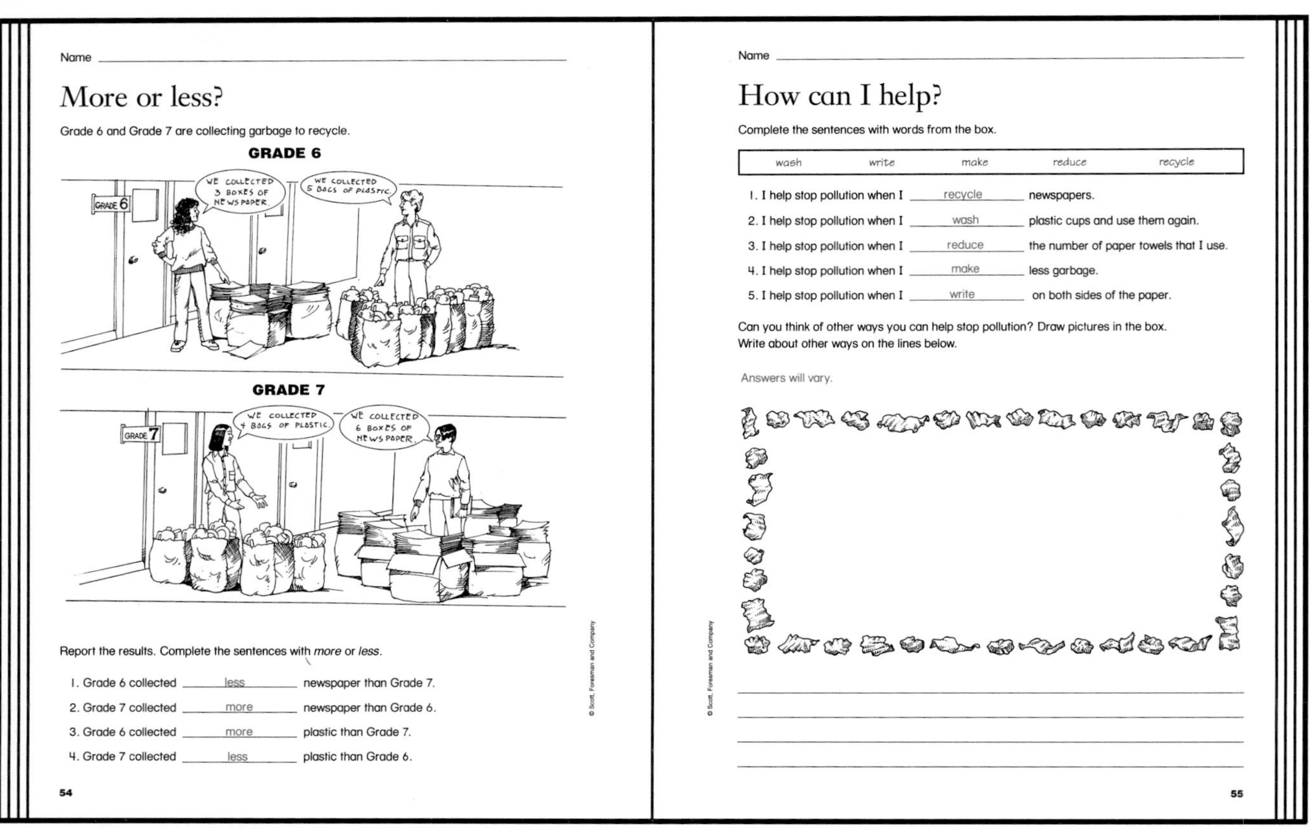

Name

More or less?

Grade 6 and Grade 7 are collecting garbage to recycle.

GRADE 6

GRADE 7

Report the results. Complete the sentences with *more* or *less*.

1. Grade 6 collected ___less___ newspaper than Grade 7.
2. Grade 7 collected ___more___ newspaper than Grade 6.
3. Grade 6 collected ___more___ plastic than Grade 7.
4. Grade 7 collected ___less___ plastic than Grade 6.

Name

How can I help?

Complete the sentences with words from the box.

wash	write	make	reduce	recycle

1. I help stop pollution when I ___recycle___ newspapers.
2. I help stop pollution when I ___wash___ plastic cups and use them again.
3. I help stop pollution when I ___reduce___ the number of paper towels that I use.
4. I help stop pollution when I ___make___ less garbage.
5. I help stop pollution when I ___write___ on both sides of the paper.

Can you think of other ways you can help stop pollution? Draw pictures in the box. Write about other ways on the lines below.

Answers will vary.

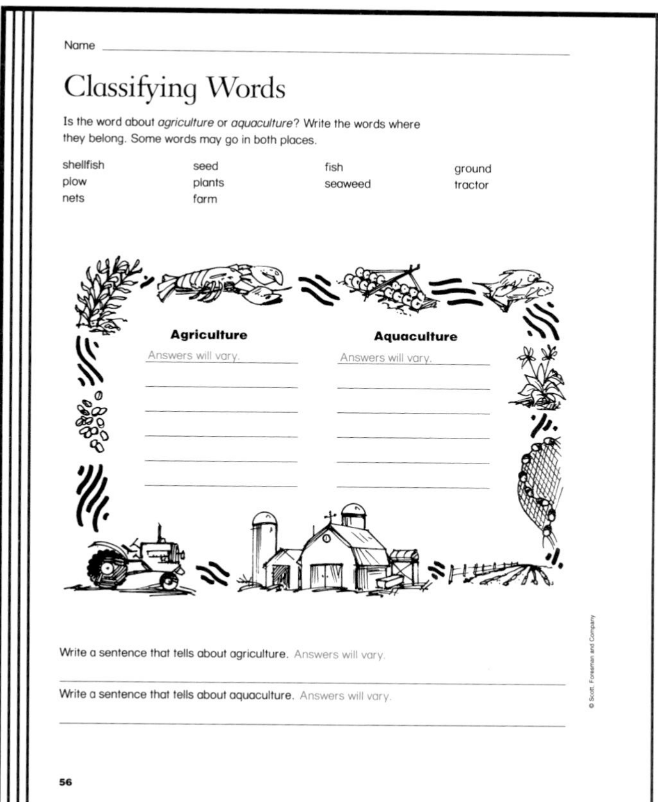

Name ______________________________

Classifying Words

Is the word about *agriculture* or *aquaculture*? Write the words where they belong. Some words may go in both places.

shellfish	seed	fish	ground
plow	plants	seaweed	tractor
nets	farm		

Agriculture	Aquaculture
Answers will vary.	Answers will vary.

Write a sentence that tells about agriculture. Answers will vary.

Write a sentence that tells about aquaculture. Answers will vary.

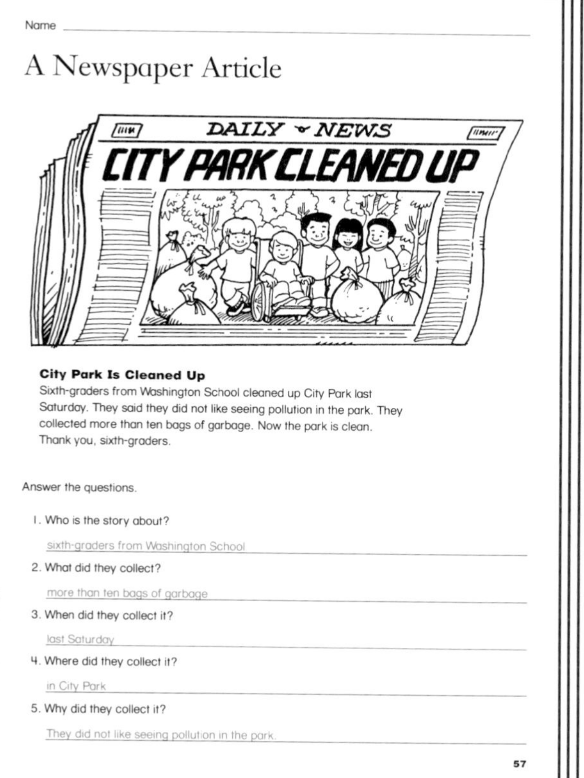

Name ______________________________

A Newspaper Article

City Park Is Cleaned Up
Sixth-graders from Washington School cleaned up City Park last Saturday. They said they did not like seeing pollution in the park. They collected more than ten bags of garbage. Now the park is clean. Thank you, sixth-graders.

Answer the questions.

1. Who is the story about?
   sixth-graders from Washington School
2. What did they collect?
   more than ten bags of garbage
3. When did they collect it?
   last Saturday
4. Where did they collect it?
   in City Park
5. Why did they collect it?
   They did not like seeing pollution in the park.

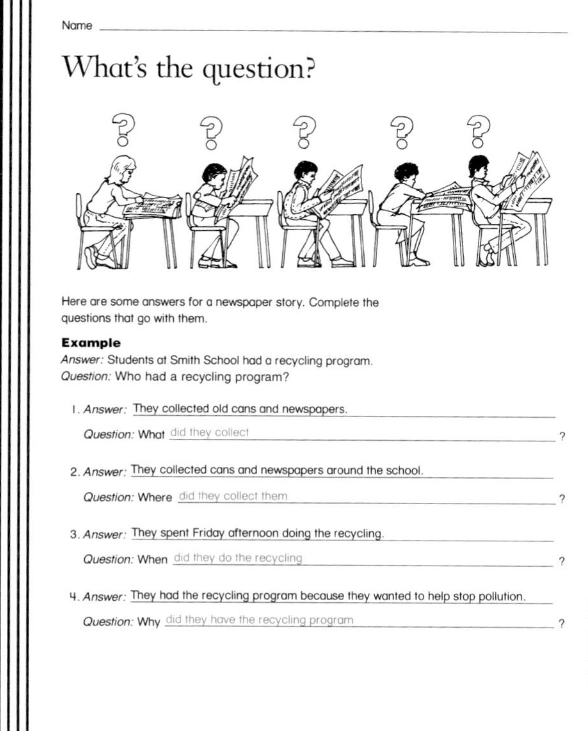

Name ______________________________

What's the question?

Here are some answers for a newspaper story. Complete the questions that go with them.

Example
Answer: Students at Smith School had a recycling program.
Question: Who had a recycling program?

1. *Answer:* They collected old cans and newspapers.
   Question: What did they collect ?
2. *Answer:* They collected cans and newspapers around the school.
   Question: Where did they collect them ?
3. *Answer:* They spent Friday afternoon doing the recycling.
   Question: When did they do the recycling ?
4. *Answer:* They had the recycling program because they wanted to help stop pollution.
   Question: Why did they have the recycling program ?

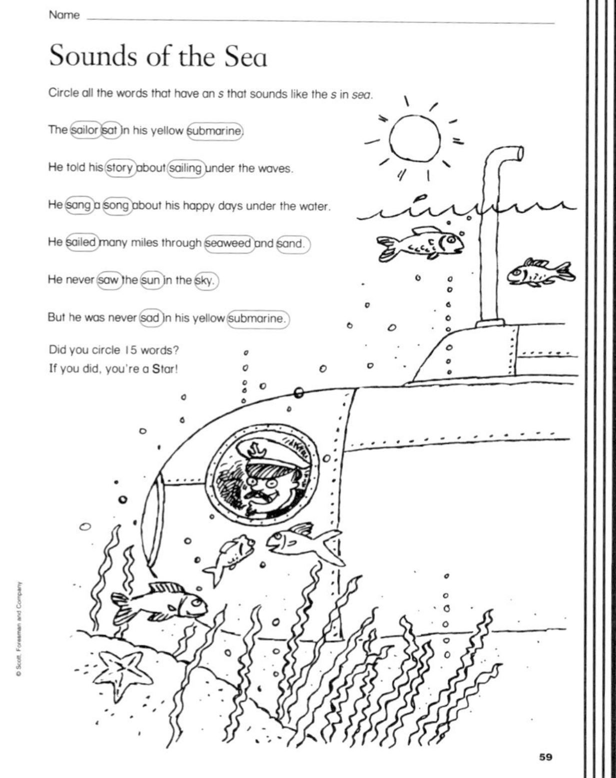

Name ______________________________

Sounds of the Sea

Circle all the words that have an *s* that sounds like the *s* in *sea*.

The sailor sat in his yellow submarine.

He told his story about sailing under the waves.

He sang a song about his happy days under the water.

He sailed many miles through seaweed and sand.

He never saw the sun in the sky.

But he was never sad in his yellow submarine.

Did you circle 15 words?
If you did, you're a Star!

UNIT 3

Preview

Activate Prior Knowledge

Use Pictures

Share pictures of various things associated with oceans (for example, a ship, waves, whales, tropical fish, a beach). Have students describe the pictures and tell or act out anything else they know about oceans. On a piece of chart paper, begin a class list of ocean words. Encourage students to contribute ocean words they already know.

Develop Language and Concepts

Present Pages 78 and 79

Introduce the words in the Word Bank and help students associate the words with the pictures. Have students describe the pictures, encouraging them to use the words from the Word Bank and from their class list.

Have students answer the questions on page 78. Invite students to discuss their knowledge of oceans even if they've only seen them in movies or on television. When you ask them, *What makes an ocean an ocean?*, try to elicit the facts that oceans are large, deep, and have salt water.

Break the class into small groups for the Talk About It activity. Supply each group with a globe and, if possible, a few pictures books or articles on the ocean to stimulate discussion.

Oceans

Word Bank

- coral reef
- salt water
- sea animals
- shore

Tell what you know.

Have you ever seen an ocean?

What makes an ocean an ocean?

Options for Reaching All Students

Beginning

Language: Words and Pictures

Have students fold a piece of paper into four sections. Ask them to choose four words that they would like to illustrate from the class list of ocean words. Have them write one word in each section of the paper and illustrate it.

Advanced

Language: Sentence Strips

Have students work in pairs. Give each pair three strips of paper. On each strip, have them write a sentence that tells about one of the pictures on page 78 or 79. Encourage them to use words from the Word Bank and from the class list of ocean words. Have them read their sentences to other pairs of students, asking them to identify the pictures to which they refer.

Mixed Ability

Video: Oceans

Show the Unit 3 portion of the video to give students an overview of the unit. You may want to replay the tape several times throughout the unit for language and concept reinforcement and development.

THEME/KEY CONCEPTS

Oceans cover most of the earth's surface. They are an important element of the environment in which we live. People need to protect the oceans.

Chapter 5

- An ocean is not simply a big body of water. It has several distinctive areas, each having its own features.
- Because of its unique characteristics, each area of the ocean supports different kinds of sea animals.

Chapter 6

- Oceans are important to the way we live. They supply food, jobs, and recreation.
- Oceans are being polluted by garbage, chemicals, and oil spills.
- If individuals, government, and industry work together, people can stop pollution of the oceans.

Talk About It

Where are the oceans in the world? What lives in the oceans?

Peer Tutoring

Language: Picture/Word Association

Have students work in teams of two. Give each team a set of ten blank cards. On five of the cards, have them write words of their choice from the Word Bank or their class list of ocean words. On the other five cards, have them illustrate the words. When they finish, have them share their cards with other teams, challenging them to match the words and illustrations.

Cooperative Language Experience

TPR: Imagery

Play a tape of the sounds of the ocean. Tell students to close their eyes and imagine that they are at the beach.

Let them imagine having water running over their feet, riding a wave, catching a fish, smelling the salt air, and walking on a beach.

Present

Activate Prior Knowledge

Review Measurement and Temperature

Ask questions to help students conceptualize measurement in feet and/or meters: *How many feet/meters wide is the classroom? How many feet/meters high is the ceiling? How many feet/meters high do you think the school building is?*

Discuss temperatures in Fahrenheit and Celsius. Ask, *What is the temperature today? Is it warm or cold? What is a warm temperature? What is a cool temprature? What is a very cold temperature?*

Develop Language and Concepts

Present Pages 80 and 81

Have students look at the picture of the ocean floor and identify any features that they can.

Before you read the text, write these words on the board: *hundred, thousand.* Model the words. Help students count by hundreds from 100 to 1,000. Write the numerals on the board as they count. Then continue counting by thousands to 10,000.

Read the text with students, pausing often to let them locate each feature as it is mentioned. Help students understand how deep each feature is by having them figure out how many times deeper it is than their school is tall. Also, discuss the variations in water temperatures, relating the water temperatures to air temperatures.

(Continued on page T81)

CHAPTER 5

Life Underwater

The Ocean Floor

Look at the map of the ocean floor. How are the ocean floor and dry land alike?

Islands rise above the ocean water. They can be the tops of volcanoes.

Coral reefs are near the shore. The water can be as shallow as 130 feet (40 meters). The temperature of the water is above 64°F (18°C).

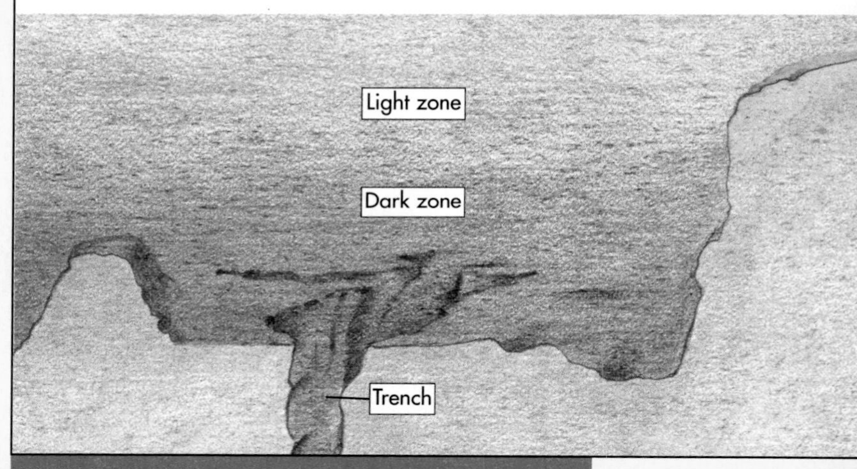

Options for Reaching All Students

Beginning

Math: Graphing

Have students make a graph on which they record the high temperatures for a week. Have students use thermometers or newspaper weather reports to obtain temperatures. Help them decide what to title the graph and give them the days of the week to copy. Display the graphs on the bulletin board.

Advanced

Math: Graphing

Have students make line graphs of the depth and temperature of the five ocean areas discussed in the text. Help them with the headings for their graphs. When they finish, have them describe the areas, reading the numbers from their graphs.

Mixed Ability

Language: Guessing Game

Have students work in pairs. Ask them make a quiz card for each of the ocean areas discussed in the text—*an island, a coral reef, the light zone, the dark zone, a trench* (using singular nouns). Have them write the name of an area on one side of the card and a clue about where it is on the other *(has colorful fish).* When they finish, have them show other pairs the clue side of their cards and

The light zone is at the top of the ocean water. The water can be as deep as 650 feet (200 meters). The temperature of the water is between 64°F and 35°F (18°C and 4°C).

The dark zone is below the light zone. The water can be as deep as 19,500 feet (6,000 meters). The temperature of the water is below 35°F (4°C).

The trenches are the deepest part of the ocean. The Mariana Trench in the Pacific Ocean is the deepest place in all the earth's oceans. It is about 35,000 feet deep or almost seven miles deep (10,668 meters).

Word Bank

- colder
- darker
- lighter
- warmer
- more food
- less food

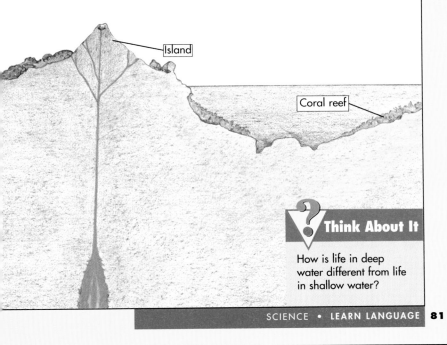

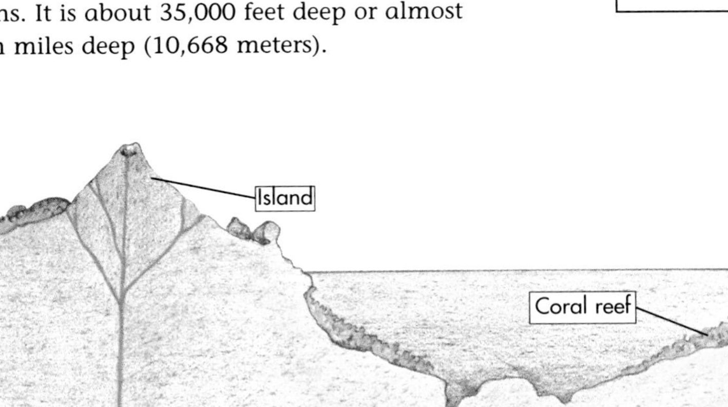

Think About It

How is life in deep water different from life in shallow water?

Language Awareness

Grammar
Comparatives with *-er*

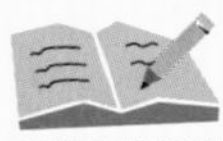
ACTIVITY BOOK

Write the word *cold* on the board. Demonstrate being a little cold, write a cool temperature on the board and say, *It is cold.* Then demonstrate being even colder and write a cooler temperature. Say, *It is colder.*

Give other illustrations of comparatives, using classroom examples; for example, *This table is bigger than that table.*

Then have students brainstorm other comparatives using classroom items. Use Activity Book page 43 for practice.

Read the words in the Word Bank with students. Prompt them to use the words to answer the Think About It question. Use Activity Book page 42 to review ocean vocabulary.

Assess 

Students should be able to

- name the different sections of the ocean
- distinguish between the water temperatures at different levels

LOOK **AHEAD**

In the next section, students will read about fish that live in the coral reefs, in the light zone, and in the dark zone.

ask, "What is it?" (As an alternative, they can show the word side of the cards and ask, "Where is it?")

Cooperative Learning Experience

Field Trip

If possible, have students visit a beach, a local aquarium, or a pet store that sells fish and aquariums. After the experience, write a class story about what the students saw, including plants and animals.

QuickCheck

Read Temperatures

Check that students understand how to read temperatures in print and that they know about Celsius and Fahrenheit thermometers. If possible, have examples of both types of temperature scales in the classroom.

Practice

Activate Prior Knowledge

Review Prior Learning

Have students orally review what they have learned about oceans. Have students name areas of the ocean and tell what they know about each one.

Start a class list of antonyms that apply to the zones, such as *dark/light, deep/shallow, cold/warm.* Present the first word and have students supply the antonym, if they can.

Develop Language and Concepts

Present Pages 82 and 83

Have students look at the pictures on the page. Then read the text with students. Help students associate the words with the pictures of the fish.

Add words from the text to the class list of antonyms, perhaps including *fast/slow, colorful/dull, many/few.* Talk about how understanding antonyms will help them understand the text.

Have students do the Write About It activity. If necessary, help them set up the chart.

Coral Reefs, Light Zones, and Dark Zones

Different kinds of animals live at different depths of the ocean. What are some differences among animals at different levels of the ocean?

Coral reefs are in warm water. The shallow water gets lots of sunlight. As many as 5,000 kinds of colorful fish live around coral reefs.

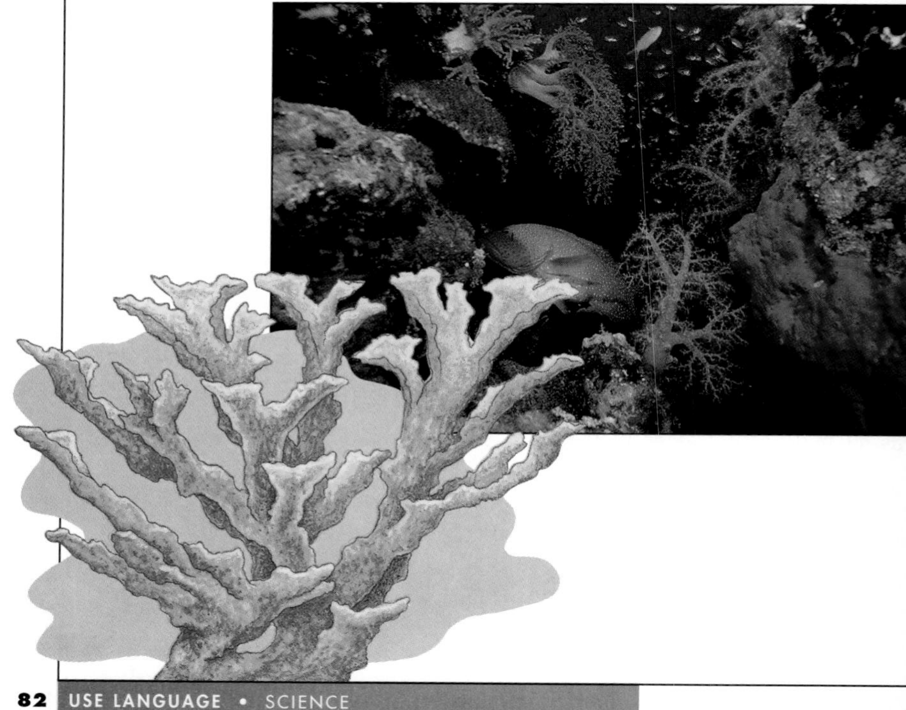

Options for Reaching All Students

Beginning

Language: Antonym Game

Have students work in two teams to prepare two sets of cards from the class antonym list. One team takes its words from the left column, the other team lists the antonyms. A member of one team holds up a card and pronounces the word, and the student holding the antonym card holds it up and pronounces the antonym.

Advanced

Language: Ocean Vocabulary

Give each student a list of phrases from the reading (for example, *cold water, shallow water, colorful fish, fish that light up, not much food*). Have them cut the phrases into strips. Write the names of the three levels of the ocean on chart paper *(coral reef, light zone, dark zone)*. Ask students to place the strips under the levels where they belong and read the phrases on the strips aloud.

Have students write a short paragraph about one level, using the phrases and other information.

The fish in the light zone have smooth bodies and large fins so they can swim fast. They need to swim fast to catch other fish or to escape their enemies. Fish in the light zones can feed on the many plants in the zone. Plants in the light zone get light from the sun to make the food they need.

Fewer fish live in the dark zone. Food is hard to find. The bodies of some dark zone fish give off light. They use the light to help them hunt or to scare off enemies. Other dark zone fish have air sacs. They can fill and empty the air sacs like balloons to help them move up and down.

Write About It

Make a chart with the three areas of the ocean. Write about each area.

Language Awareness

Grammar
Adjectives—Position and Agreement

ACTIVITY BOOK

List these phrases on the board: *warm water, cold water, colorful animal.* Explain that the words on the right name things and the words on the left describe those things. Emphasize the word order—the describing word first followed by the word it describes. Present examples of other words that describe. Use Activity Book page 44.

Model a Strategy

Identify Main Topics

Model how to find main topics:

Before I read an article, I look for the main topics. I can often find a clue to the main topic by reading the first sentence in each paragraph. In this article, the first sentence of each paragraph names a level of the ocean. So I know each paragraph is about a level of the ocean.

Assess

Use the Write About It for assessment. Students should be able to

- make a chart with the three areas of the oceans and write about each area

LOOK **AHEAD**

In the next section, students will conduct an experiment to learn why things float.

Mixed Ability

Science: Ocean Animals

Have students get illustrated books about oceans and ocean animals and read them cooperatively. Encourage the students to make a class chart with names of ocean animals other than those mentioned in the Student Book and interesting facts about them.

Cooperative Learning

Research

Have students work in groups of mixed ability. Each group should choose an aspect of ocean life to learn more about. Possibilities might be whales, sharks, tide pools, or shell fish people eat. Have them use books, encyclopedias, videos, CD-ROM, or magazines as resources. They should make an idea web showing their information or prepare a short report.

Home Connection

Experience the Ocean

Have students ask family members how they have experienced the ocean. Have them ask questions such as these: *Do they eat fish or other ocean food? Have they ever lived or vacationed near the ocean? Have they crossed an ocean?* Have students report back to class.

Practice

Activate Prior Knowledge

Use Demonstration

Have a shaker of salt and a container of fresh water. Have students taste the water and write *fresh water* on the board. Have them taste the salt and write *salt* on the board. Then add some salt to the water and ask a volunteer to taste it. Write *salt water* on the board. Ask students if they have ever tasted salt water before. Prompt that oceans have salt water.

Develop Language and Concepts

Present Pages 84 and 85

Read the activity with students. Help them understand the concept of density by showing them objects of comparable size that vary in density. Then have students perform the activity, either individually or in groups. Have them retell the steps they took to perform the activity. Then have them record their results in their notebooks, using the sentence starters shown on page 85.

Have students work in groups to answer the Talk About It questions.

Model a Strategy

Order in an Experiment

Model the steps in an experiment:

When I do an experiment, I follow the same steps: read the experiment; restate the steps

(Continued on page T85)

Why do things float?

Hold an egg and a stone of about the same size. The stone is heavier than the egg because it is denser. Density is how heavy something is for its size.

Things float if their density is less than the density of the water. Salt water is denser than fresh water. Do you think it's easier or harder to float in salt water? Try this to find out.

Things You Need

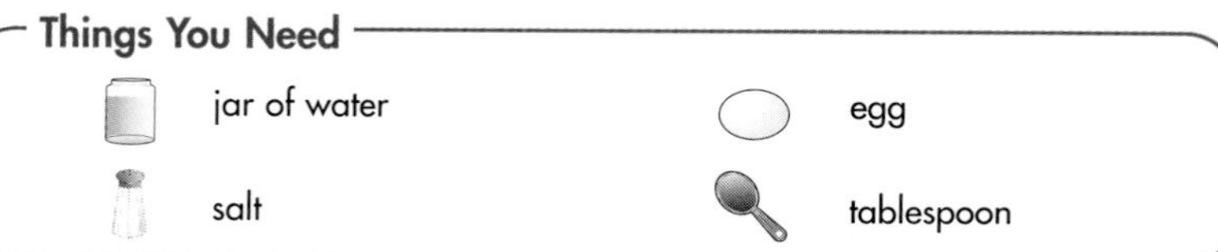

Follow these steps.

1. Use a tablespoon to place an egg into a jar of water.
2. Remove the egg from the water.
3. Add 2 to 3 tablespoons of salt to the water.

Options for Reaching All Students

Beginning

Science: Floating Items

Have students repeat the experiment with other objects and write down the results.

Advanced

Critical Thinking: Classify Picture Cards

Have students use the set of picture cards as well as magazines. Ask them to find as many cards and pictures as they can that show things that have something to do with the ocean. Perhaps the items live in the ocean, or cross the ocean, or eat things from the ocean. Have them explain what each pictured thing has to do with the ocean. Then have them group the pictures into categories, give each category a name, and tell why they grouped the categories as they did.

4. Stir the water until the salt dissolves.

5. Use the tablespoon to place the egg into the jar.

1. When I put an egg into fresh water,
2. When I put an egg into salty water,

Talk About It

An egg sinks to the bottom of the water. Which is denser, the egg or the water?

An egg floats in water. Which is denser, the egg or the water?

SCIENCE • USE LANGUAGE 85

Language Awareness

Grammar
Articles *A* and *An*

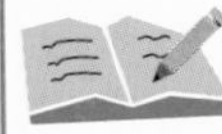

ACTIVITY BOOK

Write this sentence on the board, underlining *an* and *a: Hold an egg and a stone.* Point out that *an* is used before *egg* because *egg* begins with a vowel sound. Illustrate vowels by writing and pronouncing nouns that begin with vowel sounds and letters.

Write *This is* _____ *fish.* Have students say the sentence, using *a* or *an.* Repeat these steps several times, changing the word *fish* to other words from the unit (such as *jar, animal, zone, area, plant, island, ocean*).

Use Activity Book page 45.

in my own words; assemble the materials I need; do the experiment, taking notes as I go along; write a lab report. This helps me do thorough experiments.

Assess 

Use students' responses to the Talk About It for assessment. Students should be able to

- describe the experiment and recognize that things float more easily in salt water

LOOK **AHEAD**

In the next section, students will study a map of the oceans.

Cooperative Language Experience

Science Activity

Have students work in groups and bring in different items to put into a bowl of water. Have students predict which items will float. Have them describe the results with statements similar to those in the Talk About It activity, such as "The pen is denser than water." Write a class report about the activity.

Cooperative Learning

Floating

Have students explore the factors that affect floating and sinking, such as density and shape. Bring in fruits and vegetables. Have students weigh them and rank them from heaviest to lightest. Then have them rank them by size from biggest to smallest. Last, have them examine the shape: long, round, flat. Have students put results into a chart listing the vegetables and fruits. Then have them put each one into water to see which ones float or sink. Have students discuss what they learned and write a lab report.

Connect

Activate Prior Knowledge

Review Ocean Knowledge

Refer to the class lists of ocean words and of antonyms to review what students know about oceans. Have them review their experiment reports and tell what they learned from the experiments.

Ask students to name as many oceans as they can.

Develop Language and Concepts

Present Pages 86 and 87

ACTIVITY BOOK

Have students study the map. Model saying the names of the oceans and the continents.

Read the short introduction on page 86 with students. Then read the captions on the map with students. During the reading, invite students to locate places on the map and to have them answer the questions in the text and other questions. Add questions to help students relate one ocean to another, for example, *Is the _____ Ocean larger than the _____ Ocean?*

Use Activity Book page 46 for practice with large numbers.

Prompt discussion about personal experience with oceans by asking the Talk About It questions. Invite students who don't have personal experience to participate by telling what they imagine it would be like to be on or in an ocean.

Oceans of the World

The earth's surface is 71% water and 29% land. Most of the earth's water is in the oceans.

Name the earth's oceans.

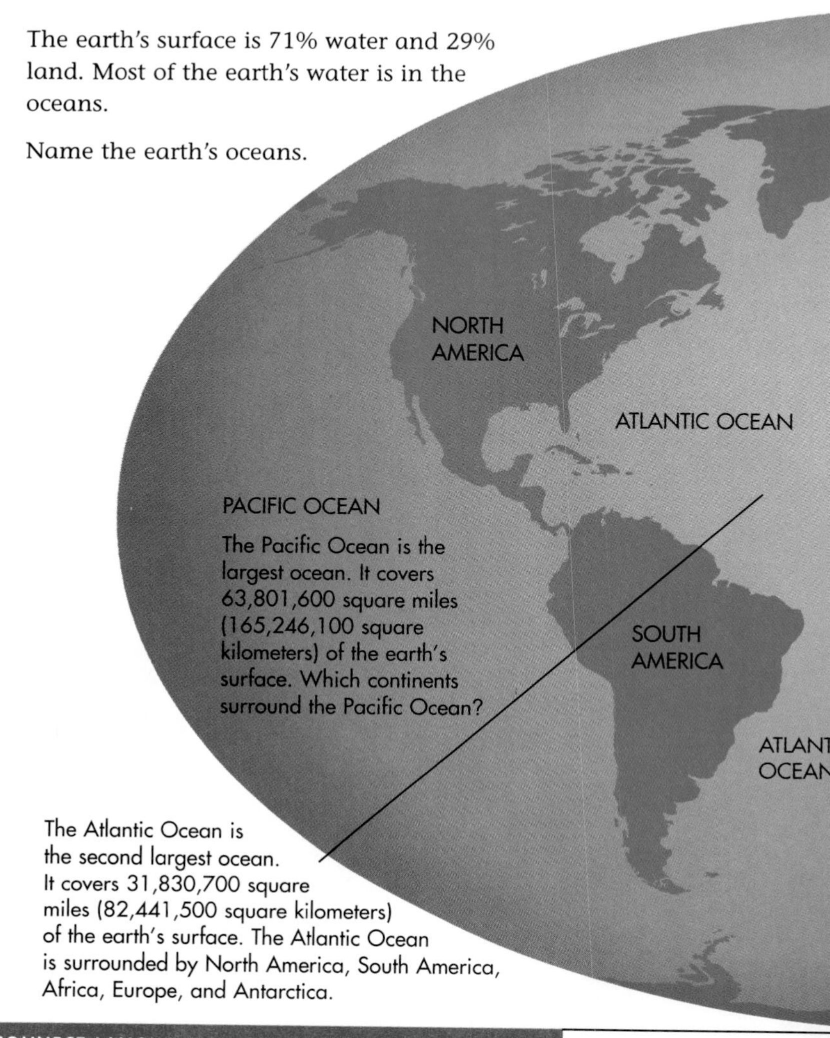

The Pacific Ocean is the largest ocean. It covers 63,801,600 square miles (165,246,100 square kilometers) of the earth's surface. Which continents surround the Pacific Ocean?

The Atlantic Ocean is the second largest ocean. It covers 31,830,700 square miles (82,441,500 square kilometers) of the earth's surface. The Atlantic Ocean is surrounded by North America, South America, Africa, Europe, and Antarctica.

Options for Reaching All Students

Beginning

Language: Guessing Game

Give students clues to oceans and have them try to guess which one you are describing:

It is bigger than the Indian Ocean. It is smaller than the Pacific Ocean.

Encourage students to make up their own clues.

Advanced

Social Studies: Countries

Have students work in groups. Give each group a world map and a globe. Assign either the Atlantic, the Pacific, or the Indian Ocean to each group and have them list all the countries that border it. Post the lists for other students to see.

Cooperative Learning

Square Feet

Have students work in groups to figure the square feet of various places in the school. Have them write down results.

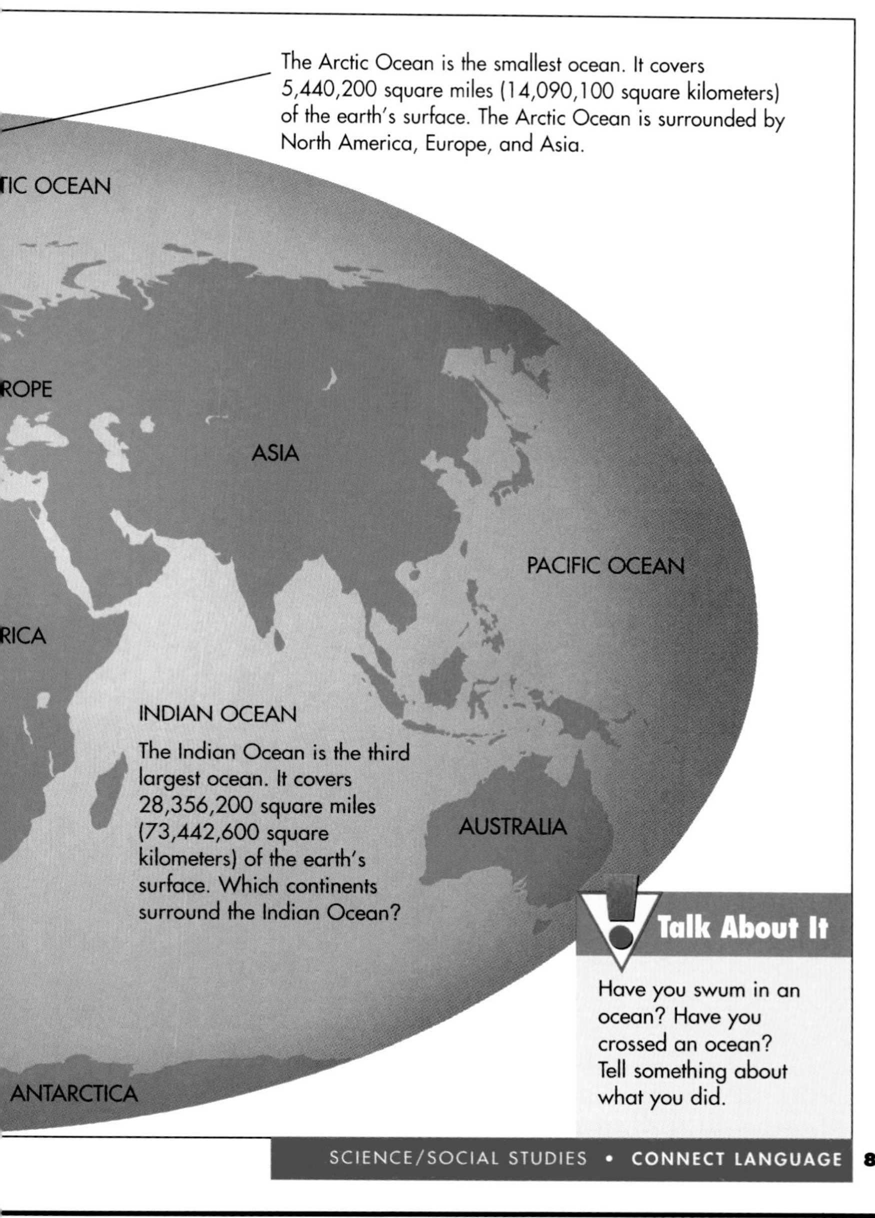
The Arctic Ocean is the smallest ocean. It covers 5,440,200 square miles (14,090,100 square kilometers) of the earth's surface. The Arctic Ocean is surrounded by North America, Europe, and Asia.
TIC OCEAN
ROPE
ASIA
PACIFIC OCEAN
RICA
INDIAN OCEAN
The Indian Ocean is the third largest ocean. It covers 28,356,200 square miles (73,442,600 square kilometers) of the earth's surface. Which continents surround the Indian Ocean?
AUSTRALIA
ANTARCTICA

Talk About It

Have you swum in an ocean? Have you crossed an ocean? Tell something about what you did.

Language Awareness

Grammar
Expressions *Surrounds/Is Surrounded By*

On the board, draw a picture of an island surrounded by water and write these sentences:

The island is surrounded by water.
Water surrounds the island.

Read the sentences. Explain that they are two ways of saying the same thing.

Then write these two sentences on the board:

The _____ is surrounded by _____.
_____ surrounds the _____.

Have students use the map in the text to make more sentences about oceans and *surround.* Use other maps and have students name places that surround another; for example, *What states surround the state you live in?*

Assess 

Students should be able to

- name some of the world's oceans

LOOK **AHEAD**

In the next section, students will read a folk tale about why the sea is salty.

QuickCheck

Large Numbers

Ask students to read large numbers. Check that they can say the numbers using millions and thousands correctly.

Writer's Workshop

Ocean Experience

Refer students to the Writer's Workshop on pages 230 to 236 of the Student Book. Have students write about their personal experiences with oceans. If students have no experience with oceans, have them choose another environment.

Connect

Activate Prior Knowledge

Relate Personal Experience

Have students tell about favorite stories from their countries that they have heard or read.

Introduce the Selection

Have students look at the pictures and discuss where they think this story takes place. Ask them to predict what the story is about.

Read the Selection

YELLOW TAPE

Read the story with students. Then read the story again and present the Reader's Tips. Play the selection on Side 1 of the Yellow Tape several times.

Model a Strategy

Use Dialogue to Evaluate Characters

Model judging characters by what they say to others and what they do:

One way to find out what characters in a story are like is to see what they say to other characters. When Jiro comes to his house. Ichiro shouts, "You again. What do you want this time?" That tells me that Ichiro may be a mean person because he won't help his brother. To find out what Jiro is like, I look at what he says when he meets the old man. Jiro says, "Good day to you, sir. Let me help you with that." That tells me that Jiro is kind. He is going to help the old man.

Language Awareness

Language Function
Greetings/Farewells

Remind students what Jiro said when he met the old man: Jiro said, "Good day to you, sir." Explain that this is a formal way of greeting.

Brainstorm a list of common greetings and list them on the board, adding to the list as needed. Elicit greetings such as *hello, hi, good morning, good afternoon, good evening.* Then brainstorm words and phrases that we say when leaving someone—*good-bye, so long, see you later, good night.* Identify those that are informal and those that are formal.

Have students role-play greeting someone, having a brief conversation, and saying something when leaving.

Teachable Moment

Folk Tales: Definition

Direct students' attention to the author line at the beginning of the story. Explain that Gail Sakurai is not the author of this story; she is only retelling it. This is a folk tale from Japan. Folk tales are stories that people have told for many years and the real authors are long forgotten. Many folk tales explain why something in the world is like it is. Have students read the title to find out what this story will explain.

Options for Reaching All Students

Beginning

TPR: Greetings Chant

TPR

Have students say and act out the following chant:

Good morning, hello, good after-noon, hi!
Good-bye, so long, see you later, bye!

Students can shake hands for greetings and wave good-bye for farewells.

Advanced

Language: Personal Word Bank

Have students choose four words from the folk tale to put into their personal word banks. They should write the word on the front of an index card and illustrate it or write a context sentence for it on the back of the card. Have students work in pairs and share their cards.

Home Connection

Folk Tales

Invite parents to come into class to tell students folk tales from their native countries. Students can also tell folk tales that they learned at home or bring in books with folk tales to share with the class.

Why the Sea Is Salty

Retold by Gail Sakurai

Reader's Tip
This folk tale is from Japan.

Language Tip
Vocabulary
Look at the words that tell about Ichiro and Jiro. Poor is the opposite of wealthy. Greedy is the opposite of generous. Mean-spirited is the opposite of kind-hearted.

Strategy Tip
Understand Plot
The words that tell about Ichiro and Jiro are opposites. The brothers are not alike. This is important in what will happen in the story.

A long time ago in Japan, there lived two brothers. Ichiro, the older brother, was wealthy, greedy, and mean-spirited. Jiro, the younger brother, was poor, generous, and kind-hearted.

It had been a hard winter for Jiro. Now the new year was approaching, and poor Jiro did not have any food to feed his family. He hated to ask his stingy older brother for help, but Jiro couldn't let his wife and children go hungry. Reluctantly, he went off to Ichiro's house.

Language Tip
Vocabulary
A stingy person does not like to share things or spend money.

Language Tip
Vocabulary
Jiro went reluctantly to his brother's house. Jiro did not want to go to his brother's house.

Strategy Tip
Understand Characters
Why do you think Jiro went reluctantly to see his brother?

"You again?" Ichiro shouted as soon as Jiro appeared at his door. "What do you want this time?"

"Please, brother, if it wouldn't trouble you too much, could you spare a little rice so my wife and children will have something to eat?"

"Not a single grain, you worthless dolt! Get out and don't come back!" Ichiro shouted.

Jiro trudged away, wondering how he was going to feed his family. Soon he came upon an old man with a bundle of firewood strapped to his back. The old fellow was stooped over from the weight of his load.

"Good day to you, sir," Jiro greeted the man. "Let me help you with that." Jiro shouldered the heavy bundle and carried it to the old man's home.

Language Tip
Vocabulary
Trudge means "to walk slowly."

Connect

Develop Language and Concepts

Present Pages 92 Through 95

Ask students to review what has happened so far in the story. Then read pages 92 through 95.

Model a Strategy

Use Pictures for Meaning

Model using pictures to define words:

Sometimes I use pictures to figure out what a word means. This story tells about a mortar, but I don't know what a mortar is. The story tells me it is something that is small and made of stone and that it is used for grinding rice. But that doesn't tell me what a mortar looks like. So I look at the pictures and find one of the old man handing a mortar to Jiro. Now I know what a mortar looks like—it looks like a small bowl.

Language Awareness

Vocabulary
Antonyms

Write these pairs of words on the board and pronounce them:

wealthy	greedy	mean
poor	generous	kind

Make up pairs of simple sentences to illustrate what each set of words means, such as *A wealthy person has a lot of money. A poor person has no money.*

Draw the a T-chart on the board and write the names Jiro and Ichiro at the top: Have students fill in the chart with the words from the board that describe each brother. Ask them to give examples from the story to support their choices—"How do you know Ichiro was wealthy?"

Teachable Moment

Folk Tales: Magic

Explain to students that folk tales often tell about something that is magic. Ask them to tell what is magic in this story and to describe what it does. If students are familiar with other folk tales, ask them about the magic in those tales.

Options for Reaching All Students

Beginning

Language: Use Pictures

Invite students to tell what is happening in the pictures in the story.

Advanced

Language: Memory Game

Have students orally compose a cumulative sentence of things they would ask for if they had a magic mortar, with one student naming something and each succeeding student adding on. (Student A: *I would like a bike.* Student B: *I would like a bike and a new house,* and so on.) When someone misses, start a new sentence.

Multicultural Connection

Breads from Other Countries

Ask students if they have ever had *manju,* barley buns with sweet bean paste, which are mentioned in the story. Explain that many countries have different kinds of breads or grain products. Invite students to bring in and share different kinds of breads or grain products that are common in their native countries.

Language Tip
Vocabulary
A mortar is a strong bowl. People use it to crush or grind things like rice or medicines into small pieces. It usually comes with a crushing tool called a pestle.

"You seem a worthy young fellow," said the old man. "Please take this as a reward for your kindness." He handed Jiro a small stone mortar, the type used for grinding rice.

"This is a magic mortar," the old fellow explained. "It will give you anything you ask for. All you have to do is turn the handle to the right and say what you want. To stop the mortar, just turn the handle to the left. Remember now—right to start and left to stop."

As soon as Jiro got home, he tried the mortar. Turning the handle to the right, he said, "Rice, please. I'd like some rice."

Rice poured out of the mortar. Soon rice covered the table and flowed onto the floor. "Whoa, stop! That's enough!" Jiro shouted.

Still the rice poured out. Finally, he remembered what the old man had said, and Jiro turned the handle to the left. The rice stopped.

Language Tip
Vocabulary
Delighted means "happy." Good fortune means "good luck."

Strategy Tip
Read On to Get Meaning
The writer uses the Japanese word manju. Read on to find out that manju is a bun, which is a piece of round bread.

"It really is magic!" cried Jiro, delighted with his good fortune.

Next he asked for *manju*. Barley buns filled with sweet bean paste poured out of the mortar until Jiro turned the handle to the left. "I can have anything I ask for," Jiro realized. "I'll be rich."

Then Jiro asked the mortar for a fine house, a horse, and a stable for the horse. In no time at all, he was the wealthiest man in the village. But he never forgot what it was like to be poor, and every day he handed out rice and manju to the villagers.

When Ichiro learned of his brother's good fortune, he was jealous. He crept up to Jiro's house and peered in the window. He watched Jiro turn the handle of the mortar to the right and ask for manju. Barley buns poured out.

"So that's how he did it," Ichiro said to himself. "It is not fair that the younger brother should have such a treasure. I am the oldest in the family—that mortar should belong to me."

Language Tip
Vocabulary
Peered means "looked."

Strategy Tip
Predict
What do you think Ichiro will do?

Connect

Develop Language and Concepts

Present Pages 96 Through 99

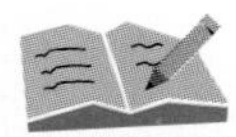
ACTIVITY BOOK

Ask students to review what has happened so far in the story and what they predicted will happen. Read pages 96 through 99 of the story. Ask students if their predictions came true. If not, what happened instead? Were they surprised? Refer back to the title of the story. Have students explain why the sea is salty. To check students' comprehension, use Activity Book page 47.

Teachable Moment

Plot: Turning Point

Have students summarize the plot of *Why the Sea is Salty*. Explain to students that most stories have a *turning point*, an event that points the way to the end of the story. Help students see that the turning point in this story comes when Ichiro decides to steal the magic mortar from Jiro. The event is the turning point because it leads to Ichiro going to sail on the sea with the mortar. The salt from the mortar is what is going to make the sea salty.

Language Awareness

Grammar

Irregular Past Tense Verbs

ACTIVITY BOOK

Explain that most verbs are made past by adding *-ed*. Write some examples on the board. Then explain that some verbs change completely when they are made past. Write examples of irregular past tense verbs from the story, such as *were, ran, had, came, found, went.* Have students find examples in the story.

Use Activity Book page 48.

Response Activities

Personal Response

Ask students to do the following: *Pretend you are Ichiro. You have received the magic mortar. What would you ask for? Would you ask for things for yourself? Would you ask for things for other people?*

Critical Response

Ask student to analyze the things that make this a folk tale. Here are some ideas to prompt students: There are very good or very bad characters. Good characters are rewarded, and bad characters are punished. The story tells about the origin of something.

Creative Response

Ask students to do the following: *How could the story have ended differently? Can you make a happy ending for the story?*

Options for Reaching All Students

Beginning

Language: Word Log

BLACKLINE MASTER

Have students complete a word log for the story. Use Blackline Master 30 in the Teacher's Resource Book.

Advanced

Language Arts: Story Telling

Have students work in groups to find another folk tale, perhaps from their native country. Have them share their story with other teams.

Mixed Ability

Drama: Role-Play

Have students act out the story. Invite them to use words from the dialogue in the story in their play. Students might want to make props and simple costumes.

Late that night, Ichiro slipped into his brother's house and stole the mortar. On his way out, he spied a stack of manju Jiro had prepared for the next day. He took several buns and placed them in his sack along with the mortar.

Ichiro ran across the fields and over the hills until he reached the sea. He found a small rowboat on the shore. He hopped into the boat and paddled away. Farther and farther out to sea he rowed. "I'll sail all the way to China. They can never catch me there," he decided.

All the rowing made Ichiro hungry. So he took out the buns and began to eat. "These manju are too sweet. They need salt. I wish I had some salt," Ichiro complained. "Ho, what am I saying? I can have anything I want—I have the magic mortar."

Ichiro pulled out the mortar and turned the handle to the right.

"Salt! Salt! Give me salt!" he said.

Salt poured out of the mortar.

"Stop! That's enough!"

Still the salt streamed into the small boat.

"I said STOP! That's enough salt! I don't need anymore!"

Language Tip
Vocabulary
Streamed means that salt flowed out quickly.

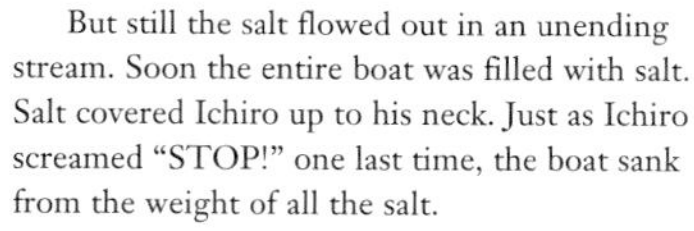

But still the salt flowed out in an unending stream. Soon the entire boat was filled with salt. Salt covered Ichiro up to his neck. Just as Ichiro screamed "STOP!" one last time, the boat sank from the weight of all the salt.

Down went the boat to the bottom of the sea. Down went Ichiro, and down went the mortar. The mortar came to rest on the sea bed, where it remains to this day still grinding salt.

Language Tip
Vocabulary
The *sea bed* is the same as the *ocean floor*.

Study Tip
Folk Tales
Folk tales are stories that people have told for many years. Some folk tales tell about how something in the world began. At the end of many folk tales, good things happen to good people, and bad things happen to bad people. Why is this story a good example of a folk tale?

Connect

Activate Prior Knowledge

Use Objects

Bring in seashells. Have students share knowledge about shells.

Develop Language and Concepts

Present Page 100

YELLOW TAPE

Read the poem with students. Help students understand the comparisons in it. Play the poem on Side 2 of the Yellow Tape and invite students to recite the poem.

Discuss the questions in Write About It. Brainstorm ideas. Have students complete the activity independently.

Language Awareness

Phonics

Long *e*; Vowel Digraphs *ea/ee*

ACTIVITY BOOK

Have students read the poem aloud and find the words that contain the sound of long *e*. Write the words on the board: *sea, green, weed.* Point out that the sound of long *e* is sometimes spelled as *ee* or *ea*.

Write these additional words from the chapter on the board: *seen, deep, reef, need, easier.* Have students underline the letters that stand for the long *e* sound.

Use Activity Book page 49.

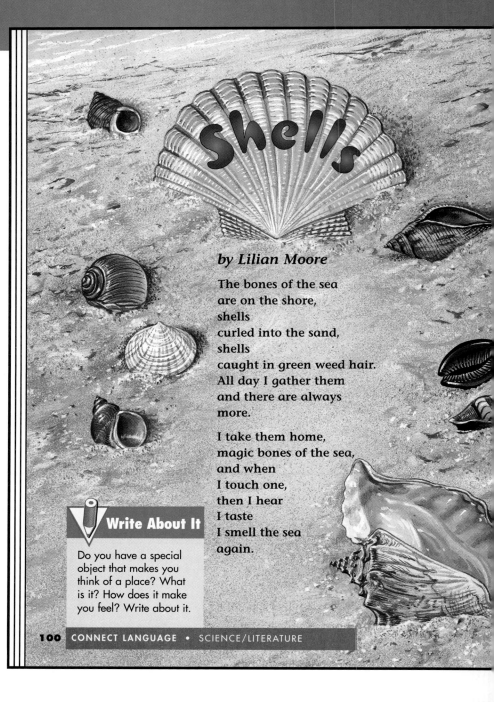

Shells

by Lilian Moore

The bones of the sea
are on the shore,
shells
curled into the sand,
shells
caught in green weed hair.
All day I gather them
and there are always
more.

I take them home,
magic bones of the sea,
and when
I touch one,
then I hear
I taste
I smell the sea
again.

Write About It

Do you have a special object that makes you think of a place? What is it? How does it make you feel? Write about it.

Options for Reaching All Students

Beginning

Language: Sensory Words

Write these words on the board: *see, touch, hear, taste, smell.* Model pointing to the part of the body that does each thing. As you point, have the students say the correct word. Then have them work in pairs, one student pointing and the other saying the word.

Advanced

Writing: Sensory Word Web

Have students make an idea web using the sensory words *see, smell, taste, feel.* Have students write the name of a place in the middle of the web; for example, the school cafeteria or a local bakery. Have them write the sensory words in circles and add word associations in additional circles.

Home Connection

Ocean Items

Have students ask family members if they have a collection of shells or other ocean items. Invite them to share them with the class.

Tell what you learned.

CHAPTER 5

1. Describe the ocean. Tell about the zones and the animals.
2. Make a word web about ocean life.

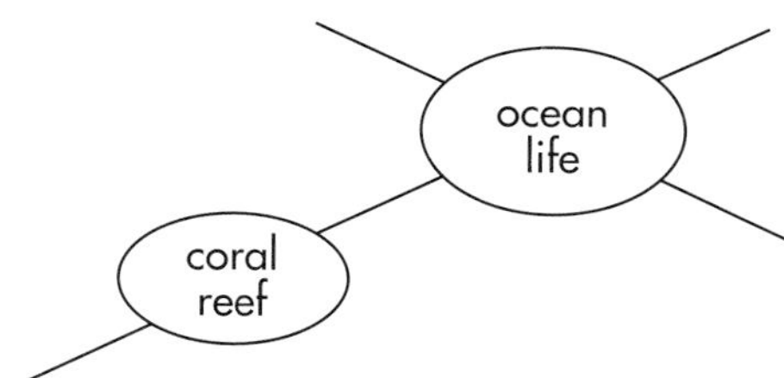

3. What lesson does the story "Why the Sea Is Salty" teach?

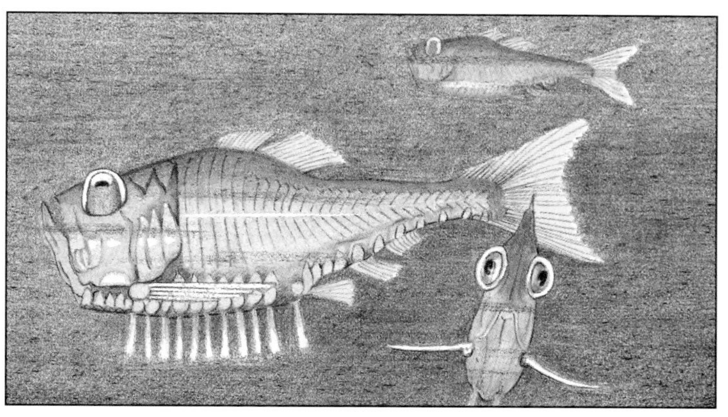

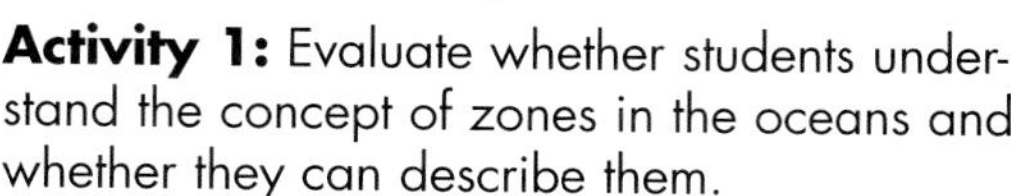

Activity 1: Evaluate whether students understand the concept of zones in the oceans and whether they can describe them.

Activity 2: Evaluate how much detail students can put into their idea webs.

Activity 3: Evaluates students' understanding of the story "Why the Sea Is Salty."

Have students complete the Chapter Self-Assessment, Blackline Master 31. Have students choose the product of one of the activities to place in their portfolios. Add the results of any rubrics, checklists, self-assessments, or portfolio assessments, Blackline Masters 2–18 and 31.

Listening Assessment

BLACKLINE MASTER

Make sure that students have a copy of Blackline Master 61, from the Teacher's Resource Book. Play the tape several times and ask students to circle the places talked about and the numbers mentioned.

WHITE TAPE

See page 78c for the tapescript.

Options for Assessment

Strategy Assessment

Identify Main Topics

Have students identify the main topic of these spreads, as well as the topics of individual paragraphs on them: pages 80 and 81and pages 82 and 83.

Writing Assessment

Ocean Book

Have students use information from the text or other sources to write interesting facts about the oceans.

Language Assessment

BLACKLINE MASTER

Use Blackline Master 60 in the Teacher's Resource Book.

Standardized Test Practice

ACTIVITY BOOK

Use pages 50 and 51. Answers: **1.** heaviness for size **2.** put egg in the jar of water **3.** to add salt to the water **4.** Is it easier or harder to float in salt water?

Preview

Activate Prior Knowledge

Brainstorm Vocabulary

With students, brainstorm ways in which they or people they know have used the ocean. Elicit responses such as *swim, ride on boats, travel, eat fish from the ocean.* Write a list on the board. Then have students look at the pictures on pages 102 and 103 to get more ideas.

Invite students to say whether they think the people in the pictures are using the oceans in a good or a bad way.

Develop Language and Concepts

Present Pages 102 and 103

Help students talk about the pictures. Present vocabulary to describe activities in the pictures: *oil/oil rig, ocean farm, hotels, fishing boat, research ship.* Discuss what each picture shows about how people use the ocean. For example, explain that people use areas near the shore to raise fish and then sell them for food; people study animal life in the ocean.

Model the words in the Word Bank and have students repeat them. Help them match the words to the pictures.

Read the question on page 102 aloud. Help students use the information they just discussed to answer the question.

(Continued on page T103)

Taking Care of the Oceans

Word Bank

- food
- fun
- jobs
- research

Tell what you know.

How do people use the oceans?

Options for Reaching All Students

Beginning

Language: Describe Pictures

Have students orally describe each of the pictures on the pages, using patterns like the following:

The boats take fish from the ocean. People eat the fish.

Oil rigs take oil from the ocean. People use the oil to run machines such as cars.

Hotels are on beaches of the ocean. People go to the beaches for fun.

Research ships go to all parts of the ocean. People study life in the ocean.

Advanced

Language: Learn Ocean Vocabulary

Present lists of vocabulary like the following and have students classify them into categories: *food from the ocean, fun in the ocean, ocean vehicles, ocean products.* Encourage them to use dictionaries for information about words they don't know:

shrimp, submarine, snorkel, tuna, pearl, goggles, lobster, drill for oil

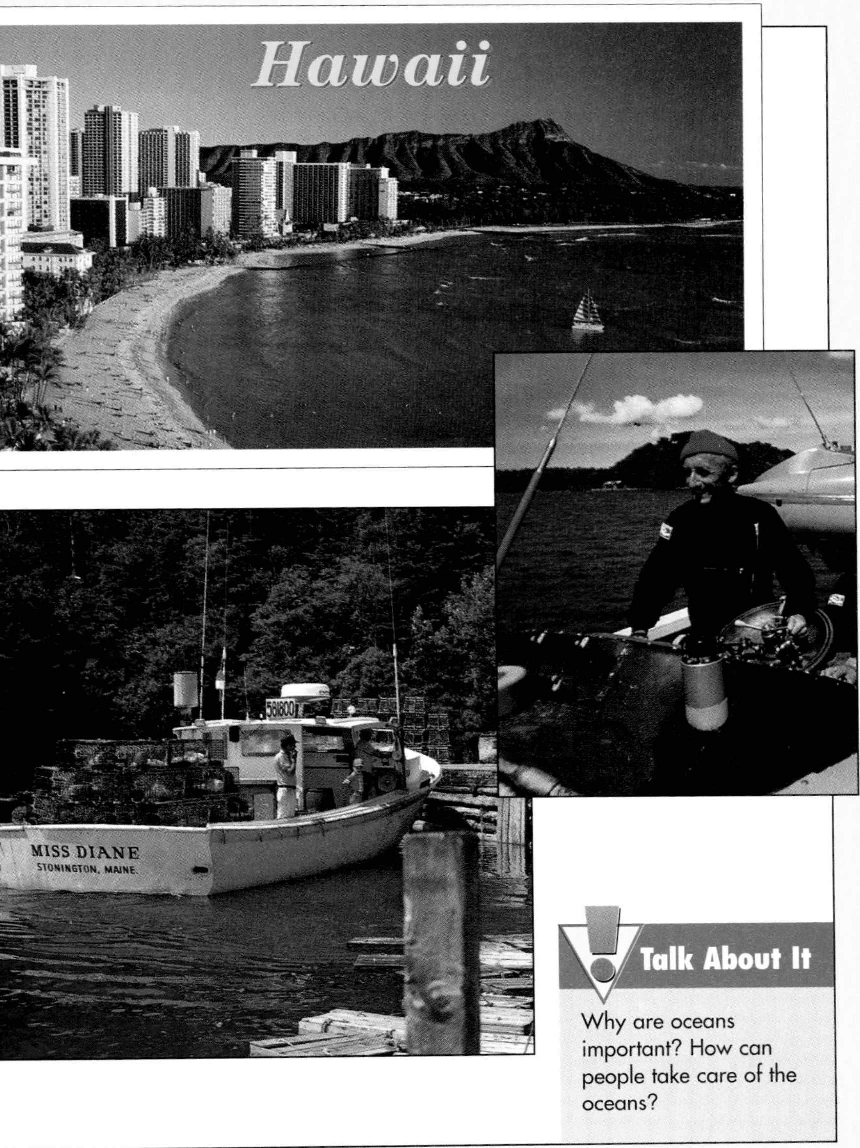
Hawaii
MISS DIANE
STONINGTON, MAINE
Talk About It
Why are oceans important? How can people take care of the oceans?
103

With the class, make a chart to organize answers to the question on page 102. On chart paper, write the title *How do people use the ocean?* Put four headings below the sentence: *Food, Fun, Jobs, Research.* Help students categorize the activities shown in the pictures and write them on the chart. Add other activities, if there are any, from the list they brainstormed earlier. Keep the chart for later reference.

Then have students answer the questions in the Talk About It activity. Prompt students to relate all uses they just discussed to explain why oceans are important to people.

Mixed Ability

TPR: Pantomime

TPR

Prepare cards with activities from pages 102 and 103 and the chart you have prepared in presenting the lesson. Have a pair of students choose a card and pantomime the activity. The other students guess what the activity is.

Cooperative Learning

Recreational Uses

Have students work in groups with pictures of different ways people use the ocean or other bodies of water for recreation. Pictures might include surfing, jet skiing, water skiing, yachting, or speed boating. Ask students if any of these uses can be harmful. Make a list of possible dangers.

Present

Activate Prior Knowledge

Visualize

Have students pretend they are walking on a beach. The sun is shining, and the water is clear and blue. How do they feel? Then all of a sudden they see soda cans, and other garbage. How do they feel?

Have students relate experiences they have had with any kind of pollution.

Develop Language and Concepts

Present Pages 104 and 105

ACTIVITY BOOK

Read the text with students. Use the pictures to help them understand the key words in the text, such as *garbage, chemicals, fertilizers, oil spill.* Bring in some chemical cleaners commonly used in households to illustrate chemicals. Make a chart to connect the information for students.

Group	Pollutant	Effect on Ocean Life
People	Garbage	Harms plants and animals
Factories	Chemicals	[Same]
Farmers	Chemicals, Fertilizers	[Same]
	Oil spill	[Same]

Use Activity Book page 52.

How do people pollute the oceans?

People **pollute** the oceans by throwing garbage on the beach or into the water. Garbage harms plants and animals in the oceans.

Factories pollute the oceans by dumping chemicals into the water. Like garbage, chemicals harm plants and animals.

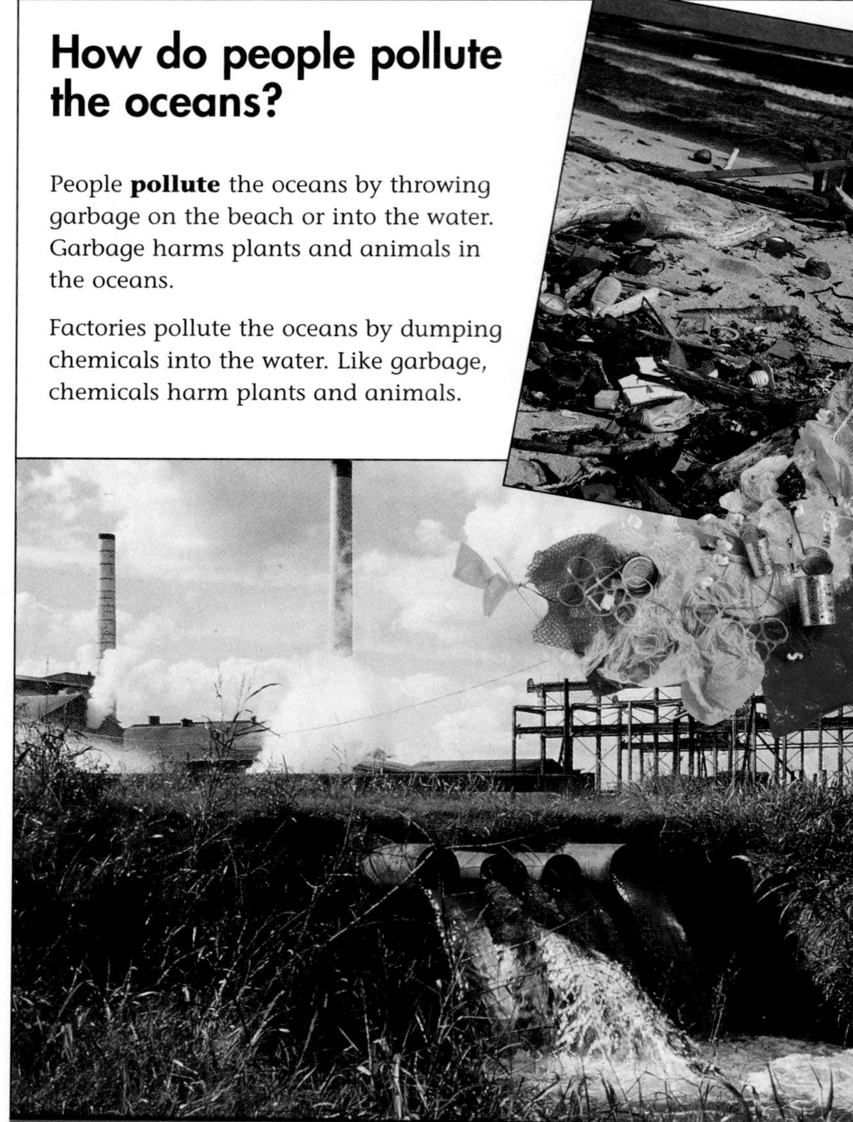

Options for Reaching All Students

Beginning

Study Skills: Find Answers in the Text

Give students a list of the groups mentioned in the article: people, factories, farmers, oil tankers. Ask students the following question for each group:

How do (farmers) pollute the ocean?

Have them find the answer in the text and read it.

Advanced

Writing: Summarize

Work with students to distinguish between *retelling* and *summarizing* an article. Point out that retelling might mean including all the details using their own words. By contrast, a summary includes main points without mentioning all the details. Use the first paragraph on page 105 as an example. Use your own words to *retell* the paragraph.

A summary could be, *Farmers use chemicals to fertilize plants and to kill insects. These can harm plants and animals.* Have students summarize in writing what they learned from reading these pages.

Farmers pollute the oceans by using chemicals to kill insects. Farmers also pollute the oceans by using chemical fertilizers to help make plants grow. The chemicals get into waterways and run into the ocean. The chemicals help farmers, but they harm ocean animals and plants.

Accidents also cause pollution. Oil tankers can pollute the ocean by spilling oil into the water. The oil can kill fish and birds. It can also kill the tiny plants and animals in the ocean that are food for larger animals.

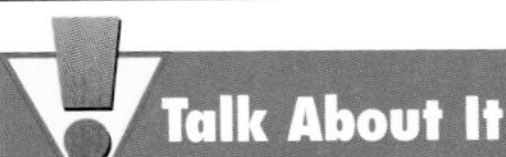

Talk About It

What are the causes of pollution? What are the effects of pollution?

Why do people pollute the oceans?

Language Awareness

Grammar
Questions with How/Answers with *By + -ing*

Ask the question *How do (factories) pollute the ocean?* Begin an answer to the question with a statement: Factories pollute the ocean by _____. (Factories pollute the ocean by dumping chemicals into the water.) Prompt a response that begins with *by* ("By dumping chemicals into the water"). Continue asking and answering questions about groups: people, factories, farmers.

Assess ✓

Use students' responses to Talk About It for assessment. Students should be able to

- name one or two groups that pollute the ocean and how they pollute it
- discuss the effects of ocean pollution

LOOK **AHEAD**

In the next section, students will learn some solutions to the problem of ocean pollution.

Mixed Ability

Social Studies: Pollution Effects

Have students look in magazines and find pictures that illustrate the effects of ocean pollution, such as animals that are caught in oil spills. Have students label their pictures.

Cooperative Language Experience

Field Trip

Take students on a walk through the neighborhood near the school. Help them identify pollutants, even if they are just paper and garbage on the streets or sidewalk. With the class, write a language experience story about the trip.

Practice

Activate Prior Knowledge
Use Prior Knowledge

Review the causes of ocean pollution that were discussed on pages 104 and 105. On the left half of a piece of chart paper, make a class list of the causes.

Develop Language and Concepts
Present Pages 106 and 107

Add a new column to the list you started in Activate Prior Knowledge. Title this column *Solutions.*

Read the text with students. Stop after each paragraph and have students discuss what it said. Have them add solutions in the appropriate places on the chart.

Present the Write About It activity to students. Point out that they have the choice of finding either effects of pollution or preventing pollution.

Use Activity Book page 53 to review vocabulary.

Model a Strategy
Use a Graphic Organizer

Model using a graphic organizer to understand information:

As a class, we made a chart that listed groups and how each could help stop pollution. This helps me understand and remember the information that I read.

Some Pollution Solutions

Governments, farmers, factories, and scientists can all help reduce pollution.

Governments can pass laws to control pollution. Governments can make factories pay money in fines for polluting water.

Farmers can stop using dangerous chemicals. Farmers can use other insects like lady bugs to eat harmful insects. Farmers can use chemicals that are less harmful to plants and animals.

106 USE LANGUAGE • SOCIAL STUDIES

Options for Reaching All Students

Beginning
Language: Alphabetize

Give each student a set of cards with these words printed on them: *government, factories, chemicals, harmful, pollution, scientists.* Have students put the cards in alphabetical order.

Advanced
Study Skills: Locate and Present Information

Lady bugs are environmentally friendly pests. Have students find information about lady bugs in the library. Have students orally present their findings to their classmates and tell where they found their information.

Mixed Ability
Critical Thinking: Look at Paper Use

Set up a separate container for waste school paper. Have students discard any school papers in that container for a week. At the end of the week, examine the contents. Provide those students who are handling the paper with plastic gloves and goggles. Have students make a pile of paper they think could have been used again. Ask them to give

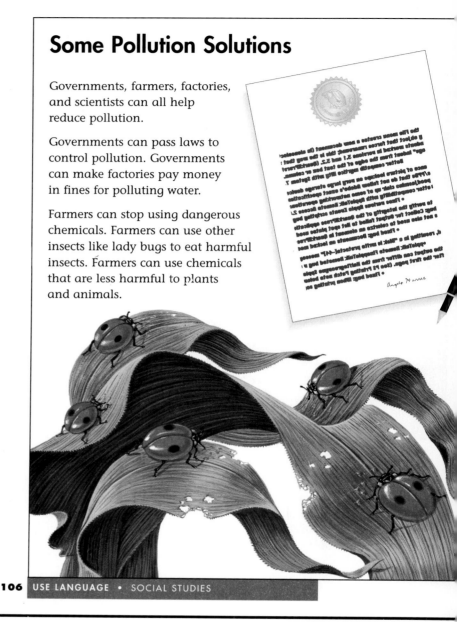

Factories can stop dumping dangerous chemicals into the water. When they finish using harmful chemicals, they can store them in special places.

Not all chemicals pollute. Scientists can find safe chemicals that do not harm plants and animals. Then factories and farmers can stop using harmful chemicals.

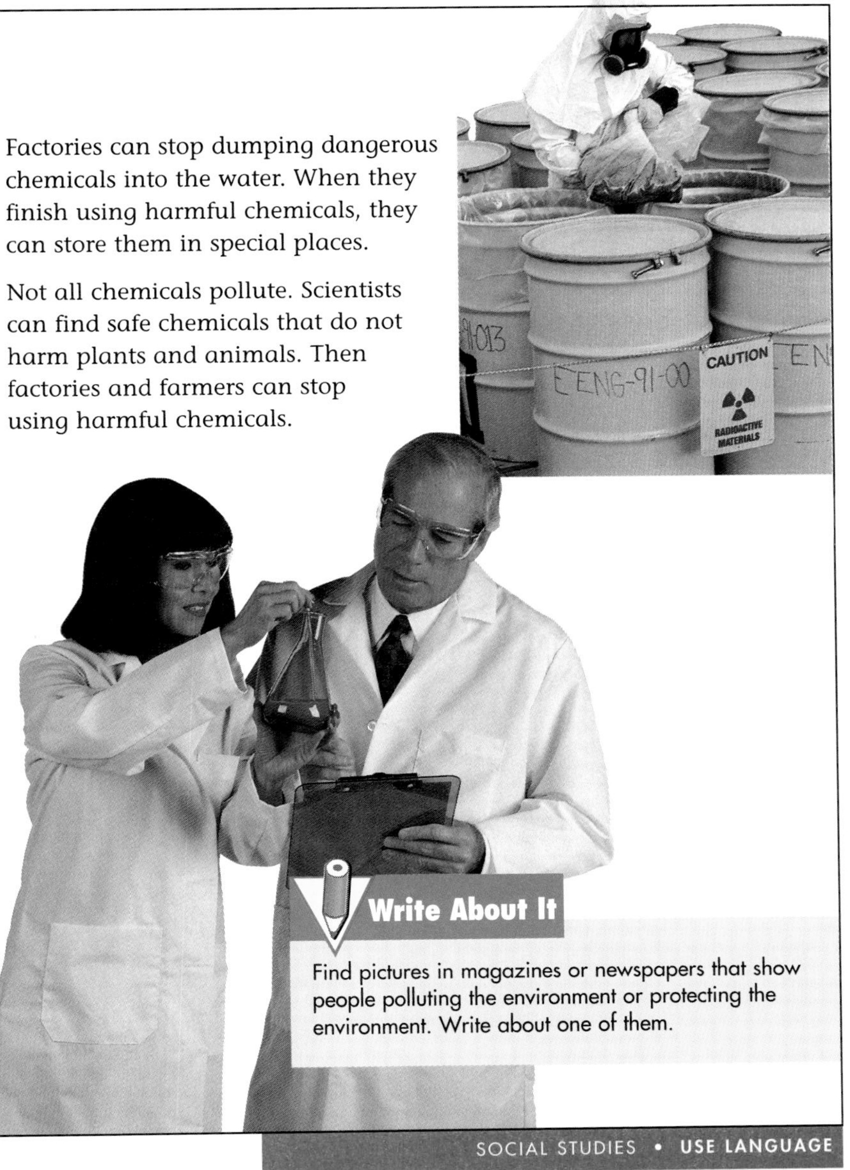

Write About It

Find pictures in magazines or newspapers that show people polluting the environment or protecting the environment. Write about one of them.

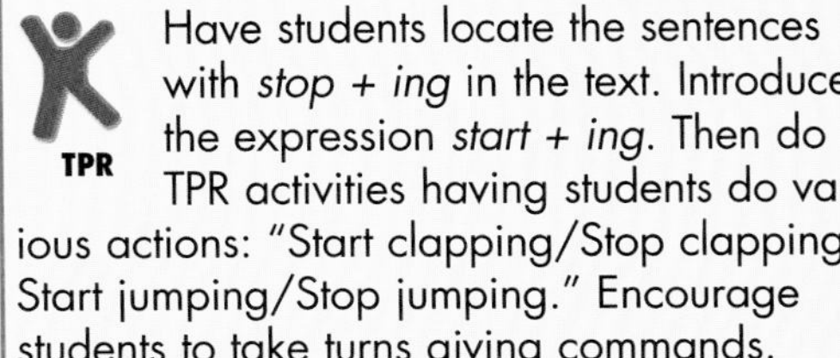

Language Awareness

Grammar

Stop/Start + ing

TPR Have students locate the sentences with *stop + ing* in the text. Introduce the expression *start + ing*. Then do TPR activities having students do various actions: "Start clapping/Stop clapping, Start jumping/Stop jumping." Encourage students to take turns giving commands.

FYI Pollutant Fact

- **Each year two million sea birds die as the result of garbage dumped into the ocean.**

Assess 

Students should be able to

- name two or three ways that groups can stop polluting the oceans

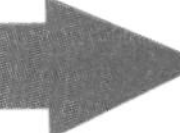

LOOK **AHEAD**

In the next section, students will learn about what they can do to help the environment.

reasons. Brainstorm ways students can help reduce waste of paper. Develop a plan. Collect school papers for another week and compare the results. Have students find out if the school participates in paper recycling. Follow-up activities could include making paper or finding out what happens to recycled paper from a recycling center.

Practice

Activate Prior Knowledge

Brainstorm Vocabulary

Bring in some antipollution posters or ads and talk about them with the students. Brainstorm a list of things they can do to help the environment (for example, *recycle, reuse, reduce, throw out, clean out, wash*). Write the words on chart paper. Add to the list during the unit.

Develop Language and Concepts

Present Pages 108 and 109

ACTIVITY BOOK

Read the text with students. Stop after each paragraph to talk about what it says. Have students explain how the pictures relate to the paragraphs. Ask students to add suggestions to those mentioned in the paragraphs.

Find a video that presents the subject of garbage and the increasing problems caused by the amount of garbage people generate. Have students identify the issues and connect them to their behavior.

Present the Try It Out activity to students. Help them to organize a plan for the Reuse It Day. Perhaps set up committees. Encourage new ideas for activities on that day.

Use Activity Book page 55 to review information on protecting the environment.

What can you do to help the environment?

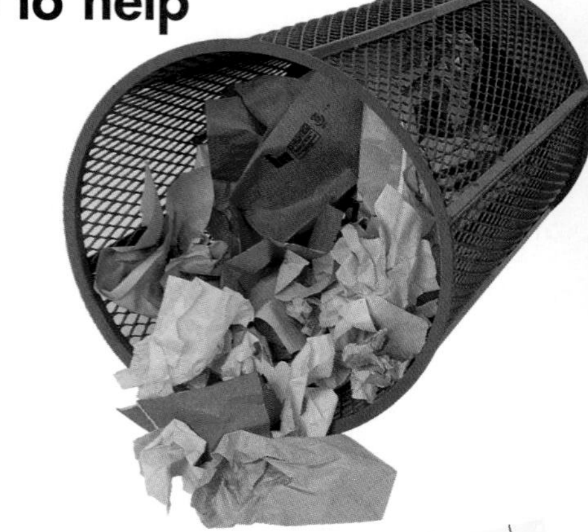

Everyone can help take care of the environment. Garbage pollutes the oceans and the land. Everyone can make less garbage. Here are some things you can do.

Reduce

Use less paper. When you write, use both sides of every sheet of paper. When you work in the kitchen, clean up with cloth rags, not with paper towels. This makes less garbage.

Reuse

Think of the things you use once and throw away. When you drink from a plastic cup, don't throw it away. Wash it and use it again.

Think of other uses for plastic things. For example, you can plant seeds in plastic bottles. When you reuse things, you make less garbage.

Options for Reaching All Students

Beginning

Writing: Materials Vocabulary

Have students find the words for materials in the text: plastic, paper. Add other materials, such as glass, wood, and cloth. Have students write sentences using the following frame:

_____ is made of _____.

An example is *A shirt is made of cloth.*

Advanced

Writing: Environmental Journal

Have students make a plan for how they will reduce the amount of garbage they make. Have them write their plan. Then have them write what they actually did in the course of a week.

Mixed Ability

Language: Classifying

Have students work in groups of three. Have them list things that they do to help the environment. They should divide their lists into three groups:

- Things That We Can *Reduce*
- Things That We Can *Reuse*
- Things That We Can *Recycle*

Also explain to students that in many communities, there are separate containers

Recycle
Materials like plastic and newspaper can be recycled. Plastic containers can be recycled to make new plastic containers. Newspapers can be recycled to make new paper. When materials are recycled, there is less garbage.

Try It Out

Plan a Reuse It Day. Bring in plastics and newspapers from home. How many different ways can you think of to use these things? Make something that reuses what you brought.

Language Awareness

Grammar
Expressions *Less* or *More*

ACTIVITY BOOK

Have students find the expression "less garbage" in the story. Point out that *less* and *more* are opposites. Demonstrate the difference in meaning with classroom examples, such as *Maria has less paper on her desk than Ruben has. Ruben has more paper on his desk than Maria has.* You might also provide prompts such as popcorn or glasses of water and have students make comparisons between two items. Note that *less* is used with noncount nouns *(less glue)*; *fewer* with count nouns (*fewer pencils*). Use Activity Book page 54.

Assess 

Students should be able to

- name ways that they can stop pollution and help protect the environment

LOOK**AHEAD** 

In the next section, students will learn about farming the water.

for paper, glass, cans, and plastic garbage. Help them list examples of things to put in each.

Cooperative Language Experience

Investigate Recycling

If possible, arrange for students to find out about plans for reducing or recycling in either your school or community. Students might go to a community recycling center or you might have a guest speaker come to class to make a visual presentation. With the class, write a language experience story about what was learned.

Home Connection

Things from the Home

Have students ask their parents about things in the home that they reuse or recycle. Invite students to bring in examples and present them to the class. These can include craft activities and things made from discarded objects.

Connect

Activate Prior Knowledge

Use Illustrations to Predict

Bring in pictures of farms. Have students look at the pictures and talk about them. Ask them what they see in the pictures, and what do farmers do? Ask students what they eat that is grown on farms.

Lead students to the idea of fish being grown on farms. How would they expect the fish farms to be different?

Develop Language and Concepts

Present Pages 110 and 111

Have students look at the pictures (a shrimp, a crab, an aquaculture farm, a shellfish hatchery) and talk about what they see.

Read the first paragraph of the article aloud. Write the words *agriculture* and *aquaculture* on the board. Make sure students understand the difference between them. Then read the rest of the article with students. Talk about the article and relate it to the pictures. Use Activity Book page 56.

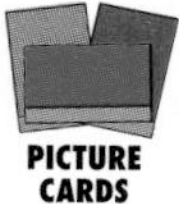

Introduce the words in the Word Bank. Use pictures such as those on Picture Cards 26 ducks, 29 farm, and 56 pumpkins to prompt discussion of farming. Then ask the Think About It questions. Encourage students to use the words from the Word Bank in their answers. Make a chart on the board of how agriculture is like aquaculture and how it is different.

Farming the Water

Growing plants and animals on land for food is called agriculture. Raising plants and animals in the water is called aquaculture.

Fish are an important source of food. The number of fish in the ocean is getting smaller. So people are farming fish.

Fish farming is raising baby fish until they grow into large adult fish. Then the fish are taken to market. They are bought and eaten.

Options for Reaching All Students

Beginning

Language: Words and Pictures

Have students find pictures of four things named in the Word Bank and label them.

Advanced

Study Skills: Research

Have students work in teams to find names and pictures of various kinds of shellfish that people eat. Examples might be clams, oysters, mussels, crabs, lobsters, scallops, or abalone. Have them make a booklet or poster on which they illustrate and label the shellfish. Illustrations may be pasted on or drawn. Display their work.

Peer Tutoring

Language: Context Sentences

Have students work in pairs of mixed ability. Provide each pair with five cards. On one side of each card, have the less advanced student write one of the words from the Word Bank. On the other side, have the more advanced student write a context sentence for the word.

On fish farms in the oceans, fish grow in large nets or cages. Ocean farms are usually in the shallow waters near the shore.

Fish farming is not new. The Chinese have been farming fish for thousands of years. In Spain, people have raised shellfish like lobster and shrimp for many years.

Each year fish farms now raise about 10.5 million tons (9.5 million metric tons) of fish. This number will get bigger and bigger.

Word Bank

- boat
- ground
- plow
- rain
- seed
- temperature
- tractor

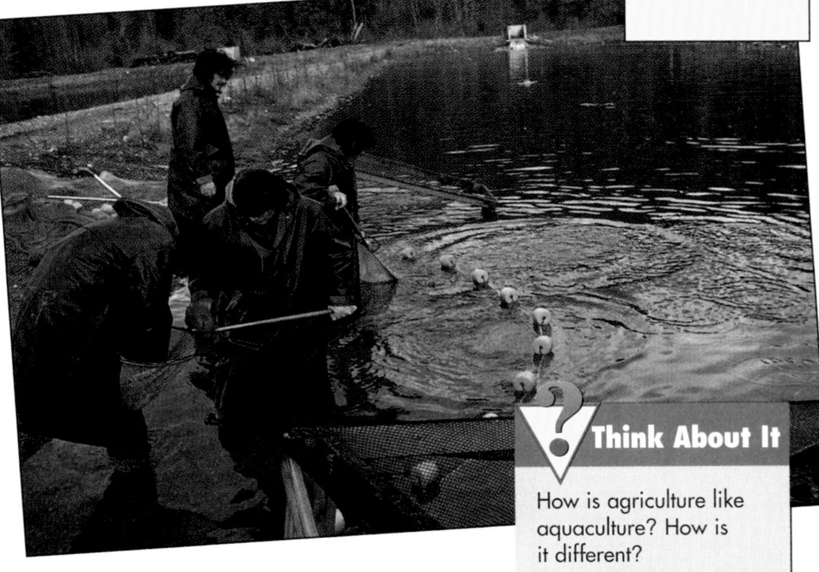

Think About It

How is agriculture like aquaculture? How is it different?

Language Awareness

Phonics
Consonant Digraph *sh*

Write the letters *sh* on the board. Model the pronunciation of the sound the digraph stands for using words such as *fish* and *shore*. Have students find all the examples of the digraph *sh* on pages 110 and 111 and read aloud the sentences in which they appear. Write examples on the board.

FYI Farming the Water Facts

- **Japan has the most productive program of sea aquaculture in the world. Seaweed is grown and dried. It is used for food and fertilizers.**
- **Only a few kinds of sea fish can be farmed successfully. Fish on farms can easily develop diseases.**

Assess 

Use students' responses to Think About It for assessment. Students should be able to

- tell some likenesses and differences between agriculture and aquaculture

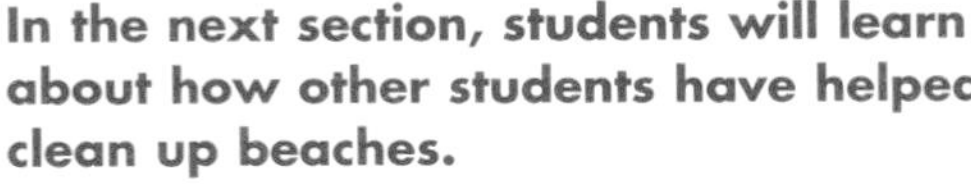

In the next section, students will learn about how other students have helped clean up beaches.

Multicultural Connection

Fish Recipes from Around the World

Use cookbooks to get information on the kinds of fish people eat around the world, how they prepare fish (fried, broiled, baked, or raw; in soups or stews, with rice), and for what meals they eat them. Invite parents to share recipes they use for preparing fish. You might arrange to bring in fish dishes from local ethnic restaurants.

Cooperative Language Experience

Field Trip

Go to a local supermarket or market that sells fish. Encourage students to learn the names of various fish available in your area. Have students find out where the fish come from. With the class, write a story about the experience.

Connect

Activate Prior Knowledge

Use Illustrations to Predict

Have students look at the pictures and identify what is happening. Invite them to talk about any experiences they have had or know about that were similar to what is occurring in the pictures. Finally, ask students to predict what the article is about.

Develop Language and Concepts

Present Pages 112 and 113

Point out that this is a newspaper article. Point out the name of the newspaper and the headline. Then read the article aloud. Use the Talk About It activity to introduce *wh-* questions and find the answers in the text. Encourage students to tell what the sixth-graders in the article did.

Model a Strategy

Find Information in a Newspaper Article

Model how to find information in a newspaper article:

When I read a newspaper article, I notice that the important general information comes near the beginning of the article. Later paragraphs give more detailed information.

★ ★ ★ ★ ★ LATEST EDITION ★ ★ ★ ★

NEIGHBORHOOD

NEWS

A Day at the Beach for Sixth-Graders

Sixth-graders from four local schools joined together last Saturday to clean up the beaches at Ocean Haven. The students divided into small groups to pick up garbage before it could wash into the ocean. They collected more than forty bags of trash during the day.

Summer tourists had left large amounts of garbage on the beach. It was littered with bottles, cans, and pieces of plastic.

"We wanted to clean our beach because we learned how garbage can harm animals," said Brian Sanders, 11, from Lincoln School.

Options for Reaching All Students

Beginning

Art: Illustration

Have students draw or describe the beach before and after the students in the article cleaned it.

Advanced

Social Studies: Community Activities

Have students work in groups to brainstorm a list of places in their communities that they could clean up or another community environmental project they could participate in. Have them share and discuss their list with other groups. Help students develop a plan to follow up.

Mixed Ability

Language: Role-Play

Have students role-play the students who participated in the cleanup described in the newspaper article, and the reporters interviewing the students. Students can use the *wh-* questions from the Talk About It and quotations in the article as prompts for the activity.

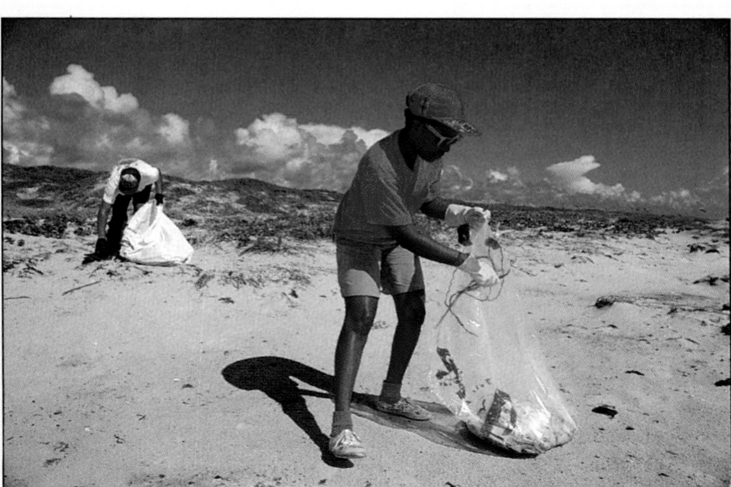

▲ Students from local schools clean up beach.

The students had learned that large pieces of plastic in the ocean can trap animals like a net. Holders for six-packs of soda can get around sea birds' necks. The birds are not able to breathe and they die.

Veronica Brown, 12, from Hawthorne School said, "It was exciting to work together and show we care about the ocean."

Talk About It

Newspaper articles answer five questions. Find the answers to these questions: who? what? when? where? why?

Language Awareness

Grammar

Wh- Questions in the Past Tense

ACTIVITY BOOK

Ask students *wh-* questions about the newspaper article and prompt responses.

Who was the subject of the article? (The sixth-grade students.)

What did the students do? (They collected garbage.)

Where did they collect the garbage? (They collected garbage at the beach.)

When did they collect garbage? (They collected garbage in September, after the summer tourists left.)

Why did they collect garbage? (They collected garbage because they wanted to help the environment.)

Then have students look back at the story *Why the Sea Is Salty* and ask and answer questions about the pictures. For example,

What did Jiro do? He asked Ichiro for rice.

Why did he ask for rice? Because he wanted to get food for his family.

Use Activity Book pages 57 and 58.

Home Connection

Cleanup Day

If possible, arrange for students and parents to participate in a cleanup day, where students help clean up a place in the school or neighborhood.

Afterwards, as a class, write about the experience in the form of a newspaper article like the one in the text.

QuickCheck

Days and Month

Check that students can name days of the week and months of the year.

Writer's Workshop

What I Did to Protect the Environment

Refer students to the Writer's Workshop on pages 230 to 236. Have students choose one experience they had in the unit related to protecting the environment and reducing garbage and write about it.

Connect

Activate Prior Knowledge

Brainstorm Vocabulary

Elicit and present ways to travel on the ocean, including the word *submarine.*

Develop Language and Concepts

Present Page 114

YELLOW TAPE

Read the song with students. Play the song on Side 2 of the Yellow Tape several times and have students sing along.

Language Awareness

Phonics
Consonant *s*

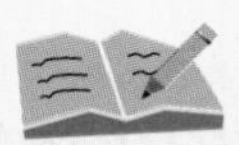
ACTIVITY BOOK

As students sing the song, have them clap every time they hear the sound of *s* as in *sea*. Then have students look at the song in the text and have them find the words written with the letter *s*. Point out that most are pronounced as the *s* in *sea,* and others are pronounced as the sound of *z* in *zoo* (*was, his,* and *waves*). Point out that the letter *s* can stand for two sounds.

Use Activity Book page 59 for further practice.

Yellow Submarine

by John Lennon and
Paul McCartney

In the town where I was born
lived a man who sailed to sea.
And he told us of his life
in the land of submarines.
So we sailed up to the sun
till we found the sea of green.
And we lived beneath the waves
in our yellow submarine.
We all live in a yellow submarine,
yellow submarine, yellow submarine.
We all live in a yellow submarine,
yellow submarine, yellow submarine.

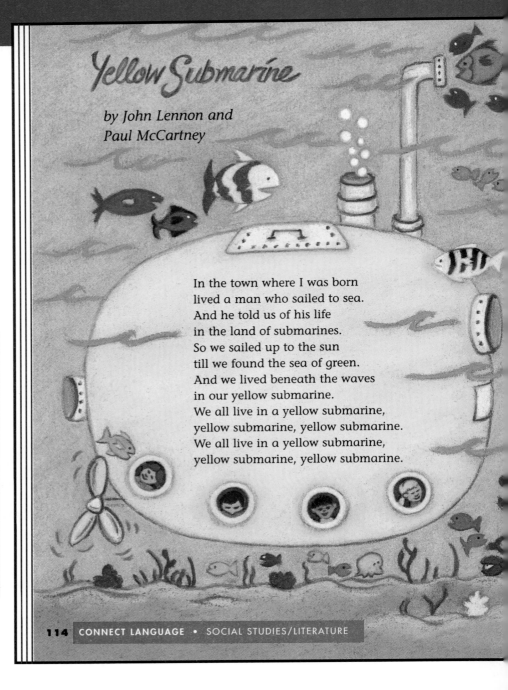

Options for Reaching All Students

Beginning

Language: Chant

Have students do the following traditional clapping chant:

A sailor went to sea, sea, sea
To see what he could see, see, see
But all that he could see, see, see
Was the bottom of the deep blue sea,
sea, sea.

Advanced

Art: Story Illustration

Have students draw their own illustration for the song—maybe what it would be like to live with a lot of people in a small submarine or what they would see outside the porthole or through the periscope.

Home Connection

Songs from Home

Have students ask other members of their families if they have any other Beatles songs. Play one or two of them for the class.

Tell what you learned.

CHAPTER 6

1. Why is the ocean important to people?

2. What are some causes of ocean pollution? What are some of the effects of ocean pollution? Make a chart.

Causes of Pollution	Effects of Pollution
Oil tankers spill oil in the ocean.	Sea birds are covered in oil and die.

3. Imagine you are the leader of a group of students who want to help protect the environment. Think of a project that the group could do in your community. Write a newspaper advertisement for the event.

Assess

Activity 1: Evaluate whether students understand that the ocean is important to people because it is a source of food (fishing and aquaculture) and a place for recreation.

Activity 2: Evaluate the number and accuracy of responses.

Activity 3: Check that students have selected a possible community project to help protect the environment.

Have students complete the Chapter Self-Assessment, Blackline Master 31. Have students choose the product of one of the activities to place in their portfolio. Add results of rubrics, self-assessments, or portfolio assessments, Blackline Masters 2–18 and 31.

Listening Assessment

BLACKLINE MASTER

Make sure each student has a copy of Blackline Master 53, from the Teacher Resource Book. Play the tape several times and ask students to circle their answers.

WHITE TAPE

See page T78d for the tapescript.

Vocabulary Assessment

Word Log

Have students try to group words from the chapter into categories: Kinds of Pollution (chemicals, garbage), Causes of Pollution (people, factories, farmers, oil tankers), Materials (plastic, paper), Ways to Protect the Environment (reduce, reuse, recycle), Basic Question Words (who, what, where, when, why). Provide students with the categories and words.

Writing Assessment

My Environmental Booklet

Have students make a booklet in which they list pollution problems and ways they can personally protect the environment.

Language Assessment

BLACKLINE MASTER

Use Blackline Master 52 in the Teacher's Resource Book.

Standardized Test Practice

ACTIVITY BOOK

Use pages 60 and 61. Answers: **1.** 56 inches **2.** cylinder **3.** November **4.** .5 inch

Wrap-Up

Activities

Environmentalism in the News

During the course of the unit, have students listen to TV and radio news reports and list issues that relate to the environment. They should list the key information: date, place, problem, or issue. For example, was there an oil spill? Are any more animals on the endangered list or are some species being saved?

Environmental Groups

Invite advanced students to contact local or national environmental groups such as Green Peace or the Sierra Club (many library books on ecology list mailing addresses and phone numbers, as might the local phone book). Encourage them to ask about how pollution affects oceans. Have them find out what can be done to help protect the ocean and other parts of the environment. Have them share the information with the class.

Oceans Game

Have students create an oceans board game. They should prepare a large map of the oceans similar to the one in the Student Book. Around the shores of the ocean, students should place squares for a game board. The path should go around the board and end in the same place. To accompany the game, they should prepare cards relating to oceans: some tell students to move forward, and some should them to move backward. For example, "There is an oil spill. Move back 5 squares. You see a whale. Move forward 3 squares." Have students play their game, trying to be the first to return the starting point.

Discussing the Theme

Have students work in small groups to discuss what they learned about oceans and recycling during this unit. Choose from the following activities to show students how much they have learned, how the information applies to their everyday lives, and how useful these types of information are to them.

- Have students tape-record a list of new words learned.
- Have students draw or find pictures that represent words they have learned. Have more advanced students label the pictures and have beginning students review the labels and pictures.
- Discuss with students how every person is responsible for oceans and the environment.
- Have groups discuss situations in which the words they have learned will be useful, for example, in social studies and science classes, when traveling, and when discussing other environments.
- Invite students to draw a picture of a time when they were on or near an ocean or another body of water. Have them use their picture to present their experience to the class.

Sharing the Project

Use the invitation form, Blackline Masters 32 and 33 in the Teacher's Resource Book, to invite family members to school for a presentation of the ocean model and recycling information.

Set up the classroom with ocean view and shoreline stations. Invite family members to view each station. Have students from each group take turns explaining their part of the ocean model.

You might want to have students prepare and distribute information they gathered while working on one or more of the activities about recycling or supporting environmental groups.

Signs of Success!

Duplicate a copy of this checklist for each student.

Name: ______________________________

Refer to the checklist below for a quick demonstration of how a student is progressing toward transitioning out of ESL instruction.

Objectives

- ☐ Names the areas of the ocean
- ☐ Names the things found in the ocean
- ☐ Compares the areas of the ocean
- ☐ Names the oceans of the world
- ☐ Tells how people use the ocean
- ☐ Tells how people pollute the ocean
- ☐ Names some solutions to pollution
- ☐ Tells how students can help the environment

Language Awareness

Understands/Uses:

- ☐ comparatives with *-er*
- ☐ adjectives—position and agreement
- ☐ expressions *surrounds/is surrounded by*
- ☐ irregular past tense verbs
- ☐ questions with *how*/answers with *by* + *-ing*
- ☐ *stop/start* + *-ing*
- ☐ expressions *less* or *more*
- ☐ *wh-* questions in the past tense

Hears/Pronounces/Reads:

- ☐ long *e*, vowel digraphs *ea/ee*
- ☐ digraph *sh*

Learning Strategies

- ☐ Identifies main topics
- ☐ Uses dialogue to evaluate character
- ☐ Uses pictures for meaning
- ☐ Uses a graphic organizer
- ☐ Finds information in a newspaper article

Comments

____

____

Planning Guide

The Roman Empire

Objectives

Tell how the ancient Romans built their empire.

Describe the ancient Romans as builders.

Discuss the nature of Roman law.

Identify Latin words in English.

Discuss contributions of the ancient Romans.

Vocabulary Focus

Words about ancient Romans such as *bridges, building, road, soldier.*

Words about buildings such as *structure, aqueduct, arena.*

Government words such as *citizen, law, vote.*

English words made from parts of Latin words such as *videotape, pregame, rewrite.*

Lesson	Content Focus	Language Awareness Objectives	Learning Strategies
Preview pp. 116–117 Tell What You Know.			
Present pp. 118–119 The Growth of Rome	Social Studies	**Grammar** Past Tense: Regular and Irregular	Read a map key.
Practice pp. 120–121 The Romans Were Builders.	Social Studies	**Grammar** Sentence Structure: The Verb *be* + an Adjective	Find the topic sentence.
Practice pp. 122–123 What Was Roman Law?	Social Studies	**Phonics** Hard and Soft *c*	
Connect pp. 124–125 Latin Words in English	Social Studies/ Language	**Vocabulary** Prefixes	Use prior knowledge.
Connect pp. 126–127 Roman Recipes	Social Studies/ Reading	**Grammar** Amounts and Container Words	Follow a recipe.
Connect p. 128 Make a Mosaic.	Social Studies/ Art	**Grammar** Plurals	
Assess p. 129 Tell What You Learned.			

Volcanoes in History

Objectives

Describe the eruption of Mount Vesuvius.

Discuss what archaeologists learned from Pompeii.

Tell what a volcano is.

Retell an ancient Roman myth.

Vocabulary Focus

Volcano words such as *explosion, fire, lightning, smoke, erupt, lava, cinder.*
Natural disaster words such as *earthquake, flood, hurricane, storm.*
Words describing volcanic action such as *rumble, grumble, blow.*

Lesson	Content Focus	Language Awareness Objectives	Learning Strategies
Preview pp. 130–131 Tell What You Know.			
Present pp. 132–133 A Volcano Erupts in A.D. 79.	Social Studies	**Grammar** Verbs and Infinitives	
Practice pp. 134–37 Vesuvius Preserves the Past.	Social Studies	**Grammar** Passive Verbs **Spelling** Consonant Blends and Digraphs with *s*	Make personal connections. Summarize to remember information.
Connect pp. 138–139 What Is a Volcano?	Social Studies/ Science	**Spelling** Capitalization: Proper Nouns	Use a graphic organizer.
Connect pp. 140–143 *An Ancient Roman Myth: The God Vulcan*	Social Studies/ Literature	**Language Function** Discourse Connectors	
Connect pp. 144–151 *Hill of Fire*	Social Studies/ Literature	**Grammar** Prepositional Phrases of Direction **Grammar** Past Tense: Regular and Irregular	Visualize a story.
Connect p. 152 "V is for Volcano"	Social Studies/ Literature	**Phonics** The Letter *V*	
Assess p. 153 Tell What You Learned.			

Resources

Chapter 7

Support Materials

PICTURE CARDS

numbers 2, 3, 11, 14, 15, 19, 21, 36, 37, 42, 44, 48, 54, 57, 60, 67

ACTIVITY BOOK

pages 82–91

VIDEO

Unti 4, The Ancient Romans

DISK

Writer's Notebook

Assessment Materials

BLACKLINE MASTER

Language Assessment, Blackline Master 70

Listening Assessment, Blackline Master, 71

CREAM TAPE

Side 1

Listening Assessment, page T129

Listen carefully. The student is talking about what she learned about the ancient Romans. Circle the items that she mentions.

The ancient Romans were good soldiers. They built a huge empire more than two thousand years ago. The empire included much of Europe, eastern Asia, and Africa. One of the most interesting things about the Romans was that they were great builders. They left many buildings that you can still see today. In several places, there are arenas built by the Romans. In the past, people went to them to see fights. Today many people go to them to hear music. Aqueducts were other interesting structures built by the Romans. They were tall structures that carried water from the country to the cities. Several of these still stand today.

Newcomer Book C

Survival language for absolute beginners. For overview, see pages xxviii–xxix.

For Extended Reading

Ancient Rome by Simon James, Viking, 1992

Numerous pictures and engaging text depict ancient Rome.

Level: Advanced

Everyday Life in Roman Times by Mike Corbishley, Franklin Watts, 1994

Descriptions of how ancient Romans cooked their meals, conducted their families, and carried out other aspects of their day-to-day lives.

Level: Beginning

A Roman Soldier edited by Claire Llewellyn, Peter Bedrick Books, 1992

The story of a young Roman soldier as he mans a fortress at Hadrian's Wall.

Level: Beginning

A Roman Villa by Jacqueline Morley, Peter Bedrick Books, 1992

Students can imagine themselves part of a wealthy Roman family as this colorful book takes them through daily life in the villa.

Level: Advanced

Science in Ancient Rome by Jacqueline Harris, Franklin Watts, 1988

How the Romans used scientific achievements from earlier civilizations to their advantage.

Level: Average

Swords and Spears and Sandals by Richard Suskind, W. W. Norton & Company, 1969

Students enter the world of the Roman legions in this informative book.

Level: Average

Related Technology

Exploring Ancient Cities, Sumeria, 1994

Explore the ancient city of Pompeii.

Chapter 8

Support Materials

pages 92–101

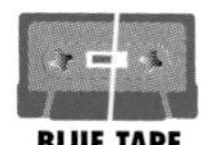

Side 1

An Ancient Roman Myth: The God Vulcan, pages T140–143

Hill of Fire, pages T144–151

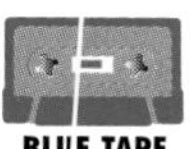

Side 2

"V Is for Volcano," page T152

Writer's Notebook

Assessment Materials

Language Assessment, Blackline Master 72

Listening Assessment, Blackline Master, 73

Side 1

Listening Assessment, page T153

Listen carefully. You are going to write down what you hear. You will hear information about ancient Rome. Then you will hear it more slowly. Begin to write. Then you will hear the information one more time. Check what you wrote.

Many things in the past were like things today. The ancient Romans had snack shops. We eat in fast food restaurants. The ancient Romans there had large arenas. They saw plays and games. We can go out to see plays and sports or we can see them at home on TV.

For Extended Reading

Hawaii Volcanoes National Park by Ruth Radlauer, Childrens Press, 1979

This book explores the beauty of this national park and its fiery volcanoes with color photographs and engaging text.

Level: Advanced

The Romans and Pompeii by Philip Steele, Dillon Press, 1994

In 79 A.D., Mount Vesuvius erupted, burying the city of Pompeii. Discover how scientists used its ruins to learn about Roman life, as well as about everyday life in the city.

Level: Average

The Secrets of Vesuvius by Sara C. Bisel, A Scholastic/Madison Press Book, 1990

An anthropologist "reads" the bones of people killed in the town of Herculaneum to learn about their lives.

Level: Average

They Survived Mount St. Helens! by Megan Stine, Random House, 1994

True accounts of the 1980 eruption of Mount St. Helens and its aftermath.

Level: Beginning

Volcano by Christopher Lampton, The Millbrook Press, 1991

Explanations of how volcanoes develop, why they erupt, and how lava enriches the soil.

Level: Average

Volcanoes and Earthquakes by Terry Jennings, Oxford University Press, 1988

Descriptions of the forces that make the earth rumble, split, and erupt, and some of the myths that used to surround these phenomena.

Level: Advanced

Related Technology

Rocks and Volcanoes, Queue, Inc., 1995
Checks for understanding and keeps a record for each student.

Project

Roman Day

This optional project can be completed over the next two chapters. In this project, students will role-play being ancient Romans. See the Unit Wrap Up, page T153a, for more ideas on sharing the project with family members.

What You'll Need

Collect and allow students access to the following:

- resource books that contain information, drawings, and diagrams of ancient Roman cities, homes, clothing, and lifestyles
- sheets for making togas and other clothing

Have available in the classroom:

- large sheets of packing box cardboard
- paints
- cardboard
- scissors
- colored construction paper
- felt-tipped markers
- glue
- newspapers
- tape
- dowels for making scrolls

Beginning the Project

Explain to students that the class will become ancient Romans for a day. Students will divide into groups for further study on one of these topics:

- dinner at home
- a day at school
- a debate in the forum or a tour of the forum
- recreation

Each group will research its topic area and make a plan for a skit or a presentation about its area of study.

Students should be encouraged to take a "You Are There" approach to their topic area, first making it come alive for themselves and then for others.

Home Involvement

Send the Letter to the Family, Blackline Masters 64–69, to families telling them that the class will re-create a day in ancient Rome as part of their study of ancient Rome. As the unit progresses, encourage home discussion of the various things people do all day now and what it might have been like in ancient Rome.

Developing Topics

Clothing

- Students will need to learn about clothing for men, women, and children. There are many project books for instructions on how to make togas and stolas.

Dinner at Home

- Who would be at dinner?
- What's on the menu?
- Where did the Romans get their food?
- Who prepared it?
- Dinner party in the dining room

The emphasis here will be on the well-to-do Roman citizen. Students can prepare a skit of the dinner party and offer narration or commentary to fill in information. Students might also give a "tour" of a Roman home or villa based on information they find in reference books.

A Day at School

- Who went to school?
- What was taught at school?
- Who taught school?
- What were boys and girls expected to know?
- What did they do when they weren't in school?
- What did they use for books?

Students can act out a classroom situation. Some of the books on Rome have pictures of a school. Students might make scrolls or writing tablets, as found in project books on the ancient Romans.

A Debate in the Forum

This might be a gathering of people from different social groups debating on who should be allowed to vote.

- Who did the Romans think should be allowed to vote?
- Why were the poor people successful in being granted the right to vote in elections?
- How did the Romans feel about women and their right to vote?

Students should develop different arguments in support of the positive and negative positions in a debate that might have taken place in the forum. They can make a back drop of a government building and steps using mural paper or appliance boxes and paint.

As an alternate, students might give a tour of a forum, commenting on the various buildings. They could use information on the Roman forum and paint a backdrop on paper.

Recreation

These could be people at arenas or theaters:

- Where were these located?
- Who went to them?
- What kind of entertainment was there?

Students could relate what they saw at the arena in the format of an on-the-spot interview.

Daily Discussion

As you progress through the unit, take a few minutes each day for one group of students to present their research on their topic. Encourage them to make bulletin board displays.

Allow students time to develop skits and dialogue as well as information to be communicated in narration. Students will also need time to prepare their clothing for Roman Day.

Encourage students to compare the details of the daily activities in ancient Rome, including household chores, personal hygiene, school, and recreation to the details of their daily activities as students in the United States.

Activity Book

Chapter 7

Name ______________________

In the Past

Fill in the blanks in the story. Use the past tense form of the word that is given.

Rome ___began___ (begin) as the home of farmers and herders. Over the years, the Romans ___conquered___ (conquer) many people. They ___learned___ (learn) how to do many things. The Romans ___built___ (build) roads and fine buildings. They ___borrowed___ (borrow) ideas from the people they ___conquered___ conquer. They ___brought___ (bring) buildings, roads, and many other things to the people they ___conquered___ (conquer). The Romans ___built___ (build) a strong empire.

Write the three most interesting things you know about the ancient Romans.
Answers will vary.

1. ______________________

2. ______________________

3. ______________________

Name ______________________

Crossword Puzzle

Fill in the crossword puzzle with the words from the list.

aqueducts
arches
arenas
army
coins
Coliseum
roads
Roman Empire
Romans
stones

			1R	O	M	2A	N	S						
3A						R								
Q						E			4A	R	5C	H	E	S
U				6R		N			R	■	O			
E			7R	O	M	A	N	E	M	P	I	R	E	
D				A		S			Y		N			
U				D							S			
8C	O	L	I	S	E	U	M							
T														
9S	T	O	N	E	S									

Down
2. places where people were entertained
3. brought water into cities
4. won battles around the Mediterranean
5. money used for trade and commerce

Across
1. lived in Rome
4. part of an aqueduct
7. controlled most of Europe
8. held 50,000 people
9. what roads were made of

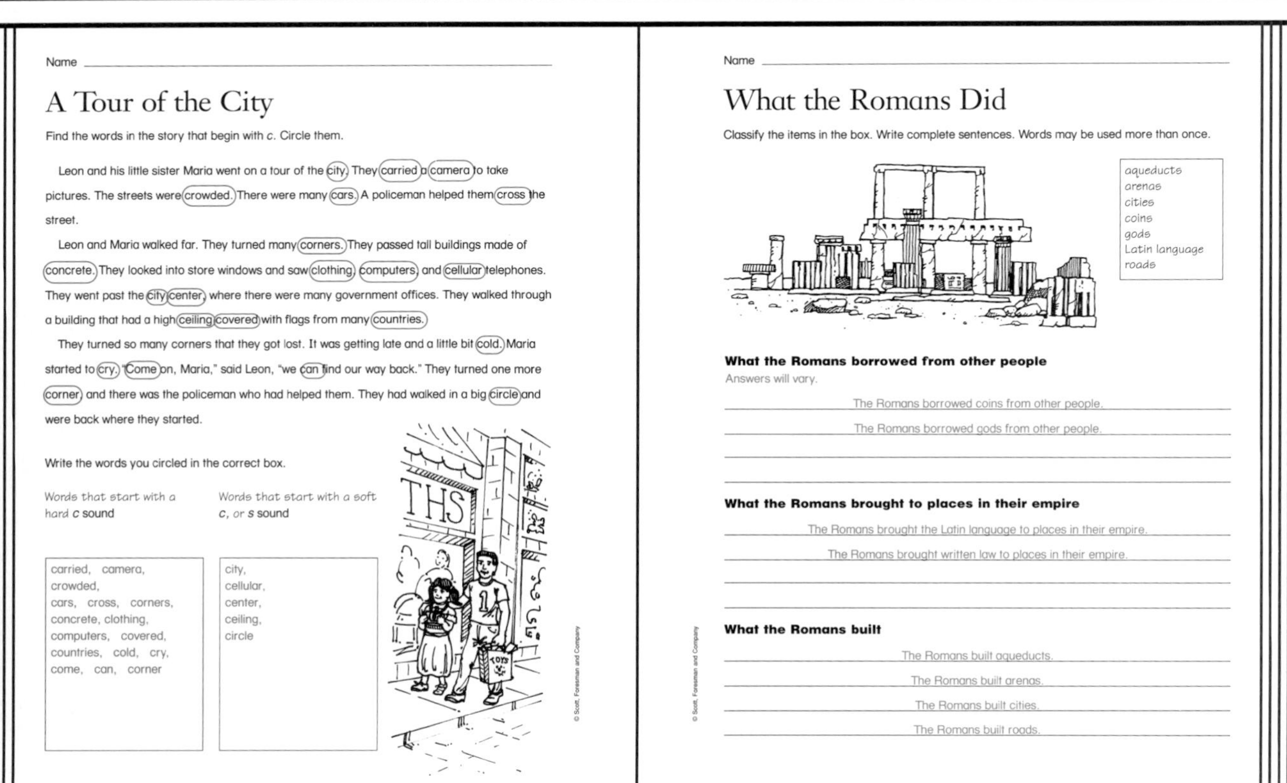

Name ______________________

A Tour of the City

Find the words in the story that begin with *c*. Circle them.

Leon and his little sister Maria went on a tour of the (city.) They (carried) a (camera) to take pictures. The streets were (crowded.) There were many (cars.) A policeman helped them (cross) the street.

Leon and Maria walked far. They turned many (corners.) They passed tall buildings made of (concrete.) They looked into store windows and saw (clothing,) (computers,) and (cellular) telephones. They went past the (city) (center,) where there were many government offices. They walked through a building that had a high (ceiling) (covered) with flags from many (countries.)

They turned so many corners that they got lost. It was getting late and a little bit (cold.) Maria started to (cry.) "(Come) on, Maria," said Leon, "we (can) find our way back." They turned one more (corner) and there was the policeman who had helped them. They had walked in a big (circle) and were back where they started.

Write the words you circled in the correct box.

Words that start with a hard *c* sound	Words that start with a soft *c*, or *s* sound
carried, camera, crowded, cars, cross, corners, concrete, clothing, computers, covered, countries, cold, cry, come, can, corner	city, cellular, center, ceiling, circle

Name ______________________

What the Romans Did

Classify the items in the box. Write complete sentences. Words may be used more than once.

aqueducts
arenas
cities
coins
gods
Latin language
roads

What the Romans borrowed from other people
Answers will vary.

The Romans borrowed coins from other people.
The Romans borrowed gods from other people.

What the Romans brought to places in their empire

The Romans brought the Latin language to places in their empire.
The Romans brought written law to places in their empire.

What the Romans built

The Romans built aqueducts.
The Romans built arenas.
The Romans built cities.
The Romans built roads.

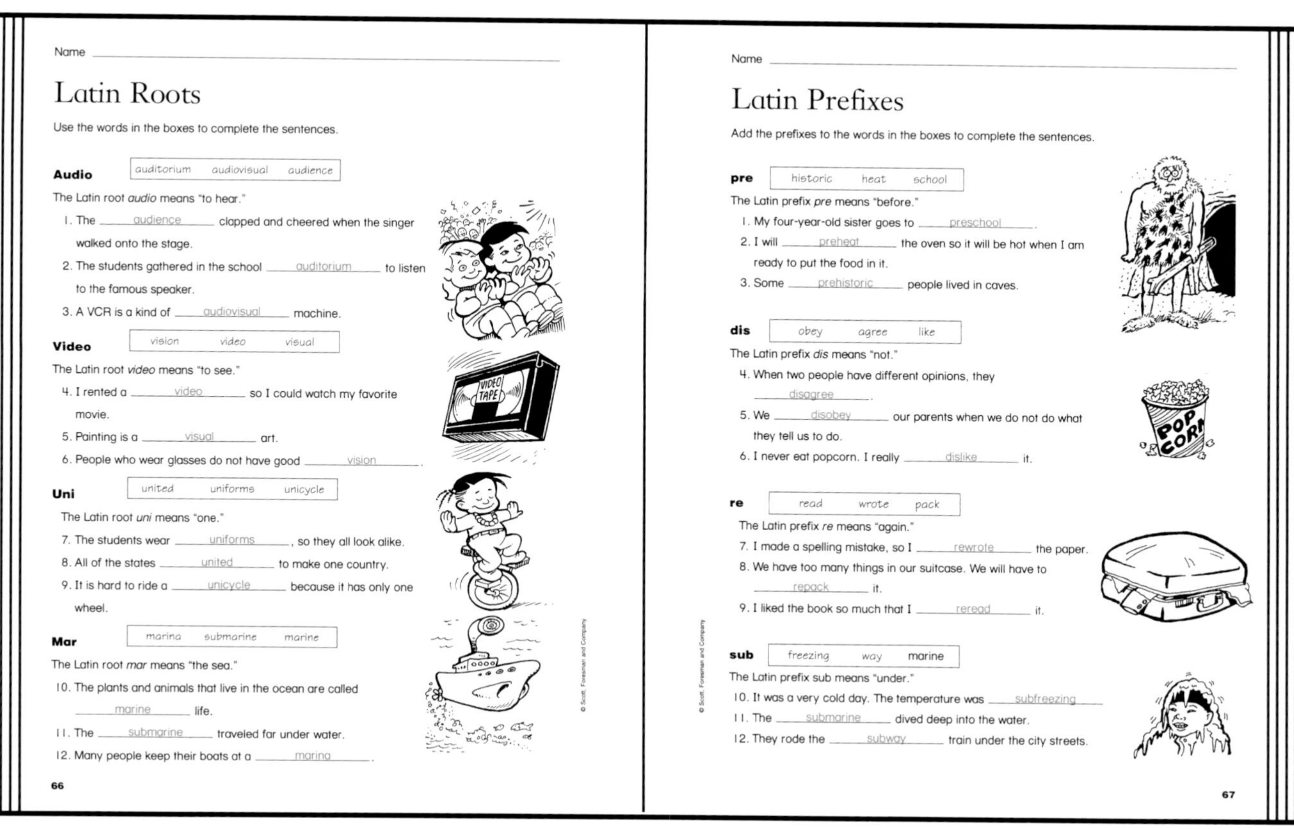

Name ______

Latin Roots

Use the words in the boxes to complete the sentences.

Audio | auditorium audiovisual audience

The Latin root *audio* means "to hear."

1. The __audience__ clapped and cheered when the singer walked onto the stage.
2. The students gathered in the school __auditorium__ to listen to the famous speaker.
3. A VCR is a kind of __audiovisual__ machine.

Video | vision video visual

The Latin root *video* means "to see."

4. I rented a __video__ so I could watch my favorite movie.
5. Painting is a __visual__ art.
6. People who wear glasses do not have good __vision__.

Uni | united uniforms unicycle

The Latin root *uni* means "one."

7. The students wear __uniforms__, so they all look alike.
8. All of the states __united__ to make one country.
9. It is hard to ride a __unicycle__ because it has only one wheel.

Mar | marina submarine marine

The Latin root *mar* means "the sea."

10. The plants and animals that live in the ocean are called __marine__ life.
11. The __submarine__ traveled far under water.
12. Many people keep their boats at a __marina__.

66

© Scott, Foresman and Company

Name ______

Latin Prefixes

Add the prefixes to the words in the boxes to complete the sentences.

pre | historic heat school

The Latin prefix *pre* means "before."

1. My four-year-old sister goes to __preschool__.
2. I will __preheat__ the oven so it will be hot when I am ready to put the food in it.
3. Some __prehistoric__ people lived in caves.

dis | obey agree like

The Latin prefix *dis* means "not."

4. When two people have different opinions, they __disagree__.
5. We __disobey__ our parents when we do not do what they tell us to do.
6. I never eat popcorn. I really __dislike__ it.

re | read wrote pack

The Latin prefix *re* means "again."

7. I made a spelling mistake, so I __rewrote__ the paper.
8. We have too many things in our suitcase. We will have to __repack__ it.
9. I liked the book so much that I __reread__ it.

sub | freezing way marine

The Latin prefix sub means "under."

10. It was a very cold day. The temperature was __subfreezing__.
11. The __submarine__ dived deep into the water.
12. They rode the __subway__ train under the city streets.

© Scott, Foresman and Company

67

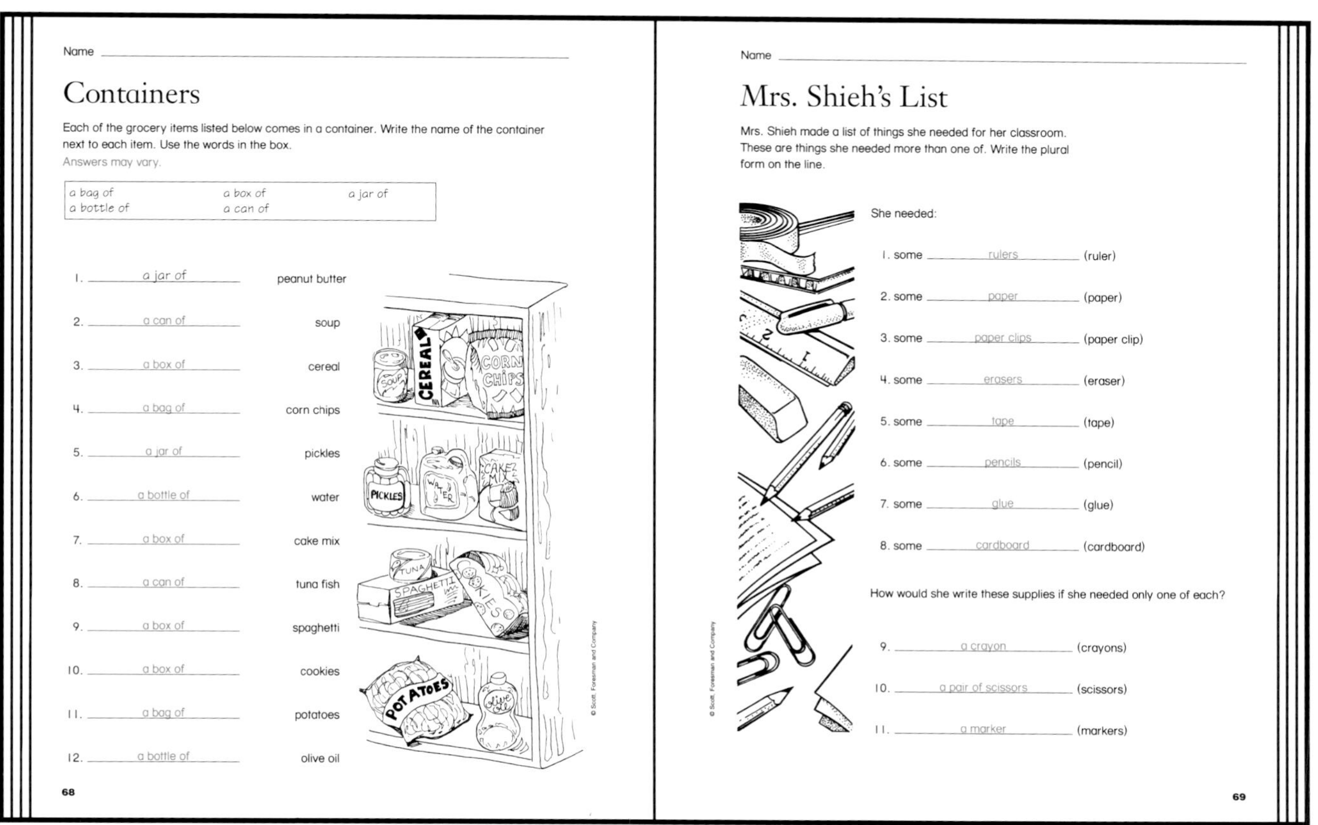

Name ______

Containers

Each of the grocery items listed below comes in a container. Write the name of the container next to each item. Use the words in the box.

Answers may vary.

a bag of	a box of	a jar of
a bottle of	a can of	

1. __a jar of__ peanut butter
2. __a can of__ soup
3. __a box of__ cereal
4. __a bag of__ corn chips
5. __a jar of__ pickles
6. __a bottle of__ water
7. __a box of__ cake mix
8. __a can of__ tuna fish
9. __a box of__ spaghetti
10. __a box of__ cookies
11. __a bag of__ potatoes
12. __a bottle of__ olive oil

© Scott, Foresman and Company

68

Name ______

Mrs. Shieh's List

Mrs. Shieh made a list of things she needed for her classroom. These are things she needed more than one of. Write the plural form on the line.

She needed:

1. some __rulers__ (ruler)
2. some __paper__ (paper)
3. some __paper clips__ (paper clip)
4. some __erasers__ (eraser)
5. some __tape__ (tape)
6. some __pencils__ (pencil)
7. some __glue__ (glue)
8. some __cardboard__ (cardboard)

How would she write these supplies if she needed only one of each?

9. __a crayon__ (crayons)
10. __a pair of scissors__ (scissors)
11. __a marker__ (markers)

© Scott, Foresman and Company

69

Activity Book

Chapter 8

Name ____________________

Mount Vesuvius

Decide whether the events in the box happened *before*, *during*, or *after* the eruption of Mount Vesuvius. Write each event under the correct heading.

A huge cloud of ash came out of the volcano.
Animals became frightened.
The earth shook.
People tried to escape.
The town of Pompeii was forgotten.
Hot rocks fell from the sky.
Water in the wells dried up.
People began to dig out Pompeii.

Before the Eruption

Animals became frightened.
The earth shook.
Water in the wells dried up.

During the Eruption

A huge cloud of ash came out of the volcano.
People tried to escape.
Hot rocks fell from the sky.

After the Eruption

The town of Pompeii was forgotten.
People began to dig out Pompeii.

Name ____________________

Facts About Pompeii

Complete these sentences with the correct form of the word in parentheses. Use the information in the box for help with some of the words (irregular verbs).

Verb	Past Participle
build	built
carry	carried
forget	forgotten
know	known
make	made

1. Pompeii's streets were made (make) of stone.
2. Water was carried (carry) to Pompeii by aqueducts.
3. Leaders were elected (elect) by the citizens.
4. Meals were cooked (cook) by slaves.
5. Colored stones were used (use) to make mosaics.
6. A square garden in the middle of a house was called (call) an atrium.
7. Rooms were built (build) around the atrium.
8. Actors were known (know) by most people in Pompeii.
9. Pompeii was covered (cover) by twelve feet of ash and rocks.
10. The town was forgotten (forget) until the 1700s.

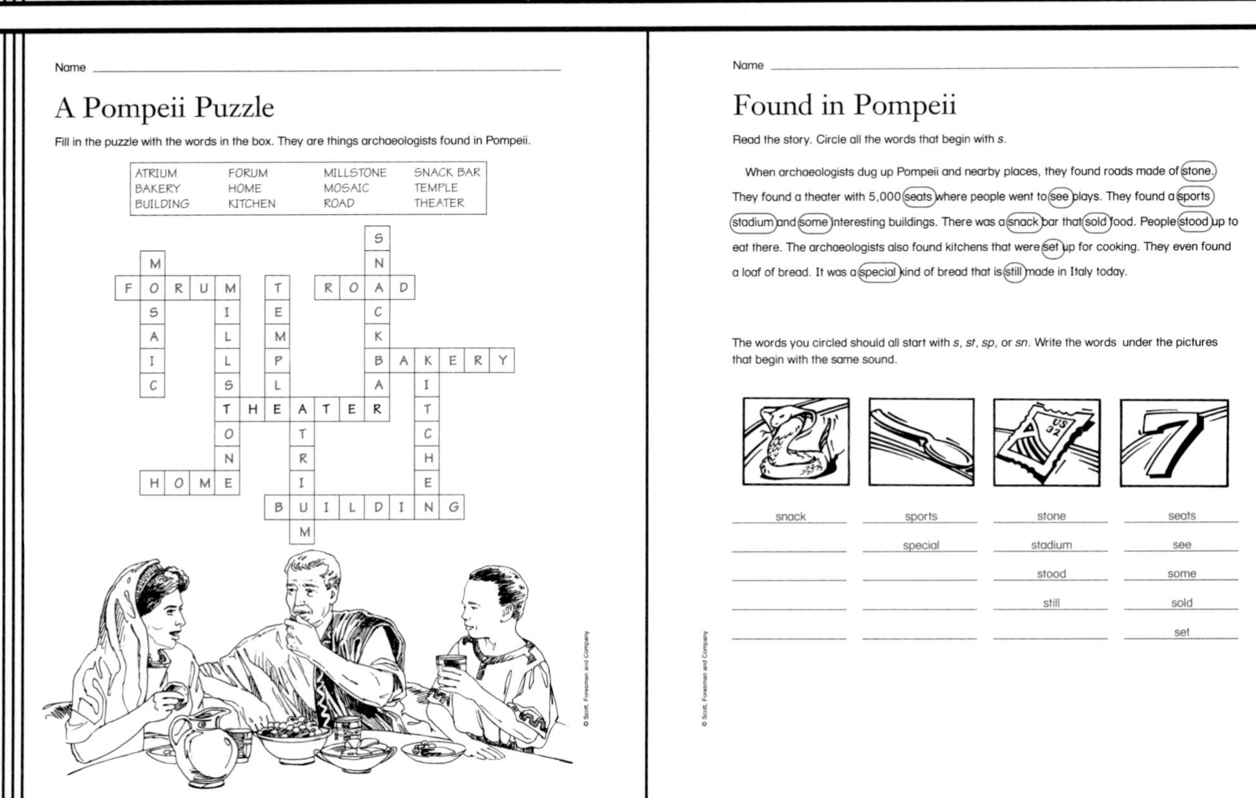

Name ____________________

A Pompeii Puzzle

Fill in the puzzle with the words in the box. They are things archaeologists found in Pompeii.

ATRIUM	FORUM	MILLSTONE	SNACK BAR
BAKERY	HOME	MOSAIC	TEMPLE
BUILDING	KITCHEN	ROAD	THEATER

Name ____________________

Found in Pompeii

Read the story. Circle all the words that begin with *s*.

When archaeologists dug up Pompeii and nearby places, they found roads made of stone. They found a theater with 5,000 seats where people went to see plays. They found a sports stadium and some interesting buildings. There was a snack bar that sold food. People stood up to eat there. The archaeologists also found kitchens that were set up for cooking. They even found a loaf of bread. It was a special kind of bread that is still made in Italy today.

The words you circled should all start with *s*, *st*, *sp*, or *sn*. Write the words under the pictures that begin with the same sound.

snack	sports	stone	seats
	special	stadium	see
		stood	some
		still	sold
			set

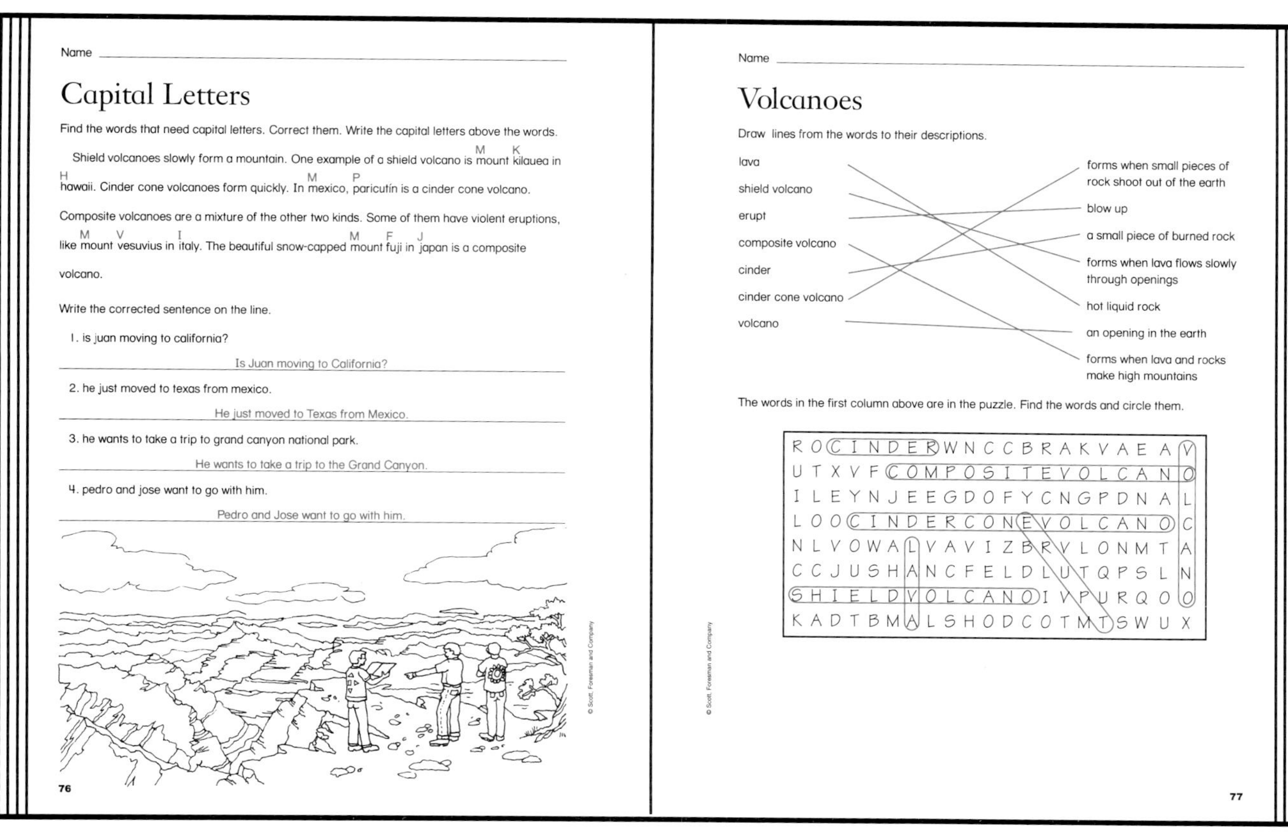

Name

Capital Letters

Find the words that need capital letters. Correct them. Write the capital letters above the words.

M K
Shield volcanoes slowly form a mountain. One example of a shield volcano is mount kilauea in
H M P
hawaii. Cinder cone volcanoes form quickly. In mexico, paricutín is a cinder cone volcano.
Composite volcanoes are a mixture of the other two kinds. Some of them have violent eruptions,
M V I M F J
like mount vesuvius in italy. The beautiful snow-capped mount fuji in japan is a composite
volcano.

Write the corrected sentence on the line.

1. is juan moving to california?
Is Juan moving to California?
2. he just moved to texas from mexico.
He just moved to Texas from Mexico.
3. he wants to take a trip to grand canyon national park.
He wants to take a trip to the Grand Canyon.
4. pedro and jose want to go with him.
Pedro and Jose want to go with him.

© Scott, Foresman and Company

76

Name

Volcanoes

Draw lines from the words to their descriptions.

lava	forms when small pieces of rock shoot out of the earth
shield volcano	blow up
erupt	a small piece of burned rock
composite volcano	forms when lava flows slowly through openings
cinder	hot liquid rock
cinder cone volcano	an opening in the earth
volcano	forms when lava and rocks make high mountains

The words in the first column above are in the puzzle. Find the words and circle them.

R O C I N D E R W N C C B R A K V A E A V
U T X V F C O M P O S I T E V O L C A N O
I L E Y N J E E G D O F Y C N G P D N A L
L O O C I N D E R C O N E V O L C A N O C
N L V O W A L V A V I Z B R V L O N M T A
C C J U S H A N C F E L D L U T Q P S L N
S H I E L D V O L C A N O I V P U R Q O O
K A D T B M A L S H O D C O T M T S W U X

© Scott, Foresman and Company

77

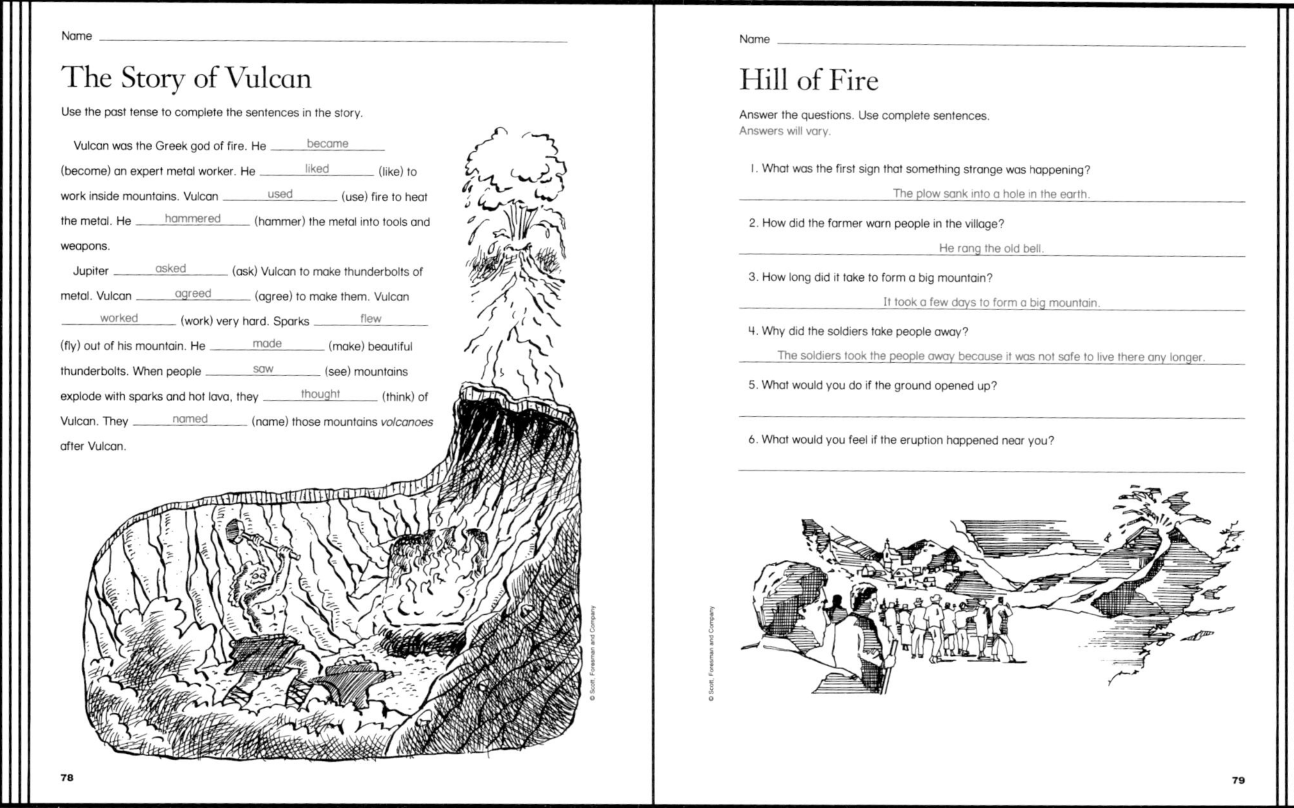

Name

The Story of Vulcan

Use the past tense to complete the sentences in the story.

Vulcan was the Greek god of fire. He became (become) an expert metal worker. He liked (like) to work inside mountains. Vulcan used (use) fire to heat the metal. He hammered (hammer) the metal into tools and weapons.

Jupiter asked (ask) Vulcan to make thunderbolts of metal. Vulcan agreed (agree) to make them. Vulcan worked (work) very hard. Sparks flew (fly) out of his mountain. He made (make) beautiful thunderbolts. When people saw (see) mountains explode with sparks and hot lava, they thought (think) of Vulcan. They named (name) those mountains *volcanoes* after Vulcan.

© Scott, Foresman and Company

78

Name

Hill of Fire

Answer the questions. Use complete sentences.
Answers will vary.

1. What was the first sign that something strange was happening?
The plow sank into a hole in the earth.
2. How did the farmer warn people in the village?
He rang the old bell.
3. How long did it take to form a big mountain?
It took a few days to form a big mountain.
4. Why did the soldiers take people away?
The soldiers took the people away because it was not safe to live there any longer.
5. What would you do if the ground opened up?
6. What would you feel if the eruption happened near you?

© Scott, Foresman and Company

79

UNIT 4

Preview

Activate Prior Knowledge

Use Pictures

Present a picture of the Coliseum in Rome. Ask students if they have ever seen a picture of this building and to speculate when it was built and why it was built. Use the picture as a springboard to lead into a discussion about the ancient Romans. Present pictures of pyramids and dinosaurs (from Unit 1) and help students to relate them chronologically to the Coliseum.

Develop Language and Concepts

Present Pages 116 and 117

Have students look at the pictures and invite any comments. Tell students that these structures were built by the ancient Romans in the city of Rome about 2,000 years ago.

Introduce the Word Bank words and help students relate them to the pictures. Have students respond to the question in Tell What You Know. Help students deduce that the ancient Romans were good soldiers, builders, and artists.

Have students answer the Talk About It questions. Help them to conclude life in Rome was similar to modern times in that there were soldiers, bridges, and buildings. Then ask about the differences between their lives and the lives of ancient Romans. Encourage them to use the pictures in the chapter to contrast such lifestyle aspects as clothing and technology.

The Ancient Romans

Word Bank

- buildings
- column
- soldiers
- stadium

Tell what you know.

These are some things from ancient Rome. What do these things tell about the ancient Romans?

Options for Reaching All Students

Beginning

Social Studies: Buildings

Collect pictures of different kinds of buildings, including houses, government buildings, churches, stores, and sports stadiums. Help students brainstorm the names for different buildings that they see. Make a list. Ask students if they have seen similar buildings in the pictures from ancient Rome. Ask them to be on the lookout for other buildings like those we have today. Have students separate the pictures into two groups: buildings they might expect to find in ancient Rome and buildings they would not expect to find in ancient Rome.

Advanced

Social Studies: Research

Have students work in groups to research Trajan's Column and the buildings in the Roman Forum. Have students create a bulletin board display with a map of the area and comments from their research.

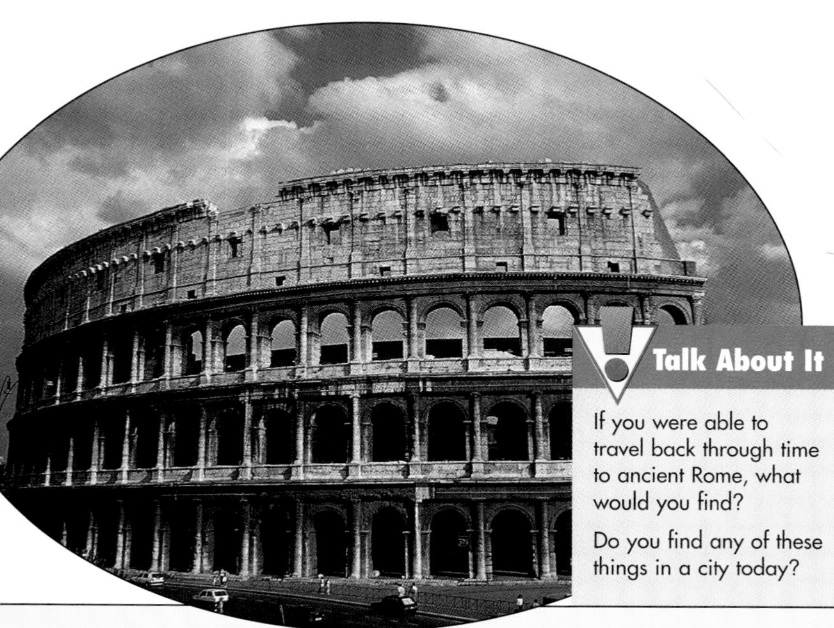

Talk About It

If you were able to travel back through time to ancient Rome, what would you find?

Do you find any of these things in a city today?

THEME/KEY CONCEPTS

The ancient Romans developed a great empire about 2000 years ago. They spread their own language and culture and learned from different cultures throughout Europe, northern Africa, and eastern Asia. They also spread their system of law and justice.

Volcanoes are a natural phenomenon. The preservation of Pompeii as a result of the eruption of the volcano Vesuvius has provided much information about the lifestyle of the ancient Romans.

Chapter 7

- The ancient Romans expanded their empire by conquering other people with their army. Then they built roads, buildings, aqueducts, and arenas throughout their empire.
- The Romans formed a republic and established laws for justice. The republic was later replaced by emperors.
- Romance languages such as Spanish come from Latin, the language of the ancient Romans. Some English words come from Latin.

Chapter 8

- There are different types of volcanoes.
- The eruption of Mount Vesuvius preserved the ancient Roman town of Pompeii.

ixed Ability

ideo: The Ancient Romans

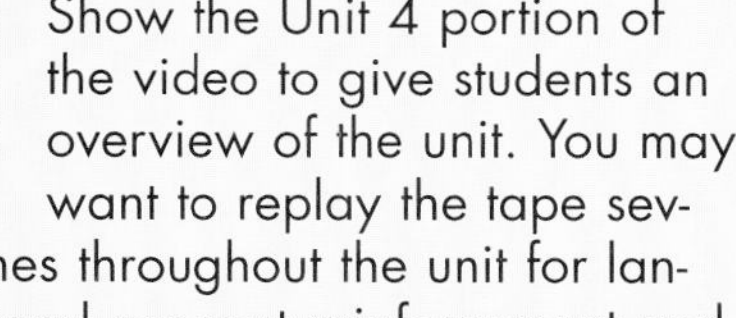

Show the Unit 4 portion of the video to give students an overview of the unit. You may want to replay the tape sev-al times throughout the unit for lan-age and concept reinforcement and velopment.

Cooperative Learning

Time Line

Have students brainstorm major dates from ancient Egypt and Greece as well as dates from the Roman Empire. Have students mark the dates of these civilizations on a time line made from adding machine tape, using a scale of two inches for each 100 years. Have more advanced students research a number of events in history and place them on the line.

Cooperative Language Experience

Sculpting

Call students' attention to the bas relief, a close-up of Trajan's Column, on page 116. Explain that a bas relief results from carving into a surface. Give each student a large bar of soap and a popsicle stick. Ask them to plan a design and to carve it on the surface of the soap, similar to bas relief.

Present

Activate Prior Knowledge

Study a Map

Ask students to study the map on page 118. Explain that the map shows the areas of the world that made up the Roman Empire. Have them locate Rome, the Mediterranean Sea, Europe, and England.

Develop Language and Concepts

Present Pages 118 and 119

Read the text with students. Help students understand that the Romans built their empire over several hundred years. Have them look at the map key and explain what the different colors indicate.

List on the board the things the Romans borrowed from other people and the things they brought to other people. Discuss the idea of cultural exchange. Help students discuss things from the United States that are in their culture and things that the United States has borrowed from their culture.

Explain how years are numbered in the Western world with 0 standing for Christ's birth and the division of dates into *b.c.* and *a.d.*

Model a Strategy

Read a Map Key

Model ways to understand a map key:

When I look at a map, I look for clues to help me use it. For example, page 118 has a color chart that tells me when Rome conquered different

(Continued on page T119)

CHAPTER 7

The Roman Empire

The Growth of Rome

The city of Rome began about 2,700 years ago. The first Romans farmed and took care of sheep and goats. From these small beginnings, the Romans built a great **empire.** They built a strong army that conquered all the land and people around the Mediterranean Sea. When the Romans were most powerful, about A.D. 116, they controlled most of Europe, including part of England.

Options for Reaching All Students

Beginning

Critical Thinking: Graphic Organizer

BLACKLINE MASTER

Have the students complete two graphic organizers to show their comprehension of the material in the text. Have them use an Idea Web (Blackline Master 20) to record four important facts about the ancient Romans. Then have them complete a T-chart (Blackline Master 22) for things the Romans borrowed and things they brought to the places they conquered.

Advanced

Critical Thinking: Cultural Exchange

Have students tell about things that they brought with them from their native country. Have them list things that they found in the United States that they did not find in their country. Have them list things from their country that they do not find in the United States. Have them discuss which things that they would like to share.

The Romans did more than win battles. They learned from the people they conquered. For example, they borrowed the idea of using coins for trade and commerce from the ancient Greeks. They even used the Greek gods, but they changed the gods' names.

The Romans also brought things and ideas to the people they conquered. They brought laws and government. They brought cities and buildings. They brought their language. These things lasted long after the Roman Empire itself had ended.

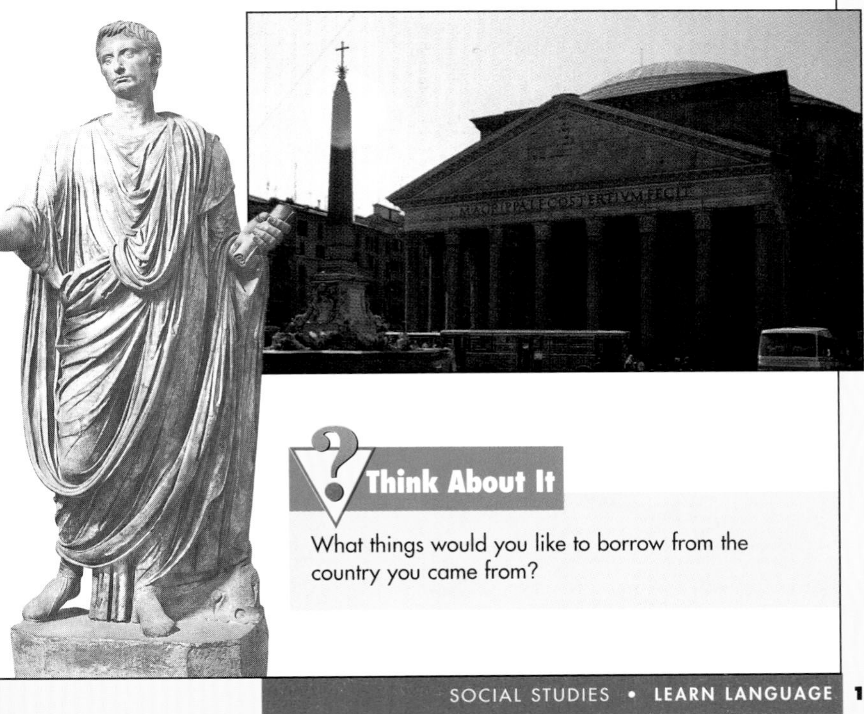

Think About It

What things would you like to borrow from the country you came from?

Language Awareness

Grammar

Past Tense: Regular and Irregular

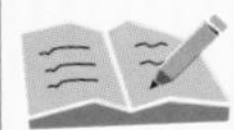

ACTIVITY BOOK

Have students look over the text to find regular past tense verbs. Examples are *farmed, used, changed, lasted,* and *ended.* Call attention to the various pronunciations of the ending: "t," "d," and "id." Then call attention to the irregular past tense verbs. Irregular verbs are *began, took care, built,* and *brought.* Invite students to tell two or three things about the ancient Romans and monitor their use of past tense. Use Activity Book page 62.

parts of the empire. Each color is a different time period. This helps me understand the growth of the Roman Empire.

Assess

Students should be able to

- briefly describe the development of the Roman empire
- list things the Romans borrowed from other people and things they brought to the people they conquered

LOOK **AHEAD**

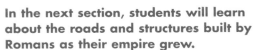

In the next section, students will learn about the roads and structures built by Romans as their empire grew.

Mixed Ability

Social Studies: Maps

Have students look at an up-to-date map of the Europe and the Mediterranean. Have students list the current names for the countries that the Romans conquered.

Home Connection

Countries' History

Have students ask their families what they know about the ancient history of their native countries. Encourage them to find out about the earliest beliefs, conquests, rulers, and other historical aspects that shaped their country. Then have them share the information with the rest of the class.

Practice

Activate Prior Knowledge

Brainstorm Vocabulary

Write the word *builders* on the board. Have them tell what builders make. Help them make a list of building words such as apartment buildings, skyscrapers, bridges, dams, roads, churches. Provide pictures, such as ones in picture dictionaries to help students' understanding.

Develop Language and Concepts

Present Pages 120 and 121

ACTIVITY BOOK

Read the text with students. As each paragraph is completed, fill in a graphic organizer with two columns—one with the heading *Building* and the other with the heading *Why was it built?* List roads, aqueducts, arenas and the reason they were built. Ask students to speculate why each of the structures was needed for the Roman Empire to grow. Point out to students that the armies built the first roads connecting Rome with a newly conquered area. Talk about the importance of a water supply for cities. Help students understand the function of an aqueduct with the diagram in the text. Ask if the arena was as important to Rome's growth as roads and water. Talk about the role of entertainment in daily life. Discuss the questions in Talk About It. Use Activity Book page 63 to review vocabulary related to the Romans.

The Romans were builders.

The Romans were good builders. Some of the things they built can still be seen today.

As the Roman Empire grew, the Romans built roads to connect the parts of their empire with Rome. Roman armies could move quickly throughout the empire on these roads.

The roads were well built. First, workers dug a ditch and filled it with stones. On top of this, they put stones that were cut to fit together closely. Many of these roads can still be seen today.

Options for Reaching All Students

Beginning

Art: Build Vocabulary

Have students plan a mural showing different kinds of buildings or things that builders build. Have them make the mural using paint, cut paper, or markers. Ask students to use the class list of building words to make labels for the buildings in their mural.

Advanced

Science: Ancient Building Methods

Have students work in groups. Assign each group the task of researching ways that heavy stones were cut, transported, and lifted in ancient times. Research will center mainly on levers, planes, and pulleys. Have each group construct a scale model or draw a diagram showing how ancient builders lifted heavy loads to great heights.

Mixed Ability

Social Studies: Research

Have students go to the library and report on two or three facts on the Roman Empire not mentioned in the text. Some might want to report on entertainment in arenas, transportation, or life in cities. Have students report the results in drawings, sentences, or paragraphs.

Romans also built tall structures called **aqueducts.** Aqueducts brought water into cities from places outside the cities. The water flowed in channels above tall arches. A few of these aqueducts still stand today.

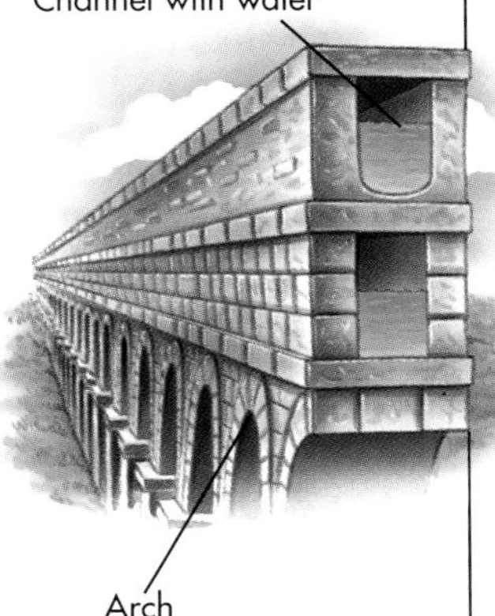

The Romans also built huge **arenas** throughout their empire. People went to these for entertainment. Fights between people and animals were popular. The large arena in Rome, called the Coliseum, held 50,000 people. People today still go to some of these arenas, to see sports events and musical performances.

Talk About It

Are there any old buildings near your school? What do they tell about the people who built them?

Should people save old things? Why?

Language Awareness

Grammar

Sentence Structure: The Verb *be* + an Adjective

Write the following sentences on the board:

The Romans were powerful.
Fights were popular.

Point out that the verb *be (was/were)* is often followed by words that describe: *powerful* describes *Romans* and *popular* describes *fights*. Invite students to make sentences to describe based on information in the text. *Aqueducts were useful. Many arenas were huge. Roman roads were strong.*

Model a Strategy

Find the Topic Sentence

Model using a topic sentence:

If I want to know what a paragraph is going to be about, the first sentence often gives a clue. In this text, the first sentence of several paragraphs names something the Romans built. The rest of the paragraph explains the thing.

Assess 

Students should be able to

- name things the Romans built

LOOK**AHEAD**

In the next section, students will read about Roman laws and citizens' rights.

Home Connection

Entertainment

Have students talk with their families about entertainment in the country their family is from. Have students share what they learn with the class.

Multicultural Connection

Old Buildings

Some cultures like the Italian culture have preserved ancient buildings and built modern cities around them. Point out that in the United States, there are preservation societies that prevent old buildings from being torn down. Despite this, many old buildings are torn down each year. Have students discuss old buildings in their native countries and how they are preserved.

Writer's Workshop

Monuments

Refer students to the Writer's Workshop on pages 230 to 236 in the Student Book. Have students write about an important monument that they have visited or that they would like to visit.

Practice

Activate Prior Knowledge

Discuss Law and Rights

Ask students why it is important to have laws. Ask, *Who is protected by laws? Who makes laws for people?*

Have students discuss rights that young people do not have. For example, in many states, a person has to be at least sixteen years old to drive. In some places, a curfew requires young people to be indoors by ten o'clock.

Discuss who has the right to vote in the United States. Explain that people who are at least eighteen years old and citizens can vote. Explain that in the past, various groups were not allowed to vote; for example, women could vote only after 1920. Also explain that *citizens* are people who are born in the United States or who have completed requirements to become naturalized citizens.

Develop Language and Concepts

Present Pages 122 and 123

ACTIVITY BOOK

Read the text with students. Ask students to define the word *rights*. Ask students what *rights* they have in school. List their answers on the board.

Discuss with students why at first only some people could vote in Rome and how that changed. Ask them why carving laws in stone and posting them was important.

Brainstorm a list of rules with the class for the Write About It activity. Use Activity Book page 65 to review the contributions of the Romans.

What was Roman law?

Early in their history, the Romans formed a republic. In a republic, **citizens** can vote. They can choose their rulers.

At first, only rich men were citizens. Then poor men demanded the right to vote. The poor men refused to serve in the army. Finally, the rulers let the poor men vote too. But women were never allowed to vote.

Poor people still felt that the law was not equal for all. So the rulers of Rome carved the laws in stone. These written laws came to be known as the Twelve Tables of Law. They were put in the forum, the center of town and of the government. Here everyone could read the laws.

Options for Reaching All Students

Beginning

Writing: Rules

Help students write rules that they followed in their old schools. Have them use the language in the Write About It as a guide.

Advanced

Social Studies: Citizenship

Have students research the requirements to become a citizen of the United States. Encourage them to interview people who have become naturalized citizens to learn about the process.

Mixed Ability

Language: Political Vocabulary

Have students make a list of words that relate to laws and politics in the chapter and use them in context sentences; for example, *republic, citizens, law, rights, rules.* Help students relate the words to current government in the United States.

It was an important step to have laws in writing. Now the law was the same for everyone, for rich people and poor people.

The stone tablets were destroyed during an attack on Rome, but the thinking behind them spread through the Roman Empire. Many nations copied the ideas of Roman law.

Write About It

Make a list of "laws" that everyone in your class follows. How do these laws help you and your classmates?

Language Awareness

Phonics
Hard and Soft *c*

ACTIVITY BOOK

Ask students to find words on pages 122 and 123 that begin with *c*, and list them on the board: *citizens, carved, came, center, could,* and *copied*. Ask them to name the sounds that *c* stands at the beginning of each word in the list. Then have them categorize each word according to its beginning sound. Ask them to identify what kind of letter follows the *c* in each of these words (a vowel). Help them find a pattern: words with *c* followed by *o* or *a* begin with a *k* sound and words with c followed by *i* or *e* begin with an *s* sound. Use Activity Book page 64.

Assess

Students should be able to

- explain the voting rights of ancient Romans
- explain how the laws of ancient Rome were changed and recorded

LOOK **AHEAD**

In the next section, students will learn about words in English that come from the Latin language of the Romans.

Cooperative Learning

Make Laws

Have all students talk about laws that govern the classroom. List those laws on chart paper. Ask students if any additional laws or changes are needed. Have students discuss and vote on any changes. Have students write the "laws" on paper that resembles stone tablets. Hang them on the wall.

QuickCheck

Past Tense

Check to see that students understand *past tense*. Ask them how most of the past tense verbs on pages 122 and 123 are formed. Check that they understand the use of *-ed* to form the past tense.

Connect

Activate Prior Knowledge

List Words

Write the names of all the languages that students speak on the board. Ask students if there are words in their languages that are similar to English words. Ask them to name them and make a separate list of them.

Develop Language and Concepts

Present Pages 124 and 125

Read the text with students. On page 124, connect the captions with the chart. For the second chart, have students use the dictionary to locate entries for the prefixes and add at least one more *pre-*, *re-*, and *uni-* word. Help students make wall charts of Latin roots, Latin prefixes, and Latin-derived words, which can be expanded as the unit progresses. Some roots are *port, duct, jus.* Talk about the questions in Think About It.

Model a Strategy

Use Prior Knowledge

Model the use of prior knowledge:

Because I have learned the meaning of special prefixes and word parts, I can use that knowledge to figure out the meanings of new words. I know that a word beginning with sub- may have something to do with below or under. I see the word subzero temperature. I can guess that is a temperature that is below zero.

Latin Words in English

Latin was the language of the ancient Romans. It was spoken all over their empire. Latin is no longer spoken, but the Spanish, French, and Italian languages come from Latin.

Some English words are made from parts of Latin words. A few of these are in the chart.

Latin Word Part	Meaning of the Latin Word Part	English Word
ped	foot	pedestrian, pedal
aqua	water	aquarium
vid	see	videotape

▲ A *pedestrian* goes places on foot. People on bicycles use their feet to push *pedals*.

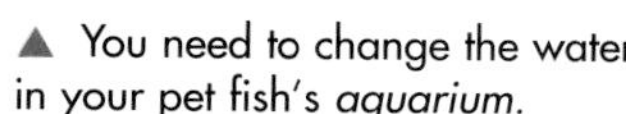

▲ You need to change the water in your pet fish's *aquarium*.

▲ You can see a *videotape* on your TV.

Options for Reaching All Students

Beginning

Language: Vocabulary

Divide students into teams. Have a student from one team act out or draw a picture that gives a clue to one of the words in the charts on pages 124 and 125 or other words they have learned in the lesson. Members of another team will use the clues to guess the word. The team that guesses the quickest gets one point. The game ends when each person has acted out a word for the other team.

Advanced

Language: Prefixes

List the following prefixes on the board: *un-, tri- , anti- , post-, sub-, trans-,* and *auto*. Have students use dictionaries and create charts similar to those in the text. When the students' charts are complete, have them cut out pictures from magazines and paste them collage-style on the chart, circling the portion of the picture that illustrates the prefix.

▲ This is Martha's room.

▲ Martha rearranged the furniture in her room.

Some English **prefixes** also come from Latin. A prefix is added to the beginning of a word. It adds to the word's meaning. For example, *re-* means "again." The word *arrange* means "to put in order." *Rearrange* means "to put in order again."

▲ Then she rearranged it once more.

Latin Prefix	Meaning	Example of English Word
pre-	before	pregame ("before the game")
re-	again	rewrite ("write again")
uni-	one	unicycle ("a bike with one wheel")

Think About It

What is the Latin word part in *aquaculture?* What do you think an aquatic animal is?

Are there any words from your native language used in English? What are they?

Does your native language use any words from English? What are they?

Language Awareness

Vocabulary
Prefixes

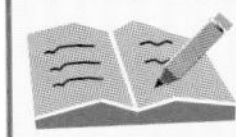

ACTIVITY BOOK

Review with students that the prefix *uni-* means "one." Then have them find the word *bicycle* in the caption at the top of page 124. Explain that *bi-* means "two" and point out that a bicycle has two wheels. Help students use dictionaries to find the meanings of these Latin prefixes: *post-, sub-, super-, dis-, inter-*. Have students write words with these prefixes and use them in sentences. Also discuss one of the most common prefixes in English, *un-*, which means "not," as in *unhappy,* but which is not of Latin origin. Use Activity Book pages 66 and 67 to review Latin prefixes and roots.

Assess

Students should be able to

- explain the importance of Latin
- show that parts of words have meanings
- show ways that languages share words

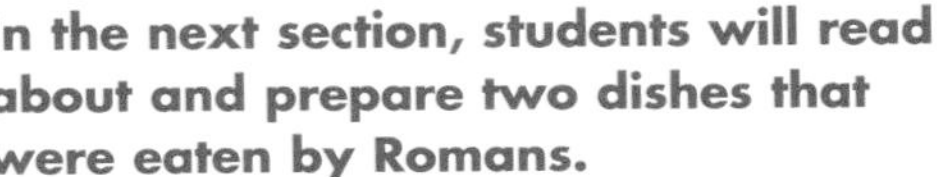

LOOK**AHEAD**

In the next section, students will read about and prepare two dishes that were eaten by Romans.

Cooperative Learning

Make a Prefix Game

Review meanings of prefixes *dis-, re-, pre-, uni-,* and *sub-*. Have students work in groups to make a card game. Have them write those prefixes on cards. On another set of cards, have students write words that can be combined with at least one of the prefixes. Have groups exchange cards, correctly match prefixes with words, and tell what the new words mean.

Connect

Activate Prior Knowledge

Brainstorm Vocabulary

Have students brainstorm lists of their favorite foods. Make a class chart of food words.

Develop Language and Concepts

Present Pages 126 and 127

Read the text with students. Explain that making a recipe requires two steps—gathering the ingredients and following the directions. Read ingredients and directions for making the salad. Clarify the meaning of words such as *break, drain, mix, toss,* and *place* by acting them out. Ask them if the recipes will make enough salad and dates to give everyone a taste. Then ask students to determine how much more or less of each ingredient is needed. Before making the salad, ask students what they think the salad will taste like: salty, sweet, bitter, or sour. Give examples of foods that fit the four senses of taste.

FYI

The dinner was the main meal for the ancient Romans. It usually consisted of three courses: an appetizer, often vegetables; a main course of fish, shellfish, or meat, together with side dishes; and a dessert of fruit, nuts, or confections. Bread and cheese were important staples.

Roman Recipes

Romans liked to eat good food. These two dishes could have been the appetizer and the dessert at a Roman banquet. Try these foods that the Romans ate.

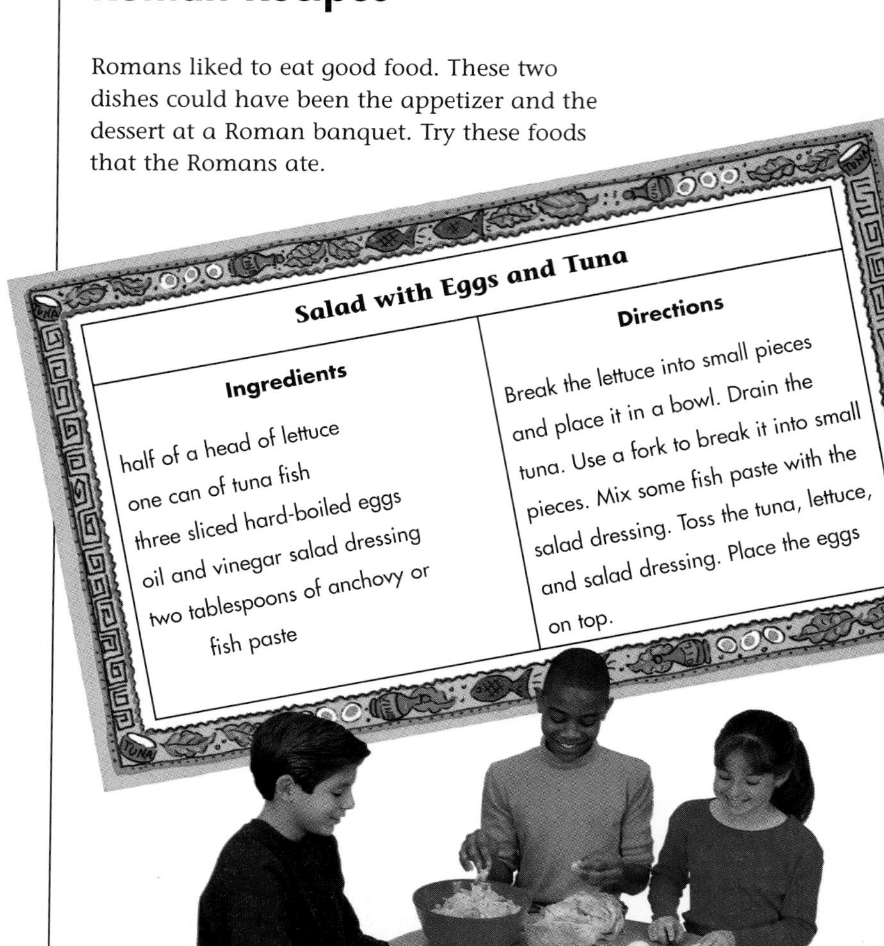

Salad with Eggs and Tuna

Ingredients	Directions
half of a head of lettuce one can of tuna fish three sliced hard-boiled eggs oil and vinegar salad dressing two tablespoons of anchovy or fish paste	Break the lettuce into small pieces and place it in a bowl. Drain the tuna. Use a fork to break it into small pieces. Mix some fish paste with the salad dressing. Toss the tuna, lettuce, and salad dressing. Place the eggs on top.

126 CONNECT LANGUAGE • SOCIAL STUDIES/READING

Options for Reaching All Students

Beginning

Language: Foods

Have students cut pictures from supermarket ads to make flash cards. Have them quiz each other and try to say both the food and package it comes in (for example, a box of eggs).

Advanced

Social Studies: Research

Have students research the foods that the ancient Romans ate and their eating customs (they ate reclining, they did not have forks, and so on).

Peer Tutoring

Language: Food Vocabulary

Give pairs of students of mixed abilities the following Picture Cards with foods: 2 apple, 11 cake, 14 carrots, 15 cheese, 19 cookies, 37 ice cream, 42 lemons/lettuce, 48 olives, 54 potatoes, 57 rice, and 67 strawberries. Students should use the cards as flash cards and work together until both can identify the foods.

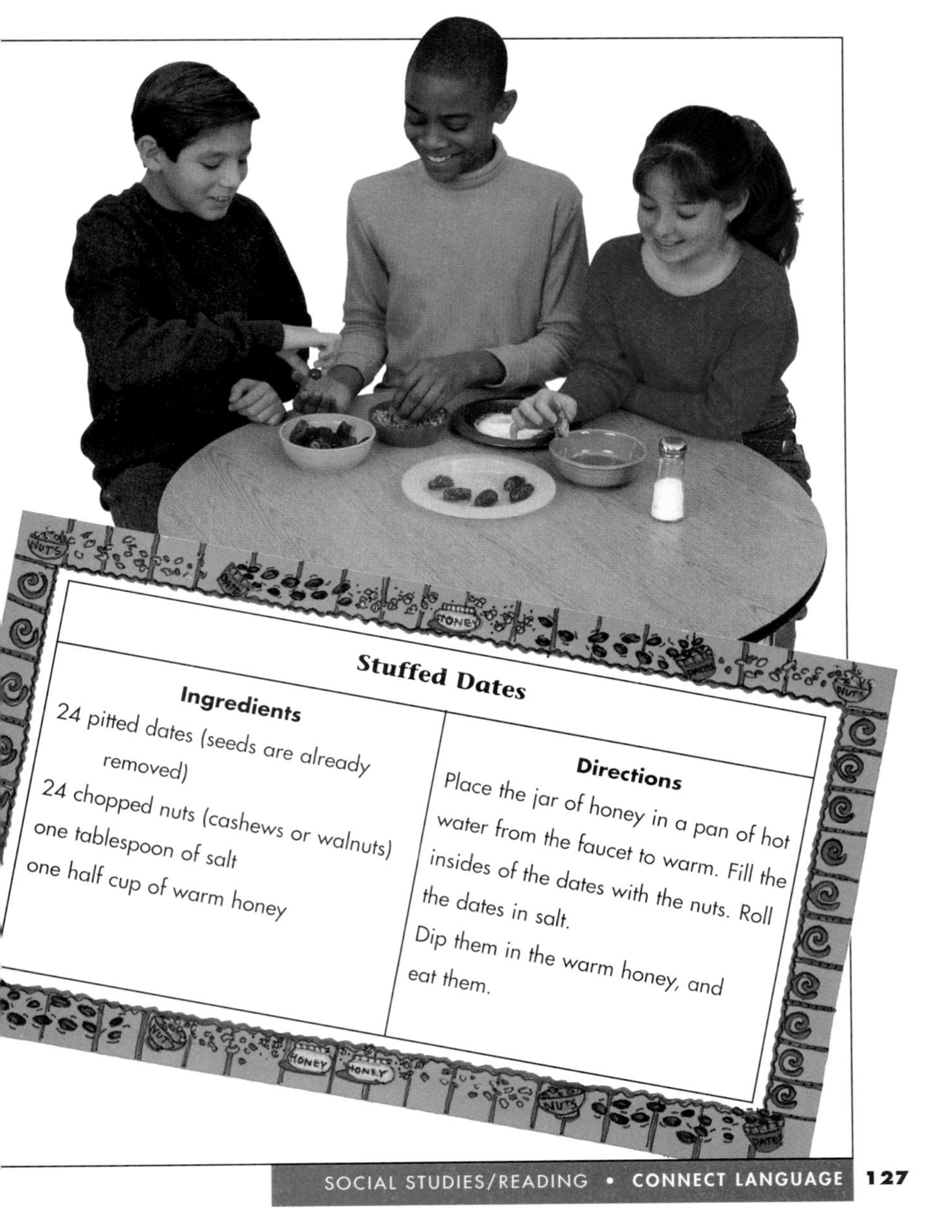

Stuffed Dates

Ingredients	Directions
24 pitted dates (seeds are already removed) 24 chopped nuts (cashews or walnuts) one tablespoon of salt one half cup of warm honey	Place the jar of honey in a pan of hot water from the faucet to warm. Fill the insides of the dates with the nuts. Roll the dates in salt. Dip them in the warm honey, and eat them.

Language Awareness

Grammar
Amount and Container Words

ACTIVITY BOOK

Have students list the measure or amounts for the ingredients in the recipes. Call students' attention to the ways amounts are indicated. The following are measurements:

one tablespoon of salt
one half cup of honey

Show measures to demonstrate the amounts. Then call attention to *a can of tuna*. Explain that a can is a container. Show other containers or pictures of other containers (for example, from supermarket ads) to expand vocabulary such as a *box* of cookies, a *bag* of chips, a *bottle* of water, a *carton* of eggs. Use Activity Book page 68.

Model a Strategy
Follow a Recipe

Model how to follow a recipe:

When I want to use a recipe to make a food, I am careful to follow directions. First I read through the recipe and gather the ingredients. Then I reread the directions to make sure I understand each step. As I make the recipe, I read and follow each direction in the order in which it is listed.

Cooperative Learning
Use a Recipe

Provide copies of real recipes for dishes students might enjoy, such as soup, a pasta dish, pizza, chili. Have each group choose a recipe. Ask them to prepare a chart showing a list of the ingredients including the amounts, steps to follow in making the recipe, and how many the recipe will serve. Ask them to adjust amounts if necessary to make enough for the class.

Cooperative Language Experience
Multicultural Food Day

Plan a Multicultural Food Day. Invite families to share a favorite food from their native land. Ask students to sign up for what they will bring. Have students plan for utensils, other necessities for eating, and a beverage. After students have eaten and cleaned up, write an experience story about Food Day. Ask students to include the countries and foods that were represented.

Connect

Activate Prior Knowledge

Brainstorm Art Media

Have students brainstorm a list of media that they have used for art projects, for example, watercolors, crayons, and oils. Discuss with them why some media are better suited for some types of art projects.

Develop Language and Concepts

Present Page 128

Read the background and directions for making a mosaic with students. Ask them where they think Romans put their mosaics. Have students work singly or in pairs to create mosaics.

Language Awareness

Grammar

Plurals

ACTIVITY BOOK

Review adding -*s* to nouns to make them plural, or mean "more than one": such as *pencil, pencils*. Point out that some nouns (noncount nouns) do not have plural forms, such as *glue*. A few words such as *scissors* have no singular forms. Help students form the singular and plural forms of nouns for classroom supplies. Use Activity Book page 69.

Make a mosaic.

The ancient Romans decorated their homes with mosaics. Mosaics are pictures made with small pieces of stone or glass.

Make your own mosaic.

Things You Need

 a large piece of cardboard

 a pencil

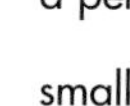 small pieces of colored paper or colored peas and beans

 glue

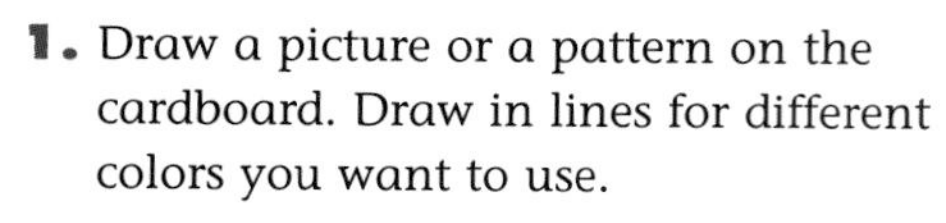 scissors

1. Draw a picture or a pattern on the cardboard. Draw in lines for different colors you want to use.
2. Put some glue on a small area of your drawing. Paste the pieces of paper or the beans onto that area. Repeat this step until your mosaic is filled in.

Options for Reaching All Students

Beginning

Language: Make a Game

PICTURE CARDS

Have students use picture cards of single objects. Students draw a card and tell how to form the plural. Other students should challenge the spelling if they question it. Use Picture Cards such as these: 3 baby, 11 butter, 15 cheese, 21 cup, 36 hot dog, 44 milk, 60 sandwich.

Advanced

Language: Give Directions

Give each students a piece of 8 1/2 X 11 inch graph paper. Distribute felt-tip markers. Tell students they must design a flag by coloring in the squares. After they have designed the flag, have them write directions and see if another student can reproduce the design.

Home Connection

Home Decoration

Asks students to bring in photos or examples of the ways that homes are decorated in their native countries.

Tell what you learned.

CHAPTER 7

1. How are the buildings of the ancient Romans like the buildings in a city today?
2. Why were the ancient Romans important?
3. English has borrowed Latin words and word parts. Give some examples of these.
4. What was the most interesting thing you learned about the ancient Romans?

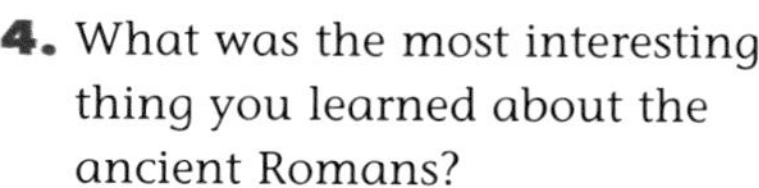

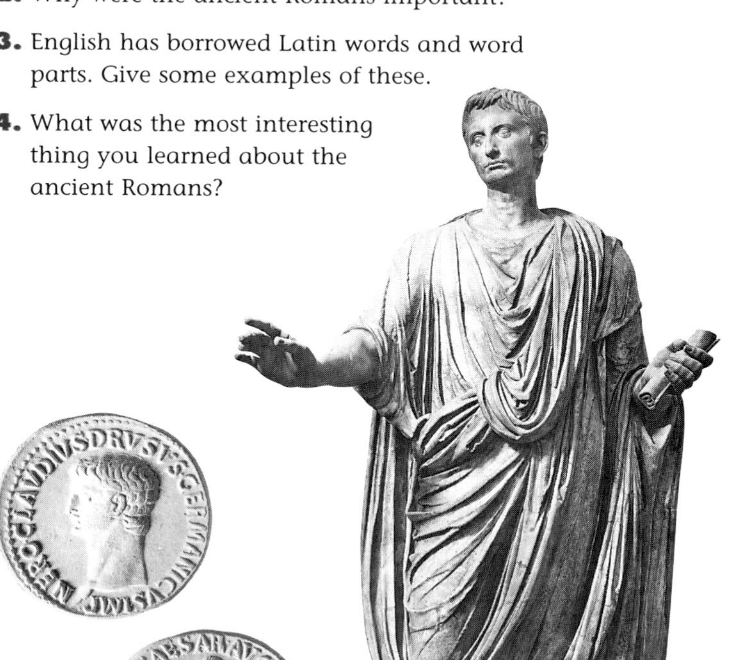

Assess

Activity 1: Evaluate whether students make parallels between ancient and modern buildings in function (arenas) and in style (use of columns).

Activity 2: Evaluate whether students can name several aspects of the legacy of the Romans, such as written law, language, and building styles and methods.

Activity 3: Check that students can name several words and word parts, either those on pages 124 and 125 or ones of their own.

Activity 4: Evaluate that students' responses show understanding of the ancient Romans.

Have students complete the Chapter Self-Assessment, Blackline Master 31. Have students choose the product of one of the activities to place in their portfolios. Add the results of any rubrics, checklists, self-assessments, or portfolio assessments, Blackline Masters 2–18 and 31.

Listening Assessment

Provide students with Blackline Master 71 from the Teacher's Resource Book. Play the tape several times and ask students to complete the activity.

See page T116c for the tapescript.

Options for Assessment

Vocabulary Assessment

New Words

Have students draw pictures of five new words they have learned. Ask them to label them and to use each word in a sentence.

Writing Assessment

Roman Booklet

Have students make a booklet in which they list the ten most important things they learned about the ancient Romans. Have students give three written examples of ways that Latin has influenced English.

Language Assessment

Use the Blackline Master 70 in the Teacher's Resource Book.

Standardized Test Practice

Use pages 70 and 71. Answers: **1.** arena where events were held **2.** the center of town **3.** citizens could vote to choose rulers **4.** structures that carried water

Preview

Activate Prior Knowledge

Relate Personal Experiences

Discuss natural disasters such as floods, earthquakes, and volcanoes with students. Encourage them to tell what they know about volcanoes. Ask if anyone has ever had an opportunity to see a volcano—active or inactive, or if they can name any volcanoes. Invite someone to draw a volcano on the board and label any parts that he or she can.

Develop Language and Concepts

Present Pages 130 and 131

Read the questions on page 130. Introduce the Word Bank words and help students use them to describe a volcano. Have students tell what the pictures show about volcanoes. Prompt responses such as they pour out fire and they can destroy things around them. Ask students to respond to the Talk About It questions. Tell students that they will be learning more about volcanoes. Develop a list of questions that students would like answered about volcanoes.

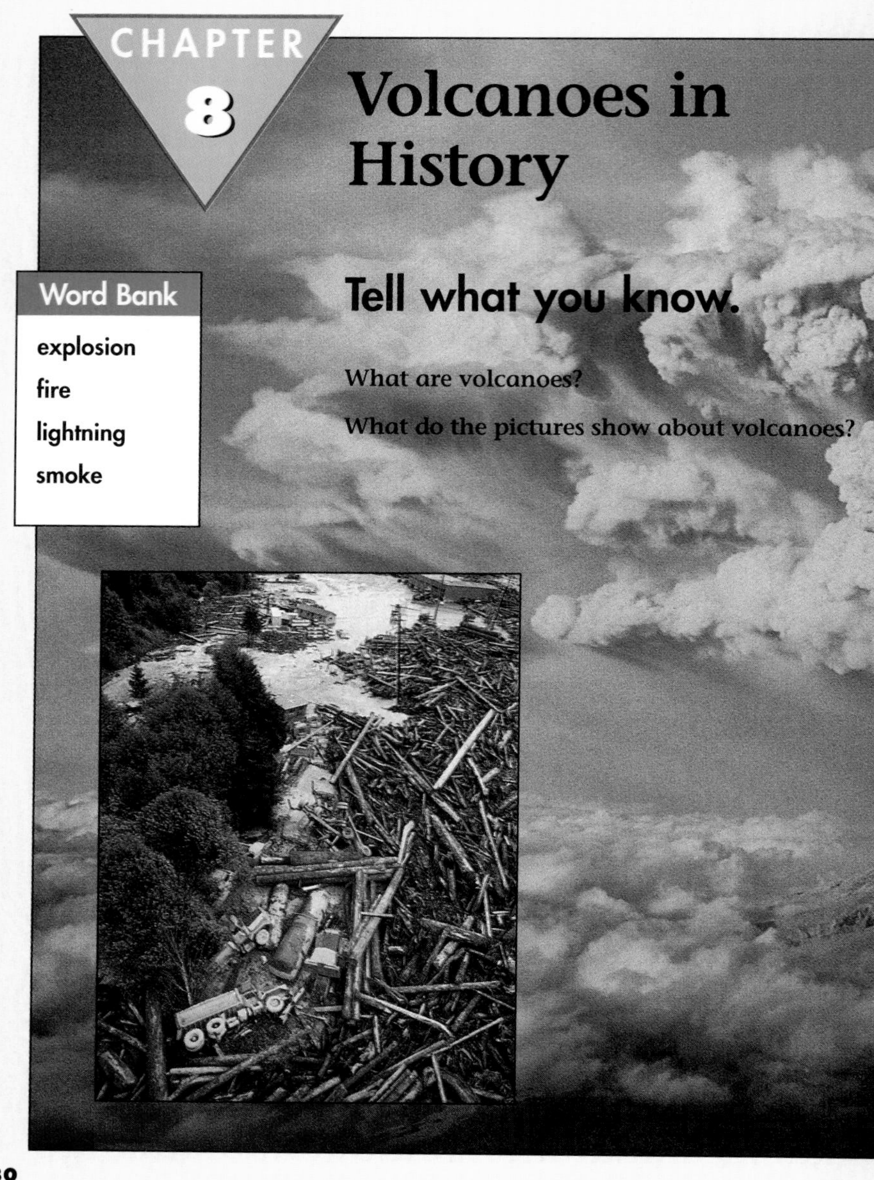

CHAPTER 8
Volcanoes in History
Word Bank
explosion
fire
lightning
smoke
Tell what you know.
What are volcanoes?
What do the pictures show about volcanoes?
130

Options for Reaching All Students

Beginning

Science: Volcano Research

Have students work with the school librarian or research materials to find out where Mount St. Helens is and when it has erupted. Have them record the dates of the eruptions on a chart and locate Mount St. Helens on a map.

Advanced

Science: Volcano Research

Have students work with the school librarian or research materials to find out about the volcanoes in the pictures in the book (Mount Etna and Hawaiian volcanoes) and two other volcanoes. They should find out where the volcanoes are located and when they last erupted.

Mixed Ability

Language: Feelings

Have students look again at the picture of Mount St. Helens erupting. Ask students to imagine that they lived near Mount St. Helens when it was erupting. Ask them what they would feel and what they would do. Help them brainstorm a list of words.

Talk About It
Would you live near a volcano? Why or why not?
Have you ever seen a volcano? What was it like?
131

FYI
The picture in the upper right is of Mount Etna in Sicily. Below it is a picture of a volcano in Hawaii. The rest of the photos are of Mount St. Helens. They show the effects of its major eruption in 1980.

Cooperative Learning

K-W-L Chart

BLACKLINE MASTER

Have students work in pairs and fill out a K-W-L chart about volcanoes. Have students add to their chart throughout the chapter. They can use Blackline Master 21.

Multicultural Connection

Natural Disasters

Review with students natural disasters that have been mentioned. Have students describe a natural disaster that happens in their native country, including the name for it in their native language. Make a list. Have students compare and contrast natural disasters and the places where they happen.

Present

Activate Prior Knowledge

Relate Personal Experiences

Review with students what they discussed about natural disasters in the previous lesson. Introduce the Word Bank words. Ask students for words for natural disasters. Students who have experienced natural disasters may want to share what happened. Invite students who have lived near an active volcano to share their own experiences and those of their family and friends.

Develop Language and Concepts

Present Pages 132 and 133

ACTIVITY BOOK

Before they read the selection, have students mark A.D. 79 on their timelines from the previous chapter and label it "Vesuvius Erupts." Introduce words that tell what came out of the volcano: *lava, ash, hot rocks,* and *poison gas.* Read the first paragraph with students. Have students locate Pompeii on the map and explain where it is in relation to Rome. Then read the rest of the lesson. Ask students to list what happened before and after the eruption. Have students complete Activity Book page 72.

Have students measure 12 feet with a tape measure (if your ceiling is not high enough, measure the distance against the wall) to find out how deep the ash and rocks were that covered Pompeii. Ask students the Talk About It question about predicting and preventing natural disasters.

A volcano erupts in A.D. 79.

Pompeii was a small town near Mount Vesuvius. The people who lived there in A.D. 79 did not know that Vesuvius was a volcano. It had been quiet for 800 years.

But Mount Vesuvius was going to **erupt.** When a volcano erupts, hot rock from deep under the earth bursts out. Hot liquid rock called **lava** often flows out of the volcano. Very tiny pieces of rock called **ash** may fill the air. Larger pieces of rock may also blow out.

▼ Mt. Vesuvius erupting in 1

Options for Reaching All Students

Beginning

Math: Subtraction

Have students use subtraction to determine how many years have passed since Mount Vesuvius erupted. Then discuss approximations with them and have them subtract to determine approximately how many years passed between the time that Mount Vesuvius erupted and the time the town was rediscovered in the 1700s.

Advanced

Language: Descriptive Writing

Ask students to imagine that they are in Pompeii at the time that strange things begin to happen prior to Mount Vesuvius's eruption. Have them decide whether they will go or stay and tell why. Have them write their thoughts as a journal entry.

Mixed Ability

Language: News Reports

Have students listen to radio and TV news reports about natural disasters and report on what they hear: where the disaster occurred and what the damage was, as well as any human-interest stories related to the disaster.

In August of A.D. 79, strange things began to happen at Pompeii. The earth shook. Animals became frightened. Water in wells dried up.

Then, on August 24, the top of Mount Vesuvius blew off. A huge cloud of ash came out of the volcano. Hot rocks fell from the sky. People tried to escape, but many were killed by the ash and the poison gas in the air. About 2,000 people died in Pompeii.

Twelve feet (four meters) of ash and rocks covered Pompeii. The town was forgotten until the 1700s. Then people began to dig it out.

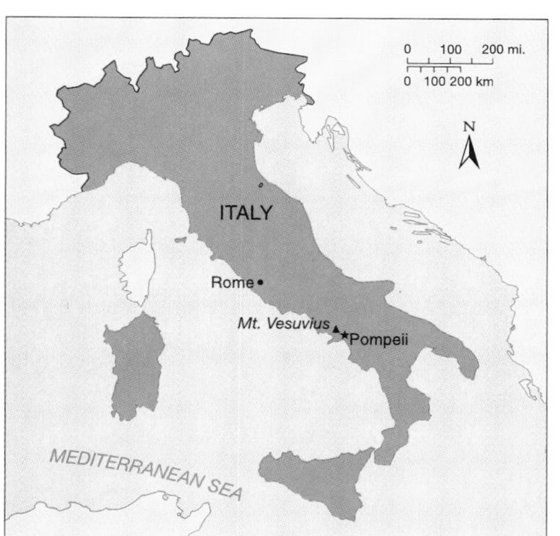

Word Bank

earthquake
flood
hurricane
storm

Talk About It

Volcanoes are just one natural disaster. What other natural disasters are there? What can people do to predict and prevent such disasters?

Language Awareness

Grammar
Verbs + Infinitives

Draw students' attention to the use of a verb plus an infinitive in the text. Write on the board:

People tried to escape.
Then people began to dig it out.

List other verbs that follow the same pattern such as *want to, learn to, hope to, need to, plan to.* Model sentences about yourself such as *I began to play the piano when I was six.* Encourage students to make similar sentences.

Assess 

Students should be able to

- explain what happened in Pompeii just before the eruption.
- describe the eruption of a volcano

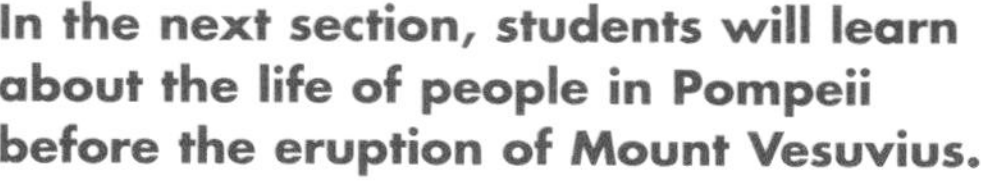

In the next section, students will learn about the life of people in Pompeii before the eruption of Mount Vesuvius.

Cooperative Language Experience

Volcano Stories

Read aloud some true accounts of people who have lived through volcanic eruptions. Several such books are available. Have students summarize the information they hear.

Home Connection

Interview

Have students interview older family members for their memories of natural disasters that occurred in their native lands. Have students share this information in an oral report to the class.

Practice

Activate Prior Knowledge

Relate Personal Knowledge

Have students talk about their town or city, describing what the center of town is like; where and what the markets or stores are like; where the theaters are; where and what the houses are like. Then discuss the roads and where water for the city comes from, and how it gets to their homes.

Develop Language and Concepts

Present Pages 134 and 135

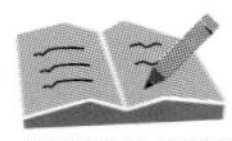
ACTIVITY BOOK

Have students study the photos on the pages and ask any questions that come to mind. Tell students that a photo essay is a combination of photographs and words. Read the text with students. Have students compare and contrast life in Pompeii to their modern life as they look at the photos and read the text. List on the board several items from the photos that are used today: roads, houses, town halls, places of worship, theaters, bakeries. Make two columns *Alike* and *Different.* Fill in the chart with students. Ask students to explain their conclusions. When the chart is finished, call on volunteers to summarize what is the same and different about life in Pompeii and modern life.

Have students do the Try It Out activity. You might use disposable cameras.

Vesuvius preserves the past.

When archaeologists dug out Pompeii and nearby places, they learned a great deal about the life of the ancient Romans. They found places just as they were when the volcano erupted in A.D. 79.

Pompeii's streets were made of stone. Some were narrow. There was only room for a donkey with baskets. Others were as wide as 23 feet (7 meters). Vehicles such as carts and chariots went down them.

Houses in ancient Rome often had a square garden in the center. This was called an atrium. The rooms were built on the four sides of the square.

Options for Reaching All Students

Beginning

Social Studies: Make Maps

Have students make a map of the school. Ask them to draw pictures of important places in the school that would help a future visitor or new students.

Advanced

Writing: Journal Entry

Have students pretend that they are visiting Pompeii with a team of archeologists. Have them write a journal entry about what they see.

Mixed Ability

Writing: Local Area Booklet

Have students prepare a booklet of stores and services near the school (such as hospitals). They should write and illustrate the booklet so that it can be used by students new to the school.

The forum was the center ▶ of town life. The government buildings were in this part of Pompeii. There was a law court. There was also a market. The most splendid buildings around the forum were temples to the gods. One was the temple of Jupiter, the king of the gods and the protector of Pompeii.

▲ This large outdoor theater in Pompeii had seats for 5,000 people. People went to see plays here. The actors in ancient times were as well known as movie stars today. Games in which animals were killed took place in a larger theater outside of Pompeii.

Try It Out

Make a record of a day in the life of your school. Take pictures. Label them and make a photo essay.

Language Awareness

Grammar
Passive Verbs

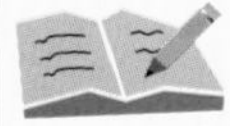

ACTIVITY BOOK

A verb is *passive* when the subject of the sentence does not do the action. Give students examples like these:

The Romans built the arena.
The arena was built by the Romans. (passive)

With the class, find and list other examples of the passive in the reading such as *Rooms were built on four sides* and list them on the board. Point out the passive is formed with the verb *be* + past participle. Point out that the past participle ends in *-ed* for regular verbs, but has a variety of forms for irregular verbs. For more practice with passive voice, have students complete Activity Book page 73.

Model a Strategy

Make Personal Connections

Model a way to make the past real:

When I read about people and places long ago, I ask myself after I finish each section: How is that like something I've seen or someplace I've been? That way, life long ago seems more real.

Cooperative Learning

Research

Have students work in groups to research one of the following topics: *Food, Clothing, Shelter, Entertainment,* in Pompeii/Rome. Groups should draw or use photos and explain their findings with labels, captions, and a brief oral presentation.

Practice

Develop Language and Concepts
Present Pages 136 and 137

Read the captions for the continuation of the photo essay. Continue to discuss with students the similarities and differences between life in Pompeii and modern life. Ask them to speculate about how archaeologists felt about the find at Pompeii. Discuss with them how such complete historical information is rare. Elicit their personal reactions to what it might have been like to live as an ancient Roman in Pompeii. Have students do the Write About It, comparing and contrasting life today and life of the ancient Romans. Use Activity Book page 74 to review content vocabulary about Roman life.

Model a Strategy
Summarize to Remember Information

Model how to summarize to remember information:

After I finished reading a section in a textbook, I always think over what I have just read. I try to ask myself, What is the important information in the text that I should remember? What information really interests me? When I stop and do this, I remember what I read better. For this photo essay, I quickly reviewed in my mind all the places that I saw pictured.

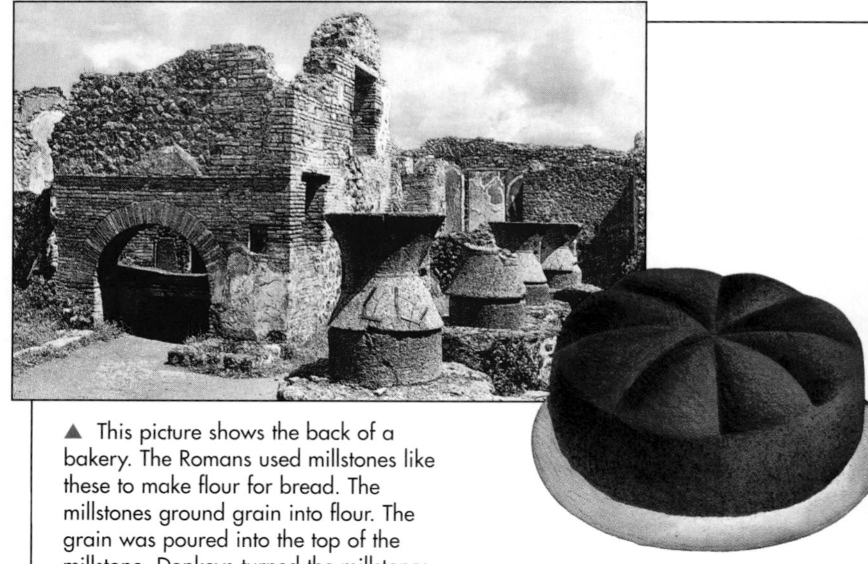

▲ This picture shows the back of a bakery. The Romans used millstones like these to make flour for bread. The millstones ground grain into flour. The grain was poured into the top of the millstone. Donkeys turned the millstones.

▲ The loaf of bread is from Pompeii. It is now as hard as rock. Round loaves of bread like these are still made in Italian bakeries.

This shop was a snack bar. People could eat while they stood up in the shop or they could take food out. This shop sold cereals and vegetables as well as hot dishes. ▶

Options for Reaching All Students

Beginning
Writing: Photo Essay

Have students look through magazines to find other examples of photo essays. Help them determine what the essay is about and then ask them to show and describe the essay to the class.

Advanced
Social Studies: Ancient Cities

Have students read other ancient sites excavated by archaeologists and list interesting things that the archaeologists have found.

Mixed Ability
Writing: Photo Essay

Have students create a photo essay of some other thing that interests them. It could be their neighborhood, a sport, artworks, clothes, and so on. Have them label or caption each of their photos and then present their photo essay to the class.

This is a kitchen set up to prepare a meal on the day the volcano erupted. Slaves would prepare food for the family using these pots and pans. ▼

▲ Glasses and dishes like these were widely used in rich people's homes.

Write About It

What things that you see in the pictures are like things people use today? What things are different?

Language Awareness

Spelling
Consonant Blends and Digraphs with *s*

ACTIVITY BOOK

Divide the class into three groups. Assign each group one of the captions and have them list the words in their caption which have an s. Then help them combine and narrow their lists to words that have consonant blends *(sn, sp, st)* and digraph *sh*: *show, millstone, still, shop, snack, sports, stadium, stood, dish,* and *slaves*. Model the pronunciation of each blend and digraph. Then ask students to list other words they know which use these blends and the digraph. For more practice, have students complete Activity Book page 75.

Assess 

Students should be able to

- explain how Pompeii helped archaeologists learn about the life of ancient Romans
- describe several aspects of the life of ancient Romans

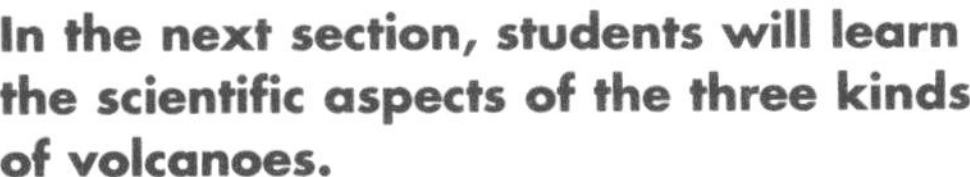

LOOK**AHEAD**

In the next section, students will learn the scientific aspects of the three kinds of volcanoes.

Cooperative Learning

Pompeii

Have students look through books about Pompeii, including picture books, and list more facts about the ancient city in addition to those in the Student Book.

Writer's Workshop

My Favorite Place

Refer students to pages 230 to 236 in the Student Book. Have students write about their favorite place to live. Is it the city or the country? Is it near the ocean or in the mountains? Students can write about places they have lived in or ones they would like to live in.

Connect

Activate Prior Knowledge

Review What Was Learned

Ask students to create a list of steps from the days leading up to the Mount Vesuvius eruption, to the aftermath. Have them use vocabulary from the preceding pages.

Develop Language and Concepts

Present Pages 138 and 139

ACTIVITY BOOK

Read the introduction with students. Discuss the definition of *volcano.* Encourage students to use the pictures and diagram to clarify their understanding of volcanoes. After you read the description of each type of volcano, stop and have a volunteer summarize the characteristics of that type of volcano. Ask students the kind of volcano in the diagram (a composite one, because of the layers). Have students complete Activity Book page 77 to review vocabulary related to volcanoes.

Model a Strategy

Use a Graphic Organizer

Model the use of a graphic organizer to keep track of major ideas and details:

When I need to keep track of information, I use a chart. In this case, I make a chart with three columns, one for each type of volcano. I put the name of each type at the top of a column. Then I will write details below. For example, for Shield Volcanoes, I write "lava flows out slowly."

What is a volcano?

Volcanoes are openings in the earth's surface. Hot rock from deep under the earth bursts out, or erupts. The eruptions cause mountains to form. The hot liquid rock that comes out of a volcano is called lava. Pieces of rock also may come out of a volcano.

▲ Paricutín in Mexico is a cinder cone volcano.

There are three kinds of volcanoes:

1. Shield volcanoes form when lava slowly flows through several openings in the earth. Over the years, the lava forms a low mountain. When a shield volcano erupts, there is not a big explosion.

2. Cinder cone volcanoes form when rocks shoot out of an opening in the earth. The rocks fall back to earth as cinders or small pieces of burned rock. The cinders form a cone-shaped mountain.

Mount Kilauea in Hawaii is a shield volcano. ▶

Options for Reaching All Students

Beginning

Art: Make Meaning with Pictures

Have students create a three-section mural, illustrating the three types of volcanoes. Have students label as many parts of the volcano as possible.

Advanced

Social Studies: Volcanoes

Have students work in three groups to find out more about each of the volcanoes shown on pages 138 and 139. They can use a map or atlas to locate Mexico, Hawaii, and Japan. Then ask them to research the eruption(s) of these volcanoes. Have them prepare a short presentation for the rest of the class.

Mixed Ability

Science: Make a Volcano

Have students work in pairs of mixed ability to make a volcano. Make sure that students take appropriate safety procedures before they do the experiment. Here are the directions.

What They Need: shallow pan, modeling clay, top of laundry detergent bottle, 1/4 cup water, 1 tablespoon of baking soda, a few drops liquid dishwashing detergent, 1/4 cup of vinegar.

3. Composite volcanoes are a mixture of the two other kinds. They form when eruptions of lava and cinders pile up to make high mountains. Some composite volcanoes have violent eruptions. Mount Vesuvius is a composite volcano.

Mount Fuji in Japan is a composite volcano.

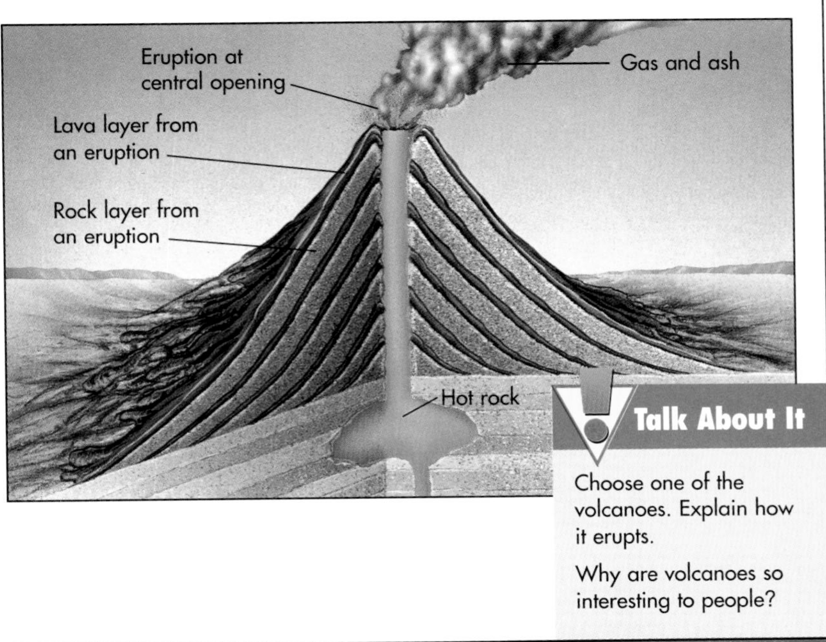

Talk About It

Choose one of the volcanoes. Explain how it erupts.

Why are volcanoes so interesting to people?

Language Awareness

Spelling
Capitalization: Proper Nouns

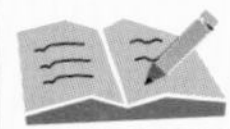

ACTIVITY BOOK

Explain or review that a *proper noun* is a specific person place or thing and that proper nouns in English begin with a capital letter. Point out that the captions on pages 138 and 139 tell about specific volcanoes and countries, whose names begin with capital letters. Encourage students to suggest other specific places they know that are proper nouns, such as the name of the school and of the town. Have volunteers write their suggestions on the board.

Assess

Use students' responses to Talk About It for assessment. Students should be able to tell about one kind of volcano.

LOOK **AHEAD**

In the next section, students will read a Roman myth about a god whose name provides the origin of the word *volcano* and a story about a Mexican farmer who had a volcano form in his field.

What To Do: Use the clay to model a volcano in the shallow pan. Scoop out hole in top and insert the laundry cap. Pour in water, baking soda, and dish-washing liquid. Stir. Pour in vinegar and watch the volcano erupt.

Cooperative Learning

Research

Have students work in groups to research volcanoes around the world. Have students add to the charts begun earlier in the chapter.

Connect

Activate Prior Knowledge

Review Learning

Review any information students know about the ancient Greek and Roman gods. Students who have completed Unit 2 should be able to give information.

Introduce the Selection

Tell students that they will be reading a Roman myth. Ask students why ancient people made up myths. Recall with students that ancient people often used myths to explain how the world works.

Language Awareness

Language Function
Discourse Connectors

Explain to students that some words help them understand the connection between ideas. For example, *After that* connects two events in sequence or gives a result. *So* indicates a result; the preceding sentence indicates the cause. *But* often suggests a contrast, something that you wouldn't think would happen. Have students find examples of these connectors in the text and read them in context. Give other examples so that students can better understand their meanings.

Read the Selection

GREEN TAPE

Read the selection with students. Read it again, presenting the Reader's Tips. Play the selection on Side 1 of the Green Tape.

Response Activities

Personal Response

Have students answer these questions:

Vulcan prefers to work and be alone. Do you know someone who is a "loner"? Why do you think that person prefers to be alone?

Critical Response

Have students answer the questions:

Think back on what you have learned about myths. How is the story of Vulcan a good example of a myth? What more do you know about myths from reading the story?

Creative Response

Vulcan liked to make things out of metal. Have students think about things that they have made or could make that they would be proud to show.

Options for Reaching All Students

Beginning

Language: Make a Story Board

Have students work in groups to produce various segments of the Vulcan myth. Each group should take one event in the story, illustrate it, and write one sentence to describe the action.

Advanced

Language: Write a Myth

Have students create their own myths. Possible questions that can produce a mythic answer might be: *Why do leaves fall from trees? Why do frogs croak? Where do hailstones come from?*

Home Connection

Myths

Have students research myths and/or gods from their native lands. Have them share this information with illustrations and an oral presentation.

An Ancient Roman Myth: The God Vulcan

Like the ancient Greeks, the ancient Romans believed in gods and goddesses. Gods made good things and bad things happen to humans. Stories about the gods and what they did are called myths.

Of all the gods and goddesses, Vulcan was the only one who was born ugly. He was the son of the most important and powerful of the Roman gods, Jupiter and Juno.

Reader's Tip
In Roman myths, the god Jupiter and his wife Juno were often fighting with each other.

Vulcan lived on Mount Olympus with the other gods and goddesses. But then one time he took his mother's side in an argument with Jupiter. In a fit of anger, Jupiter threw Vulcan from Mount Olympus. After the fall, Vulcan was lame as well as ugly. And he no longer lived with the other gods.

Vulcan became an expert at metalworking. He used fire to heat metal. Then he hammered the metal into tools for farmers or weapons for soldiers. When he hammered, sparks flew. Vulcan liked to work inside mountains. There no one would bother him.

Language Tip
Vocabulary
Lame means not being able to walk well because a person has an injured leg or foot.

After a while, Jupiter decided to use Vulcan's skill. He wanted Vulcan to make thunderbolts of metal. Jupiter planned to use the thunderbolts as a warning. They would let people know when he was unhappy with what they were doing. Vulcan agreed to make the thunderbolts. After all, Jupiter was the most powerful god.

Vulcan worked hard. Sparks flew out of his mountain night and day. The thunderbolts that Vulcan made were very beautiful and very frightening. Jupiter was quite pleased with them. After that, Vulcan was again welcome at Mount Olympus.

But Vulcan kept on doing his beautiful metal work. He was happiest when he was inside a mountain working over a fire.

When people saw a mountain explode with smoke, sparks, and hot lava, they thought Vulcan was inside the mountain working. So they called mountains that threw out fire volcanoes after Vulcan, the god of fire.

Strategy Tip
Stop and Think
This myth tells the origin of two things in nature. What are they?

Connect

Activate Prior Knowledge

Review Vocabulary

Ask students what words they can think of to describe the activity of a volcano. List their answers on the board.

Introduce the Selection

Before they read the selection, ask students to study the illustrations. Ask students whether the story takes place in the country or in the city. Ask students whether the story happened now or in ancient times or in a time not too long ago. Tell them that the story they are about to read happened in Mexico in 1943. Have them do the math to find out how long ago the story took place. Talk with students about differences between a nonfiction account and a story based on real events. Tell them that this story uses events that really happened but makes up characters. These characters may be like real people who lived through the event, but they are not actual people.

FYI

This story is excerpted from the book *Hill of Fire* by Thomas Lewis (1971) published by Harper and Row.

Read the Selection

GREEN TAPE

Read the selection with students. Then read it again, presenting the Reader's Tips. Play the story on Side 1 of the Green Tape.

Language Awareness

Grammar

Prepositional Phrases of Direction

Call students' attention to direction words. Read sentences with prepositions of directions, such as *Fire and smoke came from the ground.* Have volunteers illustrate them on the board or pantomime them. Other possibilities are *to, toward, inside, out of.*

Options for Reaching All Students

Beginning

Language Arts: Plot

Ask pairs of students to write the main events of the story on separate pieces of paper. Have them mix up the pieces and give them to another pair, who puts them in order.

Advanced

Writing: Create a Myth

Have students work in groups to develop a myth about the hole in the ground told from the point of view of Vulcan. Tell the students that the plow opened a hole in Vulcan's underground workshop. The students' myth should tell what Vulcan did and why.

Cooperative Learning

History: Natural Disasters

Have students work in groups to research—using the encyclopedia, the World Almanac, or books on weather—other natural disasters such as earthquakes, tornadoes, hurricanes, and floods. Have them report on some of the effects of the disasters. Have them find out about people's efforts to predict such disasters.

Hill of Fire

by Thomas P. Lewis

Reader's Tip
This story takes place in Mexico. When the story begins, a young boy, Pablo, is helping his father to plow the family's cornfield.

The ox pulled, and the plow turned up the soil. Suddenly the plow stopped. The farmer and his son pushed, and the ox pulled, but the plow did not move. It sank into the earth. It went down, down, down into a little hole.

The little hole became a bigger hole. There was a noise deep under the ground, as if something big had growled.

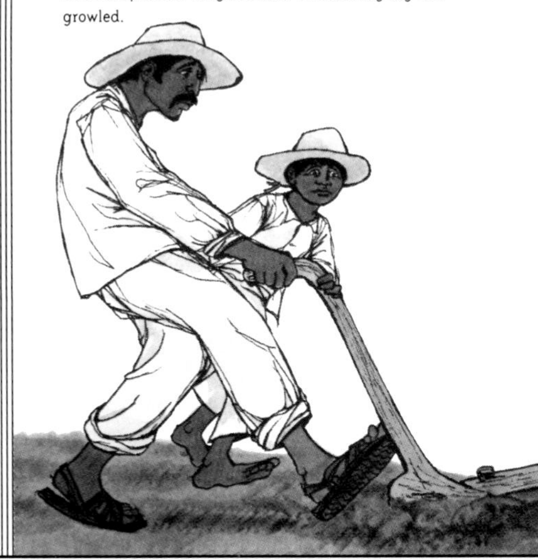

The farmer looked. Pablo looked. The ox turned its head. White smoke came from the hole in the ground.

"Run!" said the farmer. "Run!"

There was a loud CRACK, and the earth opened wide. The farmer ran, Pablo ran, and the ox ran too. Fire and smoke came from the ground.

The farmer ran all the way to the village. He ran inside the church and rang the old bell.

The other farmers came from their fields. People came out of their houses. "Look!" said the farmer. "Look there!"

Language Tip
Sound Words
Some words in English are sound words. *Crack* means a sound like the one you make when you say the word. As you read on, look for another sound word.

That night no one slept. Everyone watched the fire in the sky. It came from where the farmer's field had been.

There was a loud BOOM, and another, and another. Hot lava came out of the earth. Steaming lava spread over the ground, through the trees. It came toward the farmer's house. It came toward the village. Pieces of burning stone flew in the air.

Strategy Tip
Stop and Think
Use what you learned in this chapter. What do you think is happening? How do you know?

Strategy Tip
Stop and Think
Why did no one sleep that night?

Strategy Tip
Personification
Authors sometimes compare things and animals to people. Here the author says the earth was coughing. Coughing is an action that people do.

Connect

Develop Language and Concepts

Present Pages 148 Through 153

ACTIVITY BOOK

Ask students to describe what has happened so far in the story. Have students describe the process or the steps in the formation of the volcano. Ask, *Why do the people think the crosses will protect them? How or to whom might the people pray to be saved from a volcano?*

After students have read the story, have them complete Activity Book page 79 to check comprehension.

Language Awareness

Grammar

Past Tense: Regular and Irregular

Review the past tense. Have students look for examples of verbs that use *-ed* to form past tense: *carried, prayed,* and *stopped.* Point out the spelling rules. Then, ask them to look for more examples of irregular past tense: *flew, led, went, came, rode,* and *gave.*

Model a Strategy

Visualize a Story

Model a way to visualize a story to improve comprehension:

When I read, I try to picture in my mind the events that are happening. This part of the story tells about the volcano growing and farming. I try to picture all the things that are happening—the sound of the boom, the animals running, the feel of the burning ash.

Response Activities

Personal Response

The farmer, the boy, and the people in the village have a noteworthy experience: they see the formation of a volcano. Have students write about a noteworthy or interesting experience they have had.

Critical Response

The people in the village call the volcano "The Monster" as though it were alive. Ask students why they think the people thought of the volcano as a monster.

Creative Response

The story uses description to help the reader experience the formation of the volcano. For example, sound words are used. Have students write a description of something they have experienced; for example, attending a sports event. Help them revise their description and add words that help the reader "see" the experience.

Options for Reaching All Students

Beginning

Language Arts: Motivation

Have students imagine that they have to flee like the villagers. They can only take a backpack with their most precious items. What they can put in the backpack is all they can have from their home. Have students draw and label the items that they would take.

Advanced

Language Arts: Point of View

Have students work in groups and retell the story from any of the following points of view: the ox, the volcano, the farmer's son as an old man remembering the incident, or one of the soldiers who made the villagers leave.

Mixed Ability

Language: Role-Play

Have students role-play an interview from a news reporter and Pablo and his father. The reporter asks about what happened in the field and how the volcano grew.

Language Tip
Vocabulary
A *burro* is a small donkey.

Study Tip
Use What You Know
As you read any story, use what you know to help understand it better. As you read this story, you can use what you know about volcanoes and volcano eruptions to help you understand what is happening in the story.

The earth was coughing. Every time it coughed, the hill of fire grew bigger. In a few days the hill was as big as a mountain. And every few minutes there was a loud BOOM. Squirrels and rabbits ran, and birds flew away from the fire. People led their burros and their oxen to safety.

Pieces of burning ash flew everywhere. The farmer and his neighbors put wet cloths over their noses to keep out the smoke.

Some of the people went close to the steaming lava. They carried big crosses. They prayed for the fire to stop. The farmer and Pablo watched from the side of a hill.

When the booming stopped and the fires grew smaller, the farmer's house was gone. The school was gone. The market was gone. Half the village was gone.

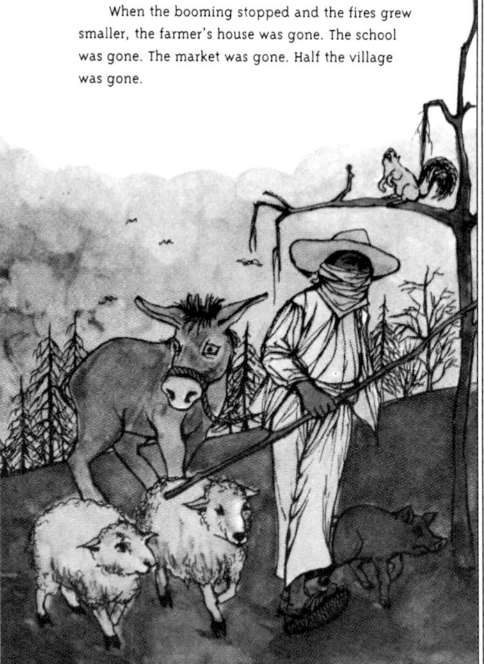

Strategy Tip
Cause and Effect
In this part of the story, the author is talking about the effects of the volcano. What are they? Find them in the story.

Strategy Tip
Stop and Think
Why do the soldiers laugh? Did the farmer really cause the volcano to erupt and form?

Language Tip
Vocabulary
Amigo is the Spanish word for friend.

One day some men in uniform came in cars and trucks.

"So you are the one with the plow that opened up the earth," they said to the farmer.

They laughed.

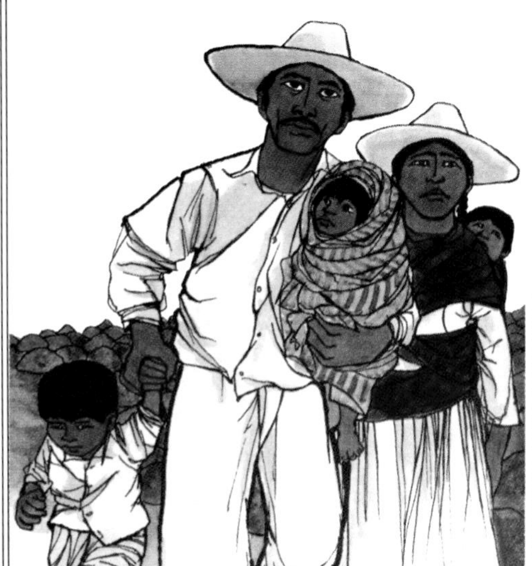

"You are lucky to be alive, *amigo.*"

The soldiers looked at the village. "Everyone must go!" the captain said. "It is not safe to live here any longer." The farmer and his wife and Pablo and all the people of the village went with the soldiers. They rode away in the trucks.

The farmer found a new house. It was bigger than the one they lived in before.

It was not far from the old one. But it was far enough away to be safe from *El Monstruo,* which means "The Monster." That is the name the people gave to the great volcano.

Reader's Tip
This story is based on a true event. The volcano Paricutín in Mexico began to form in 1943 from a hole in a cornfield. When the volcano stopped erupting in 1952, it was 1,345 feet (410 meters) tall. It is a cinder cone volcano.

Connect

Activate Prior Knowledge

Brainstorm Vocabulary

Have students list words to describe a volcanic eruption.

Develop Language and Concepts

Present Page 152

GREEN TAPE

Read the poem with students. Ask them what words make the volcano seem like a person. Explain the meaning of *rumble* and *grumble* as words that suggest sounds. Play the poem on Side 2 of the Green Tape several times and invite students to join in the recitation.

Language Awareness

Phonics
The Letter *v*

Review the sound the letter *v* stands for with students. Have them practice putting their front teeth to their lower lips to say the sound. Next, have them brainstorm a list of words they know that have the letter *v* in them. Then help them categorize where the *v* sound comes in the word: beginning, middle, or end.

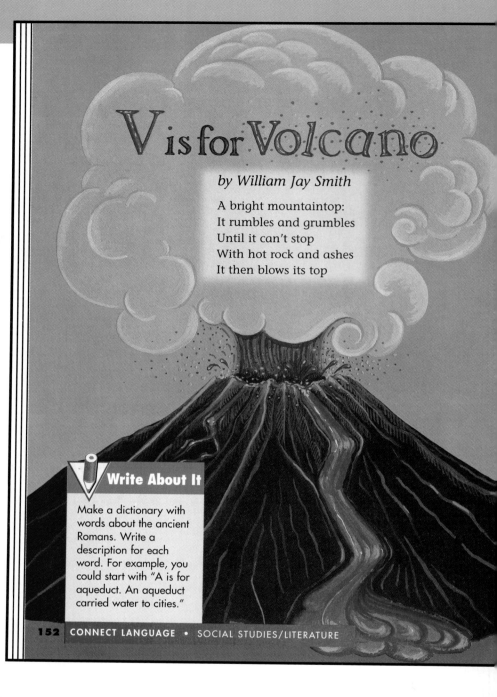

V is for Volcano

by William Jay Smith

A bright mountaintop:
It rumbles and grumbles
Until it can't stop
With hot rock and ashes
It then blows its top

Write About It

Make a dictionary with words about the ancient Romans. Write a description for each word. For example, you could start with "A is for aqueduct. An aqueduct carried water to cities."

Options for Reaching All Students

Beginning

Language: Alphabet Books

Have students make personal alphabet books. Present examples to students (there are some at all levels of sophistication). Students can choose to have all the words relate to one theme or pick their favorite words that begin with the letters.

Advanced

Language: Write a Story Book

Have students write a simple children's story—one or two sentences per page—about a child who sees a hole in his backyard and discovers that the hole is making angry, rumbling noises. What happens next? Does the yard begin to rise? Do houses in the neighborhood slide off the volcano?

Mixed Ability

Language: Poetry

Have students work in groups to create a selection of various "volcano" poems. Forms might include: the shape of a volcano with the interior from the top down made of words, phrases, then sentences telling about volcanoes; the word *volcano* written vertically, using each letter in the word as a letter in a word or phrase about volcanoes.

Tell what you learned.

CHAPTER 8

1. Imagine that you are a reporter for a newspaper in a town near Pompeii. Tell about the volcano blowing up.
2. Pretend you are a tour guide for Pompeii. Make an advertisement for your tour. Draw pictures of the places and artifacts you show. Label the pictures. What do those places and artifacts tell you about the people who lived there?
3. In the story "Hill of Fire," the boy and his father had to move to a new place. Why do you think they chose to stay nearby?
4. Create a city. What would you include?

Assess

Activity 1: Evaluate the detail and accuracy of their responses from before, during, and after the eruption.

Activity 2: Evaluate students' knowledge of places, and artifacts, as well as of the lives of people who lived there.

Activity 3: Check to see if student responses take into consideration the people, the setting, and the events that happened.

Activity 4: Evaluate students' ability to connect personal experience and what they learned in this unit about cities.

Have students complete the Chapter Self-Assessment, Blackline Master 31. Have students choose the product of one of the activities to place in their portfolios. Add the results of any rubrics, checklists, self-assessments, or portfolio assessments, Blackline Masters 2–18 and 31.

Listening Assessment

BLACKLINE MASTER

Make sure each student has a copy of Blackline Master 73, from the Teacher's Resource Book. Play the tape several times. Ask students to write down the sentences they hear dictated.

CREAM TAPE

See page T116d for the tapescript.

Options for Assessment

Vocabulary Assessment

Play Pictionary

Ask students to review vocabulary from the chapter and create a list of words, writing them on individual slips of paper. Then divide students into teams and have them play "pictionary:" they select a word and then draw a picture of it, one piece of the drawing at a time, the team who guesses it first wins a point.

Writing Assessment

Write a Letter

Have students imagine that they have witnessed a volcano eruption. Ask them to write a letter to a friend describing what they saw, heard, and smelled.

Language Assessment

BLACKLINE MASTER

Use the Blackline Master 72 in the Teacher's Resource Book.

Standardized Test Practice

ACTIVITY BOOK

Use pages 80 and 81. Answers: **1.** $43.75 **2.** 243 **3.** $69.80 **4.** 1 2/3 hours

Wrap-Up

Activities

Compare and Contrast

Take time to talk about similarities and differences between the ancient Romans and our society today. Help them to consider both the differences in technology and the many things about their lives that are parts of peoples lives today. Make a Venn diagram with them, showing differences and similarities. Ask students what they would most like to do or see if they could visit ancient Rome for a day.

Latin Language

Present students with several Latin roots and words derived from them in English. Have students make trees with the various words on the "branches." The students should look in a dictionary to find the definition the word, write it down, and illustrate the word in a related context sentence and accompanying drawing. Examples are *amor/amicus "love"/"friend" (amiable, amorous), dict "say" (dictate, dictation, predict).*

Discussing the Theme

Review with students the information they learned about Roman life. Choose from the following activities that will demonstrate to them how much they have learned about Roman life, how life was similar to modern-day life:

- Have students tape-record a list of new words learned.
- Have students gather the photographs and drawings they collected in their research. Have them label pictures or drawings and make a bulletin board display.
- Have students study a map of their city or town, locating the marketplaces, churches, bridges, courthouses, and any other structures discussed in the unit.
- Discuss the fact that there are still ruins of ancient buildings all over the world. Ask students to describe old buildings and ruins they know about in the United States and in their native countries.

Sharing the Project

Use the invitation form, Blackline Masters 32–33, to invite family members to school for Roman Day.

In an organized audience setting, have each group of students present the part of Roman life that they researched. Encourage them to use the vocabulary they learned in the unit to describe the many aspects of life of the ancient Romans. Also encourage them to use the pictures and drawings on the bulletin board to draw comparisons between ancient Roman and modern times.

Encourage informal question-and-answer style discussion among families and students about life for the ancient Romans.

For refreshments you may ask volunteers to fix the dishes included in the unit: salad with eggs and tuna, and stuffed dates.

Signs of Success!

Duplicate a copy of this checklist for each student.

Name: ____

Refer to the checklist below for a quick demonstration of how a student is progressing toward transitioning out of ESL instruction.

Objectives

- ☐ Understands the ancient Romans and their contributions
- ☐ Tells how the Romans built their empire
- ☐ Describes the ancient Romans as builders
- ☐ Identifies Latin words in English
- ☐ Describes a volcano
- ☐ Discusses what archaeologists learned from Pompeii
- ☐ Retells an ancient Roman myth

Language Awareness

Understands/Uses:

- ☐ past tense: regular and irregular
- ☐ quantity words: *many, few, some*
- ☐ prefixes
- ☐ amounts and container words
- ☐ plurals
- ☐ verbs and infinitives
- ☐ passive verbs
- ☐ capitalization: proper nouns
- ☐ prepositional phrases of direction

Hears/Pronounces/Reads:

- ☐ hard and soft *c*
- ☐ consonant blends and digraphs with *s*
- ☐ the letter *v*

Learning Strategies:

- ☐ Reads a map key
- ☐ Finds the topic sentence
- ☐ Activates prior knowledge
- ☐ Makes personal connections
- ☐ Summarizes to remember information
- ☐ Uses a graphic organizer

Comments

____

Planning Guide

What Makes Things Move?

Objectives

Explain why objects move.

Identify everyday activities that use motion.

Experiment with friction and gravity.

Explain why things move and why they stop.

Vocabulary Focus

Motion words, such as *blow, hit, kick, throw.*
Words for everyday action, such as *eat, sleep.*
Words to describe motion, such as *slower, fastest, stronger.*

Lesson	Content Focus	Language Awareness Objectives	Learning Strategies
Preview pp. 154–155 Tell What You Know.			
Present pp. 156–157 What Makes Things Move?	Science	**Grammar** Present Tense	
Practice pp. 158–159 Friction	Science	**Vocabulary** Shape Words	
Practice pp. 160–161 Gravity	Science	**Grammar** Comparisons with *-er*	Predict.
Connect pp. 162–163 Can Friction and Gravity Change a Marble Race?	Science/Math	**Grammar** Superlatives with *-est*	Monitor work.
Connect pp. 164–171 *The Tug Of War*	Science/Literature	**Spelling** Quotation Marks for Dialogue **Vocabulary** Action Words	Use context clues to find meaning.
Connect p. 172 "There's Motion Everywhere"	Science/Literature	**Spelling** Rhyming Words with Different Spellings	
Assess p. 173 Tell What You Learned.			

Physics of Roller Coasters

Objectives

Explain how a roller coaster works.

Experiment with the forces that make a roller coaster run.

Learn about synonyms in English and the use of a thesaurus.

Vocabulary Focus

Words that describe one's feelings on a roller coaster ride, such as *exciting, fun, scary.*

Words related to roller coasters, such as *curve, twist.*

Things that affect how far a roller coaster goes, such as *gravity, friction, energy.*

Words that mean to move quickly, such as *rush, zoom,* or to move slowly, such as *inch, crawl.*

Lesson	Content Focus	Language Awareness Objectives	Learning Strategies
Preview pp. 174–175 Tell What You Know.			
Present pp. 176–177 How Does a Roller Coaster Work?	Science	**Grammar** Words That Show a Sequence	
Practice pp. 178–179 What Things Affect How Far a Roller Coaster Goes?	Science	**Vocabulary** Expressions with *up*	
Practice pp. 180–181 What Forces Work Together on a Roller Coaster?	Science	**Grammar** Conditional Sentences	Visualize.
Connect pp. 182–183 Can a Taller Roller Coaster Give You a Longer Ride?	Science/Math	**Vocabulary** Math Words for Averaging	How to read a chart.
Connect pp. 184–187 Riding the Scream Machine	Science/ Reading	**Language Function** Express Excitement	Understand words with multiple meanings.
Connect pp. 188–189 Using a Thesaurus	Science/ Reading	**Vocabulary** Synonyms and Antonyms	Use word groups to remember new words.
Connect p. 190 "Let's Twist Again"	Science/ Literature	**Vocabulary** Slang	
Assess p. 191 Tell What You Learned.			

Resources

Chapter 9

Support Materials

PICTURE CARDS

numbers 3, 4, 5, 17, 18, 22, 24, 40, 53, 61, 62, 63, 68

ACTIVITY BOOK

pages 82-91

VIDEO

Unti 5, The Physics of Fun

BLUE TAPE

Side 1

The Tug Of War, pages T164–T171

BLUE TAPE

Side 2

"There's Motion Everywhere," page T172

DISK

Writer's Notebook

Assessment Materials

BLACKLINE MASTER

Language Assessment, Blackline Master 80

Listening Assessment, Blackline Master 81

CREAM TAPE

Side 1

Listening Assessment, page T173

Listen carefully and follow the directions.

1. Circle the drawing that shows a force making something move.
2. Friction is a force that slows things down. Circle the drawing that shows friction slowing something down.
3. Circle a picture that shows gravity pulling something to the ground.

Newcomer Book C

Survival language for absolute beginners. For overview, see pages xxviii–xxix.

For Extended Reading

Isaac Newton, Reluctant Genius by D.C. Ipsen, Enslow Publishers, Inc., 1985

A biography of the seventeenth century English scientist who developed the theory of gravity, discovered the secret of light and color, and formulated the system of calculus.

Level: Average

Let's Investigate Force and Motion by Robin Kerrod, Marshal Cavendish, 1994

Simple experiments to help students understand the principles behind natural forces and the motions they create.

Level: Advanced

Muscles to Machines by Neil Ardley, Gloucester Press, 1990

Discusses how our bodies and machines use the same properties of motion to function.

Level: Average

Understanding Movement by Ralph Hancock, Silver Burdett Company, 1984

How and why things move, from animals, to wheels, to spacecrafts.

Level: Advanced

Why Doesn't the Earth Fall Up? by Vicki Cobb, Lodestar Books, 1988

Students learn the answer to this and eight other "not such dumb questions about motion" as the explore Newton's laws of motion, gravity, centrifugal force, and other principles of movement.

Level: Beginning

Related Technology

Wild Science Arcade, Binary Zoo, Broderbund, 1993

Learning physics was never more fun!

Chapter 10

Support Materials

ACTIVITY BOOK

pages 92-101

BLUE TAPE

Side 2

"Let's Twist Again," page T190

DISK

Writer's Notebook

Assessment Materials

BLACKLINE MASTER

Language Assessment, Blackline Master 82

Listening Assessment, Blackline Master 83

CREAM TAPE

Side 2

Listening Assessment, page T191

Listen carefully.

Joe went on a roller coaster ride. Follow the directions and mark the pictures that show what happened on his ride.

The roller coaster went slowly up the first hill. Joe could hear the click of the motor pulling the train. Put an X on the picture that shows the roller coaster going up the first hill.

The roller coaster zoomed down the hill and around the first loop. Circle the picture that shows the roller coaster going around the loop.

The roller coaster came down the last hill and came to a stop. Draw a line through the picture that shows the end of the roller coaster ride.

Look at the pictures. Put a 1 by the picture that happened first. Put a 2 by the picture that happened second. Put a 3 by the picture that happened last.

For Extended Reading

Machines by David Glover B.Sc., Ph.D., Thomas Learning, 1993

Simple experiments that show parts of machines and how they use the laws of motion and force to work.

Level: Average

Making Mad Machines by Jen Green, Gloucester Press, 1992

Students learn the properties of physics by making planes, cars, and other machines using things from around their houses.

Level: Beginning

Simple Slopes by Andrew Dunn, Thomas Learning, 1993

Readers will be surprised to discover how much of everyday life rests on principles of physics involved in simple slopes.

Level: Beginning

Young Engineer in the Factory by Malcolm Dixon, The Bookwright Press, 1983

More simple experiments illustrating the properties of motion at work in everyday objects.

Level: Advanced

Related Technology

Fun School in Time!, Expert Software, 1995

Visit Fantasy Funfair and explore roller coasters and physics.

Project

Physics in Action

This optional project can be completed over the next two chapters. In this project, students will be studying movement and the laws of movement as demonstrated in playground activities. They will make a photo essay and caption or narrate their pictures. See the Unit Wrap-Up, page T191a, for more ideas on sharing the project with family members.

What You'll Need

Collect the following kinds of items to set up the Physics in Action project:

Materials
- chart paper
- markers
- camera or video camera

Beginning the Project

Locate a playground with as much interesting and varied equipment and play space as possible. Take students on a get-acquainted trip. Tell them that they will be starting a project in connection with their study of the physics of motion. They will photograph everyday activities in a playground or sports facility. They will record the actions on film, name the action, and then describe how the activities illustrate laws of physics and energy, relating to motion, gravity, and friction. Explain that the purpose of the get-acquainted trip is to let them explore the facility so that they can plan the ways in which they will use it for the project.

Home Involvement

Send the Letter to the Family, Blackline Masters 74 through 79, to families to solicit their participation in collecting materials for the physics project. They will be asked to provide sports equipment to assist in the project.

Planning and Continuing the Project

Have students plan what playground experiences they are going to record and how they will record them. As they begin to record, help them verbalize the principles of physics involved.

In addition, encourage students to do simple science experiments as typically found in books of experiments for elementary and middle school students. Encourage them to identify what kind of motion each experiment demonstrates. Have them set up a station for each experiment so that friction, gravity, and so forth can be demonstrated for visitors. Discuss with them an appropriate order for the stations to show motion from starting to stopping (force, then friction).

Daily Discussion

Take a few minutes each day for discussion to practice vocabulary learned in conjunction with physics and experiments. At the end of the unit, have students discuss ways motion is part of their daily lives. See page T191a for ideas about sharing the Physics Fair with families and friends when the unit is completed.

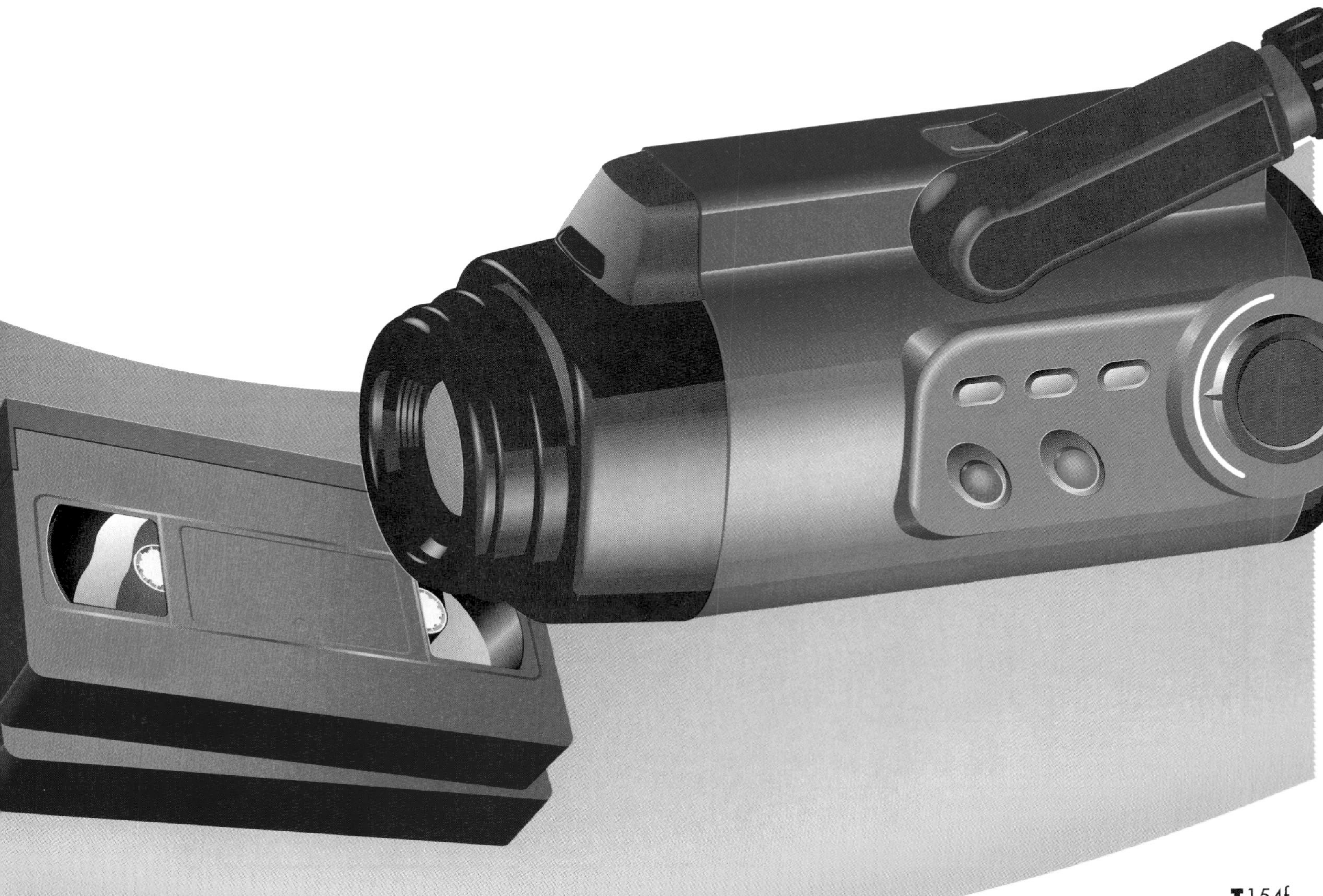

Activity Book Chapter 9

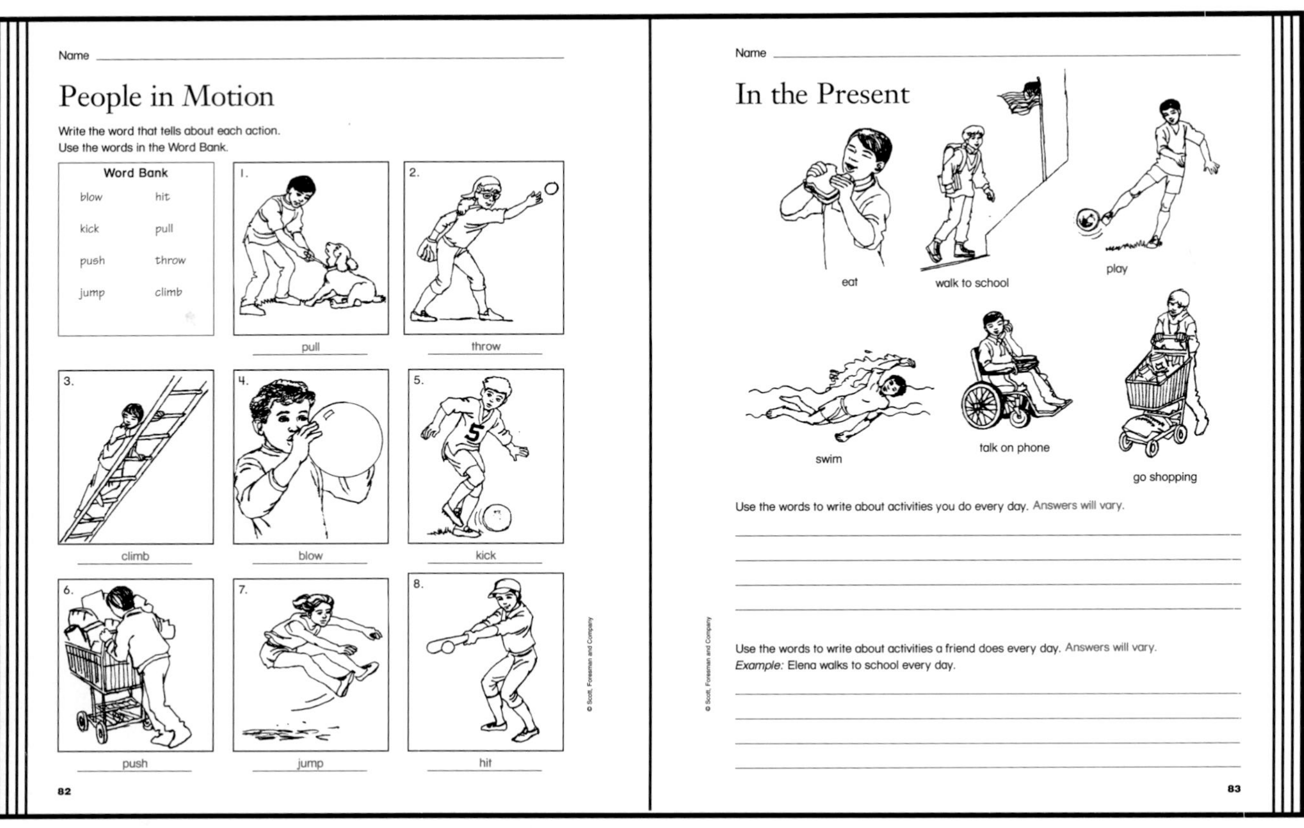

Name
People in Motion
Write the word that tells about each action.
Use the words in the Word Bank.
Word Bank
blow hit
kick pull
push throw
jump climb
1. pull
2. throw
3. climb
4. blow
5. kick
6. push
7. jump
8. hit
82
Name
In the Present
eat
walk to school
play
swim
talk on phone
go shopping
Use the words to write about activities you do every day. Answers will vary.
Use the words to write about activities a friend does every day. Answers will vary.
Example: Elena walks to school every day.
83

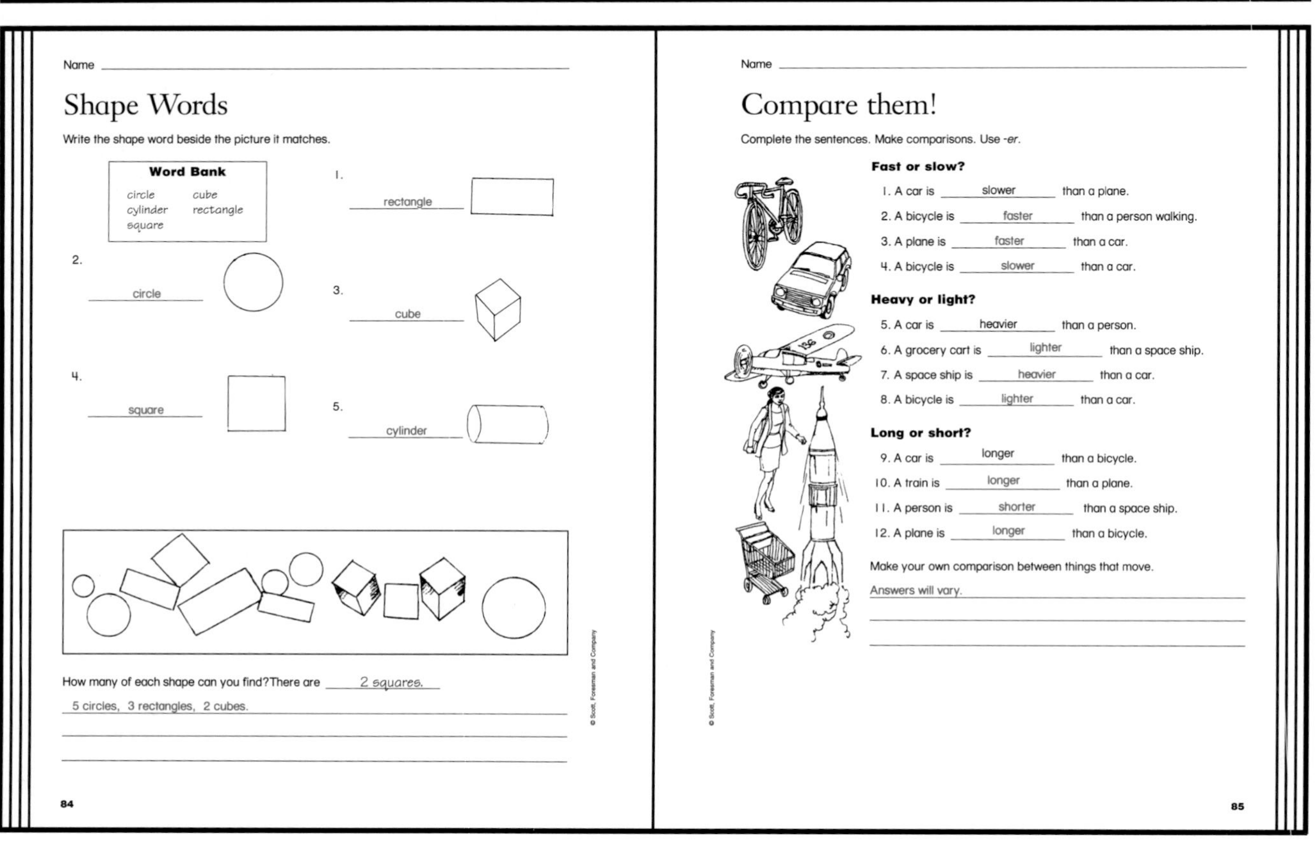

Name
Shape Words
Write the shape word beside the picture it matches.
Word Bank
circle cube
cylinder rectangle
square
1. rectangle
2. circle
3. cube
4. square
5. cylinder
How many of each shape can you find? There are 2 squares.
5 circles, 3 rectangles, 2 cubes.
84
Name
Compare them!
Complete the sentences. Make comparisons. Use -er.
Fast or slow?
1. A car is slower than a plane.
2. A bicycle is faster than a person walking.
3. A plane is faster than a car.
4. A bicycle is slower than a car.
Heavy or light?
5. A car is heavier than a person.
6. A grocery cart is lighter than a space ship.
7. A space ship is heavier than a car.
8. A bicycle is lighter than a car.
Long or short?
9. A car is longer than a bicycle.
10. A train is longer than a plane.
11. A person is shorter than a space ship.
12. A plane is longer than a bicycle.
Make your own comparison between things that move.
Answers will vary.
85

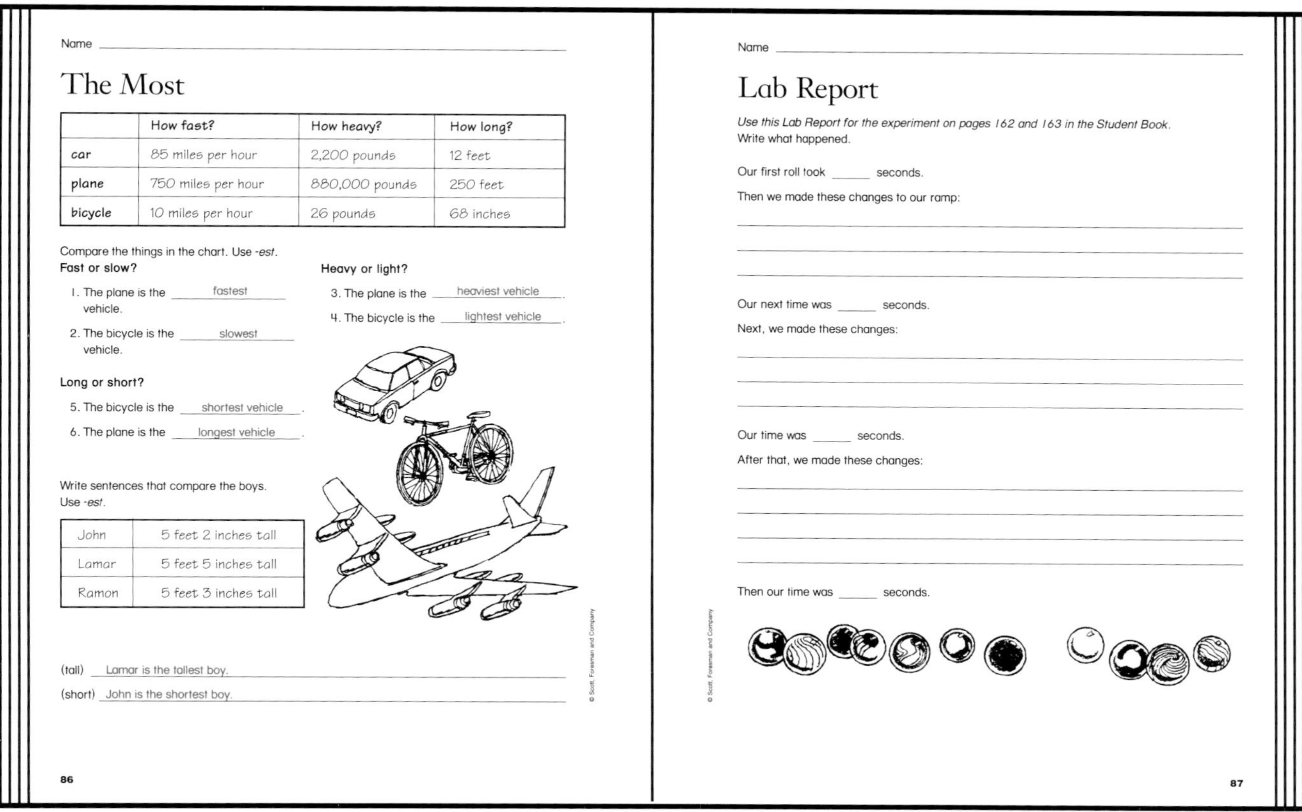

Name ______________________

The Most

	How fast?	How heavy?	How long?
car	85 miles per hour	2,200 pounds	12 feet
plane	750 miles per hour	880,000 pounds	250 feet
bicycle	10 miles per hour	26 pounds	68 inches

Compare the things in the chart. Use *-est*.

Fast or slow?

1. The plane is the ___fastest___ vehicle.
2. The bicycle is the ___slowest___ vehicle.

Heavy or light?

3. The plane is the ___heaviest vehicle___.
4. The bicycle is the ___lightest vehicle___.

Long or short?

5. The bicycle is the ___shortest vehicle___.
6. The plane is the ___longest vehicle___.

Write sentences that compare the boys. Use *-est*.

John	5 feet 2 inches tall
Lamar	5 feet 5 inches tall
Ramon	5 feet 3 inches tall

(tall) ___Lamar is the tallest boy.___

(short) ___John is the shortest boy.___

Name ______________________

Lab Report

Use this Lab Report for the experiment on pages 162 and 163 in the Student Book.
Write what happened.

Our first roll took ______ seconds.

Then we made these changes to our ramp:

____

Our next time was ______ seconds.

Next, we made these changes:

____

Our time was ______ seconds.

After that, we made these changes:

____

Then our time was ______ seconds.

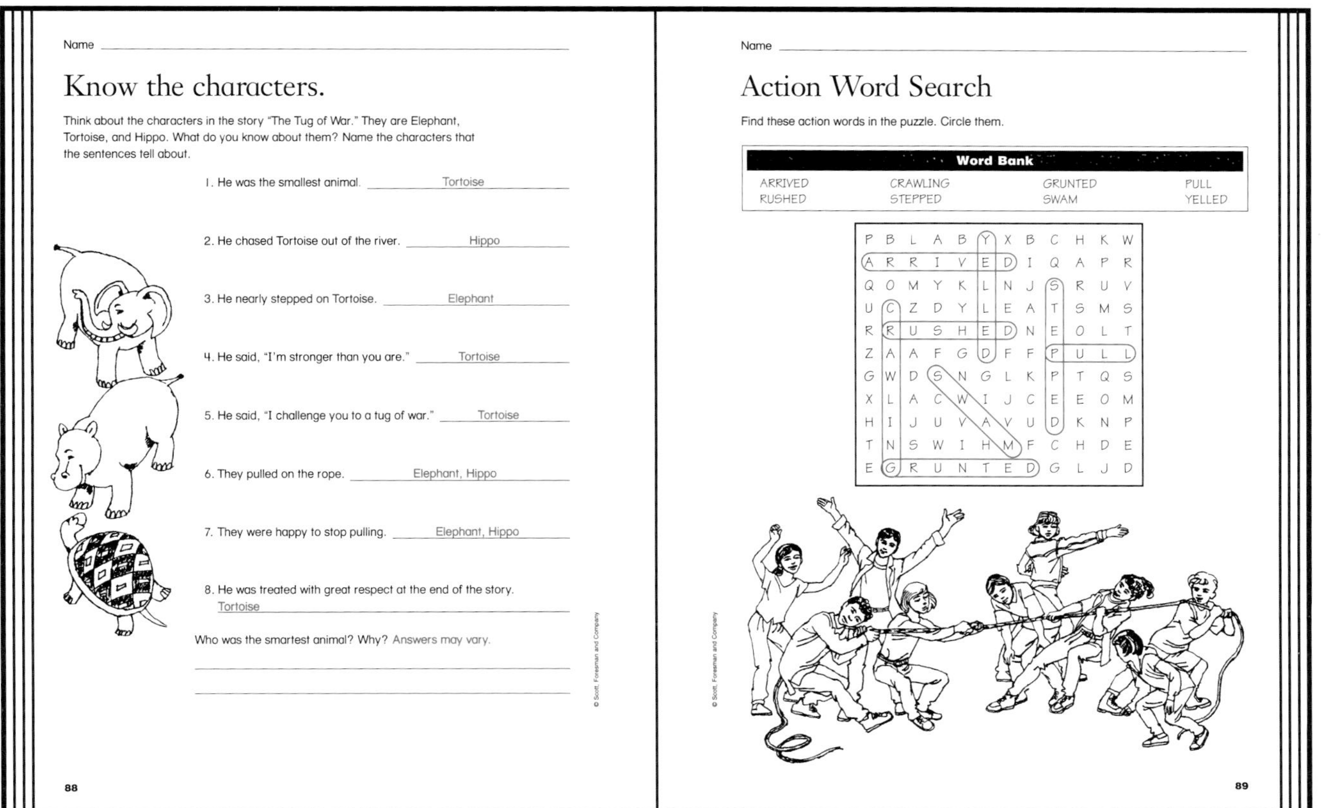

Name ______________________

Know the characters.

Think about the characters in the story "The Tug of War." They are Elephant, Tortoise, and Hippo. What do you know about them? Name the characters that the sentences tell about.

1. He was the smallest animal. ___Tortoise___
2. He chased Tortoise out of the river. ___Hippo___
3. He nearly stepped on Tortoise. ___Elephant___
4. He said, "I'm stronger than you are." ___Tortoise___
5. He said, "I challenge you to a tug of war." ___Tortoise___
6. They pulled on the rope. ___Elephant, Hippo___
7. They were happy to stop pulling. ___Elephant, Hippo___
8. He was treated with great respect at the end of the story. ___Tortoise___

Who was the smartest animal? Why? Answers may vary.

____

Name ______________________

Action Word Search

Find these action words in the puzzle. Circle them.

Word Bank

ARRIVED	CRAWLING	GRUNTED	PULL
RUSHED	STEPPED	SWAM	YELLED

P	B	L	A	B	Y	X	B	C	H	K	W
A	R	R	I	V	E	D	I	Q	A	P	R
Q	O	M	Y	K	L	N	J	S	R	U	V
U	C	Z	D	Y	L	E	A	T	S	M	S
R	R	U	S	H	E	D	N	E	O	L	T
Z	A	A	F	G	D	F	F	P	U	L	L
G	W	D	S	N	G	L	K	P	T	Q	S
X	L	A	C	W	I	J	C	E	E	O	M
H	I	J	U	V	A	V	U	D	K	N	P
T	N	S	W	I	H	M	F	C	H	D	E
E	G	R	U	N	T	E	D	G	L	J	D

Activity Book

Chapter 10

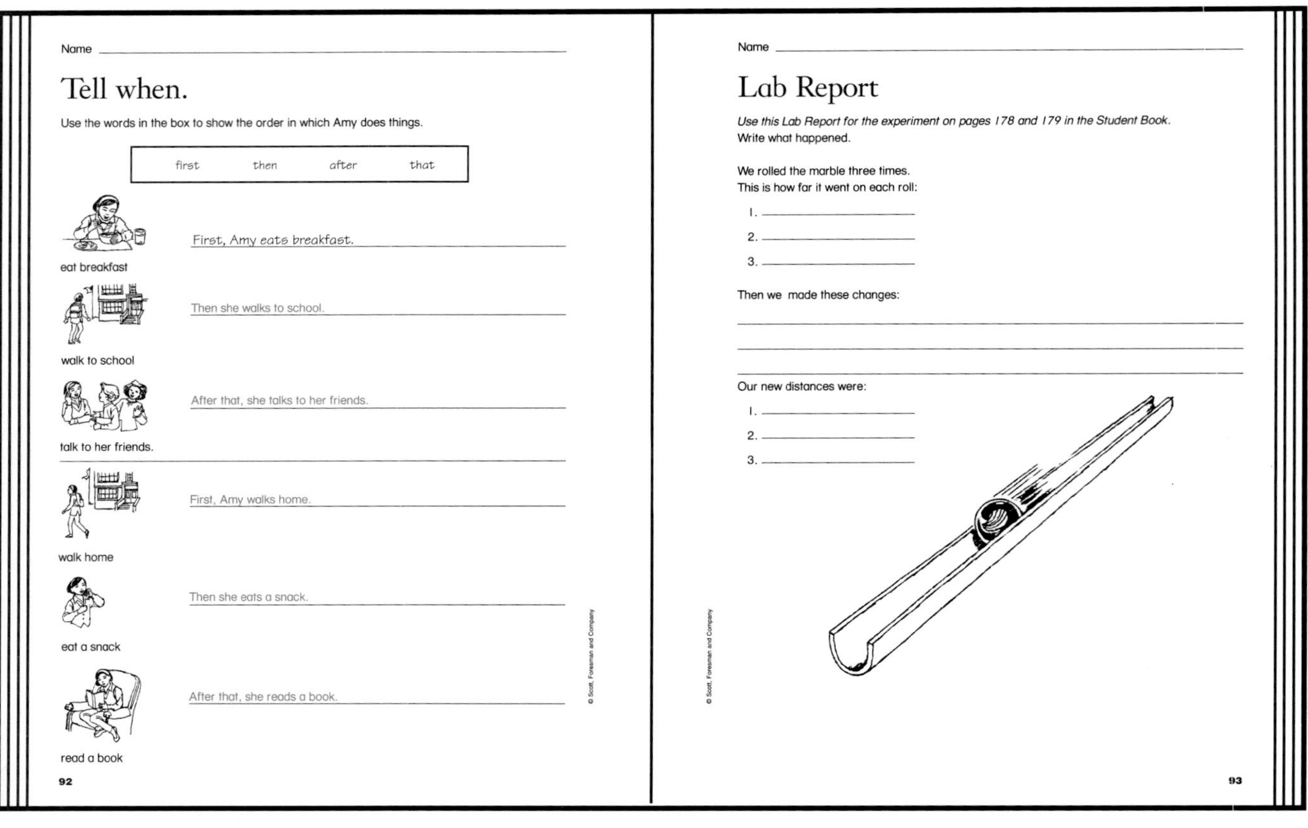

Name
Tell when.
Use the words in the box to show the order in which Amy does things.
first then after that
eat breakfast
First, Amy eats breakfast.
walk to school
Then she walks to school.
talk to her friends.
After that, she talks to her friends.
walk home
First, Amy walks home.
eat a snack
Then she eats a snack.
read a book
After that, she reads a book.
92
© Scott, Foresman and Company
Name
Lab Report
Use this Lab Report for the experiment on pages 178 and 179 in the Student Book.
Write what happened.
We rolled the marble three times.
This is how far it went on each roll:
1.
2.
3.
Then we made these changes:
Our new distances were:
1.
2.
3.
93

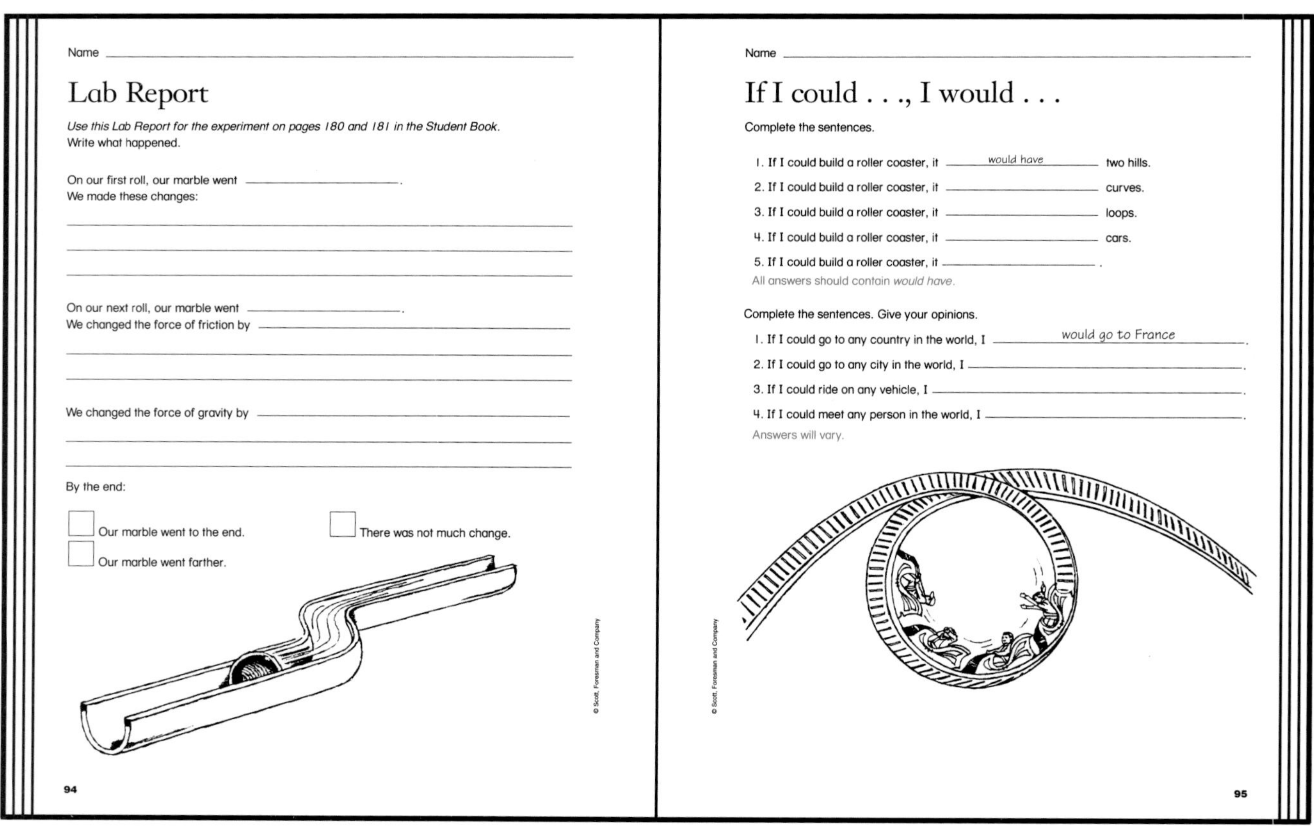

Name
Lab Report
Use this Lab Report for the experiment on pages 180 and 181 in the Student Book.
Write what happened.
On our first roll, our marble went
We made these changes:
On our next roll, our marble went
We changed the force of friction by
We changed the force of gravity by
By the end:
Our marble went to the end.
Our marble went farther.
There was not much change.
94
Name
If I could . . ., I would . . .
Complete the sentences.
1. If I could build a roller coaster, it would have two hills.
2. If I could build a roller coaster, it curves.
3. If I could build a roller coaster, it loops.
4. If I could build a roller coaster, it cars.
5. If I could build a roller coaster, it .
All answers should contain would have.
Complete the sentences. Give your opinions.
1. If I could go to any country in the world, I would go to France.
2. If I could go to any city in the world, I .
3. If I could ride on any vehicle, I .
4. If I could meet any person in the world, I .
Answers will vary.
95

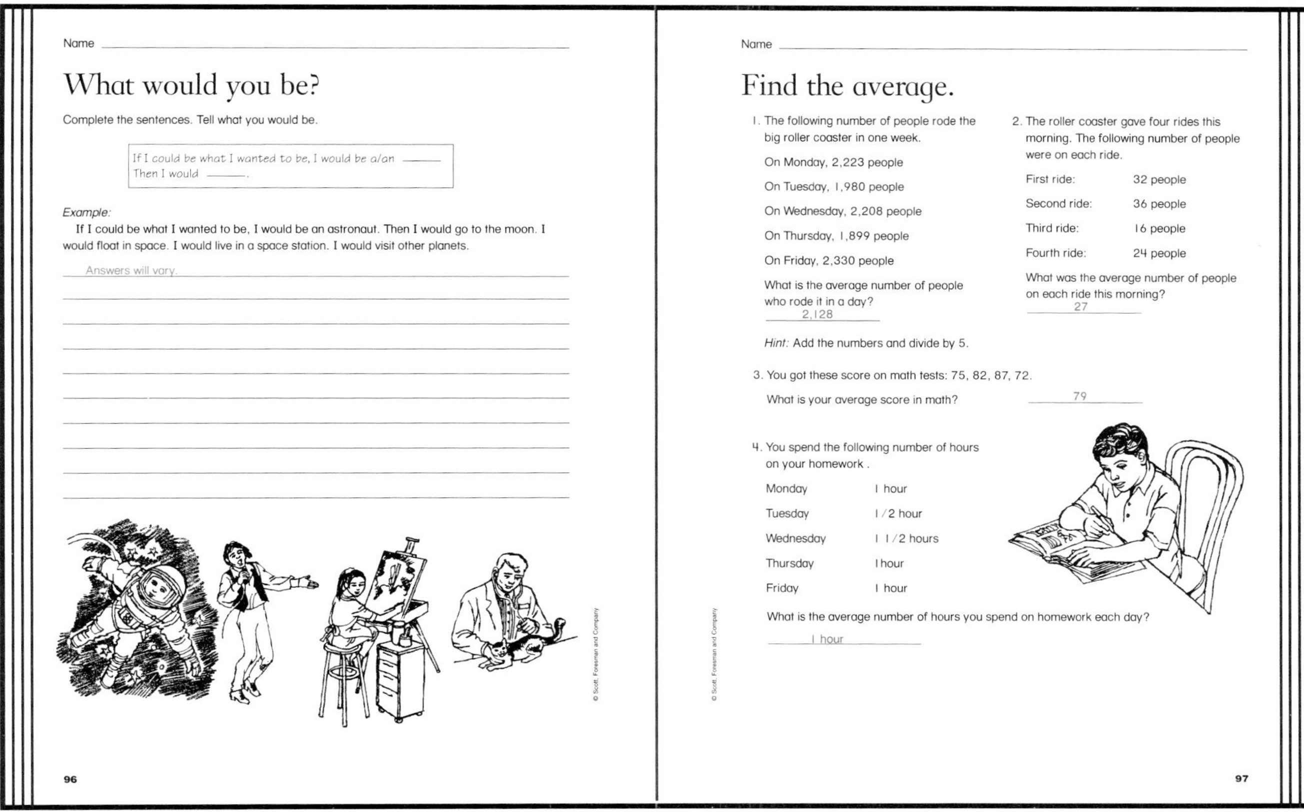

Name ______

What would you be?

Complete the sentences. Tell what you would be.

If I could be what I wanted to be, I would be a/an ______
Then I would ______.

Example:

If I could be what I wanted to be, I would be an astronaut. Then I would go to the moon. I would float in space. I would live in a space station. I would visit other planets.

Answers will vary.

Name ______

Find the average.

1. The following number of people rode the big roller coaster in one week.

   On Monday, 2,223 people

   On Tuesday, 1,980 people

   On Wednesday, 2,208 people

   On Thursday, 1,899 people

   On Friday, 2,330 people

   What is the average number of people who rode it in a day? 2,128

   Hint: Add the numbers and divide by 5.

2. The roller coaster gave four rides this morning. The following number of people were on each ride.

First ride:	32 people
Second ride:	36 people
Third ride:	16 people
Fourth ride:	24 people

   What was the average number of people on each ride this morning? 27

3. You got these score on math tests: 75, 82, 87, 72.

   What is your average score in math? 79

4. You spend the following number of hours on your homework.

Monday	1 hour
Tuesday	1/2 hour
Wednesday	1 1/2 hours
Thursday	1 hour
Friday	1 hour

   What is the average number of hours you spend on homework each day? 1 hour

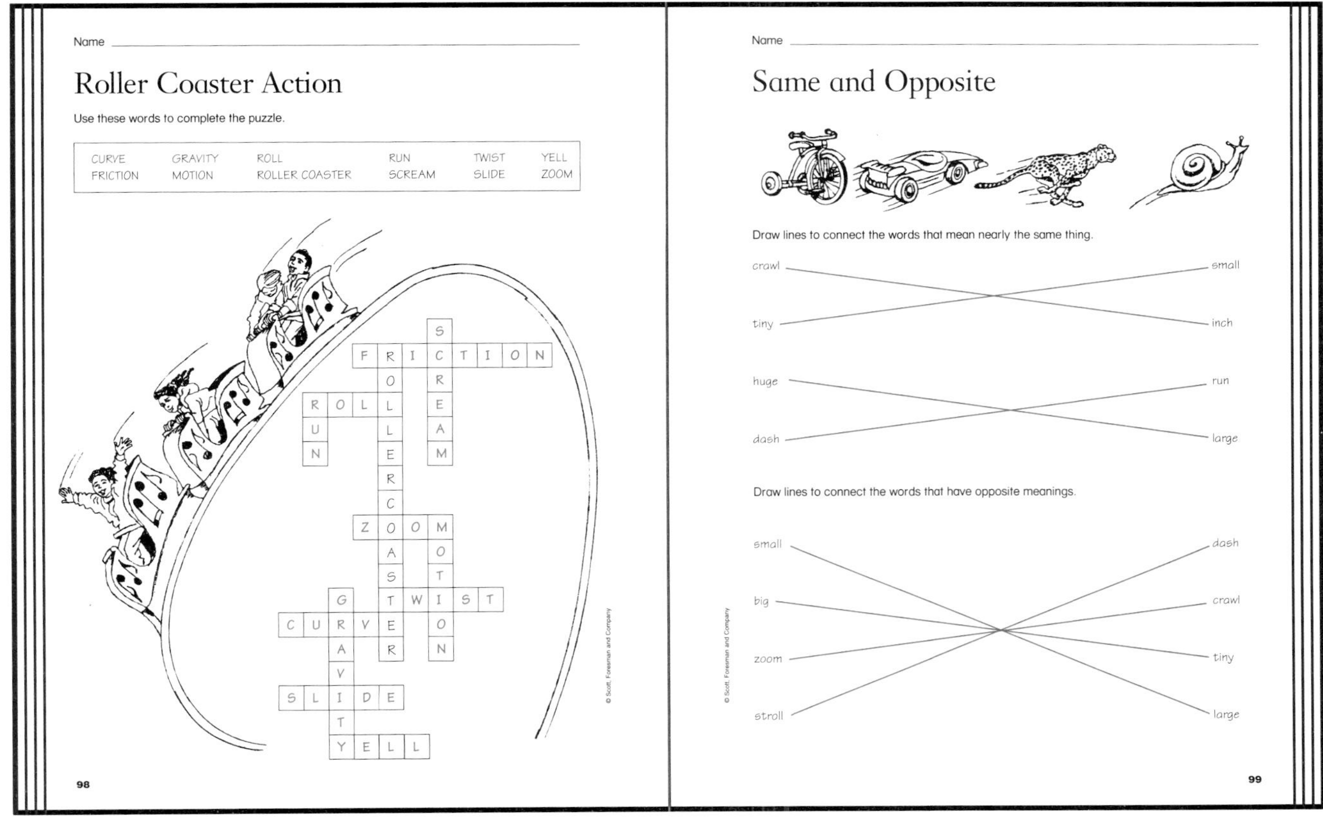

Name ______

Roller Coaster Action

Use these words to complete the puzzle.

CURVE	GRAVITY	ROLL	RUN	TWIST	YELL
FRICTION	MOTION	ROLLER COASTER	SCREAM	SLIDE	ZOOM

Name ______

Same and Opposite

Draw lines to connect the words that mean nearly the same thing.

crawl	small
tiny	inch
huge	run
dash	large

Draw lines to connect the words that have opposite meanings.

small	dash
big	crawl
zoom	tiny
stroll	large

UNIT 5

Preview

Activate Prior Knowledge
Demonstrate

TPR

Ask students to act out ways to make a ball move, using a nerf ball. Present words such as *push, roll, throw, kick, bounce, drop.*

Ask students to name as many ways to move as they can. Encourage them to explore a range of motion, including their own actions and movement, small moving objects, moving vehicles, and motion in nature. Make a list of actions on the board.

Develop Language and Concepts
Present Pages 154 and 155

TPR

Introduce the words in the Word Bank by acting them out. Have students look at the pictures on pages 154 and 155. Ask them to find examples of each motion in the Word Bank. Introduce the motion words in Tell What You Know. Have students act out *start, stop, go up,* and *fall* to be sure they understand the meanings. Read the questions on page 154 with the students. Ask them to answer the questions. Add any new motion words to the list. Read the Talk About It questions with students. Help them understand the concept of relationship between how hard a ball is kicked and how far it will go. Encourage them to explore the relationship with the nerf ball.

The Physics of Fun

Word Bank

blow
hit
kick
pull
push
throw

Tell what you know.

What makes things start moving?

What makes things stop moving?

What makes things go up in the air?

What makes things fall to the ground?

Options for Reaching All Students

Beginning
Language: Pantomime

TPR

Write the Word Bank words on cards. Review the words with students. Have each student draw a card and act out the word.

Advanced
Critical Thinking: Apply Concepts

Have students work together in pairs to come up with a list of classroom objects that move by outside force. (Windows are pushed open, doors are pulled open, chairs are lifted and carried, and so on).

Mixed Ability
Video: Physics of Fun

VIDEO

Show the Unit 5 portion of the video to give students an overview of the unit. You may want to replay the tape several times throughout the unit for language and concept reinforcement and development.

Talk About It

What is the relationship between how hard you kick a ball and how fast and how far the ball will go?

155

THEME/KEY CONCEPTS

In this unit, students will learn about the physics of energy. This is done through hands-on experiments and scientific explanations. This is a good opportunity for students to develop language connected with movement.

Chapter 9

- Concepts from Newton's First Law of Motion are introduced: an object in motion tends to stay in motion; an object not in motion tends to stay still.
- Friction and gravity are forces that affect motion.

Chapter 10

- Concepts from the first chapter are applied to roller coasters, showing the relationship between energy, the motion of the roller coaster, and friction and gravity.
- People relate to roller coasters with a variety of responses, but many are attracted to them.
- There are many synonyms in English, and a reference tool called a thesaurus helps distinguish among their meanings.

Cooperative Learning

People in Action

Use pictures of people from the Picture Cards with occupations: 3 artist, 17 clown, 18 cook, 22 dance, 24 doctor, 53 police officer, 61 secretary. Have pairs of students work together to list words related to the occupations. Then have students act out the ways these people might move. Add any new motion words to the class list.

Present

Activate Prior Knowledge

Brainstorm Vocabulary

Ask students to name some physical activities they have done in the past twenty-four hours. Write their responses on chart paper to make a class list.

Develop Language and Concepts

Present Pages 156 and 157

ACTIVITY BOOK

Ask students to think about an object that is not moving; for example, a ball at rest. Ask them what it takes to get the ball moving. Explain the term *outside force.* A ball needs an outside force to set it in motion. Ask students to suggest different ways to make the ball move.

Ask students what stops a thing from moving once it is moving. Let them experiment with the nerf ball. If they throw a ball and someone catches it, the ball stops moving. Tell students they will be learning about other things that slow down movement.

Read pages 156 and 157 with students.

Introduce the words in the Word Bank. Use the Talk About It question with students. Add any new motion words to the class list.

Use Activity Book page 82.

CHAPTER 9

What makes things move?

Motion

Children run and jump. Animals swim and climb trees. The Earth is moving too. All of this is **motion.**

You start an object in motion by using an outside **force.** A force is a push, pull, or kick that starts something moving. Wind and water are forces too.

Options for Reaching All Students

Beginning

Language: Action Words

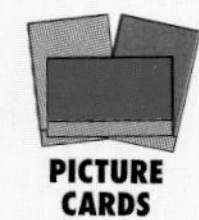
PICTURE CARDS

Invite students to look at and name Picture Cards of objects for outdoor activities, such as 4 ball, 5 bike, 40 kite, 62 skate, 63 slide, and 68 swing. Ask them to identify an action or force used with the object. For example I *throw a ball.* I *fly a kite.* Help students Make a list of verbs.

Advanced

Language: Play and Action

Ask students to think about all the different ways to move while playing their favorite games. Help them make a list.

Mixed Ability

Language: Make a Schedule

Pair students of mixed ability to make daily schedules of their routines and times, such as when they have school subjects. Help students brainstorm a list of common activities.

When something is in motion, it stays moving until an outside force stops it. When you run down a hill, you can't stop quickly. Your legs keep taking you forward. When you throw a ball, it does not stop exactly where it lands. It rolls on.

Word Bank

eat
jump
run
walk

Talk About It

Tell about some activities you do every day. How do they use motion?

Language Awareness

Grammar
Present Tense

ACTIVITY BOOK

Write the following verbs on the board: *eat, jump, run, walk*. After pronouncing them, explain that the present tense is used to talk about facts or things they do everyday. For example:

I walk to school everyday.
I jump rope after school.
I eat lunch at school.

Have students practice using the present tense by making up sentences about their daily routine. Then introduce the third person singular form by having students report routines of classmates.

Use Activity Book page 83.

Assess 

Use students' responses to Talk About It for assessment. They should be able to

- give an example of motion
- give an example of an outside force

LOOK**AHEAD**

In the next section, students will learn about the force of friction.

Peer Tutoring

Critical Thinking: Retelling the Main Idea

Have students work in pairs of mixed ability to review and retell the main idea of the reading.

Ask them to come up with forces that start and stop things from moving.

Cooperative Language Experience

Field Trip

Have students take a walk around the school and observe actions. Encourage students to be on the look out for different kinds of action. As a class, write a story about the experience.

Writer's Workshop

A Typical Day

Refer students to the Writer's Workshop on pages 230 to 236 of the Student Book. Have them write about a typical school day.

Practice

Activate Prior Knowledge

Demonstrate

Ask students what they do when they want to stop a pencil from rolling off a desk. Discuss other ways to stop things from moving. Ask students to give other examples of stopping motion. Use the nerf ball. Ask students to think of ways to stop it from moving. Examples might be catching the ball or blocking the ball.

Develop Language and Concepts

Present Pages 158 and 159

Roll a marble over two different surfaces—a bare table top and a table with a cloth towel on it. Have students observe the differences between the two examples. Read page 158 with students and discuss the scientific explanation of *friction.*

Next, read through the steps of the experiment for students. Have them retell the steps to make sure they understand the procedure before they begin. You may wish to remind students that they are monitoring their understanding. Ask students to copy the chart on page 159 and record their findings. Discuss with students that rough objects cause more friction than smooth objects and that is why their movement is slower. Also the wooden board is rougher than the metal sheet, so objects move more smoothly down the metal sheet. Help students complete the science report. Have students do the Write About It.

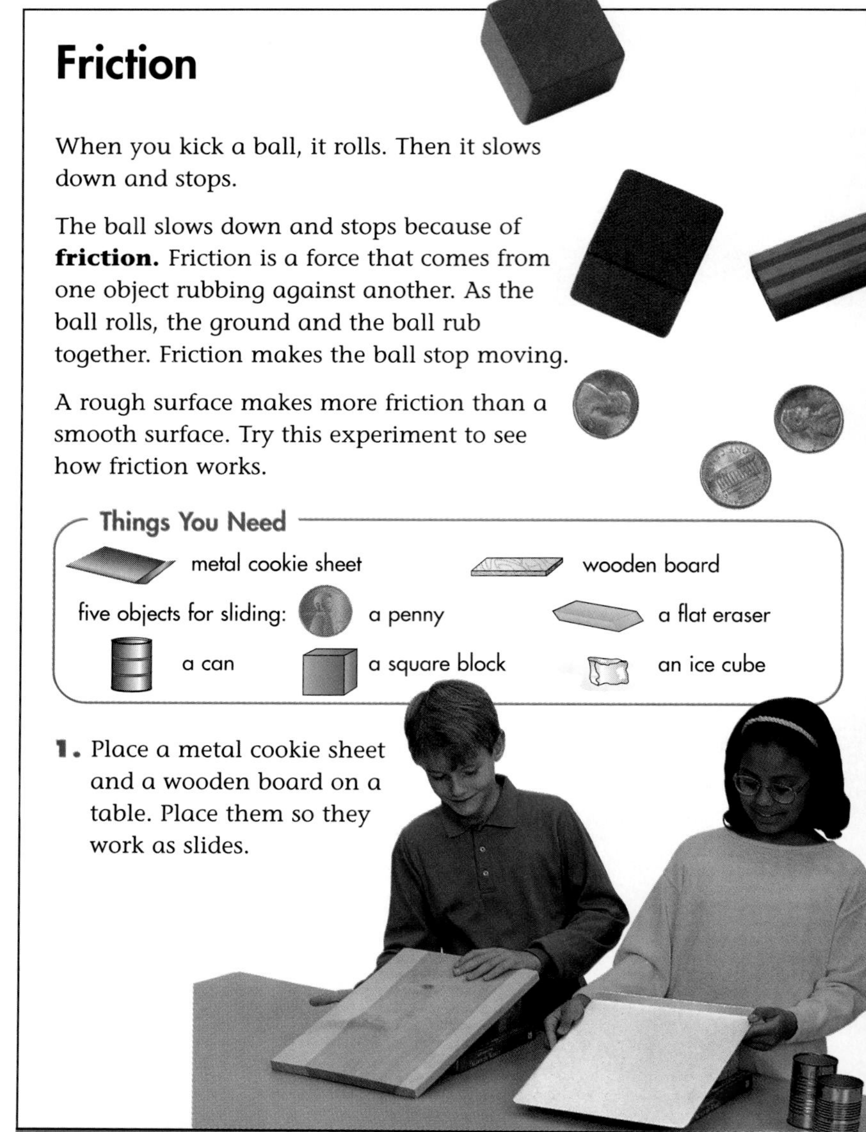

Friction

When you kick a ball, it rolls. Then it slows down and stops.

The ball slows down and stops because of **friction.** Friction is a force that comes from one object rubbing against another. As the ball rolls, the ground and the ball rub together. Friction makes the ball stop moving.

A rough surface makes more friction than a smooth surface. Try this experiment to see how friction works.

Things You Need

- metal cookie sheet
- wooden board
- five objects for sliding: a penny, a flat eraser, a can, a square block, an ice cube

1. Place a metal cookie sheet and a wooden board on a table. Place them so they work as slides.

158 USE LANGUAGE • SCIENCE

Options for Reaching All Students

Beginning

Math: Shape Words

Review the shapes and shape names with students. Have them go on a shape hunt to find as many examples of those shapes as they can in the environment.

Advanced

Art: Shape Art

Ask students to draw a design. Provide students with compasses for drawing circles, rulers for drawing straight lines, or shapes to outline. Have them incorporate as many shapes as they can into an artistic design.

Cooperative Language Experience

Science Experiment: Weight and Friction

Pair students and provide them with scales. Have them weigh three match boxes, each one filled with a different material. Have them slide the boxes down a slide such as those in the experiment. Have them observe the force of friction. Ask students to record the weight and make a statement

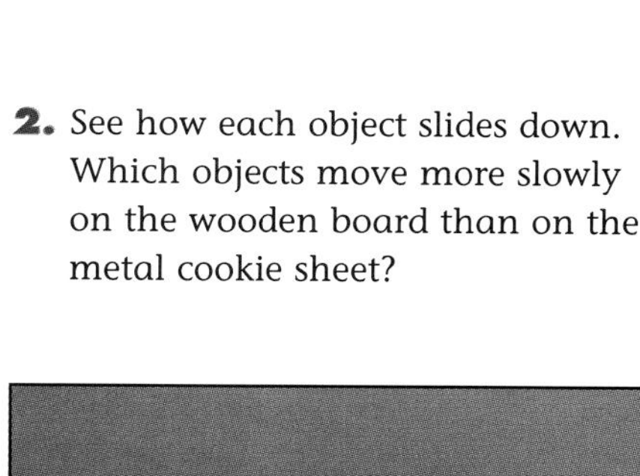

My Record
These are smooth objects:
These are rough objects:
Does the coin move more slowly on wood or on metal?
Try the other objects.

2. See how each object slides down. Which objects move more slowly on the wooden board than on the metal cookie sheet?

3. Talk about the results in class. Answer these questions: Do rough objects move faster or slower than smooth objects? Do objects move more slowly down the metal cookie sheet or the wooden board? Why?

Write About It

Think of other examples from your everyday life that show friction. Draw pictures of them and label them.

Language Awareness

Vocabulary
Shape Words

ACTIVITY BOOK

Introduce words for two-dimensional shapes using materials from the activity, such as *circle* (outline of the penny), *rectangle* (outline of the eraser), and *square* (one side of the block). Students can trace the objects. Then introduce the words for three-dimensional shapes, such as cylinder (can), cube.

Make a shape chart. Have students draw and label pictures that show the shapes. Use Activity Book page 84.

FYI Newton's Laws of Motion

One of Newton's Laws is the Law of Inertia. Inertia is the tendency of an object at rest to stay at rest unless acted upon by an outside force. An object will tend to stay in motion until acted upon by an outside force.

Assess

Use the students' responses in the experiment chart for assessment. Students should be able to give an example of friction.

LOOK**AHEAD**

In the next section, students will conduct an experiment on gravity.

about the relationship between weight and how fast or slow each one moved.

Cooperative Learning

Science Activities

Provide students with simple experiments relating to friction from science activity books. Have students work in groups to do the activity and write up results. Have them share their results with the class.

Home Connection

Repeat the Experiment

Encourage students to repeat the experiment at home with the help of family using household objects. Invite them to report the results back to the class.

Practice

Activate Prior Knowledge

Demonstrate

Present different objects and have students speculate about the weight of each. Have a scale available to weigh small objects. Have students speculate about the weight of objects such as an elephant (8,000 pounds) or a jet plane (880,000 pounds).

Develop Language and Concepts

Present Pages 160 and 161

Have students look at the pictures on page 160. Invite students to explain what is happening to the plate in the picture. Read page 160 with students.

Next, read the steps of the activity on page 161. Ask students to retell the steps in their own words. Have students predict the outcome of the experiment and write the responses on the board. Refer back to their predictions after the activity.

Then have students work in pairs to do the experiment. Encourage them to discuss the procedure as they are working and to observe what is happening. Both objects should fall at the same speed, but the heavier ball should make more of an impact because of its weight.

Have students make predictions before they do the experiment with the feather and marker in the Talk About It activity. Have students do the experiment. Discuss the results. The air resistance makes the feather fall more slowly.

Gravity

When you kick a ball into the air, what brings it back to the ground? One answer is **gravity.** Gravity is a force. It pulls everything down to the ground.

When you walk, you stay on the ground because of gravity. Without gravity, things would float in the air like astronauts in space.

Options for Reaching All Students

Beginning

Math: Graph Weights

Provide students with weights of different things such as an elephant, a hippo, a car, and so on. Have students make a bar graph and compare the weights of the things.

Advanced

Science: Research Space Travel

Have students look in encyclopedias and books to make a time line about space travel.

Cooperative Learning Experience

Science: Experiment with Gravity

Have students do an experiment in which they see how air resistance affects how objects fall. Have students follow this procedure:

Fold a piece of aluminum foil in half and cut on the fold line, making two identical rectangles. Have students hold the foil pieces at the same height.

Do heavy things fall faster than light things? Try this experiment to see how gravity works.

Things You Need

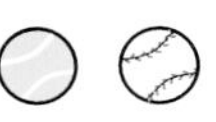 two balls—a light one and a heavy one

 modeling clay

 metal cookie sheet

 rolling pin

1. Put a metal cookie sheet on the ground.
2. Hold the two balls the same distance above the cookie sheet.
3. Drop the balls at exactly the same time. Listen carefully. Do the balls fall at the same rate of speed?
4. Roll out the clay on the cookie sheet. Drop the two balls again. What do you see in the clay? Which ball fell with greater force?

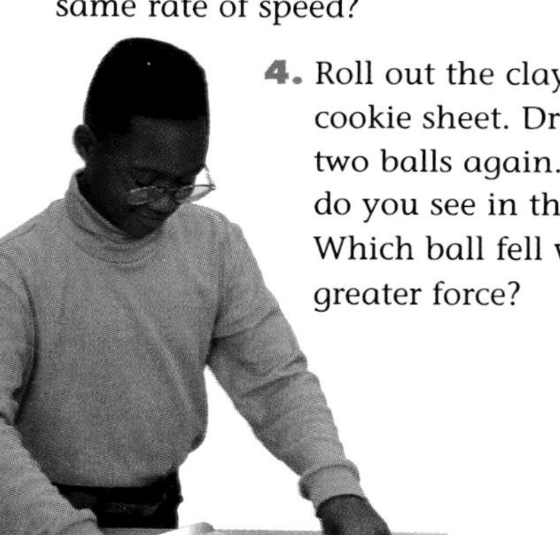

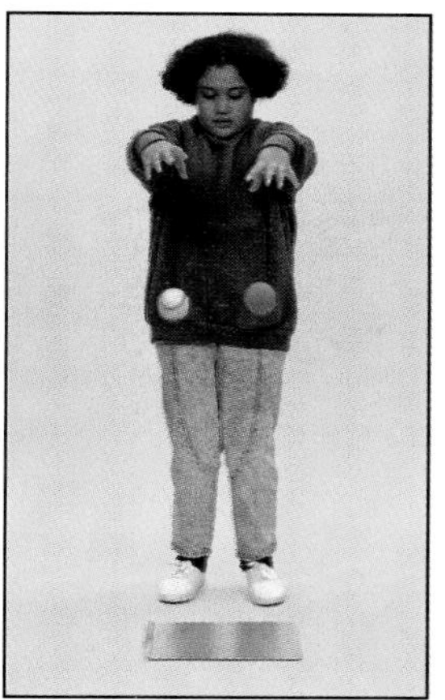

Think About It

Will a feather and a marker fall at the same rate of speed? Make a prediction and try it. Talk about the results.

Model a Strategy

Predict

Model a strategy for predicting:

Before I do an experiment, I predict what is going to happen. I use what I know about science to make my prediction.

Language Awareness

Grammar

Comparisons with *-er*

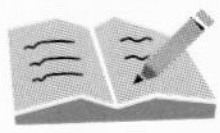

ACTIVITY BOOK

Have students run their fingers over a piece of sand paper and a wet bar of soap. Tell students that they can compare two things to each other by using words ending in *-er:*

The sandpaper is rougher than the soap.
The soap is smoother than the sandpaper.

Use classroom objects to demonstrate comparisons such as *long* and *short.* Have students make simple comparative sentences using the *-er* ending, such as *The pencil is longer than the crayon.* Use Activity Book page 85.

Assess

Students should be able to explain what gravity is and how it works.

LOOK**AHEAD**

In the next section, students will examine how friction and gravity work together.

Predict which piece will reach the floor first. One piece may land a little earlier or later than the other. But, with several tries, the pieces will often land at the same time. Crumble one piece into a small ball. Hold the ball and the other piece at the same height. Drop them at the same time. Predict which one will land on the floor first. The ball will reach the floor first even though both pieces contain the same amount of foil. Why does this happen? Both pieces are pulled to the ground by gravity. The uncrumpled foil meets more air resistance as it falls. If there were no air resistance, both pieces would reach the ground at the same time.

Connect

Activate Prior Knowledge

Use Pictures to Predict

Invite students to look at the pictures and point out where they think two forces of motion, friction and gravity, are affecting what is happening.

Develop Language and Concepts

Present Pages 162 and 163

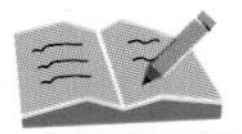
ACTIVITY BOOK

In this activity, students will predict and discover how friction and gravity work together to affect motion.

Read the introduction with students. Discuss the concept that friction and gravity work together to change the motion of moving objects.

Next, review the instructions for the activity and encourage students to ask questions to check their understanding. Have students retell the steps in their own words.

For safety, make sure students immediately pick up anything they might have dropped. All students should wear safety goggles. Students may need help placing the ramps so that marble falls on the ramp below; stops may need to be added to the ends of ramps.

Help students develop a procedure for recording results. Activity Book page 87 can be used for this purpose.

Can friction and gravity change a marble race?

Friction and gravity slow down moving objects. Try this experiment to see how they slow down marbles. Work with a team.

Things You Need

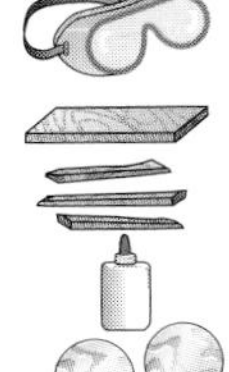

- goggles
- wood board
- wood strips
- white glue
- marbles

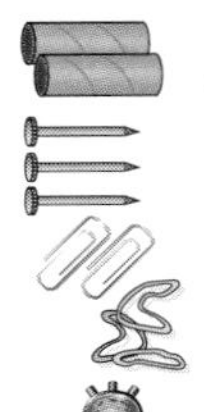

- cardboard tubes
- nails
- paper clips
- rubber bands
- stopwatch

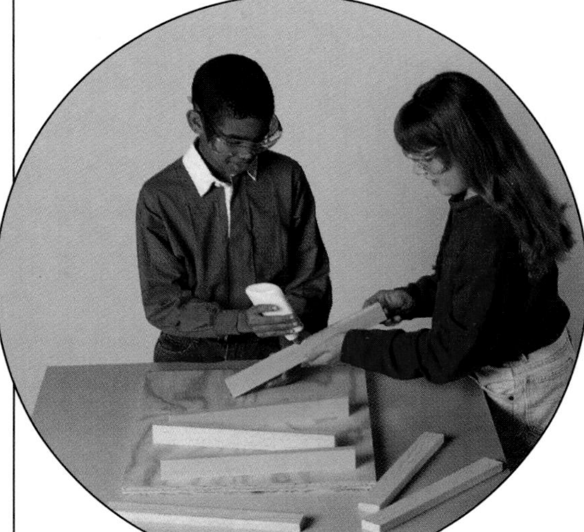

1. Get a flat board. It will work as a slide.
2. Use wood strips to make a ramp. Glue the strips to the board. Let the glue dry.
3. Roll a marble down the ramp. Use a stopwatch to time it.

Options for Reaching All Students

Beginning

Critical Thinking: Friction and Gravity Diagram

Have students use knowledge and experience they gained from performing the experiment to draw a track in which the marbles will fall slowly.

Advanced

Critical Thinking: Predicting

Provide students with a hypothetical question: Would a marble go faster if it drops straight down, or rolls down a steep angle? Let them explore the question and discuss their findings. (Answer: A marble goes faster when it drops straight down because any rolling action produces friction which slows it down.)

Mixed Ability

Science: Be an Inventor

Have students work in pairs of mixed ability to invent a new machine that uses the laws of gravity and friction. They may draw it and then tell how to use it. Display the machines on the bulletin board.

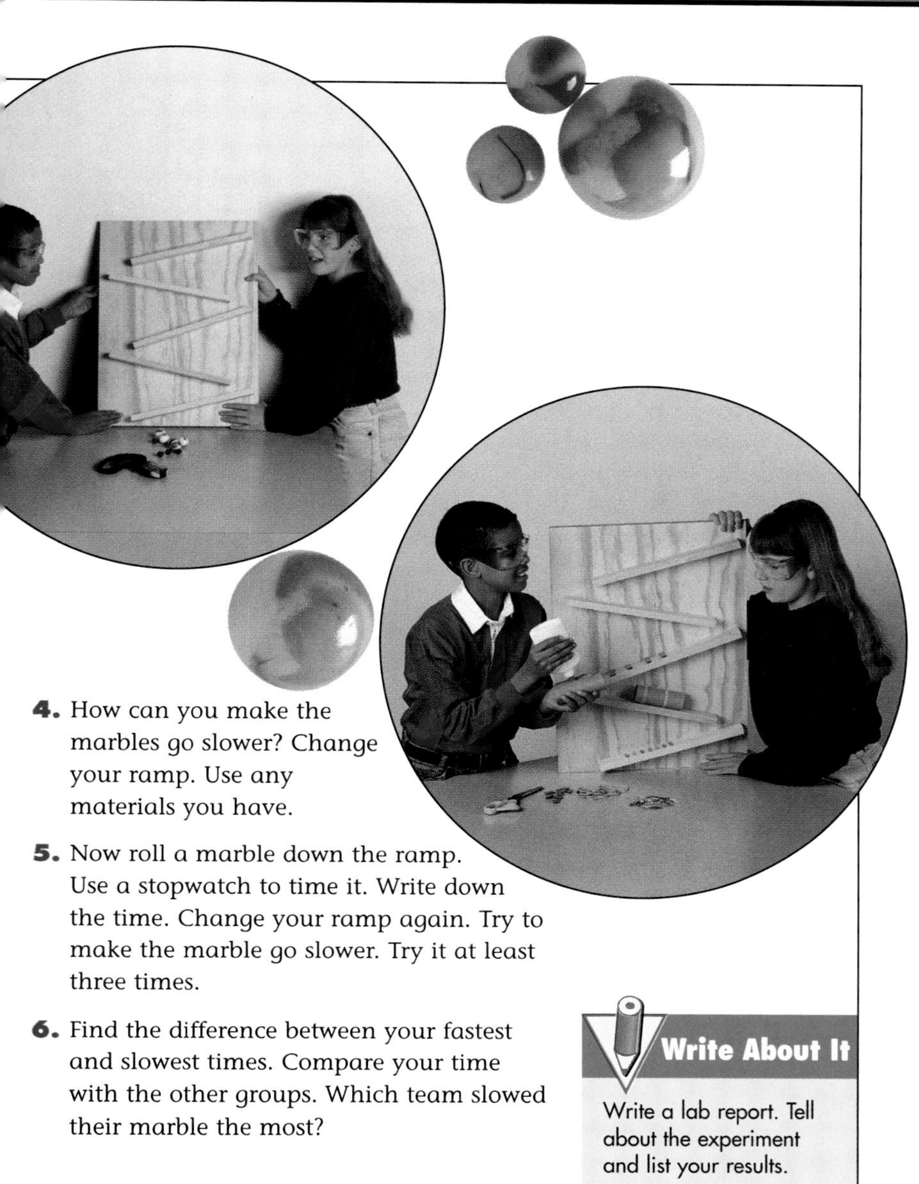

4. How can you make the marbles go slower? Change your ramp. Use any materials you have.
5. Now roll a marble down the ramp. Use a stopwatch to time it. Write down the time. Change your ramp again. Try to make the marble go slower. Try it at least three times.
6. Find the difference between your fastest and slowest times. Compare your time with the other groups. Which team slowed their marble the most?

Write About It

Write a lab report. Tell about the experiment and list your results.

Model a Strategy

Monitor Work

Model a strategy for monitoring one's work:

I know it is important to check my understanding and progress while doing any activity. I need to stop and ask myself, " Do I understand what I am doing?" and "Have I done all the steps I need to do?"

Language Awareness

Grammar
Superlatives with *-est*

Review comparing two items by adding *-er* with students. Make sentences with *longer* and *shorter*. Add a third item. Point out to students that one way of making comparisons between three or more items, is to add *-est* to an adjective. Ask students which item is the longest and which item is the shortest. Ask students to make comparisons using classroom objects. Use Activity Book page 86.

Assess 

Students should be able to tell how friction and gravity can slow down movement.

LOOK**AHEAD** 

In the next section, students read a folk tale in which the action of pulling is important.

QuickCheck

Comparatives

Check students' use of *-er* and *-est* endings on adjectives as they discuss the results of the experiment, comparing the three marbles in each try.

Connect

Activate Prior Knowledge

Use Pictures to Predict

Have students look at the pictures and the title of the story. Ask questions such as these:

- What do you think this story is about?
- Where do you think this story takes place?

Introduce the Selection

Read the title and the author's name with students. Ask them if they know what a tug of war is. Read the first vocabulary tip with them to present the meaning.

Read the Selection

BLUE TAPE

Read through the story once, using the illustrations to clarify meaning. Then read the story again and use the tips to help students with reading strategies and understanding content. Have students describe how they use each stategy tip. Play Side 1 of the Blue Tape. Let students listen to the tape of the story as often as they want.

Identify and discuss the characters with students.

Model a Strategy

Use Context Clues to Find Meaning

Model the use of context clues to find meaning:

When I see a word that I don't understand, I read the sentence again. I look for other words that can help me understand the word better. For example, I know that "lumbering fool" on page 165 is an insult by the elephant's reaction.

Language Awareness

Spelling
Quotation Marks for Dialogue

Point out Tortoise's response to Elephant's threats, "I challenge you to a contest of strength, a tug of war," on page 166. Explain to students that quotation marks are used in dialogue to show words that a character actually says to another character or to the reader. Students can work in pairs to find other examples of words a character says to someone on pages 164 through 167. Point out that each new paragraph usually signals that a different character is speaking.

Teachable Moment

Literature: Animal Tales

Ask students: *What is a folk tale?* Write their responses on chart paper. Make sure they understand that every culture has its own folk tales. Some tales involve animals and teach about human behavior. As they read, ask students to think about what kind of behavior *The Tug of War* teaches.

Options for Reaching All Students

Beginning

Language Arts: Pantomime

TPR

In groups of three, have students choose characters from the story *The Tug of War*. Ask them to review what their character says and does in the story. Then have them pantomime those things the character does.

Advanced

Writing: Find the Events

Ask students to list the main events in the story.

Home Connection

Animal Folk Tales

Invite students to ask their families to tell a folk tale with animals they know from childhood. Encourage students to share the story with the class or ask family members to come and tell the story. You can make a class book of animal folk tales.

The Tug Of War

by Pleasant DeSpain

Vocabulary Tip
Language
Tug of war is a game of motion. People play it by pulling on both ends of a rope. The winner is the one who can pull the hardest.

ONCE LONG AGO Tortoise was crawling along a jungle trail. He had just been chased out of the river by Hippo and was not in a friendly mood. Suddenly, Elephant rushed across the path and nearly stepped on Tortoise.

"Watch where you're going, you big, lumbering fool!" cried Tortoise.

Elephant did not like to be insulted and replied, "You watch where you're going, tiny Tortoise, and also watch your sharp tongue. It could get you into trouble."

"You don't frighten me," said Tortoise defiantly. "I'm stronger than you realize. In fact, I'm as strong as you."

"No, you're not!" trumpeted Elephant. "You are too small to have my strength, and if you don't apologize for your silly boasts, I'm going to step on you!"

Strategy Tip
Make Inferences
You can use what you know about the story to help you figure out a new word or expression. What does Elephant mean when he says Tortoise has a "sharp tongue"?

Language Tip
Vocabulary
When people talk about how good they are at doing something, they are making a boast.

"I have a better idea," said Tortoise, as he took hold of a stout vine. "I challenge you to a contest of strength, a tug-of-war. You hold one end of this long vine with your trunk and I'll go down to the river with the other end. I will try to pull you into the water and you will try to pull me into the jungle. When I yell, 'Pull, O mighty beast, pull!' the contest begins."

"Very well," agreed Elephant, "it will be fun to make a fool of you."

Tortoise took the other end of the vine and disappeared into the thick jungle growth. When he arrived at the river's edge, he called, "Hippo! Hippo! Stick your head out of the water if you're brave enough!"

The huge hippo slowly surfaced and swam over to Tortoise. "Are you calling me, little one?"

"Yes, big one," answered Tortoise. "You chased me out of the river earlier today, and now I'm mad. You think that you're strong because of your size. I'm going to show you that I, too, am strong."

Language Tip
Vocabulary
Hippo is a short form of *hippopotamus*.

Connect

Develop Language and Concepts

Present Pages 168 Through 171

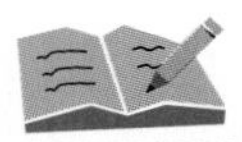

Have students retell the story to this point. Discuss with them how briefly retelling what has happened will help them better understand what they are hearing or reading. Using Activity Book page 88 to check students' comprehension.

When students have become familiar with the story, use it for a Readers' Theater experience. Assign each character as a role for a student and also assign a narrator. Review dialogue with students so that they understand which parts of the story they will be reading. When students have had an opportunity to rehearse their parts, perform the story.

Language Awareness

Vocabulary
Action Words

Review action words with students. Help them to find and act out examples of action words on pages 168 through 171. For instance, *pulled, laughed, yelled, grunted, caught one's breath, chased.* Encourage students to act out other words from the story.

Use Activity Book Page 89 for practice with action words.

Response Activities

Personal Response

Have students answer these questions:

How did you feel when Tortoise won the tug of war? Why? Which character reminded you most of yourself? Have you ever acted like Hippo, Tortoise, or Elephant?

Critical Response

Have students answer these questions:

Folk tales similar to this are found in many different countries and places. What does the tale teach? Why do you think it is told all over the world? Do you know any folk tales like this one?

Creative Response

Ask students to describe what will happen the next time Tortoise meets Elephant on the path, or meets Hippo at the river.

Options for Reaching All Students

Beginning

Writing: Story Chart

Help students complete the Story Elements Chart, Blackline Master 25 in the Teacher's Resource Book, in which they list characters and main story events.

Advanced

Science: Research Animal Facts

Have students research and find two interesting real-life facts about the three kinds of animals in the story: a hippo, an elephant, and a tortoise.

Mixed Ability

Critical Thinking: Compare Characters

Have students work in pairs of mixed ability to compare Elephant and Hippo. Ask them how they are the same, and how they are different.

Strategy Tip
Make Inferences
What does Hippo mean when he tells Tortoise that his words are bigger than his shell?

Strategy Tip
Stop and Think
Why do you think Tortoise challenges Hippo?

Hippo was amused by Tortoise's angry speech and said, "Your words are bigger than your shell, little friend. How can you prove such a boast?"

"By challenging you to a tug of war!" said Tortoise. "You take this end of the vine in your mouth and I'll go into the jungle and take up the other end. You try to pull me into the river, and I'll try to pull you out of it. I'll yell, 'Pull, O mighty beast, pull!' when I'm ready."

Hippo laughed and said, "I agree. It will be fun to teach you some manners."

Hippo bit on the end of the vine and Tortoise walked back into the trees. Then he yelled in his loudest voice, "Pull, O mighty beast, pull!"

Both Elephant and Hippo began to pull, and they pulled and pulled with all of their strength, but neither could gain on the other.

Strategy Tip
Understand Vocabulary
Use the other words in the sentence to guess the meaning of *yelled*.

"Tortoise is as strong as Hippo!" thought Elephant as he grunted and pulled even harder.

"Tortoise is as strong as Elephant!" thought Hippo as he strained and pulled harder still.

When he could see that Elephant and Hippo were growing very tired, Tortoise yelled, "Stop, stop! Let's call it a tie. I'm afraid that the vine will break!"

Both of the large beasts were happy to stop pulling.

Strategy Tip
Make a Picture
Make a picture in your mind of Elephant and Hippo on page 170 of the story. What makes this part of the story funny?

Language Tip
Vocabulary
A *tie* happens when a game ends and there is no winner. No one loses, but no one wins.

Tortoise ran to Elephant, and as soon as Elephant caught his breath, he said, "You are strong, friend Tortoise, and I will be careful of where I step from now on."

Then Tortoise went down to the river and Hippo said, "I'm sorry for chasing you out of the water, little friend. You are much too strong to be joked with."

Tortoise was treated with great respect from that time forth.

Study Tip
Trickster Tales
Many folk tales have tricksters. A trickster can be an animal or a person. Tricksters try to fool others. They think they are smart. Who is the trickster in this story? How does the trickster fool the others?

Connect

Activate Prior Knowledge

Review Vocabulary

Briefly review motion vocabulary and action words with students.

Develop Language and Concepts

Present Page 172

Read the poem first and review any words that students might not understand. Explain that microbes are among the smallest living things and specks are tiny pieces of dust in the air. Play the poem on Side 2 of the Blue Tape several times and encourage students to recite the poem along with the tape.

Language Awareness

Spelling
Rhyming Words with Different Spellings

Have students look at the words at the end of lines. Tell them that poems often have rhyming words at the end of lines. Help them find the rhyming words:

everywhere, air
too, through, new

Explain to them that endings of words can sound the same but be spelled differently.

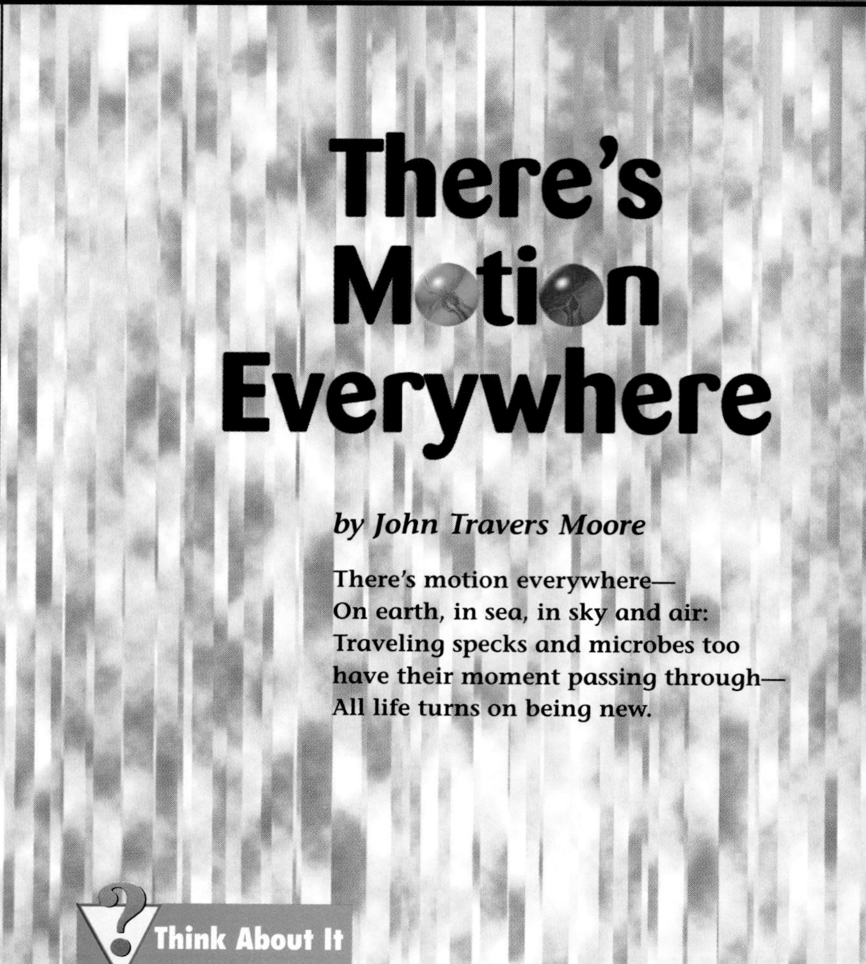

There's Motion Everywhere

by John Travers Moore

There's motion everywhere—
On earth, in sea, in sky and air:
Traveling specks and microbes too
have their moment passing through—
All life turns on being new.

Think About It

The author of the poem writes that there is motion on earth, in the sea, and in the air. What examples can you give to show that the author is right?

Options for Reaching All Students

Beginning

Art: Collage

Ask students to work in pairs. Have them collect magazine pictures that show motion. Encourage them to select pictures that show a variety of types of motion and a variety of places where it is occurring. Have them arrange the pictures as a collage that shows there is motion everywhere.

Advanced

Writing: Poetry in Motion

Have students write a concrete poem whose shape illustrates its contents. Provide examples on the board: such as the words *throw a ball* in the trajectory of ball being thrown, *bounce* in the shape of words going to the ground and coming back up.

Tell what you learned.

CHAPTER 9

1. Draw a picture of one way to make an object move. Label your picture.
2. How do gravity and friction work to stop a baseball?
3. Draw a picture of what your classroom might look like if there were no force of gravity.
4. People often are afraid of other people who are a lot bigger than they are. Was Tortoise afraid of Elephant and Hippo? How do you know?
5. Play a tug-of-war game. What forces of motion do you use in a tug of war?

Assess

Activity 1: Students should be able to show a force that makes an object move.

Activity 2: Evaluate whether students understand two concepts—friction slows everything down by rubbing, and gravity is a pulling action toward the ground.

Activity 3: Check that students understand that gravity keeps everything on the ground.

Activity 4: Evaluate students' understanding that size and muscle strength are not the only strengths. They should see that Tortoise was very much in charge and was not afraid.

Activity 5: Check that students understand that two opposing pulling forces are involved.

Have students complete the Chapter Self-Assessment, Blackline Master 31. Have students choose the product of one of the activities to place in their portfolio. Add results of rubrics, self-assessments, or portfolio assessments, Blackline Masters 2–18 and 31.

Listening Assessment

BLACKLINE MASTER

Make sure that each student has a copy of Blackline Master 81 from the Teacher's Resource Book. Play the tape several times and have students complete the activity.

CREAM TAPE

See page T154c for the tapescript.

Options for Assessment

Vocabulary Assessment

Charades

Make word cards with motion words from the chapter. Each student chooses a motion card and acts out the word. The other students try to guess the word and to write it down.

Writing Assessment

Experiment Reports

Have students choose one of the experiments from this chapter and write about it.

Language Assessment

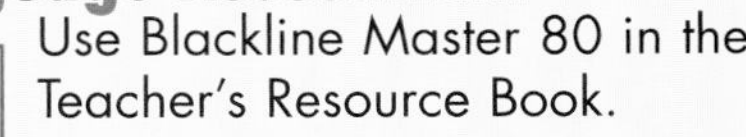

BLACKLINE MASTER

Use Blackline Master 80 in the Teacher's Resource Book.

Standardized Test Practice

ACTIVITY BOOK

Use pages 90 and 91.
Answers: **1.** the ice is too smooth for much friction to occur **2.** float **3.** friction **4.** gravity

Preview

Activate Prior Knowledge

Use Pictures

Use pictures showing experiences that could be described with the words in the Word Bank. Introduce those words. Ask students to talk about scary or exciting experiences they have had. Then use pictures to introduce the topic of roller coasters. Ask students to share their experiences of amusement parks. Ask, *What rides have you been on? How did those rides make you feel?* Use the Word Bank words *fun, exciting, safe,* and *scary.*

Develop Language and Concepts

Present Pages 174 and 175

BLACKLINE MASTER

Invite students to look at the pictures on pages 174 and 175 of people riding roller coasters. Encourage them to come up with their own words to describe roller coasters and how it feels to ride one. Have students respond to Tell What You Know questions. Start a list of words that describe feelings. Then talk about what they would see or hear on a roller coaster. Use the Talk About It questions to help students brainstorm words. Ask them why some people will not ride on roller coasters. Ask students to share their words with the class. Have students work in pairs and create a T-chart, Blackline Master 22, with the categories *Good Things About Roller Coasters* and *Bad Things About Roller Coasters.*

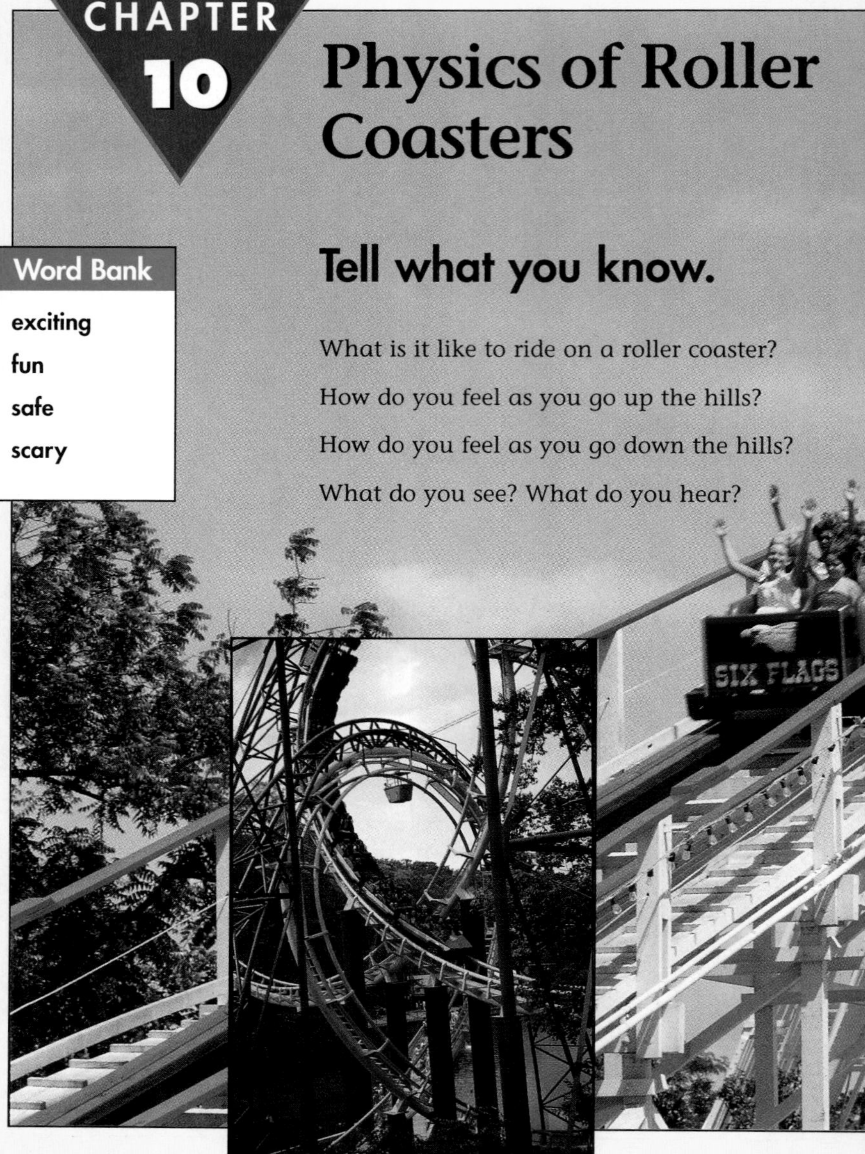

CHAPTER 10

Physics of Roller Coasters

Word Bank

exciting
fun
safe
scary

Tell what you know.

What is it like to ride on a roller coaster?

How do you feel as you go up the hills?

How do you feel as you go down the hills?

What do you see? What do you hear?

174

Options for Reaching All Students

Beginning

Language: Roller Coaster Ride

Ask students to draw a picture of a roller coaster or a similar ride they have been on. Have them write as many words as possible to describe the different emotions one ride brings. For example, *During my ride on a roller coaster I am scared, happy, excited, thrilled,* and so on.

Advanced

Critical Thinking: Predict

Tell students that they are going to design their ideal roller coaster. Have them make diagrams of that coaster. Encourage them to label as many parts as they can. Then ask them to predict what parts of a roller coaster are affected by laws of motion. Have them hold onto their predictions to see if they were right.

Mixed Ability

Language: Emotion Words

TPR

Make cards with the words *fun, exciting, safe,* and *scary.* With students in groups, have each one draw a card and act it out for others to guess.

Talk About It

What do you like best about riding on a roller coaster? What don't you like?

Why do people like roller coasters?

FYI: Roller Coaster

Roller coasters are designed by using the laws of motion. Engines give roller coaster trains the energy to go up the first hill. Then they stop and go according to the laws of momentum, inertia, and forces of gravity and friction. Centrifugal force allows them to go around loops while riders stay in their seats.

Home Connection

Family Interview

Ask students to interview their family members to learn of stories about exciting adventures they may have had. Invite students to share their interviews with the class.

Present

Activate Prior Knowledge

Review Vocabulary

Ask students to share their knowledge about the way a bicycle moves. Ask students these questions:

- What makes a bicycle start moving?
- What happens when a bicycle goes down a hill?
- Then what happens when it comes to flat ground?
- What happens when it goes up a hill?

Develop Language and Concepts

Present Pages 176 and 177

Write these words on the board: *zoom, twist, curve, hill,* and *loop*. Help students use the text and pictures to define these words.

Read pages 176 and 177 with students and ask them to pay special attention to any new information on the forces of motion.

After reading the page, discuss with students what it means to build up energy. Compare how the roller coaster works with a bicycle.

Suggest that students think of their own experiences with physical activity. These can include bicycle riding or in-line skating. What does it feel like to build up energy? Write students' responses on a chart.

How does a roller coaster work?

A roller coaster is fun and scary. First, it goes slowly up, up, up a big hill. Then it zooms and twists down a track.

A roller coaster train needs a motor to climb the first hill. After that, it runs because of the forces of motion.

The train goes down the first hill because of gravity. As it zooms down the hill, it builds up **energy** from the motion. Energy is the ability to do work.

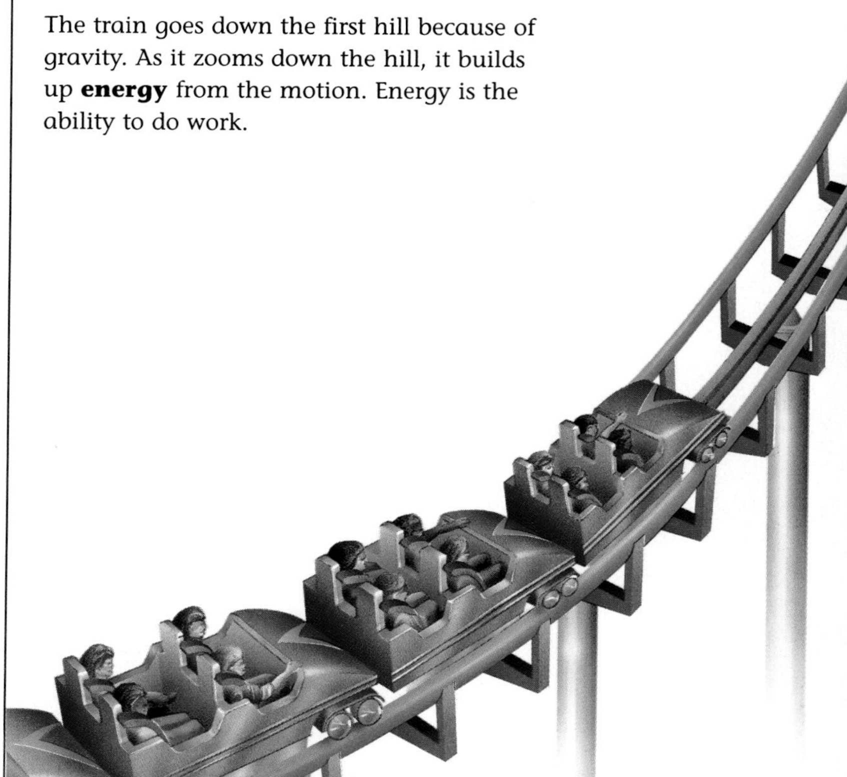

Options for Reaching All Students

Beginning

Language: Chant

Have students sing rounds while they chant the words *The roller coaster zooms up the hill and loops around the curves. It goes and goes on energy, until there's none to burn.* They can clap their hands when the say particular words, such as *zoom* or *roller coaster*, in order to reinforce vocabulary and concepts.

Advanced

Critical Thinking: Diagram a Ride

Ask students to diagram a roller coaster ride and indicate where the train would pick up energy and where it would expend energy. Encourage them to predict where the train would gather the most energy and where it would expend the most energy.

Mixed Ability

Critical Thinking: Getting Around

Pair students in mixed ability and have them invent a new form of transportation using what they know about energy and motion.

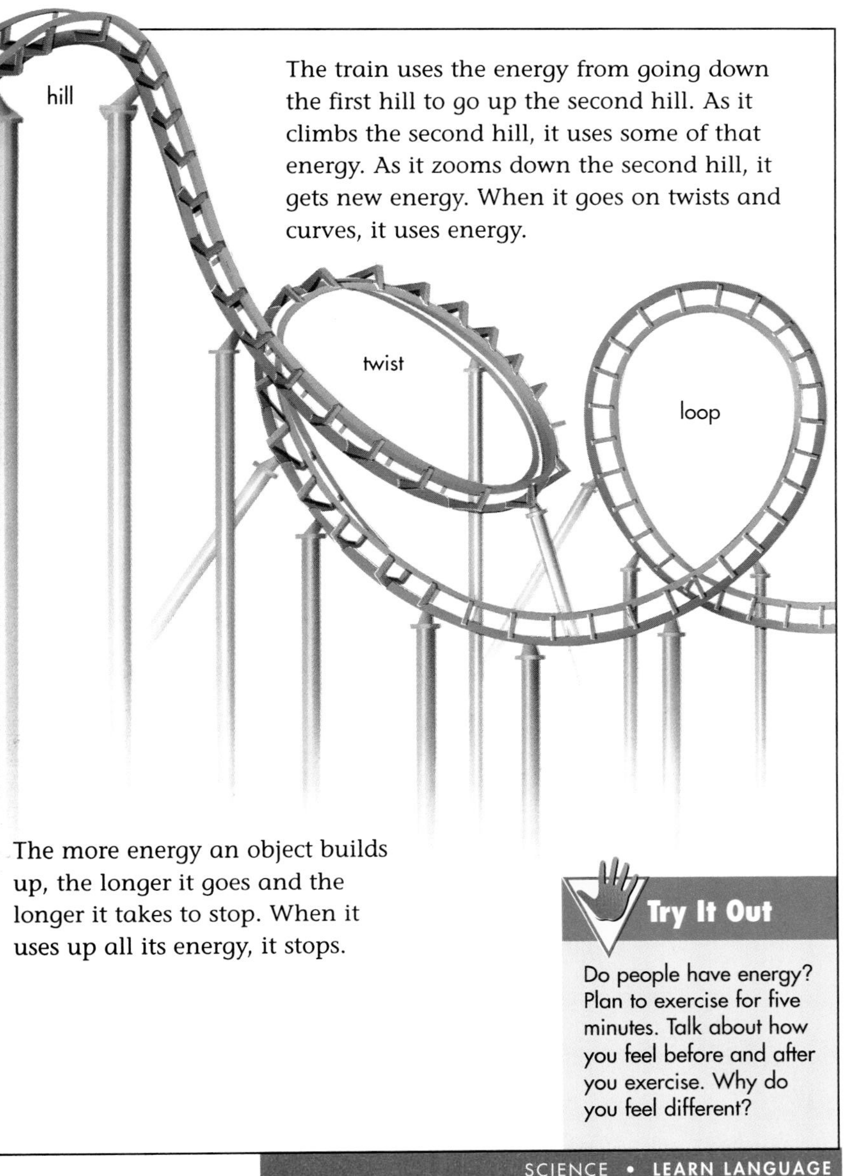

The train uses the energy from going down the first hill to go up the second hill. As it climbs the second hill, it uses some of that energy. As it zooms down the second hill, it gets new energy. When it goes on twists and curves, it uses energy.

The more energy an object builds up, the longer it goes and the longer it takes to stop. When it uses up all its energy, it stops.

Try It Out

Do people have energy? Plan to exercise for five minutes. Talk about how you feel before and after you exercise. Why do you feel different?

Language Awareness

Grammar
Words That Show a Sequence

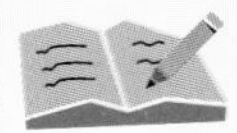

ACTIVITY BOOK

Direct students' attention to the steps involved in a roller coaster ride.

Point out to students that these steps occur consecutively, or one after the other, as opposed to simultaneously, or all at once. Point out the adverbs that indicate order in time; *first, then, after that.* Model an example of their use by giving an example of your daily activities and invite students to make their own sentences.

Use Activity Book page 92.

Assess

Use students' responses to Try It Out for assessment. Students should be able to

- tell what energy is (ability to do work)
- show how objects in motion gain energy
- show how objects in motion expend energy

LOOK **AHEAD**

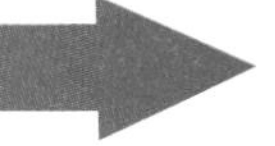

In the next section, students will learn how the laws of motion apply to a roller coaster ride.

Cooperative Language Experience

Field Trip

Take students to a constuction site. Help them identify forces of motion in construction equipment, tools, and workers. Have students write a story about the trip and what they learned about energy.

Practice

Activate Prior Knowledge

Start a K-W-L Chart

Find out what students know about how a roller coaster works. Use the information to make a K-W-L Chart:

K: What We Know	A roller coaster runs on energy.
W: What We Want to Find Out	What affects how far a roller coaster goes?
L: What We Learned	

Complete the chart at the end of the lesson.

Develop Language and Concepts

Present Pages 178 and 179

ACTIVITY BOOK

Read the activity to the students. Tell students they will do a science experiment. Have students work in small groups. Have one student from each group retell the steps to make sure everyone understands the procedure.

Ask students to look for similarities between a roller coaster and a marble track as they do the activity. Have them record results. Activity Book page 93 can be used to record results.

FYI: Pipe Insulation
Pipe insulation is inexpensive and can be found at a local hardware store. You might want to get foam rubber because it's easy to bend and to tape. Before class begins, cut the insulation in half.

What things affect how far a roller coaster goes?

A roller coaster runs on energy. Gravity and friction affect how a roller coaster runs.

Work with a group. Do an experiment to see how gravity, friction, and energy work.

Things You Need

- foam insulation pipe, cut in half the long way
- masking tape
- marble

1. Put the pieces of pipe together to make a marble track 12 feet (4 meters) long.
2. Place one end of the track against the wall. The top of the track should be 6 inches (15 centimeters) off the ground. Make the track straight. Tape it in place.

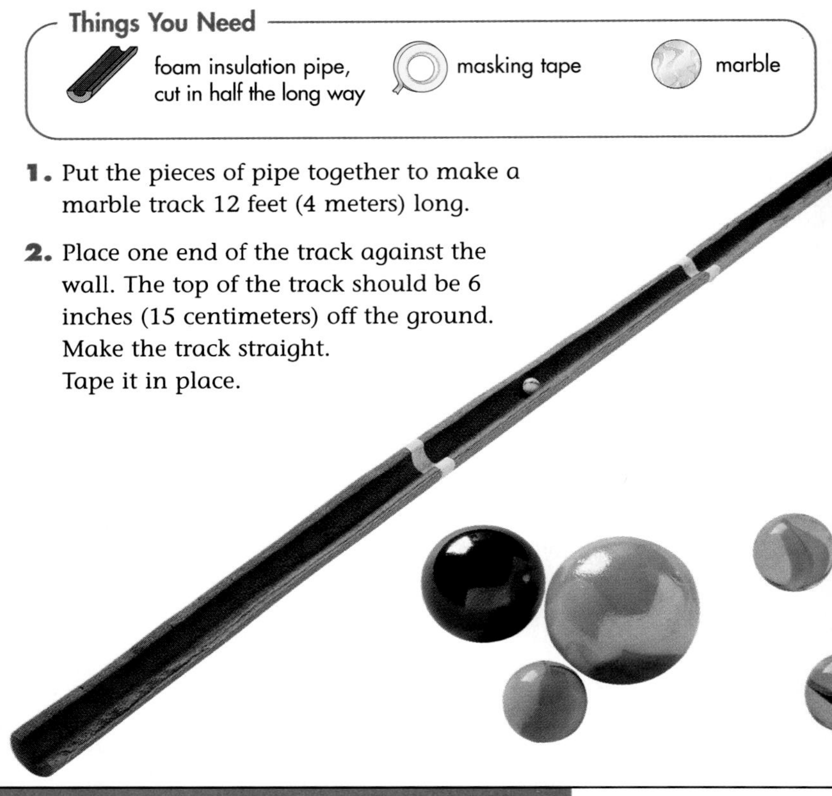

Options for Reaching All Students

Beginning

Language: Use Pictures

PICTURE CARDS

Display Picture Cards of vehicles. Invite students to choose a vehicle and illustrate how forces of motion help it operate. For example, a sail boat runs on energy from wind and water current. A motor supplies the energy for a car or bus. Then students can illustrate it and label the forces of motion. (Picture card numbers: 1 airplane, 5 bike, 6 boat, 10 bus, 13 car, 29 fire engine, 59 sailboats)

Advanced

Science: Physics of Everyday Activities

Ask students to think of other common instances of gravity, friction, and motion in their lives. Have each student create a chart with the headings *Gravity, Friction,* and *Motion.* Have them fill in the charts with examples from ordinary activities. For example, under motion, a student might write *riding my bike down a hill;* under gravity, *throwing a penny*

3. Put the marble at the top of the track. Let it roll down the track. Where does the marble stop? Mark the place with a piece of tape.

4. Roll the marble down the track again three times. Number each tape.

Can you make the marble roll farther? What happens if you use a curvy track? What happens if you make the beginning of the track higher? Think of other things with your group. Try them.

Write About It

Write a lab report showing what you did and your results.

Language Awareness

Vocabulary
Exprssions with *up*

Call students' attention to the expressions *builds up* and *uses up*. Point out that there are many expressions in English with up. After the word add the idea of "completely": When you use up your energy, you have no more energy. Adding up after a verb gives it a special meaning. Help students list and define expressions with *up, such as get up, pick up.*

Assess

Use students' lab reports from Write About It to see if students understand

- that a roller coaster travels farther when it builds up more energy
- that a roller coaster comes to a stop because it uses up all its energy

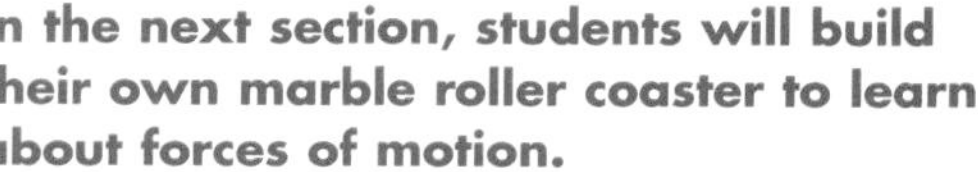

In the next section, students will build their own marble roller coaster to learn about forces of motion.

in a fountain; under friction, *scraping my knee on the pavement.*

Cooperative Learning Experience

Share Experiment Results

Ask students of mixed ability to work in pairs. Invite students to brainstorm what they learned from the activity and write about it in a group experience story.

Writer's Workshop

A Roller Coaster Ride

Refer students to the Writer's Workshop on pages 230 to 236 in the Student Book. Have students write about an exciting experience they have had, such as riding on a roller coaster.

Practice

Activate Prior Knowledge

Brainstorm Vocabulary

Show students a picture of an amusement park. Ask students to name their favorite amusement park rides. Encourage them to analyze why these rides are fun. Direct their attention to elements such as height, speed, loops, and curves.

Develop Language and Concepts

Present Pages 180 and 181

Read the introduction to the activity with the students. Brainstorm what their ideal roller coaster would look like. Write their responses on the board. Ask students to work in small groups to build their own marble track.

Remind students to take notes and look for answers to the questions listed in Talk About It on page 181. Make sure the students understand that the energy that a roller coaster builds up going down the first slope influences how much energy it has for the length of the track. Activity Book page 94 can be used to record results.

Model a Strategy

Visualize

Model ways that visualizing can be helpful:

When I am getting ready to plan an activity, such as building a roller coaster, I make pictures in my mind of possible results of the activity. Visualizing helps me to get ideas for carrying out the project.

What forces work together on a roller coaster?

Think about your ideal roller coaster. What would it look like? Would it have hills, loops, or curves? Work in a group to build your own marble coaster. Put all your ideas together. Start with the insulation pipe from the last experiment. Add any materials you have.

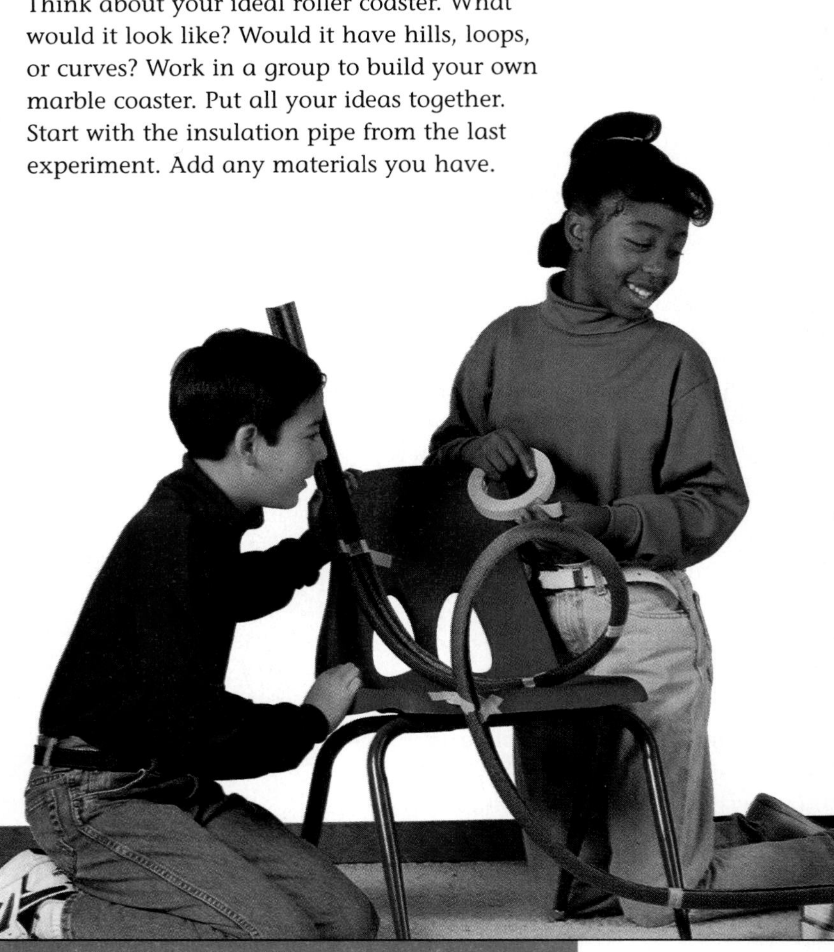

Options for Reaching All Students

Beginning

Science: Retelling

Have students retell the results of the activity to a partner from another group. Encourage students to demonstrate what they did, how they changed the marble track, and their conclusions from the experiment. Students can use their lab reports and diagrams to help them.

Advanced

Critical Thinking Making Predictions

Have students make predictions about what part of a roller coaster helps it build up energy, and where it loses energy. Students should base their predictions on what they learned from the marble track. Ask them to diagram it and write their predictions down.

Mixed Ability

Art: Amusement Park

Pair students of mixed ability. Have them draw the different rides at an amusement park. Ask them to label as many forces of motion at work as possible.

Roll your marble down the track. You may find the marble does not have enough energy to go all the way up the second hill. Together decide how you can make the marble build up more energy to make it go all the way to the end of the track.

Share what you learned with the class.

Write about the results.

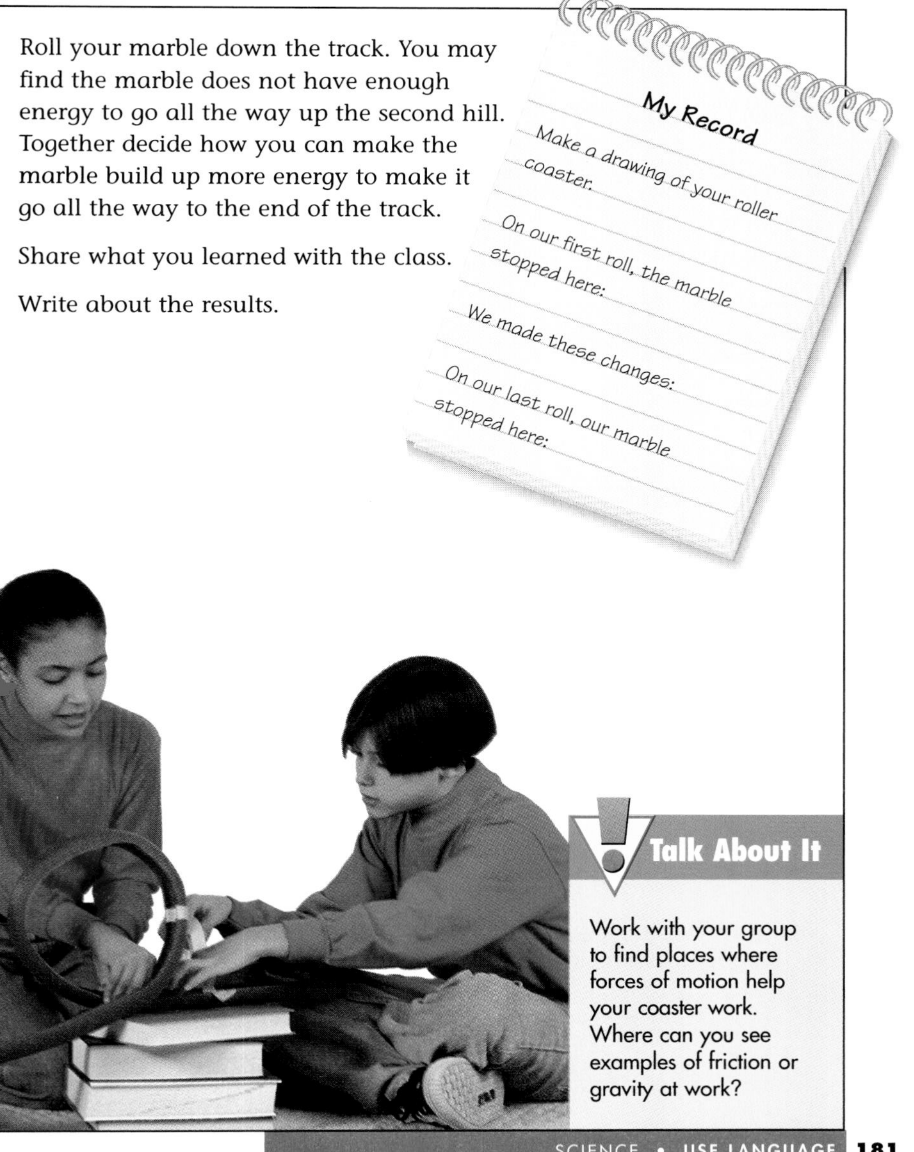

My Record
Make a drawing of your roller coaster.
On our first roll, the marble stopped here:
We made these changes:
On our last roll, our marble stopped here:

Talk About It

Work with your group to find places where forces of motion help your coaster work. Where can you see examples of friction or gravity at work?

Language Awareness

Grammar
Conditional Sentences

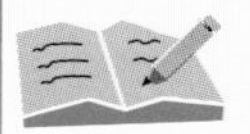
ACTIVITY BOOK

Write the following sentence on the board:

If you could build your own roller coaster, what would it look like?

Explain that *if* clauses are used to talk about situations and things that we think about or imagine. For example, *If I could go to an amusement park, I would ride the roller coaster all day.*

Provide students with sentence starters to complete such as *If I could fly, I would _____.* *If I could drive a car, I would _____.* Use Activity Book pages 95 and 96.

Assess 

Use students' responses to Talk About It for assessment. Students should be able to tell what they learned from the activity.

LOOK**AHEAD**

In the next section, students will calculate the relationship between height and length of a roller coaster.

Peer Tutoring

Language: Conditional Sentences

Have students work in pairs with mixed ability to complete sentences.

The form they should use is:

If I could, I would be _____ so that I could _____.

Give them some examples, such as

If I could, I would be an astronaut, so I could go in space.

Brainstorm a few examples with them before they begin working in pairs.

QuickCheck

Comparatives and Superlatives

Check that students use comparatives and superlatives correctly when they report the results of their experiments.

Connect

Activate Prior Knowledge

Use Illustrations to Predict

Have students look at the chart and read the lesson title. Ask them what information this chart might include. Invite students to make predictions about the activity.

Review with students the meanings of the words *height, length,* and *average*. Measure the heights of several students and then help them to find the average height.

Develop Language and Concepts

Present Pages 182 and 183

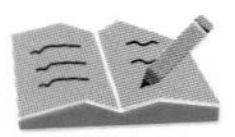

Read the introduction and the chart with students, calling their attention to the various roller coaster names. Review the information given about each roller coaster.

Ask if any student has ridden one of these tall roller coasters. How long was the ride? Do higher roller coasters give rides that are longer? Shorter? The same? Students should look at the information and see that higher roller coasters provide longer rides. Ask them to why. (The trains are able to build up more energy.)

Read the questions on page 183 with students and ask them to solve the math problems. Use Activity Book page 97 for more practice with averages. Use Activity Book page 98 for review of chapter vocabulary.

Can a taller coaster give you a longer ride?

The chart shows the height and length of four roller coasters. Compare these numbers.

Roller Coaster	Place	Height of First Hill	Length of Track
American Eagle	Six Flags, IL	39 meters	1,400 meters
Colossus	Six Flags, CA	35 meters	1,300 meters
The Twister	Blitch Gardens, CO	30 meters	900 meters
The Riverside Cyclone	Riverside Park, MA	33 meters	1,000 meters

Answer these questions:

1. How long is the longest roller coaster?
2. How long is the roller coaster with the shortest first hill?
3. How does the height of the hill affect the length of the track?

Options for Reaching All Students

Beginning

Math: Chart a Marble Run

Invite students to make a bar graph that displays the results of their marble runs down the track. Have them show the height of the track and the length of the run. If you have access to a computer, the students can make their graph on a computer.

Advanced

Math: Graph Height and Length

Help students visualize the relationship of height to length of the roller coasters by making a diagram of each one. Have them use a scale of one square for every five meters of length.

Students will need to fasten pages of graph paper together to allow for the length. Have them color in the appropriate number of squares for each measurement.

Cooperative Learning

Math: Height and Length

Have students use the track and marbles from previous activities. Have them start with a straight track at a height of seven centimeters, roll the marble, and mark how far the marble goes with a piece of tape. Have them repeat the procedure three times. Each time they should raise the starting point by 5 centimeters. Ask them to record their results and share them with the class.

What is the relationship between the height of the first hill and the length of the track?

1. Find how far each roller coaster goes for a meter of its height. For example, The Twister is 30 meters high and 900 meters long. You can find how far it goes for each meter of its height by dividing the height into the length. The Twister goes 30 meters for each meter of its height.

$30\overline{)900}$

2. Find the answer for each of the coasters. When you have figured out each answer, find the average of all four. You will have the average distance a coaster travels for each meter of height.

Try It Out

Use the average distance for each meter of height. If you build a coaster with a hill that is 42 meters high, how far will the roller coaster go?

Language Awareness

Vocabulary
Math Words for Averaging

Work with students to introduce them to English terms for the steps they use in computing averages. Work through an averaging problem with them using these terms: *entries, add, divide,* and *results.* Tell students the items to be averaged are *entries.* Then they add the numbers for each *entry* and *divide* by the number of entries. The *result* is the average.

Model a Strategy

How to Read a Chart

Model how to read a chart:

I use the categories at the top of a chart to understand what information is being given. I can use a ruler as a guide to help me line up the information with its correct heading in the side column.

Assess

Students should be able to predict that the roller coaster in Try It Out would be longer than the other coasters.

LOOK**AHEAD**

In the next section, students will read an article on roller coaster enthusiasts.

Ask them to infer why height makes such a difference in how far the marble goes.

Connect

Activate Prior Knowledge

Use the Title and Pictures to Predict

Have students look at the title of this article and the pictures. Ask questions such as:

- What do you think this article is about?
- What is a "Scream Machine"?
- What is happening in this picture?

Develop Language and Concepts

Present Pages 184 Through 187

Look at the title with students. Ask them to infer why a roller coaster would be called a scream machine. Ask them if they think the name is a good one. Ask them why they think so.

Model a Strategy

Words with Multiple Meanings

Model ways to understand words in context:

Many words in English have two or more meanings. I find this confusing. To know which way a word is being used, I look at the context clues to help me. For example, a record *can be the written results of an experiment. When I do an experiment, I keep a* record *of the results. The article says Richard Rodriguez set a* record *for the longest ride on a roller coaster. The next sentence helps me to figure out that* record *means something no one else had ever done before.*

Language Awareness

Language Function
Express Excitement

Point out that certain words can be used to express a tone or feeling. Words such as *thrilling, exciting,* and *scary* describe emotion. There are also interjections such as *Wow! Super! Ooh!* Provide a list. Have students role-play using the words in exciting situations.

Response Activities

Personal Response

Have students tell their reactions to the people described in the story. Do they think it would be fun to ride many roller coasters or to spend a long time on one roller coaster?

Critical Response

Have students divide the magazine article into sections: introduction, middle, and end. Where do they divide them? Ask what two topics the middle itself talks about.

Creative Response

Have students think of an unusual activity that they would really like to do similar to riding a roller coaster for a long time. Have them explain what it would be and describe the experience.

Options for Reaching All Students

Beginning

Language: Role-play an Interview

Help students practice interviewing another person. Encourage them to plan with these questions: *What do I want to find out? What questions do I want to ask?*

Have them work in pairs to role-play an interview with Richard Roderiguez. Have each pair evaluate the questions they asked after the role-play.

Advanced

Writing: Point of View

Invite students to work in their journals. Have them write entries from the point of view of Richard Rodriguez. Encourage them to imagine how it feels to ride a roller coaster for four days. Start them off with the following:

Day One: Today is the most exciting day of my life. I am determined to set a record! I . . .

Mixed Ability

Language: Interview

Have students interview each other to find out what was the most exciting and scary experience they ever had. Students can share their interview with the class.

Riding the Scream Machine

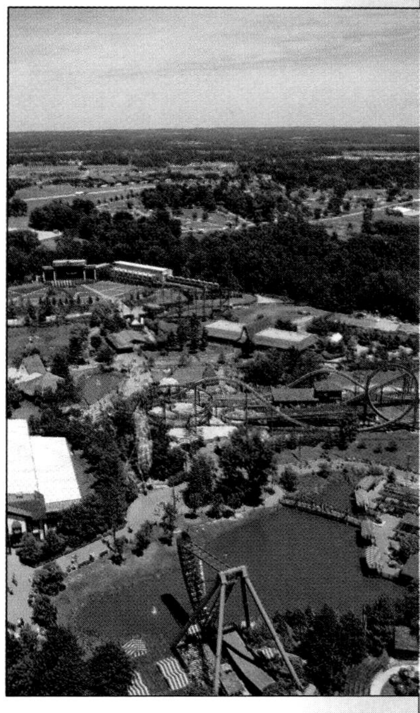

Why do people love roller coasters? Why do they look for the exciting feeling they get as they zoom down the track?

Ask Michael Api. He started riding the roller coasters soon after he started to walk. By the age of nine, he had ridden 62 different roller coasters. His 14-year-old brother, Robert, has already ridden more than 140 coasters. The brothers want to ride even more roller coasters.

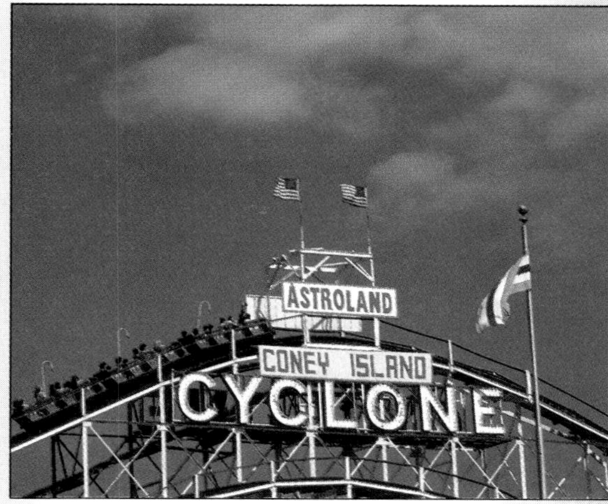

Other lovers of roller coasters take the same ride many times. Ask Richard Rodriguez. He rode Cyclone, a famous roller coaster at Coney Island in New York, for four days. Actually, he spent 103 hours and 55 minutes taking rides on the roller coaster.

That was a record. No one had ridden a coaster for such a long time.

Ask Carl Eichelman. He rode the famous Beast roller coaster at King's Island Park in Cincinnati, Ohio. He rode this scream machine 4,022 times during a five-year period. That's a lot of hours of thrills.

Many people are not as interested in roller coasters as Michael, Richard, and Carl.

But most riders like scary and exciting rides. As a result, new roller coasters are going up in many places.

These new coasters are even bigger and more exciting.

One example is the Dragon Mountain roller coaster. It is the highest steel coaster in North America. It is at Marineland Park in Niagara Falls, Canada. Riders go down a 186-foot (57-meter) drop and zoom around two vertical loops. The roller coaster passes through a copy of a volcano with lava inside it. Then it passes behind a small copy of Niagara Falls. The ride lasts only 3 minutes and 12 seconds, but it is full of excitement.

So if you ever get the chance, take that roller coaster ride. You may never want to get off.

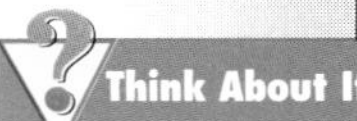

Think about how you would feel after riding a roller coaster for three days. Draw a picture of the way you would feel and share it with your classmates.

Connect

Activate Prior Knowledge

Use a Thesaurus

Present students with a dictionary and a thesaurus and allow them to examine each. Talk about different things they notice about the two books. It is best to use an illustrated thesaurus designed for elementary school students.

Develop Language and Concepts

Present Pages 188 and 189

Have students read the introduction on page 188, and then ask them why someone would use a thesaurus. Explain that writers often use different words with similar meanings to make their writings more interesting and specific. Use these sentences as examples. Ask students to visualize each one.

He walked to the bus.
He dashed to catch the bus.
He strolled to the bus stop.

Read the rest of the page together. Ask students to choose three words that have similar meanings and make their own sentences using these words.

Students can start a class thesaurus to add to the end of each unit. If there is a computer available, you can create a class thesaurus on the computer and print it for class use.

Using a Thesaurus

A **thesaurus** is a book that lists words that are alike in meaning. This part of a thesaurus has words that mean "to move."

A thesaurus can help you with your writing. You can find other words to use in place of a word that you have used again and again.

To move quickly

Dash means to move quickly. It often means to take a short, quick run.

The boy *dashed* to catch the bus.

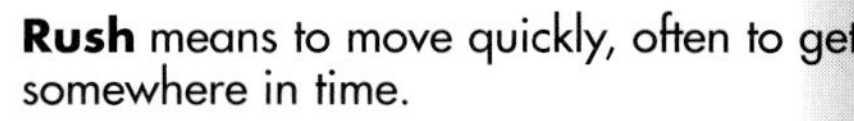

Rush means to move quickly, often to get somewhere in time.

The passengers *rushed* to catch the train.

Zoom means to move at high speed, often in a car or other vehicle.

The cars *zoomed* down the highway.

Options for Reaching All Students

Beginning

Language: Motion Words

Write the words from the thesaurus on cards. Invite students to pick cards and act them out for the group to guess.

Advanced

Writing: A New Thesaurus Entry

Have students work in pairs with a thesaurus to find words similar to one of the following: *happy, scared, tired, good.* Encourage them to make a list, illustrate the new words, and write context sentences.

Mixed Ability

Language: Use a Thesaurus

TPR

Have students work in groups, look through a thesaurus, and find an entry that interests them. Have them write down three or four synonyms and illustrate them or act them out.

To move slowly

Crawl means to move forward on one's hands and knees.

The baby *crawled* to get the toy.

Crawl can also mean to move slowly.

The cars *crawled* down the street.

Inch means to move very slowly, about an inch at a time.

We *inched* our way forward to the ticket booth.

Lumber means to move slowly, as if one were carrying a lot of weight.

The old truck *lumbered* up the mountain road.

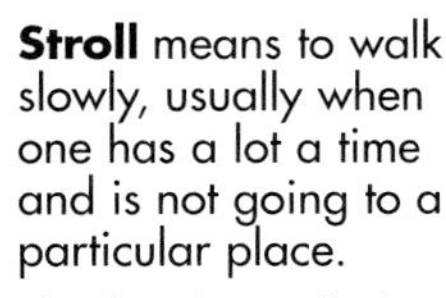

Stroll means to walk slowly, usually when one has a lot a time and is not going to a particular place.

The family *strolled* through the park.

Write About It

Look back at the story "The Tug of War." Find the motion words on page 164. Which ones mean to move quickly? Which ones mean to move slowly?

Language Awareness

Vocabulary
Synonyms and Antonyms

ACTIVITY BOOK

Look at the thesaurus lesson pages with students. Help them to see that the words for *move quickly* are synonyms, and are antonyms for *move slowly*. Use the words *large* and *small* to introduce more synonyms and antonyms; for example, *small, tiny; big, huge, gigantic*. Brainstorm synonyms and antonyms with students. Use a thesaurus with students to add to the list.

Use Activity Book page 99 for more practice with synonyms and antonyms.

Model a Strategy

Use Word Groups to Remember New Words

Model a way to remember new words:

When I want to remember a new word, I think of groups of words I know that are like it. For example, if the word is *delighted*, I think of *happy*, a word that I know. *Delighted* is another way to describe happy feelings. That helps me remember the new word.

Cooperative Learning

Make a Thesaurus

Invite students to work in small groups to brainstorm and create their own thesaurus page using words of motion they have learned in the unit or the ones on the pages. Encourage them to alphabetize the list. Ask them to illustrate new words and write context sentences.

Connect

Activate Prior Knowledge

Use Pictures to Predict

Have students look at the picture illustrating the song lyrics. Ask questions such as:

What do you think this song is about? What is the difference between the twists in a roller coaster and a person twisting?

Develop Language and Concepts

Present Page 190

Introduce the song "Let's Twist Again" by reading the lyrics once. Then play the Blue Tape, Side 2, and invite students to listen to the music and rhythm of the lyrics. Next, replay the tape and invite students to sing along.

Language Awareness

Vocabulary

Slang

Direct students' attention to the words *yeah* and *baby* in the song. Explain that *yeah* is an informal form of *yes,* and *baby* is an informal word for *girl friend,* and both words are known as slang. Help students brainstorm other slang words that they know from songs. Explain that slang may be appropriate in talking to a close friend, but should be avoided in writing or talking to a teacher.

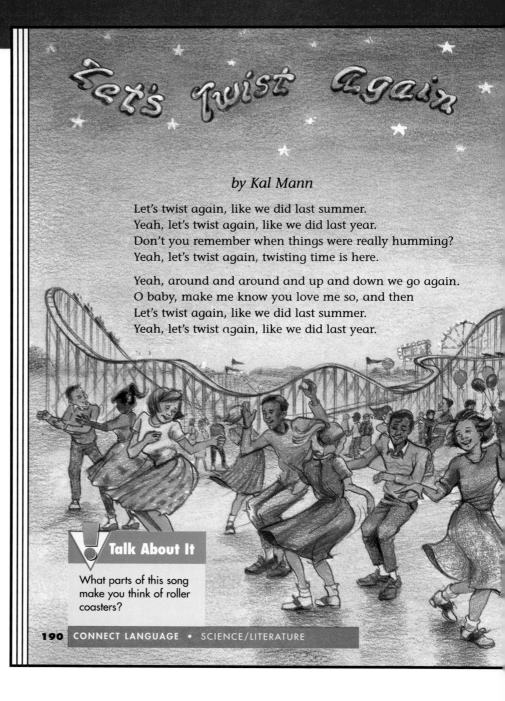

Let's Twist Again

by Kal Mann

Let's twist again, like we did last summer.
Yeah, let's twist again, like we did last year.
Don't you remember when things were really humming?
Yeah, let's twist again, twisting time is here.

Yeah, around and around and up and down we go again.
O baby, make me know you love me so, and then
Let's twist again, like we did last summer.
Yeah, let's twist again, like we did last year.

Talk About It

What parts of this song make you think of roller coasters?

Options for Reaching All Students

Beginning

Language: Chant

TPR

Have students chant the lyrics to the song "Let's Twist Again." Ask them to get up and twist every time they sing, "around and around and around we go."

Advanced

Language: Point of View

Have students brainstorm a list of motion words that describe a roller coaster ride from a rider's point of view. Ask them top act out the words for other classmates to guess.

Cooperative Learning

Music

Have students work in groups. Ask each group to write their own version of *Let's Twist Again*. Review some action words with students. They need to choose an action to substitute for *twist*. Otherwise, the song remains the same. Have students b rainstorm a few possibilities before working with their group. Invite them to be humorous. Have them share their results with the class.

Tell what you learned.

CHAPTER 10

1. How do roller coasters work? What makes them move?
2. How can friction and gravity affect how a roller coaster works?
3. You are going to plan a roller coaster. How would it look? Draw a picture. Explain how it works.
4. Tell about one thing you learned about motion that you did not know before.

Assess

Activity 1: Assess students' ability to describe how a roller coaster works.

Activity 2: Evaluate students' understanding of how friction and gravity affect motion.

Activity 3: Evaluate student's understanding of gaining and using energy.

Activity 4: Evaluate that responses show understanding of motion.

Have students complete the Chapter Self-Assessment, Blackline Master 31. Have students choose the product of one of the activities to place in their portfolios. Add results of rubrics, self-assessments, or portfolio assessments, Blackline Masters 2–18 and 31.

Listening Assessment

BLACKLINE MASTER

Make sure that each student has a copy of Blackline Master 83, from the Teacher's Resource Book. Play the tape several times and ask students to follow the directions for marking answers.

CREAM TAPE

See page T154d for the tapescript.

Options for Assessment

Vocabulary Assessment

Balance

Have students work in pairs with a T-chart for motion words. One side of the T-chart should be words for *moves quickly;* the other should be words for *moves slowly*. All the words on one side are synonyms, the words on the other side are antonyms. One student picks a motion word. The other student must balance that with an antonym for that word.

Writing Assessment

Experiment Results

Have students write about something they did on their roller coaster projects and how that changed the project.

Language Assessment

BLACKLINE MASTER

Use Blackline Master 82 in the Teacher's Resource Book.

Standardized Test Practice

ACTIVITY BOOK

Use pages 100 and 101. Answers: **1.** subtract the area of the pool from the area of the concrete **2.** the number of students attending **3.** 70/3 = S/15 **4.** 1/3

Wrap-Up

Activities

Motion Mural

Have students use books and magazines to find pictures of motion. When they have enough examples, ask them to plan a mural that shows a continuum of motion. Place examples of force toward the left of the mural and examples of friction toward the right. Invite them to choose their own media (paint, markers, crayons, blueprint style) for their mural.

Simple Machines

Have students learn more about motion as demonstrated by simple machines: the lever, the wheel and axle, the pulley, the inclined plane, the wedge, the screw, and gears. Have them research each simple machine, prepare a report, and present it to the rest of the class, using pictures, diagrams, or prototypes.

Motion and Machines at Work

Invite students to research motion at work in the world of construction. Have them contact a construction company, contractor, or engineer and plan a visit to a site where machines are using force to build. Encourage them to observe and ask questions about moving large construction pieces and machinery. Have them draw pictures to report their findings, labeling them as appropriate.

Discussing the Theme

Have students work in small groups to discuss their progress during this unit about physics. Choose from the following activities that will demonstrate to them how much they have learned, how the information applies to their everyday lives, and how useful these types of information are to them.

- Have students tape-record a list of new words learned.
- Have students draw or find pictures that represent words they have learned. Have more advanced students label the pictures and have beginning students review the labels and pictures.
- Discuss with students how motion and the relationship between motion and basic activity is part of everyone's life.
- Have groups discuss situations in which the words they have learned will be useful, for example, in science classes, as they plan activities and as they observe and discuss any type of motion.
- Invite students to draw a picture of a time they were on a roller coaster and label it with the words of motion.

Sharing the Project

Use the invitation form, Blackline Masters 32 and 33, to invite family members to school for a presentation of Physics in Action.

Set up the classroom so that family members can view the photographs or videotape. Also have stations for experiments for family members to visit, if students have done this part of the project. Have students from each group take turns demonstrating and explaining the experiments.

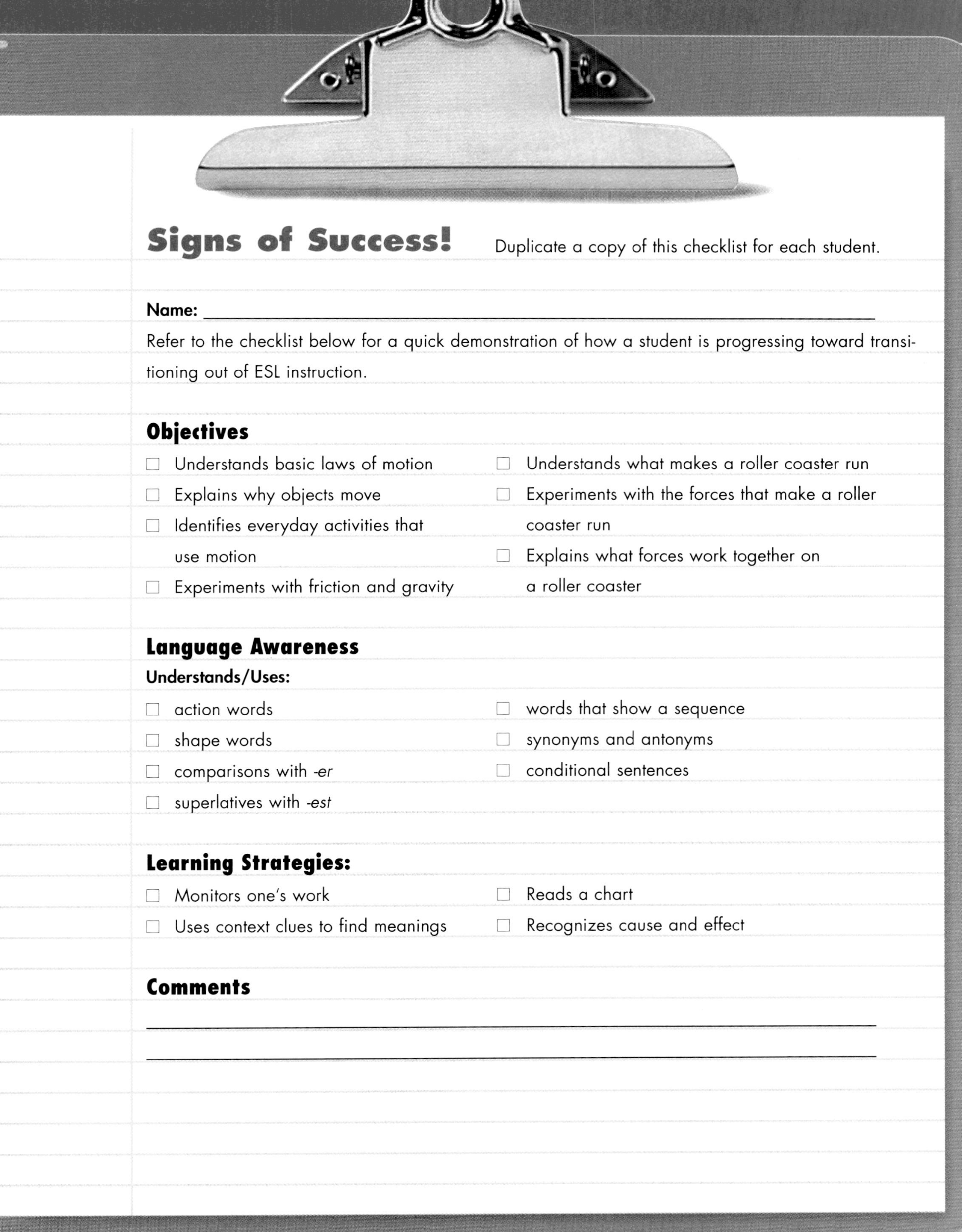

Signs of Success!

Duplicate a copy of this checklist for each student.

Name: ______________________________

Refer to the checklist below for a quick demonstration of how a student is progressing toward transitioning out of ESL instruction.

Objectives

- ☐ Understands basic laws of motion
- ☐ Explains why objects move
- ☐ Identifies everyday activities that use motion
- ☐ Experiments with friction and gravity
- ☐ Understands what makes a roller coaster run
- ☐ Experiments with the forces that make a roller coaster run
- ☐ Explains what forces work together on a roller coaster

Language Awareness

Understands/Uses:

- ☐ action words
- ☐ shape words
- ☐ comparisons with *-er*
- ☐ superlatives with *-est*
- ☐ words that show a sequence
- ☐ synonyms and antonyms
- ☐ conditional sentences

Learning Strategies:

- ☐ Monitors one's work
- ☐ Uses context clues to find meanings
- ☐ Reads a chart
- ☐ Recognizes cause and effect

Comments

____

____

Planning Guide

Handling Stress

Objectives

Describe some of the physical effects of stress.

Identify situations that cause stress.

Name ways to deal with stress.

Discuss school and differences among schools attended.

Vocabulary Focus

Types of feelings associated with stress, such as *sad, happy, angry, excited, nervous.*
Parts of the body that respond to stress, such as *heart, lungs, stomach, glands.*
Words for clothing such as *shirts, sweaters, dresses, coats, earrings.*
Words for food such as *corn, meat, peppers, onions, gravy.*

Lesson	Content Focus	Language Awareness Objectives	Learning Strategies
Preview pp. 192–193 Tell What You Know.			
Present pp. 194–195 What Is Stress?	Health	**Grammar** *May*	
Practice pp. 196–197 What Causes Stress?	Health	**Grammar** *Have to*	Paraphrase/retell.
Practice pp. 198–199 How Can You Deal with Stress?	Health	**Spelling** End Punctuation	Solve a problem.
Connect pp. 200–201 Ask For Help	Health/ Language Arts	**Language Function** Giving Advice	State main idea.
Connect pp. 202–209 *In the Year of the Boar and Jackie Robinson*	Health/ Language Arts	**Language Function** Greetings/ Introductions **Grammar** Infinitives: Telling "Why"	Identify with characters.
Connect pp. 210–213 *Schools in Japan and the United States*	Health/ Reading	**Language Function** Stating Rules: *have to, can't, not allowed to*	Compare and contrast.
Connect p. 214 "You Can Do Better."	Health/ Literature	**Grammar** Comparisons: *Good/Better/Best*	
Assess p. 215 Tell What You Learned.			

CHAPTER 12

Getting Information

Objectives

Describe sources of information.

Tell how to use an encyclopedia as a reference tool.

Describe information found in magazines.

Describe information found in newspapers.

Use graphic organizers to connect information.

Vocabulary Focus

Sources of information, such as *computer, encyclopedia, magazine, newspaper.*

Information words, such as *reference tool, topics, facts, organize.*

Newspaper words, such as *events, current, sections, article, feature.*

Question words such as *who, what, where, when, why.*

Lesson	Content Focus	Language Awareness Objectives	Learning Strategies
Preview pp. 216–217 Tell What You Know.			
Present pp. 218–219 Encyclopedias	Study Skills	**Grammar** Appositives	Understand chronology.
Practice pp. 220–221 Magazines	Study Skills	**Spelling** Punctuation: Quotation Marks	Understand magazine articles.
Practice pp. 222–223 Newspapers	Study Skills	**Grammar** Questions and Answers	Consider the source.
Connect pp. 224–225 Write to Learn	Study Skills/ Language	**Spelling** Punctuation: Colon	Use graphic organizers.
Connect pp. 226–227 Interviews	Study Skills/ Reading	**Grammar** *Wh-* Questions	Read on to get meaning.
Connect p. 228 "Aprender el inglés"/"Learning English"	Study Skills/ Literature	**Vocabulary** Cognates	
Assess p. 229 Tell What You Learned.			

Resources

Chapter 11

Support Materials

ACTIVITY BOOK

pages 102–111

VIDEO

Unit 6, Dealing with Change

PURPLE TAPE

Side 1

In the Year of the Boar and Jackie Robinson, pages T202–T209

PURPLE TAPE

Side 2

"You Can Do Better," page T214

DISK

Writer's Notebook

Assessment Materials

BLACKLINE MASTER

Language Assessment, Blackline Master 90

Listening Assessment, Blackline Master 91

CREAM TAPE

Side 2

Listening Assessment, page T215

Listen carefully. You will hear about students who feel stressed out. Match each student with the problem that he or she has. Draw lines to the pictures.

Student 1: Mariko and her sister argue all the time. Mariko gets angry because her sister uses her things without asking. Her sister gets angry because Mariko leaves their room in a mess. Mariko made a list of their problems. She and her sister talked about them. Mariko agreed to clean up their room if her sister would stop using her things.

Student 2: Juan wants to play on the basketball team. He went to practice a couple of times, but he didn't play very well. He didn't make many baskets. Juan was stressed out. He decided to quit the basketball team.

Newcomer Book C

Survival language for absolute beginners. For overview, see pages xxvii–xxix.

For Extended Reading

Almost a Hero by Clyde Robert Bulla, E. P. Dutton, 1981

When he has to go back to the place that caused him pain in his childhood, a young man learns an important lesson.

Level: Beginning

The Best Friends Book by Arlene Erlbach, Free Spirit Publishing, 1995

Real best friends tell their stories and give ideas about what you can do with your best friend.

Level: Average

Can I Help How I Feel? by Carl V. Morrison, M.D., Atheneum, 1976

Discover how to avoid stress, anger and other negative emotions that can only make your life more difficult.

Level: Advanced

Open the Door and See All the People by Clyde Robert Bulla, Thomas Y. Crowell Company, 1972

A family deals with moving and meeting new friends.

Level: Beginning

Starring Dorothy Kane by Judith Casely, Greenwillow Books, 1992

Follow Dorothy on her adventures as she learns to adjust to her new school.

Level: Average

Related Technology

Compton's Interactive Encyclopedia, Compton's New Media, 1996

Research the causes of stress; how does it affect you?

Chapter 12

Support Materials

ACTIVITY BOOK

pages 112–121

PURPLE TAPE

Side 2

"Aprender el inglés," page T228

DISK

Writer's Notebook

Assessment Materials

BLACKLINE MASTER

Language Assessment, Blackline Master 92

Listening Assesment, Blackline Master 93

CREAM TAPE

Side 2

Listening Assessment, page T229

Listen carefully. You will write a list of words. First, you will hear the words. Then you will hear them again more slowly. Begin to write them down. Then you will hear them one more time. Check what you wrote. Finally, rewrite the list of words in alphabetical order.

newspaper
facts
information
people
places
things
article

For Extended Reading

Book by Karen Brookfield, Alfred A. Knopf, 1993

A detailed look at the creation and functions of books, and how these elements have changed over time.

Level: Advanced

Extra! Extra! The Who, What, Where, When, and Why of Newspapers by Linda Granfield, Orchard Books, 1993

An introduction to and overview of newspapers.

Level: Beginning

How to Read a Newspaper by Helen H. Carey, Franklin Watts, 1983

Look at the components of a newspaper and learn how to use them as reference tools.

Level: Beginning

How to Use Primary Sources by Helen H. Carey and Judith E. Greenberg, Franklin Watts, 1983

Learn how to access direct information from museums, libraries, and numerous kinds of documents.

Level: Average

The News Media by Ruth and Mike Wolverton, Franklin Watts, 1981

A description of how news media writers develop their stories.

Level: Average

Related Technology

Encarta 95, Microsoft, 1995

User-friendly research report creation tool.

Project

Life in School

This optional project can be completed over the next two chapters. In this two-part project, students will act out scenes relating to school that can cause stress. They will also make a school magazine. See the Unit Wrap Up, page T230a, for more ideas on sharing the project with family members.

What You'll Need

Collect materials for making props, costumes, and scenery:

- a sheet or curtain
- a roll of Kraft brown paper
- construction paper
- cardboard and oak tag
- fabric
- paints, crayons, and magic markers
- string or yarn
- needles and thread
- safety pins
- scissors
- makeup
- computer or typewriter
- camera
- photocopier

Beginning the Project

Divide the class into small groups. Explain that each group will plan and perform its own short play about situations that can cause stress. Have students brainstorm situations. Have each group choose a theme, such as one of the following:

- the first day in school
- speaking in front of a group
- getting along with friends or family
- getting poor grades

Remind them to gather ideas for their play as they progress through the unit.

Tell students that they will also be writing and publishing a class magazine about life in school. Help them brainstorm ideas for a theme, title, and articles for the magazine.

Home Involvement

Send the Letter to the Family, Blackline Masters 84–89 in the Teacher's Resource Book, to families, explaining that the class will be studying various aspects of change, including handling stress. The letter suggests that family members discuss with students some changes they have faced since coming to the United States and how they have coped with them.

Daily Discussion

Take a few minutes each day to talk about the plays. Give the groups time to brainstorm ideas, write dialogue, and rehearse. Assure students that stories and dialogue can be very simple. Encourage groups to develop dialogue through repeated rehearsals and to use vocabulary from the unit. Tell students that the plays can be based on the personal or family experiences of group members or can be purely fictional. In either case, the plays should include facts presented in the unit. As the groups progress with their plays, set aside class time for the preparation of props and scenery.

Also take a few minutes each day to talk about the magazine. Give students time to brainstorm about the magazine's articles, design, length, and cover. Possible topics include school programs and subjects, after-school clubs and activities, issues of concern to students, and profiles of school personalities, such as the principal, president of the student council, or cafeteria manage, and resources available in the library.

Theater Jobs

Discuss the jobs involved in producing a play, as listed below. Groups should decide how the responsibilities will be divided and shared among group members.

- Writers prepare either a script for actors to memorize or an outline that actors can improvise from.
- Actors perform the roles in a play.
- The director helps actors develop their roles and makes technical decisions, such as how to light the play and how to switch from scene to scene.
- Set designers create the scenery and props for a play.
- Costume designers develop ideas for costumes and accessories.

Information About Magazines

Discuss the parts of a magazine, such as the cover, table of contents, articles, photographs, drawings, and cartoons. Explain the steps in producing a magazine: planning, writing, editing, illustrating, designing, typesetting, proofreading, and copying. Let students volunteer for the steps that interest them most, or make appropriate assignments.

Activity Book Chapter 11

Name

Telling About Emotions

Read the following situations. Imagine what the person may feel in each situation. Write a sentence to describe the person's feelings. Use *may* in each sentence. Use the words in the box to describe emotions.

afraid	excited	nervous	worried
angry	happy	sad	

1. Louisa is moving to a new country. She is leaving her friends behind. She will not see them for a very long time.
   Louisa may feel sad. Answers may vary.
2. Hector received a low grade in math. He knows that his mother wants him to get a good grade. Hector is sitting on the back steps of his house before showing his mother his progress report.
   Hector may feel worried.
3. Mitsu hears strange noises in the back yard. She goes to find her father.
   Mitsu may feel afraid.
4. Frances and Isabel practiced for weeks. Today are the tryouts for the school play.
   Frances and Isabel may feel nervous.
5. Isabel's report is on the top of her desk. Alex and his friends are fooling around, and they accidentally spill water on her report.
   Isabel may feel angry. Alex and his friends may be worried.
6. Tomorrow Angela is flying to Guatemala to visit her family. She hasn't seen her cousins during the past year.
   Angela may feel excited/happy.
7. Sandra is going to go to a summer camp for a month. It is the first time she is traveling without her parents.
   Sandra may feel excited/nervous.

Name

Reacting to Stress

Think of the correct word to complete each sentence. Then write the word in the crossword puzzle.

Across

1. ______ may send a chemical called adrenaline through the body.
3. Perspiration may appear on the ______.
5. ______ may race through the body.
6. The ______ may beat faster.

Down

2. The ______ may breathe faster.
3. The ______ may slow down or speed up digestion.
4. The ______ may feel dry.

Answers: 1 Across GLANDS; 3 Across SKIN; 5 Across BLOOD; 6 Across HEART; 2 Down LUNGS; 3 Down STOMACH; 4 Down MOUTH

Name

I have to . . .

Read the following sentences. They tell about things people have to do when they move to a new country. If it is something that adults would have to do, write *adults*. If it is something that children would have to do, write *children*. If it is something that adults and children would both have to do, write *both*.

1. You have to learn new ways of doing things. both
2. You may have to get new jobs. adults
3. You have to go to a new school. children
4. You have to make new friends. both
5. You may have to learn a new language. both
6. You may have to worry about money. adults
7. You have to fix up your new home. both
8. You have to find a new place to buy clothes. both

Write three sentences about things you have to do at home. Be sure to use *have to* in your sentences.

Answers will vary.

Now write three sentences about things that you have to do at school.

Answers will vary.

Name

End Punctuation

This is an entry from a student's journal. Place the proper punctuation at the end of each sentence. Use periods, question marks, or exclamation points.

Did you ever have a day when everything just went wrong ? I woke up late . I burned my toast . I missed the bus . I had to run to school in the rain . I forgot my homework . What a bad day ! What else can go wrong ? When school is over, I am going to go home and go to bed . I am so glad that tomorrow is a new day .

Below is a letter that Renée wrote to a friend. Add the proper punctuation at the end of each sentence.

Dear Catherine,

How are you ? Today was my first day in my new school . I was very nervous . My new school is huge . All the students were very nice . But there were so many students . Will I ever learn all their names ?

My teacher's name is Mrs. Williams . She told me that she lived in France for two years . Can you believe that ? She even speaks French . What a surprise !

Did you get my last letter ? Please write soon .

Sincerely,

Renée

Name ______________________________

What's the answer?

Read the following letter to Sally, the advice columnist. Then answer the questions below.

Dear Sally:

I want to get a dog. But my sister wants to get a cat. My mother says that until we agree, we can't have a pet at all. What should I do?

Margaret, Age 12

Answers will vary.

1. What is Margaret's problem?

2. Is this a problem Margaret can do something about?

3. What advice would you give to Margaret to help her solve this problem?

Write a letter back to Margaret.

Name ______________________________

The First Day at School

The following sentences are about the story "In the Year of the Boar and Jackie Robinson." Some of the sentences are correct and some are incorrect. Correct any statements that are wrong.

1. Shirley had just moved to the United States from Japan.
   Shirley had just moved to the United States from China.
2. The children in Shirley's new school had to wear ugly uniforms.
   The children in Shirley's new school did not have to wear uniforms.
3. Shirley was taller than most of her new classmates.
   Shirley was shorter than most of her new classmates.
4. Shirley liked her new teacher, Mrs. Rappaport, right away.
5. Shirley did not understand English very well.
6. She went with her new friends to a Chinese restaurant for lunch.
   She went with her new friends to a store and bought a sandwich for lunch.
7. Her new friends played marbles after lunch.
8. Shirley had a terrible time at lunch.
   Shirley had a great time at lunch.

What did you do on your first day at your present school? Was your day like Shirley's day?

Name ______________________________

What's for lunch?

Look at the lunches in the pictures below. List the things that are in each lunch. Use all the words in the box.

Info Box

apple	bowl of
hamburger	can of
hot dog	carton of
milk	glass of
orange juice	slice of
pizza	
potato chips	
salad	
sandwich	
soda	
soup	
tacos	

1. sandwich; glass of milk; apple
2. a slice of pizza; can of soda
3. hot dog; potato chips; carton of orange juice
4. bowl of soup; tacos
5. salad; hamburger

What is your favorite lunch? Write about it.

Answers will vary.

Name ______________________________

Old and New

Think about the differences between schools in the country where you were born and the school you go to now. Fill in the chart. Answers will vary.

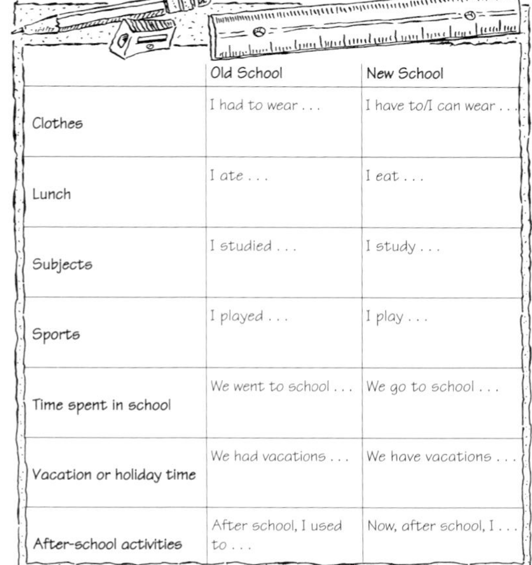

	Old School	New School
Clothes	I had to wear . . .	I have to/I can wear . . .
Lunch	I ate . . .	I eat . . .
Subjects	I studied . . .	I study . . .
Sports	I played . . .	I play . . .
Time spent in school	We went to school . . .	We go to school . . .
Vacation or holiday time	We had vacations . . .	We have vacations . . .
After-school activities	After school, I used to . . .	Now, after school, I . . .

What's the same about the schools? What's different? On a separate sheet of paper, write about how the schools are alike and how they are different.

Activity Book

Chapter 12

Name

A Famous Person

Read the encyclopedia article about Susan B. Anthony. One hundred years ago in the United States and many other countries, men could vote, but women could not. People like Susan B. Anthony fought so that women could also vote.

Susan B. Anthony (1820-1906) was an important person in the fight for women's voting rights. She was born in Massachusetts, but her family moved to New York in 1826. She studied and became a school teacher. In 1854, she joined the fight against slavery. In 1872, she led her first protest for women's voting rights. She led a group of women to a place where men were voting, and she tried to vote. She was arrested for her action. She continued to fight for the next thirty-four years to gain voting rights for women. Her hard work helped achieve the passage of the Nineteenth Amendment to the United States Constitution in 1920. This amendment gained women the right to vote.

Draw a line from each sentence to its place on the time line.

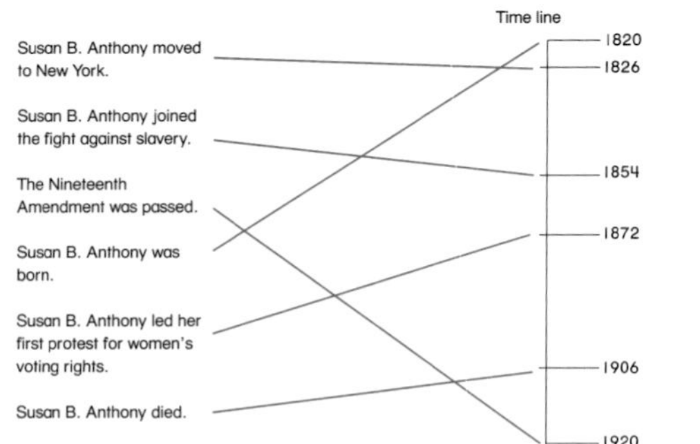

Time line
Susan B. Anthony moved to New York.
Susan B. Anthony joined the fight against slavery.
The Nineteenth Amendment was passed.
Susan B. Anthony was born.
Susan B. Anthony led her first protest for women's voting rights.
Susan B. Anthony died.
1820
1826
1854
1872
1906
1920

Name

My Magazine Log

Look at several magazines. Then choose two and answer the following questions. Answers will vary.

SPORT
STAR

Name of magazine: ______

Description of magazine: ______

Articles I looked at: ______

The article that interested me most: ______

I liked that article the most because ______

I chose this magazine because ______

Name of magazine: ______

Description of magazine: ______

Articles I looked at: ______

The article I that interested me most: ______

I liked that article the most because ______

I chose this magazine because ______

Name

Understanding the News

Read the newspaper article and then answer the questions.

Springfield's Thanksgiving Day Parade

Nov. 23—Thousands of people of all ages lined the streets of downtown Springfield for the annual Thanksgiving Day Parade. People began arriving as early as 7 a.m. to get good places to see the parade in the freezing cold morning. When the parade began at 9 a.m., the temperature was still a chilly 28°. But the weather was sunny as the more than 20 bands and 40 floats marched down the main street of the city. As usual, the huge balloons in the shape of famous people and cartoon characters were the most popular feature in the parade.

Mayor Howard Hopkins could not be in the judge's stand because of a bad case of the flu. The chief of police, James Garcia, chose the best float instead.

Answers may vary.

1. What event took place?
   The event was the Thanksgiving Day Parade.
2. Where did it happen?
   The event took place in downtown Springfield.
3. When did it happen?
   The event took place on Thanksgiving.
4. Why was there a parade?
   The parade is an annual event to celebrate Thanksgiving.
5. Who watched it?
   Thousands of people of all ages watched the parade.
6. What was in the parade?
   There were bands, floats, and huge balloons in the parade.

Find a newspaper article that interests you. Write about *who, what, where, when,* and *why.*

Name

Getting Information

What tool would you use to complete each of the following assignments? Choose from the list below.

Info Box		
encyclopedia	newspaper	textbook
magazine	computer	interview

Answers may vary.

1. Find out what the weather will be like in your city or town tomorrow.
   newspaper, computer
2. Find out where your teacher grew up and went to school.
   interview
3. Write a report about the history of your state.
   encyclopedia
4. Read an article about athletes who are preparing for the Olympics.
   magazine, computer, newspaper
5. Find out how to change temperatures from Fahrenheit to Celsius.
   textbook
6. Find out about current events in Russia.
   newspaper
7. Learn the rules of punctuation in the English language.
   textbook
8. Find facts about the life of George Washington.
   encyclopedia, computer
9. Find out what a student in another state is studying in math class.
   computer

Name

A Fighter for Rights

Read the encyclopedia article about Martin Luther King, Jr. He fought for full rights for all people. But he fought with words, not fists. He himself was an African American.

Martin Luther King , Jr.,(1929–1968) was a leader of the civil rights movement in the United States from the middle of the 1950s until 1968.

King's father and grandfather were ministers. King received his degree as a minister in 1951. In 1955, King became important in the fight for equal treatment of all people. He helped win the right for African American people to sit anywhere they wanted on buses.

He believed he could win equal rights by peaceful means. He took part in a march on Washington in 1963. There he made a famous speech titled "I Have a Dream." He said he believed that Americans could create a society where people were not judged by the color of their skin. In 1964, he won the Nobel Peace Prize. His work helped win passage of the Civil Rights Act of 1964 and the Voting Rights Act of 1965. These laws protect the rights of all Americans.

King was shot and killed in 1968. In 1986, Congress set a national holiday in his honor. It is celebrated the third Monday in January.

Now complete the graphic organizer. Answers may vary.

Martin Luther King, Jr.			
Early Life	What He Believed	What He Did	Accomplishments
King studied and became a minister.	King believed that he could help win equal rights for all Americans by peaceful means.	He fought to help win the right for African Americans to sit any place on buses. He spoke and fought for equal and fair treatment for all.	King helped to win the right for African Americans to sit any place on buses. His work helped to pass the Civil Rights Act of 1964 and the Voting Rights Act of 1965. These laws helped win equal rights for all.

Name

Use a graphic organizer.

Choose the most interesting article you have read as you have studied this chapter. Read that article again. Now write the four most interesting things you learned in the graphic organizer below. Answers will vary.

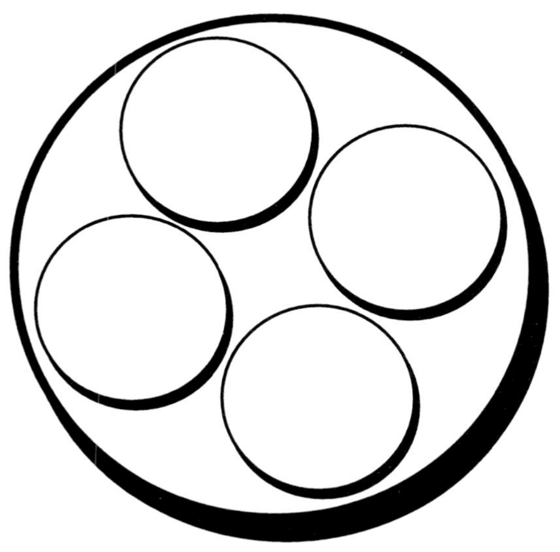

Name

Asking Questions

To get information, interviewers ask questions. Think back to the interview with Jorge, on page 227 in the Student Book. Here are some of Jorge's answers. Write the question that you think the interviewer may have asked to get each answer.

Example:

Jorge's answer: Almost from the day I came here, I worked.

Interviewer's question: When did you start working?

Answers may vary.

1. Jorge's answer: "First I worked in a restaurant. Now I work at a video store."
   Interviewer's question: Where do you work?
2. Jorge's answer: "At the video store I make four dollars an hour."
   Interviewer's question: How much money do you make?
3. Jorge's answer: "I work from right after school until 8:30 at night."
   Interviewer's question: When do you work?
4. Jorge's answer: "I don't eat dinner until I go home, around 9:30."
   Interviewer's question: When do you eat dinner?
5. Jorge's answer: "I go to bed around eleven or twelve."
   Interviewer's question: When do you go to bed?
6. Jorge's answer: "I spend an hour or two on homework each night."
   Interviewer's question: How much time do you spend on homework?
7. Jorge's answer: "My average for the whole year is eighty-something."
   Interviewer's question: What are your grades in school?
8. Jorge's answer: "I buy things for my family and I save some money."
   Interviewer's questions: What do you do with your money?

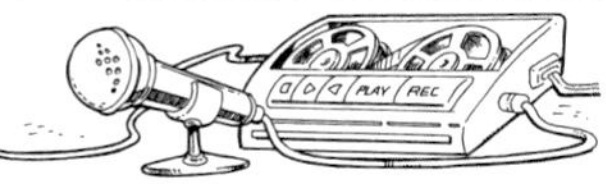

What person would you like to interview? What questions would you ask? Write them.

Name

Information Please Crossword

What words would complete the sentences? Use the answers to solve the crossword puzzle.

Across

6. An ______ has information about a large number of topics.
7. A dictionary is a handy ______ tool.

Down

1. The ______ has information about events that are currently happening.
2. On a ______, you can read an encyclopedia without turning a page.
3. Students use a ______ in the classroom to get information.
4. I can buy the same ______ with new pictures and information every month.
5. A reporter would use an ______ to get information about a famous person.

1 N						2 C		3 T			4 M				5 I				
6 E	N	C	Y	C	L	O	P	E	D	I	A				N				
W						M		X			G				T				
S						P		T			A				E				
P						U		B			Z				R				
A						T		O			I				V				
P						E		O			N				I				
E						R		K		7 R	E	F	E	R	E	N	C	E	
R															W				

UNIT 6

Preview

Activate Prior Knowledge

Relate Personal Experiences

Begin with a discussion that allows students to share their own experiences with changes in their lives. Start by giving examples from your own experiences, including times you moved and the emotions you felt. The difficulties with change will probably arouse many feelings, both good and unpleasant, in many of the students. Allow them to express their feelings as well as their experiences, as the unit will deal with both the feelings and the facts of changes.

Develop Language and Concepts

Present Pages 192 and 193

Have students look at the pictures and ask them what they know about the settings depicted there and what they think is happening. Encourage them to contrast or relate their own experiences with what they see. Help the students use the Word Bank words to describe what they see in the pictures. Present the World Bank words to students by describing situations in which people might feel the emotions, such as those pictured. Illustrate them with more examples of situations, as well as facial expressions and gestures that might accompany the emotions.

Help students discuss answers to the questions in Talk About It. Then have students work in small groups to compare their personal experiences.

Dealing with Change

Tell what you know.

What is happening in each picture?

How do you think each person feels?

Options for Reaching All Students

Beginning

Language: Say What You Feel

Make a card for each student with one of the Word Bank words written on it. Have students form a circle and have each hold a card so that the others can see it. Choose someone to start. The student says "I am _____," completing the sentence with the word on his or her card. Then he or she says "_____ is _____," choosing another student at random and saying the word on that person's card. For example, "I am sad. LaToya is nervous." The chosen student then takes his or her turn. Encourage students to use appropriate intonation and body language. Extend the activity by having students exchange cards after everyone has had a turn.

Advanced

Language: Write About Feelings

Invite students to imagine that their favorite team has just won the world championship. How would the students feel? What if the team had lost? Have students write short paragraphs describing their reactions in both situations.

Word Bank

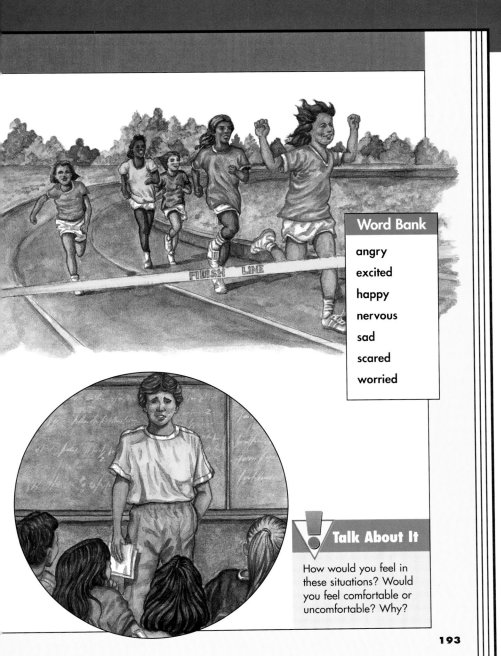

angry
excited
happy
nervous
sad
scared
worried

Talk About It

How would you feel in these situations? Would you feel comfortable or uncomfortable? Why?

THEME/KEY CONCEPTS

In this unit, the theme of change is developed through an examination of how people handle change on a personal level and a discussion of where to go to understand changes in our world. Students will learn about the causes and nature of stress and ways to deal with it. They will also study how to get information, as a means to help them get control over their environment, as well as to improve their academic skills.

Chapter 11

- Difficult situations, as well as pleasant ones, can cause stress.
- People experience many changes and difficult situations in their lives.
- There are a number of ways that people use to handle stress and problems.

Chapter 12

- There are many ways to gather and understand information in the world around us.
- Encyclopedias, magazines, newspapers, writing things down, and interviews are among the ways to process information.

FYI

The pictures show, from bottom left, starting in a new school, moving, winning a race, talking in front of a group.

Mixed Ability

Video: Dealing with Change

VIDEO

Show the Unit 6 portion of the video to give students an overview of the unit. You may want to replay the tape several times throughout the unit for language and concept reinforcement and development.

Peer Tutoring

Language: Words and Pictures

Form pairs of mixed-ability students. Have them use words from the Word Bank and find pictures in magazines that illustrate the words. Have them label each picture with a word that expresses feelings and write a sentence about the picture.

Cooperative Learning

Body Language

TPR

Write the words from the Word Bank on separate cards. Show the cards to students one at a time. Show a variety of facial expressions and gestures that could accompany each emotion. Have students indicate ways that they might express the same emotion nonverbally in their culture. Have students compare and contrast gestures and expressions.

Present

Activate Prior Knowledge

Brainstorm Vocabulary

Have students brainstorm words for parts of the body. Help them be aware of the inside of their bodies:

- Have them place hands on rib cages and take a deep breath. (They are feeling their lungs fill with air.)
- Have them place fingers against the side of the neck to feel their pulse beating. (They are feeling their hearts pumping.)

Develop Language and Concepts

Present Pages 194 and 195

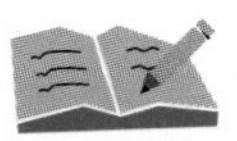

Have the students recall emotion words, and ask them how their bodies reacted to a situation that was scary or exciting. Ask, *Did your heart beat faster? Did your breathing change? Did you perspire or feel sick?* Encourage them to share experiences. Read the text with students. Have students look at the drawing. Explain that it shows how different parts of the body can react to stress. Use TPR to model the body's physical reaction to stress. For example, breathe rapidly to show how the lungs breathe faster.

Help students brainstorm situations in which they have both benefited from and been harmed by stress. Have them answer the Think About It question. Use Activity Book page 103 to review basic vocabulary.

Handling Stress

What is stress?

Stress is what happens to your body when you are in a difficult situation. It happens when you feel a strong emotion. The emotion may be pleasant or unpleasant. You can feel signs of stress when you are worried, afraid, excited, or happy.

Everyone feels stress at one time or another. But things that cause you stress may not cause much stress to another person.

Stress can be helpful. When you run in a race, you want to win. The stress you feel helps you run faster. It makes you more alert.

Too much stress can be harmful to your body Too much stress can make you tired and nervous. Too much stress makes it harder for your body to fight sickness.

WORRY

Options for Reaching All Students

Beginning

Science: Anatomical Drawings

Provide students with simple anatomical drawings from science and health textbooks. Have them work in pairs to draw or trace the picture and label the internal body parts, such as lungs, heart, glands, liver, brain.

Advanced

Writing: Stressful Situations

Have the students write a short paragraph about a time when they experienced "negative" stress and a time they experienced "positive" stress. Instruct them to include their physical, as well as their emotional, reactions in their paragraphs.

Mixed Ability

Language: Role-Play

Have students pick situations from the list they developed of positive and negative stress to act out. Have students write in groups of two or three and act out the situation before the class.

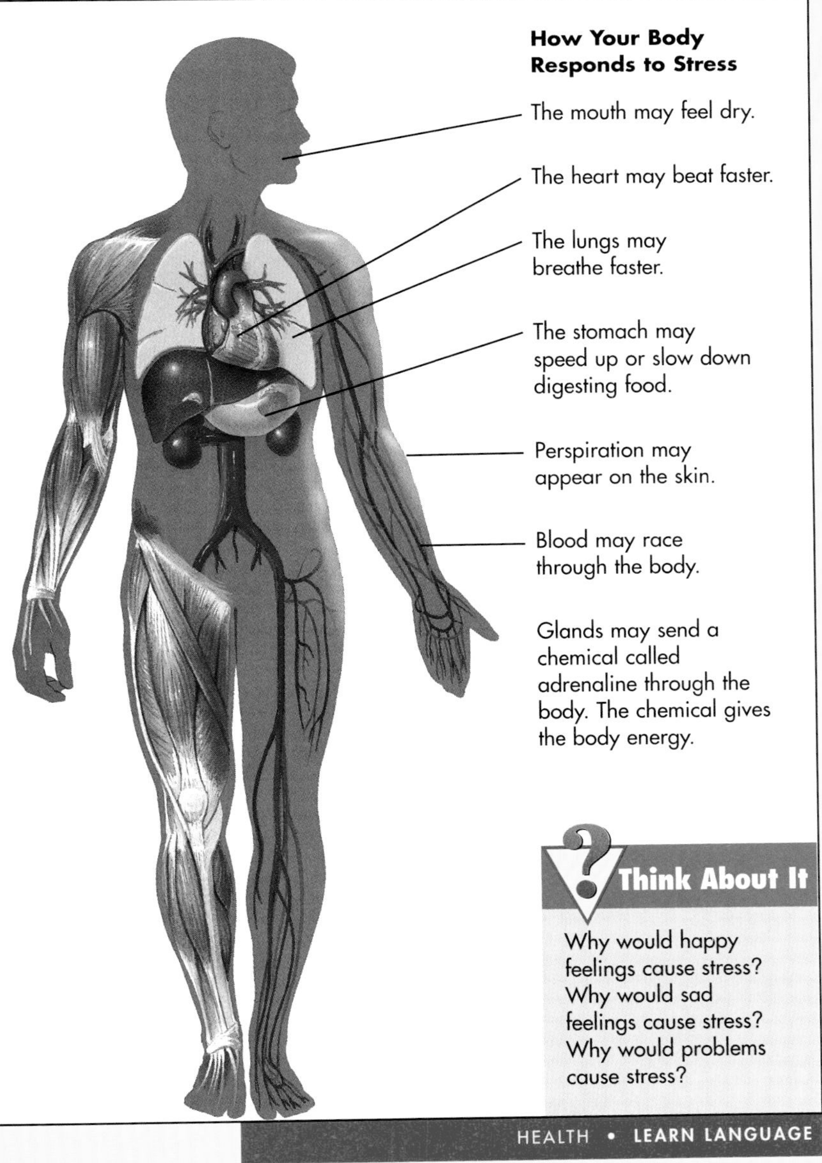

How Your Body Responds to Stress
The mouth may feel dry.
The heart may beat faster.
The lungs may breathe faster.
The stomach may speed up or slow down digesting food.
Perspiration may appear on the skin.
Blood may race through the body.
Glands may send a chemical called adrenaline through the body. The chemical gives the body energy.

Think About It

Why would happy feelings cause stress? Why would sad feelings cause stress? Why would problems cause stress?

Language Awareness

Grammar

May

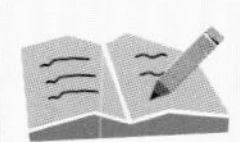
ACTIVITY BOOK

Tell the students that the word *may* is often used to describe something that could or could not happen. Have students review the captions on the diagram and point out the use of *may*. Explain that some of the body reactions will occur and some will not occur at any one time. Have students look back at the pictures on pages 192 and 193 and invite them to speculate about how each student may feel and why. For example, the boy may feel nervous because he is talking in front of a group. Use Activity Book page 102 to practice *may* and emotion words.

Assess

Students should be able to

- define stress
- tell about some of the physical effects of stress

LOOK**AHEAD**

In the next section, students will learn why changes might cause stress.

Multicultural Connection

Language: You Say, I Say

List the following words on the board: *head, heart, mouth, stomach, blood, skin, knees,* and *hands*. Have students copy the list. Invite students to write words in their native language beside their English equivalents. Then have them share their lists with other students in small groups.

QuickCheck

Pronouns

Check to make sure that pronouns in the text are understood. Ask the students to find a sentence that uses *it*, and check whether they know what the word *it* replaces.

Practice

Activate Prior Knowledge

Start a K-W-L Chart

Find out what students know about the causes of stress. Ask questions such as these:

- Do you know some things that might cause stress? Have you ever felt stress? What caused this feeling?

Use the information to make a K-W-L chart:

K: What We Know	Meeting new people may be stressful.
W: What We Want to Find Out	How do people deal with stress?
L: What We Learned	

Continue to add to the chart throughout the lesson.

Develop Language and Concepts

Present Pages 196 and 197

Have students look at the pictures. Help them discuss what the students in the pictures are experiencing by using words from the preceding lessons. Read the pages with students and lead a discussion of similar experiences in students' lives and how students were affected by those experiences.

What causes stress?

The changes people experience in life can cause stress.

Moving to a New Place

Moving to a new place can cause stress. You miss the family and friends you left behind. You have to learn new ways of doing things. You might even have to learn a new language.

Your whole family might feel stress. They may have to get new jobs. They may worry about money.

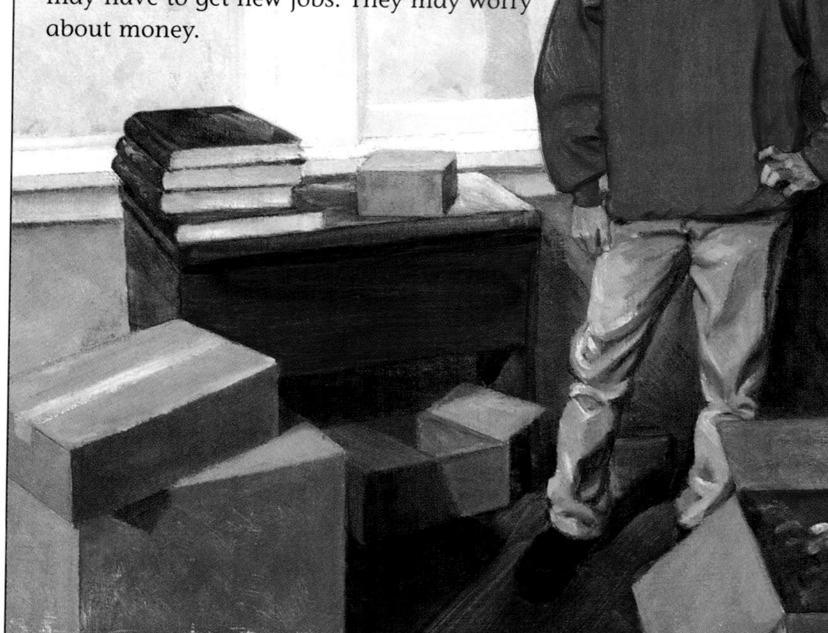

Options for Reaching All Students

Beginning

Art: Stress Collage

Have students look through old magazines for pictures of people in stressful situations. Have them create a stress collage. Then talk about what is causing the stress in each picture. Help them identify what feelings they think the people in the pictures are having as a result of their stress.

Advanced

Language: Stress Skits

TPR Have students work in teams. Ask each team to choose a stressful situation listed in the book and develop a skit to act it out. Have groups present their skits to the class, and invite other students to help come up with solutions for how to handle the stressful situation.

Multicultural Connection

Deal with Stress

Encourage students to discuss stress and its causes at home. Ask them to find out whether their family thinks stress-causing situations are the same in the United States as they were in their native countries. Encourage students to share responses with the class.

Going to a New School

Going to a new school can cause stress. You might worry about whether you will be able to do the schoolwork. You might worry about whether you will make friends. You might worry about whether the other students will like your clothes. If you speak a different language, you may worry whether you will understand the teacher and be able to study in English.

The stress in new situations does not have to be negative. You might see such changes as a chance to really do your best. The stress you feel might help you to do this.

Some Common Causes of Stress
Arguing with parents about rules
Arguing with brothers or sisters
Having a friendship begin or end
Having trouble with a school subject

Write About It

Make a list of things that have made you feel stress. Then put them in order. Write the thing that caused the most stress at the top.

Language Awareness

Grammar

Have to

ACTIVITY BOOK

Call attention to the phrases *you have to* and *they have to* in the text. Explain that this is one way to express something we must do, or something that is required. Ask students to think of other things they "have to" do at school and at home. Use Activity Book page 104.

Model a Strategy

Paraphrase/Retell

Model retelling for understanding:

This page states several reasons for feeling stress. Telling someone about what I read helps me to remember and understand ideas: "I read that changes, such as moving to a new place or going to a new school, can cause stress."

Assess

Use responses to the Write About It activity for assessment. Students should be able to

- list situations that cause them stress

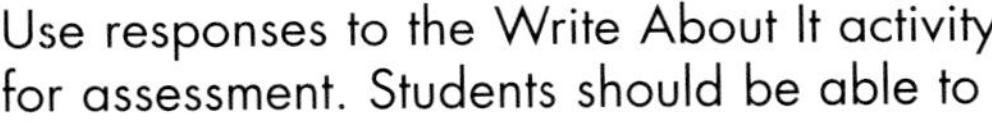

LOOK**AHEAD**

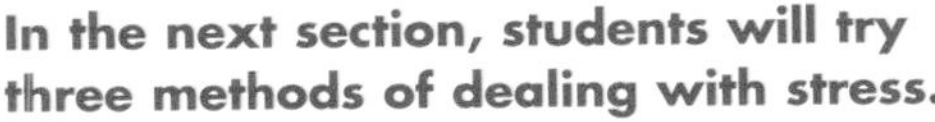

In the next section, students will try three methods of dealing with stress.

Practice

Activate Prior Knowledge

Brainstorm Ways to Relax

Ask students to think about what they do to relax. Write their ideas on chart paper and add to the list throughout the lesson.

Develop Language and Concepts

Present Pages 198 and 199

TPR

Invite students to look at the pictures. Explain that the students in the pictures are engaged in different ways of dealing with stress. Read the text with students.

Incorporate TPR to enhance students' understanding: Lead students through the breathing and smiling exercises. Discuss and perform other physical relaxation techniques. Help students make a list of their problems as suggested in the article, first classifying problems as solvable or unsolvable, then listing steps for dealing with each solvable problem.

Model a Strategy

Solve a Problem

Model a strategy for problem solving:

If I can't make a problem go away, I can do something to help with my fears. I worry about keeping up in school when I don't understand the language. I could tape-record parts of my classes and find a student who speaks my language and English to help me understand.

How can you deal with stress?

Your room is a mess. You have a math test in two days. Your mother is mad at you because you were late getting home. You feel stressed out. There are many ways to handle too much stress. Here are three ideas.

Do breathing exercises.

One way of dealing with stress is to relax. This exercise will help you relax.

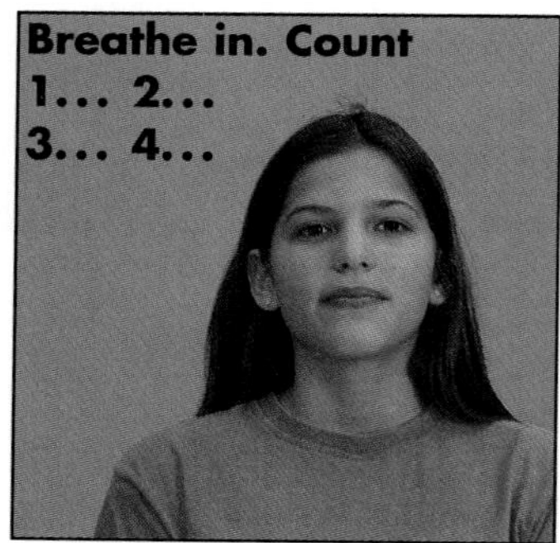
Breathe in. Count
1... 2...
3... 4...

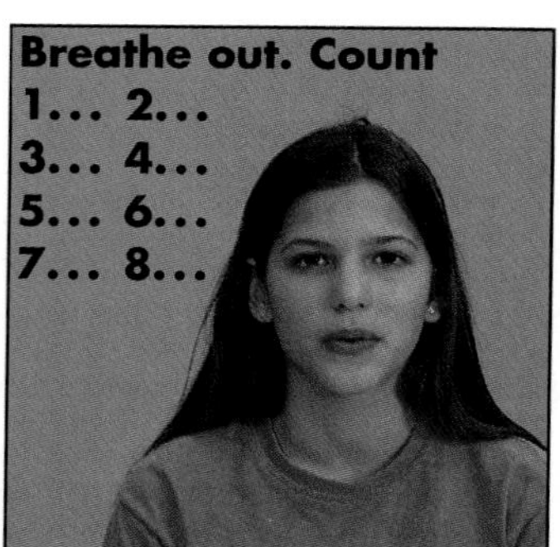
Breathe out. Count
1... 2...
3... 4...
5... 6...
7... 8...

1. Sit or lie in a comfortable position.
2. Breathe in through your nose as deeply as you can. Count to four while you hold your breath.
3. Then breathe out through your mouth. Count to eight.
4. Do this exercise three or four times.

Options for Reaching All Students

Beginning

Language: Words and Body Language

TPR

Write the words *smile, frown, yawn, glare, sob, squint,* and *giggle* on the board. Say each word aloud and model the action for students. Then say the words again in random order, having the students give the appropriate physical response.

Advanced

Critical Thinking: Evaluate Relaxation Techniques

Have students work in groups to brainstorm relaxation methods for dealing with stress. Ask groups to look in health books for additional techniques. Encourage groups to practice each technique. Have them list the ways to relax and rank them according to those they think are most effective. Ask them to give reasons for their choices.

Mixed Ability

Language: Jokes

Provide students with joke books. Have them work in small groups to read the jokes. Have more advanced students explain the meaning of the jokes to the less advanced students. Mention that jokes in English often depend on word play and words having double meaning. Explain any jokes that students want you to explain.

Make a list.

What are your problems? Make a list.

- Are there problems that you cannot do anything about? Try to forget them.
- Put the other problems in order. Try to deal with them one at a time.

Luke: Hey, Mom, I got 100 today!
Mom: That's great. What did you get 100 in?
Luke: Three subjects: a 30 in math, a 20 in history, and a 50 in English.

Try laughing.

Did you know that laughing can help you cut down on stress? Give a big smile and notice how the muscles in your face relax.

Try It Out

Find some jokes that make you laugh. Share one with a classmate. What is his or her response?

Language Awareness

Spelling
End Punctuation

ACTIVITY BOOK

Write a period, question mark, and exclamation mark on the board. Invite students to find examples in the text. Explain that most sentences end with periods. Sentences that end in question marks usually call for answers. They often begin with question words or with *do/did* or *is/are/was/were.* Exclamation points are used to show emotion. Model reading sentences in the text with appropriate intonation and invite students to repeat them. Note *wh-* questions have a falling intonation, while *yes-no* questions have rising intonation.

Use Activity Book page 105.

Assess

Students should be able to

- name ways to deal with stress

LOOK**AHEAD**

In the next section, students will read about reducing stress by sharing problems with others.

Cooperative Language Experience

Social Studies: Eastern Philosophy

Bring in a beginning yoga videotape. Explain that the yoga exercises arise from Indian philosophy and religion, and that many people today practice the yoga system of exercises for mind and body relaxation. Lead students in performing some of the simpler yoga exercises demonstrated in the video.

Home Connection

Ways to Handle Stress

Have students interview adults at home about their ways of reducing stress, noting both current ways as well as those they may have used in their native lands.

Multicultural Connection

Jokes and Humorous Stories

Invite students to ask family members about common jokes and humorous stories in their native countries. Have students share the jokes with the class.

Connect

Activate Prior Knowledge

Relate Personal Experiences

Lead students in a discussion of the different persons and places they turn to for advice and help.

Develop Language and Concepts

Present Pages 200 and 201

Show letters to advice columnists, preferably ones written by students, which can be found in newspapers and magazines. Ask if students have ever read any such letters.

Read the text with students. Have students brainstorm problems students of their age have. Find one that is common to all or most of them. Write a letter about the problem as a class. Focus students' attention on the letters in English: salutation (Dear . . .), body of letter, complimentary close, signature. Then help students make a clear, written statement of the problem. As a follow-up, have the students see how many solutions they can devise, and have small groups write responses.

Have students do the Talk About It activity. Suggest problems with getting advice from strangers as well as advantages. Use Activity Book page 106 for more practice in writing advice letters.

Ask for help.

Handling a problem by yourself can add to the stress you feel. Sometimes it helps to share your problem with someone else. Putting your problem into words can help you to see it in a new way.

Sometimes people write to the newspaper for advice. Read the following advice column from a newspaper.

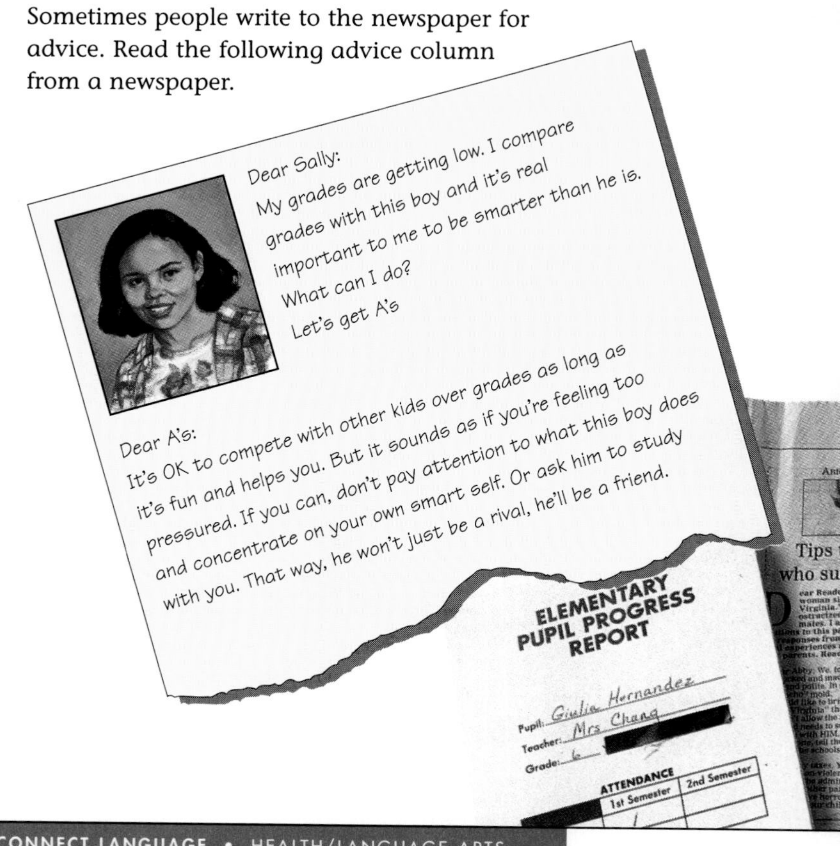

Dear Sally:
My grades are getting low. I compare grades with this boy and it's real important to me to be smarter than he is. What can I do?
Let's get A's

Dear A's:
It's OK to compete with other kids over grades as long as it's fun and helps you. But it sounds as if you're feeling too pressured. If you can, don't pay attention to what this boy does and concentrate on your own smart self. Or ask him to study with you. That way, he won't just be a rival, he'll be a friend.

Options for Reaching All Students

Beginning

Writing: Advice Letter

Have students work in small groups to write an advice letter to a columnist. They should choose one of the problems brainstormed during the class discussion. Help them with language as needed and monitor their use of correct form for writing letters.

Advanced

Language: Role-Play Giving and Getting Advice

Have the students work in two teams to role-play giving and getting advice. First, have each group brainstorm to agree on a problem they all share, have had experience with, or all understand. Have one of students in each group write the problem in one or two sentences. When each team has developed their problem, have them exchange "problems," and let each group brainstorm a solution for the other group. Then have each group share their advice with the other.

Here is another letter to Sally:

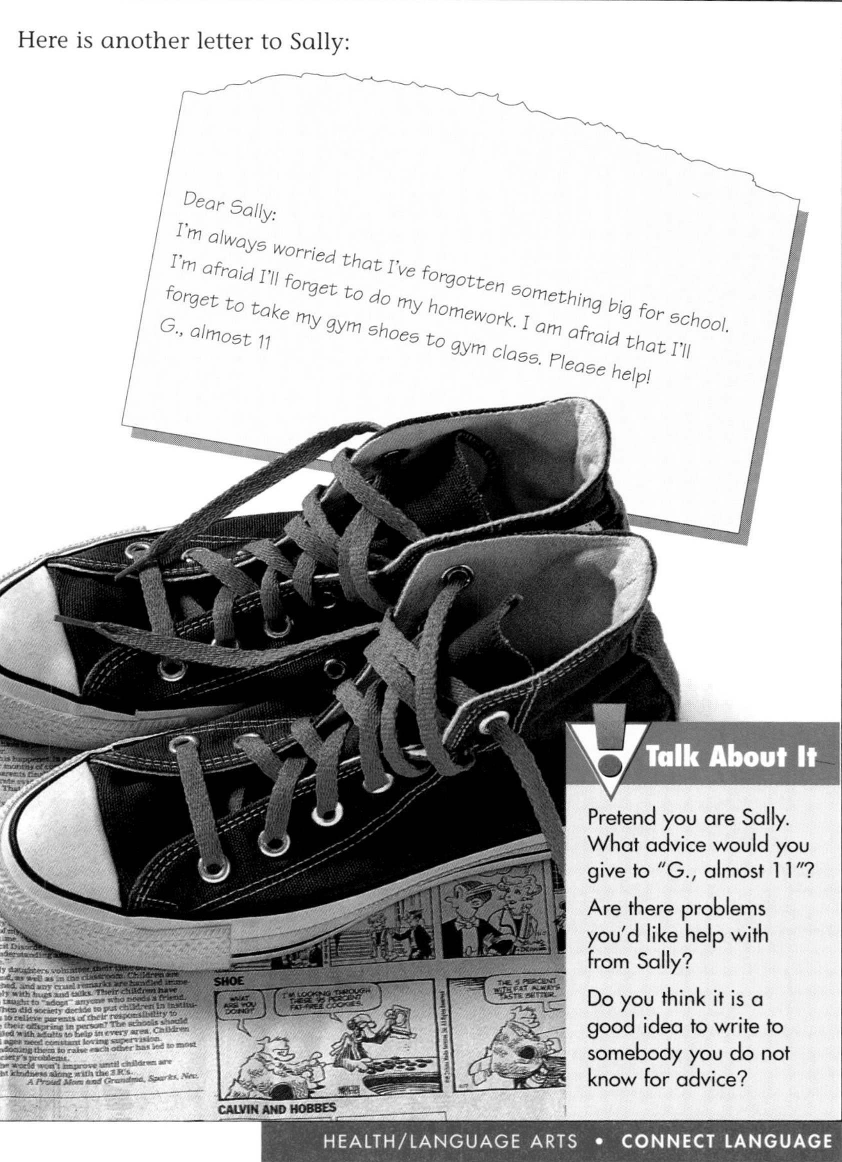

Dear Sally:
I'm always worried that I've forgotten something big for school. I'm afraid I'll forget to do my homework. I am afraid that I'll forget to take my gym shoes to gym class. Please help!
G., almost 11

Talk About It

Pretend you are Sally. What advice would you give to "G., almost 11"?

Are there problems you'd like help with from Sally?

Do you think it is a good idea to write to somebody you do not know for advice?

Language Awareness

Language Function
Giving Advice

Present phrases to give advice:

You should study more.
You shouldn't worry so much.
You ought to go out more.
You need to watch less TV.

Have students work in small groups to discuss the problems brought up in the class, giving advice for the problems.

Model a Strategy

State Main Idea

Model how to state the main idea:

When I write letters and many assignments for school, I know I need to state the problem or issue at the beginning of what I write. This is the pattern that people expect in English. When I look at the letters in the text, I see that the writers stated their problem in the first sentences.

Assess

Students should be able to

- discuss ways to get advice
- read and write letters of advice

LOOK**AHEAD**

In the next section, students will read a story that describes a Chinese girl's first day at school in the United States.

Mixed Ability

Writing: Write Advice

Bring in copies of several letters to advice columnists with the advice removed. Distribute the letters to small groups of students and have them write brief letters in response. Then have them compare their response to the one given in the newspaper.

Cooperative Language Experience

Identify School and Community Resources

Help students distinguish differences among problems. Everyone has problems that cause stress from day to day. Identify some problems that might benefit from professional help. These might be problems related to employment, finances, housing, emotions, or health. As newcomers to the community, students may be unaware of resources that are available to them. Develop a plan to acquaint students with these resources. Alternatives might be inviting individuals to visit the classroom to talk about community resources such as counseling services. If appropriate, take a trip to a center or a facility. Have students write a language experience story about what they learned.

Connect

Activate Prior Knowledge
Relate Personal Experiences

Invite students to discuss their first day at their current school or their first day at school in the United States. Encourage them to describe how they felt.

Introduce the Selection
Have students look at the pictures in the story. Ask questions such as these:

- What do you think the story is about? How do you know?
- Who do you think is the main character?

Read the Selection

PURPLE TAPE

Help students read the title of the story, the author's name, and the first Reader's Tip. Read the story with students. Then read the story again, presenting the Reader's Tips. Play the tape of the story on Side 1 of the Purple Tape several times.

Model a Strategy
Identify with Characters

Model how to identify with characters to understand stories better:

As I read the story, I try to think about what the main character Shirley is feeling. I think that she is nervous in her new school. I remember feeling strange in a new school myself, and I think I know how she feels.

Language Awareness

Language Functions
Greetings/Introductions

Point out to students the part of the story where the class says "Hi, Shirley!" Shirley answers this greeting by replying "Hi!" She also bows deeply. Explain that "hi" is an informal and friendly form of greeting. Discuss greetings such as "How are you?" and "What's happening?" and the situations in which they are used. Encourage them to suggest other English ways to ask "How are you?" that they may have heard. Then present the formulas for introductions in English such as "This is . . ." and "Nice to meet you" or "How do you do?" Have students practice greetings and introductions in English.

Teachable Moment
Simile

Direct students to the paragraph describing the students in Shirley's class. Explain the author's use of *simile*, such as "their faces were white, like clean plates" and "others were as thin as chopsticks." Help students to understand what trait the author is emphasizing when comparing a face to a plate or a child to chopsticks. Explain that *similes* most often contain the words *like* or *as*.

Options for Reaching All Students

Beginning
Language: Introductions
Have students practice making introductions and greetings. Have them choose to be fictional or famous people and write their names on a card that they pin to their clothing. Then have them perform the introductions and greetings.

Advanced
Writing: Write a Letter
Have students write letters to a friend who still lives in their native land. The letter should describe what their new classmates look like and the clothes they wear. The letter would also tell the friend what things the students miss about their old school.

Mixed Ability
Language: Clothing Vocabulary
Have students work in pairs of mixed ability and identify words that describe students' clothing in the first two pages of the story, such as *stripes, squares, or varied colors*. Have them draw pictures of the different kinds of decoration. Then have students look at clothing catalogues and describe clothing.

In the Year of the Boar and Jackie Robinson

by Bette Bao Lord

Reader's Tip
This reading is from a longer book. This part of the story tells of a young Chinese girl's first day at school in the United States. Her mother has taken her to the principal's office. Now the girl, Shirley, is going to meet her new teacher and classmates.

The principal then led her to class. The room was large, with windows up to the ceiling. Row after row of students, each one unlike the next. Some faces were white, like clean plates; others black like ebony. Some were in-between shades. A few were spotted all over. One boy was as big around as a water jar. Several others were as thin as chopsticks.

▲ Bette Bao Lord

No one wore a uniform of blue, like hers. There were sweaters with animals on them, shirts with stripes and shirts with squares, dresses in colors as varied as Grand-grand Uncle's paints. Three girls even wore earrings.

Strategy Tip
Understand Comparisons
When Shirley sees her new classmates, she compares them to things she is familiar with from her home in China. A water jar is big and round. Chopsticks are thin wooden sticks used for eating.

Strategy Tip
Stop and Think
What things about the children's clothes surprise Shirley? Why do you think they surprise her?

Strategy Tip
Stop and Think
What is the principal doing? What is she telling the other children?

Reader's Tip
Amitabha! is an expression of surprise that Shirley uses.

Reader's Tip
Shirley's mother said that Shirley was an ambassador. Shirley was representing her native country, China, to people in the United States. So that's why Shirley calls herself an ambassador. Here Shirley is thinking that she would like a pair of high-heeled shoes so that she would be tall like the other children.

Strategy Tip
Stop and Think
What did Shirley guess?

While Shirley looked about, the principal had been making a speech. Suddenly it ended with "Shirley Temple Wong." The class stood up and waved.

Amitabha! They were all so tall. Even Water Jar was a head taller than she. For a fleeting moment she wondered if Mother would consider buying an ambassador a pair of high-heeled shoes.

"Hi, Shirley!" The class shouted.

Shirley bowed deeply. Then, taking a guess, she replied, "Hi!"

The teacher introduced herself and showed the new pupil to a front-row seat. Shirley liked her right away, although she had a most difficult name, Mrs. Rappaport. She was a tiny woman with dainty bones and fiery red hair brushed skyward. Shirley thought that in her previous life she must have been a bird, a cardinal perhaps. Yet she commanded respect, for no student talked out of turn.

Language Tip
Vocabulary
Dainty means "tiny."

Language Tip
Vocabulary
A *cardinal* is a red bird. The feathers on the top of its head rise up to a point.

Language Tip
Idiom
To talk out of turn means "to talk when you are not allowed to talk."

Connect

Develop Language and Concepts

Present Pages 206 Through 209

Have students retell the story, and encourage them to relate to Shirley's experience by discussing their own experiences with new situations. Help them understand that it is often natural to feel different, left out, or strange in a new situation. Use Activity Book page 107 to check students' comprehension of the story. Use Activity Book page 108 to review food vocabulary.

Language Awareness

Grammar
Infinitives: Telling "Why"

Call students' attention to the first sentence on page 206. Help students find words to tell why Shirley leaned forward—to catch the meaning. Explain to students that *to catch the meaning* tells why. Help them find the infinitive on page 207: *to pick up coats.* Ask them to tell what this explains (why they went back to the classroom). Then have them offer other infinitive explanations to situations you present, such as why they wear coats (to stay warm).

Teachable Moment

Point of View

Explain to students the difference between first person and third person point of view in stories. In the first person, the story teller is "I." Point out that while this story is in the third person (there is no "I"), the reader really sees events from the point of view of Shirley. The author always tells what Shirley is thinking about other people but does not tell what other people are thinking about Shirley.

Response Activities

Personal Response

Shirley is trying to understand all the new ways of behavior she encounters. Have the students share their own similar experiences. Encourage them to share their feelings about these experiences.

Critical Response

In this story, the author tells what Shirley is thinking, but doesn't tell what the other characters are thinking. Did the author make a mistake by leaving this out? What point is the author making by only presenting Shirley's point of view?

Creative Response

The author describes people and things through Shirley's eyes. The reader understands that Shirley has never seen anything like this before. Have students pretend that they are like Shirley in the story and have just arrived in their classroom. Have students describe what they see.

Options for Reaching All Students

Beginning

Writing: Things Here

Have students list things such as foods and clothing they found in the United States that were not as common in their native lands. Encourage them to cut pictures from magazines to illustrate their words.

Advanced

Writing: My First Day

Have students write about a first day at school, either at this school or a school in their native countries.

Mixed Ability

Body Language: Nonverbal Communication

Write on the board:

wink, roll your eyes up, raise one or two eyebrows, scratch your head, shake your head up and down

Demonstrate and explain what these gestures mean in the United States. Ask students if there are similar gestures with similar meanings in their native cultures.

Throughout the lessons, Shirley leaned forward, barely touching her seat, to catch the meaning, but the words sounded like gurgling water. Now and then, when Mrs. Rappaport looked her way, she opened and shut her eyes as the principal had done, to show friendship.

At lunchtime, Shirley went with the class to the school cafeteria, but before she could pick up a tray, several boys and girls waved for her to follow them. They were smiling, so she went along.

Reader's Tip
The principal had winked at Shirley to make her feel comfortable. Now Shirley thinks that it is a good thing to wink at people. But Shirley closes both eyes, instead of one, when she winks.

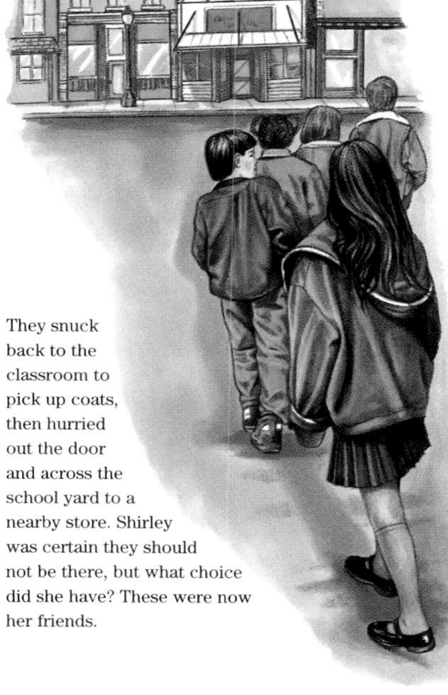

They snuck back to the classroom to pick up coats, then hurried out the door and across the school yard to a nearby store. Shirley was certain they should not be there, but what choice did she have? These were now her friends.

Strategy Tip
Put Yourself in the Story
Shirley thinks that the other students are doing something wrong, but she decides to follow them. What would you do?

One by one they gave their lunch money to the store owner, whom they called "Mr. P." In return, he gave each a bottle of orange-colored water, bread twice the size of an ear of corn oozing with meat balls, peppers, onions, and hot red gravy, and a large piece of brown paper to lay on the icy sidewalk and sit upon.

While they ate, everyone except Shirley played marbles or cards and traded bottle caps and pictures of men swinging a stick or wearing one huge glove. It was the best lunch Shirley had ever had.

Reader's Tip
The pictures of men swinging a bat and wearing gloves are baseball cards. These cards have pictures of major league baseball players and information about these players. Many children collect these cards.

Strategy Tip
Put Yourself in the Story
Why do you think that Shirley says it is the best lunch she ever had?

Connect

Activate Prior Knowledge

Review Vocabulary

Have students look at the pictures. Have them speculate as to what is being compared. Encourage students to share their experiences when they entered a new school in a foreign country.

Introduce the Selection

Help students read the title and the author's name. Read the essay with students several times and use the Reader's Tips.

Language Awareness

Language Function

Stating Rules: *have to, can't, not allowed to*

Point out some of the school rules mentioned on pages 210 to 213. Point out words and phrases such as *have to, can't, are not allowed to.* Then ask students to find examples of rules on the pages and to note how the rules are stated. Then ask them to name rules they have to follow, using the language they have learned.

Model a Strategy

Compare and Contrast

Model comparing and contrasting:

To compare and contrast, I look for what is the same and different. As I read about school in Japan, I think about what is the same and different in my school. I think about what I wear to school, what days I go to school, and when and how long my vacations are. I can write a list or talk about what is the same and different for each of these things. Sometimes I like to use a Venn diagram or a chart to help me see the differences more clearly.

ACTIVITY BOOK

Have students compare and contrast their current and former schools by completing Activity Book page 109.

Teachable Moment

Conclusion

Have students read the selection again. Point out that the author does not place values on the differences—she doesn't say that Japanese or American schools are better than the other. Her conclusion states that she is lucky to be part of both countries. An author's conclusion should be supported by what he or she has previously written.

FYI

This essay was written by a student in an ESL class taught by Mrs. Ann Newcomer at the Wilson Vance Elementary school in Findlay, Ohio.

Options for Reaching All Students

Beginning

Language: Compare Clothing

PICTURE CARDS

Have students work in pairs and use Picture Cards 7 boots, 17 coat, 26 dress, 34 hats, 38 jeans, 50 pants, 60 scarf, 62 skirt, 65 sneakers, socks, 68 sweater, 61 secretary (earrings, necklaces, rings) to study vocabulary. Then have them cut pictures from magazines and label clothing.

Advanced

Critical Thinking: Compare Lunches

Provide students with a copy of the Food Pyramid. Have them classify which food groups the lunches on pages 210 and 211 are in and decide which is the more healthful lunch. Alternatively, they could compare typical school lunches in their native countries with typical school lunches in the United States.

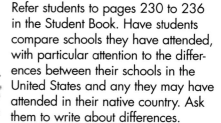

Writer's Workshop

Writing About Schools

Refer students to pages 230 to 236 in the Student Book. Have students compare schools they have attended, with particular attention to the differences between their schools in the United States and any they may have attended in their native country. Ask them to write about differences.

Schools in Japan and the United States

by Sayo Yamaguchi

Reader's Tip
This story was written by a young girl from Japan who is going to school in the United States. She tells her ideas about the differences between Japanese schools and schools in the United States.

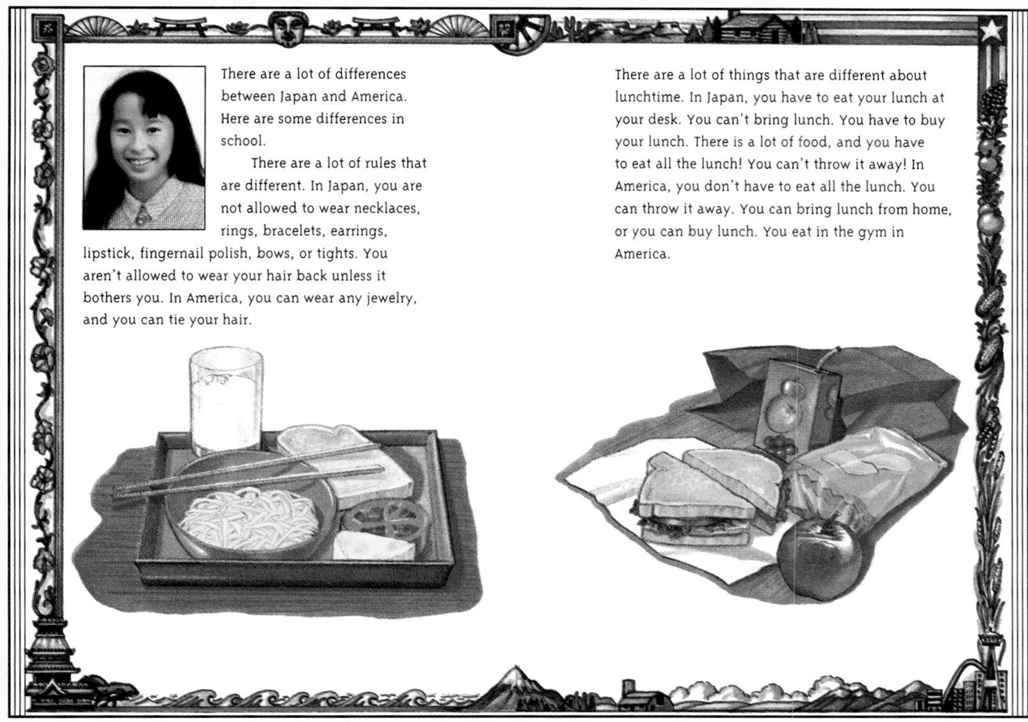

There are a lot of differences between Japan and America. Here are some differences in school.

There are a lot of rules that are different. In Japan, you are not allowed to wear necklaces, rings, bracelets, earrings, lipstick, fingernail polish, bows, or tights. You aren't allowed to wear your hair back unless it bothers you. In America, you can wear any jewelry, and you can tie your hair.

There are a lot of things that are different about lunchtime. In Japan, you have to eat your lunch at your desk. You can't bring lunch. You have to buy your lunch. There is a lot of food, and you have to eat all the lunch! You can't throw it away! In America, you don't have to eat all the lunch. You can throw it away. You can bring lunch from home, or you can buy lunch. You eat in the gym in America.

There are a lot of differences in elementary school. In Japan, you wear uniforms to school on Monday, Tuesday, Wednesday, Thursday, and Friday. You go to school for three hours on Saturday, but you don't have to wear your uniform. You usually go to kindergarten for three years. In America, you only go to kindergarten for a year. You don't go to school on Saturday, and you don't wear uniforms either.

In Japan, vacations are short. In winter and spring, you only have one or two weeks. In summer, you have one or two months. In America, you have more vacations. In winter, there are two weeks. Spring vacation is about one week. In summer, you have three months.

There are a lot of differences between schools in America and Japan. I think I am lucky to be a part of both countries.

Study Tip
Compare and Contrast
Writers often compare and contrast things. In this essay, the student contrasts school in Japan with school in the United States. What things about school in the two countries does she compare?

Connect

Activate Prior Knowledge

Using Pictures to Predict

Have students look at the picture. Ask, *What is the girl doing? How does she feel? What do you think the poem is about?*

Develop Language and Concepts

Present Page 214

Read the poem several times with students. Then play Side 2 of the Purple Tape several times. Remind students that they have learned several ways of coping with stress. Have students form small groups to discuss suggestions for helping the student in the poem.

Language Awareness

Grammar
Comparisons: *Good/Better/Best*

Review comparative forms and superlative forms with students, using classroom items: *This bookbag is big. This bookbag is bigger than that one. This is the biggest of all.* Then list lunches. Have students make judgments about lunches they like, using *good, better, best,* and the same structure pattern as above.

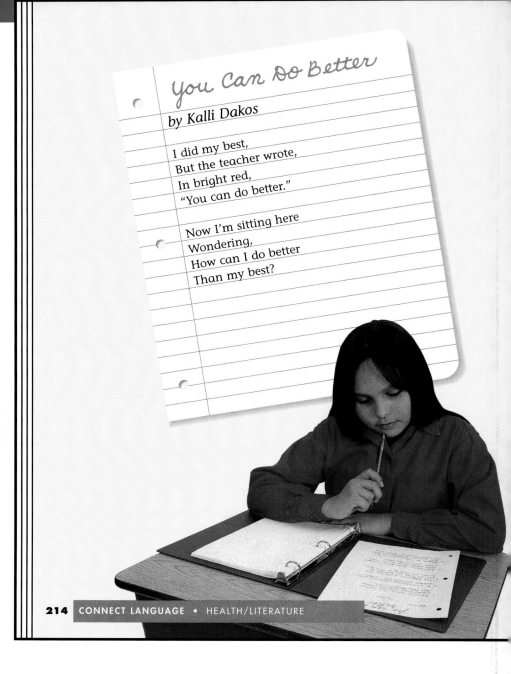

You Can Do Better

by Kalli Dakos

I did my best,
But the teacher wrote,
In bright red,
"You can do better."

Now I'm sitting here
Wondering,
How can I do better
Than my best?

Options for Reaching All Students

Beginning

Language: Pronunciation

Have students do a choral reading of the poem. Then have them tape-record their reading, and listen for places to improve pronunciation and intonation.

Advanced

Writing: Give Advice

Have students work in groups of three and list advice to a student about how to get better grades in school.

Tell what you learned.

CHAPTER 11

1. How does the body react to stress? What happens?
2. What situations can cause stress?
3. How can you deal with stress?
4. Think over the story. What problems did Shirley have on her first day of school in a new country? Did you have similar problems?
5. What is the most important thing you learned in this chapter?

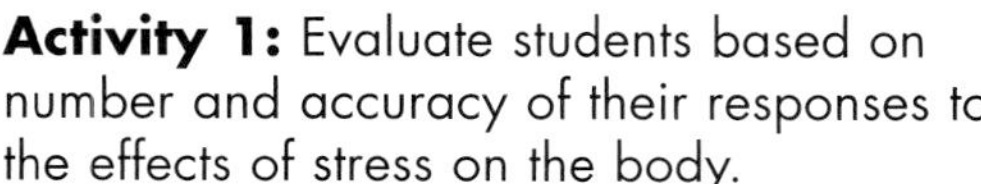

Assess

Activity 1: Evaluate students based on number and accuracy of their responses to the effects of stress on the body.

Activity 2: Students should be able to relate both positive and negative situations.

Activity 3: Students should identify relaxation exercises, classifying problems, humor, and asking for help.

Activity 4: Evaluate whether students can compare their experiences to Shirley's.

Activity 5: Evaluate students' ability to explain the reasons for their choices.

Have students complete the Chapter Self-Assessment, Blackline Master 31. Have students choose the product of one of the activities to include in their portfolios. Add the results of any rubrics, checklists, self-assessments, or portfolio assessments, Blackline Masters 2–18 and 31.

Listening Assessment

BLACKLINE MASTER

Make sure that students have a copy of Blackline Master 91 from the Teacher's Resource Book. Play the tape several times and have students complete the activity.

CREAM TAPE

See page 192c for the tapescript.

Options for Assessment

Vocabulary Assessment

Classes of Words

Have students write as many words as they can in each of the following categories: "Emotions," "Parts of the Body," and "Situations That Cause Stress."

Writing Assessment

Personal Profiles

Have students write two autobiographical profiles. The first describes their first day of school in the United States. The second describes themselves in the present.

Language Assessment

BLACKLINE MASTER

Use Blackline Master 90 in the Teacher's Resource Book.

Standardized Test Practice

ACTIVITY BOOK

Use pages 110 and 111. Answers: **1.** Shirley went to a new school in the United States. On the first day she was scared . . . **2.** Shirley made friends with her classmates and had the best lunch of her life.

Preview

Activate Prior Knowledge

Demonstrate Reference Materials

Bring in copies of reference materials such as picture encyclopedias, kids' almanacs, atlases, newspapers, and magazines. Ask students if they know about or have used similar materials. Ask students whether they can name each type of reference material and predict what kind of information it contains.

Develop Language and Concepts

Present Pages 216 and 217

Read the questions and help students associate words in the Word Bank with the pictures on the pages. Ask students whether they have ever used these sources to get information. Ask students to answer the first question in Tell What You Know: *How do people you know get their information?*

Ask students to think about how people got their information a hundred years ago. Have them answer the second question based on what they know.

Explain to students that some people call the present era the "Information Age." That is because the revolution in the development of computers and advancements in telecommunications have made vast amounts of information available to individuals at speeds unprecedented in history.

CHAPTER 12

Getting Information

Tell what you know.

What sources of information do people use?

What changes have there been in the ways people can get information?

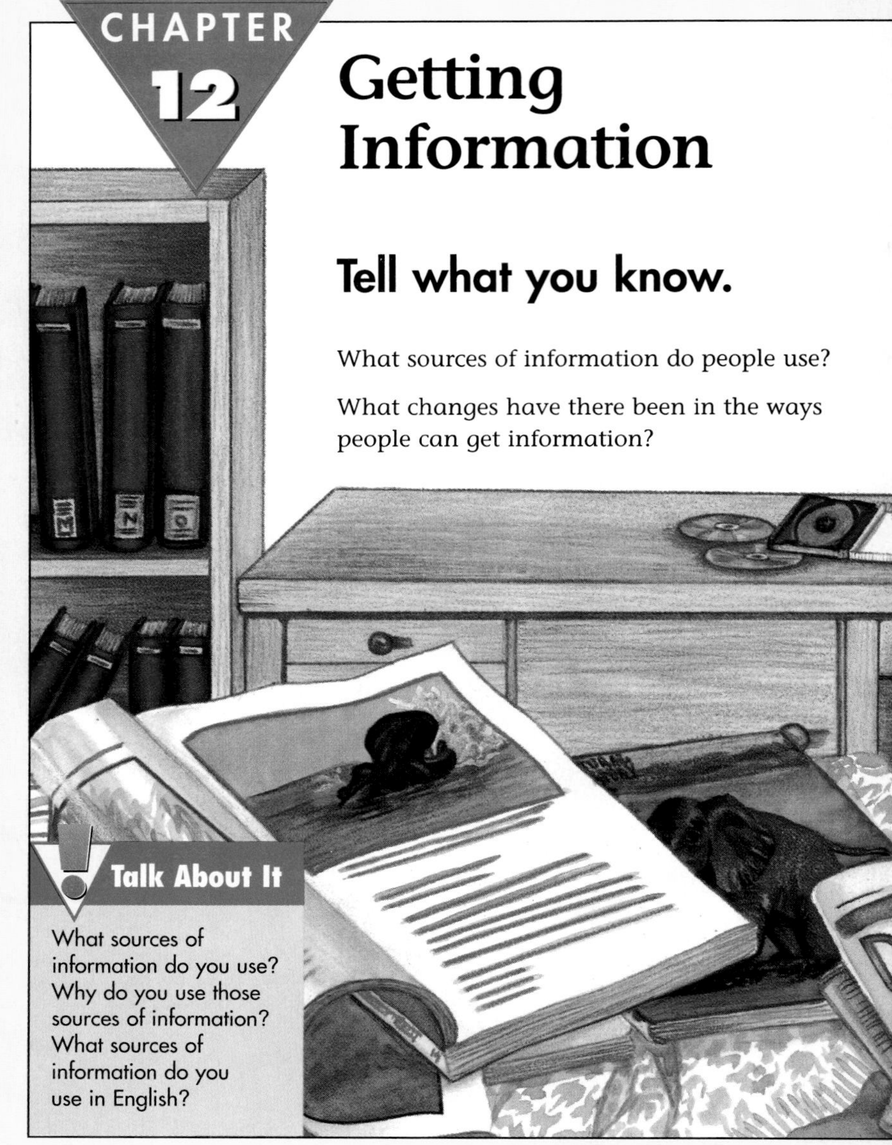

Talk About It

What sources of information do you use? Why do you use those sources of information? What sources of information do you use in English?

Options for Reaching All Students

Beginning

Language: Categorize

Remind the students that there are many ways of communicating that are so new that even their parents did not have them at their age. Find as many pictures of ways of communicating as you can using the list below. Make cards with these words on them. Have students match the cards with the pictures and then post them in one of two columns set up on the board: *Yes* and *No*. "Yes" is for yes, their parents had these ways to communicate, and "No" for those their parents did not have when they were growing up:

telephone; cellular phone; television; cable television; newspaper; personal computer; fax; magazine; beeper; radio

Advanced

Critical Thinking: Compare and Contrast

Have pairs of students write a paragraph comparing today's telephone to those made in 1960. They should compare and contrast at least three attributes such as size, functions, and portability. Have them do the same for computers and television. Explain how to get information about the older versions through newspaper files at the library.

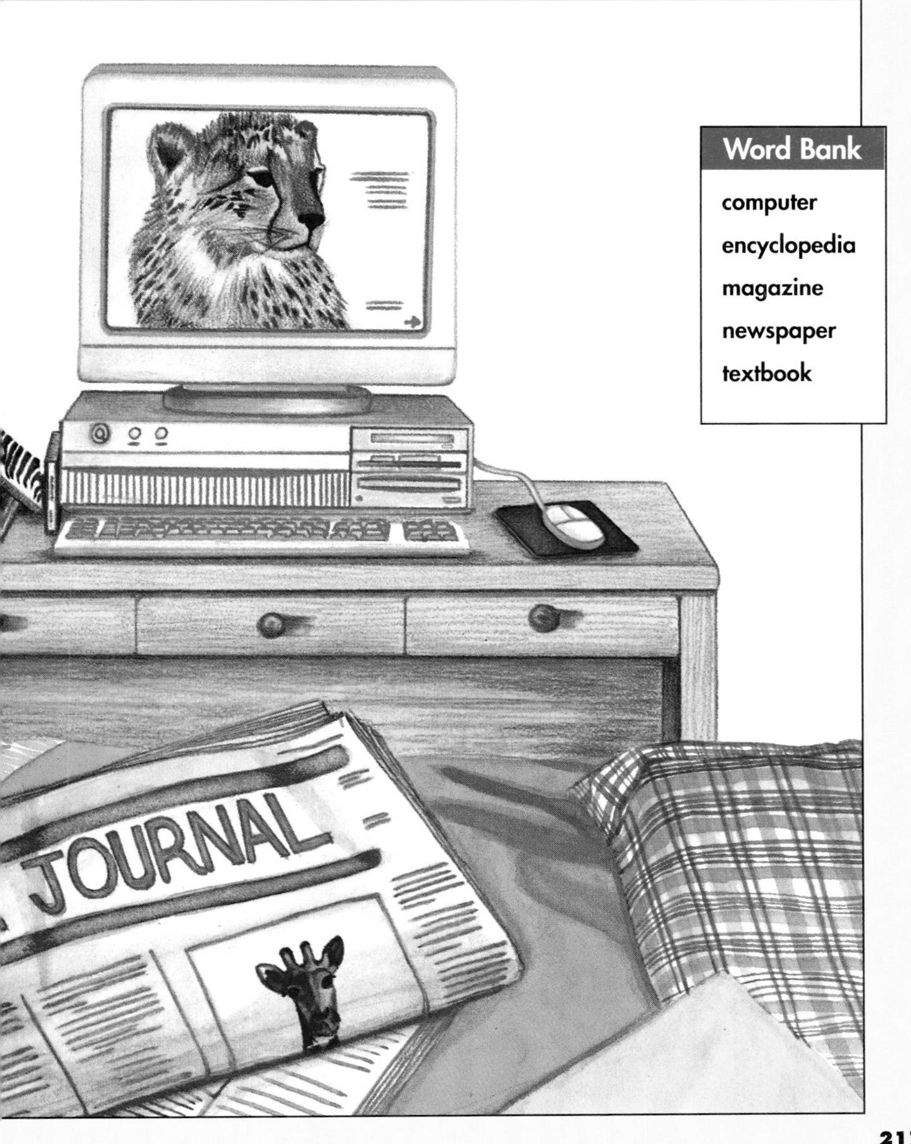

Word Bank
computer
encyclopedia
magazine
newspaper
textbook
JOURNAL

217

Help students understand that the speedy and ample availability of information has made the world a much smaller place. Let students know that they can easily find and understand information about changes in the world that affect their lives. They only have to learn where to look. Discuss the Talk About It questions with students.

Mixed Ability

Art: Time Line

Invite students to work in pairs of mixed ability to make an invention time line on chart paper, using cutouts from magazines or other sources. They should place pictures of the following along the time line in their proper places: computer, printing press, modern encyclopedia, television, telephone, radio, telegraph. Have advanced students research encyclopedias to learn the dates of the inventions' appearance.

Home Connection

Communication

Have students interview their parents or other adults about the inventions and devices that are in common use now that the adults didn't have when they were the student's age. Have students share the results with the class.

Present

Activate Prior Knowledge

Brainstorm Vocabulary

Bring in volumes of different encyclopedias. Include picture encyclopedias, from which even beginning students can get information if just in graphic form. Have students suggest what kinds of information they might find in an encyclopedia and list them on chart paper, adding to the list throughout the lesson.

Develop Language and Concepts

Present Pages 218 and 219

Read the text with students. Provide examples of information that can be found in encyclopedias, such as biographies as well as science and geographical facts. Help students understand which information might have changed since the book was printed (recent news events, population figures) versus information that would be mostly unchanged (stories of historical people's lives, stories of past inventions).

Model a Strategy

Understand Chronology

Model rereading to understand sequence:

As I read this article, I find the date Roosevelt got sick with polio. The article also tells me that he served as President from 1933 to 1945. By rereading the material, I can tell that he got polio before he became President.

ACTIVITY BOOK

Have students complete Activity Book page 112 to focus on chronology.

Encyclopedias

When you need the answer to almost any question, look in an encyclopedia. An encyclopedia is a good **reference tool.** It has information about a large number of topics. It has information about people, places, and things. It is full of facts. It has a great deal of information on events and people who lived in the past.

Roosevelt, Franklin Delano (1882–1945)
Franklin Delano Roosevelt was the 32nd president of the United States. He served longer than any other president—over 12 years—from 1933 to 1945. He was called "FDR" for short.

He was born in 1882, in Hyde Park, New York, to a wealthy family. In 1921, he got sick with polio. Even though he was crippled for life and could no longer walk well, he went on to do great things. He was one of America's greatest presidents.

He led the United States through the Great Depression, a time when millions of people had no jobs and little money. He said, "The only thing we have to fear is fear itself." He started many government programs, such as Social Security, that helped older people and sick people.

As commander-in-chief, he led the United States on its way to victory in World War II.

He died suddenly of a cerebral hemorrhage in 1945.

Options for Reaching All Students

Beginning

Language: Alphabetical Order

Have students write words on separate index cards. Help students alphabetize the words. Have students read the cards aloud as they alphabetize them. Then have each student select a word, look it up in a dictionary, and give the definition.

Advanced

Critical Thinking: Article Organization

Have students look at articles on the same topic in several different encyclopedias and compare the information presented. Also have students categorize the type of information that is commonly given for different types of articles; for example, biographies and descriptions of countries.

Peer Tutoring

Language: Summarize

Have students work in pairs of mixed ability. Have students make a list of the information they remember from the encyclopedia article. Ask them to put the information in chronological order.

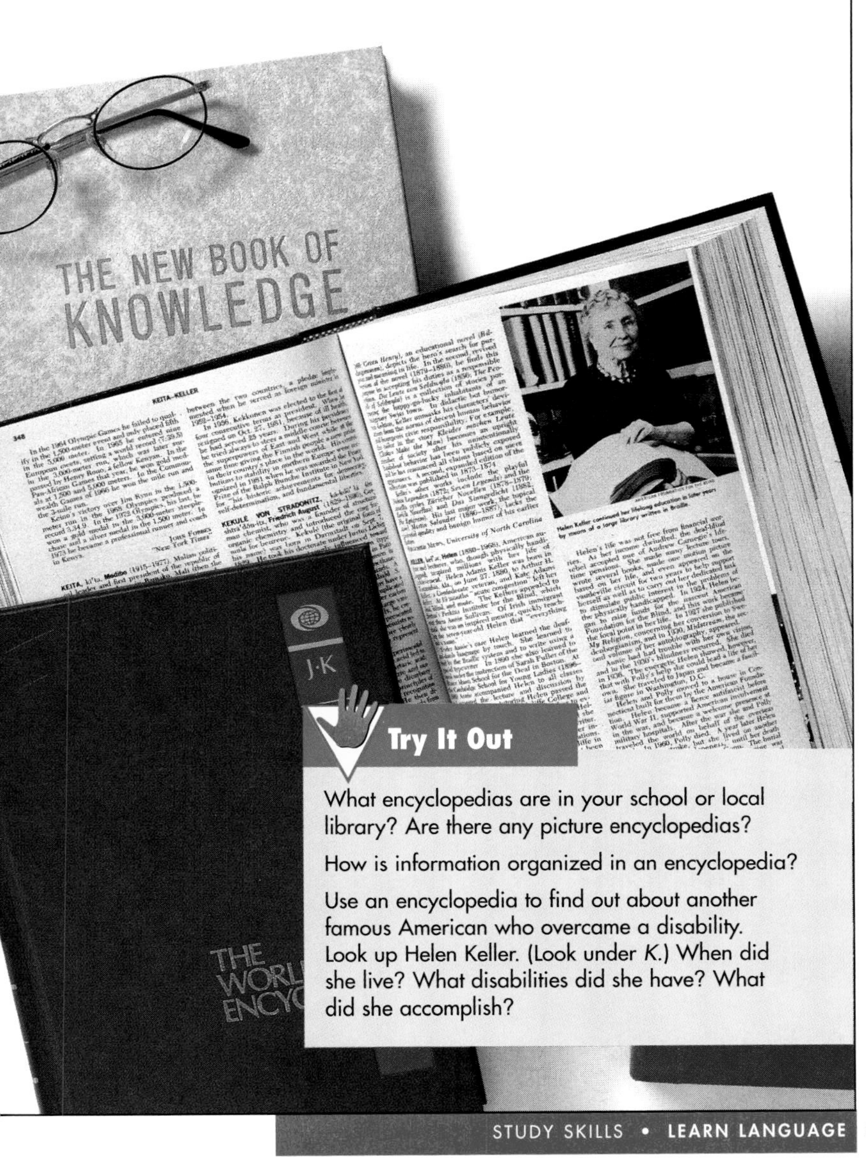

Try It Out

What encyclopedias are in your school or local library? Are there any picture encyclopedias?

How is information organized in an encyclopedia?

Use an encyclopedia to find out about another famous American who overcame a disability. Look up Helen Keller. (Look under *K*.) When did she live? What disabilities did she have? What did she accomplish?

Language Awareness

Grammar
Appositives

Call students' attention to the sentence about the Great Depression in the encyclopedia entry. Tell them that sometimes commas are used to set off information that explains something. In this case, "a time when millions of people had no jobs and little money" gives the definition of the *Great Depression*. Encourage students to look for appositives in their reading.

Assess 

Have students answer the questions and perform the activities in Try It Out for assessment. Students should be able to

- describe different types of encyclopedias and explain how they organize information
- find information by using an encyclopedia

LOOK**AHEAD**

In the next section, students will learn about magazines and their uses.

Cooperative Language Experience

Library Visit

Make a K-W-L chart with the class about ways of communicating. Focus students' attention on things they want to learn. Have students work in pairs of mixed ability to research one item on the list, using the school library as an information resource. Have them prepare by listing some of the basic ways they can use the library for research and discovery: encyclopedias and other reference works, the card catalog, online resources, the reader's assistant at the library, and so on. Have them think about which library resources will be most useful. Then have them work to find the information they want to discover by using library resources. On returning to class, have students share their experience, reinforcing the productive ways they used the library and suggesting better ways in cases that were only partly successful.

Practice

Activate Prior Knowledge

Demonstrate Magazines

Find out what students know about magazines. Bring in examples of magazines for students, such as *Time Magazine for Children, Sports Illustrated for Kids, National Geographic World, Zillions,* and so on.

Ask them to name magazines they know and list the titles on the board, or give students a chance to look at the materials you have brought. Help students to discuss the areas of interest covered by each magazine.

Develop Language and Concepts

Present Pages 220 and 221

ACTIVITY BOOK

Read the pages several times with students. Make sure they know that magazines are more current than encyclopedias. Explain that magazines spend a great amount of time, money, and effort to design covers and page layouts that will make their product stand out from their competitors' on the newsstand. Have students do Activity Book page 113.

Magazines

Magazines come out every week or every month. The information they have is more recent than the information in encyclopedias. Articles are written in an interesting way to attract the reader. Often it is fun just to look at the pictures in a magazine.

Many magazines focus on one subject area. For example, there are magazines with articles only about sports. There are magazines for students of your age.

Options for Reaching All Students

Beginning

Language: Table of Contents

Bring in several copies of an issue of a magazine for students. On the board, write three topics covered by the magazine. Have students work in small groups to read the table of contents and find the page on which the articles begin. Have them locate the articles in the magazine.

Advanced

Reading: Explore a Magazine

Collect copies of magazines for young people. Possibilities include *Sports Illustrated for Kids, Zillions, National Geographic World, Time Magazine for Kids, Cricket,* and *Ranger Rick.* Have students work in pairs and choose a magazine they think looks appealing. Have them read the table of contents and look through the magazine carefully. Ask them to figure out the general subject area and intended audience for the magazine. Have them look for special sections that are repeated in other issues. Have them choose an article to read. When they have completed their exploration, have them share what they learned with the group.

A Real Success Story

Success, then a problem, then success. That's the story of Gloria Estefan, singer with the hit group Miami Sound Machine.

The Cuban-born singer and songwriter became famous in the 1980s. Her group attracted millions of listeners with the sounds of Hispanic music—salsa, samba, and conga.

Then Estefan was in a terrible car accident. Her back was broken.

Doctors operated and put a metal rod down Estefan's back. Estefan was in constant pain. She says that she was depressed only once. "The beginning was the worst, the low point." She could only lift her foot an inch off the ground.

Slowly she managed to walk on her own. Now she is back on stage singing and dancing. And her albums sell thousands of copies.

Try It Out

Go to a school or local library. Look at the magazines. Are there any magazines that interest you? What are they?

STUDY SKILLS • USE LANGUAGE 221

Language Awareness

Spelling

Punctuation: Quotation Marks

Point out the sentence in *quotation marks* in the article. Explain to students that quotation marks in an interview are used to set off things the person being interviewed actually said. The article doesn't specifically tell who the quote is from. However, the reader can tell it is from Gloria Estefan because the surrounding sentences discuss things she said.

Model a Strategy

Understand Magazine Articles

Model how to understand the organization of magazine articles:

When I read magazine articles, I notice that many times the author starts with interesting information that makes me want to read on. In this story, I have to get to the second sentence to know that this article is going to be about the life of Gloria Estefan.

Assess ✓

Students should be able to

- find and name magazines that interest them

LOOK **AHEAD**

In the next section, students will learn about newspapers.

Cooperative Language Experience

Visit a Newsstand

Take students to visit a well-stocked newsstand or magazine store. Divide the class into teams to cover separate sections of the stand or store and look through magazines. Have the class write a language experience story about the visit.

Multicultural Connection

Music

Have students work in small groups to discuss the three types of Hispanic music mentioned in the excerpt. Bring in samples of each if possible. Also have students bring in samples of music from their native lands to share with the class. Encourage students to discuss differences and similarities.

QuickCheck

Possessives

Point out the possessives in the article: *Estefan's*. Check whether students are forming possessives correctly. Help those needing practice form possessives of both proper and common nouns. Review rules for forming the possessive forms of plurals and words ending in *-s*.

Practice

Activate Prior Knowledge

Start a K-W-L Chart

Find out what students know about newspapers. Ask students questions such as these:

- Do you read newspapers?
- What information do you look for?

Use the information to make a K-W-L chart:

K: What We Know	Newspapers provide information about news of the day.
W: What We Want to Find Out	What are the parts of a newspaper?
L: What We Learned	

Complete the chart at the end of the lesson.

Develop Language and Concepts

Present Pages 222 and 223

Read the pages with students. Explain that the list of questions is also known as the 5Ws. Use Activity Book page 114.

Help students brainstorm sources of information more current than newspapers. Are there reasons to prefer a newspaper over a more current source? A magazine over a newspaper? An encyclopedia over a magazine?

To review sources of information, use Activity Book page 115.

Newspapers

The newspaper has information about events that are currently happening.

Volcano Erupts and Travel Is Disrupted

NEW ZEALAND—September 26

Mount Ruapehu has begun to throw out ash, steam, and rocks the size of cars. Dr. Sidney Simons, a geologist and expert on volcanoes, told reporters that a major eruption could occur at any time. He has asked the government to take action to keep people safe.

The government has stopped certain kinds of travel. Airplanes are not allowed to fly near the mountain because the ash may clog their engines, causing the engines to stop working. Train travel in the area has been stopped because the train track runs near the side of the mountain. Ash and mud could fall on the tracks.

People in the area can expect heavy ash to fall. One local resident told reporters, "I'm leaving! It's too stressful to stay here any longer." Many more people may decide to leave the area.

Options for Reaching All Students

Beginning

Language: Newspaper Headlines

Bring in multiple copies of the same newspaper edition. Give one to each student. At random, choose articles that are continued further inside. Have students turn to that page. Read the headline aloud to students. Students must then find the correct page where the article is continued and be the first to call out the correct headline on that page. Each first-place answerer receives one point. Then have students tell what they think the articles are going to be about.

Advanced

Advanced: Cub Reporter

Set the scene in this way: Put a cardigan sweater on the back of your chair. Have a colleague enter the classroom unannounced, grab the sweater, then quickly leave. Have students work in pairs to write a news story describing the event and answering the questions who, what, where, when, and why.

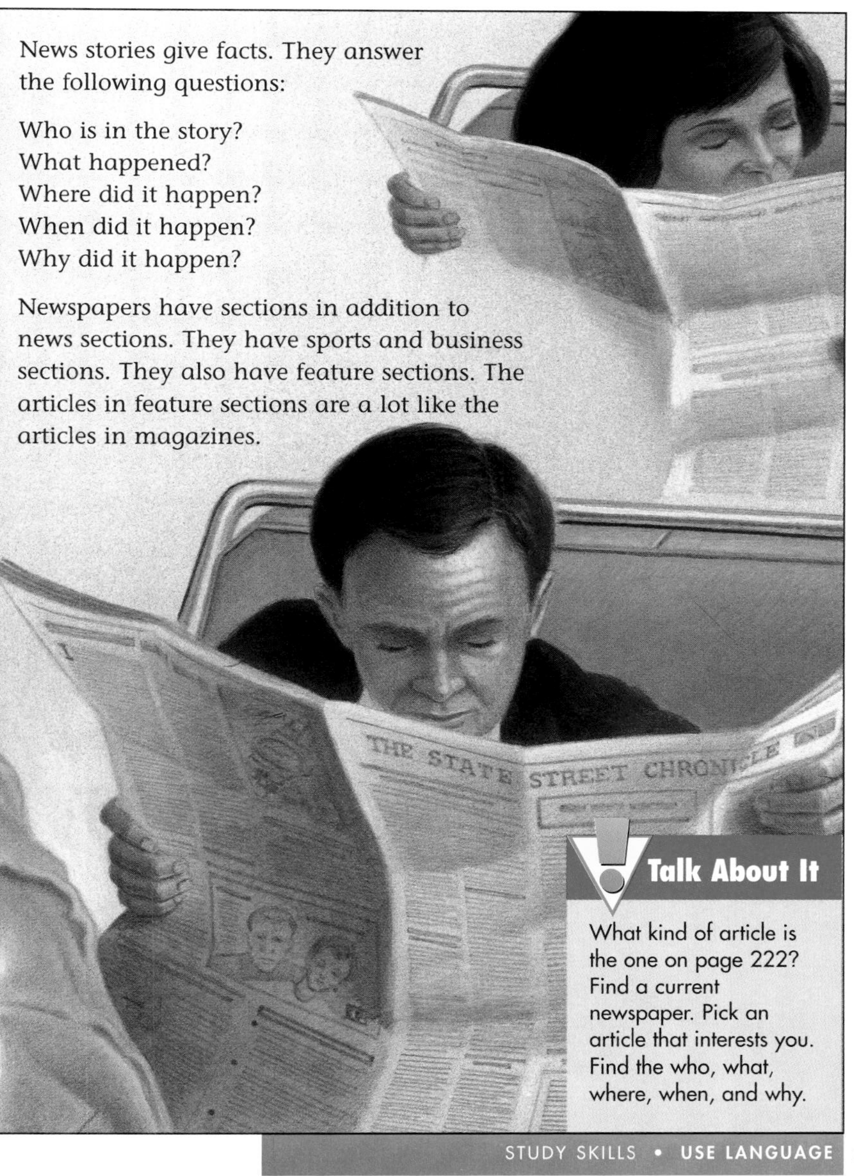

News stories give facts. They answer the following questions:

Who is in the story?
What happened?
Where did it happen?
When did it happen?
Why did it happen?

Newspapers have sections in addition to news sections. They have sports and business sections. They also have feature sections. The articles in feature sections are a lot like the articles in magazines.

Talk About It

What kind of article is the one on page 222? Find a current newspaper. Pick an article that interests you. Find the who, what, where, when, and why.

Language Awareness

Grammar
Questions and Answers

Provide students with different articles from recent newspapers. Have them use the questions on page 223 and work in pairs. Each one asks the other one the questions about his or her article and then gives an oral summary of the other's news article.

Model a Strategy

Evaluate an Article

Model evaluating an article:

The article states that news stories answer the questions who, what, where, when, and why. I can generalize that all news stories answer these questions. I can apply this knowledge to any newspaper article in order to evaluate whether it is a good news story.

Assess 

Use students' responses to Talk About It for assessment. Students should be able to

- find the "5Ws" in a newspaper article

LOOK**AHEAD** 

In the next section, students will use graphic organizers to help remember and connect information.

Mixed Ability

Study Skills: Comparing Sources

Have students work in pairs of mixed ability to make a chart with the headings *Encyclopedia, Magazine*, and *Newspaper*. Have them make a side column of categories such as *Type of Information* or *How Often Published.* Encourage students to fill in their charts based on what they have learned.

Cooperative Learning

Class Newspaper

Have students put together a class newspaper. Have the class as a whole decide on a title and the sections and kinds of information the newspaper will include. Assign students various tasks: editors, designers, writers, typists.

Home Connection

Newspaper of Record

Have students interview those at home who read newspapers. They should ask which newspapers are read and the reasons for choosing them. Have students report their findings in small groups.

Connect

Activate Prior Knowledge

Demonstrate Graphic Organizers

BLACKLINE MASTER

Pass out copies of Idea Webs, Venn Diagrams, and Story Charts, Blackline Masters 20, 23, 24, and 25, and have students discuss what they know about graphic organizers. Explain that a graphic organizer is a pictorial representation of information. Have them look at the specific diagrams and tell about some of the specific information they can use them for.

Develop Language and Concepts

Present Pages 224 and 225

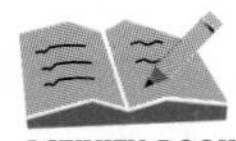

ACTIVITY BOOK

Read the text with students. Have students work in pairs of mixed ability to discuss the two organizers. They should discuss the differences between the organizers and try to understand why they are different. Help them note that the pie chart is a simpler form of organizer that helps them take notes about important facts but doesn't connect them.

For additional practice with graphic organizers, have students complete Activity Book pages 116 and 117.

Write to learn.

Writing down information you read is useful. Writing can help you remember ideas. Thinking about the connections between ideas can help you understand what you read better.

Graphic organizers can help you organize pieces of information and find connections between them.

This graphic organizer has main topics about the life of Franklin Roosevelt: Early Life, Problems, Accomplishments. Under each topic is related information.

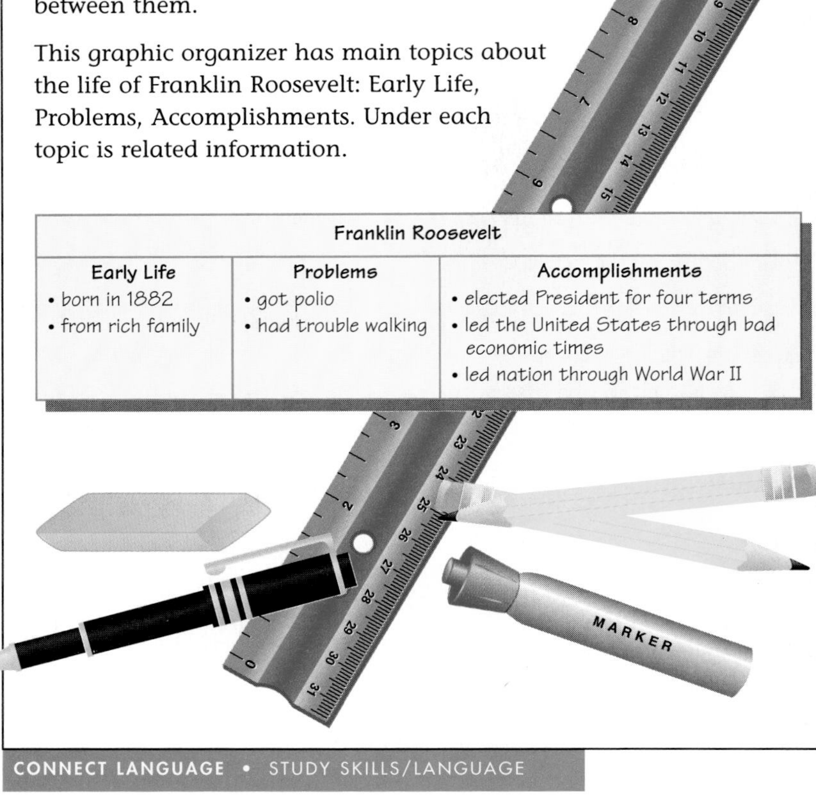

Franklin Roosevelt		
Early Life	**Problems**	**Accomplishments**
• born in 1882 • from rich family	• got polio • had trouble walking	• elected President for four terms • led the United States through bad economic times • led nation through World War II

Options for Reaching All Students

Beginning

Language: Use Graphic Organizers

Choose a current story from a magazine or newspaper that will be of interest to your students You may want to find an article about music or sports, depending on the makeup of the class, their backgrounds, and their experience. Choose an article that lends itself to being expressed in a graphic organizer: record sales or popularity polls for rock groups, comparative season records and other statistics for favorite sports teams, and so on. Have students discuss which kind of graphic organizer would be most useful for expressing the information in the article. Then have them work in small groups to complete one.

Advanced

Writing: Use a Graphic Organizer

Have students use the same type of organizer as for Franklin Roosevelt, but instead fill it by using information obtained about Helen Keller. Then have students fill the chart with information about themselves. Invite students to form pairs and exchange their personal charts. Each student analyzes the other's organizer and orally summarizes the information.

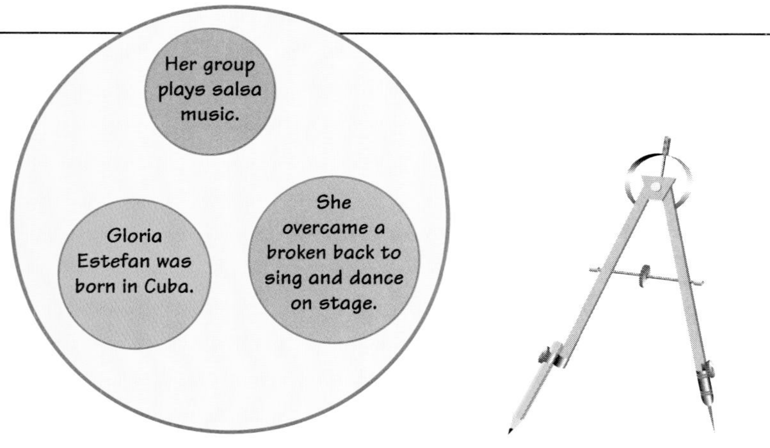

Her group plays salsa music.
Gloria Estefan was born in Cuba.
She overcame a broken back to sing and dance on stage.

Sometimes it is helpful just to write down four or five facts that you find interesting about something you have read. This graphic organizer has facts about Gloria Estefan.

Write About It

Look at the newspaper article on page 222. Use a graphic organizer to remember important information from it.

Choose a topic that interests you. Find an encyclopedia, magazine, or newspaper article about it. Write down important or interesting information from it in a graphic organizer.

Language Awareness

Spelling
Punctuation: Colon

Call attention to the last paragraph on page 224. Ask students to name the *colon*, if they can. Tell them that colons are used in several ways. Here it introduces a list. Help them read the list. Then have them produce sentences with lists, while you write them on the board.

Model a Strategy

Use Graphic Organizers

Model the uses of graphic organizers:

I have learned when it is best to use different kinds of graphic organizers. When I want to brainstorm ideas, an idea web is good to use. When I want to remember information in textbooks, the Main Idea and Supporting Details are often useful. When I read fiction stories, story charts are useful. Graphic organizers help me remember information I have read.

Assess

Use students' responses to Write About It for assessment. Students should be able to

- use a graphic organizer correctly

LOOK**AHEAD**

In the next section, students will read an interview of a young Cuban immigrant.

Cooperative Language Learning

Graphics in Newspapers and Magazines

Point out that much information in newspapers is summarized in pictures; for example, papers such as *USA Today* have these as a regular feature. Help students collect examples of these graphics and organize them into categories. Then have students choose one format to summarize information about the class.

Multicultural Connection

Famous People

Have students create a graphic organizer chart like the one on page 224. Then have them select a famous person from their native land and fill in the same type of information provided about Franklin Roosevelt. Have students meet in small groups to exchange their charts.

Writer's Workshop

What I Learned

Refer students to the Writer's Workshop on pages 230 to 236 in the Student Book. Have students use an encyclopedia, magazine, newspaper article, or online sources to research a topic. Ask them to write a paragraph of two or three interesting things they learned about the topic.

Connect

Activate Prior Knowledge

Review Themes

Explain to students that this article is taken from an interview with a young immigrant. Use a discussion topic such as the following to activate what students already know: *Share some of the feelings you had when you moved to a new country.* Review with students the effects of changes on people's lifestyles and emotions.

Develop Language and Concepts

Present Pages 226 and 227

ACTIVITY BOOK Help students read the introduction to the article. Read the interview several times with students. Have them offer their impressions of the interview. Discuss with them the conversational tone of the interview. Help them compare and contrast the interview to other information articles. Ask them what kinds of interviews interest them most, for example: sports figures, television, film and music celebrities, political figures, or "ordinary" people.

To review sources of information, use Activity Book page 119.

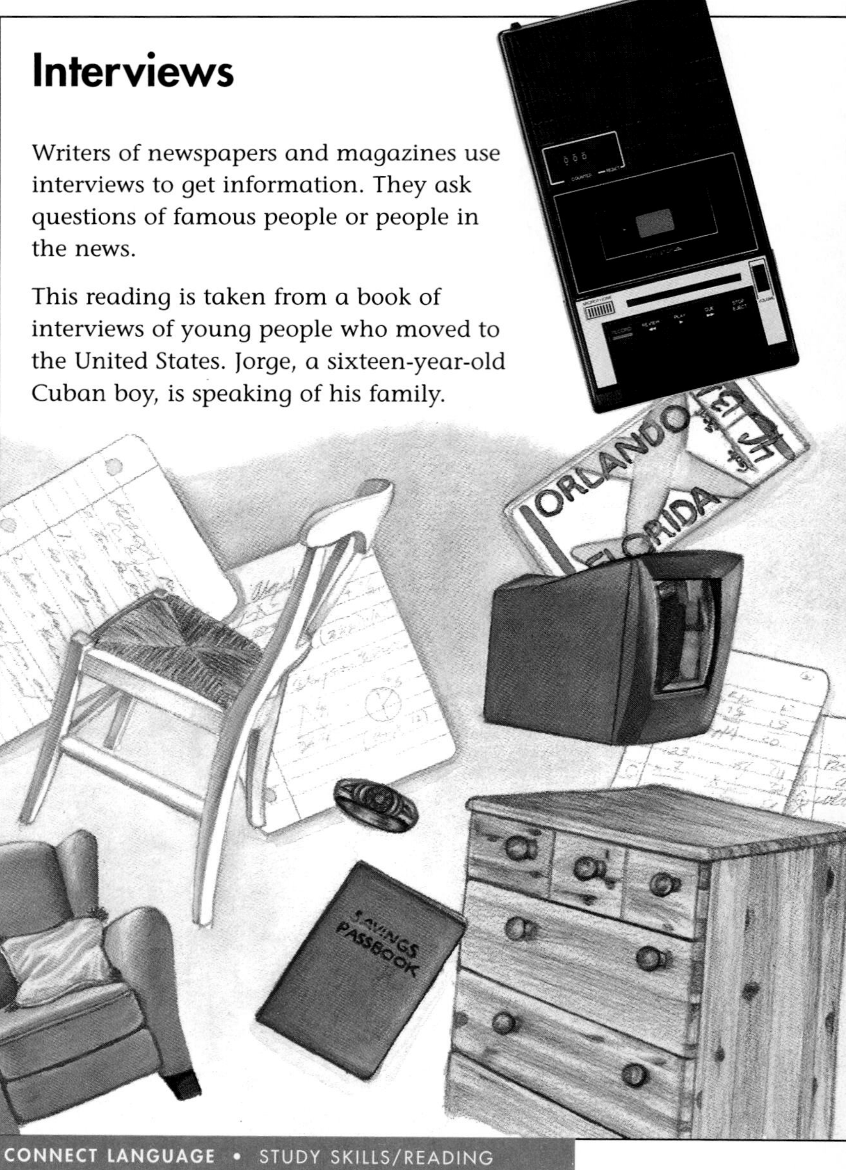

Interviews

Writers of newspapers and magazines use interviews to get information. They ask questions of famous people or people in the news.

This reading is taken from a book of interviews of young people who moved to the United States. Jorge, a sixteen-year-old Cuban boy, is speaking of his family.

226 CONNECT LANGUAGE • STUDY SKILLS/READING

Options for Reaching All Students

Beginning

Language: Schedule

Review with students the activities mentioned in the interview. Have them create a schedule of their own day. Then have them create a list of what they have accomplished since coming to the United States.

Advanced

Language: Interview

Have students work in pairs. Each partner takes a turn interviewing the other. Students should ask questions about the other student's activities on that day, taking notes as answers are given. After both interviews are completed, have students write a story describing what the interviewee said.

Mixed Ability

Math: Time Clock

Have students work in pairs of mixed ability to answer the following questions: How much time does Jorge have to get from school to work? How long does he work per day? How long does it take for him to get home from work? How long does it take to eat his dinner?

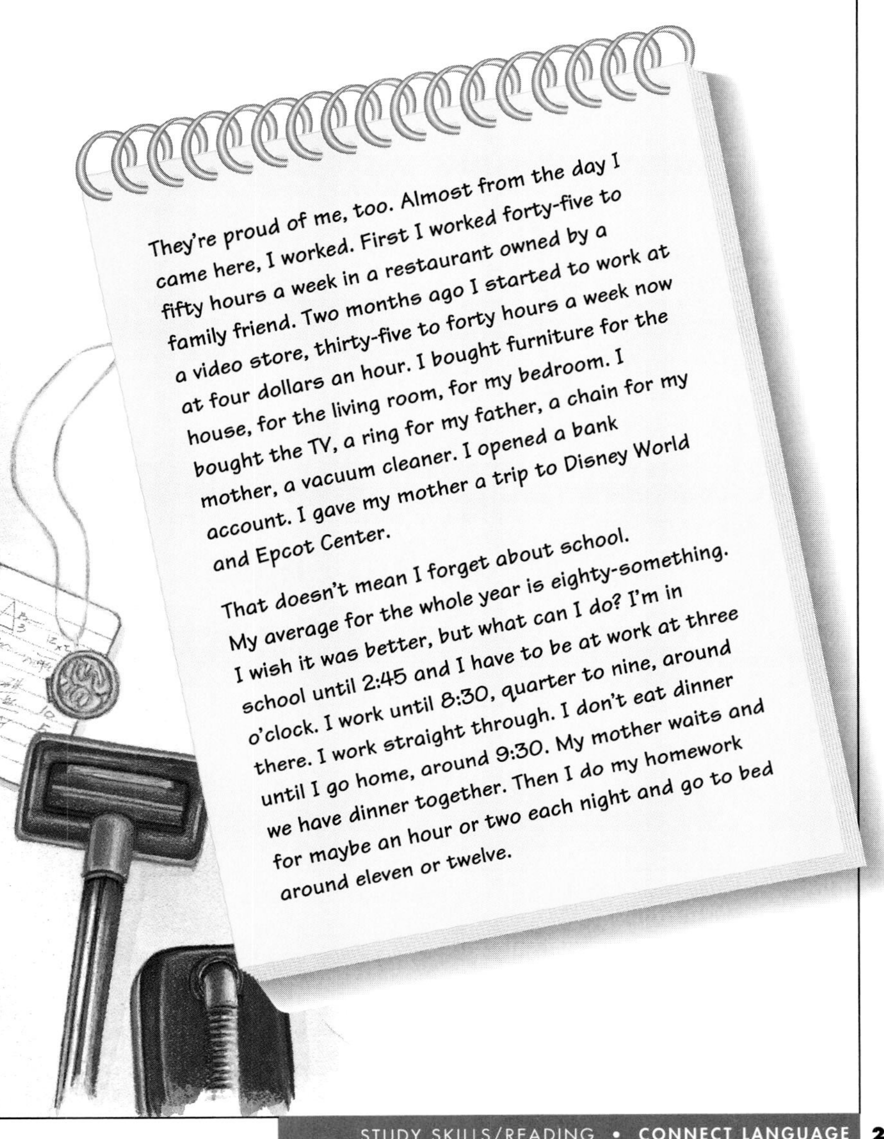

They're proud of me, too. Almost from the day I came here, I worked. First I worked forty-five to fifty hours a week in a restaurant owned by a family friend. Two months ago I started to work at a video store, thirty-five to forty hours a week now at four dollars an hour. I bought furniture for the house, for the living room, for my bedroom. I bought the TV, a ring for my father, a chain for my mother, a vacuum cleaner. I opened a bank account. I gave my mother a trip to Disney World and Epcot Center.

That doesn't mean I forget about school. My average for the whole year is eighty-something. I wish it was better, but what can I do? I'm in school until 2:45 and I have to be at work at three o'clock. I work until 8:30, quarter to nine, around there. I work straight through. I don't eat dinner until I go home, around 9:30. My mother waits and we have dinner together. Then I do my homework for maybe an hour or two each night and go to bed around eleven or twelve.

Language Awareness

Grammar
Wh- Questions

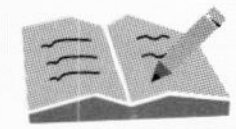

Review with students *who, what, when,* and *where* questions. Ask them to tell what information is gained by each kind of question (*when–time, where–place, who–people*, and so on). Reread the interview. Then help students determine what questions might have been asked of Jorge in order for him to give the information that he did. Write them on the board. Use Activity Book page 118.

Then have students think of someone they would like to interview and write down questions they would ask the person.

Model a Strategy
Read On to Get Meaning

Model reading on to get the meaning of pronouns:

When I read, I see pronouns such as *they, he, she.* Usually I need to go back in the story to figure out who the people are. But this interview begins with the pronoun *they.* I have to read on to get meaning. After I finish reading the first paragraph, I stop and ask myself, *Who are the "they"?* I can conclude that *they* must be Jorge's mother and father. He mentions them in the first paragraph.

Connect

Activate Prior Knowledge

Review Vocabulary

Ask students whether it has been hard to learn English. Read the English title of the poem. Ask students what they think the poem is about.

Develop Language and Concepts

Present Page 228

PURPLE TAPE

Read the English translation of the poem several times—the author feels his native language expresses himself best. Then have Spanish-speaking students read the original Spanish version. Ask Spanish-speaking students to tell which version of the poem they prefer and why. Have students look for similar words and differences in spelling and conventions between the two languages. Play the poem on Side 2 of the Purple Tape.

Language Awareness

Vocabulary
Cognates

Explain that many words in English are similar to words in other languages. Remind students that in Unit 4 they learned that many English words have their origins in Latin. Have students look for similar words in the English and Spanish versions of the poem (*lenguaje/language, persona/person).*

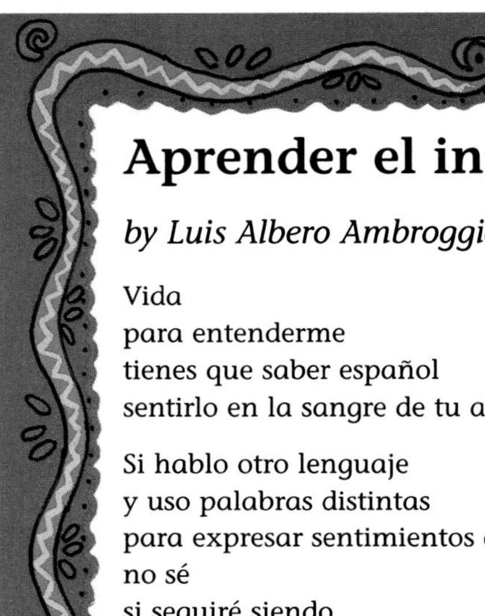

Aprender el inglés

by Luis Albero Ambroggio

Vida
para entenderme
tienes que saber español
sentirlo en la sangre de tu alma.

Si hablo otro lenguaje
y uso palabras distintas
para expresar sentimientos que nunca cambiarán
no sé
si seguiré siendo
la misma persona.

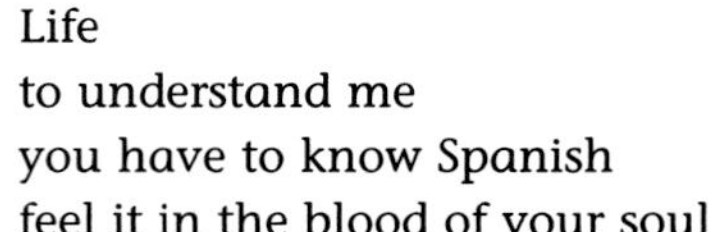

Learning English

Translated by Lori M. Carlson

Life
to understand me
you have to know Spanish
feel it in the blood of your soul.

If I speak another language
and use different words
for feelings that will always stay the same
I don't know
If I'll continue being
the same person.

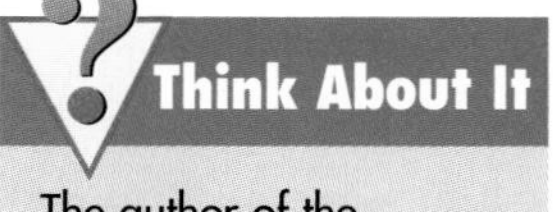

Think About It

The author of the poem says that he can only express himself completely in his native language. Do you have trouble getting information in English? What ways can you help yourself get information?

Options for Reaching All Students

Beginning

Advanced: Borrowing Words

Explain that sometimes English adopts words from other languages. Write the words *adobe, bronco, burro, fiesta, rodeo,* and *taco* on the board. Explain their meanings to students. Then have students match them to these similar-meaning words on a piece of paper: *party, sandwich, donkey, brick, horse,* and *show.*

Advanced

Advanced: Write a Poem

Have students write poems on any subject they choose. Have them write the poem first in English, then in their native language. Invite them to share their poems in small groups.

CHAPTER 12

Tell what you learned.

1. What sources of information did you use as you studied this chapter? What was the most interesting thing you read?
2. What is the most important thing you learned on your own as you studied this chapter?

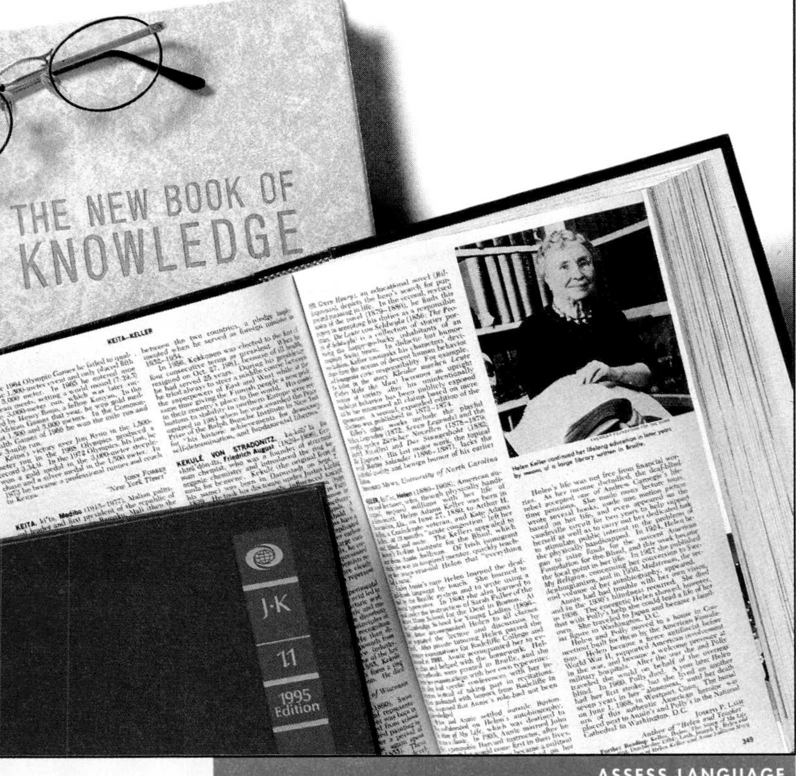

THE NEW BOOK OF KNOWLEDGE
J·K
11
1995 Edition

Assess

Activity 1: Students should name encyclopedias, magazines, newspapers, graphic organizers, and interviews. Students should offer reasons for finding their choices interesting.

Activity 2: Students should discuss something they learned independently and offer reasons for its importance.

Have students complete the Chapter Self-Assessment, Blackline Master 31. Have students choose a product from one of the activities to include in their portfolios. Add the results of any rubrics, checklists, self-assessments, portfolio assessments, Blackline Masters 2–18 and 31.

Listening Assessment

BLACKLINE MASTER

Make sure that students have a copy of Blackline Master 93 from the Teacher's Resource Book. Have students complete the dictation and put the words in alphabetical order.

CREAM TAPE

See page 192d for the tapescript.

Strategy Assessment

Understand Articles

Provide a newspaper or magazine article for students to read. Discuss with them how what they learned in this chapter can help them read the article and remember important information. Encourage them to use strategies such as reading on, using chronology, and producing a graphic organizer.

Writing Assessment

Write "How-To" Instructions

Have students select one source of information they have learned about. Then ask them to explain how to use the information source and what information it contains.

Language Assessment

BLACKLINE MASTER

Use Blackline Master 92 in the Teacher's Resource Book.

Standardized Test Practice

ACTIVITY BOOK

Use pages 120 and 121. Answers: **1.** $33.00 **2.** 200 **3.** between $1.50 and $2.00 **4.** 12

Wrap-Up

Activities

Advertisements

Have each student create an advertisement for a product that relieves stress. Encourage them to create visual aids, write a jingle, or create a sample of their product to make their advertisement more convincing. Some examples might be an easy chair, a massage, a yoga class, a trip to Hawaii.

Magazine Rack Display

Have each student bring a copy of a favorite article from a magazine for display on a large bulletin board. Invite students to make presentations about their articles on an ongoing basis, explaining why they found the article interesting.

Fact Hunt

Give students a list of questions for which you have found the answers in reference materials that are available in the school or that are on hand in the school library. The facts can be on famous people, historical events, current events, locations, and so on. Try to get a variety of topics that can be best researched in a variety of reference sources such as the ones the students studied in the unit. Give students the list and have them see how many answers they can find within a given time period. Have prizes for winners.

Discussing the Theme

Review with students what they have learned about handling stress and getting information. Choose from the following activities that will demonstrate to students how much they have learned and how useful the information is:

- Have students tape-record a list of new words learned.
- Have students discuss the sources of information they studied. Were there any particular books they found most interesting?
- Have students discuss how what they learned in the unit will be useful to them in school in the future. Focus particularly on reference sources.

Sharing the Project

Use the invitation form, Blackline Masters 32–33, to invite family members to school to see the students' plays.

Provide class time for dress rehearsals. After the rehearsals, help students critique each other's plays.

Help students create a name for their theater group, such as "The Less Stress Players," and make simple programs listing the plays and the students involved in each. You might have students write brief biographies to include in the program. Photocopy the programs for distribution at the performance.

Have students prepare the class magazine for distribution at the performance and to other students at school. Invite students to work on more than one aspect of the magazine. Provide class time for students to work together to write, edit, illustrate, and design the articles. Have more advanced students do the final editing and proofreading. Beginning students can do the copying, collating, and stapling.

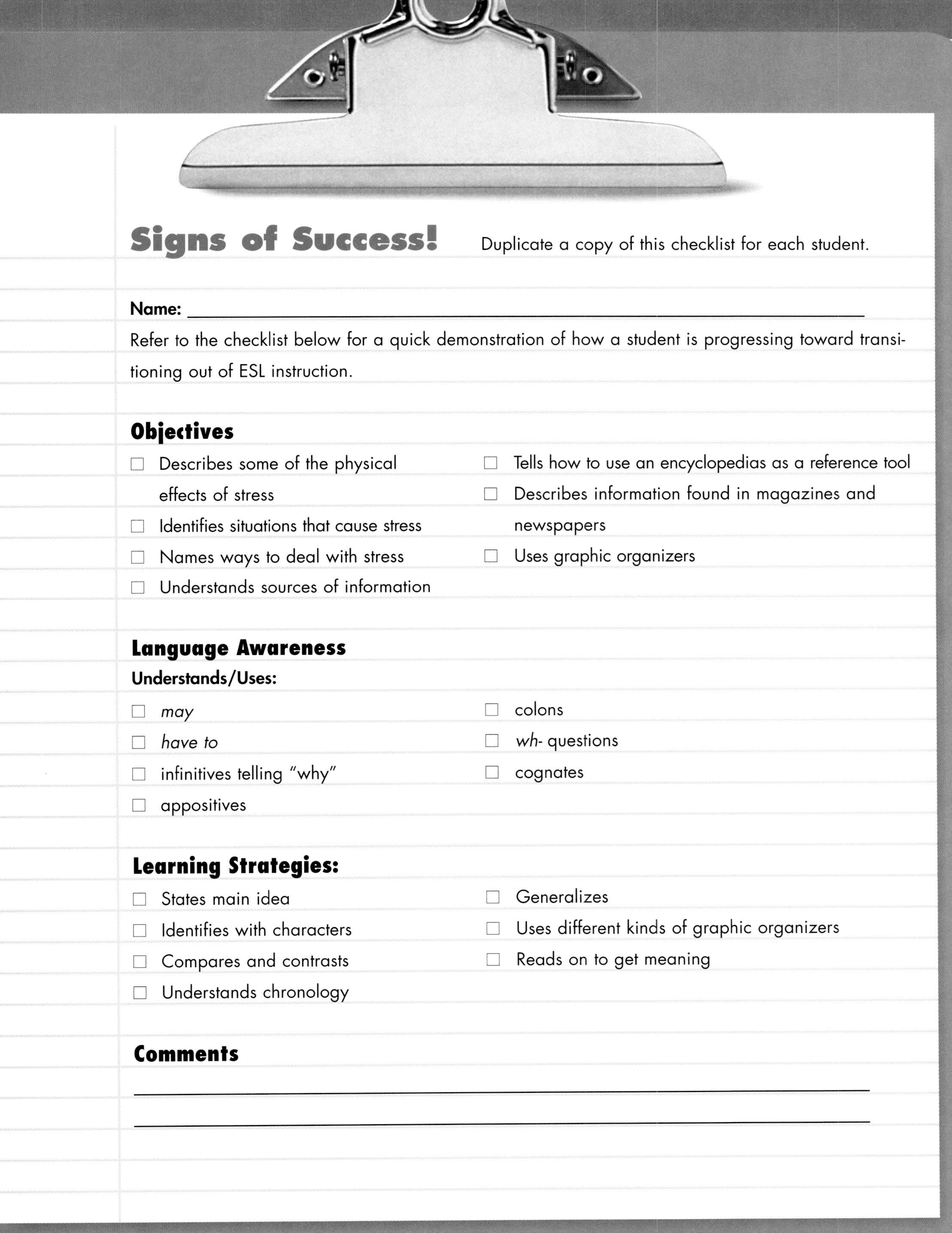

Signs of Success!

Duplicate a copy of this checklist for each student.

Name: ____

Refer to the checklist below for a quick demonstration of how a student is progressing toward transitioning out of ESL instruction.

Objectives

- ☐ Describes some of the physical effects of stress
- ☐ Identifies situations that cause stress
- ☐ Names ways to deal with stress
- ☐ Understands sources of information
- ☐ Tells how to use an encyclopedias as a reference tool
- ☐ Describes information found in magazines and newspapers
- ☐ Uses graphic organizers

Language Awareness

Understands/Uses:

- ☐ *may*
- ☐ *have to*
- ☐ infinitives telling "why"
- ☐ appositives
- ☐ colons
- ☐ *wh-* questions
- ☐ cognates

Learning Strategies:

- ☐ States main idea
- ☐ Identifies with characters
- ☐ Compares and contrasts
- ☐ Understands chronology
- ☐ Generalizes
- ☐ Uses different kinds of graphic organizers
- ☐ Reads on to get meaning

Comments

____

____

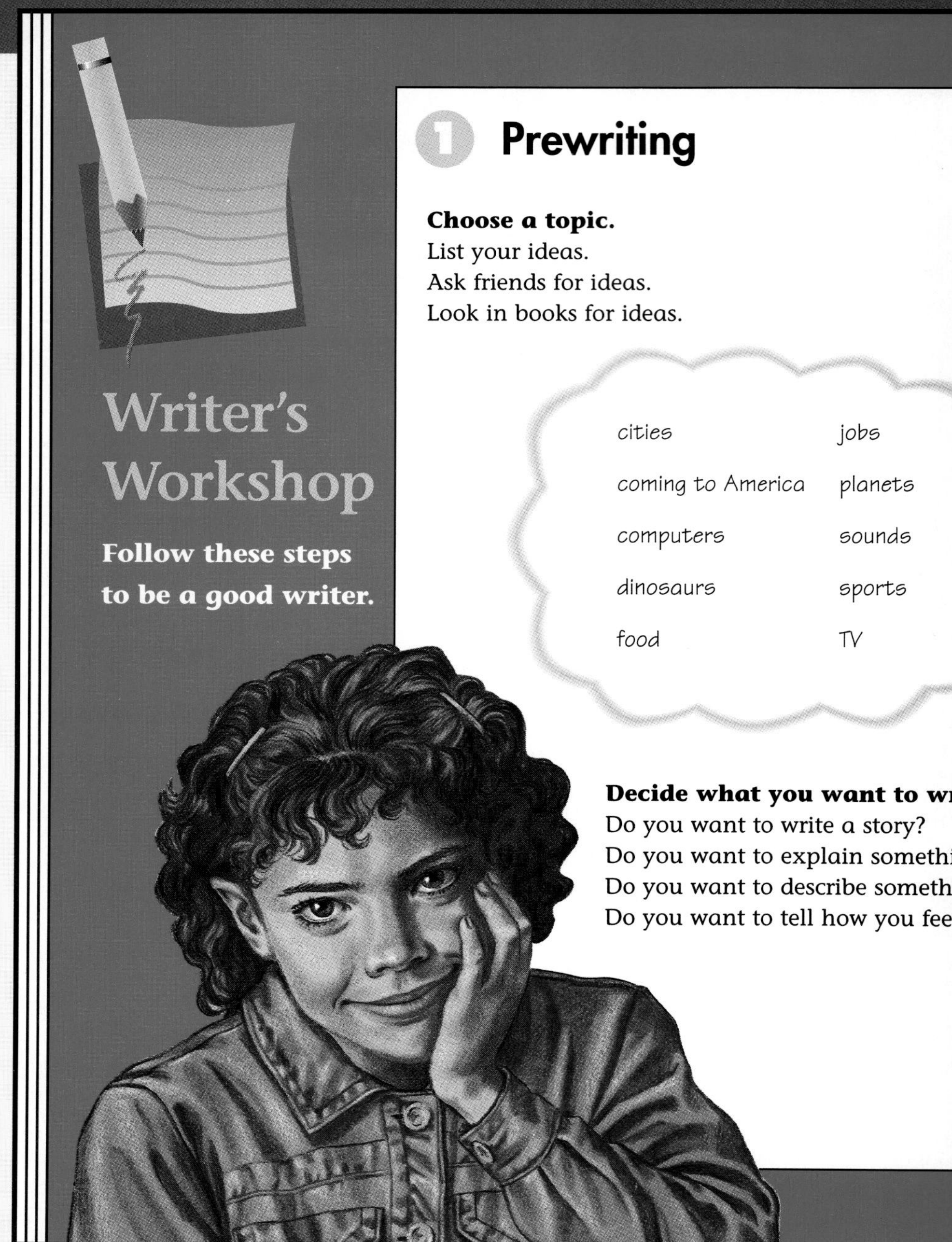
Writer's Workshop
Follow these steps to be a good writer.
1 Prewriting
Choose a topic.
List your ideas.
Ask friends for ideas.
Look in books for ideas.
cities
jobs
coming to America
planets
computers
sounds
dinosaurs
sports
food
TV
Decide what you want to wr
Do you want to write a story?
Do you want to explain somethi
Do you want to describe somethi
Do you want to tell how you feel

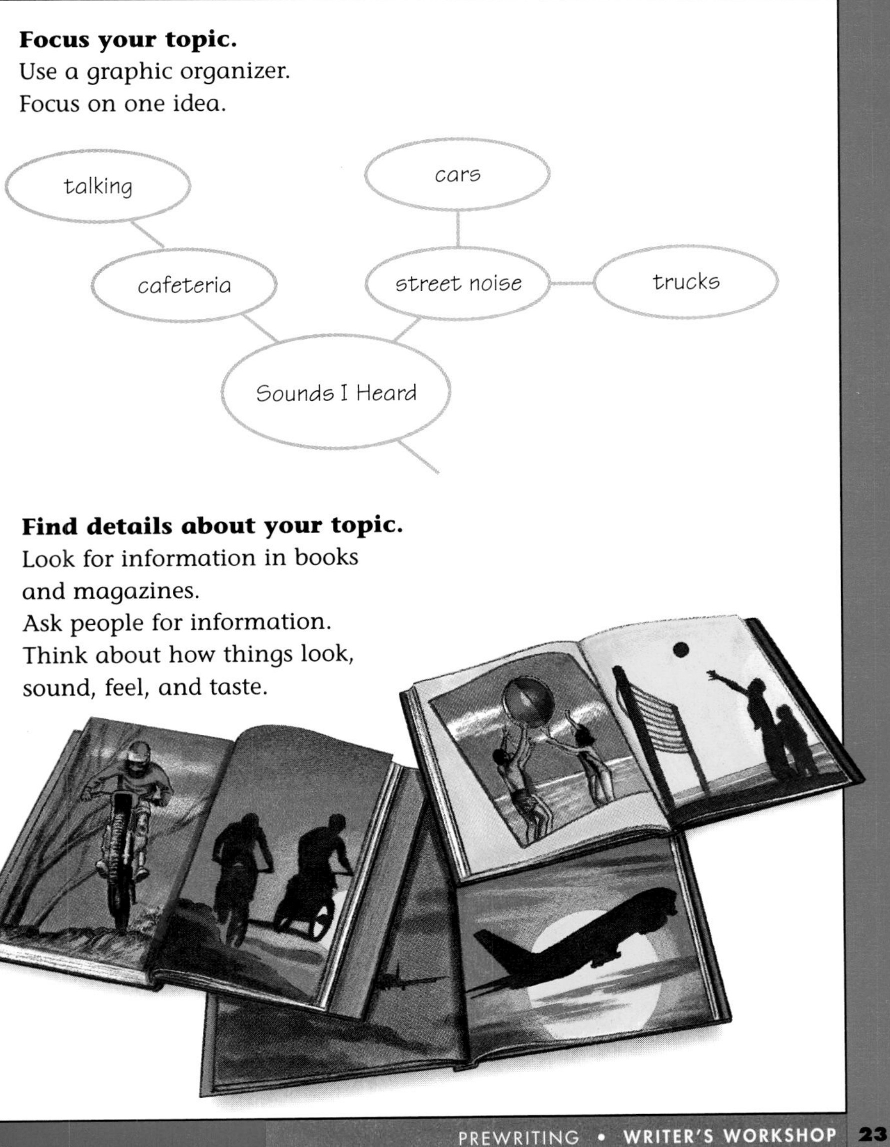

Focus your topic.
Use a graphic organizer.
Focus on one idea.

Find details about your topic.
Look for information in books and magazines.
Ask people for information.
Think about how things look, sound, feel, and taste.

Drafting

Get what you need.
Get paper and pencils.
Get your graphic organizer.
Sit in a comfortable place.

Set a goal.
How much will you write now?

Read your notes.
What do you want to say first?

Keep writing.
Write down all your ideas.
Don't worry about spelling and punctuation now.

Sounds I Heard

I see many cars and truks on the streets Some cars were honking ther horns. I saw a tall building too.

At school the peeple in the cafeteria were very noisy they was talking. In muzic class, everyone was singing. After school, I walked by a park. the grant Park Orchestra was playing muzic there I liked the drums and the trupets.

I want play the the drums some day. I like Loud sounds.

3 Revising

Read what you wrote. Ask yourself:
Does my story have a beginning, a middle, and an end?
Is my information correct?
What parts should I keep?
What parts should I leave out?

Talk with someone.
Show your writing to a friend or your teacher.
Do your readers understand your writing?

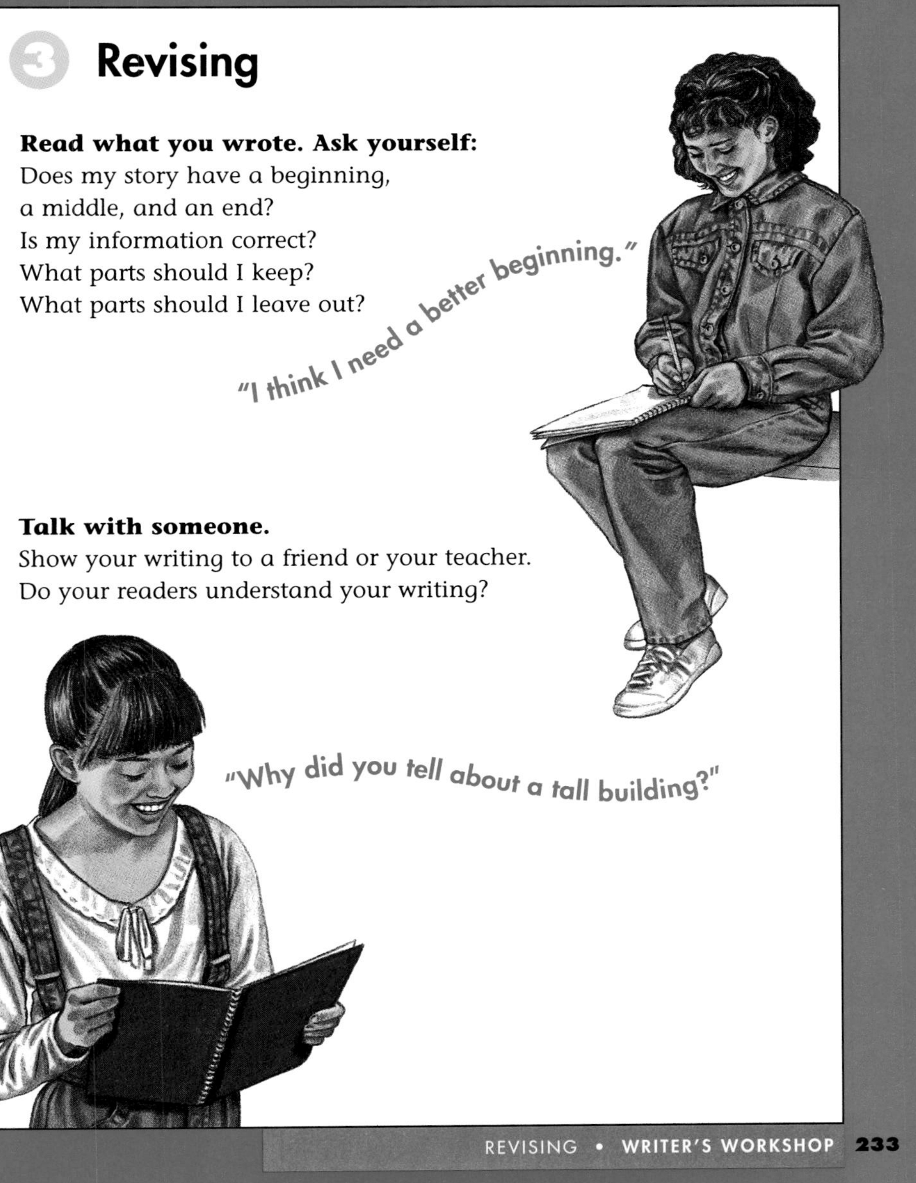

"I think I need a better beginning."
"Why did you tell about a tall building?"

Proofreading

Check your spelling.
Look in a dictionary or ask for help.

Look for capital letters.

Look for correct punctuation.

Make a new copy.

≡	**Make a capital.**
/	**Make a small letter.**
∧	**Add something.**
℘	**Take out something.**
⊙	**Add a period.**
¶	

Sounds I Heard

Yesterday I hear many sounds. I see many cars and truks on the streets Some cars were honking ther horns.

At school the peple in the cafeteria were very noisy they was talking. In muzic class, everyone was singing. After school, I walked by a park. the grant Park Orchestra was playing muzic there I liked the drums and the trupets.

I want play the the drums some day. I like Loud sounds.

5 Presenting

Share your writing.
Read it aloud to your family or classmates. Make a book. Lend the book to your family or classmates.

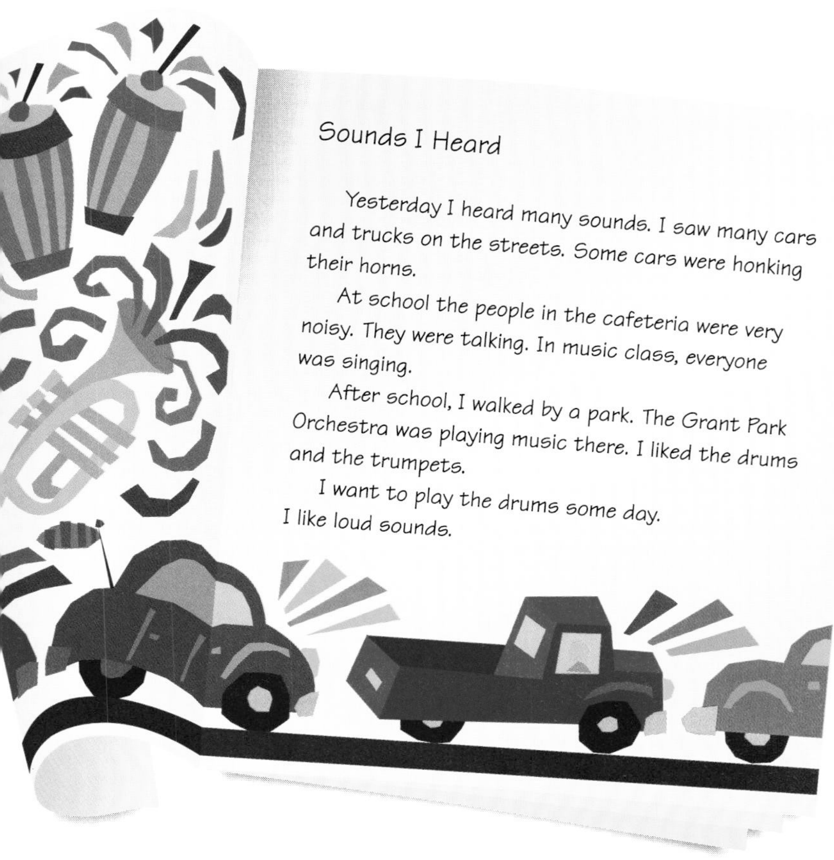

Sounds I Heard

Yesterday I heard many sounds. I saw many cars and trucks on the streets. Some cars were honking their horns.

At school the people in the cafeteria were very noisy. They were talking. In music class, everyone was singing.

After school, I walked by a park. The Grant Park Orchestra was playing music there. I liked the drums and the trumpets.

I want to play the drums some day. I like loud sounds.

What a Good Writer Can Do

- I can plan before I write.
- I can write about things I know. I can write about my family, my school, and myself.
- I can write stories with a beginning, a middle, and an end.
- I can ask others to read my work.
- I can write in complete sentences.
- I can put periods at the ends of sentences.
- I can make my handwriting easy to read.

ScottForesman

Scope and Sequence

SCOPE AND SEQUENCE 1

Chapter		Objectives	Content Focus	Language Awareness Objectives	Learning Strategies
1	**Families**	Tell who is in a family; tell what families do; tell how families change.	social studies, science, literature	plurals, pronouns, present tense, capital letters, initial *f*, color words	Use what you know; predict content.
2	**Growing and Changing**	Tell new things children can do as they grow; tell how children and animals grow and change.	social studies, science, literature	adjectives that mean "more," plurals, prepositions *in* and *on*, color words, proper nouns, offering to do something, typographical devices	Use picture clues; use pictures to get meaning; recognize main idea; draw conclusions.
3	**At School**	Tell how children get to school; tell what's seen at school; name rules; tell what's done at school.	social studies, math, literature	pronouns—*I* and *we*, days of the week, question words, *many*, contractions, initial *m*, initial *c* /k/, initial *d*, greetings	Use pictures; recognize patterns; understand a process; paraphrase/retell.
4	**Learning**	Name some things done alone and some things done in a group; name things practiced at school; tell how children feel at school; tell what's learned in school.	social studies, health, literature	infinitives, verbs, verb— *can*, pronouns, multiple meanings—*like, if*	Understand cause and effect; recognize repetition.
5	**Neighbors**	Tell where people live; tell what neighbors are; tell what a community is; tell how maps help people.	social studies, math, literature	question words, initial *n*, capitalization, opposites, initial *p*, words for noises, position words, initial *s*, initial *r*, rhyming words	Use a map; use brainstorming; use what you know; make inferences; draw conclusions.
6	**Animals and Their Homes**	Name places where animals live; name animals that live in trees, in ponds, and in fields; name animals that can be pets; tell how to care for pets.	science, math, literature	prepositional phrases, initial *t*, verbs, number and verbs, initial *w*, names for animal babies, future tense, initial *h*	Reread; use pictures; visualize word problems; make predictions based on prior knowledge.
7	**How You Can Feel Safe**	Name places where safety is important; name people who help keep others safe; name rules that help people stay safe.	health, math, literature	word families, verbs + *-er*, multiple meanings, rules, initial soft *g*, short *i*, word order, question mark, exclamation mark	Use what you know; compare and contrast; use predicting; use selective attention; recognize reality and fantasy; make predictions.

Chapter	Objectives	Content Focus	Language Awareness Objectives	Learning Strategies
8 **How You Can Feel Healthy**	Tell benefits of exercising; name ways to keep clean and healthy; name foods that assist growth and good health.	health, math, literature	adjectives with *-y*, pronoun *they,* antonyms, count vs. noncount nouns, days of the week, period, short *a,* expressing gratitude	Use picture cards; use a chart; use finding the total; make predictions based on prior knowledge.
9 **Using Our Senses**	Tell how to take care of the eyes and ears; tell how to make high and low sounds; tell what body part is used for each sense.	health, science, literature	verbs, antonyms, plural forms, giving instructions, capital letters, short *o,* multiple meanings—*went,* places in a house, past tense	Use imagining; recognize cause and effect; make predictions; recognize reality and fantasy; draw conclusions.
10 **How We See and Hear**	Compare how people and animals see; compare how people and animals hear; compare things seen and heard.	science, math, literature	expression *very well,* capitalization and punctuation, numerals and number words, questions and answers, short *u,* rhyming words	Use prior knowledge; follow directions.
11 **The Four Seasons**	Name the four seasons; name the months of the year; tell how the weather changes from season to season; tell what seasonal things people do; tell how people dress for the weather.	science, social studies, literature	phrases, root words, consonant blend *cl,* capitalization/punctuation, adjectives, contractions	Predict content; get information; understand that numbers show sequence; compare and contrast.
12 **Trees**	Tell ways people can save and protect trees; tell ways people use trees; tell why people and animals need trees.	social studies, science, literature	long *a,* period and question mark, opposites, verbs, pronoun—*they,* color words, superlatives, adjectives of size—*small/long/wide*	Use pictures for meaning; visualize; use planning; understand type conventions; use context clues.

SCOPE AND SEQUENCE 2

Chapter		Objectives	Content Focus	Language Awareness Objectives	Learning Strategies
1	**People and Places**	Name different kinds of groups; tell what different groups do; name places in the community; tell what people do in each place; name states in the U.S.; begin recognizing animal groups and their places.	social studies, science, literature	present tense; sentence patterns; capitalization; irregular plurals; rhyming words with long *a, e,* and *i;* informal English expression *OK;* statements showing approval	Use picture details; read maps; use pictures for meaning; recognize fact and fantasy; summarize.
2	**Animals and Their Habitats**	Name animals and some of their attributes; understand what animals need from their habitats.	science, math, literature	subject/verb agreement, short *a,* explaining choices, comparatives, similes, rhyme	Use pictures for meaning; understand patterns; understand main idea; count how many; remember details.
3	**How People Work**	Name community workers; tell how workers help us; name workplaces; tell what people's "needs" are; tell the difference between *needs* and *wants;* tell what animals' needs are.	social studies, science, literature	verbs, related words, words *needs* and *wants,* contractions, rhyme	Use pictures for meaning; use title to predict; note repeated words; find a way to classify; use what you know.
4	**What Animals Do**	Tell ways animals work; tell how animals protect themselves; tell how protective coloration works.	science, math, literature	subject/verb agreement; consonant blends *sm, sk,* and *spr;* giving directions; punctuation; contractions; verbs; describing; rhyme	Recognize main idea; recognize sentence patterns; follow directions; understand specialized language; use prior knowledge; use pictures to get meaning; summarize.
5	**How We Have Fun**	Name toys and games; name ways to play alone and to play with friends; tell how to get exercise while playing; name ways that exercise is good for you; tell what parts of the body are used with different exercises.	health, math, literature	final consonant *s /z/,* long *i,* number and present progressive tense, irregular past tense, future tense, pronouns, contractions, addressing family members and friends	Visualize; use imagery; recognize cause and effect; use pictures for meaning.
6	**How Things Move**	Tell what things can be pushed or pulled; understand *force;* tell what magnets do; tell about play involving pushing and pulling.	science, social studies, literature	consonant blend *tr,* adjectives, prepositions, present progressive, future tense, imperatives	Use picture clues; ask questions for information; use word structure; use context clues.

Chapter		Objectives	Content Focus	Language Awareness Objectives	Learning Strategies
7	**Plants We Eat**	Name the parts of plants; tell what each part of a plant does; name plants we eat; tell which parts of plants we eat; name grains and foods made from grains.	science, social studies, literature	consonant blends *st* and *str, a few* and *a lot (of),* count vs. noncount nouns, passive expressions; sentence patterns, nouns and verbs; long *o* spelled *ow* and *oa*	Use pictures for meaning; see that numerals show sequence; find a way to classify; locate patterns; understand a process; summarize.
8	**Where We Buy Food**	Tell where fruits and vegetables are grown; tell where foods are purchased; tell which foods can be purchased in which places; name kinds of restaurants.	social studies, math, literature	phrases, capitalization, making requests, numerals and number words, possessives, pronouns	Preview text; monitor meaning; plan to read orally; use pictures and text; use context clues.
9	**Night and Day**	Name things in the sky; tell what causes night and day; tell about the sun; tell about the moon; tell why a calendar is important.	science, social studies, literature	homophones, compound words, expressing time, irregular past tense, comparatives, similes, describing, pattern and rhyme	Use a diagram; generalize; predict; make comparisons; use context; use prior knowledge.
10	**Long Ago and Today**	Tell about the first people in North America; tell about Spanish settlers of North America; tell about Pilgrims; name U.S. holidays.	social studies, math, literature	telling why, time expressions, ordinal numbers, questions and answer, present tense, onomatopoeia	Understand chronology; use a calendar; summarize.
11	**Where We Find Water**	Name sources of water; tell how some bodies of water differ; find bodies of water on a map; tell what happens when there is too much or too little water; tell how water can be saved.	social studies, science, literature	adjectives, capitalization, expressions of amount, long *a,* short *u,* possessives, informal expressions, short and long *i*	Use context clues; use a map; visualize; preview a story; recognize cause and effect; paraphrase/retell.
12	**Water and the Weather**	Tell how rain makes people feel; tell about clouds; tell where rain comes from; tell about water vapor; tell about the water cycle.	science, math, literature	related words, forming questions, prepositional phrases, comparatives, punctuation, compound words	Check inferences; self-assess; preview directions; solve problems.

SCOPE AND SEQUENCE 3

Chapter		Objectives	Content Focus	Language Awareness Objectives	Learning Strategies
1	**The Farm and the City**	Tell what farmers do; identify products that come from a farm; tell how wheat is grown; read a thermometer.	social studies, science, literature	singular and plural nouns, subject-verb agreement—*is/are,* simple present tense, recognize commands, /p/ and /b/	Use time expressions; follow directions; recognize patterns in English.
2	**Life in the City**	Tell about a community; name services and goods in a city; solve math story problems; name parts of a city; name state capitols; name the five food groups.	social studies, math, health, literature	sentence structure, consonant sounds /g/ and /k/, capitalization of proper nouns, numbers as words, slang/informal English, extending an invitation, present progressive tense	Reread; use a map; read a chart; recognize opinions; type conventions; draw conclusions.
3	**How You Use Light**	Name lights used in the past and today; read a time line of lights; tell uses of lights in a community; explain how people use their eyes to see.	social studies, science literature	words in a series, time words, *when* and *where,* the sound of long *i,* contractions, rhyme	Recognize time and sequence; use a time line; visualize; use a diagram.
4	**What Light Can Do**	Tell what light can and cannot move through; identify what makes light bend and bounce back; use a prism to see rainbow colors; put on a shadow play.	science, social studies, literature	*some, all,* or *none;* prepositions of location *on, in, under;* commands; nouns as adjectives; communicating with sounds; expressing the same idea with different expressions; plurals of words ending in -y; alliteration	Explain a process; use pictures for meaning; paraphrase; use different expressions with the same meaning.
5	**How You Make Sound**	Tell how sound is made; demonstrate vibrations; tell how sounds are different; name musical instruments from around the world.	science, social studies, literature	the *v* sound, *can* and *can't,* adjectives, the pronoun *it,* past tense, long *a* and short *a,* rhyme, onomatopoeia	Record information; recognize sentence patterns; use type conventions; understand specialized vocabulary.
6	**How You Use Sound**	Tell how you hear sound; name parts of the ear; tell how ears help animals survive; find out how well you hear; name inventions in communication.	science, social studies, literature	the sound of *ear,* singular/plural agreement—*has/have, you* as understood subject in commands, *can* + verb + complement, *so . . . that,* long *o* and short *o*	Read a diagram; set a purpose for reading; recognize main idea; distinguish between fact and opinion.
7	**Plants, Animals, and Climate**	Describe the climate of deserts and forests; tell how a cactus can live in the desert; tell how animals live in a forest; tell how veterinarians help animals.	science, social studies, literature	*some* or *other;* adjectives; long *e;* pronouns *he, she, they; many, most, some* and *all, they* and *them; once, twice;* words for the senses	Compare and contrast; use a Venn diagram; use picture captions; reread sentences.

Chapter		Objectives	Content Focus	Language Awareness Objectives	Learning Strategies
8	**Weather and People**	Tell how weather affects the way people live; tell how people dress for the weather; identify climates in various parts of the world; tell how to stay healthy in hot weather; tell how to stay healthy in cold weather.	social studies, health, literature	antonyms; infinitives of purpose; consonant blends *sl, pl, cl;* commands; similies; quantity expressions	Recognize cause—effect relationships; recognize main idea; use a map key; use pictures for meaning.
9	**What Shelters Are Made Of**	Name materials used to build homes; tell how people found building materials long ago; tell how homes changed over time; name steps in building a beaver lodge.	social studies, science, literature	beginning and ending consonant sounds *st* and *ch, house* or *home,* past tense verbs ending in *t,* sequence words, short *i* and long *i,* identify a sentence and punctuation, parenthetical expressions	Recognize a pattern; read a time line; use numbers; learn information.
10	**How Shelters Are Built**	Name tools and materials and tell how they are used; tell how bricks and glass are made; name simple machines; name shapes in houses.	science, math, literature	forms of *build, /ks/,* subject-verb agreement *is* and *are,* show possibility—*can be,* phrases that tell *where* and *when*	Reread to understand; understand a process; use pictures for meaning.
11	**Changing the Earth**	Tell how people affect the environment; tell about a local habitat; tell how children can save a rain forest; name endangered or extinct animals write a letter to an environmental group.	science, social studies, literature	special singular and plural nouns, consonant blends—*str* and *thr,* context and picture clues, *when* clauses, making requests, possessive adjectives	Set a purpose for reading; use pictures to follow directions; use context clues; take notes.
12	**Pollution**	Name causes of water pollution; name ways to prevent water pollution; tell how to find out how clean the air is; tell how recycling works; name things that can be recycled; tell what people can do to prevent pollution.	science, social studies, literature	gerunds, sounds /h/ and /j/, conjunctions—*and,* verbs with *up, was going to,* prepositions—*under, above,* adverbs of degree—*very, too*	Paraphrase; draw conclusions; recognize language patterns; recognize supporting details; use prior knowledge to predict.

SCOPE AND SEQUENCE 4

Chapter		Objectives	Content Focus	Language Awareness Objectives	Learning Strategies
1	**The American West Today**	Name the states and landforms in the West; name crops farmers grow in the West; describe ranching, fishing, and mining in the West.	social studies, science, literature	singular and plural nouns; verbs; /m/ and /n/; simple present tense; place an order; antonyms	Use a map key; recognize a pattern; read money amounts.
2	**Settling the West**	Explain why people went west; describe the trip west; tell what settlers took with them; talk about the Oregon Trail; talk about the dangers and benefits of prairie fires.	social studies, science, literature	*want* + infinitive; household items; /w/; habitual *would*; quotation marks; recount past activities; exclamations; metaphors	Set a purpose for reading; visualize; use pictures for meaning; recognize a personal title.
3	**You Are a Living Thing!**	Explain that all living things are made of cells; describe how cells grow; tell why living things need energy; demonstrate that yeast is a living thing; tell how people communicate.	science, social studies, literature	/k/ and /s/ spelled *c;* simple present vs. present progressive tense; questions with *what* and *how;* onomatopoeia; describe activities with other people; using *cannot*	Use pictures for meaning; classify to understand; use chronology to understand.
4	**Living in Your Ecosystem**	Define an ecosystem; explain how an ecosystem works; make an ecosystem; use bat facts to solve math problems.	science, math, literature	compare with *as* + adjective + *as;* conjunctions *when* and *as;* diphthong /oi/; *how many* and *how much;* prepositions of location; noun phrases with *who;* express obligation	Use labels to understand; prepare for an activity; use pictures for word meaning; visualize a relationship.
5	**The First Americans**	Name some American Indian shelters and the resources used to build them; identify the parts of a buffalo and how they were used; describe American Indian crafts; tell what an archaeologist does; name some materials that are good insulators.	social studies, science, literature	pronoun *they;* sentence patterns with *use . . . for;* present perfect tense; sequence words *first, second, third, last;* deductions with *must be;* /j/; fraction words	Classify information; use numerals for sequence; predict content; use context clues; visualize story details.
6	**The Aztec Indians**	Name some crops that Aztec farmers grew; describe Aztec arts and crafts; name foods that come from the Aztecs; explain how the Aztec calendar worked.	social studies, math, literature	past tense verbs; consonant blend *st;* expressing preference; *before* and *after;* adverbs; *I am . . .*	Use context clues; set a purpose for reading; paraphrase.

Chapter		Objectives	Content Focus	Language Awareness Objectives	Learning Strategies
7	**You Are What You Eat!**	Explain that people need food for energy; describe a balanced diet; describe a food pyramid; tell where foods grow.	health, social studies, literature	compare past abilities to present abilities with *can/couldn't;* expressing people's needs; *yes/no* questions with *did;* adverbs *well* and *poorly;* /ü/ and /yü/; /fr/	Use graphics for information.
8	**Let's Eat!**	Use a diagram to explain digestion; tell what saliva does; explain why people feel hungry; describe how people learned about vitamins.	science, social studies, literature	words for parts of the body; *when* clauses; *yes/no* questions with *do/does;* /v/ and /b/; express obligation; prepositional phrases; foreign words; *I like* + noun vs. *I like* + infinitive	Understand specialized vocabulary; use phonetic spellings; use pictures for meaning; read to find information.
9	**Life in the Rain Forest**	Tell where rain forests grow; name types of species that live in a rain forest; describe a food chain in a rain forest; tell the history of rubber.	science, social studies, literature	prepositions *above, below, along, through;* give examples with *such as;* pronoun referents; /l/ and /r/; comparisons; frequency expressions; present and past tenses	Identify main idea; use pictures for meaning; use a map key; use punctuation to read.
10	**Using Our Forests**	Tell why people need trees; explain why people need rain forests; find rain forest products; describe a rain forest scientist; tell how people are trying to save the rain forests.	social studies, science, literature	consonant blends *gr* and *tr;* past tense of irregular verbs; possibility—*might;* present progressive tense; use *please*	Use graphics to compare; use prior knowledge.
11	**Regions of Our Country**	Identify directions on a map; name regions of the U.S.; read a map; make a map; recognize state symbols.	social studies, science, literature	form plurals; capitalization of proper nouns; /sh/; expressions of amount *some, most, each, a lot of;* polite requests; rhyme scheme	Use sources of information; recognize patterns.
12	**State Histories**	Tell events in the history of California; read a time line; read a population bar graph; read a population line graph.	social studies, math, literature	ordinal numbers; irregular past-tense verbs; prefix—*re;* comparatives and superlatives; digraph *th;* express wants; /kw/; contractions	Read time lines; use prior knowledge; read a line graph; use pictures for meaning; understand author's point of view.

SCOPE AND SEQUENCE 5

Chapter		Objectives	Content Focus	Language Awareness Objectives	Learning Strategies
1	**The Science of Sound**	Tell what sound is; tell how people hear; make and use an ear trumpet; read a decibel graph.	science, math, literature	The *v* sound, singular and plural nouns, action words as directions, comparatives, rhyming sounds, the long *o* sound	Recognize cause and effect; use a graph; use pictures to predict.
2	**Uses of Sound**	Make sounds of different pitch; tell how musical instruments make sound; make a musical instrument; name events people celebrate with music.	science, social studies, literature	superlatives; passive voice expressions; count vs. non-count nouns; the sound /ng/ in the final position; time expressions; suffixes *-er, -ist;* idioms	Use a graph; use classification; work cooperatively; use pictures for meaning; use intonation.
3	**The Earth Is Not Flat!**	Tell why the Indies were important; identify Columbus and describe his voyage; tell about the meeting of Columbus and the Taino people; explain how a compass works.	social studies, science, literature	use language for buying, selling, and trading; past tense verbs; word origins; digraphs in the final position, *-sh, -th;* verb tenses; asking questions; expressions of frequency	Use pictures for meaning; visualize; make inferences; make a model to understand meaning.
4	**The Aztecs and the Spaniards**	Describe the Aztec city of Tenochtitlán; explain how Cortés conquered the Aztecs; name the parts of a horse; make an Aztec sun god mask.	social studies, science, literature	prepositions *in, on;* saying dates; / ėr/ sound spelled *er, ir, ear, or;* making general statements; verbs in directions; rhythm and rhyme	Identify main idea; use patterns; understand a process.
5	**Precious Water**	Explain differences between fresh water and salt water; tell why living things need water; name ways people use water; do an experiment with salty water.	social studies, science, literature	capitalization of proper nouns; infinitives; use of *as;* the pronoun *it;* /y/ in *Yaya* vs. /j/ in *magical;* the sound /v/; clauses with *that*	Find a topic sentence; read on to get meaning; recognize supporting details; record observations; summarize.
6	**The Forms of Water**	Name the forms of water; explain the water cycle; do a water cycle experiment; describe water sources in the Sahara Desert.	science, social studies, literature	Sounds for *s,* the *-tion* ending, long vowel sounds, simple present tense for presenting facts; asking questions	Use pictures for meaning; use context to get meaning; follow directions; use imagery to understand poetry.
7	**Coming to America**	Name countries from which settlers came; tell why setters came to America; tell about a journey to America; describe a beaver.	social studies, science, literature	time expressions; short *a,* long *a;* past progressive tense; describing; transportation words; *there is, there are*	Visualize story details; formulate opinions; summarize.

Chapter	Objectives	Content Focus	Language Awareness Objectives	Learning Strategies
8 **Life in the Colonies**	Tell something about Jamestown; become familiar with the names of the thirteen colonies; tell something about the New England, Middle, and Southern Colonies; read a graph on tobacco exports.	social studies, math, literature	infinitives; names of languages; past tense of irregular verbs; comparisons— *more, less*; compound sentences; comparisons—*as* + adjective + *as;* short *i* and long *i*	Recognize cause and effect; use a Venn Diagram; read a bar graph; make predictions; use context clues; paraphrasing.
9 **What Do You Read?**	Tell why people read; name materials people read; identify the parts of a front page; identify the sections of a newspaper; use word clues to solve story problems.	language arts, math, literature	infinitives; letter-sound correspondence—*f, ph, th;* report information; clauses with *that;* use of *do;* make exclamations	Use pictures to answer questions; read story problems; decode unfamiliar words.
10 **What Makes a Good Story?**	Define setting, characters, and plot; read a plot diagram; write a plot diagram; tell about storytelling around the world.	language arts, social studies, literature	subject/verb agreement—*is, are;* present tense verbs; question marks; the sound *s* spelled *c;* idioms; consonant digraph—*sh*; contractions; expressing approval and disapproval; rhyming words	Recall the plot; make a plot diagram; skim and scan; use pictures for meaning; ask questions to understand word meanings.
11 **Problems with England**	Tell that America's thirteen colonies belonged to England; explain why some colonists were angry with England; describe what happened at the Boston Tea Party; write and solve a sales tax problem.	social studies, math, literature	*only/many,* idioms, irregular past tense, the short *e* sound, sound words, indefinite pronouns and adverbs, the present perfect tense, long and short *i*	Draw conclusions; take notes; recognize point of view; follow directions.
12 **The War for Independence**	Identify Thomas Jefferson as the writer of the Declaration of Independence; identify George Washington and describe conditions at Valley Forge; tell what happened at the Battle of Yorktown; use capital letters; name important beliefs in the Declaration of Independence.	social studies, language arts, literature	pronouns—*they, he, it;* describe conditions; sounds *or* and *ar;* capitalization of proper nouns; adjective/pronoun—*these*	Summarize; use a time line; generalize; read on to get meaning.

SCOPE AND SEQUENCE 6

Chapter		Objectives	Content Focus	Language Awareness Objectives	Learning Strategies
1	**Digging Up Fossils**	Describe dinosaurs; tell how scientists learn about dinosaurs; tell when dinosaurs lived; compare old and new ideas about dinosaurs.	science, art, literature	plurals; the idiom *turn into; before* and *after;* consonant *p;* consonant blends *pl* and *pr;* past tense of *to be;* antonyms; conjunctions *or* and *and;* synonyms	Use headings; recognize patterns; read a chart; use action words in directions; find details; remember details.
2	**Digging Up Ancient Objects**	Name ancient Egyptian artifacts; tell how archeologists learn about the past; tell about ancient Egyptian burial; tell about King Tut's tomb; tell about hieroglyphics.	social studies, language arts, reading, literature	letters *f* and *ph;* past tense; expressions *years old/years ago;* numbers; quantity words *all/most/many/several;* rhyme	Use diagrams for meaning; keep track of chronology.
3	**Types of Fitness**	Name various types of physical fitness; describe steps one must take to be fit; identify body parts; understand and use commands in exercises; make a fitness plan; talk about games played around the world.	health, social studies, literature	*when* clauses; number words; gerunds; present tense; initial consonants *b* and *f;* contractions	Rehearse steps; read a chart; use reference resources; use techniques to memorize.
4	**Olympic Challenges**	Describe the history of the Olympic Games; explain how the modern games differ from the ancient Olympics; name various Olympic events; identify skills Olympic athletes need; explain the nature of Greek myths.	social studies, math, literature	irregular past tense; expression *such as;* ordinal numbers; superlatives; subject pronouns; real conditional sentences; regular past tense; punctuation rules	Use a map; categorize information; predict before and during reading.
5	**Life Underwater**	Name the areas of the ocean; name the things found in the ocean; compare the areas of the ocean; tell why things float; name the oceans of the world.	science social studies, literature	comparatives with *-er;* adjectives —position and agreement; articles *a* and *an;* expressions *surrounds/ is surrounded by;* antonyms; irregular past tense verbs long *e;* vowel digraphs *ea/ee*	Identify main topics; follow order in an experiment; use dialogue to evaluate character; use pictures for meaning.
6	**Taking Care of the Ocean**	Tell how people use the ocean; tell how people pollute the ocean; name some solutions to pollution; tell how students can help the environment; tell about aquaculture.	social studies, science, reading, literature	questions with *how;* answers with *by + -ing; stop/start + -ing;* expressions *less* and *more;* consonant digraph *sh; wh-* questions in the past tense; consonant *s*	Use a graphic organizer; find information in a newspaper article.

Chapter		Objectives	Content Focus	Language Awareness Objectives	Learning Strategies
7	**The Roman Empire**	Tell how the ancient Romans built their empire; describe the ancient Romans as builders; discuss the nature of Roman law; identify Latin words in English; discuss contributions of the ancient Romans.	social studies, language, reading, art	regular and irregular past tense; the verb *be* + adjective; hard and soft *c;* prefixes; amounts and container words; plurals	Read a map key; find the topic sentence; use prior knowledge; follow a recipe.
8	**Volcanoes in History**	Describe the eruption of Mount Vesuvius; discuss what archaeologists learned from Pompeii; tell what a volcano is; retell an ancient Roman myth.	social studies, science, literature	verbs and infinitives; passive verbs; consonant blends and digraphs with *s;* capitalization of proper nouns; discourse connectors; prepositional phrases of direction; regular and irregular past tense; letter *v*	Make personal connections; summarize to remember information; use a graphic organizer; visualize a story.
9	**What Makes Things Move?**	Explain why objects move; identify everyday activities that use motion; experiment with friction and gravity; explain why things move and why they stop.	science, math, literature	present tense; shape words; comparisons with *-er;* superlatives with *-est;* quotation marks for dialogue; action words; rhyming words with different spellings	Predict, monitor one's work; use context clues to find meaning.
10	**Physics of Roller Coasters**	Explain how a roller coaster works; experiment with the forces that make a roller coaster run; learn about synonyms and the use of a thesaurus.	science, math, reading, literature	words that show a sequence; expressions with *up;* conditional sentences; math words for averaging; express excitement; synonyms and antonyms; slang	Visualize; how to read a chart; understand words with multiple meanings; use word groups to remember new words.
11	**Handling Stress**	Describe some of the physical effects of stress; identify situations that cause stress; name ways to deal with stress; discuss school and differences among schools attended.	health, language arts, reading, literature	may; *have to;* end punctuation; giving advice; greetings and introductions; infinitives; telling "why"; stating rules; comparisons *good/better/best*	Paraphrase/retell; solve a problem; state main idea; identify with characters; compare and contrast.
12	**Getting Information**	Describe sources of information; tell how to use an encyclopedia as a reference tool; describe information found in magazines and newspapers; use graphic organizers to connect information.	study skills, language, reading, literature	appositives; quotation marks; questions and answers; colon; *wh-* questions; cognates	Understand chronology; understand magazine articles; consider the source; use graphic organizers; read on to get meaning.

Chapter		Objectives	Content Focus	Language Awareness Objectives	Learning Strategies
1	**Immigration Then and Now**	Give reasons why people immigrate; tell about the first settlers in North America; name the early English and Spanish settlements in the United States; tell where later immigrants to the United States came from.	social studies, literature, math	infinitive answers to *why* questions; past tense; expression *such as*; verbs *increase/decrease*; dialogue; action verbs; expressions *there was/there were*; short *a*	Make a time line; read large numbers; visualize the story.
2	**Gifts from Many Lands**	Tell how immigrants have brought their culture to the US; tell how people borrow customs and language from other groups; describe how different ethnic groups celebrate; identify place names from other cultures.	social studies, language arts, reading, literature	information questions; *when* clauses; words for nationalities ending in *-ese* and *-an;* capitalization; imperatives; vowel digraphs *oo* and *ou*	Use cognates; use paragraphs to follow meaning.
3	**How the Eyes Work**	Identify parts of the eye and how they work together; explain how pictures are formed and transmitted to the brain; compare human eyes to those of bees; learn idioms about eyes and seeing.	science, language arts, literature	position words; present tense: third person singular; hard and soft *c;* gerunds; negative present tense; greetings and farewells	Read science vocabulary; use a diagram to get meaning; follow steps compare and contrast.
4	**Looking at Colors**	Name different kinds of radiant energy; describe how light is comprised of different colors with different wavelengths; explain where rainbows come from; tell how artists use color to affect the viewer's mood.	science, art, literature	the conjunction *but;* present perfect tense; position of adjectives; *all/most/many/some/several/few;* past tense; *sh, sl,* and *sp;* words that describe sequence; *like* used for comparison	Scan text to predict content; read a scientific process; use diagrams to visualize; identify values; understand italics.
5	**Life in the Middle Ages**	Name classes of people during the Middle Ages; describe life in a castle; explain how a boy became a knight; tell about the legend of King Arthur.	social studies, health, literature, art	negative past tense; pronouns; gerunds; frequency adverbs; antonyms; sentence structure; future expressions; possessive forms	Recognize patterns in text; use reader's tips; make inferences; analyze a legend.
6	**Trade in the Middle Ages**	Describe how people traveled in the Middle Ages; tell how towns grew during the Middle Ages; identify products Europeans imported and exported during the Middle Ages; explain how the Black Death spread through Europe.	social studies, health, literature	names of occupations ending in *-er;* verbs + infinitives; past perfect tense; irregular past tense verbs ending in *-aught* and *-ought;* giving reasons with *because* and *so that*	Track cause and effect; use maps; revise predictions and self-correct; understand the use of italics.

Chapter	Objectives	Content Focus	Language Awareness Objectives	Learning Strategies
7 **Reading Stories**	Tell about types of reading materials; identify story elements; tell about story genres; tell how scientists test ideas.	language arts, science, literature	question words; irregular plurals; *may/might; yes/no* questions; use of italics for emphasis; interjections; long *e:* vowel digraphs *ie/ea;* contractions	Use an idea web; identify genres; use pictures to get meaning; identify story elements; identify a fantasy.
8 **Writing Stories**	Tell about languages and alphabets; tell about the parts of a dictionary; name types of writing; tell about different kinds of writers; write about yourself.	language arts, careers, reading literature	capitalization of place names, languages, nationalities, and book titles; words with multiple meanings; common punctuation; verbs that express necessity; words that describe people; long *o:* vowel digraphs *ow, oa*	Look up words in a dictionary; prepare to write.
9 **Mysteries in History**	Tell about the Inca civilization in South America; describe the end of the Inca civilization; tell about the historical site of Machu Picchu; describe various features of the Andes Mountains.	social studies, science, literature	position of adjectives; passive voice; cause and effect with *so* and *since;* comparatives and superlatives with *-er* and *-est;* real conditionals; expressing opinions; present and past tense; express likes and dislikes	Keep track of main ideas; use maps; use selective attention; take notes on main ideas.
10 **How Science Solves Mysteries**	Describe the process scientists use to solve mysteries; explain hypotheses scientists have about whales' songs; tell about the mystery of Loch Ness.	science, math, reading, literature	*why* questions; digraphs *ch* and *tch*; cause and effect; math vocabulary; connecting words *however* and *but;* sensory words	Paraphrase; read math problems; follow arguments.
11 **Desert Life**	Describe conditions found in the desert; name deserts of the world; tell how plants, animals, and people survive in the desert; name animals that live in the desert.	science, social studies, literature	adjectives ending in *-y;* present tense; ordinal numbers, prepositions of time; *because* clauses; negatives; intensifiers; long *a*	Identify main and supporting ideas; use information to understand characters' feelings; visualize.
12 **Water in the Desert**	Describe how plants and animals adapt to lack of water and to sudden rainfalls; explain how cities, towns, and farms get water; identify ways to conserve water; describe other solutions to the water shortage problem.	science, math, reading, literature	present tense: third person singular and negative; appostives; transitions; questions about amounts; *start/stop* + gerund; vowel digraphs *aw* and *al*	Read diagrams; guess word meanings; use context clues.

Chapter	Objectives	Content Focus	Language Awareness Objectives	Learning Strategies
1 **Growing Up**	Name physical characteristics family members share; describe the growth of boys and girls between ages 9 and 15; tell how heredity influences growth; name foods from the different food groups.	health, math, reading, literature	comparatives; present tense *has/have* and *is/are;* plural forms; possessive adjectives; superlatives; opposites	Understand key words; use a chart; understand directions.
2 **Life Cycles of Plants**	Name the parts of a plant; name the four main parts of a flower; describe the life cycle of a plant; tell how plants and animals are interdependent; identify parts of plants that people can eat.	science, math, literature, reading	words that describe; initial consonant *p;* consonant blends *pl* and *pr;* count and noncount nouns; position words; capitalization of place names; expressing intention with *going to* or *will;* past tense; punctuation	Use pictures for meaning; follow a sequence; make inferences; recognize cause and effect; visualize story details.
3 **Changing Weather**	Name kinds of weather; tell what makes weather change; tell how we know that air has weight; tell what causes storms; use weather idioms and sayings.	science, language arts, literature	conjunctions *and* and *or;* imperatives; present tense; adjectives that end in *-y; he/she/they;* past tense; *ou* and *ow*	Follow directions; track cause and effect; infer word meaning; understand story elements; read on to get meaning.
4 **Predicting the Weather**	Name the ways we get information about weather; tell about meteorologists; tell about the tools meteorologists use; tell who uses weather forecasts; read a weather map.	science, math, reading, literature	future with *will;* the expression *use (it) to;* clauses with *so* to express purpose; *there is/there are;* future with *going to;* the letter *l;* long *a*	Use a graphic organizer; understand specialized vocabulary; recognize text organization; use a map key.
5 **The United States Before the Civil War**	Describe the prewar economies of the North and the South; tell about slavery and the abolitionist movement; talk about Harriet Tubman and the Underground Railroad.	social studies, math, reading, literature	words that contrast; passive voice; italics for titles; expressions for comparison; past tense; contractions	Recognize supporting details; use encyclopedias; understand textbook explanations.
6 **War Between North and South**	Tell how people were affected by the war; describe the results of the war; name the leaders and some famous people of the war; tell how the songs of the era describe the times; tell how literature describes the war.	social studies, music, literature	use commas in numbers; stating opinions; occupation words ending in *-er* and *-ist;* future tenses with *will* and *going to;* action words; words that paint pictures; position words; prefix *un-*	Understand chronology and biographies; understand characters' feelings; summarize events.

Chapter		Objectives	Content Focus	Language Awareness Objectives	Learning Strategies
7	**The Sun**	Describe the solar system; explain why space appears to be black; tell how ancient peoples interpreted the universe; cite some literary examples that were inspired by the Sun and moon.	science, social studies, literature	prepositions of position; words for big; *little* vs. *few;* nationalities ending in *-ese* and *-an;* homonyms; synonyms	Read a diagram.
8	**The Planets**	Describe different physical characteristics of the planets; describe some major events in the history of space exploration; name idioms that relate to space.	science, math, literature, language arts	present tense to state general facts; comparatives; dates; *before* and *after;* unreal conditions; words that describe; ordinal numbers; superlatives; idioms	Use charts to make comparisons; read a time line.
9	**Settling the West**	Tell how, why, and when immigrants and and other settlers moved to the West; describe a prairie home and life there in the late 1800s; recognize problems caused by increased contact between settlers and Indians.	social studies, science, literature	capitalization of place names; the suffix *-less;* passive voice; amount words *many/few/little;* quotation marks with unattributed dialogue; negatives; long *o*	Use maps in textbooks; scan; use previously learned information; use a dictionary to increase vocabulary.
10	**Industry Changed the Nation**	Describe the Industrial Revolution; identify some U.S. industrial leaders and inventors; tell about the causes and effects of the reform movement; describe the life of Andrew Carnegie; sing songs of the Industrial Revolution.	social studies, math, literature	expressions of time; appositives; phrase *because of;* question formation; recognize unreal conditions; rhyming words; making requests	Read on to get meaning; use a time line; predict content; compare and contrast.
11	**Citizenship**	Describe the requirements for becoming a naturalized citizen and the meaning of good citizenship; tell about the Statue of Liberty, Ellis Island, and immigration experiences there.	social studies, math, reading, literature	*by* + gerund; answers to *how* questions; expressions with *must* and *have to;* spelling rules for gerunds; present perfect tense; silent letters in words; words with double *ss;* use of *would;* words that rhyme	Use a Venn diagram; understand the use of bulleted text.
12	**Government**	Describe the U.S. as a democracy; name the three branches of government; discuss the Constitution and some key amendments; list some views on the meaning of the U.S.	social studies, math, literature	*or* to signal appositives or explanations; colons; two-word verbs with *out;* present perfect tense with *since*; speech fillers; consonant blends	Understand text organization; use charts to get meaning; use a time line.

NOTES